Rick Steves'
FRANCE
2003

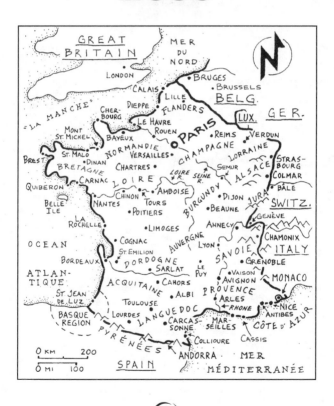

D. M. HUNT LIBRARY
FALLS VILLAGE, CONN. 06031

AVALON TRAVEL

Other ATP travel guidebooks by Rick Steves
Rick Steves' Best of Europe
Rick Steves' Europe Through the Back Door
Rick Steves' Europe 101: History and Art for the Traveler (with Gene Openshaw)
Rick Steves' Mona Winks: Self-Guided Tours of Europe's Top Museums
   (with Gene Openshaw)
Rick Steves' Postcards from Europe
Rick Steves' Germany, Austria & Switzerland
Rick Steves' Great Britain
Rick Steves' Ireland (with Pat O'Connor)
Rick Steves' Italy
Rick Steves' Scandinavia
Rick Steves' Spain & Portugal
Rick Steves' Amsterdam, Bruges & Brussels (with Gene Openshaw)
Rick Steves' Florence (with Gene Openshaw)
Rick Steves' London (with Gene Openshaw)
Rick Steves' Paris (with Steve Smith and Gene Openshaw)
Rick Steves' Rome (with Gene Openshaw)
Rick Steves' Venice (with Gene Openshaw)
Rick Steves' Phrase Books: French, German, Italian, Portuguese,
   Spanish, and French/Italian/German

Thanks to Steve's wife, Karen Lewis Smith, for her help covering French cuisine, and to Steve's son Travis for help with children's activities.

Avalon Travel Publishing, 1400 65th Street, Suite 250, Emeryville, CA 94608

Printed in the USA by R.R. Donnelley Norwest, Inc. First printing January 2003. Distributed to the book trade by Publishers Group West.

For the latest on Rick's lectures, guidebooks, tours, and public television series, contact Europe Through the Back Door, Box 2009, Edmonds, WA 98020, 425/771-8303, fax 425/771-0833, www.ricksteves.com, or e-mail: rick@ricksteves.com.

ISBN 1-56691-463-9 • ISSN 1084-4406

Europe Through the Back Door Managing Editor: Risa Laib
Europe Through the Back Door Editors: Jill Hodges, Cameron Hewitt
Avalon Travel Publishing Editor: Mia Lipman
Avalon Travel Publishing Series Manager: Laura Mazer
Copy Editor: Leslie Miller
Research Assistance: Kristen Kusnic, Chris Coleman
Production & Typesetting: Kathleen Sparkes, White Hart Design
Cover Design: Janine Lehmann
Interior Design: Linda Braun
Maps & Graphics: David C. Hoerlein, Rhonda Pelikan, Zoey Platt
Cover photo: Arc de Triomphe, Paris © Jeff Greenberg/Unicorn Stock Photos
Front matter color photos: p. i, Provence © Paul Orcutt; p. viii, Mont Saint
   Michel © Julie Coen

CONTENTS

Top Destinations in France

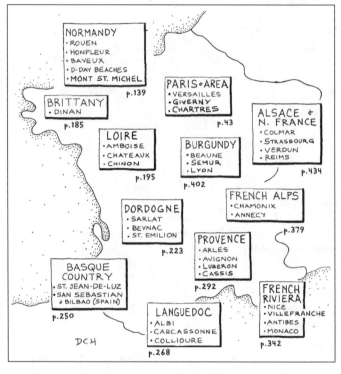

NORMANDY
- ROUEN
- HONFLEUR
- BAYEUX
- D-DAY BEACHES
- MONT ST. MICHEL

p.139

BRITTANY
- DINAN

p.185

PARIS & AREA
- VERSAILLES
- GIVERNY
- CHARTRES

p.43

ALSACE & N. FRANCE
- COLMAR
- STRASBOURG
- VERDUN
- REIMS

p.434

LOIRE
- AMBOISE
- CHATEAUX
- CHINON

p.195

BURGUNDY
- BEAUNE
- SEMUR
- LYON

p.402

FRENCH ALPS
- CHAMONIX
- ANNECY

p.379

DORDOGNE
- SARLAT
- BEYNAC
- ST. EMILION

p.223

PROVENCE
- ARLES
- AVIGNON
- LUBERON
- CASSIS

p.292

BASQUE COUNTRY
- ST. JEAN-DE-LUZ
- SAN SEBASTIAN & BILBAO (SPAIN)

p.250

FRENCH RIVIERA
- NICE
- VILLEFRANCHE
- ANTIBES
- MONACO

p.342

LANGUEDOC
- ALBI
- CARCASSONNE
- COLLIOURE

p.268

DCH

INTRODUCTION

You've made a great choice. France is Europe's most diverse, tasty, and, in many ways, exciting country to explore. It's a multi-faceted cultural fondue.

France is nearly as big as Texas, with 58 million people and more than 500 different cheeses. *Diversité* is a French forte. This country features three distinct mountain ranges (the Alps, the Pyrenees, and the Central), the different-as-night-and-day Atlantic and Mediterranean coastlines, cosmopolitan cities (such as Paris, Lyon, and Nice—all featured in this book), and sleepy villages. From its Swiss-like Alps to its *molto* Italian Riviera, and from the Spanish Pyrenees to *das* German Alsace, you can stay in France, feel like you've sampled much of Europe, and never be more than a short stroll from a good *vin rouge*.

Throughout 15 years of tour-guiding and working on this book together, Rick Steves and Francophile Steve Smith have worked hard to discover and describe France's most interesting destinations, giving you tips on how to use your time and money most efficiently. Each of our recommended destinations is a dripping forkful (complete with instructions on how to enjoy the full flavor without burning your tongue).

This book covers the predictable biggies and mixes in a healthy dose of "Back Door" intimacy. Along with seeing the Eiffel Tower, Mont St. Michel, and the French Riviera, you'll take a bike tour of the Loire, marvel at 15,000-year-old cave paintings, and ride a canoe down the lazy Dordogne River. You'll find a *magnifique* hill-town perch to catch a Provençal sunset, ride Europe's highest mountain lift over the alps, and touch the quiet Romanesque soul of village Burgundy. Just as important, you'll meet the intriguing people who run your hotel or bed-and-breakfast.

Rick Steves' France is a tour guide in your pocket—actually, two tour guides in your pocket. Destinations covered in this book are balanced to include the most famous cities and intimate villages, from jet-setting beach resorts to the traditional heartland. We've been selective, including only the most exciting sights and romantic villages. For example, there are *beaucoup de* beautiful châteaux in the Loire region. We recommend just the best. And while there are dozens of Loire towns where you could base yourself, we recommend only the top two.

The best is, of course, only our opinion. But after more than 25 busy years of travel writing, lecturing, tour-guiding, and Francophilia between us, we've developed a sixth sense for what touches the traveler's imagination.

This Information Is Accurate and Up-to-Date

This book is completely updated every year. Most publishers of guidebooks that cover a region from top to bottom can afford an update only every two or three years (and even then, it's often by letter). Since this book is selective, covering only the places we think make the top month of sightseeing, we can update it each summer. Of course, even with an annual update, things change. But, if you're traveling with the current edition of this book, we guarantee you're using the most up-to-date information available in print (for the latest, see www.ricksteves.com/update). This book will help you have an inexpensive, hassle-free trip. Use this year's edition. Saving a few bucks by traveling on old information is not smart. If you're packing an old book, you'll learn the seriousness of your mistake...in France. Your trip costs at least $10 per waking hour. Your time is valuable. This guidebook saves lots of time.

Planning Your Trip

This book is organized by destination. Each of these destinations is a mini-vacation on its own, filled with exciting sights and homey, affordable places to stay. For each chapter, you'll find the following:

Planning Your Time, a suggested schedule with thoughts on how to best use your limited time.

Orientation material, including tourist information, city transportation, and an easy-to-read map designed to make the text clear and your arrival smooth.

Sights with ratings: ▲▲▲—Don't miss; ▲▲—Try hard to see; ▲—Worthwhile if you can make it; No rating—Worth knowing about.

Sleeping and **Eating**, with our favorite hotels and restaurants, from budget bargains to worthwhile splurges.

Transportation Connections to nearby destinations by train and route tips for drivers.

The handy **appendix** includes telephone tips, a festival calendar, a climate chart, French survival phrases, and a brief stroll through French history.

Browse through this book, choose your favorite destinations, and link them up. You'll travel like a temporary local, getting the absolute most out of every mile, minute, and dollar. You won't waste time on mediocre sights because, unlike other guidebooks, we cover only the best. Since your major financial pitfall is lousy, expensive hotels, we've worked hard to assemble the best accommodation values for each stop. As you travel the route we know and love, we're happy you'll be meeting some of our favorite French people.

Trip Costs

Five components make up your total trip cost: airfare, surface transportation, room and board, sightseeing/entertainment, and shopping/miscellany.

Airfare: Don't try to sort through the mess. Find and use a good travel agent. A basic round-trip United States-to-Paris flight costs $700 to $1,100 (even cheaper in winter), depending on where you fly from and when. Always consider saving time and money in Europe by flying "open jaw" (into one city and out of another). Flying into Nice and out of Paris costs roughly the same as flying round-trip to Paris. (Many find relaxed, Mediterranean Nice far easier than Paris as a starting point for their trip.) You can find cheaper round-trip flights from the United States to London or Amsterdam, but the cost of train tickets (to get you back to London or Amsterdam for your flight home) eliminate most of your savings.

Within France, inexpensive flights can get you from Paris or Nice to all major cities, such as Strasbourg, Toulouse, Lyon, and Bordeaux.

Surface Transportation: For a three-week whirlwind trip of our recommended destinations, allow $500 per person for public transportation (trains and key buses), or $600 per person (based on 2 people sharing) for a three-week car rental, tolls, gas, and insurance. Car rental is cheapest if arranged from the United States. Train passes are normally available only outside of Europe. You may save money by simply buying tickets as you go (see "Transportation," below).

Room and Board: You can thrive in France on $75 a day per person for room and board (allow $85 a day for Paris). A $75-a-day budget allows $10 for lunch, $20 for dinner, and $45 for lodging (based on 2 people splitting the cost of a $90 double room that includes breakfast). That's definitely doable. Students and tightwads do it on $45 a day ($25 per bed, $20 for meals and snacks). But budget sleeping and eating requires the skills and information covered later in this chapter (and in much greater depth in *Rick Steves' Europe Through the Back Door*).

Sightseeing and Entertainment: In big cities, figure $5 to $8 per major sight (Arc de Triomphe-$7, Louvre-$7.50), $2 for minor ones (climbing church towers), $10 for guided walks, and $25 for bus tours and splurge experiences (concerts in Paris' Sainte-Chapelle or a ride on the Chamonix gondola). An overall average of $15 a day works for most. Don't skimp here. After all, this category directly powers most of the experiences all the other expenses are designed to make possible.

Shopping and Miscellany: Figure $2 per ice-cream cone,

coffee, or soft drink. Shopping can vary in cost from nearly nothing to a small fortune. Good budget travelers find that this category has little to do with assembling a trip full of lifelong and wonderful memories.

Prices, Times, and Discounts

The prices in this book, as well as the hours and telephone numbers, are accurate as of mid-2002. But Europe is always changing, and we know you'll understand that this, like any other guidebook, starts to yellow even before it's printed.

In Europe, you'll be using the 24-hour clock. After 12:00 noon, keep going—13:00, 14:00, and so on. For anything over 12, subtract 12 and add p.m. (for example, 14:00 is 2 p.m.).

While discounts for sights and transportation generally are not listed in this book, seniors (60 and over) and students (with International Student Identification Cards; contact STA Travel, below) may get discounts—but only by asking. Those under 18 nearly always receive generous discounts. Teachers with an International Teacher ID Card are also given discounts or free admission to many sights. To get a Teacher or Student ID Card, contact STA Travel (U.S. tel. 800/777-0112, www .statravel.com or www.isic.org).

Exchange Rates

We've priced things throughout this book in the local currency: the euro.

> 1 euro (€) = about $1.

One euro is broken down into 100 cents. You'll find coins ranging from 1 cent to 2 euros, and bills from 5 euros to 500 euros.

When to Go

Late spring and fall are best, with generally good weather and lighter crowds (except during holiday weekends—for details, see "Holiday Weekends" on page 8)—though summer brings festivals, reliable weather, and long opening hours at sights. Europeans vacation in July and August, jamming the Riviera and the Alps (worst July 15–Aug 20), but leaving the rest of the country reasonably tranquil. And, while many French businesses close in August, the traveler hardly notices. Winter travel is fine for Paris, but you'll find smaller cities and villages buttoned up tight. Winter weather is gray, noticeably milder in the south (unless the wind is blowing), and colder and wetter in the north. Sights and tourist information offices keep shorter hours, and some tourist activities (like English-language castle tours) vanish altogether.

Thanks to France's relatively mild climate, fields of flowers greet the traveler much of the year:

April–May: Brilliant yellow colza (rapeseed) crops bloom, mostly in the north. Wild red poppies *(coquelicots)* begin sprouting in the south.

June: Red poppies pop up throughout the country. Lavender begins to bloom in the hills of Provence, generally during the last week of the month.

July: Lavender is in full swing in Provence, and sunflowers are awakening. Cities, towns, and villages everywhere overflow with carefully tended flowers.

August–September: Sunflowers flourish, north and south.

October: In the latter half of the month, the countryside glistens with fall colors, as most trees are deciduous. Vineyards go for the gold.

Sightseeing Priorities

Depending on the length of your trip, here are our recommended priorities.

3 days:	Paris and, if you like, Versailles
5 days, add:	Normandy
7 days, add:	The Loire
10 days, add:	Dordogne, Carcassonne
15 days, add:	Provence, the Riviera
18 days, add:	Burgundy, Chamonix
21 days, add:	Alsace, Champagne
23 days, add:	Basque Country

For a day-by-day itinerary of this three-week trip—geared for drivers and train travelers—see "Whirlwind Three-Week Trip," below.

Red Tape and Business Hours

You need a passport, but no visa or shots, to travel in France.

You'll find much of rural France closed weekdays from noon to 14:00 (lunch is sacred). On Sunday and during the numerous holidays (see below), most businesses are closed (family is sacred), though small markets such as *boulangeries* (bakeries) are open until noon, and museums are open all day. On Monday, many businesses are closed until 14:00 and often all day. Smaller towns are often quiet and downright boring on Sundays and Mondays. Saturdays are like weekdays. Note that on any day, sights stop admitting people 30 to 60 minutes before they close.

Whirlwind (Kamikaze) Three-Week Trip of France by Car or Train

Day By Car

1   Fly into Paris, pick up car, visit Giverny and/or Rouen, overnight in Honfleur (save Paris sightseeing for end of trip).

2   9:00–Depart Honfleur, 10:00–Caen World War II Museum, 12:30–Drive to Arromanches for lunch and museum, 15:30–American cemetery, 17:00–Pointe du Hoc, 17:45–German cemetery, dinner and overnight in Bayeux.

3   9:00–Bayeux tapestry and church, 12:00–Drive to Dinan, 13:00–Arrive in Dinan for a quick look at Brittany, 17:00–Drive to Mont St. Michel, sleep on Mont St. Michel.

4   10:00–Drive to Loire, 14:30–Tour Chambord, 17:00–Arrive in Amboise, sleep in Amboise.

5   8:45–Depart Amboise, 9:00–Chenonceaux, 11:30–Cheverny château and lunch, 14:00–Possible stop in Chaumont, back in Amboise for Leonardo's house and free time in town, sleep in Amboise.

6   8:30–Depart Amboise, short stop in Chauvigny, lunch at Mortemart, 13:30–Oradour-sur-Glane, 14:30–Drive to Beynac, 17:30–Wander Beynac or tour its castle, dinner and overnight in Beynac.

7   9:00–Browse the town and market of Sarlat, 12:00–Font-de-Gaume tour, 14:00–More caves, castles, or canoe extravaganza, dinner and sleep in Beynac.

8   9:00–Depart Beynac, 10:00–Short stop at Cahors bridge, 12:30–Arrive in Albi, have lunch, 14:00–Tour church and Toulouse-Lautrec Museum, 16:00–Depart for Carcassonne, 18:00–Explore, have dinner, and sleep in Carcassonne.

9   10:30–Depart Carcassonne, 11:00–Lastours castles or Minerve, 15:30–Pont du Gard, 16:30–Drive to Arles, 17:30–Set up for evening in Arles.

10   All day for Arles and Avignon, evening back in Arles.

11   8:30–Depart Arles, 9:00–Les Baux, 11:00–Depart Les Baux, 12:00–Lunch and wander in Isle sur la Sorgue, 14:00–Luberon hill-town drive, 16:00–Depart for the Riviera, 19:00–Arrive in Nice or Antibes.

12   Sightsee in Nice and Monaco, then sleep in Nice or Antibes.

13 Morning free, 12:00–Drive north, sleep in Lyon.

14 Morning drive north, long stop in Annecy, in afternoon arrive in Chamonix. With clear weather, do Aiguille du Midi.

15 All day for the Alps.

16 9:00–Depart Chamonix, 12:00–Lunch in Brançion, 14:00–Depart, 15:00–Arrive in Beaune for Hôtel Dieu and wine-tasting, sleep in Beaune.

17 9:00–Depart for Burgundy village treats or get to Alsace early. Arrive in Colmar after 3.5-hour drive.

18 9:00–Unterlinden Museum, 10:00–Free in town, 14:00–Wine Road villages, evening back in Colmar.

19 8:00–Depart Colmar, 12:00–Lunch, tour Verdun battlefield, 15:00–Depart, 16:00–Arrive Reims, church and champagne, 18:00–Turn in car at Reims, picnic-dinner celebration on train to Paris, 21:00–Collapse in Paris hotel.

20 Sightsee Paris, trip over.

continued on next page

Whirlwind Trip (continued)
Day By Train and Bus
All times are approximate. Fewer buses and trains run on Sunday.

1   Fly into Paris, find your hotel, go for an afternoon walk.

2   All day to sightsee in Paris.

3   Head to Giverny in morning (about 8:00, depart Paris by train to Vernon, check bags at station, then bus or taxi to Giverny), early afternoon train to Rouen (check bags at station), sightsee there, then head to Honfleur (from Rouen, take late afternoon train to Le Havre—about 16:15—then catch bus to Honfleur—about 17:30), sleep in Honfleur.

4   Morning in Honfleur, midday bus to Caen, then train to Bayeux, see tapestries in the afternoon. Sleep in Bayeux.

5   All day for D-Day beaches by minivan excursion or one-day car rental, late afternoon train (about 17:00) to Pontorson, taxi to Mont St. Michel, sleep on Mont St. Michel.

6   Tour abbey and walk around the island, 11:00–Bus to Pontorson, 12:00–Train to Caen, transfer to Tours, transfer to Amboise, sleep in Amboise.

7   All day to tour the Loire, sleep in Amboise.

8   Early-morning train to Sarlat (with transfers at Tours and Bordeaux St. Jean), afternoon in Sarlat, sleep in Sarlat or Beynac (note: it's possible to visit Oradour-sur-Glane on this day; see Amboise and Sarlat transportation connections on pages 209 and 234).

9   All day in the Dordogne, morning train to Les Eyzies (Grotte de Font-de-Gaume), taxi back, afternoon canoe trip, sleep in Sarlat or Beynac.

Holiday Weekends
Be wary of holiday weekends, which make many places busier than summer with crowded trains, roadways, and hotels. The French are experts at the four-day getaway, and you're no match when it comes to driving and hotel-finding during these peak periods. In 2003, these dates will be busy anywhere: Easter week (April 19–26), Labor Day weekend (May 1–4), VE Day (May 8–10), Ascension weekend (May 29–31), Pentecost weekend (June 7–9), Bastille Day (July 14), Assumption (Aug 15), All Saints' Day weekend (Oct 30–Nov 1), Armistice Day (Nov 11), and the winter holidays (late Dec–early Jan). Many sights close on the actual holiday (check with the local TI).

10 Morning train to Carcassonne (transfer in Souillac or Bordeaux and in Toulouse), afternoon wall walk, sleep in Carcassonne.

11 Morning train to Arles, sightsee and sleep in Arles.

12 Morning train to Nîmes, late-morning bus to Pont du Gard (about 11:00), early-afternoon bus from Pont du Gard to Avignon (about 13:30), afternoon in Avignon, evening train back to Arles, sleep in Arles.

13 Morning bus to Les Baux (about 8:30), midday return to Arles, afternoon train to Nice, stroll the promenade, sleep on the Riviera.

14 Morning in Nice's old city, bus to Monaco, see casino and Changing of the Guard, return to Nice for beach time or Chagall museum, sleep in Nice.

15 Take a vacation from your vacation and spend a day on the beach. Spend part of the day in Antibes or take the bus to St. Paul-de-Vence.

16 Choose between urban or rural: Morning train to Lyon, visit Lyon, sleep there. Or take the scenic train to Digne/Grenoble and sleep in a remote mountain village en route (see "Inland Hill Towns of the Riviera," page 376).

17 Morning in Lyon, midday train to Annecy, visit Annecy, late-afternoon train to Chamonix, sleep in Chamonix. Or train from your remote village to Grenoble and Annecy (visit if time allows), then train to Chamonix.

18 All day to hike in the Alps, sleep in Chamonix.

19 Train to Colmar, sleep in Colmar.

20 All day in Alsace, sleep in Colmar (or evening train to Paris if you must leave the next day).

21 Train to Paris.

Banking

Bring your ATM, credit, or debit card, along with a couple hundred dollars in cash as a backup. Traveler's checks are a waste of your time and money.

The best and easiest way to get cash in euros is to use the omnipresent French bank machines (always open, lower fees, quick processing; you'll need a PIN code—numbers only, no letters—with your Visa or MasterCard). Before you go, verify with your bank that your card will work. Bring two cards in case one gets damaged. "Cash machines" in French are signed *distributeur des billets*, but the French just say "distributeur"

(pron. dee-stree-bew-toor); look also for signs indicating *point
d'argent* (pron. pwan dar-zhahn).

Just like at home, credit or debit cards work easily at hotels,
restaurants, and shops, but small businesses (like bed-and-breakfasts) accept payment only in local currency. Smart travelers function with hard local cash.

VAT Refunds for Shoppers

Wrapped into the purchase price of your French souvenirs is a
Value Added Tax (VAT) of 16.4 percent. If you make a purchase
of more than €175 in France at a store that participates in the
VAT refund scheme, you're entitled to get most of that tax back.
Personally, we've never felt that VAT refunds are worth the
hassle, but if you do, here's the scoop.

If you're lucky, the merchant will subtract the tax when you
make your purchase (this is more likely to occur if the store ships
the goods to your home). Otherwise, you'll need to:

Get the paperwork. Have the merchant completely fill out
the necessary refund document, called a "cheque." You'll have to
present your passport at the store.

Have your cheque(s) stamped at the border at your last stop
in the European Union by the customs agent who deals with
VAT refunds. It's best to keep your purchases in your carry-on
for viewing, but if they're too large or dangerous (such as knives)
to carry on, then track down the proper customs agent to inspect
them before you check your bag. You're not supposed to use
your purchased goods before you leave. If you show up at customs wearing your chic new outfit, officials might look the other
way—or deny you a refund.

To collect your refund, you'll need to return your stamped
documents to the retailer or its representative. Many merchants
work with a service, such as Global Refund or Cashback, which
have offices at major airports, ports, or border crossings. These services, which extract a 4 percent fee, can refund your money immediately in your currency of choice or credit your card (within 2 billing
cycles). If you have to deal directly with the retailer, mail the store
your stamped documents and then wait. It could take months.

The Language Barrier and
That French Attitude

You've no doubt heard that the French are "mean and cold and
refuse to speak English." This is an out-of-date preconception
left over from the de Gaulle days. The French are as sincere
as any other people. Parisians are no more disagreeable than
New Yorkers. And, without any doubt, the French speak more

English than Americans speak French. Be reasonable in your expectations: Waiters are paid to be efficient, not chatty. And small-town French postal clerks are every bit as speedy, cheery, and multilingual as ours are back home.

The biggest mistake most Americans make when traveling in France is trying to do too much with limited time. Hurried, impatient travelers who miss the subtle pleasures of people-watching from a sun-dappled café and taking walks in the countryside often misinterpret French attitudes. By slowing your pace and making an effort to understand French culture, you're much more likely to have a richer experience. The French take great pride in their culture, clinging to their belief in cultural superiority despite the fact that they're no longer a world superpower. Let's face it—it's tough to keep on smiling when you've been crushed by a Big Mac, Mickey-Moused by Disney, and drowned in instant coffee.

Your hosts are cold only if you decide to see them that way. Polite and formal, they respect the fine points of culture and tradition. In France, strolling down the street with a big grin on your face (and saying hello to people you don't know) is a sign of senility, not friendliness (seriously). They think that Americans, while friendly, are hesitant to pursue more serious friendships. Recognize sincerity and look for kindness. Give them the benefit of the doubt.

Communication difficulties are exaggerated. To hurdle the language barrier, bring a small English/French dictionary, a phrase book (look for ours), a menu reader, and a good supply of patience. If you learn only five phrases, learn and use these: *bonjour* (good day), *pardon* (pardon me), *s'il vous plaît* (please), *merci* (thank you), and *au revoir* (good-bye). The French place great importance on politeness. Begin every encounter with "*Bonjour, madame/monsieur*" and end every encounter with "*Au revoir, madame/monsieur.*"

The French are language perfectionists—they take their language (and other languages) seriously. They often speak more English than they let on. This isn't a tourist-baiting tactic, but timidity on their part to speak another language less than fluently. Start any conversation with "*Bonjour, madame/monsieur. Parlez-vous anglais?*" and hope they speak more English than you speak French. In transactions, a small notepad and pen minimize misunderstandings about prices. Have vendors write down the price.

Travel Smart

Your trip to France is like a complex play—easier to follow and really appreciate on a second viewing. While no one does the same trip twice to gain that advantage, reading this book in its entirety before your trip accomplishes much the same thing.

Reread this book as you travel, and visit local tourist

information offices. Upon arrival in a new town, lay the ground-work for a smooth departure. Slow down and ask questions. Most locals are eager to tell you about their town's history and point you in their idea of the right direction. Buy a phone card and use it for reservations and confirmations. Wear your money belt. Those who expect to travel smart, do.

Train travelers: Look for the tips on trains and buses later in this chapter. Drivers: Read our driving tips and study the examples of road signs in this chapter.

Maximize rootedness by minimizing one-night stands. Mix intense and relaxed periods. Every trip (and every traveler) needs at least a few slack days. Pace yourself. Assume you will return.

As you peruse this book, note special days (holidays, festivals, market days, and days when sights are closed). Plan ahead for laundry, post office chores, picnics, and Sundays (particularly if traveling by train). Sundays have pros and cons, as they do for travelers in the United States (special events and weekly markets, limited hours, shops and banks closed, limited public transportation, no rush hours). Saturdays are virtually weekdays. Popular places are even more popular on weekends and inundated on three-day weekends (most common in May).

Tourist Information

Except in Paris, the tourist information office is your best first stop in any new city. If you're arriving in town after the office closes, try calling ahead or picking up a map in a neighboring town. In this book, we refer to tourist offices as TIs (for Tourist Information). Throughout France, you'll find TIs are usually well-organized and have English-speaking staff. Most will help you find a room by calling hotels (for a small fee) or giving you a complete listing of available bed-and-breakfasts. Towns with a lot of tourism generally have English-speaking guides available for private hire (about $100 for a 2-hr guided town walk).

The French call TIs by different names. *Office de Tourisme* and *Bureau de Tourisme* are used in cities, while *Syndicat d'Initiative* or *Information Touristique* are used in small towns. Also look for *Accueil* signs in airports and at popular sights. These are info booths staffed with seasonal helpers who provide tourists with limited, though generally sufficient, information. TIs are often closed from noon to 14:00.

Tourist Offices, U.S. Addresses

France's national tourist offices in the United States are a wealth of information. Before your trip, request any specific information you may want (such as city maps and schedules of upcoming festivals).

French Government Tourist Office: For questions and brochures (on regions, barging, and the wine country), call 410/286-8310. Ask for the Discovery Guide. Materials delivered in 4–6 weeks are free; there's a $4 shipping fee for information delivered in 5–10 days.

They share a Web site, www.franceguide.com, and their offices are...

In New York: 444 Madison Ave., 16th floor, New York, NY 10022, fax 212/838-7855, e-mail: info@francetourism.com.

In Illinois: 676 N. Michigan Ave. #3360, Chicago, IL 60611-2819, fax 312/337-6339, e-mail: fgto@mcs.net.

In California: 9454 Wilshire Blvd. #715, Beverly Hills, CA 90212, fax 310/276-2835, e-mail: fgto@gte.net.

Recommended Guidebooks

Consider some supplemental travel information, especially if you're traveling beyond our recommended destinations. Considering the improvements they'll make in your $3,000 vacation, $25 or $35 for extra maps and books is money well spent. One simple budget tip can easily save the price of an extra guidebook.

France: Lonely Planet's *France* is well-researched, with good maps and hotel recommendations for low- to moderate-budget travelers (but it's not updated annually). The highly opinionated, annually updated *Let's Go: France* (St. Martin's Press) is ideal for students and vagabonds. The popular, skinny, green Michelin guides are dry but informative, especially for drivers. They're known for their city and sightseeing maps and for their concise, helpful information on all major sights. English editions, covering most of the regions you'll want to visit, are sold in France for about €13 (or $20 in the U.S.). Consider *Rick Steves' Paris* (see below). Of the multitude of other guidebooks on France and Paris, many are high on facts and low on opinion, guts, or personality. To better understand the French, read *French or Foe* (by Polly Platt) and *Fragile Glory* (by Richard Bernstein). *The Course of French History* (by Pierre Goubert) provides a reasonably succinct and readable summary of French history.

Rick Steves' Books and Videos

Rick Steves' Europe Through the Back Door 2003 gives you budget travel tips on minimizing jet lag, packing light, planning your itinerary, traveling by car or train, finding budget beds without reservations, changing money, avoiding rip-offs, outsmarting thieves, using cell phones, hurdling the language barrier, staying healthy, taking great photographs, using your bidet, and lots more. The book also includes chapters on 35 of Rick's favorite "Back Doors."

Rick Steves' Country Guides are a series of eight

guidebooks—including this book—covering the Best of Europe, Great Britain, Ireland, Germany/Austria/Switzerland, Italy, Spain/ Portugal, and Scandinavia. All are updated annually; most are available in bookstores in December, the rest in January.

Rick's **City Guides** feature Rome, Venice, Florence, Paris, London, and—new for 2003—*Rick Steves' Amsterdam, Bruges & Brussels*. These practical guides offer in-depth coverage of the sights, hotels, restaurants, and nightlife in these grand cities along with illustrated tours of their great museums. They're updated annually and come out in December and January.

Rick Steves' Europe 101: History and Art for the Traveler (with Gene Openshaw, 2000) gives you the story of Europe's people, history, and art. Written for smart people who were sleeping in their history and art classes before they knew they were going to Europe, *101* really helps Europe's sights come alive.

Rick Steves' Mona Winks (with Gene Openshaw, 2001) gives you fun, easy-to-follow, self-guided tours of Europe's top 25 museums and cultural sites, including Paris' Louvre, Orsay, Rodin Museum, Palace of Versailles, and a walk through historic Paris.

The *Rick Steves' French Phrase Book* is a fun, practical tool for independent budget travelers. This handy book has everything you'll need while traveling in France, including a menu decoder, conversational starters for connecting with locals, and an easy-to-follow telephone template for making hotel reservations.

Rick's new public television series, *Rick Steves' Europe*, keeps churning out shows. Of 82 episodes (from the new series and from *Travels in Europe with Rick Steves*), three shows are on Paris and seven are on other parts of France. These air nationally on public television and the Travel Channel. They're also available in information-packed home videos and DVDs (order online at www.ricksteves.com or call us at 425/771-8303 for our free newsletter/catalog).

Rick Steves' Postcards from Europe, Rick's autobiographical book, packs 25 years of travel anecdotes and insights into the ultimate 2,000-mile European adventure. Through his guidebooks, Rick shares his favorite European discoveries with you. *Postcards* (set partly in France) introduces you to his favorite European friends.

All of Rick's books are published by Avalon Travel Publishing (www.travelmatters.com).

Maps

The black-and-white maps in this book, drawn by Dave Hoerlein, are concise and simple. Dave, who is well-traveled in France, designed the maps to help you locate recommended places and reach

TIs, where you'll find more in-depth maps (often free) of cities or regions. Also see the handy color city and Métro maps in this book.

Consider the new Rick Steves' France Planning Map, which shows France on one side and Paris on the other. Designed for the traveler, it lists sightseeing destinations prominently. For an all-Europe trip, consider the Rick Steves' Europe Planning Map (order either map online at www.ricksteves.com, or call 425/771-8303 for our free newsletter/catalog).

Don't skimp on maps. Michelin maps are available throughout France at bookstores, newsstands, and gas stations (for €5, half the U.S. price). Train travelers can do fine with Michelin's #989 France map (1:1,000,000). For better detail, pick up the yellow 1:200,000-scale maps as you travel. Drivers should consider the soft-cover Michelin France atlas (the entire country at 1:200,000, well-organized in a $20 book with an index and maps of major cities). Learn the Michelin key to get the most sightseeing value out of their maps.

Tours of France by Rick Steves and Steve Smith

Travel agents can tell you about all the normal tours, but they won't tell you about ours. At Europe Through the Back Door, we organize and lead tours covering the highlights of this book. Choose from "Paris and the Heart of France" (14 days), "Provence and the South of France" (15 days), and the "Best of Village France" (18 days). These depart each year from April through October, are limited to 22 to 26 people per group, and have two guides and big, roomy buses. We also offer one-week getaways to Paris (20 people maximum). For details, call us at 425/771-8303 or check www.ricksteves.com.

Transportation

By Car or Train?

Cars are best for three or more traveling together (especially families with small kids), those packing heavy, and those scouring the countryside. Trains and buses are best for solo travelers, blitz tourists, and city-to-city travelers. Train stations are usually centrally located in cities, making hotel-hunting and sightseeing easy. But because so many of your destinations are likely to be small places, such as Honfleur, Mont St. Michel, D-Day beaches, Loire châteaux, Dordogne caves, and villages in Provence and Burgundy, trains and buses require great patience, planning, and time. If relying on public transportation, seriously evaluate the value of a train or bus detour and focus on fewer key destinations.

The French Rail System

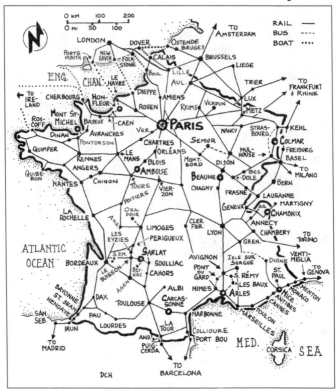

Trains

France's rail system (SNCF) sets the pace in Europe. Its super TGV (*train à grande vitesse*; pron. tay zhay vay) system has inspired bullet trains throughout the world. The TGV runs at 170 to 220 mph. Its rails are fused into one long, continuous track for a faster and smoother ride. The TGV has changed commuting patterns in much of France and put most of the country within day-trip distance of Paris. The Eurostar English Channel tunnel train to Britain and the Thalys bullet train to Brussels are two more links in the grand European train system of the 21st century. The fastest TGV Mediterranean line opened in 2001, with trains screaming from Paris' city center and Charles de Gaulle airport to Avignon (in Provence) in 2.5 hours.

Schedules change by season, weekday, and weekend. Verify train schedules shown in this book (to study ahead on the Web,

Cost of Rail Passes

Prices listed are for 2002. My free *Rick Steves' Guide to European Railpasses* has the latest on 2003 prices. To get the railpass guide, call us at 425/771-8303 or visit www.ricksteves.com/rail. France-only passes are not valid on Thalys or Paris-Berlin night train.

FRANCE FLEXIPASS

	Adult 1st class	Adult 2nd class	Senior 1st class	Youth 1st class	Youth 2nd class
Any 4 days in 1 month	$240	$210	$224	$170	$148
Extra rail days (max 6)	30	30	30	25	18

Seniors 60+, Youth under 26. Kids 4–11 half adult fare.

FRANCE FLEXI SAVERPASS

	Adult 1st cl.	Adult 2nd cl.	Senior 1st cl.
Any 4 days in 1 month	$196	$171	$179
Extra rail days (max 6)	25	25	20

Prices are per person for two or more traveling together. OK to mix kids and adults (kids 4–11 half adult fare) but senior rates (age 60+) cannot be mixed with adults or kids on the same pass.

France: The map shows approximate point-to-point one-way 2nd class rail fares in $US. 1st class costs 50% more. Add up fares for your itinerary to see if a railpass will save you money.

FRANCE RAIL & DRIVE PASS

Any 3 days of rail and 2 days of Avis rental car in 1 month.

Car category	1st cl	2nd cl	Extra car day
Economy	$205	$175	$37
Compact	215	185	47
Intermediate	225	195	51
Small automatic	237	205	67

Rail and Drive prices are approximate per person, two traveling together. Solo travelers pay about $100 extra, third and fourth members of a group need only buy the equivalent flexi railpass. Extra rail days (7 max) cost $30 per day for first or second class. You can add up to 6 extra car days. To order a France Rail & Drive pass, call your travel agent or Rail Europe at 800/438-7245.

EURAIL SELECTPASSES

This pass covers travel in three adjacent countries (for instance: France–Benelux–Germany). For additional country choices in 2003, visit www.ricksteves.com/rail.

	1st cl Selectpass	1st cl Saverpass	2nd cl Youthpass
5 days in 2 months	$346	$294	$243
6 days in 2 months	380	322	266
8 days in 2 months	444	378	310
10 days in 2 months	502	428	352

Saverpass: price is per person for 2 or more adults traveling together at all times.
Youthpasses: Under age 26 only. Kids 4-11 pay half adult fare; under 4: free.

Train Tips

- Arrive at the station with plenty of time before your departure to find the right platform, confirm connections, and so on. In small towns, your train may depart before the station opens; go directly to the tracks and find the overhead sign that confirms your train stops at that track.
- Check schedules in advance. Upon arrival at a station, find out your departure possibilities. Large stations have a separate information window or office; at small stations, the regular ticket office gives information.
- Write the date on your "flexi" pass each day you travel.
- Validate tickets (not passes) and reservations in orange machines before boarding. If you're traveling with a pass and have a reservation for a certain trip, you must validate the reservation.
- Before getting on a train, confirm that it's going where you think it is. For example, ask the conductor or any local passenger, *"À Bayeux?"* (pron. ah Bayeux; meaning, "To Bayeux?").
- Some trains split cars en route. Make sure your train car is continuing to your destination by asking, *"Cette voiture va à Bayeux?"* (pron. set vwa-ture vah ah Bayeux; meaning, "This car goes to Bayeux?").
- If a seat is reserved, it will be labeled *réservé*, with the cities to and from which it is reserved.
- Verify with the conductor all transfers you must make (*"Correspondance à?"*; meaning, "Transfer where?").

check http://bahn.hafas.de/bin/query.exe/en). The nationwide information line for train schedules and reservations is tel. 08 36 35 35 35 or 08 92 35 35 39 (the message prompts you to push "9" for a sales agent—ask for an English-speaking agent and hope for the best). This incredibly helpful, timesaving service costs €0.35 per minute from anywhere in France (call to confirm schedules and make TGV reservations, allow 5 min per call). The time and energy you save easily justifies the telephone torture, particularly when making seat reservations (phoned reservations must be picked up at least 30 min prior to departure). Bigger stations have helpful information agents (often in red vests) roaming the station and/or at *Accueil* offices or booths. They're capable of answering rail questions more quickly than the information or ticket windows.

You can save big money with a France Railpass (available only outside France, through travel agents, or Europe Through the Back

- To guard against theft, keep your bags right overhead; don't store them on the racks at the end of the car.
- Note your arrival time so you'll be ready to get off.
- Use the trains' free WCs before you get off (a bird in the hand...).

Bus Tips
- Read the train tips above and use those that apply.
- TIs often have regional bus schedules and can help plan your trip.
- Service is sparse on Sunday. Wednesday bus schedules are often different during the school year.
- Be at stops at least five minutes early.
- On schedules, *en semaine* means Monday through Saturday.

Key Phrases
- *Bonjour, monsieur/madame, parlez vous anglais?* Pronounced: bohn-zhoor, muhs-yur/mah-dahm, par-lay-voo ahn-glay? Meaning: Hello, sir/madame, do you speak English?
- *Je voudrais un départ pour* ___ (destination), *pour le* ___ (date), *vers* ___ (general time of day), *la plus direct possible.* Pronounced: zhuh voo-dray day-par poor ___ (destination), poor luh ___ (date), vayr ___ (time), lah ploo dee-rek poh-see-bluh. Meaning/Example: I would like a departure for Amboise, on 23 May, about 9:00, the most direct way possible.

Door; call us at 425/771-8303 for our free railpass guide, or find it at www.ricksteves.com). For roughly the cost of a Paris–Avignon–Paris ticket, the France Railpass offers four days of travel (within a month) anywhere in France. You can add up to six additional days for the cost of a two-hour ride each. (The Flexi Saver gives 2 people traveling together a 20 percent discount.) Each day of use allows you to take as many trips as you want in a 24-hour period (you could go from Paris to Chartres, see the cathedral, then continue to Avignon, stay a few hours, and end in Nice—though we don't recommend it). Buy second-class tickets in France for shorter trips and spend your valuable railpass days wisely.

If traveling *sans* railpass, inquire about the many point-to-point discount fares possible (for youths, those over 60, married couples, families, travel during off-peak hours, and more). While Eurailers over 26 automatically travel first class, those buying individual tickets should remember that second-class tickets, available to people of any age, provide the same transportation for 33 percent less (and many regional trains to less-trafficked places often have only second-class cars). Adults (but not seniors) also have a choice of first or second class with the France Railpass.

Reservations, while generally unnecessary for non-TGV trains, are advisable during busy times (e.g., Fri and Sun afternoons, weekday rush hours, and particularly holiday weekends; see "Holiday Weekends," above). Reservations are required for any TGV train (usually about €3, more during peak periods) and for *couchettes* (berths, €15) on night trains. Even railpass-holders need reservations for the TGV trains. To avoid the more expensive reservation fees, avoid traveling at peak times; ask at the station. Validate (*composter*, pron. cohm-poh-stay) all train tickets and reservations in the orange machines located before the platforms. (Do not *composte* your railpass—but do validate it at a ticket window before the first time you use it.) Watch others and imitate.

For mixing train and bike travel, ask at stations for information booklets *(Train + Velo)*.

Cars, Rail 'n' Drive Passes, and Buses

Car rental is cheapest if arranged in advance through your home-town travel agent. The best rates are weekly, with unlimited mileage or leasing (see below). You can pick up and drop off in moderate to larger cities anytime. Big companies have offices in more cities and towns. Small rental companies can be cheaper, but aren't as flexible.

You can rent a car on the spot just about anywhere. In many cases, this is a worthwhile splurge. All you need is your American driver's license, plus money (about €60/day, with 100 kilometers/60 miles included). If you only want a car for a day (e.g., for D-Day beaches or Loire châteaux-hopping), you'll find it cheaper to take care of in France, as most U.S.-arranged rentals have a three-day minimum (which is still cheaper than 2 days of a car rental arranged in Europe).

When you drive a rental car, you are liable for its replacement value. CDW (Collision-Damage Waiver) insurance gives you the peace of mind that comes with zero- or low-deductible coverage for about $15 a day. A few "gold" credit cards provide this coverage for free if you use their card for the rental; quiz your credit-card company on the worst-case scenario. Or consider the $6-a-day policy offered by Travel Guard (U.S. tel. 800/826-1300, www.travelguard.com).

For a trip of three weeks or more, leasing is a bargain. By technically buying and then selling back the car, you save lots of money on tax and insurance (CDW is included). Leasing, which you should arrange from the United States, usually requires a 22-day minimum contract, but Europe by Car leases cars in France for as few as 17 days for $500 (U.S. tel. 800/223-1516, www.europebycar.com).

Rail 'n' drive passes allow you to mix car and train travel economically (available only outside of France, from your travel agent). Generally, big-city connections are best done by train, and rural regions are best done by car. With a rail 'n' drive pass, you get an economic "flexi" railpass with "flexi" car days. This allows you to combine rail and drive into one pass—you can take advantage of the high speed and comfort of the TGV trains for longer trips, and rent a car for as little as one day at a time for those regions that are difficult to get around in without one (such as the Loire, the Dordogne, and Provence), all for a very reasonable package price. Within the same country, you can pick up a car in one city and drop it off in another city without problems. While you're only required to reserve the first car day, it's safer to reserve all days, as cars are not always available on short notice.

Regional buses take over where the trains stop. You can get nearly anywhere by rail and bus if you're well-organized, patient, and allow enough time. Review our bus schedule information and always verify times at the local tourist office or bus station, calling ahead when possible. A few bus lines are run by SNCF (France's rail system) and are included with your railpass (show your railpass at the station to get a free bus ticket), but most bus lines are independent of the rail system and are not covered by railpasses. Train stations often have bus information where train-to-bus connections are important—and vice versa for bus companies. On Sunday, regional bus service virtually disappears.

Regional minivan excursions offer organized day tours of regions where bus and train service is useless. For the D-Day beaches, châteaux of the Loire Valley, Dordogne Valley villages and caves, Languedoc, the *Route du Vin* in the Alsace, and wine-tasting in Burgundy, we list companies providing this helpful service at reasonable rates. Some of these minivan excursions offer just transportation between the sights; others add a running commentary and regional history.

Driving

An international driver's license is not necessary in France. Seat belts are mandatory, and children under age 10 must be in the back seat. Gas *(essence)* is expensive—about $4.50 per gallon. Diesel *(gazole)* is less—about $3.50 per gallon. Rent a diesel car if you can. Gas is most expensive on autoroutes and cheapest at big

Driving in France: Distance and Time

supermarkets (closed at night and on Sunday). Many gas stations close on Sunday.

Go metric. A liter is about a quart, four to a gallon. A kilometer is six-tenths of a mile. We figure kilometers to miles by cutting them in half and adding back 10 percent of the original (120 km: 60 + 12 = 72 miles, 300 km: 150 + 30 = 180 miles).

Four hours of autoroute tolls cost about €20, but the alternative to these super "feeways" is often being marooned in rural traffic. Autoroutes usually save enough time, gas, and nausea to justify the splurge. Mix high-speed "autorouting" with scenic country-road rambling (be careful of sluggish tractors on country roads). You'll usually take a ticket when entering an autoroute and pay when you leave, though shorter sections have periodic unmanned toll booths, which you can pay by dropping coins into a basket (change given; keep a good supply of coins in your ashtray)

Quick-and-Dirty Road Sign Translation

Céder le Passage:	Yield
Centre Commercial:	Grouping of large, suburban stores (not city center)
Centre-Ville:	City center
Doublage Interdit:	No passing
Feu:	Traffic signal
Horadateur:	Remote parking meter, usually at the end of the block
Parc de Stationnement:	Parking lot
Parking Interdit/ Stationnement Interdit:	No parking
Priorité à Droite:	Right-of-way
Rue Pietonne:	Pedestrian-only street
Sauf Riverains:	Local access only

Signs Unique to Autoroutes:

Bouchon:	Traffic jam ahead
Fluide:	No slowing ahead, fluid conditions
Peage:	Toll
Telepeage:	Toll booths—for locals with automatic toll payment only
Toutes Directions:	All directions (leaving city)
Autres Directions:	Other directions (leaving city)

or by inserting a credit card. Autoroute gas stations usually come with well-stocked mini-marts, clean rest rooms, sandwiches, maps, local products, and cheap coffee (€1). Many have small cafés or more elaborate cafeterias with reasonable prices.

Roads are classified into departmental (D), national (N), and autoroutes (A). D routes (usually yellow lines on maps) are slow and often the most scenic. N routes (usually red lines) are the fastest after autoroutes (orange lines). Green road signs are for national routes; blue are for autoroutes. There are plenty of good facilities, gas stations, and rest stops along most French roads.

Here are a few French road tips: In city centers, traffic merging from the right normally has the right-of-way *(priorité à droite)*, though cars entering the many suburban roundabouts must yield *(cedez le passage)*. When navigating through cities, approach intersections cautiously, stow the map, and follow the signs to *Centre-ville* (downtown) and from there to the tourist information office *(Office de Tourisme)*. When leaving or just passing through, follow

Standard European Road Signs

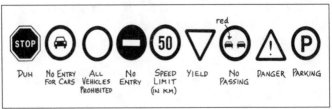

the signs for *Toutes Directions* or *Autres Directions* (meaning any-where else) until you see a sign for your specific destination. While locals are eating (12:00–14:00), many sights (and gas stations) are closed, so you can make great time driving. The French drive fast and live to tailgate.

Parking is a headache in the larger cities, and theft is a prob-lem throughout France. Ask your hotelier for ideas, and pay to park at well-patrolled lots (blue P signs direct you to parking lots in French cities). Most parking structures require that you take a ticket and prepay at a machine just before leaving (your first hour is often free—ask). Or use the curbside metered park-ing (usually free 12:30–14:00, 19:00–9:00, and in August). Look for a small machine selling time (called *horadateur*, usually 1 per block), plug in a few coins (about €1 gets an hour), push the green button, and get a receipt showing the amount of time you have, then display it inside your windshield. Keep a pile of coins in your ashtray for parking meters, public rest rooms, launderettes, and short stints on autoroutes.

Biking

Throughout France, you'll find areas where public transportation is limited and where bicycle touring is a good idea for some. For many, biking is a romantic notion that is less so after the first hill—realistically evaluate your physical condition and understand the limitations bikes present. We've listed bike-rental shops where appropriate. The TI will always have addresses. For a good tour-ing bike, allow about €10 for a half day and €16 for a full day. Pay more for better equipment; generally the best is available through bike shops, not at TIs or train stations. If you haven't been on a bike in a while, start with an easy ride.

Telephones, Mail, and E-mail

You cannot travel smartly in France without using the telephone—to reserve and confirm hotel rooms, make restaurant reservations, check sightseeing plans, and call home. You'll want a locally purchased phone card *(une carte téléphonique)*. Phone cards have effectively replaced coin-operated phones in France. There are two basic types: a *télécarte* must be inserted into the telephone and can only be used in a public phone booth; a *carte téléphonique à code* has a scratch-off PIN code that can be used from any phone. Either card can be purchased at any post office and from most tobacco shops *(tabacs)*, which you'll find everywhere in France, including at train stations and airports. These cards will only work in France. You can't use a French card to make calls from Switzerland.

When you use a ***télécarte***, simply take the phone off the hook, insert the prepaid card, wait for a dial tone, and dial away. The price of the call (local or international) is automatically deducted while you talk. There are two denominations: *une petite* costs about €7; *une grande* about €15.

There are a variety of prepaid **PIN cards** *(carte téléphonique à code)* that work like PIN cards sold in the United States, allowing you to dial from the comfort of your hotel (or anywhere else). These cards all work the same way and are simple to use, once you learn the rules. Dial the access number listed on the card, then follow the prompts, dialing your scratch-to-reveal Personal Identification Number (PIN) and finally the number you want to call. (You often need to press the pound key—#—after each step, e.g., after entering your PIN and again after the number you want to dial.) The *Carte Kertel* (pron. care-tel) and *Carte 365* are the most common (€7 and €15 denominations available). There's also an international card *(le Ticket de Téléphone International)* that offers cheaper rates for international calls. While per-minute rates for these PIN cards are cheaper than an insertable *télécarte*, it's slower to use (more numbers to dial)—so local calls are quicker with a *télécarte* from a phone booth.

Calling Card Services: Since direct-dialing rates have dropped, calling cards (offered by AT&T, MCI, and Sprint) are no longer the good value they used to be. In fact, they are a rip-off. You'll likely pay $3 for the first minute with a $4 connection fee; if you get an answering machine, it'll cost you $7 to say, "Sorry I missed you." Simply dialing direct (even from your hotel room) is generally a much better deal.

Dialing Direct: France has a direct-dial, 10-digit telephone system. There are no area codes. To call to or from anywhere in France, including Paris, dial the 10 numbers directly.

To call France from another country, start with the international access code of the country you're calling from (00 for European countries and 011 from the U.S. and Canada), dial France's country code (33), and then drop the initial zero of the 10-digit local number and dial the remaining nine digits. For example, the phone number of one of our favorite hotels in Paris is 01 47 05 49 15. To call it from home, dial 011-33-1 47 05 49 15.

To dial out of France, start your call with its international code (00), then dial the country code of the country you're calling. To call our office in the United States, dial 00 (France's international access code), 1 (U.S. country code), then 425/771-8303 (our area code plus local number).

For a list of **international access codes and country codes**, see the appendix. European time is six/nine hours ahead of the East/West Coast of the United States.

Cell Phones: Many travelers in France buy cheapie cell phones—about $70 on up—to make local and international calls. The cheapest phones work only in the country where they're sold; the pricier phones work throughout Europe (but it'll cost you about $40 per country to outfit the phone with the necessary chip and prepaid phone time). Because of their expense, cell phones are most economical for travelers staying in one country for two weeks or more.

If you're interested, stop by one of the ubiquitous phone shops or at a cell-phone counter at a department store. Find an English-speaking clerk to help you. Confirm with the clerk whether the phone works only in France or throughout Europe. To understand all the extras, get a brand that has instructions in English. Make sure the clerk shows you how to use the phone—practice making a call to the store or, for fun, to the clerk's personal cell phone. You'll need to pick out a policy; different policies offer, say, better rates for making calls at night or for calling cell phones rather than fixed phones, etc. We get the basic fixed rate: a straight 30 cents per minute to the United States and 15 cents per minute to any fixed or cell phone in the home country at any hour. Receiving calls is generally free. When you run out of calling time, buy more time at a newsstand. Upon arrival in a different country, purchase a new chip (which comes with a new phone number). Remember, if you're on a tight budget, skip cell phones and buy PIN phone cards instead.

Mail: The hours of post offices (called PTT for Postal, Telegraph, and Telephone) vary, though most are open weekdays from 8:00 to 19:00 and Saturday mornings from 8:00 to 12:00. Small-town PTTs open at 9:00 and close for lunch from 12:00 to 14:00. Stamps and phone cards are also sold at *tabac* (tobacco) shops. It costs about €0.70 to mail a postcard to the United States.

To arrange for mail delivery, reserve a few hotels along your route in advance and give their addresses to friends, or use American Express Company's mail services, free for AmEx cardholders (and for a minimal fee to others). Allow 10 days for a letter to arrive. Phoning and e-mailing are so easy that we've dispensed with mail stops altogether.

E-mail: E-mail use among French hoteliers is increasing. We've listed e-mail addresses when possible. Some family-run pensions can become overwhelmed by the volume of e-mail they receive, so be patient if you don't get an immediate response. Internet service providers (ISPs) can change with alarming frequency, so if your e-mail message to a hotel bounces back, use a search engine (such as www.google.com) to search for the hotel name and see if it has a new Web site—and if that doesn't work, fax or call the hotel.

Cybercafés and little hole-in-the-wall Internet access shops (offering a few computers, no food, and cheap prices) are popular in most cities. If the extension dot-com (.com) doesn't work at the end of a URL, try .fr for France.

If traveling with a laptop and modem, you'll need an ISP that has local phone numbers for each country you'll visit. While an American modem cable plugs into European phone jacks, you may have to tweak your settings to make your computer recognize a pulse instead of the U.S. dial tone. Bring a phone jack tester that reverses line polarity as needed.

Sleeping

Accommodations are a good value and easy to find. Choose from one- to three-star hotels (two stars is our mainstay), bed-and-breakfasts, hostels, and campgrounds. We like places that are clean, small, central, traditional, inexpensive, friendly, and not listed in other guidebooks. Most places we list have at least five of these seven virtues.

Hotels

In this book, the price for a double room will range from €30 (very simple, toilet and shower down the hall) to €150 (maximum plumbing and more), with most clustering around €65. Rates are higher in Paris and other popular cities.

Most hotels have lots of doubles and a few singles, triples, and quads. While groups sleep cheap, traveling alone can be expensive. Singles (except for the rare closet-type rooms that fit only 1 twin bed) are simply doubles used by one person—so they cost about the same as a double. Because rooms with double beds and showers are cheaper than rooms with twin beds and baths, room prices vary within each hotel. A triple and a double are often the same room, with a small double bed and a sliver single, so a third person sleeps very cheaply. Quad rooms usually have two double beds. Hotels cannot legally allow more in the room than what's shown on their price list.

Sleep Code

To give maximum information in a minimum of space, we use these codes to describe accommodations listed in this book. Prices listed are per room, not per person.

- **S** = Single room (or price for one person in a double).
- **D** = Double or Twin. French double beds can be very small.
- **T** = Triple (generally a double bed with a single).
- **Q** = Quad (usually two double beds).
- **b** = Private bathroom with toilet and shower or tub.
- **s** = Private shower or tub only. (The toilet is down the hall.)
- **CC** = Accepts credit cards (Visa and MasterCard, rarely American Express).
- **no CC** = Does not accept credit cards; pay in local cash.
- **SE** = Speaks English. This code is used only when it seems predictable that you'll encounter English-speaking staff.
- **NSE** = Does not speak English. Used only when it's unlikely you'll encounter English-speaking staff.
- ***** = French hotel rating system, ranging from zero to four stars.

According to this code, a couple staying at a "Db-€70, CC, SE" hotel would pay a total of 70 euros (about $70) for a double room with a private bathroom. The hotel accepts credit cards or cash in payment, and the staff speaks English.

Receptionists often don't mention the cheaper rooms (they assume you want a private bathroom). Study the price list on the Web site or posted at the desk. Understand it. You can save as much as €20–25 by finding the increasingly rare room without a private shower or toilet *(une chambre sans douche* or *sans WC)*. You will save less (about €15) on a room with a toilet but no shower *(une chambre avec cabinet de toilette)*. Some hotels charge for down-the-hall showers. A room with a bathtub *(salle de bain)* costs €5–10 more than a room with a shower *(douche)* and is generally larger. Hotels often have more rooms with tubs than showers and are inclined to give you a room with a tub (which the French prefer).

A double bed *(grand lit)* is €5–10 cheaper than twins *(deux petits lits)*, though rooms with twin beds tend to be larger, and French double beds are generally smaller than American double beds. Hotels rarely offer queen-size beds *(un lit de 160,* meaning a bed that's 160 centimeters wide—most doubles are 140). To see if a hotel has queen-size beds, ask, *"Avez-vous un lit de cent-soixante?"* (pron. ah-vay-voo uh lee duh sahn-swah-sahnt). Some hotels push two twins together with king-size sheets and blankets.

If you prefer a double bed (instead of twins) and a shower (instead of a tub), you need to ask for it—and you'll save up to €20. If you're willing to take either twins or a double, ask generically for a *chambre pour deux* (room for two) to avoid being needlessly turned away.

The French have a simple hotel rating system based on amenities (0–4 stars, indicated in this book by * through ****). One star is simple, two has most of the comforts, and three is generally a two-star with a minibar and fancier lobby. Four stars offer more luxury than you have time to appreciate. One- and two-star hotels are the best budget values, though some three-star hotels (and even a few 4-star hotels) can justify the extra cost. Lately, the star system has become less reliable. Unclassified hotels (no stars) can be bargains or depressing dumps. Look before you leap, and lay before you pay (upon departure).

Hotels in France must charge a daily tax *(taxe du séjour)* that is normally added to the bill. It varies from €0.50 to €1 per day per person depending on the hotel's number of stars. While some hotels include it in the price list, most add it to your bill.

You'll almost always have the option of breakfast at your hotel, which is pleasant and convenient, but, at €5–10, it's more than the price of breakfast at the corner café, and with less ambience (though you get more coffee at your hotel). Some hotels offer only the classic continental breakfast for about €5–7, but others offer buffet breakfasts for about €8–10 (cereal, yogurt, fruit, cheese, croissants, juice, and hard-boiled eggs)—which we usually spring for. While hotels hope you'll buy their breakfast, it's optional unless otherwise noted.

Some hotels strongly encourage their peak-season guests to take half pension; that is, breakfast and either lunch or dinner. By law, they can't require you to take half pension unless you are staying three or more nights, but, in effect, many do during summer. While the food is usually good, it limits your ability to shop around. We've indicated where we think *demi pension* is a good value.

France is littered with sterile, ultramodern hotels, usually located on cheap land just outside of town, providing drivers with low-stress accommodations. The antiseptically clean and cheap Formule 1 and ETAP chains (€24–40/room for up to 3 people), the more attractive Ibis hotels (€50–70 for a double), and the cushier Mercure and Novotels hotels (€70–110 for a double) are all run by the same company, Accor. While far from quaint, these can be a good value; check their Web site at www .accorhotels.com. A smaller, up-and-coming chain, Kyriad, has its act together, offering good prices and quality (toll-free tel. 08 25 00 30 03, from overseas tel. 01 64 62 46 46, www.kyriad.com; these telephone numbers also work for 8 other affiliated chains, includ- ing Clarine, Climat, and Campanile). For a long listing of various hotels throughout France, see www.france.com.

Rooms are safe. Still, keep cameras and money out of sight. Towels aren't routinely replaced every day; drip-dry and conserve. If that Lincoln-log pillow isn't your idea of comfort, American- style pillows (and extra blankets) may be in the closet or available on request. For a pillow, ask for *un oreiller, s'il vous plaît* (pron. uhn oar-ray-yay, see voo play).

Some hoteliers will ask you to sign their *Livre d'Or* (a book for client comments). They take this seriously and enjoy reading your remarks.

Making Reservations

It's possible to travel at any time of year without reservations, but, given the high stakes and the quality of the gems I've found for this book, I'd recommend making reservations. You can call long in advance from home, or grab rooms a few days to a week in advance as you travel. (If you have difficulty, ask the fluent receptionist at your current hotel to call for you.) If you like more spontaneity (or if you're traveling off-season), you might make a habit of calling between 9:00 and 10:00 on the day you plan to arrive, when the hotel clerk knows who'll be checking out and just which rooms will be available. I've taken great pains to list tele- phone numbers with long distance instructions (see "Telephones," above; also see the appendix). Use a public phone, the convenient PIN telephone cards, or your cell phone. Most hotels listed here are accustomed to English-only speakers. A hotel receptionist will trust you and hold a room until 16:00 without a deposit, though some will ask for a credit-card number.

If you know where you want to stay each day (and you don't need or want flexibility), reserve your rooms a month or two in advance from home. This is particularly smart for Paris and dur- ing holidays (see "Holiday Weekends," above). To reserve from home, telephone first to confirm availability, then fax or e-mail your formal request. Phone and fax costs are reasonable, e-mail is a steal, and simple English is usually fine. To fax, use the handy form in the appendix (or find it online at www.ricksteves.com /reservation). If you don't get an answer to your fax request, consider that a "no." (Many little places get 20 faxes a day after they're full, and they can't afford to respond.)

A two-night stay in August would be "2 nights, 16/8/03 to 18/8/03" (Europeans write the date in this order—day/month/year—and hotel jargon uses your day of departure).

If you receive a response from the hotel stating its rates and room availability, it's not a confirmation. You must confirm that you indeed want a room at the given rate. One night's deposit is generally required. A credit-card number is often accepted as a deposit (though you may need to send a signed traveler's check or, rarely, a bank draft in the local currency). To make things easier on yourself and the hotel, be sure you really intend to stay at the hotel on the dates you requested. These family-run businesses lose money if they turn away customers while holding a room for someone who doesn't show up. Understandably, some hotels bill no-shows for one night. *If you must cancel, give at least two days' notice.* Long distance is cheap and easy from public phone booths. Don't let these people down—I promised you'd call and cancel if for some reason you won't show up.

Reconfirm your reservations a few days in advance for safety. Don't needlessly confirm rooms through the tourist office; they'll take a commission.

Bed-and-Breakfasts (Chambres d'hôte)

B&Bs offer double the cultural intimacy for a good deal less than most hotel rooms. This book and local tourist offices list B&Bs. *Chambres d'hôte* (CH) are found mainly in the smaller towns and the countryside. They are listed by the owner's family name. While some post small *Chambres* or *Chambres d'hôte* signs in their front windows, many are found only through the local tourist office. We list reliable CHs that offer a good value and/or unique experience (such as CHs in renovated mills, châteaux, and wine *domaines*). Most have private bathrooms in all rooms. Doubles with breakfast generally cost between €35 and €50, fancier ones €60 to €70 (breakfast may or may not be included—ask). While your hosts may not speak English, they will almost always be enthusiastic and pleasant.

Hostels (Auberge de Jeunesse)

Hostels charge about €14 per bed. Get a hostel card before you go (contact Hostelling International, 202/783-6161, www.hiayh.org). Travelers of any age are welcome if they don't mind dorm-style accommodations or meeting other travelers. Travelers without a hostel card can generally spend the night for a small extra "one-night membership" fee. Cheap meals are sometimes available, and kitchen facilities are usually provided for do-it-yourselfers. Expect youth

Tips on Tipping

Tipping *(donner un pourboire)* in France isn't as automatic and generous as it is in the United States, but for special service, tips are appreciated, if not expected. As in the United States, the proper amount depends on your resources, tipping philosophy, and the circumstance—but some general guidelines apply.

Restaurants: Almost all restaurants include tax and a 15 percent service charge *(service compris)* in their prices, but it's polite to round up for a drink or meal well-served. This bonus tip is usually about 5 percent of the bill (e.g., if your bill is €19, leave €20). For exceptional service, tip up to 10 percent. In the rare case where service is not included (the menu would state *service non compris* or *s.n.c.*), a 15 percent tip is appropriate. When you hand your payment plus a tip to your waiter, you can say, *"C'est bon"* (pron. say bohn), meaning, "It's good." It's best to tip in cash even if you pay with your credit card. Otherwise, the tip may never reach your server. If you order your food at a counter, don't tip.

Taxis: To tip a cabbie, round up. For a typical ride, round up to the next euro on the fare (to pay a €13 fare, give €14); for a long ride, to the nearest 5 (for a €51 fare, give €55). If the cabbie hauls your bags and zips you to the airport to help you catch your flight, you might want to toss in a little more—but not more than €5. If you feel like you're being driven in circles or otherwise ripped off, skip the tip.

Special services: Tour guides at public sites sometimes hold out their hands for tips after they give their spiel; if we've already paid for the tour, we don't tip extra, though some tourists do give a euro or two, particularly for a job well done. If the tour was free (e.g., the abbey of Mont St. Michel), then we tip the guide €1 to €2 per person. We don't tip at hotels, but if you do, give the porter a euro for carrying bags and leave a couple of euros in your room at the end of your stay for the maid if the room was kept clean. In general, if someone in the service industry does a super job for you, a tip of a couple of euros is appropriate . . . but not required.

When in doubt, ask. If you're not sure whether (or how much) to tip for a service, ask your hotelier or the TI; they'll fill you in on how it's done on their turf.

groups in spring, crowds in the summer, snoring, and incredible variability in quality from one hostel to the next. Family rooms are sometimes available on request, but it's basically boys' dorms and girls' dorms. You usually can't check in before 17:00 and must be out by 10:00. There is often a 23:00 curfew. Official hostels are marked with a triangular sign that shows a house and a tree.

Camping

In Europe, camping is more of a social than an environmental experience. It's a great way for American travelers to make European friends. Camping costs about €13 per campsite per night, and almost every destination recommended in this book has a campground within a reasonable walk or bus ride from the town center and train station. A tent and sleeping bag are all you need. Many campgrounds have small grocery stores and washing machines, and some even come with discos and miniature golf. Hot showers are better at campgrounds than at many hotels. Local TIs have camping information. You'll find more detailed information in the annually updated *Michelin Camping/Caravanning Guide*, available in the United States and at most French bookstores.

Eating in France

The French eat long and well. Relaxed lunches, three-hour dinners, and endless hours sitting in outdoor cafés are the norm. They have a legislated 35-hour workweek and a self-imposed 36-hour eat-week. Local cafés, cuisine, and wines should become a highlight of any French adventure—sightseeing for your palate. Even if the rest of you is sleeping in cheap hotels, let your taste buds travel first class in France. (They can go coach in England.) You can eat well without going broke—but choose carefully: You're just as likely to blow a small fortune on a mediocre meal as you are to dine wonderfully for €20.

Breakfast

Petit déjeuner (pron. puh-tee day-zhuh-nay) is typically café au lait, hot chocolate, or tea; a roll with butter and marmalade; and a croissant. While breakfasts are available at your hotel (about €5–7), they're cheaper at corner cafés (but don't come with coffee refills). It's fine to buy a croissant or roll at a bakery and eat it with your cup of coffee at a café. Better still, some bakeries offer worthwhile breakfast deals with juice, a croissant, and coffee or tea for about €3 (try the bakery chain La Brioche Dorée). Breakfast buffets at hotels are becoming more common, with cereal, yogurt, fruit, cheese, croissants, juice, and hard-boiled eggs (a few euros extra—and well worth it). If the urge for a morning egg gets the

Say Cheese!

The origin of cheese goes back thousands of years to when someone decided to curdle milk. The French consider cheese essential to daily life and have established an extensive market for their creations.

There are more than 500 different cheeses from various regions of France, but only 35 of them qualify for the strict AOC (Appellation d'Origine Contrôlée) standards first established in the 15th century. These guidelines are similar to those prescribed for quality wine-making and assure consistent production methods.

In French restaurants, the cheese plate is served just before (or instead of) dessert. Cheese not only helps with digestion, it gives you a great chance to sample regional varieties. Traditionally, a cheese plate has a selection of about five cheeses, such as:

Camembert de Normandie: Pale yellow, creamy, and slightly salty.

Bleu d'Auvergne: Sticky, moist, and crumbly.

Saint Nectaire: Thick rind, but solid and creamy inside.

Crottins de Chavignol: A cylindrical, alpine goat cheese (also served in a hot goat cheese salad).

Munster: A pliable, slightly sticky cheese with a pungent aroma and bold flavor. Benedictine monks prohibited from eating meat created it in the 12th century.

If you'd like "A little of each, please," say, *"Un peu de chaque, s'il vous plaît"* (pron. uh puh duh shahk see voo play). If you serve yourself from the cheese plate, abide by French etiquette and keep the traditional shape of the cheese. Don't be gauche by digging out the inside of the wedge of Brie. Politely shave off a slice from the side of the cheese or cut small wedges.

best of you, drop into a café and order *une omelette* or *oeufs sur le plat* (fried eggs). You could also buy or bring plastic bowls and spoons from home, buy a box of cereal and a small box of milk, and eat in your room before heading out for coffee.

Picnics

For most lunches—*déjeuner* (pron. day-zhuh-nay)—we picnic or munch a take-away sandwich from a *boulangerie* (bakery) or a crêpe from a *crêperie*.

Picnics can be first-class affairs and adventures in high cuisine. Be daring. Try the smelly cheeses, ugly pâtés, sissy quiches, and

Get an assortment of cheese and host your own classy wine-and-cheese tasting. Visit a *fromagerie* (cheese shop) and experiment. Ask for a *fromage de la région* (of the region), and specify *doux* (mild), *fort* (sharp), *chèvre* (goat), or *bleu* (blue). Say *"Je peux goûter un peu"* (pron. zhuh puh goo-tay uh puh) if you'd like to taste a little.

Here are a few kinds to try: **Port Salut** comes in a sweet, soft wedge. **Beaufort** is a huge, disk-shaped, Gruyère-style cheese, made since Roman times from the milk of an ancient breed of alpine cow. One wheel takes about 130 gallons of milk and needs at least four months to ripen. **Roquefort**—strong, crumbly, and blue-veined—is made exclusively from Lacaune sheep's milk. **Boursault** is a rich, triple-cream, cow's milk cheese. Some cheeses are good enough to be named after the city they come from, such as **Pont l'Evêque,** which has had the same creamy, slightly sweet flavor since the Middle Ages. The rich **Liverot** has a strong smell likened to "the town drains running down to the sea." Its nickname, *le colonel,* comes from its stripes, made by the bands of paper that hold its form while it ages. *Fromage au cendré,* a cheese coated with ash from burned grapevine roots, is ash-ually better than it sounds. **Cantal,** from the Auvergne, is a mild, nutty, cheddar-like cheese, dating back more than 2,000 years. In Provence, the sheep's milk cheese named **Brousse** is creamy and fresh. *Chèvre* (goat cheese) may be rolled in pepper, herbs, or spices, or wrapped in leaves to protect it from mold.

Whether it's fresh or aged in caves, cooked or raw, double- or triple-cream, pasteurized or not, farm-made or mass-produced, cow's, sheep's, or goat's milk... in France, *c'est fromage.*

baby yogurts. Local shopkeepers are accustomed to selling small quantities of produce. Try the tasty salads-to-go and ask for a plastic fork *(une fourchette en plastique;* pron. oon foor-shet en plah-steek). A small container is *une barquette* (pron. oon bar-ket).

Gather supplies early; you'll want to visit several small stores to assemble a complete meal, and many close at noon (see also "Market Day," below). Look for a *boulangerie,* a *crémerie* (cheeses), a charcuterie (deli items, meats, and pâtés), an *épicerie* or *alimentation* (small grocery with veggies, drinks, and so on), and a pâtisserie (delicious pastries). Open-air markets *(marchés)* are fun and photogenic and close at about 13:00 (many are listed in this book; local TIs have complete lists). Local *supermarchés* offer less color and cost, more efficiency, and adequate quality. Department stores often have supermarkets in the basement. On the outskirts of cities, you'll find the monster *hypermarchés*. Drop in for a glimpse of hyper-France in action.

Market Day (Jour du Marché)

Market days are a big deal throughout France. They have been a central feature of life in rural areas since the Middle Ages. No single event better symbolizes the French preoccupation with fresh products and their strong ties to the small farmer than the weekly market. It's said that locals mark their calendars with the arrival of fresh produce. Notice the signs as you enter towns indicating the *jours du marché* (essential information to any civilized soul, and a reminder to nonlocals not to park on the streets the night before).

Most *marchés* take place once a week in the town's main square and, if large enough, spill into nearby streets. Markets combine fresh produce; tastings of wine and other locally produced beverages (such as brandies and ciders); and a smattering of nonperishable items, such as knives, berets, kitchen goods, and cheap clothing. The bigger the market, the greater the overall selection—particularly for nonperishable goods. Bigger towns (such as Beaune and Arles) may have two weekly markets, one for produce and another for nonperishable goods; in other towns, the second weekly market may simply be a smaller version of the main market day. Biggest market days are usually on weekends, so that everyone can go.

Providing far more than fresh produce, market day is a weekly chance to resume friendships and get current on gossip. Here, locals can catch up on Henri's barn renovation, see photos of Jacqueline's new grandchild, and relax over *un café* with an old friend. Dogs are tethered to café tables while friends exchange kisses. Tether yourself to a café table and observe: three cheek-kisses for good friends (left-right-left), a fourth for friends you haven't seen in a while. You should never be in a hurry on market day. Allow the crowd to set your pace. Observe the interaction between vendor and client, then think of your home supermarket routine.

All perishable items are sold direct from the producers—no middlemen, no Visa cards, just really fresh produce. Most vendors follow a weekly circuit of markets they feel work best for them, and most show up every market day, year in and year out. Notice how much fun they have chatting up their customers and each other. Many speak enough English to allow you to learn about their product. Space rental is cheap (about €5–10, depending on the size). Markets end by 13:00—in time for lunch, allowing the town to reclaim its streets and squares.

Café Culture

French cafés (or brasseries) provide light meals and a refuge from museum and church overload. They are carefully positioned places from which to watch the river of local life flow by.

Cafés generally open by 7:00, but closing times vary wildly (later in cities, earlier in smaller towns). Unlike at restaurants, food is served throughout the day—so if you want a late lunch or an early dinner, find a café.

It's easier to sit and feel comfortable in a café when you know the system. Check the price list first. Prices, which must be posted prominently, vary wildly between cafés (main-square cafés are more expensive than those on small alleys). Cafés charge different prices for the same drink, depending upon where you want to be seated. Prices are posted: *comptoir* (counter/bar) and the more expensive *salle* (seated). Don't pay for your drink at the bar if you want to sit at a table (as you might do at home).

Your waiter probably won't overwhelm you with friendliness. Notice how hard they work. They almost never stop. Cozying up to clients (French or foreign) is probably the last thing on their minds.

The standard menu items are the *croque monsieur* (grilled ham and cheese sandwich) and *croque madame* (*monsieur* with a fried egg on top). The *salade composée* (pron. sah-lahd cohm-poh-zay) is a hearty chef's salad. To get salad dressing on the side, order *la sauce à côté* (pron. lah sohs ah coat-ay). Sandwiches are least expensive but plain and much better at the *boulangerie* (bakery). To get more than a piece of ham (*jambon*, pron. zhahm-bohn) on a baguette, order a sandwich *jambon-crudité* (pron. crew-dee-tay), which means garnished with lettuce, tomatoes, cucumbers, and so on. Omelettes come lonely on a plate with a basket of bread. The *plat du jour* (daily €9–12 special) is your fast, hearty hot plate. Regardless of what you order, bread is free; to get more, just hold up your bread basket and ask, "*Encore, s'il vous plaît.*"

If you order coffee, here's the lingo:

- *un express* (pron. uh nex-press) = shot of espresso
- *une noisette* (pron. oon nwah-zette) = espresso with a shot of milk
- café au lait = coffee with lots of milk. Also called *un grand crème* (pron. uh grahn krem; big) or *un petit crème* (pron. uh puh-tee krem; average)
- *un grand café noir* (pron. uh grahn kah-fay nwar) = cup of coffee, closest to American style
- *un décaffiné* (pron. uh day-kah-fee-nay) = decaf; can modify any of the above drinks

By law, the waiter must give you a glass of tap water with your coffee if you request it; ask for *un verre d'eau, s'il vous plaît*

(pron. uh vayr dough, see voo play). For more café drink suggestions, see "Drinks," below.

Restaurants

Choose restaurants filled with locals, not places with big neon signs
boasting, "We Speak English." Consider our suggestions and your
hotelier's opinion, but trust your instinct. If the menu *(la carte)*
isn't posted outside, move along. Refer to our restaurant recommendations to get a sense of what a reasonable meal should cost.

French restaurants open for dinner at 19:00 and are typically
most crowded about 20:30 (the early bird gets the table). Last
seating is usually about 21:00, or 22:00 in cities (even later in
Paris) and possibly earlier in small villages during the off-season.
When lunch is served at restaurants, it generally begins at 11:30
and goes until 14:00, with last orders taken around 13:30.

La carte is the menu; if you ask for *le menu*, you'll get a fixed-
price meal. This fixed-price *menu* gives you a choice of soup,
appetizer, or salad *(entrée);* a choice of three or four main courses
(plat principal) with vegetables; plus a cheese course and/or a choice
of desserts. (The same *menu* can cost €6 more at dinner.) Most
restaurants offer a reasonable *menu-enfant* (kids' menu). Service is
included, but wine or drinks are generally extra. Wines are often
listed in a separate *carte des vins;* ask for *un vin ordinaire* (pron.
uh van or-din-air) if all you want is table wine.

If you'd prefer ordering à la carte, ask the waiter for help in
deciphering *la carte*. Go with the waiter's recommendations and
anything *de la maison* (of the house), unless it's organ meat *(tripes,
rognons, andouillette*—yuck). Galloping gourmets should bring a
menu translator (the *Marling Menu Master* is excellent).

Remember, the *entrée* is the first course and *le plat principal*
is the main course. The *plat du jour* (€9–12 plate of the day),
mentioned in "Café Culture," above, is served all day at bistros
and cafés but only at lunch (when available) at restaurants. Soft
drinks and beer cost €2–3, and a bottle or carafe of house wine—
invariably good enough for Rick Steves, if not always Steve Smith—
costs €6–11. To get a waiter's attention, say, "*S'il vous plaît.*"

Restaurants are almost always a better value in the countryside than in Paris. If you're driving, look for red-and-blue *Relais
Routier* decals, indicating that the place is recommended by the
truckers' union.

Drinks

In stores, unrefrigerated soft drinks, bottled water, and beer are
one-third the price of cold drinks. Milk, bottled water, and boxed
fruit juice are the cheapest drinks. Avoid buying drinks to go at

streetside stands; you'll find them far cheaper in a shop. Try to keep a water bottle with you. Water quenches your thirst better and cheaper than anything you'll find in a store or café. We drink tap water throughout France, filling our bottles in hotel rooms as we go.

The French often order bottled water with their meal (*eau minérale;* pron. oh mee-nay-rahl). If you'd rather get a free pitcher of tap water, ask for *une carafe d'eau* (pron. oon kah-rahf doh). Otherwise, you may unwittingly buy bottled water.

To save money when ordering a beer at a café or restaurant, ask for a beer on tap (*une pression;* pron. oon pres-yon) or, cheapest, the house draft beer (*un demi;* pron. uh duh-mee); either is less expensive than a bottled beer. House wine is cheaper by the "pitcher" (*pichet;* pron. pee-shay) than a bottle (*bouteille;* pron. boo-teh-ee). If all you want is a glass of wine (about €2–4), ask for *un verre de vin* (pron. uh vehr duh van).

You could drink away your children's inheritance if you're not careful. The most famous wines are the most expensive, while lesser-known tastealikes remain a bargain (see our regional suggestions in each chapter). For a refreshing before-dinner drink, try a *kir* (pron. keer): a thumb's level of *crème de cassis* (black currant liqueur) topped with white wine. If you like brandy, try a *marc* (regional brandy, e.g., *marc de Bourgogne)* or an Armagnac, cognac's cheaper twin brother. Pastis, the standard aperitif, is a sweet anise or licorice drink that comes on the rocks with a glass of water. Cut it to taste with lots of water. France's best beer is Alsatian; also try Krônenburg or the heavier Pelfort. *Une panaché* (pron. pan-a-shay) is a very refreshing French shandy (lemonade and beer). For a fun, bright, nonalcoholic drink, order *un diablo menthe* (7-Up with mint syrup). The ice cubes melted after the last Yankee tour group left.

Traveling with Kids

France is young-kid-friendly, partly because so much of it is rural. (Our teenagers, on the other hand, tend to prefer cities). Our kids' favorite places have been Mont St. Michel, the Alps, Loire châteaux, Carcassonne, and Paris (especially the Eiffel Tower and Seine River boat ride)—and any hotel with a pool (see below). To make your trip fun for everyone in the family, mix heavy-duty sights with kids' activities (playing miniature golf, renting bikes, and riding the little tourist trains popular in many towns). While Disneyland Paris is the predictable draw, our kids had more fun for half the expense simply by enjoying the rides in the Tuileries Gardens in downtown Paris. If you're in France near Bastille Day, remember that firecracker stands pop up everywhere on the days leading up to July 14. Putting on their own fireworks show can be a highlight for teenagers.

Minimize hotel changes by planning three-day stops. Aim for hotels with attached restaurants, so the kids can go back to the room and play while you finish a pleasant dinner. We've listed public pools in many places (especially the south), but be warned: Public pools in France commonly require a small, Speedo-like bathing suit for boys and men (my son's American-style swim trunks didn't do)—though they usually have these little suits to loan.

For breakfast, croissants are a hit. For lunch and dinner, rather than fast food, we developed a knack for finding *crêperies*—plenty of kid-friendly stuffings for both savory and dessert crêpes. It's easy to find fast food places and restaurants with kids' menus, but we travel with a plastic container of peanut butter brought from home and smuggle small jars of jam from breakfast for food emergencies.

Swap baby-sitting duties with your partner if one of you wants to take in an extra sight. Kids homesick for friends can keep in easy touch with cheap international phone cards (a dollar buys 10 minutes of time for catching up). Internet cafés are a godsend for parents with teenagers.

For memories that will last long after the trip, keep a family journal. Pack a small diary and a glue stick. While relaxing at a café over a *citron pressé* (lemonade), take turns writing the day's events and include mementos such as ticket stubs from museums, postcards, or a stalk of lavender.

Stranger in a Strange Land

We travel all the way to Europe to enjoy differences—to become temporary locals. You'll experience frustrations. Certain truths that we find "God-given" or "self-evident," such as cold beer, ice in drinks, bottomless cups of coffee, hot showers, and bigger being better, are suddenly not so true. One of the benefits of travel is the eye-opening realization that there are logical, civil, and even better alternatives. The fact that Americans treat time as a commodity can lead to frustrations when dealing with other cultures. For instance, while an American "spends" or "wastes" time, a French person merely "passes" it. You will find no cup holders in French cars—drinks are meant to be enjoyed slowly, with friends. A willingness to go local (and at a local tempo) ensures that you'll enjoy a full dose of European hospitality.

If there is a negative aspect to the European image of Americans, it's that we can appear big, loud, aggressive, impolite, rich, and a bit naive. While Europeans look bemusedly at some of our Yankee excesses—and worriedly at others—they nearly always afford us individual travelers all the warmth we deserve.

Back Door Manners

While updating this book, we heard over and over again that our readers are considerate and fun to have as guests. Thank you for traveling as temporary locals who are sensitive to the culture. It's fun to follow you in our travels.

Send Us a Postcard, Drop Us a Line

If you enjoy a successful trip with the help of this book and would like to share your discoveries, please fill out and send the survey at the end of this book to us at Europe Through the Back Door, Box 2009, Edmonds, WA 98020. We personally read and value all feedback. Thanks in advance—it helps a lot.

For our latest travel information, tap into our Web site: www.ricksteves.com. For any updates to this book, check www.ricksteves.com/update. Rick's e-mail address is rick @ricksteves.com. Anyone is welcome to request a free issue of our *Back Door* quarterly newsletter.

Judging from all the positive feedback and happy postcards we receive from travelers who have used this book, it's safe to assume you'll enjoy a great, affordable vacation—with the finesse of an independent, experienced traveler.

From this point, "we" (your co-authors) will shed our respective egos and become "I."

Thanks, and *bon voyage!*

BACK DOOR TRAVEL PHILOSOPHY
by Rick Steves, author of *Europe Through the Back Door*

Travel is intensified living—maximum thrills per minute and one of the last great sources of legal adventure. Travel is freedom. It's recess, and we need it.

Experiencing the real Europe requires catching it by surprise, going casual . . . "through the Back Door."

Affording travel is a matter of priorities. (Make do with the old car.) You can travel—simply, safely, and comfortably—anywhere in Europe for $80 a day plus transportation costs. In many ways, spending more money only builds a thicker wall between you and what you came to see. Europe is a cultural carnival, and, time after time, you'll find that its best acts are free and the best seats are the cheap ones.

A tight budget forces you to travel close to the ground, meeting and communicating with the people, not relying on service with a purchased smile. Never sacrifice sleep, nutrition, safety, or cleanliness in the name of budget. Simply enjoy the local-style alternatives to expensive hotels and restaurants.

Extroverts have more fun. If your trip is low on magic moments, kick yourself and make things happen. If you don't enjoy a place, maybe you don't know enough about it. Seek the truth. Recognize tourist traps. Give a culture the benefit of your open mind. See things as different but not better or worse. Any culture has much to share.

Of course, travel, like the world, is a series of hills and valleys. Be fanatically positive and militantly optimistic. If something's not to your liking, change your liking. Travel is addictive. It can make you a happier American, as well as a citizen of the world. Our Earth is home to six billion equally important people. It's humbling to travel and find that people don't envy Americans. They like us, but, with all due respect, they wouldn't trade passports.

Globe-trotting destroys ethnocentricity. It helps you understand and appreciate different cultures. Travel changes people. It broadens perspectives and teaches new ways to measure quality of life. Many travelers toss aside their hometown blinders. Their prized souvenirs are the strands of different cultures they decide to knit into their own character. The world is a cultural yarn shop. And Back Door Travelers are weaving the ultimate tapestry.

Come on, join in!

PARIS

Paris offers sweeping boulevards, sleepy parks, world-class art galleries, chatty crêpe stands, Napoleon's body, sleek shopping malls, the Eiffel Tower, and people-watching from outdoor cafés. Climb the Notre-Dame and the Eiffel Tower, cruise the Seine and the Champs-Elysées, and master the Louvre and Orsay Museums. Save some after-dark energy for one of the world's most romantic cities. Many people fall in love with Paris. Some see the essentials and flee, overwhelmed by the huge city. With the proper approach and a good orientation, you'll fall head over heels for Europe's capital.

Planning Your Time: Paris in One, Two, or Three Days

Day 1
Morning: Follow "Historic Core of Paris" Walk (see "Sights," below), featuring Ile de la Cité, Notre-Dame, Latin Quarter, and Sainte-Chapelle (consider lunch at nearby Samaritaine view café).
Afternoon: Visit the Pompidou Center (at least from the outside), then walk to the Marais neighborhood, visit the place des Vosges, and consider touring any of three museums nearby: Carnavalet Museum (city history), Jewish Art and History Museum, or Picasso Museum.
Evening: Cruise Seine River or take illuminated Paris by Night bus tour.

Day 2
Morning: Visit Arc de Triomphe, then walk down the Champs-Elysées to the Tuileries Garden.
Afternoon: Have lunch in the Tuileries (several lunch cafés in the park), then tour the Louvre.

Daily Reminder

Monday: These sights are closed today—Orsay, Rodin, Marmottan, Montmartre, Carnavalet, Catacombs, Giverny, and Versailles; the Louvre is more crowded because of this, but the Denon wing (with *Mona Lisa*, Venus de Milo, and more) stays open until 21:45. Napoleon's Tomb is closed the first Monday of the month. Some small stores don't open until 14:00. Street markets, such as rue Cler and rue Mouffetard, are dead today. Some banks are closed. It's discount night at most cinemas.

Tuesday: Many museums are closed today, including the Louvre, Picasso, Cluny, and Pompidou Center. The Eiffel Tower, Orsay, and Versailles are particularly busy today.

Wednesday: All sights are open (Louvre until 21:45). The weekly *Pariscope* magazine comes out today. School is out, so many kids' sights are busy. Some cinemas offer discounts.

Thursday: All sights are open (except the Sewer Tour). The Orsay is open until 21:45. Department stores are open late.

Friday: All sights are open (except the Sewer Tour). Afternoon trains and roads leaving Paris are crowded; TGV reservation fees are higher.

Saturday: All sights are open (except the Jewish Art and History Museum). The fountains run at Versailles (July–Sept). Department stores are busy. The Jewish Quarter is quiet.

Sunday: Some museums are two-thirds price all day and/or free the first Sunday of the month, thus more crowded (e.g., Louvre, Orsay, Rodin, Cluny, Pompidou, and Picasso). The fountains run at Versailles (early April–early Oct). Most of Paris' stores are closed, but shoppers find relief in the Marais' lively Jewish Quarter—and in Bercy Village, where many stores are open. Look for organ concerts at St. Sulpice and possibly other churches. The American Church sometimes offers a free evening concert at 18:00 (Sept–May only). Most recommended restaurants in the rue Cler neighborhood are closed for dinner.

Evening: Enjoy Trocadero scene and twilight ride up the Eiffel Tower.

Day 3

Morning: Tour the Orsay Museum.
Afternoon: Either tour the nearby Rodin Museum and Napoleon's Tomb or visit Versailles (take RER train direct from Orsay).
Evening: Visit Montmartre and Sacré-Coeur.

Orientation

Paris is split in half by the Seine River, divided into 20 *arrondisse-ments* (proud and independent governmental jurisdictions), and circled by a ring-road freeway (the *périphérique*). You'll find Paris easier to navigate if you know which side of the river you're on, which *arrondissement* you're in, and which subway (Métro) stop you're closest to. If you're north of the river (the top half of any city map), you're on the Right Bank *(rive droite)*. If you're south of it, you're on the Left Bank *(rive gauche)*. Most of your sight-seeing will take place within five blocks of the river.

Arrondissements are numbered, starting at Notre-Dame (ground zero) and moving in a clockwise spiral out to the ring road. The last two digits in a Parisian zip code are the *arron-dissement* number. The notation for the Métro stop is "Mo." In Parisian jargon, Napoleon's tomb is on *la rive gauche* (the Left Bank) in the *7ème* (7th *arrondissement*), zip code 75007, Mo: Invalides. Paris Métro stops are used as a standard aid in giving directions, even for those not using the Métro. As you're tracking down addresses, these definitions will help: *place* (square), *rue* (road), and *pont* (bridge).

Tourist Information

Avoid the Paris tourist offices, which are long on lines, short on information, and charge for maps. This book, *Pariscope* magazine (see below), and one of the free maps available at any hotel (plus the sights and Métro maps at the front of this book) are all you need. The main TI is at 127 avenue des **Champs-Elysées** (daily 9:00–20:00, tel. 08 36 92 31 12—phone tree), and the other, less crowded TIs are at **Gare de Lyon** (daily 8:00–20:00), the **Eiffel Tower** (May–Sept daily 11:00–18:42, yes, 18:42, closed off-season, tel. 01 45 51 22 15), and the **Louvre** (Wed–Mon 10:00–19:00, closed Tue). Both **airports** have handy TIs (called ADP) with long hours and short lines (see "Transportation Connec-tions," below). For a complete list of museum hours and sched-uled English-language museum tours, pick up the free *Musées, Monuments Historiques, et Expositions* booklet from any museum.

Pariscope: *Pariscope* weekly magazine (or one of its clones, €0.50 at any newsstand) lists museum hours, art exhibits, con-certs, music festivals, plays, movies, and nightclubs. Smart tour guides and sightseers rely on this for all the latest (in French, www.pariscope.fr).

Web Sites: Here's a short list of sites that I find entertain-ing and, at times, useful: www.bonjourparis.com (a newsy site that claims to offer a virtual trip to Paris, with interactive French les-sons, tips on wine and food, and news on the latest Parisian trends),

The Paris Museum Pass

In Paris, there are two classes of sightseers—those with a Paris museum pass, and those who stand in line. Serious sightseers save time and money by getting the pass.

Most of the sights listed in this chapter are covered by the Paris museum pass, except for the Eiffel Tower, Montparnasse Tower, Marmottan Museum, Garnier Opéra, Notre-Dame treasury, Jacquemart-André Museum, Jewish Art and History Museum, Grande Arche de la Défense, Jeu de Paume Exhibition Hall, Catacombs, *Paris Story* film, and the ladies of Pigalle. Outside Paris, the pass covers the châteaux of Versailles, Chantilly, and Fontainebleau.

The pass pays for itself in two admissions and gets you into most sights without lining up (1 day-€15, 3 consecutive days-€30, 5 consecutive days-€45, no youth or senior discount). It's sold at museums, main Métro stations (including Ecole Militaire and Bastille stations), and TIs (even at the airports). Try to avoid buying the pass at a major museum (such as the Louvre), where supply can be spotty and lines long.

The pass isn't activated until the first time you use it (you enter the date on the pass). Think and read ahead to make the most of your pass, since some museums are free (e.g., Carnavalet, the Petit Palais, and Victor Hugo's House), many are discounted on Sundays, and your pass must be used on consecutive days.

The pass isn't worth buying for children, as most museums are free for those under 18. Note that kids can skip the lines with their passholder parents.

The free museum and monuments directory that comes with your pass lists the latest hours, phone numbers, and specifics on

www.paris-touristoffice.com (the official site for Paris' TIs, offering practical information on hotels, special events, museums, children's activities, fashion, nightlife, and more), and www.paris-anglo.com (similar to bonjourparis.com, with informative stories about visiting Paris, plus a directory of over 2,500 English-speaking businesses).

Maps: While Paris is littered with free maps, they don't show all the streets. You may want the huge Michelin #10 map of Paris. For an extended stay, I prefer the pocket-size, street-indexed *Paris Pratique* (€6), with an easy-to-use Métro map.

Bookstores: There are many English-language bookstores in Paris where you can pick up guidebooks (for nearly double what kids pay. The cutoff age for free entry ranges from five to 18. Most major art museums let young people under 18 in for free, but anyone over age five has to pay to tour the sewers—go figure.

Included sights (and admission prices without the pass) you're likely to visit: Louvre (€7.50), Orsay (€7), Sainte-Chapelle (€5.50), Arc de Triomphe (€7), Les Invalides Museums/Napoleon's Tomb (€6), Conciergerie (€5.50), Panthéon (€5.50), Sewer Tour (€4), Cluny Museum (€7), Pompidou Center (€5.50), Notre-Dame towers (€5.50) and crypt (€3.50), Picasso Museum (€5.50), Rodin Museum (€5), and the Cité des Sciences et l'Industrie museum (€9). Outside Paris, the pass covers the Palace of Versailles (€7.50) and its Trianons (€5); Château of Fontainebleau (€5.50); and Château of Chantilly (€6).

Tally up what you want to see—and remember, an advantage of the pass is that you skip to the front of some lines, saving hours of waiting, especially in summer (though everyone must pass through the slow-moving metal-detector lines at some sights, and a few places, such as Notre-Dame's tower, can't accommodate a bypass lane). With the pass you'll pop freely into sights that you're walking by (even for a few minutes) that might otherwise not be worth the expense (e.g., Notre-Dame crypt, Conciergerie, Picasso Museum, and the Panthéon).

Museum Strategy: Arriving 20 minutes before major museums open is line-time well spent. Remember, most museums require you to check day packs and coats, and important museums have metal detectors that will slow your entry. If you're still ahead of the pack when you enter, consider hustling to the most popular works first.

their American prices). A few of the best: Shakespeare & Company (daily 12:00–24:00, some used travel books, 37 rue de la Bûcherie, across the river from Notre-Dame, tel. 01 43 26 96 50), W. H. Smith (248 rue de Rivoli, Mo: Concorde, tel. 01 44 77 88 99), and Brentanos (37 avenue de L'Opéra, Mo: Opéra, tel. 01 42 61 52 50). The friendly Red Wheelbarrow Bookstore in the Marais neighborhood sells Rick Steves' books (13 rue Charles V, Mo: St. Paul, tel. 01 42 77 42 17).

American Church: The American Church is a nerve center for the American émigré community. It distributes a free, handy, and insightful monthly English-language newspaper called the *Paris Voice* (with useful reviews of concerts, plays, and current events;

Paris Overview

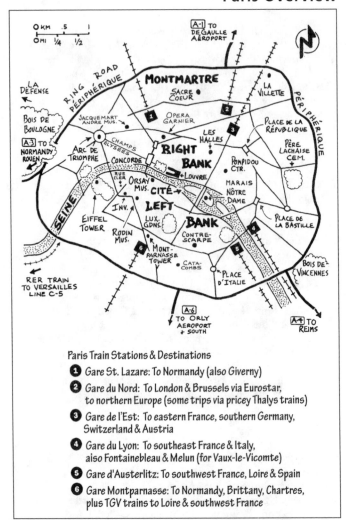

Paris Train Stations & Destinations

1 Gare St. Lazare: To Normandy (also Giverny)

2 Gare du Nord: To London & Brussels via Eurostar, to northern Europe (some trips via pricey Thalys trains)

3 Gare de l'Est: To eastern France, southern Germany, Switzerland & Austria

4 Gare du Lyon: To southeast France & Italy, also Fontainebleau & Melun (for Vaux-le-Vicomte)

5 Gare d'Austerlitz: To southwest France, Loire & Spain

6 Gare Montparnasse: To Normandy, Brittany, Chartres, plus TGV trains to Loire & southwest France

available at about 200 locations in Paris, http://parisvoice.com) and an advertisement paper called *France—U.S.A. Contacts* (full of useful information for those seeking work or long-term housing). The church faces the river between the Eiffel Tower and Orsay Museum (reception open Mon–Sat 9:30–22:30, Sun 9:00–19:30, 65 quai d'Orsay, Mo: Invalides, tel. 01 40 62 05 00).

Arrival in Paris

By Train: Paris has six train stations, all connected by Métro, bus, and taxi. All have ATMs, banks or change offices, information desks, telephones, cafés, lockers *(consigne automatique)*, newsstands, and clever pickpockets. Hop the Métro to your hotel (see "Getting around Paris," below).

By Plane: For detailed information on getting from Paris' airports to downtown Paris (and vice versa), see "Transportation Connections" at the end of this chapter.

Helpful Hints

Theft Alert: Pickpockets seem more numerous and determined than ever. Métro and RER lines that serve popular sights are infested with thieves. Wear a money belt, put your wallet in your front pocket, loop your day bag over your shoulders (consider wearing it in front), and keep a tight grip on a purse or shopping bag. If you're out late, avoid the riverfront quays if the lighting is dim and pedestrian activity minimal.

Useful Telephone Numbers: American Hospital—01 46 41 25 25, English-speaking pharmacy—01 45 62 02 41 (Pharmacie les Champs, open 24 hrs, 84 avenue des Champs-Elysées, Mo: George V), Police—17, U.S. Embassy—01 43 12 22 22, Paris and France directory assistance—12 (see appendix for additional numbers).

Street Safety: Be careful on foot! Parisian drivers are notorious for ignoring pedestrians. Look both ways, as many streets are one-way, and be careful of seemingly quiet bus/taxi lanes. Don't assume you have the right of way, even in a crosswalk. When crossing a street, keep your pace constant and don't stop suddenly. By law, drivers must miss pedestrians by one meter/three feet (1.5 meters/5 feet in the countryside). Drivers carefully calculate your speed and won't hit you, provided you don't alter your route or pace.

Watch out for a lesser hazard: *merde*. Parisian dogs decorate the city's sidewalks with 16 tons of droppings a day. People get injured by slipping in it.

Toilets: Carry small change for pay toilets, or walk into any sidewalk café like you own the place and find the toilet in the back. The toilets in museums are free and generally the best you'll find, and if you have a museum pass, you can drop into almost any museum for the clean toilets. Modern, super-sanitary, street-booth toilets provide both relief and a memory (coins required, don't leave small children inside unattended). Keep some toilet paper or tissues with you, as some toilets are poorly supplied.

Getting around Paris

By Métro

By Métro: Europe's best subway is divided into two systems—the Métro (for puddle-jumping everywhere in Paris; see map in this book) and the RER (connects suburban destinations with a few stops in central Paris). You'll use the Métro for almost all your trips (daily from 5:30 until 00:30). Occasionally, you'll find the RER more convenient, as it makes fewer stops (like an express bus).

Tickets and Passes: In Paris, you're never more than a 10-minute walk from a Métro station. One ticket takes you anywhere in the system with unlimited transfers. Save 40 percent by buying a *carnet* (pron. car-nay) of 10 tickets for €10 at any Métro station (a single ticket is €1.40, kids 4–10 pay €5 for a *carnet*). Métro tickets work on city buses, though one ticket cannot be used as a transfer between subway and bus. If you're staying in Paris for a week or more, consider the *Carte Orange* (pron. kart oh-rahnzh), which gives you free run of the bus and Métro system for one week (about €15, ask for *Carte Orange Coupon Vert* and supply a passport-size photo) or a month (about €50, ask for *Carte Orange Coupon Orange*). These passes cover only central Paris; you can pay more for passes covering regional destinations (such as Versailles). The weekly pass begins Monday and ends Sunday, and the monthly pass is valid from the first to last day of the month, so midweek or mid-month pass purchases aren't worthwhile. All passes can be purchased at any Métro station, most of which have photo booths where you can get the photo required for the pass. While some Métro agents may hesitate to sell you *Carte Orange* passes because you're not a resident (and encourage you to buy the bad-value *Paris Visite* pass instead), *Carte Orange* passes are definitely not limited to residents; if you're refused, simply go to another station to buy your pass. The overpriced *Paris Visite* passes were designed for tourists, offering minor reductions at minor sights but costing more than a *carnet* of 10 tickets or a *Carte Orange* (1 day-€9, 2 days-€14, 3 days-€19, 5 days-€28).

How the Métro works: To get to your destination, determine the closest "Mo" stop and which line or lines will get you there. The lines have numbers, but they're best known by their direction or end-of-the-line stop. (For example, the La Défense/Château de Vincennes line runs between La Défense in the west and Vincennes in the east.) Once in the Métro station, you'll see blue-and-white signs directing you to the train going in your direction (e.g., *direction: La Défense*). Insert your ticket in the automatic turnstile, pass through, and reclaim and keep your ticket until you exit the system. Fare inspectors regularly check

Paris

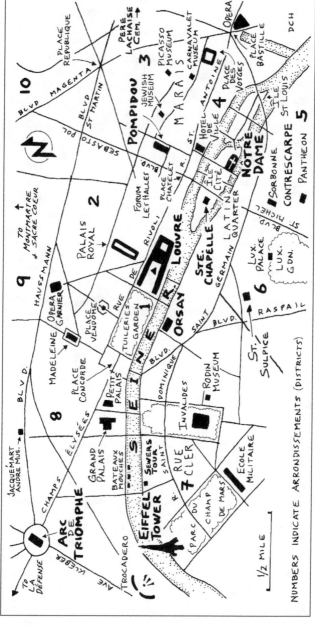

NUMBERS INDICATE ARRONDISSEMENTS (DISTRICTS)

1/2 MILE

Key Words for the Métro and RER

- *direction* (pron. dee-rek-see-ohn): direction
- *ligne* (pron. leen-yuh): line
- *correspondance* (pron. kor-res-pohn-dahns): transfer
- *sortie* (pron. sor-tee): exit
- *carnet* (pron. car-nay): cheap set of 10 tickets
- *Pardon, madame/monsieur* (pron. par-dohn, mah-dahm/ mes-yur): Excuse me, lady/bud.
- *Je descend* (pron. juh day-sahn): I'm getting off.
- *Donnez-moi mon porte-feuille!* (pron. dohn-nay-mwuh mohn port-foo-ay): Give me back my wallet!

Etiquette
- When waiting at the platform, get out of the way of those exiting the train. Board only once everyone is off.
- Avoid using the hinged seats when the car is jammed; they take up valuable standing space.
- In a crowded train, try not to block the exit. If you're blocking the door when the train stops, step out of the car and to the side, let others off, then get back on.
- Talk softly in the cars. Listen to how quietly Parisians can communicate and follow their lead.
- When leaving or entering a station, hold the door open for the person behind you.
- On escalators, stand on the right and pass on the left.

for cheaters and accept absolutely no excuses from anyone. I repeat, keep that ticket until you leave the Métro system. Also keep in mind that if you travel beyond the center city, you'll need to buy an RER ticket for your destination before you get on the RER (see below for details).

Transfers are free and can be made wherever lines cross. When you transfer, look for the orange *correspondance* (connections) signs when you exit your first train, then follow the proper direction sign.

While the Métro whisks you quickly from one point to another, be prepared to walk significant distances within the stations to reach your platform (most noticeable when you transfer). Escalators are usually available for vertical movement, but they are not always in working order. To avoid excessive walking, try to avoid transferring at these stations: Montparnasse, Chatelet/Les Halles, Etoile, Gare du Nord, and Bastille.

Before you head for the *sortie* (exit), check the helpful *plan du quartier* (map of the neighborhood) to get your bearings, locate your destination, and decide which *sortie* you want. At stops with several *sorties*, you can save lots of walking by choosing the best exit.

After you exit the system, toss or tear your ticket so you don't confuse it with your unused tickets. Used and unused tickets look virtually identical.

Thieves spend their days in the Métro. Be on guard. For example, if your pocket is picked as you pass through a turnstile, you end up stuck on the wrong side while the thief strolls away. Any jostle or commotion (especially when boarding or leaving trains) is likely the sign of a thief or team of thieves in action.

Paris has a huge homeless population and higher than 11 percent unemployment, so expect a warm Métro welcome from panhandlers, musicians, and those selling magazines produced by the homeless community.

By RER: The RER (Réseau Express Régionale; pron. air-ay-air) is the suburban train system serving destinations such as Versailles, Disneyland Paris, and the airports. These routes, indicated by thick lines on your subway map, are identified by letters A, B, C, and so on. The RER works like the Métro, but can be speedier (if it serves your destination directly) because it makes only a few stops within the city. One Métro ticket is all you need for RER rides within central Paris. You can transfer between the Métro and RER systems with the same ticket. Unlike the Métro, you need to insert your ticket in a turnstile to exit the RER system, and also unlike the Métro, signage can vary between RER stations, meaning you have to pay attention and verify that you're heading the right direction (RER lines often split at the end of the line leading to different signed *destinations*—study your map or confirm with a local and you'll do fine). To travel outside the city (to Versailles or the airport, for example), you'll need to buy a separate, more expensive ticket at the station window before boarding; make sure your stop is served by checking the signs over the train platform. Not all trains serve all stops. If you see "*toutes les gares*" on the platform sign describing your train, it means the train will stop at all of the stations.

By City Bus: The trickier bus system is worth figuring out. Métro tickets are good on both bus and Métro, though you can't use the same ticket to transfer between the two systems. One ticket gets you anywhere in central Paris, but if you leave the city center (shown as zone 1 on the diagram on board the bus), you must validate a second ticket. While the Métro shuts down about 00:30, some buses continue much later. Schedules are posted at bus stops.

Handy bus-system maps (*plan des autobus*) are available in any Métro station and are provided in your *Paris Pratique* map book if you invest €6.

Big system maps, posted at each bus and Métro stop, display the routes. Individual route diagrams show the exact routes of the lines serving that stop. Major stops are painted on the side of each bus. Enter through the front doors. Punch your Métro ticket in the machine behind the driver, or pay the higher cash fare. Get off the bus using the rear door. Even if you're not certain you've figured it out, do some joyriding (outside of rush hour). Lines #24, #63, and #69 are Paris' most scenic routes and make a great introduction to the city. Bus #69 is particularly handy, running between the Eiffel Tower, rue Cler (recommended hotels), Orsay, Louvre, Marais (recommended hotels), and the Père Lachaise Cemetery. The handiest bus routes are listed for each hotel area recommended (see "Sleeping," below).

By Taxi: Parisian taxis are reasonable—especially for couples and families. The meters are tamper-proof. Fares and supplements (described in English on the back windows) are straightforward. There's a €5 minimum. A 10-minute ride costs about €8 (versus €1 to get anywhere in town on the Métro). You can try waving one down, but it's easier to ask for the nearest taxi stand (*Où est une station de taxi?*; pron. oo ay oon stah-see-ohn duh taxi). Taxi stands are indicated by a circled T on many city maps, including Michelin's #10 Paris. A typical taxi takes three people (maybe 4 if you're polite and pay €2.50 extra); groups of up to five can use a *grand taxi*, which must be booked in advance (ask your hotel to call). If a taxi is summoned by phone, the meter starts as soon as the call is received—adding €3 or €4 to the bill. Higher rates are charged at night from 19:00 to 7:00, all day Sunday, and to either airport. There's a €1 charge for each piece of baggage and for train station pick-ups. To tip, round up to the next euro (minimum €0.50). Taxis are tough to find on Friday and Saturday nights, especially after the Métro closes (around 00:30). If you need to catch a train or flight early in the morning, consider booking a taxi the night before.

Organized Tours of Paris

Bus Tours—Paris Vision offers handy bus tours of Paris, day and night (advertised in hotel lobbies); their "Paris Illumination" tour is much more interesting (see "Nightlife in Paris," below). Far better daytime bus tours are the hop-on, hop-off double-decker bus services connecting Paris' main sights while providing running commentary (ideal in good weather when you can sit on top; see also Bâtobus under "Boat Tours" below).

Two companies provide hop-on, hop-off bus service: L'Open Tours and Les Cars Rouges (pick up their brochures showing routes and stops from any TI or on their buses). **L'Open Tours**, which uses yellow buses, provides more extensive coverage and offers three different routes rolling by most of the important sights in Paris (the Paris Grand Tour offers the best introduction). Tickets are good for any route. Buy your tickets from the driver (€25/1-day ticket, €27/2-day ticket, kids 4–11 pay €12.50 for 1 or 2 days, 20 percent less if you have a *Carte Orange* Métro pass). Two or three buses depart hourly from about 10:00 to 18:00; expect to wait 10 to 20 minutes at each stop (stops can be tricky to find). You can hop off at any stop, then catch a later bus following the same circuit. You'll see these bright yellow topless double-decker buses all over town—pick one up at the first important sight you visit, or start your tour at the Eiffel Tower stop (the first street on non-river side of the tower, tel. 01 42 66 56 56). **Les Cars Rouges'** bright red buses offer largely the same service with fewer stops on a single, Grand Tour Route for less money (2-day tickets, €22-adult, €11-kids 4–12, tel. 01 53 95 39 53).

Boat Tours—Several companies offer one-hour boat cruises on the Seine (by far, best at night). The huge, mass-production **Bâteaux-Mouches** boats depart every 20 to 30 minutes from pont de l'Alma's right bank and right in front of the Eiffel Tower, and are convenient to rue Cler hotels (€7.50, €4.50 for ages 4–12, daily 10:00–22:30, useless taped explanations in 6 languages and tour groups by the dozens, tel. 01 40 76 99 99). The smaller and more intimate **Vedettes de pont Neuf** depart only once an hour from the center of pont Neuf (twice an hour after dark), but they come with a live guide giving explanations in French and English and are convenient to Marais and Contrescarpe hotels (€9.50, €5 for ages 4–12, tel. 01 46 33 98 38).

From April through October, **Bâtobus** operates hop-on, hop-off boats on the Seine, connecting eight popular stops every 15 to 25 minutes: Eiffel Tower, Champs-Elysées, Orsay/place de la Concorde, Louvre, Notre-Dame, St. Germain-des-Prés, Hôtel de Ville, and Jardin des Plantes. Pick up a schedule at any stop (or TI) and use them as a scenic alternative to the Métro. Tickets are available for one day (€10, €5.50 under 12) and two days (€12.50, €6.50 under 12); boats run from 10:00 to 19:00, and until 21:00 June through September, www.batobus.com.

Paris Canal departs twice daily for three-hour, one-way cruises between the Orsay and Parc de la Vilette. You'll cruise up the Seine then along a quiet canal through nontouristy Paris, accompanied by English explanations (€17, €9.50 for kids 4–11, €12.50 for ages 12–25, tel. 01 42 40 96 97); the one-way trips depart at 9:30 from quai Anatole France (near the Orsay), and from Parc de la Vilette (at Folie des Visites du Parc) at 14:30.

Canauxrama offers a 2.5-hour cruise on a peaceful canal without the Seine in sight, starting from place de la Bastille and ending at Bassin de la Vilette, near Métro stop Stalingrad (€14, €9 for kids, €11 for seniors and students, departs at 9:45 and 14:30 across from Bastille Opéra, just below boulevard de la Bastille, opposite #50, where the canal meets place de la Bastille, tel. 01 42 39 15 00).

Paris Walking Tours—This company offers a variety of excellent two-hour walks, led by British or American guides, nearly daily for €10 (tel. 01 48 09 21 40 for recorded schedule in English, fax 01 42 43 75 51, see www.paris-walks.com for their complete schedule). Tours focus on the Marais, Montmartre, Ile de la Cité and Ile St. Louis, and Hemingway's Paris. Ask about their family-friendly tours. Call ahead a day or two to learn their schedule and starting point. No reservations are required. These are thoughtfully prepared, relaxing, and humorous. Don't hesitate to stand close to the guide to hear.

Private Guide Service—For many, Paris merits hiring a Parisian as your personal guide. Two excellent licensed local guides who freelance for individuals and families are Arnaud Servignat, who runs Accueil-France-Paris-Guide (also does car tours of country-side around Paris, tel. 06 72 77 94 50, fax 01 42 57 00 38, e-mail: arnotour@noos.fr or franceparisguide@noos.fr), and Marianne Siegler (€150/4 hrs, €250/day, reserve in advance if possible, tel. 01 42 52 32 51).

Bike Tours—**Mike's Bullfrog Bike Tours** attract a younger crowd for its three- to four-hour rolls through Paris (€20, May–Nov daily at 11:00, also at 15:30 June–July, no CC, in English, no bikes or reservations needed, meet at south pillar of Eiffel Tower, cellular 06 09 98 08 60, www.mikesbiketours.com).

Excursion Tours—Many companies offer minivan and big bus tours to regional sights, including all of the day trips described in this book. **Paris Walking Tours** are the best, with informative though infrequent tours of the Impressionist artist retreats of Giverny and Auvers-sur-Oise (€47–56, includes admissions, tel. 01 48 09 21 40 for recording in English, fax 01 42 43 75 51, www.paris-walks.com).

Paris Vision offers mass-produced, full-size bus and minivan tours to several popular regional destinations, including the Loire Valley, Champagne region, D-Day beaches, and Mont St. Michel. Their minivan tours are more expensive but more personal, given in English, and offer pick up at your hotel (€130–200/person). The full-size bus tours are multilingual and cost about half the price of a minivan tour—worth it for some simply for the ease of transportation to the sights (full-size buses depart from 214 rue de Rivoli, Mo: Tuileries, tel. 01 42 60 30 01, fax 01 42 86 95 36, www.parisvision.com).

Sights—The "Historic Core of Paris" Walk

(This information is distilled from the Historic Paris Walk chapter in *Rick Steves' Mona Winks*, by Gene Openshaw and Rick Steves.)

Allow four hours for this self-guided tour, including sight-seeing. Start where the city did—on the Ile de la Cité. Face Notre-Dame and follow the dotted line on the "Core of Paris" map (see page 58). To get to Notre-Dame, ride the Métro to Cité, Hôtel de Ville, or St. Michel and walk to the big square facing the...

▲▲**Notre-Dame Cathedral**—This 700-year-old cathedral is packed with history and tourists. Study its sculpture and windows, take in a Mass, eavesdrop on guides, and walk all around the outside (free, daily 8:00–18:45; treasury-€2.50, not covered by museum pass, daily 9:30–17:30; ask about free English tours, normally Wed and Thu at 12:00 and Sat at 14:30; Mo: Cité, Hôtel de Ville, or St. Michel). Climb to the top for a great view of the city; you get 400 steps for only €5.50 (daily April–Sept 9:30–19:30, until 21:00 July–Aug on Sat and Sun, Oct–March 10:00–17:30, last entry 45 min before closing, covered by museum pass though you can't bypass line, arrive early to avoid long lines). There are clean €0.50 toilets in front of the church near Charlemagne's statue.

The **cathedral facade** is worth a close look. The church is dedicated to "Our Lady" (Notre-Dame). Mary is center stage—cradling Jesus, surrounded by the halo of the rose window. Adam is on the left and Eve is on the right.

Below Mary and above the arches is a row of 28 statues known as the Kings of Judah. During the French Revolution, these biblical kings were mistaken for the hated French kings. The citizens stormed the church, crying, "Off with their heads!" All were decapitated, but have since been recapitated.

Speaking of decapitation, look at the carving above the doorway on the left. The man with his head in his hands is St. Denis. Back when there was a Roman temple on this spot, Christianity began making converts. The fourth-century bishop of Roman Paris, Denis, was beheaded. But these early Christians were hard to keep down. The man who would become St. Denis got up, tucked his head under his arm, and headed north until he found just the right place to meet his maker: Montmartre. (Although the name "Montmartre" comes from the Roman "Mount of Mars,"

Core of Paris

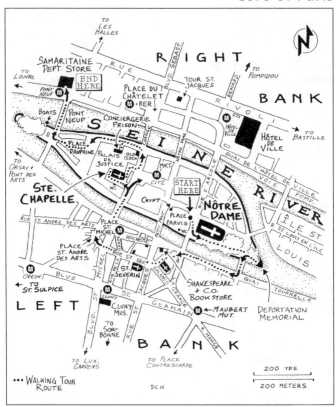

later generations—thinking of their beheaded patron St. Denis—
preferred a less pagan version, "Mount of Martyrs.") The Parisians
were convinced of this miracle, Christianity gained ground, and a
church soon replaced the pagan temple.

Medieval art was OK if it embellished the house of God and
told Bible stories. For a fine example, move to the base of the central column (at the foot of Mary, about where the head of St. Denis
could spit if he was real good). Working around from the left, find
God telling a barely created Eve, "Have fun, but no apples." Next,
the sexiest serpent I've ever seen makes apples à la mode. Finally,
Adam and Eve, now ashamed of their nakedness, are expelled by
an angel. This is a tiny example in a church covered with meaning.

Now move to the right and study the carving above the **central portal**. It's the end of the world, and Christ sits on the throne

of Judgment (just under the arches, holding his hands up). Below
him an angel and a demon weigh souls in the balance. The "good"
stand to the left, looking up to heaven. The "bad" ones to the
right are chained up and led off to...Versailles on a Tuesday.
The "ugly" ones must be the crazy sculpted demons to the right,
at the base of the arch.

Wander through the interior. You'll be routed around the
ambulatory, much as medieval pilgrims would have been. Don't
miss the rose windows filling each of the transepts. Back outside,
walk around the church through the park on the riverside for a
close look at the flying buttresses.

The neo-Gothic, 90-meter/300-foot **spire** is a product of the
1860 reconstruction. Around its base are apostles and evangelists
(the green men) as well as Viollet-le-Duc, the architect in charge
of the work. Notice how the apostles look outward, blessing the
city, while the architect (at top, seen from behind the church)
looks up, admiring his spire.

The archaeological **crypt** is a worthwhile 15-minute stop
with your museum pass (€3.50, Tue–Sun 10:00–18:00, closed
Mon, enter 100 meters/330 feet in front of church). You'll see
Roman ruins, trace the street plan of the medieval village, and
see diagrams of how the earliest Paris grew and grew, all thoughtfully explained in English.

If you're hungry near Notre-Dame, the nearby Ile St. Louis
has inexpensive *crêperies* and grocery stores open daily on its main
drag. Plan a picnic for the quiet, bench-filled park immediately
behind the church (public WC available).

Behind Notre-Dame, squeeze through the tourist buses, cross
the street, and enter the iron gate into the park at the tip of the
island. Look for the stairs and head down to reach...

▲▲**Deportation Memorial (Mémorial de la Déportation)**—
This memorial to the 200,000 French victims of the Nazi concentration camps draws you into their experience. As you descend
the steps, the city around you disappears. Surrounded by walls,
you have become a prisoner. Your only freedom is your view of
the sky and the tantalizing glimpse of the river below.

Enter the single-file chamber ahead. Inside, the circular
plaque in the floor reads, "They descended into the mouth of the
earth and they did not return." A hallway stretches in front of you,
lined with 200,000 lighted crystals, one for each French citizen
that died. Flickering at the far end is the eternal flame of hope.
The tomb of the unknown deportee lies at your feet. Above, the
inscription reads, "Dedicated to the living memory of the 200,000
French deportees sleeping in the night and the fog, exterminated
in the Nazi concentration camps."

Above the exit as you leave is the message you'll find at all Nazi sights: "Forgive, but never forget." (Free, April–Sept daily 10:00–12:00 & 14:00–19:00, Oct–March daily 10:00–12:00 & 14:00–17:00, east tip of the island Ile de la Cité, behind Notre-Dame and near Ile St. Louis, Mo: Cité.)

Ile St. Louis—Look across the river to the Ile St. Louis. If the Ile de la Cité is a tug laden with the history of Paris, it's towing this classy little residential dinghy laden only with boutiques, famous sorbet shops, and restaurants (see "Eating in Paris," below). This island wasn't developed until much later (18th century). What was a swampy mess is now harmonious Parisian architecture. The pedestrian bridge, pont Saint Louis, connects the two islands, leading right to rue Saint Louis en l'Ile. This spine of the island is lined with interesting shops. A short stroll takes you to the famous Berthillon ice-cream parlor (#31). Loop back to the pedestrian bridge along the parklike quays (walk north to the river and turn left). This walk is about as peaceful and romantic as Paris gets.

Before walking to the opposite end of the Ile de la Cité, loop through the Latin Quarter (as indicated on the map). From the Deportation Memorial cross the bridge onto the Left Bank and enjoy the riverside view of the Notre-Dame and window shop among the green book stalls, browsing through used books, vintage posters, and souvenirs. At the little park and church (over the bridge from the front of Notre-Dame), venture inland a few blocks, basically arcing through the Latin Quarter and returning to the island two bridges down at place St. Michel.

▲**Latin Quarter**—This area, which gets its name from the language used here when it was an exclusive medieval university district, lies between Luxembourg Garden and the Seine, centering around the Sorbonne University and boulevards St. Germain and St. Michel. This is the core of the Left Bank—it's crowded with international eateries, far-out bookshops, street singers, and jazz clubs. For colorful wandering and café sitting, afternoons and evenings are best (Mo: St. Michel).

Along rue Saint-Severin, you can still see the shadow of the medieval sewer system (the street slopes into a central channel of bricks). In the days before plumbing and toilets, when people still went to the river or neighborhood wells for their water, "flushing" meant throwing it out the window. Certain times of day were flushing times. Maids on the fourth floor would holler, "*Garde de l'eau!*" ("Look out for the water!") and heave it into the streets, where it would eventually be washed down into the Seine.

Consider a visit to the Cluny Museum for its medieval art and unicorn tapestries (listed under "Sights—Southeast Paris," below).

Place St. Michel (facing the St. Michel bridge) is the traditional core of the Left Bank's artsy, liberal, hippie, bohemian district of poets, philosophers, winos, and tourists. In less-commercial times, place St. Michel was a gathering point for the city's malcontents and misfits. Here, in 1871, the citizens took the streets from the government troops, set up barricades *Les Mis*–style, and established the Paris Commune. During World War II, the locals rose up against their Nazi oppressors (read the plaques by St. Michel fountain). And in the spring of 1968, a time of social upheaval all over the world, young students—battling riot batons and tear gas—took over the square and demanded change.

From place St. Michel, look across the river and find the spire of Sainte-Chapelle church and its weathervane angel (below). Cross the river on pont St. Michel and continue along boulevard du Palais. On your left, you'll see the high-security doorway to Sainte-Chapelle. But first, continue another 30 meters/100 feet and turn right at a wide pedestrian street, the rue de Lutèce.

Cité "Métropolitain" Stop—Of the 141 original turn-of-the-19th-century subway entrances, this is one of 17 survivors preserved as national art treasures. The curvy, plantlike ironwork is a textbook example of Art Nouveau, the style that rebelled against the erector-set squareness of the Industrial Age (e.g., Mr. Eiffel's tower).

The flower market here on place Louis Lepine is a pleasant detour. On Sundays, this square chirps with a busy bird market. And across the way is the Prefecture de Police, where Inspector Clouseau of *Pink Panther* fame used to work, and where the local resistance fighters took the first building from the Nazis in August 1944, leading to the Allied liberation of Paris a week later.

Pause here to admire the view. Sainte-Chapelle is a pearl in an ugly architectural oyster, part of a complex of buildings that includes the Palace of Justice (to the right of Sainte-Chapelle, behind the fancy gates). Return to the entrance of Sainte-Chapelle. Everyone needs to pass through a metal detector to get in. Free toilets are ahead on the left. The line into the church may be long. (Museum passholders can go directly in; pick up the excellent English info sheet.) Enter the humble ground floor of...

▲▲▲Sainte-Chapelle—This triumph of Gothic church architecture is a cathedral of glass like no other. It was speedily built from 1242 to 1248 for Louis IX (the only French king who is now a saint) to house the supposed Crown of Thorns. Its architectural harmony is due to the fact that it was completed under the direction of one architect in only six years—unheard of in Gothic times. (Notre-Dame took more than 200 years to build.)

The design clearly shows an Old Regime approach to worship. The basement was for staff and other common folk. Royal

Christians worshiped upstairs. The ground-floor paint job, a 19th-century restoration, is a reasonably accurate copy of the original.

Climb the spiral staircase to the **Chapelle Haute**. Fill the place with choral music, crank up the sunshine, face the top of the altar, and really believe that the Crown of Thorns was there, and this becomes one awesome space.

"Let there be light." In the Bible, it's clear: Light is divine. Light shining through stained glass was a symbol of God's grace shining down to earth. Gothic architects used their new technology to turn dark stone buildings into lanterns of light. The glory of Gothic shines brighter here than in any other church.

There are 15 separate panels of stained glass (6,500 square feet—two-thirds of it 13th-century original), with more than 1,100 different scenes, mostly from the Bible. In medieval times, scenes like these helped teach Bible stories to the illiterate.

The altar was raised up high to better display the relic—the Crown of Thorns—around which this chapel was built. The supposed crown cost King Louis three times as much as this church. Today, it is kept in the Notre-Dame treasury and shown only on Good Friday.

Louis' little private viewing window is in the wall to the right of the altar. Louis, both saintly and shy, liked to go to church without dealing with the rigors of public royal life. Here, he could worship still dressed in his jammies.

Lay your camera on the ground and shoot the ceiling. Those ribs growing out of the slender columns are the essence of Gothic.

Books in the gift shop explain the stained glass in English. There are concerts (€16–25) almost every summer evening (€5.50, €8 combo-ticket covers Conciergerie, both covered by museum pass, daily 9:30–18:00, Mo: Cité, tel. 01 44 07 12 38 for concert information).

Palais de Justice—Back outside, as you walk around the church exterior, look down and notice how much Paris has risen in the 800 years since Sainte-Chapelle was built. You're in a huge complex of buildings that has housed the local government since ancient Roman times. It was the site of the original Gothic palace of the early kings of France. The only surviving medieval parts are the Sainte-Chapelle church and the Conciergerie prison.

Most of the site is now covered by the giant Palais de Justice, home of France's supreme court (built in 1776). "*Liberté, Egalité, Fraternité,*" emblazoned over the doors, is a reminder that this was also the headquarters of the Revolutionary government.

Now pass through the big iron gate to the noisy boulevard du Palais and turn left (toward the Right Bank). On the corner is the site of the oldest public clock in the city (built in 1334). While the present clock is said to be Baroque, it somehow still manages to keep accurate time.

Turn left onto quai de l'Horologe, and walk along the river. The round medieval tower just ahead marks the entrance to the Conciergerie. Pop in to visit the courtyard and lobby (free). Step past the serious-looking guard into the courtyard.

Conciergerie—This former prison is a gloomy place. Kings used it to torture and execute failed assassins. The leaders of the Revolution put it to similar good use. The tower next to the entrance, called "the babbler," was named for the painful sounds that leaked from it.

Look at the stark lettering above the doorways. This was a no-nonsense revolutionary time. Everything, even lettering, was subjected to the test of reason. No frills, or we chop 'em off.

Step inside; the lobby, with an English-language history display, is free. Marie-Antoinette was imprisoned here. During a busy eight-month period in the Revolution, she was one of 2,600 prisoners kept here on the way to the guillotine. The interior, with its huge vaulted and pillared rooms, echoes with history but is pretty barren (€5.50, €8 combo-ticket covers Sainte-Chapelle, both covered by museum pass, daily April–Sept 9:30–18:30, Oct–March 10:00–17:00, good English descriptions). You can see Marie-Antoinette's cell, housing a collection of her mementos. In another room, a list of those made "a foot shorter at the top" by the "national razor" includes ex-King Louis XVI, Charlotte Corday (who murdered Marat in his bathtub), and the chief revolutionary who got a taste of his own medicine, Maximilien Robespierre.

Back outside, wink at the flak-proof-vested guard, and turn left. Listen for babbles and continue your walk along the river. Across the river you can see the rooftop observatory—flags flapping—of the Samaritaine department store, where this walk will end. At the first corner, veer left past France's supreme-court building and into a sleepy triangular square called place Dauphine. Marvel at how such quaintness could be lodged in the midst of such greatness as you walk through the park to the end of the island. At the equestrian statue of Henry IV, turn right onto the bridge and take refuge in one of the nooks on the Eiffel Tower side.

Pont Neuf—This "new bridge" is now Paris' oldest. Built during Henry IV's reign (around 1600), its 12 arches span the widest part of the river. The fine view includes the park on the tip of the island (note Seine tour boats), the Orsay Museum, and the Louvre. These turrets were originally for vendors and street entertainers. In the days of Henry IV, who originated the promise of "a chicken in every pot," this would have been a lively scene.

Directly over the river, the first building you'll hit on the Right Bank is the venerable old department store, Samaritaine. ▲**Samaritaine Department Store Viewpoint**—Enter the store and go to the rooftop. Ride the glass elevator from near the pont Neuf entrance to the ninth floor (you'll be greeted by a WC—check out the sink). Pass the 10th-floor *terrasse* (with café) for the 11th-floor panorama (€2, tight spiral staircase; watch your head). Quiz yourself. Working counterclockwise, find the Eiffel Tower, Invalides/Napoleon's Tomb, Montparnasse Tower, Henry IV statue on the tip of the island, Sorbonne University, the dome of the Panthéon, Sainte-Chapelle, Notre-Dame, Hôtel de Ville (city hall), Pompidou Center, Sacré-Coeur, Opéra, and the Louvre. The Champs-Elysées leads to the Arc de Triomphe. Shadowing that—even bigger, while two times as distant—is the Grande Arche de la Défense. You'll find light, reasonably priced, and incredibly scenic meals on the breezy 10th-floor terrace, and there's a supermarket in the basement (daily 9:30–19:00, Mo: Pont Neuf, tel. 01 40 41 20 20).

Sights—Paris Museums near the Tuileries Garden

The newly renovated Tuileries Garden was once private property of kings and queens. Paris' grandest public park links these museums.
▲▲▲**Louvre**—This is Europe's oldest, biggest, greatest, and maybe most crowded museum. There is no grander entry than through the pyramid, but metal detectors create a long line at times.

There are several ways to avoid the line. Museum passholders can use the group entrance in the pedestrian passageway between the pyramid and rue de Rivoli (facing the pyramid with your back to the Tuileries Garden, go to your left, which is north; under the arches, you'll find the entrance and escalator down). Otherwise, you can enter the Louvre underground directly from the Métro stop Palais Royal/Musée du Louvre (exit following signs to Musée du Louvre) or from the Carrousel shopping mall, which is connected to the museum. Enter the mall at 99 rue de Rivoli (the door with the red awning, daily 8:30–23:00). The taxi stand is across rue de Rivoli next to the Métro station.

Pick up the free "Louvre Handbook" in English at the information desk under the pyramid as you enter. Don't try to cover the entire museum. Consider taking a tour (see "Tours," below).

Self-Guided Tour: Start in the Denon wing and visit the highlights, in the following order (thanks to Gene Openshaw for his help with this).

Wander through the **ancient Greek and Roman works** to see the Parthenon frieze, Pompeii mosaics, Etruscan sarcophagi, and Roman portrait busts. You can't miss lovely Venus de Milo

Paris Museums near the Tuileries Garden

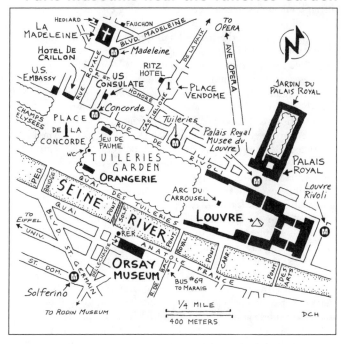

(*Aphrodite*). This goddess of love (c. 100 B.C., from the Greek island of Milos) created a sensation when she was discovered in 1820. Most "Greek" statues are actually later Roman copies, but Venus is a rare Greek original. She, like Golden Age Greeks, epitomizes stability, beauty, and balance. Later Greek art was Hellenistic, adding motion and drama. For a good example, see the exciting Winged Victory of Samothrace (*Victoire de Samothrace*, on the landing). This statue of a woman with wings, poised on the prow of a ship, once stood on a hilltop to commemorate a great naval victory. This is the Venus de Milo gone Hellenistic.

The **Italian collection** is on the other side of the Winged Victory. The key to Renaissance painting was realism, and for the Italians "realism" was spelled "3-D." Painters were inspired by the realism and balanced beauty of Greek sculpture. Painting a 3-D world on a 2-D surface is tough, and after a millennium of Dark Ages, artists were rusty. Living in a religious age, they painted mostly altarpieces full of saints, angels, Madonnas-and-bambinos, and crucifixes floating in an ethereal gold-leaf heaven. Gradually, though, they brought these otherworldly scenes down to earth. The Italian collection—including *Mona Lisa*—is scattered throughout rooms *(salles)* 3 and 4, in the long Grand Gallery, and in adjoining rooms.

Two masters of the Italian High Renaissance (1500–1600) were Raphael (see his *La Belle Jardinière*, showing the *Madonna, Child, and John the Baptist)* and Leonardo da Vinci. The Louvre has the greatest collection of Leonardos in the world—five of them, including the exquisite *Virgin, Child, and St. Anne,* the neighboring *Madonna of the Rocks,* and the androgynous *John the Baptist.* His most famous, of course, is *Mona.*

Leonardo was already an old man when François I invited him to France. Determined to pack light, he took only a few paintings. One was a portrait of a Lisa del Giocondo, the wife of a wealthy Florentine merchant. When Leonardo arrived, François immediately fell in love with the painting, making it the centerpiece of the small collection of Italian masterpieces that would, in three centuries, become the Louvre museum. He called it *La Gioconda.* We know it as a contraction of the Italian for "my lady Lisa"—*Mona Lisa.* Warning: François was impressed, but *Mona* may disappoint you. She's smaller and darker than you'd expect, engulfed in a huge room, and hidden behind a glaring pane of glass.

Mona's overall mood is one of balance and serenity, but there's also an element of mystery. Her smile and long-distance beauty are subtle and elusive, tempting but always just out of reach, like strands of a street singer's melody drifting through the Métro tunnel. *Mona* doesn't knock your socks off, but she winks at the patient viewer.

Now for something **neoclassical**. Notice the fine work, such as *Coronation of Napoleon* by J. L. David, near *Mona* in the Salle Daru. Neoclassicism, once the rage in France (1780–1850), usually features Greek subjects, patriotic sentiment, and a clean, simple style. After Napoleon quickly conquered most of Europe, he insisted on being made emperor (not merely king) of this "New Rome." He staged an elaborate coronation ceremony in Paris, and rather than let the pope crown him, he crowned himself. The setting is the Notre-Dame cathedral, with Greek columns and Roman arches thrown in for effect. Napoleon's mom was also added, since she couldn't make it to the ceremony. A key on the frame describes who's who in the picture.

The **Romantic** collection, in an adjacent room (Salle Mollien), has works by Géricault *(Raft of the Medusa)* and Delacroix *(Liberty at the Barricades).* Romanticism, with an emphasis on motion and emotion, is the complete flip side of neoclassicism, though they both flourished in the early 1800s. Delacroix's *Liberty,* commemorating the stirrings of democracy in France, is also a fitting tribute to the Louvre, the first museum opened to the common rabble of humanity. The good things in life don't belong only to a small wealthy part of society, but to all. The motto of France is *"Liberté, Egalité, Fraternité"*—liberty, equality, and brotherhood.

Exit the room at the far end (past the café) and go downstairs, where you'll bump into the bum of a large, twisting male nude who looks like he's just waking up after a thousand-year nap. The two *Slaves* (c. 1513) by Michelangelo Buonarroti are a fitting end to this museum—works that bridge the ancient and modern worlds. Michelangelo, like his fellow Renaissance artists, learned from the Greeks. The perfect anatomy, twisting poses, and idealized faces look like they could have been done 2,000 years earlier. Michelangelo said that his purpose was to carve away the marble to reveal the figures God put inside. The *Rebellious Slave*, fighting against his bondage, shows the agony of that process and the ecstasy of the result.

Cost: €7.50, €5 after 15:00 and on Sunday, free on first Sunday of month and for those under 18, covered by museum pass. Tickets good all day. Reentry allowed. Tel. 01 40 20 51 51, recorded info tel. 01 40 20 53 17 (www.louvre.fr).

Hours: Wed–Mon 9:00–18:00, closed Tue. All wings open Wed until 21:45. On Mon, only the Denon wing is open until 21:45, but it contains the biggies: *Mona Lisa*, Venus de Milo, and more. Galleries start closing 30 minutes early. Closed Jan 1, Easter, May 1, Nov 1, and Dec 25. Crowds are worst on Sun, Mon, Wed, and mornings. Save money by visiting after 15:00.

Tours: The 90-minute English-language tours, which leave six times daily except Tuesday, when the museum is closed, and Sunday, boil this overwhelming museum down to size (normally at 11:00, 14:00, and 15:45, €3 plus your entry ticket, tour tel. 01 40 20 52 63). Clever €5 digital audioguides (after ticket booths, at top of stairs) give you a receiver and a directory of about 130 masterpieces, allowing you to dial a (rather dull) commentary on included works as you stumble upon them. Rick Steves' and Gene Openshaw's museum guidebook, *Rick Steves' Mona Winks* (buy in United States), includes a self-guided tour of the Louvre.

Louvre Complex: The newly renovated Richelieu wing and the underground shopping-mall extension add the finishing touches to Le Grand Louvre Project (which started in 1989 with the pyramid entrance). To explore this most recent extension of the Louvre, enter through the pyramid, walk toward the inverted pyramid, and uncover a post office, a handy TI and SNCF (train tickets) office, glittering boutiques and a dizzying assortment of good-value eateries (up the escalator), and the Palais-Royal Métro entrance. Stairs at the far end take you right into the Tuileries Garden, a perfect antidote to the stuffy, crowded rooms of the Louvre.

▲▲▲**Orsay Museum**—The Musée d'Orsay (pron. mew-zay dor-say) houses French art of the 1800s (specifically, art from 1848 to 1914), picking up where the Louvre leaves off. For us, that means Impressionism. The Orsay houses the best general collection anywhere of Manet, Monet, Renoir, Degas, van Gogh, Cézanne, and Gauguin.

The museum shows art that is also both old and new, conservative and revolutionary. You'll start on the ground floor with the Conservatives and the early rebels who paved the way for the Impressionists, then head upstairs to see how a few visionary young artists bucked the system and revolutionized the art world, paving the way for the 20th century.

For most visitors, the most important part of the museum is the upstairs Impressionist collection. Here, you can study many pictures you've probably seen in books, such as Manet's *Luncheon on the Grass*, Renoir's *Dance at the Moulin de la Galette*, Monet's *Gare St. Lazare*, *Whistler's Mother*, van Gogh's *Church at Auvers*, and Cezanne's *Card Players*. As you approach these beautiful, easy-to-enjoy paintings, remember that there is more to this art than meets the eye.

Impressionism 101: The camera threatened to make artists obsolete. A painter's original function was to record reality faithfully, like a journalist. Now a machine could capture a better likeness faster than you could say Etch A Sketch.

But true art is more than just painted reality. It gives us reality from the artist's point of view, putting a personal stamp on the work. It records not only a scene—a camera can do that—but the artist's impressions of that scene. Impressions are often fleeting, so the artist has to work quickly.

The Impressionist painters rejected camera-like detail for a quick style more suited to capturing the passing moment. Feeling stifled by the rigid rules and stuffy atmosphere of the Academy, the Impressionists took as their motto, "out of the studio, into the open air." They grabbed their berets and scarves and took excursions to the country, setting up their easels on riverbanks and hillsides or sketching in cafés and dance halls. Gods, goddesses, nymphs, and fantasy scenes were out; common people and rural landscapes were in.

The quick style and simple subjects were ridiculed and called childish by the "experts." Rejected by the Salon, the Impressionists staged their own exhibition in 1874. They brashly took their name from an insult thrown at them by a critic, who laughed at one of Monet's impressions of a sunrise. During the next decade, they exhibited their own work independently. The public, opposed at first, was slowly drawn in by the simplicity, color, and vibrancy of Impressionist art.

Cost: €7; €5 after 16:15, on Sun, and for ages 18 to 25; free for youth under 18 and for anyone first Sun of month; covered by museum pass. Tickets are good all day. Museum passholders can enter to the left of the main entrance (during the renovation, they can walk to the front of the line and show their passes).

Hours: June 20–Sept 20: Tue–Sun 9:00–18:00; Sept 21–June 19: Tue–Sat 10:00–18:00, Sun 9:00–18:00; Thu until 21:45 all year, always closed Mon. Last entrance is 45 minutes before closing. The Impressionist Galleries start closing at 17:15, frustrating many unwary visitors. Note that the Orsay is crowded on Tue, when the Louvre is closed.

Tours: Live English-language tours of the Orsay usually run daily (except Sun) at 11:30. The 90-minute tours cost €6 and are also available on audioguide (€5). Tours in English focusing on the Impressionists are offered Tuesdays at 14:30 and Thursdays at 18:30 (sometimes also on other days, €6).

Cafés: The museum has a cheap café on the fourth floor, and the elegant Salon de Thé du Musée is on the second floor (good salad bar).

Location: The Orsay sits above the RER-C stop called Musée d'Orsay. The nearest Métro stop is Solferino, three blocks south of the Orsay. Bus #69 from the Marais and rue Cler neighborhoods stops at the museum on the river side (Quai Anatole France).

In the summer of 2003, the main entry to the Orsay will be reopened after renovation. Until then, visitors are admitted through a temporary entry facing the river.

Jeu de Paume—Previously home to the Impressionist art collection now located in the Orsay, the Jeu de Paume now hosts rotating exhibits of top contemporary artists (€6, not covered by museum pass, Tue 12:00–21:30, Wed–Fri 12:00–19:00, Sat–Sun 10:00–19:00, closed Mon, on place de la Concorde, just inside Tuileries Garden on rue de Rivoli side, Mo: Concorde).

L'Orangerie—This excellent Impressionist museum is closed until 2004. The small, quiet, and often-overlooked museum houses Monet's water lilies, many famous Renoirs, and a scattering of other great Impressionist works. The breezy, round rooms of water lilies are two of the most enjoyable rooms in Paris (located in Tuileries Garden near place de la Concorde, Mo: Concorde).

Sights—Southwest Paris: The Eiffel Tower Neighborhood

▲▲▲**Eiffel Tower (La Tour Eiffel)**—It's crowded and expensive, but worth the trouble. Go early (by 8:45) or late in the day (after 20:00 in summer, otherwise 18:00) to avoid most crowds; weekends are worst. The Pilier Nord (north pillar) has the biggest

Eiffel Tower to Les Invalides

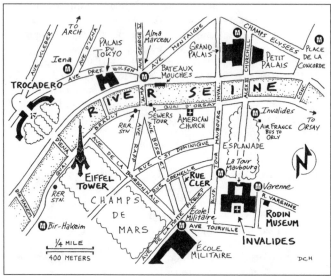

elevator and, therefore, the fastest-moving line. It takes two elevators to get to the top (transfer at level 2), which means two lines and very long waits if you don't go early or late. A TI/ticket booth is between the Pilier Nord and Pilier Est (east pillar). The stairs (yes, you can walk up partway) are next to the Jules Verne restaurant entrance. A sign in the jam-packed elevator reminds you to beware of pickpockets.

The tower is 300 meters/1,000 feet tall, 15 centimeters/6 inches taller in hot weather, covers 2.5 acres, and requires 50 tons of paint. Its 7,000 tons of metal are spread out so well at the base that it's no heavier per square inch than a linebacker on tiptoes. Visitors to Paris may find *Mona Lisa* to be less than expected, but the Eiffel Tower rarely disappoints, even in an era of skyscrapers.

Built one hundred years after the French Revolution (and in the midst of an Industrial one), the tower served no function but to impress. Bridge-builder Gustave Eiffel won the contest for the 1889 Centennial World's Fair by beating out such rival proposals as a giant guillotine. To a generation hooked on technology, the tower was the marvel of the age, a symbol of progress and of man's ingenuity. To others, it was a cloned-sheep monstrosity. The writer Guy de Maupassant routinely ate lunch in the tower just so he wouldn't have to look at it.

Delicate and graceful when seen from afar, it's massive—

even a bit scary—from close up. You don't appreciate the size until you walk toward it; like a mountain, it seems so close but takes forever to reach. There are three observation platforms at 60, 120, and 270 meters (200, 400, and 900 feet); the higher you go, the more you pay. Each requires a separate elevator (and line), so plan on at least 90 minutes if you want to go to the top and back. The view from the 120-meter-high (400 feet) second level is plenty. As you ascend through the metal beams, imagine being a worker, perched high above nothing, riveting this giant erector set together. On top, all of Paris lies before you, with a panorama guide. On a good day, you can see for 65 kilometers/40 miles.

The first level has exhibits, a post office (daily 10:00–19:00, cancellation stamp will read Eiffel Tower), snack bar, WCs, and souvenirs. Read the informative signs (in English) describing the major monuments, see the entertaining free movie on the history of the tower, and don't miss a century of fireworks including the entire millennium blast on video. Then consider a drink or a sandwich overlooking all of Paris at the snack café (outdoor tables in summer) or at the city's best view bar/restaurant, **Altitude 95** (€19–28 lunches, €46 dinners, dinner seatings at 19:00 and 21:00, reserve well ahead for a view table; before you ascend to dine, drop by the booth between the north *(nord)* and east *(est)* pillars to buy your Eiffel Tower ticket and pick up a pass that enables you to skip the line; tel. 01 45 55 20 04, fax 01 47 05 94 40).

The second level has the best views (walk up the stairway to get above the netting), a small cafeteria, WCs, and an Internet gimmick to have your photo at the Eiffel Tower sent into cyberspace (La Gallerie des Visiteurs).

It costs €4 to go to the first level, €7 to the second, and €10 to go all the way for the 270-meter/900-foot view (not covered by museum pass). On a budget? You can climb the stairs to the second level for only €3 (March–Sept daily 9:00–24:00, Oct–Feb 9:30–23:00, last entry 1 hour before closing, shorter lines at night, Mo: Trocadero, RER: Champ de Mars, tel. 01 44 11 23 23).

The best place to view the tower is from Trocadéro Square to the north (a 10-min walk across the river, and a happening scene at night). Consider arriving at the Trocadéro Métro stop, then walking toward the tower. Another great viewpoint is the long, grassy field, le Champ de Mars, to the south (after about 20:00, the gendarmes look the other way as Parisians stretch out or picnic on the grass). However impressive it may be by day, it's an awesome thing to see at twilight, when the tower becomes engorged with light, and virile Paris lies back and lets night be on top.

▲**Paris Sewer Tour (Egouts)**—This quick and easy visit takes you along a few hundred meters of underground water tunnel lined with interesting displays, well described in English, explaining the evolution of the world's longest sewer system. (If you straightened out Paris' sewers, they would reach beyond Istanbul.) Don't miss the slideshow, the fine WCs just beyond the gift shop, and the occasional tour in English (€4, covered by museum pass, Sat–Wed 11:00–17:00, closed Thu–Fri, where pont de l'Alma greets the Left Bank, Mo: Alma Marceau, RER: Pont de l'Alma, tel. 01 47 05 10 29).

▲▲**Napoleon's Tomb and Army Museum (Les Invalides)**—The emperor lies majestically dead inside several coffins under a grand dome—a goose-bumping pilgrimage for historians. Napoleon is surrounded by the tombs of other French war heroes and a fine military museum in Hôtel des Invalides. Check out the interesting World War II wing. Follow signs to the "crypt" to find Roman Empire–style reliefs listing the accomplishments of Napoleon's administration. The restored dome glitters with 26 pounds of gold (€6, students and kids 12–17–€5, under 12 free, daily April–Sept 9:00–17:45, mid-June–mid-Sept until 18:45, Oct–March 10:00–16:45; closed first Mon of month; open 30 min longer Sun, Napoleon's Tomb open 45 min longer daily June 15–Sept 15, closed Jan 1, May 1, Nov 1, and Dec 25, Mo: La Tour Maubourg or Varennes, tel. 01 44 42 37 72).

▲▲**Rodin Museum (Musée Rodin)**—This user-friendly museum is filled with passionate works by the greatest sculptor since Michelangelo. See *The Kiss, The Thinker, The Gates of Hell*, and many more. Don't miss the room full of work by Rodin's student and mistress, Camille Claudel (€5, €3 on Sun and for students, free for youth under 18 and for anyone first Sun of month; covered by museum pass; €1 for gardens only, which may be Paris' best deal as many works are well displayed in the beautiful gardens; April–Sept Tue–Sun 9:30–17:45, closed Mon, gardens close 18:45, Oct–March Tue–Sun 9:30–17:00, closed Mon, gardens close 16:45; near Napoleon's Tomb, 77 rue de Varennes, Mo: Varennes, tel. 01 44 18 61 10). There's a good self-serve cafeteria as well as idyllic picnic spots in the family-friendly back garden.

▲▲**Marmottan Museum (Musée Marmottan)**—In this private, intimate, less-visited museum, you'll find more than 100 paintings by Claude Monet (thanks to his son Michel), including the *Impressions of a Sunrise* painting that gave the movement its start—and name (€6.50, not covered by museum pass, Tue–Sun 10:00–18:00, closed Mon, 2 rue Louis Boilly, Mo: La Muette, follow museum signs 6 blocks through a delightful kid-filled park, tel. 01 44 96 50 33). Nearby is one of Paris' most pleasant shopping streets, the rue de Passy (from La Muette Métro stop).

Sights—Southeast Paris: The Latin Quarter

▲**Latin Quarter (Quartier Latin)**—This Left Bank neighborhood, just opposite Notre-Dame, is the Latin Quarter. (For more information and a walking tour, see the "Historic Core of Paris Walk," above.) This was a center of Roman Paris. But its touristic fame relates to the Latin Quarter's intriguing artsy, bohemian character. This was perhaps Europe's leading university district in the Middle Ages—home, since the 13th century, to the prestigious Sorbonne University. Back then, Latin was the language of higher education. And, since students here came from all over Europe, Latin served as their linguistic common denominator. Locals referred to the quarter by its language: Latin. In modern times, this was the center of Paris' café culture. The neighborhood's main boulevards (St. Michel and St. Germain) are lined with cafés—once the haunts of great poets and philosophers but now the hangout of tired tourists. While still youthful and artsy, the area has become a tourist ghetto filled with cheap North African eateries.

▲▲**Cluny Museum (Musée National du Moyen Age)**—This treasure trove of medieval art fills the old Roman baths, offering close-up looks at stained glass, Notre-Dame carvings, fine goldsmithing and jewelry, and rooms of tapestries—the best of which is the exquisite *Lady with the Unicorn*. In five panels, a delicate-as-medieval-can-be noble lady introduces a delighted unicorn to the senses of taste, hearing, sight, smell, and touch (€7, €5.50 on Sun, free first Sun of month, covered by museum pass, Wed–Mon 9:15–17:45, closed Tue, near corner of boulevards St. Michel and St. Germain, Mo: Cluny, tel. 01 53 73 78 00).

St. Germain-des-Prés—A church was first built on this site in A.D. 452. The church you see today was constructed in 1163. The area around the church hops at night with fire eaters, mimes, and scads of artists (Mo: St. Germain-des-Prés).

▲**St. Sulpice Organ Concert**—For pipe-organ enthusiasts, this is a delight. The Grand-Orgue at St. Sulpice has a rich history, with a succession of 12 world-class organists (including Widor and Dupré) going back 300 years. Widor started the tradition of opening the loft to visitors after the 10:30 service on Sundays. Daniel Roth continues to welcome guests in three languages while playing five keyboards at once. The 10:30 Sunday Mass is followed by a high-powered 25-minute recital at 11:40. Then, just after noon, the small, unmarked door is opened (left of entry as you face the rear). Visitors scamper like 16th notes up spiral stairs, past the 18th-century StairMasters that were used to fill the bellows, into a world of 7,000 pipes, where they can watch the master play during the next Mass.

Latin Quarter

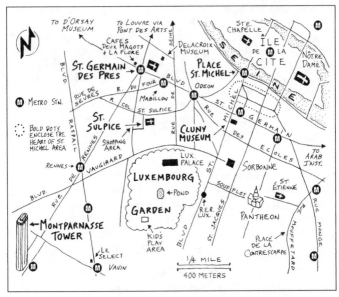

You'll generally have 30 minutes to kill (there's a plush lounge) before the organ plays; visitors can leave at any time. If late or rushed, show up around 12:30 and wait at the little door. As someone leaves, you can slip in (Mo: St. Sulpice or Mabillon). The Luxembourg Garden and St. Germain market are both nearby and open daily (the St. Germain market is between St. Sulpice and Métro stop Mabillon on rue Clément).

▲▲**Luxembourg Garden (Jardin du Luxembourg)**—Paris' most beautiful, interesting, and enjoyable garden/park/recreational area is a great place to watch Parisians at rest and play. These private gardens are property of the French Senate (housed in the château) and have special rules governing their use (e.g., where cards can be played, where dogs can be walked, where joggers can run, when and where music can be played). The brilliant flower beds are completely changed three times a year, and the boxed trees are brought out of the orangerie in May. Challenge the card and chess players to a game (near the tennis courts), or find a free chair near the main pond and take a breather. Notice any pigeons? The story goes that a poor Ernest Hemingway used to hand-hunt (read: strangle) them here. Paris Walking Tours offers a good tour of the park (see "Organized Tours of Paris," page 54).

The grand, neoclassical-domed Panthéon, now a mausoleum

housing the tombs of several great Frenchmen, is a block away and only worth entering if you have a museum pass. The park is open until dusk (Mo: Odéon, RER: Luxembourg).

If you enjoy the Luxembourg Garden and want to see more, visit the nearby, colorful Jardin des Plantes (Mo: Jussieu or Gare d'Austerlitz, RER: Luxembourg) and the more elegant Parc Monceau (Mo: Monceau).

Montparnasse Tower (La Tour Montparnasse)—This 59-floor superscraper is cheaper and easier to get to the top of than the Eiffel Tower, and has the added bonus of one of Paris' best views—since the Eiffel Tower is in it, and the Montparnasse Tower isn't. Buy the photo guide to the city, then go to the rooftop and orient yourself (€8, not covered by museum pass, daily in summer 9:30–23:30, off-season 10:00–22:00, disappointing after dark, entrance on rue l'Arrivé, Mo: Montparnasse). The tower is an efficient stop when combined with a day trip to Chartres, which begins at the Montparnasse train station.

▲**Catacombs**—These underground tunnels contain the anonymous bones of six million permanent Parisians. In 1785, the Revolutionary government of Paris decided to make its congested city more spacious and sanitary by emptying the city cemeteries (which traditionally surrounded churches) into an official ossuary. The perfect locale was the many kilometers of underground tunnels from limestone quarries, which were, at that time, just outside the city. For decades, priests led ceremonial processions of black-veiled, bone-laden carts into the quarries, where the bones were stacked into piles 1.5 meters/5 feet high and as much as 24 meters/80 feet deep behind neat walls of skull-studded tibiae. Each transfer was completed with the placement of a plaque indicating the church and district from which that stack of bones came and the date they arrived.

From the entry of the catacombs, a spiral staircase leads 18 meters/60 feet down. Then you begin a 1.5-kilometer-long (1 mile) subterranean walk. After several blocks of empty passageways, you ignore a sign announcing: "Halt, this is the empire of the dead." Along the way, plaques encourage visitors to reflect upon their destiny: "Happy is he who is forever faced with the hour of his death and prepares himself for the end every day." You emerge far from where you entered, with white, limestone-covered toes, telling anyone in the know you've been underground gawking at bones. Note to wanna-be Hamlets: An attendant checks your bag at the exit for stolen souvenirs. A flashlight is handy (€5, not covered by museum pass, 1 place Denfert-Rochereau, Mo: Denfert-Rochereau, Wed–Sun 9:00–16:00, Tue 11:00–16:00, closed Mon, tel. 01 43 22 47 63).

Sights—Northwest Paris

▲▲**Place de la Concorde and the Champs-Elysées**—This famous boulevard is Paris' backbone, and has the greatest concentration of traffic. All of France seems to converge on the place de la Concorde, the city's largest square. It was here that the guillotine took the lives of thousands—including King Louis XVI and Marie-Antoinette. Back then it was called the place de la Revolution.

Catherine de' Medici wanted a place to drive her carriage, so she started draining the swamp that would become the Champs-Elysées. Napoleon put on the final touches, and it's been the place to be seen ever since. The Tour de France bicycle race ends here, as do all parades (French or foe) of any significance. While the boulevard has become a bit hamburgerized, a walk here is a must. Take the Métro to the Arc de Triomphe (Mo: Etoile) and saunter down the Champs-Elysées (Métro stops every few blocks: FDR, George V, and Etoile).

▲▲▲**Arc de Triomphe**—Napoleon had the magnificent Arc de Triomphe commissioned to commemorate his victory at the Battle of Austerlitz. There's no triumphal arch bigger (50 meters/164 feet high, 40 meters/130 feet wide). And, with 12 converging boulevards, there's no traffic circle more thrilling to experience—either behind the wheel or on foot (take the underpass). An elevator or a spiral staircase leads to a cute museum about the arch and a grand view from the top, even after dark (€7, covered by museum pass, April–Sept daily 10:00–23:00, Oct–March daily 10:00–22:30, Mo: Etoile, use underpass to reach arch, tel. 01 55 37 73 77).

▲**Old Opera House (Le Palais Garnier)**—This grand palace of the belle époque was built for Napoleon III and finished in 1875. (After completing this project, the architect—Garnier—went south to do the casino in Monte Carlo.) From the grand avenue de l'Opéra, once lined with Paris' most fashionable haunts, the newly restored facade seems to say "all power to the wealthy." While huge, the actual theater seats only 2,000. The real show was before and after, when the elite of Paris—out to see and be seen—strutted their elegant stuff in the extravagant lobbies. Think of the grand marble stairway as a theater itself. As you wander the halls and gawk at the decor, imagine the place filled with the beautiful people of the day. The massive foundations straddle an underground lake (creating the mysterious world of the *Phantom of the Opera*). Tourists can peek from two boxes into the actual red velvet theater to see Marc Chagall's colorful ceiling (1964) playfully dancing around the eight-ton chandelier. Note the box seats next to the stage—the most expensive in the house, with an obstructed view of the stage but just right if you're there only to be seen. The elitism of this place prompted Mitterand to have a people's opera house built in the 1980s (symbolically, on place de la Bastille, where the French Revolution started in 1789). This left the Garnier Opéra home only to a ballet and occasional concerts (usually no performances mid-July–mid-Sept). While the library/museum is of interest to opera buffs, anyone will enjoy the second-floor grand foyer and Salon du Glacier, iced with decor typical of 1900 (€6, not covered by museum pass, daily 10:00–17:00 except when in use for performance, €10 English tours summers only, normally at 12:00 and 14:00, 90 min, includes entry, call to confirm; enter through the front off place de l'Opéra, Mo: Opéra, tel. 01 40 01 22 53). American Express and the *Paris Story* film are on the left side of the opera, and the venerable Galeries Lafayette department store is just behind.

Paris Story Film—This entertaining film gives a good and painless overview of Paris' turbulent and brilliant past, covering 2,000 years in 45 fast-moving minutes. The theater's wide-screen projection and cushy chairs provide an ideal break from bad weather and sore feet and make it fun with kids (€8, kids 6–18-€5, families with 2 kids and 2 parents-€21, not covered by museum pass, claim a 20 percent discount with this book, shows are on the hour daily 9:00–19:00, next to opera at 11 rue Scribe, Mo: Opéra, tel. 01 42 66 62 06).

▲▲**Jacquemart-André Museum (Musée Jacquemart-André)**— This thoroughly enjoyable museum showcases the lavish home of a wealthy, art-loving, 19th-century Parisian couple. After wandering the grand boulevards, you now get inside for an intimate look at the lifestyles of the Parisian rich and fabulous. Edouard André and his wife, Nélie Jacquemart—who had no children—spent their lives and fortunes designing, building, and then decorating a sumptuous mansion. What makes this visit so rewarding is the fine audioguide tour (in English, free with admission). The place is strewn with paintings by Rembrandt, Botticelli, Uccello, Mantegna, Bellini, Boucher, and Fragonard—enough to make a painting gallery famous. Plan on spending an hour with the audioguide (€8, not covered by museum pass, daily 10:00–18:00, elegant café, 158 boulevard Haussmann, Mo: Miromesnil, tel. 01 42 89 04 91).

▲**Grande Arche de la Défense**—On the outskirts of Paris, the centerpiece of Paris' ambitious skyscraper complex (La Défense) is the Grande Arche. Inaugurated in 1989 on the 200th anniversary of the French Revolution, it was dedicated to human rights and brotherhood. The place is big—38 floors holding offices for 30,000 people on more than 200 acres. Notre-Dame Cathedral could fit under its arch. The complex at La Défense is an interesting study in 1960s land-use planning. More than 100,000 workers commute here daily, directing lots of business and development away from downtown and allowing central Paris to retain its more elegant feel. This makes sense to most Parisians, regardless of whatever else they feel about this controversial complex. You will enjoy city views from the Arche elevator (€7, under 18-€5.50, not covered by museum pass, daily 10:00–19:00, includes a film on its construction and art exhibits, RER or Mo: La Défense, follow signs to Grande Arche or get off 1 stop earlier at Esplanade de la Défense and walk through the interesting business complex, tel. 01 49 07 27 57).

Sights—North Paris: Montmartre

▲▲**Sacré-Coeur and Montmartre**—This Byzantine-looking church, while only 130 years old, is impressive (daily until 23:00). One block from the church, the place du Tertre was the haunt of Toulouse-Lautrec and the original bohemians. Today, it's mobbed with tourists and unoriginal bohemians, but it's still fun (go early in the morning to beat the crowds). Take the Métro to the Anvers stop (1 Métro ticket buys your way up the funicular and avoids the stairs) or the closer but less scenic Abbesses stop. A taxi to the top of the hill saves time and avoids sweat.

Pigalle—Paris' red-light district, the infamous "Pig Alley," is at the foot of butte Montmartre. *Ooh la la.* It's more shocking than dangerous. Walk from place Pigalle to place Blanche, teasing desperate barkers and fast-talking temptresses. In bars, a €150 bottle of cheap champagne comes with a friend. Stick to the bigger streets, hang on to your wallet, and exercise good judgment. Cancan can cost a fortune, as can con artists in topless bars. After dark, countless tour buses line the streets, reminding us that tour guides make big bucks by bringing their groups to touristy nightclubs like the famous Moulin Rouge (Mo: Pigalle or Abbesses).

Sights—Northeast Paris: Marais Neighborhood and More

The Marais neighborhood extends along the Right Bank of the Seine from the Pompidou Center to the Bastille. It contains more pre-revolutionary lanes and buildings than anywhere else in town and is more atmospheric than touristy. It's medieval Paris. This is how much of the city looked until, in the mid-1800s, Napoleon III had Baron Haussmann blast out the narrow streets to construct broad boulevards (wide enough for the guns and ranks of the army, too wide for revolutionary barricades), creating modern Paris. Originally a swamp *(marais)* during the reign of Henry IV, this area became the hometown of the French aristocracy. In the 17th century, big shots built their private mansions *(hôtels)*, close to Henry's place des Vosges. When strolling the Marais, stick to the

Marais Neighborhood

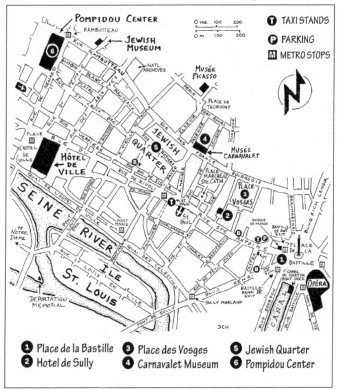

O yds. 100 200
O m 100 200

T TAXI STANDS
P PARKING
M METRO STOPS

❶ Place de la Bastille   ❸ Place des Vosges   ❺ Jewish Quarter
❷ Hotel de Sully   ❹ Carnavalet Museum   ❻ Pompidou Center

west-east axis formed by rue Sainte Croix de la Bretonnerie,
rue des Rosiers (heart of Paris' Jewish community), and rue
St. Antoine. On Sunday afternoons, this trendy area pulses with
shoppers and café crowds.

▲**Place des Vosges**—Study the architecture in this grand square:
nine pavilions per side. Some of the brickwork is real, some is fake.
Walk to the center, where Louis XIII sits on a horse surrounded
by locals enjoying their community park. Children frolic in the
sandbox, lovers warm benches, and pigeons guard their fountains
while trees shade this retreat from the glare of the big city. Henry
IV built this centerpiece of the Marais in 1605. As hoped, this
turned the Marais into Paris' most exclusive neighborhood. As the
nobility flocked to Versailles in a later age, this too was a magnet
for the rich and powerful of France. With the Revolution, the aristocratic elegance of this quarter became working-class, filled with

gritty shops, artisans, immigrants, and Jews. **Victor Hugo** lived at #6, and you can visit his house (free, Tue–Sun 10:00–17:40, closed Mon, 6 place des Vosges, tel. 01 42 72 10 16). Leave the place des Vosges through the doorway at southwest corner of the square (near the 3-star Michelin restaurant, l'Ambroisie) and pass through the elegant **Hôtel de Sully** (great example of a Marais mansion) to rue St. Antoine.

▲▲**Pompidou Center**—Europe's greatest collection of far-out modern art, the Musée National d'Art Moderne, is housed on the top floor of this newly renovated and colorful exoskeletal building. Once ahead of its time, this 20th-century (remember that century?) art has been waiting for the world to catch up with it. After so many Madonnas-and-Children, a piano smashed to bits and glued to the wall is refreshing (€5.50, audioguide-€4, Wed–Mon 11:00–21:00, closed Tue and May 1, to use escalator you need a ticket for the museum or a museum pass, good mezzanine-level café is cheaper than cafés outside, Mo: Rambuteau, tel. 01 44 78 12 33).

The Pompidou Center and its square are lively, with lots of people, street theater, and activity inside and out—a perpetual street fair. Kids of any age enjoy the fun, colorful fountains (called *Homage to Stravinsky*) on the square.

▲▲**Jewish Art and History Museum (Musée d'Art et Histoire du Judaïsme)**—This fascinating museum is located in a beautifully restored Marais mansion and tells the story of Judaism throughout Europe, from the Roman destruction of Jerusalem to the theft of famous artworks during World War II. Helpful, free audioguides and many English explanations make this an enjoyable history lesson (red numbers on small signs indicate the number you should press on your audioguide). Move along at your own speed. The museum illustrates the cultural unity maintained by this continually dispersed population. You'll learn about the history of Jewish traditions from bar mitzvahs to menorahs, and see exquisite traditional costumes and objects around which daily life revolved. Don't miss the explanation of "the Dreyfus affair," a major event in early 1900 French politics. You'll also see photographs of and paintings by famous Jewish artists, including Chagall, Modigliani, and Soutine. A small but moving section is devoted to the deportation of Jews from Paris (€6.50, ages 18–26-€4, under 18 free, not covered by museum pass, Mon–Fri 11:00–18:00, Sun 10:00–18:00, closed Sat, 71 rue du Temple, Mo: Rambuteau or Hôtel de Ville a few blocks farther away, tel. 01 53 01 86 60).

▲**Picasso Museum (Musée Picasso)**—Hidden in a far corner of the Marais and worth ▲▲▲ if you're a Picasso fan, this museum contains the world's largest collection of Picasso's paintings, sculptures, sketches, and ceramics, and includes his small collection of Impressionist art. The art is well-displayed in a fine old mansion with a peaceful garden café. The room-by-room English introductions help make sense of Picasso's work—from the Lautrec-like portraits at the beginning of his career, to his gray-brown Cubist period, to his Salvador Dalí–like finish. The well-done €3 English guidebook helps Picassophiles appreciate the context of his art and learn more about his interesting life. Most will be happy reading the posted English explanations while moving at a steady pace through the museum—the ground and first floors satisfied my curiosity (€5.50, free first Sun of month, covered by museum pass, Wed–Mon 9:30–18:00, closes at 17:30 Oct–March, closed Tue, 5 rue Thorigny, Mo: St. Paul or Chemin Vert, tel. 01 42 71 25 21).

▲▲**Carnavalet Museum**—The tumultuous history of Paris is well-displayed in this converted Marais mansion. Unfortunately, explanations are in French only, but many displays are fairly self-explanatory. You'll see paintings of Parisian scenes, French Revolution paraphernalia, old Parisian store signs, a small guillotine, a model of 16th-century Ile de la Cité (notice the bridge houses), and rooms full of 15th-century Parisian furniture (free, Tue–Sun 10:00–18:00, closed Mon, 23 rue de Sévigné, Mo: St. Paul, tel. 01 44 59 58 58).

▲**Promenade Plantée Park**—This three-kilometer-long (2 miles), narrow garden walk on a viaduct was once a railroad and is now a joy. It runs from place de la Bastille (Mo: Bastille) along avenue Daumesnil to Saint-Mandé (Mo: Michel Bizot). Part of the park is elevated. At times, you'll walk along the street until you pick up the next segment. To reach the park from place de la Bastille, take avenue Daumesnil (past opera building) to the intersection with avenue Ledru Rollin; walk up the stairs and through the gate (free, opens Mon–Fri at 8:00, Sat–Sun at 9:00, closes at sunset). The shops below the viaduct's arches make for entertaining window-shopping.

▲**Père Lachaise Cemetery (Cimetière Père Lachaise)**— Littered with the tombstones of many of the city's most illustrious dead, this is your best one-stop look at the fascinating, romantic world of "permanent Parisians." More like a small city, the place is confusing, but maps will direct you to the graves of Chopin, Molière, Edith Piaf, Oscar Wilde, Gertrude Stein, Jim Morrison, and Héloïse and Abelard. In section 92, a series of statues memorializing World War II makes the French war experience a bit more real (helpful €1.50 maps at flower store near entry, closes at dusk, across street from Métro stop, Mo: Père Lachaise or bus #69).

Shopping Parisian-Style

Even staunch anti-shoppers may be tempted to partake of chic Paris. Wandering among the elegant and outrageous boutiques provides a break from the heavy halls of the Louvre, and, if you approach it right, a little cultural enlightenment.

Here are some tips for avoiding *faux pas* and making the most of the experience.

French Etiquette: Before you enter a Parisian store, remember the following points.

• In small stores, always greet the clerk by saying *Bonjour*, plus the appropriate title *(Madame, Mademoiselle, or Monsieur)*. When leaving, say, *Au revoir, Madame/Mademoiselle/Monsieur*.

• The customer is not always right. In fact, figure the clerk is doing you a favor by waiting on you.

• Except for in department stores, it's not normal for the customer to handle clothing. Ask first.

• Observe French shoppers. Then imitate.

Department Stores: Like cafés, department stores were invented here (surprisingly, not in America). Parisian department stores, monuments to a more relaxed and elegant era, begin with their spectacular perfume sections. Helpful information desks are usually nearby (pick up the handy store floor plan in English). Most stores have a good selection of souvenirs and toys at fair prices and reasonable restaurants; some have great view terraces. Choose from these four great Parisian department stores: Galeries Lafayette (behind old Opéra Garnier, Mo: Opéra), Printemps (next door to Galeries Lafayette), Bon Marché (Mo: Sèvres-Babylone), and Samaritaine (near pont Neuf, Mo: Pont Neuf). Forum des Halles is a huge subterranean shopping center (Mo: Les Halles).

Boutiques: I enjoy window-shopping, pausing at cafés, and observing the rhythm of neighborhood life. While the shops are more intimate, sales clerks are more formal—mind your manners. Here are four very different areas to explore:

A stroll from Sèvres-Babylone to St. Sulpice allows you to sample smart, classic clothing boutiques while enjoying one of Paris' prettier neighborhoods—for sustenance along the way, there's La Maison du Chocolat at 19 rue de Sèvres, selling handmade chocolates in exquisitely wrapped boxes.

The ritzy streets connecting place de la Madeleine and place Vendôme form a miracle mile of gourmet food shops, jewelry stores, four-star hotels, perfumeries, and exclusive clothing boutiques. Fauchon's, on place Madeleine, is a bastion of over-the-top food products, hawking €7,000 bottles of Cognac (who buys this stuff?). Hediard's, across the square from Fauchon's, is an older, more appealing, and accessible gourmet food shop. Next door, La Maison des Truffes sells black mushrooms for about €180 a pound, and white truffles from Italy for €2,500 a pound.

For more eclectic, avant-garde stores, peruse the artsy shops between the Pompidou Center and place des Vosges in the Marais.

For a contemporary, more casual, and less frenetic shopping experience, and to see Paris' latest urban renewal project, take the Métro to Bercy Village, a once-thriving wine warehouse district that has been transformed into an outdoor shopping mall (Mo: Cour St. Emilion).

Flea Markets: Paris hosts several sprawling weekend flea markets (*marché aux puces*, pron. mar-shay oh poos; literally translated, since *puce* is French for flea). These oversized garage sales date back to the Middle Ages, when middlemen would sell old, flea-infested clothes and discarded possessions of the wealthy at bargain prices to eager peasants. Today, some travelers find them claustrophobic, crowded, monster versions of those back home, though others find their French diamonds-in-the-rough and return happy.

The Puces St. Ouen (pron. poos sahn-wahn) is the biggest and oldest of them all, with more than 2,000 vendors selling everything from flamingos to faucets (Sat 9:00–18:30, Sun–Mon 10:00–18:30, Mo: Porte de Clingancourt).

Street Markets: Several traffic-free street markets overflow with flowers, produce, fish vendors, and butchers, illustrating how most Parisians shopped before there were supermarkets and department stores. Good market streets include the rue Cler (Mo: Ecole Militaire), rue Montorgueil (Mo: Etienne Marcel), rue Mouffetard (Mo: Cardinal Lemoine or Censier-Daubenton), and rue Daguerre (Mo: Denfert-Rochereau). Browse these markets to collect a classy picnic (open daily except Sun afternoons and Mon, also closed for lunch 13:00–15:00).

Souvenir Shops: Avoid souvenir carts in front of famous monuments. Prices and selection are better in shops and department stores. The riverfront stalls near Notre-Dame sell a variety of used books, magazines, and tourist paraphernalia in the most romantic setting.

Whether you indulge in a new wardrobe, an artsy poster, or just one luscious pastry, you'll find that a shopping excursion provides a priceless slice of Parisian life.

Disappointments de Paris

Here are a few negatives to help you manage your limited time:

La Madeleine is a big, stark, neoclassical church with a post-card facade and a postbox interior. The famous aristocratic deli behind the church, Fauchon, is elegant, but so are many others handier to your hotel.

Paris' **Panthéon** (nothing like Rome's) is another stark neo-classical edifice, filled with the mortal remains of great Frenchmen who mean little to the average American tourist.

The **Bastille** is Paris' most famous non-sight. The square is there, but confused tourists look everywhere and can't find the famous prison of Revolution fame. The building's gone and the square is good only as a jumping-off point for Promenade Plantée Park (see "Sights—Northeast Paris," above).

Finally, the **Latin Quarter** is a frail shadow of its characteris-tic self. It's more Tunisian, Greek, and Woolworth's than old-time Paris. The café life that turned on Hemingway and endeared the "boul' Miche" and boulevard St. Germain to so many poets is also trampled by modern commercialism.

Palace of Versailles

Every king's dream, Versailles was the residence of the French king and the cultural heartbeat of Europe for about 100 years—until the Revolution of 1789 ended the notion that God depu-tized some people to rule for Him on Earth. Louis XIV spent half a year's income of Europe's richest country turning his dad's hunting lodge into a palace fit for a divine monarch. Louis XV and Louis XVI spent much of the 18th century gilding Louis XIV's lily. In 1837, about 50 years after the royal family was evicted, King Louis Philippe opened the palace as a museum. Europe's next-best palaces are Versailles wannabes.

Information: A helpful TI is just past Sofitel Hôtel on your walk from the station to the palace (May–Sept daily 9:00–19:00, Oct–April daily 9:00–18:00, tel. 01 39 24 88 88, www.chateauversailles.fr). You'll also find information booths inside the château (doors A, B-2, and C) and, in peak season, kiosks scattered around the courtyard. The useful brochure "Versailles Orientation Guide" explains your sightseeing options. A baggage check is available at door A.

Cost: €7.50 (main palace and both Trianons are covered by museum pass); €5.50 after 15:30, under 18 free (the palace is also theoretically free for all teachers, professors, and architecture students). Admission is payable at entrances A, C, and D. Tours cost extra (see "Touring Versailles," below). The Grand and Petit Trianons cost €5 together, €3 after 15:30 (both covered

Versailles

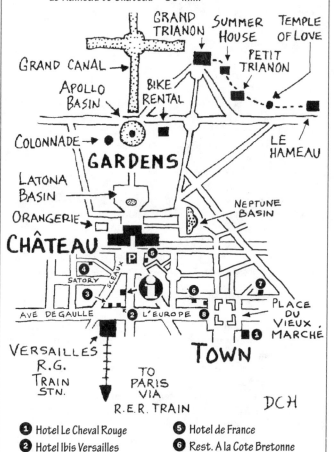

WALKING TIMES

Train Stn to Chateau = 10 min.
Chateau to Grand Trianon = 30 min.
Grand Trianon to Le Hameau = 20 min.
Le Hameau to Chateau = 30 min.

GRAND TRIANON   SUMMER HOUSE   TEMPLE OF LOVE

GRAND CANAL →   PETIT TRIANON

APOLLO BASIN   BIKE RENTAL

COLONNADE →   LE HAMEAU

GARDENS

LATONA BASIN

ORANGERIE →   NEPTUNE BASIN

CHÂTEAU

SATORY   SCEAUX

AVE DE GAULLE   L'EUROPE   PLACE DU VIEUX MARCHÉ

TOWN

VERSAILLES R.G. TRAIN STN.

TO PARIS VIA R.E.R. TRAIN

DCH

- ❶ Hotel Le Cheval Rouge
- ❷ Hotel Ibis Versailles
- ❸ Hotel du Palais
- ❹ Hotel d'Angleterre
- ❺ Hotel de France
- ❻ Rest. A la Cote Bretonne
- ❼ Rest. Fenetres sur Cour
- ❽ Rest. La Boeuf a la Mode

Entrances to Versailles

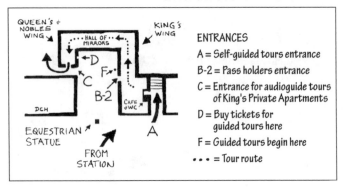

QUEEN'S +
NOBLES
WING

KING'S
WING

HALL OF
MIRRORS

D

F

C

B-2

DCH

CAFE
JWC

EQUESTRIAN
STATUE

A

FROM
STATION

ENTRANCES

A = Self-guided tours entrance

B-2 = Pass holders entrance

C = Entrance for audioguide tours
of King's Private Apartments

D = Buy tickets for
guided tours here

F = Guided tours begin here

• • • = Tour route

by museum pass). The gardens, which usually cost €3, are €5.50 on fountain "spray days" on summer weekends (gardens not covered by museum pass, see "Fountain Spectacles," below).

If you don't have a museum pass, consider getting the Versailles Pass, which covers your entrance, gives you priority access (no lines) to everything, and includes an audioguide (€21, sold at Versailles train station, RER stations that serve Versailles, and at FNAC department stores).

Hours: The **palace** is open April–Oct Tue–Sun 9:00–18:30, Nov–March Tue–Sun 9:00–17:30, closed Mon (last entry 30 min before closing). The **Grand and Petit Trianon Palaces** are open daily April–Oct 12:00–18:00, Nov–March 12:00–17:00, closed Mon. The **garden** is open daily from 7:00 to sunset (as late as 21:30).

In summer, Versailles is especially crowded around 10:00 and 13:00, and all day Tue and Sun. Remember, the crowds gave Marie-Antoinette a pain in the neck, too, so relax and let them eat cake. For fewer crowds, go early or late: Either arrive by 9:00 (when the palace opens, touring the palace first, then the gardens) or after 15:30 (you'll get a reduced entry ticket, but you'll miss the last guided tours of the day, which generally depart at 15:00). If you arrive midday, see the gardens first and the palace later, at 15:00. The gardens and palace are great late. On my last visit, I was the only tourist in the Hall of Mirrors at 18:00... even on a Tuesday.

Touring Versailles: Versailles' highlights are the State Apartments, the lavish King's Private Apartments, the Opera House, and the magnificent Hall of Mirrors. Most visitors are satisfied with a spin through the State Apartments, the gardens, and the Trianon Palaces. Versailles aficionados should spend the time (and money) to see the King's Private Apartments, which can be visited only with an audioguide or live guide (neither tour covered by museum pass).

Guided tours—You may select a one-hour guided tour from a variety of themes, such as the daily life of a king or the lives of such lesser-known nobles as the well-coiffed Madame de Pompadour (€4, join first English tour available). Or consider the 90-minute tour (€6) of the King's Private Apartments (Louis XV, Louis XVI, and Marie-Antoinette) and the chapel. This tour, which is the only way visitors can see the Opera House, can be long depending upon the quality of your guide.

For a live tour, make reservations at entrance D immediately upon arrival, as tours can sell out by 13:00 (first tours generally begin at 10:00, last tours depart usually at 15:00 but as late as 16:00). Guided tours begin at entrance F. The price of any tour is added to the €7.50 entry fee to Versailles (entry covered by museum pass, tours extra).

If you don't have a museum pass or Versailles Pass, and you think you might want to take a guided tour after you've seen the palace on your own, remember to keep your ticket to prove you've already paid for admission.

Audioguide tours—There are two informative but dry audioguide tours. One covers the State Apartments (€4, includes Hall of Mirrors and queen's bedchamber; start at entrance A or, if you have a museum pass, entrance B-2). The other includes more of the King's Private Apartments (Louis XIV) and a sampling of nobles' chambers (€4, entrance C). Both audioguide tours are sold until one hour before closing and are available at each entrance.

Self-guided tour—To tour the palace on your own, join the line at entrance A if you need to pay admission. Those with a museum pass are allowed in through entrance B-2 without a wait. Enter the palace and take a one-way walk through the State Apartments from the King's Wing, through the Hall of Mirrors, and out via the Queen's and Nobles' Wing.

The Hall of Mirrors was the ultimate hall of the day— 75 meters/250 feet long, with 17 arched mirrors matching 17 windows with royal garden views, 24 gilded candelabra, eight busts of Roman emperors, and eight classical-style statues (7 are ancient originals). The ceiling is decorated with stories of Louis' triumphs. Imagine this place filled with silk gowns and powdered wigs, lit by thousands of candles. The mirrors— a luxurious rarity at the time—were a reflection of a time when aristocrats felt good about their looks and their fortunes. In another age altogether, this was the room in which the Treaty of Versailles was signed, ending World War I.

Before going downstairs at the end, take a stroll clockwise around the long room filled with the great battles of France murals. If you don't have *Rick Steves' Paris* or *Rick Steves' Mona Winks*, the guidebook called *The Châteaux, The Gardens, and Trianon* gives a room-by-room rundown.

Fountain Spectacles: Classical music fills the king's back-yard, and the garden's fountains are in full squirt, on Sat July–Sept and on Sun early April–early Oct (schedule for both days: 11:00–12:00 & 15:30–17:00 & 17:20–17:30). On these "spray days," the gardens cost €5.50 (not covered by museum pass, ask for a map of fountains). Louis had his engineers literally reroute a river to fuel these fountains. Even by today's standards, they are impressive. Pick up the helpful brochure of the fountain show ("Les Grandes Eaux Musicales") at any information booth for a guide to the fountains. Also ask about the impressive *Les Fêtes de Nuit* nighttime spectacle (some Sat, July–mid-Sept).

Getting around the Gardens: It's a 30-minute hike from the palace, down the canal, past the two mini-palaces to the Hamlet. You can rent bikes (€6/hr). The fast-looking, slow-moving tourist train leaves from behind the château and serves the Grand Canal and the Trianon Palaces (€5, 4/hr, 4 stops, you can hop on and off as you like; nearly worthless commentary).

Palace Gardens: The gardens offer a world of royal amuse-ments. Outside the palace is *l'orangerie*. Louis, the only person who could grow oranges in Paris, had a mobile orange grove that could be wheeled in and out of his greenhouses according to the weather. A promenade leads from the palace to the Grand Canal, an artificial lake that, in Louis' day, was a mini-sea with nine ships, including a 32-cannon warship. France's royalty used to float up and down the canal in Venetian gondolas.

While Louis cleverly used palace life at Versailles to "domes-ticate" his nobility, turning otherwise meddlesome nobles into groveling socialites, all this pomp and ceremony hampered the royal family as well. For an escape from the public life at Versailles, they built more intimate palaces as retreats in their garden. Before the Revolution there was plenty of space to retreat—the grounds were enclosed by a 40-kilometer-long (25 miles) fence.

The beautifully restored **Grand Trianon Palace** is as sump-tuous as the main palace, but much smaller. With its pastel-pink colonnade and more human scale, this is a place you'd like to call home. The nearby **Petit Trianon**, which has a fine neoclas-sical exterior and a skippable interior, was Marie-Antoinette's favorite residence (€5 for both Trianons, €3 after 15:30, covered by museum pass, daily April–Oct 12:00–18:00, Nov–March 12:00–17:00, closed Mon).

You can almost see princesses bobbing gaily in the branches as you walk through the enchanting forest, past the white marble temple of love (1778) to the queen's fake-peasant **Hamlet** (*le Hameau;* interior not tourable). Palace life really got to Marie-Antoinette. Sort of a back-to-basics queen, she retreated further and further from her blue-blooded reality. Her happiest days were spent at the Hamlet, under a bonnet, tending her perfumed sheep and her manicured gardens in a thatch-happy wonderland.

Cafés: The cafeteria and WCs are next to door A. You'll find a sandwich kiosk and a decent restaurant are at the canal in the garden. For more recommendations, see "Eating in Versailles," page 129. A handy McDonald's is immediately across from the train station (WC without crowds).

Trip Length: Allow two hours for the palace and two for the gardens. Including two hours to cover your round-trip transit time, it's a six-hour day trip from Paris.

Getting There: Take the **RER-C train** (€5 round-trip, 30 min one-way) to Versailles R.G. or "Rive Gauche"—not Versailles C.H., which is farther from the palace. Trains named "Vick" leave about five times an hour for the palace from these RER stops: Gare d'Austerlitz, St. Michel, Musée d'Orsay, Invalides, Pont de l'Alma, and Champ de Mars. Any train named Vick goes to Versailles; don't board other trains. Get off at the last stop (Versailles Rive Gauche), turn right out of the station, and turn left at the first boulevard. It's a 10-minute walk to the palace.

Your Eurailpass covers this inexpensive trip, but it uses up a valuable "flexi" day. If you really want to use your railpass, consider seeing Versailles on your way in to or out of Paris. To get free passage, show your railpass at an SNCF ticket window—for example, at the Les Invalides or Musée d'Orsay RER stops—and get a *contremarque de passage*. Keep this ticket to exit the system.

When returning from Versailles, look through the windows past the turnstiles for the departure board. Any train leaving Versailles serves all downtown Paris RER line C stops (they're marked on the schedule as stopping at "*toutes les gares jusqu'à Austerlitz*," meaning "all stations until Austerlitz").

Taxis for the 30-minute ride between Versailles and Paris cost about €25.

To reach Versailles from Paris by **car**, get on the *périphérique* freeway that circles Paris and take the toll-free autoroute A-13 toward Rouen. Follow signs into Versailles, then look for Château signs and park in the huge lot in front of the palace (pay lot). The drive takes about 30 minutes one-way.

Town of Versailles (zip code: 78000): After the palace closes and the tourists go, the prosperous, wholesome town of Versailles feels a long way from Paris. The central market thrives on place du Marché on Sunday, Tuesday, and Friday until 13:00 (leaving the RER station, turn right and walk 10 min). Consider the wisdom of picking up or dropping your rental car in Versailles rather than in Paris. In Versailles, the Hertz and Avis offices are at Gare des Chantiers (Versailles C.H., served by Paris' Montparnasse station). Versailles makes a fine home base; see Versailles accommodations and recommended restaurants under "Sleeping" and "Eating," below.

More Day Trips from Paris

Chartres

Chartres and its cathedral make a ▲▲▲ day trip.

In 1194, a terrible fire destroyed the church at Chartres that housed the much-venerated veil of Mary. With almost unbelievably good fortune, the monks found the veil miraculously preserved in the ashes. Money poured in for the building of a bigger and better cathedral—decorated with 2,000 carved figures and some of France's best stained glass. The cathedral feels too large for the city because it was designed to accommodate huge crowds of pilgrims. One of those pilgrims, an impressed Napoleon, declared after a visit in 1811: "Chartres is no place for an atheist." Rodin called it the "Acropolis of France." British Francophile Malcolm Miller or his assistant give great "Appreciation of Gothic" tours Monday through Saturday, usually at noon and 14:45 (verify times in advance, no tours off-season, tel. 02 37 28 15 58, fax 02 37 28 33 03). Each €10 tour is different; many people stay for both tours. Just show up at the church (daily 7:00–19:00).

Explore Chartres' pleasant city center and discover the picnic-friendly park behind the cathedral. The helpful TI, next to the cathedral, has a map with a self-guided tour of Chartres (Mon–Sat 9:00–19:00, Sun 9:30–17:30, tel. 02 37 18 26 26).

Getting There: Chartres is a one-hour train trip from the Gare Montparnasse (about €11.50 one-way, 10/day).

Sleeping in Chartres: To stay overnight, try the comfy **Hôtel Chatelet***** with its welcoming lobby and its spotless, spacious, well-furnished rooms (Sb-€65–75, Db-€72–83, extra person-€10, streetside rooms are cheaper, CC, 6 avenue Jehan de Beauce, tel. 02 37 21 78 00, fax 02 37 36 23 01, e-mail: hchatel@club-internet.fr). **Hôtel Jehan de Beauce**** is basic, but clean and quiet, with some tiny bathrooms (S-€31, D-€40, Ds-€43, Db-€54, Tb-€62, CC, 19 avenue Jehan de Beauce, tel. 02 37 21 01 41, fax 02 37 21 59 10). **Trois Lys** *crêperie* makes good and cheap crêpes just across the river on pont Boujou (3 rue de la Porte Guillaume, tel. 02 37 28 42 02).

Chartres

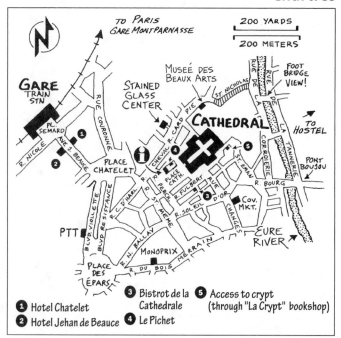

1 Hotel Chatelet
2 Hotel Jehan de Beauce
3 Bistrot de la Cathedrale
4 Le Pichet
5 Access to crypt (through "La Crypt" bookshop)

Giverny

Monet spent 43 of his most creative years here (1883–1926). His gardens and home, a ▲ sight, are unfortunately split by a busy road and are very popular with tourists. Buy your ticket, walk through the gardens, and take the underpass into the artist's famous lily pad land. The path leads you over the Japanese Bridge, under weeping willows, and past countless scenes that leave artists aching for an easel. Back on the other side, stroll through his more robust, structured garden and his mildly interesting home. The jammed gift shop at the exit is Monet's actual skylit studio.

While lines may be long and tour groups may trample the flowers, true fans still find magic in those lily pads. Minimize crowds by arriving before 10:00 (get in line) or after 16:00 (€5.50, €4 for gardens only, April–Oct Tue–Sun 10:00–18:00, closed Mon and Nov–March, tel. 02 32 51 94 65).

Take the Rouen-bound train from Paris' Gare St. Lazare station to Vernon (about €22 round-trip, long gaps in service, know schedule before you go). From the Vernon train station to Monet's garden (4 km/2.5 miles one-way), you have three good options (bus, taxi, and

Paris Day Trips

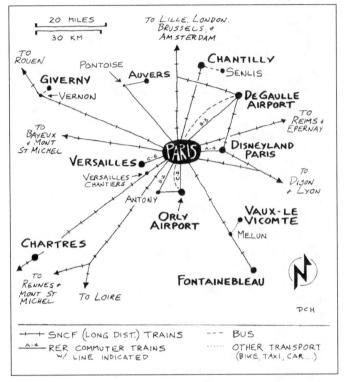

bike). The Vernon–Giverny **bus** is scheduled to meet most trains (4/day, make sure the driver knows you plan to return by bus and on which trip, otherwise he may not make the last Giverny pickup). If you miss the last bus, find others to share a **taxi** (about €11 for up to 3, €12 for 4, tel. 06 07 34 36 68, 06 76 08 50 78, or 02 32 21 31 31). The ticket office at Monet's home in Giverny has bus schedules and can call a taxi if you don't see one waiting by the bus stop (see taxi phone numbers above). The bus stop is on the main road from Vernon, just below Monet's home. You can also rent a **bike** at the bar opposite the train station (€12, tel. 02 32 21 16 01), and follow a paved bike path *(piste cyclable)* that runs along an abandoned railroad right-of-way (the bike path begins across the river from Vernon in Veronnet).

Big tour companies do a Giverny day trip from Paris for around €65. Ask at your hotel.

The **Musée de l'Art Americain** (American Art Museum,

turn left when leaving Monet's place and walk 100 meters) is devoted to American artists who followed Claude to Giverny. Giverny had a great influence on American artists of Monet's day. This bright, modern gallery—with a good little Mary Cassatt section—is well-explained in English (same price and hours as Monet's home), though its most appealing feature might be its garden café.

Sleeping in Giverny: To sleep two blocks from Monet's home, try the adorable **Hôtel La Musardiere**** (Db-€50–66, Tb-€65–75, CC, 132 rue Claude Monet, 27620 Giverny, tel. 02 32 21 03 18, fax 02 32 21 60 00). You'll find a café and sandwich stand near the entry to Monet's home, but the garden café at the overlooked American Impressionist Museum is better—peaceful, and surrounded by gardens Monet would appreciate (€9 salads, picnics possible at the far end).

Disneyland Paris

Europe's Disneyland, a ▲▲ sight, is basically a modern remake of California's, with most of the same rides and smiles. The main difference is that Mickey Mouse speaks French (and you can buy wine with your lunch). My kids went ducky. Locals love it. It's worth a day if Paris is handier than Florida or California. Crowds are a problem (tel. 01 64 74 30 00 for the latest). If possible, avoid Saturday, Sunday, Wednesday, school holidays, and July and August. After dinner, crowds are gone, and you'll walk right onto rides that had a 45-minute wait three hours earlier. The free FASTPASS system is a worthwhile timesaver for popular rides (reserve a time to go on a ride when you buy your ticket at the gate). You'll also save time by buying your tickets ahead (at airport TIs, over 100 Métro stations, or along the Champs-Elysées at the TI, Disney Store, or Virgin Megastore). Food is fun and not outrageously priced. (Still, many smuggle in a picnic.)

The hours and prices for Disneyland Paris are listed below. **Walt Disney Studios:** The new zone, opened in 2002 next to the 10-year-old Disneyland Paris, has a Hollywood focus that aims at an older crowd with animation, special effects, and movie magic "rides." The Aerosmith Rock 'n' Roller Coaster is nothing special. The highlight is the Stunt Show Spectacular, filling a huge back-lot stadium five times a day for 45 minutes of car chases and thriller filming tips. An actual movie sequence is filmed with stunt drivers, audience bit players, and brash MTV-style hosts.

Cost and Hours: Disneyland Paris and Walt Disney Studios share the same hours, contact information, and prices—which you pay separately. Only the three-day passes (called "Hopper" tickets) include entry to both parks. From March 31 through Nov 5, adults pay €38 for one day (€72 for 2 days, €99 for 3-day "Hopper" ticket) and kids ages 3–11 pay €29 for one day (€56 for 2 days, €80 for 3-day "Hopper" ticket). Regular prices are about 25 percent less off-season. Kids under three are always free. On summer evenings (17:00–23:00) at the Disneyland Park only, everyone pays €19. The only budget deal (and, I think, the only way the Walt Disney Studios are worth visiting) is to pay for a full-price Walt Disney Studios ticket, which gets you into the Disneyland Park for free during the last three hours of that day when lines at rides are nearly nonexistent (April–June daily 9:00–20:00, July–Aug daily 9:00–23:00, Sept–March Mon–Fri 10:00–20:00, Sat–Sun 9:00–20:00, tel. 01 60 30 60 30, www.disneylandparis.com).

Sleeping at Disneyland Paris: Most are better off sleeping in reality (Paris), though with direct buses and freeways to both airports, Disneyland makes a convenient first- or last-night stop. Seven different Disney-owned hotels offer accommodations at or near the park in all price ranges. The cheapest is **Davy Crockett,** but you'll need a car. **Hôtel Sante Fe**** offers the best value, with shuttle service to the park every 12 minutes (Db-€214 includes breakfast and 2-day park pass, CC). The most expensive is **Disneyland Hotel****,** right at the park entry (Db-€427 for the same deal, CC). To reserve any Disneyland hotel, call 01 60 30 60 30, fax 01 60 30 60 65, or check www.disneylandparis.com. The prices you'll be quoted include entry to the park.

Transportation Connections— Disneyland Paris

By train: TGV trains connect Disneyland directly with **Charles de Gaulle airport** (10 min), the **Loire Valley** (1.5 hrs, Tours-St. Pierre des Corps station, 15 min from Amboise), **Avignon** (3 hrs, TGV station), **Lyon** (2 hrs, Part Dieu station), and **Nice** (6 hrs, main station).

By RER: The slick, one-hour RER trip is the best way to Disneyland from downtown Paris. Take RER line A-4 to Marne-la-Vallee-Chessy (from Etoile, Auber/Opera, Chatelet, and Gare de Lyon stations, about €7.50 each way, hrly, drops you 1 hour later right in the park). The last train back to Paris leaves shortly after midnight. Be sure to get a ticket that is good on both the RER and Métro; returning, remember to use your RER ticket for your Métro connection in Paris.

By bus: Both airports have direct shuttle buses to Disneyland Paris (€13, daily 8:30–19:45, every 45 min).

By car: Disneyland is about 40 minutes east of Paris on the A-4 autoroute (direction Nancy/Metz, exit #14). Parking is €7 per day at the park.

Nightlife in Paris

Paris is brilliant after dark. Save energy from your day's sight-seeing and get out at night. Whether it's a concert at Sainte-Chapelle, an elevator up the Arc de Triomphe, or a late-night café, experience the city of light lit. If a **Seine River cruise** appeals, see "Organized Tours of Paris," page 54.

Pariscope magazine (see "Tourist Information," above), offers a complete weekly listing of music, cinema, theater, opera, and other special events. *Paris Voice* newspaper, in English, has a monthly review of Paris entertainment (available at any English-language bookstore, French-American establishments, or the American Church, www.parisvoice.com).

Music

Jazz Clubs: With a lively mix of American, French, and interna-tional musicians, Paris has been an internationally acclaimed jazz capital since World War II. You'll pay €6–24 to enter a jazz club (a drink may be included; if not, expect to pay €5–9 per drink; beer is cheapest). See *Pariscope* magazine under "Musique" for listings; or, better yet, check out the American Church's *Paris Voice* paper for a good monthly review, or drop by the clubs to check out their calendars posted on the front door. Music starts after 21:00 in most clubs. Some offer dinner concerts from about 20:30 on. Here are several good bets:

Caveau de la Huchette, a characteristic old jazz club, fills an ancient Latin Quarter cellar with live jazz and frenzied dancing every night (€9 weekday, €12 weekend admission, €5 drinks, Tue–Sun 21:30–2:30 or later, closed Mon, 5 rue de la Huchette, Mo: St. Michel, recorded info tel. 01 43 26 65 05).

For a hotbed of late-night activity and jazz, go to the two-block-long rue des Lombards, at boulevard Sebastopol, midway between the river and Pompidou Center (Mo: Chatelet). **Au Duc des Lombards**, right at the corner, is one of the most popular and respected jazz clubs in Paris, with concerts gener-ally at 21:00 (42 rue des Lombards, tel. 01 42 33 22 88). **Le Sunside** offers more traditional jazz—Dixieland and big band—and fewer crowds, with concerts generally at 21:00 (60 rue des Lombards, tel. 01 40 26 21 25).

At the more down-to-earth and mellow **Le Cave du Franc Pinot**, you can enjoy a glass of chardonnay at the main-floor wine bar, then drop downstairs for a cool jazz scene (good dinner-and-jazz values as well, located on Ile St. Louis where pont Marie meets the island, 1 quai de Bourbon, Mo: Pont Marie, tel. 01 46 33 60 64).

Classical Concerts: For classical music on any night, con-sult *Pariscope* magazine; the "Musique" section under "Concerts

Classiques" lists concerts (free and fee). Look for posters at the churches. Churches that regularly host concerts (usually March–Nov) include St. Sulpice, St. Germain-des-Prés, Basilique de Madeleine, St. Eustache, St. Julien-le-Pauvre, and Sainte-Chapelle. It's worth the €16–25 entry for the pleasure of hearing Mozart surrounded by the stained glass of the tiny Sainte-Chapelle (it's unheated—bring a sweater). Look also for daytime concerts in parks, such as the Luxembourg Garden. Even the Galeries Lafayette department store offers concerts. Many concerts are free *(entrée libre)*, such as the Sunday atelier concert sponsored by the American Church (18:00, not every week, Sept–May, 65 quai d'Orsay, Mo: Invalides, RER: Pont de l'Alma, tel. 01 40 62 05 00).

Opera: Paris is home to two well-respected opera venues. The Opéra de la Bastille is a massive, modern opera house that dominates place de la Bastille. Come here for state-of-the-art special effects and modern interpretations of classic ballets and operas. In the spirit of this everyman's opera, unsold seats go on sale at a big discount to seniors and students 15 minutes before the show (Mo: Bastille, tel. 01 43 43 96 96). The Opéra Garnier, Paris' first opera house, hosts opera and ballet performances. Come here for less expensive tickets and grand belle époque decor (Mo: Opéra, tel. 01 44 73 13 99). For tickets, call 01 44 73 13 00, go to the opera ticket offices (open 11:00–18:00), or reserve on the Web at www.opera-de-paris.org (for both operas).

Bus Tours

Paris Illumination Tours, run by Paris Vision, connect all the great illuminated sights of Paris with a 100-minute bus tour in 12 languages. Double-decker buses have huge windows, but customers continuing to the overrated Moulin Rouge get the most desirable front seats.

You'll stampede along with a United Nations of tourists, get an audioguide, and listen to a tape-recorded spiel (interesting, but occasionally hard to hear). Uninspired as it is, this tour provides an entertaining first-night overview of the city at its floodlit and scenic best (bring your city map to stay oriented as you go). Left-side seats are marginally better. Visibility is fine in the rain. You're always on the bus, except for one five-minute cigarette break at the Eiffel Tower viewpoint (adults-€23, kids under 11 ride free, departures at 20:30 nightly all year, also at 21:30 April–Oct only, departs from Paris Vision office at 214 rue de Rivoli, across the street from Mo: Tuileries).

The same company will take you on the same route for twice the price by minivan—pickup is at your hotel, the driver is a qualified guide, and there's a maximum of seven clients (adult-€46, kids ages 4–11-€23).

These trips are sold through your hotel (brochures in lobby) or at Paris Vision (214 rue de Rivoli, tel. for bus and minivans 01 42 60 30 01, fax 01 42 86 95 36, www.parisvision.com).

Sleeping in Paris
(€1 = about $1, country code: 33)
Sleep Code: **S** = Single, **D** = Double/Twin, **T** = Triple, **Q** = Quad, **b** = bathroom, **s** = shower only, **CC** = Credit Cards accepted, **no CC** = Credit Cards not accepted, * = French hotel rating system (0–4 stars).

To help you sort easily through these listings, I've divided the rooms into three categories based on the price for a standard double room with bath:

Higher Priced—Most rooms more than €140.
Moderately Priced—Most rooms €140 or less.
Lower Priced—Most rooms €100 or less.

I've focused on three safe, handy, and colorful neighborhoods: rue Cler, Marais, and Contrescarpe. For each, I list good hotels, helpful hints, and restaurants (see "Eating in Paris," below). Before reserving, read the descriptions of the three neighborhoods closely. Each offers different pros and cons, and your neighborhood is as important as your hotel for the success of your trip.

Reserve ahead for Paris, the sooner the better. Conventions clog Paris in September (worst), October, May, and June (very tough). In August, when Paris is quiet, some hotels offer lower rates to fill their rooms (if you're planning to visit Paris in the summer, the extra expense of an air-conditioned room can be money well spent). Most hotels accept telephone reservations, require prepayment with a credit-card number, and prefer a faxed follow-up to be sure everything is in order. For more information, see "Making Reservations" in this book's introduction.

French hotels are rated by stars (indicated in this book by a *). One star is simple, two has most of the comforts, three is generally a two-star with a minibar and fancier lobby, and four is luxurious. Hotels with two or more stars are required to have an English-speaking staff. Nearly all hotels listed here will have someone who speaks English.

Old, characteristic, budget Parisian hotels have always been cramped. Retrofitted with elevators, toilets, and private showers (as most are today), they are even more cramped. Even three-star hotel rooms are small and often not worth the extra expense in Paris. Some hotels include the hotel tax (*taxe du séjour*, about €0.50–1 per person per day), though most will add this to your bill.

Recommended hotels have an elevator unless otherwise noted. Quad rooms usually have two double beds. Because rooms with double beds and showers are cheaper than rooms with twin beds and baths, room prices vary within each hotel.

You can save as much as €20–25 by finding the increasingly rare room without a private shower, though some hotels charge for down-the-hall showers. Singles (except for the rare closet-type rooms that fit only 1 twin bed) are simply doubles used by one person. They rent for only a little less than a double.

Continental breakfasts average €6, buffet breakfasts (baked goods, cereal, yogurt, and fruit) cost €8 to €10. Café or picnic breakfasts are cheaper, but hotels usually give unlimited coffee.

Get advice from your hotel for safe parking (consider long-term parking at Orly Airport and taxi in). Meters are free in August. Garages are plentiful (€14–23/day, with special rates through some hotels). Self-serve launderettes are common; ask your hotelier for the nearest one (*Où est un laverie automatique?*; pron. ooh ay uh lah-vay-ree auto-mah-teek).

If you have any trouble finding a room using our listings, try this Web site: www.parishotel.com. You can select from various neighborhood areas (e.g., Eiffel Tower area), give the dates of your visit and preferred price range, and presto—they'll list options with rates. You'll find the hotels listed in this book to be better located and objectively reviewed, though as a last resort, this online service is handy.

Rue Cler Orientation

Rue Cler, a village-like pedestrian street, is safe and tidy, and makes me feel like I must have been a poodle in a previous life. How such coziness lodged itself between the high-powered government district and the wealthy Eiffel Tower and Invalides areas, I'll never know. This is a neighborhood of wide, tree-lined boulevards, stately apartment buildings, and lots of Americans. The American Church, American library, American University, and many of my readers call this area home.

Become a local at a rue Cler café for breakfast or join the afternoon crowd for *une bière pression* (a draft beer). On rue Cler, you can eat and browse your way through a street full of tart shops, delis, cheeseries, and colorful outdoor produce stalls. For an after-dinner cruise on the Seine, it's just a short walk to the river and the Bâteaux-Mouches (see "Organized Tours of Paris," above).

Your neighborhood **TI** is at the Eiffel Tower (May–Sept daily 11:00–18:42, no kidding, tel. 01 45 51 22 15). There's a **post office** at the end of rue Cler on avenue de la Motte Piquet, and a handy **SNCF office** at 78 rue St. Dominique (Mon–Fri

9:00–19:00, Sat 10:00–12:20 & 14:00–18:00, closed Sun). Rue
St. Dominique is the area's boutique-browsing street. The
Epicerie de la Tour **grocery** is open until midnight (197 rue
de Grenelle). **Cyber World Café** is at 20 rue de l'Exposition
(open daily, tel. 01 53 59 96 54).

The **American Church and College** is the community
center for Americans living in Paris and should be one of your
first stops if you're planning to stay awhile (reception open Mon–
Sat 9:00–22:00, Sun 9:00–19:30, 65 quai d'Orsay, tel. 01 40 62
05 00). Pick up copies of the *Paris Voice* for a monthly review of
Paris entertainment, and *France-U.S.A. Contacts* for information
on housing and employment through the community of 30,000
Americans living in Paris. The interdenominational service at
11:00 on Sunday, the coffee hour after church, and the free Sunday concerts (18:00, not every week, Sept–May only) are a great
way to make some friends and get a taste of émigré life in Paris.
Afternoon *boules* (lawn bowling) on the esplanade des Invalides
is a relaxing spectator sport. Look for the dirt area to the upper
right as you face the Invalides.

Key **Métro** stops are Ecole Militaire, La Tour Maubourg,
and Invalides. The **RER-C** line runs along the river, serving
Versailles to the west and the Orsay Museum, Latin Quarter
(St. Michel stop), and Austerlitz train station to the east (in rue
Cler area, use Pont de l'Alma or Invalides RER stops). Smart
travelers take advantage of these helpful **bus routes:** Line #69
runs along rue St. Dominique and serves Les Invalides, Orsay,
Louvre, Marais, and Père Lachaise Cemetery. Line #63 runs
along the river (the Quai d'Orsay), serving the Latin Quarter
along boulevard St. Germain to the east, and the Trocadero and
the Musée Marmottan to the west. Line #92 runs along avenue
Bosquet north to the Champs-Elysées and Arc de Triomphe and
south to the Montparnasse Tower. Line #87 runs on avenue de la
Bourdonnais and serves St. Sulpice, Luxembourg Garden, and
the Sèvres-Babylone shopping area. Line #28 runs on boulevard
La Tour Maubourg and serves the St. Lazare station.

Sleeping in the Rue Cler Neighborhood
(7th arrondissement, Mo: Ecole Militaire, zip code: 75007)

Rue Cler is the glue that holds this pleasant neighborhood together.
From here, you can walk to the Eiffel Tower, Napoleon's Tomb,
the Seine, and the Orsay and Rodin Museums. Hotels here are relatively spacious and a great value, considering the elegance of the
neighborhood and the high prices of the more cramped hotels in
the trendy Marais.

Rue Cler Hotels

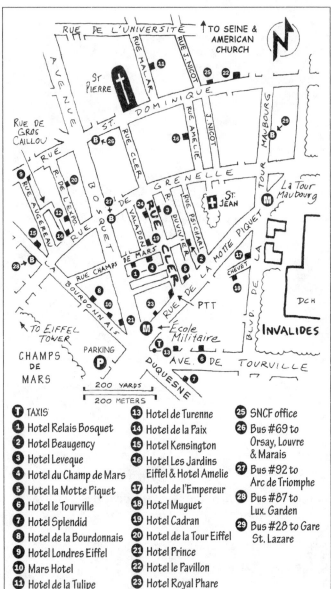

T TAXIS
1 Hotel Relais Bosquet
2 Hotel Beaugency
3 Hotel Leveque
4 Hotel du Champ de Mars
5 Hotel la Motte Piquet
6 Hotel le Tourville
7 Hotel Splendid
8 Hotel de la Bourdonnais
9 Hotel Londres Eiffel
10 Mars Hotel
11 Hotel de la Tulipe
12 Hotel de l'Alma

13 Hotel de Turenne
14 Hotel de la Paix
15 Hotel Kensington
16 Hotel Les Jardins Eiffel & Hotel Amelie
17 Hotel de l'Empereur
18 Hotel Muguet
19 Hotel Cadran
20 Hotel de la Tour Eiffel
21 Hotel Prince
22 Hotel le Pavillon
23 Hotel Royal Phare
24 Hotel la Serre

25 SNCF office
26 Bus #69 to Orsay, Louvre & Marais
27 Bus #92 to Arc de Triomphe
28 Bus #87 to Lux. Garden
29 Bus #28 to Gare St. Lazare

Many of my readers stay in this neighborhood. If you want to disappear into Paris, choose a hotel away from the rue Cler, or in the other neighborhoods I list. And if nightlife matters, sleep elsewhere. The first five hotels listed below are within Camembert-smelling distance of rue Cler; the others are within a five- to 10-minute stroll.

Sleeping in the Heart of Rue Cler

HIGHER PRICED
Hôtel Relais Bosquet*** is modern, spacious, and a bit upscale, with snazzy, air-conditioned rooms, electric darkness blinds, and big beds. Gerard and his staff are polite, formal, and friendly (Sb-€125–146, standard Db-€140, spacious Db-€160, extra bed-€30, CC, parking-€14, 19 rue de Champ de Mars, tel. 01 47 05 25 45, fax 01 45 55 08 24, www.relaisbosquet.com).

MODERATELY PRICED
Hôtel Beaugency***, on a quieter street a short block off rue Cler, has 30 small but comfortable rooms, a lobby you can stretch out in, and friendly Chantal in charge. When I have tour groups in Paris, this is my first choice for their home base (Sb-€104, Db-€111, Tb-€127, CC, buffet breakfast, 21 rue Duvivier, tel. 01 47 05 01 63, fax 01 45 51 04 96, www.hotel-beaugency.com).

LOWER PRICED
Warning: The first two hotels listed here—while the best value—are overrun with my readers (book long in advance . . . or avoid).

Hôtel Leveque** is ideally located, with a helpful staff (Pascale and Christophe SE), a singing maid, and a Starship Enterprise elevator. It's a classic old hotel with well-designed rooms that have all the comforts (S–€53, Db-€84–91, Tb-€114 for two adults and one child only, breakfast-€7, first breakfast free for readers of this book, CC, air-con, 29 rue Cler, tel. 01 47 05 49 15, fax 01 45 50 49 36, check room availability on Web site, www.hotel-leveque.com, e-mail: info@hotelleveque.com).

Hôtel du Champ de Mars**, with charming pastel rooms and helpful English-speaking owners Françoise and Stephane, is a homier rue Cler option. This plush little hotel has a Provence-style, small-town feel from top to bottom. Rooms are small, but comfortable and a good value. Single rooms can work as tiny doubles (Sb-€66, Db-€72–76, Tb-€92, CC, 30 meters/100 feet off rue Cler at 7 rue de Champ de Mars, tel. 01 45 51 52 30, fax 01 45 51 64 36, www.hotel-du-champ-de-mars.com, e-mail: stg@club-internet.fr).

Hôtel la Motte Piquet**, at the end of rue Cler, is reasonable and spotless and comes with a cheery welcome from Daniele. Most of its 18 cozy rooms face a busy street, but the twins are on the quieter rue Cler (Ss-€57, Sb-€60–64, Db-€73–81, CC, 30 avenue de la Motte Piquet, tel. 01 47 05 09 57, fax 01 47 05 74 36).

Sleeping near Rue Cler
The following listings are a five- to 10-minute walk from rue Cler.

HIGHER PRICED
Hôtel le Tourville**** is the most classy and expensive of my rue Cler listings. This four-star place is surprisingly intimate and friendly, from its designer lobby and vaulted breakfast area to its pretty but small pastel rooms (small standard Db-€145, superior Db-€215, Db with private terrace-€240, junior suite for 3–4 people-€310, extra bed-€17, CC, air-con, 16 avenue de Tourville, Mo: Ecole Militaire, tel. 01 47 05 62 62, fax 01 47 05 43 90, e-mail: hotel@tourville.com).

Hôtel Splendid*** is Art Deco mod, friendly, and worth your while if you land one of its suites with great Eiffel Tower views (Db-€124–146, Db suite-€205–220, CC, 29 avenue Tourville, tel. 01 45 51 24 77, fax 01 44 18 94 60, e-mail: splendid@club-internet.fr).

Hôtel de la Bourdonnais*** is a *très* Parisian place, mixing slightly faded Old World elegance with professional service and mostly spacious rooms (their smaller rooms can be cramped, confirm that room is not small, Sb-€120, Db-€150, Tb-€160, Qb-€180, 5-person suite-€210, CC, air-con, 111 avenue de la Bourdonnais, tel. 01 47 05 45 42, fax 01 45 55 75 54, www .hotellabourdonnais.fr).

MODERATELY PRICED
Hôtel Londres Eiffel*** is my closest listing to the Eiffel Tower and Champs de Mars park. It offers immaculate, warmly decorated rooms, cozy public spaces, and Internet access. The helpful staff take good care of their guests (Sb-€93–102, Db-€105–115, Tb-€137, extra bed-€17, CC, use handy bus #69 or the RER Alma stop, 1 rue Augerau, tel. 01 45 51 63 02, fax 01 47 05 28 96, www.londres-eiffel.com).

Eber-Mars Hôtel** , with helpful owner Jean-Marc, is a good midrange value with larger-than-average rooms and a beam-me-up-Jacques, coffin-sized elevator (small Db-€75, large Db-€90–110, Tb-€130, extra bed-€20, CC, 117 avenue de la Bourdonnais, tel. 01 47 05 42 30, fax 01 47 05 45 91).

Hôtel de la Tulipe*** is a unique place two blocks from rue Cler toward the river, with a seductive wood-beamed lounge and a peaceful, leafy courtyard. Its artistically decorated rooms (each one different) come with small, stylish bathrooms (Db-€105–135, Tb-€160, CC, no elevator, 33 rue Malar, tel. 01 45 51 67 21, fax 01 47 53 96 37, www.hoteldelatulipe.com).

Hôtel de l'Alma*** is well-located on "restaurant row," with good rooms, but small bathrooms and reasonable rates (Db-€100–115, CC, 32 rue de l'Exposition, tel. 01 47 05 45 70, fax 01 45 51 84 47, e-mail: almahotel@minitel.net, Carine SE).

LOWER PRICED
Hôtel de Turenne**, with sufficiently comfortable, air-conditioned rooms, is a good value when it's hot. It also has five truly single rooms (Sb-€61, Db-€71–81, Tb-€96, extra bed-€9.50, CC, 20 avenue de Tourville, tel. 01 47 05 99 92, fax 01 45 56 06 04, e-mail: hotel.turenne.paris7@wanadoo.fr).

Hôtel de la Paix**, a smart hotel located away from the fray on a quiet little street, offers 23 plush, well-designed rooms for a good value (Sb-€61, Db-€80, big Db-€91, Tb-€11, CC, fine buffet breakfast, Internet access, 19 rue du Gros-Caillou, tel. 01 45 51 86 17, fax 01 45 55 93 28, e-mail: hotel.de.lapaix @wanadoo.fr).

Hôtel Kensington** is impersonal and has teeny rooms, but is a fair value (Sb-€53, Db-€67–82, CC, 79 avenue de la Bourdonnais, tel. 01 47 05 74 00, fax 01 47 05 25 81, www .hotel-kensington.com).

Sleeping near Métro: La Tour Maubourg
The next three listings are within two blocks of the intersection of avenue de la Motte Piquet and Les Invalides.

HIGHER PRICED
Hôtel Les Jardins Eiffel*** feels like a modern motel, but earns its three stars with professional service, a spacious lobby, an outdoor patio, and 80 comfortable, air-conditioned rooms—some with private balconies (ask for a room *avec petit balcon*). Even better: Readers of this book get free buffet breakfasts (Db-€130–160, extra bed-€21 or free for a child, CC, parking-€17/day, 8 rue Amelie, tel. 01 47 05 46 21, fax 01 45 55 28 08, e-mail: eiffel@unimedia.fr, Marie SE).

LOWER PRICED
Roomy **Hôtel de l'Empereur**** lacks personality, but is a fine value. Its 38 pleasant, woody rooms come with sturdy furniture and all the comforts except air-conditioning. Streetside rooms

have views but some noise; fifth-floor rooms have small balconies and Napoleonic views (Sb-€70–75, Db-€75–85, Tb-€105, Qb-€120, CC, 2 rue Chevert, tel. 01 45 55 88 02, fax 01 45 51 88 54, www.hotelempereur.com, Petra SE).

Hôtel Muguet**, a peaceful and clean hotel, gives you three-star comfort for the price of two. The remarkably spacious hotel offers 48 sharp, air-conditioned rooms and a small garden courtyard. The hands-on owner, Catherine, gives her guests a peaceful and secure home in Paris (Sb-€85, Db-€95–103, Tb-€130, CC, 11 rue Chevert, tel. 01 47 05 05 93, fax 01 45 50 25 37, www.hotelmuguet.com).

Lesser Values
Given this fine area, these are acceptable last choices.

HIGHER PRICED

Perfectly located **Hôtel Cadran***** has a shiny lobby, but no charm and tight, narrow, overpriced rooms (Db-€148–165, CC, air-con, 10 rue du Champs de Mars, tel. 01 40 62 67 00, fax 01 40 62 67 13, www.hotelducadran.com).

LOWER PRICED

Hôtel de la Tour Eiffel** is a modest little place with fair-priced rooms but cheap furnishings and foam mattresses (Sb-€65, Db-€80, Tb-€100, CC, 17 rue de l'Exposition, tel. 01 47 05 14 75, fax 01 47 53 99 46, Muriel SE). **Hôtel Prince****, just across avenue Bosquet from the Ecole Militaire Métro stop, has good-enough rooms, many overlooking a busy street (Sb-€70, Db-€82–105, CC, 66 avenue Bosquet, tel. 01 47 05 40 90, fax 01 47 53 06 62, www.hotel-paris-prince .com). **Hôtel le Pavillon**** is quiet, with basic rooms, no elevator, and cramped halls in a charming location (Sb-€72, Db-€80, Tb, Qb, or Quint/b-€105, CC, 54 rue St. Dominique, tel. 01 45 51 42 87, fax 01 45 51 32 79, e-mail: patrickpavillon@aol .com). **Hôtel Royal Phare**** is very simple (Db-€61–74, CC, facing Ecole Militaire Métro stop, 40 avenue de la Motte Piquet, tel. 01 47 05 57 30, fax 01 45 51 64 41, www.hotel -royalphare-paris.com). **Hôtel Amelie**** is another possibility (Db-€95, CC, 5 rue Amelie, tel. 01 45 51 74 75, fax 01 45 56 93 55). The basic **Hôtel La Serre*** has a good location on rue Cler, but generates readers' complaints for its rude staff and bizarre hotel practices—you can't see a room in advance or get a refund (Db-€90, CC, 24 rue Cler, across from Hôtel Leveque, Mo: Ecole Militaire, tel. 01 47 05 52 33, fax 01 40 62 95 66).

Marais Orientation

Those interested in a more Soho–Greenwich Village locale should make the Marais their Parisian home. Only 15 years ago, it was a forgotten Parisian backwater, but now the Marais is one of Paris' most popular residential, tourist, and shopping areas. This is jumbled, medieval Paris at its finest, where elegant stone mansions sit alongside trendy bars, antique shops, and fashion-conscious boutiques. The streets are a fascinating parade of artists, students, tourists, immigrants, and babies in strollers munching baguettes—and the Marais is also known as a hub of the Parisian gay and lesbian scene. This area is *sans* doubt livelier (and louder) than the rue Cler area.

In the Marais, you have these sights at your fingertips: Picasso Museum, Carnavalet Museum, Victor Hugo House, Jewish Art and History Museum, and the Pompidou Center (modern art). You're also a manageable walk from Paris' two islands (Ile St. Louis and Ile de la Cité), where you'll find Notre-Dame and Sainte-Chapelle. The Opera de la Bastille, Promenade Plantée Park, place des Vosges (Paris' oldest square), Jewish Quarter (rue des Rosiers), and nightlife-packed rue de Lappe are also nearby. Two good open markets lie nearby: the sprawl-ing Marché Bastille on place Bastille (Thu and Sun until 12:30) and the more intimate Marché de la place d'Aligre (daily 9:00–12:00, a few blocks behind opera on place d'Aligre).

The nearest **TIs** are in the Louvre (Wed–Mon 10:00–19:00, closed Tue) and Gare de Lyon (daily 8:00–20:00, tel. 08 92 68 31 12, wait for English recording). Most banks and other ser-vices are on the main drag, rue de Rivoli/St. Antoine. For your Parisian Sears, find the **BHV** next to Hôtel de Ville. Marais **post offices** are on rue Castex and on the corner of rues Pavée and Francs Bourgeois.

Métro service is excellent to the Marais neighborhood, with direct service to the Louvre, Champs-Elysées, Arc de Triomphe, and four major train stations: Gare du Lyon, Gare du Nord, Gare de l'Est and Gare d'Austerlitz. Key Métro stops in the Marais are, from east to west: Bastille, St. Paul, and Hôtel de Ville (Sully Mor-land, Pont Marie, and Rambuteau stops are also handy). There are also several helpful **bus routes:** Line #69 on rue St. Antoine takes you to the Louvre, Orsay, Rodin, and Napoleon's Tomb and ends at the Eiffel Tower. Line #86 runs down boulevard Henri IV, cross-ing Ile St. Louis and serving the Latin Quarter along boulevard St. Germain. Line #96 runs on rues Turenne and Francois Miron and serves the Louvre and boulevard St. Germain (near Luxem-bourg Garden). Line #65 serves the train stations d'Austerlitz, Est, and Nord from place de la Bastille.

You'll find **taxi stands** on place Bastille, on the north side of rue St. Antoine (where it meets rue Castex), and on the south side of rue St. Antoine (in front of St. Paul Church).

Sleeping in the Marais Neighborhood
(4th arrondissement, Mo: St. Paul or Bastille, zip code: 75004)

The Marais runs from the Pompidou Center to the Bastille (a 15-min walk), with most hotels located a few blocks north of the main east-west drag, rue de Rivoli/St. Antoine (one street with two names). It's about 15 minutes on foot from any hotel in this area to Notre-Dame, Ile St. Louis, and the Latin Quarter. Strolling home (day or night) from Notre-Dame along the Ile St. Louis is marvelous.

MODERATELY PRICED

Hôtel Castex***, on a quiet street near the Bastille, is completely renovating and upgrading to three stars in early 2003, with the addition of an elevator, air-conditioning, and brand-spanking-new rooms (estimated new prices: Sb-€100, Db-€120, Tb-€140, CC, closed until March, just off place de la Bastille and rue St. Antoine, 5 rue Castex, Mo: Bastille, tel. 01 42 72 31 52, fax 01 42 72 57 91, www.castexhotel.com, e-mail: info@castexhotel.com).

Hôtel Bastille Speria***, a short block off the Bastille, offers business-type service. The 42 plain but cheery rooms have air-conditioning, thin walls, and curiously cheap and sweaty foam mattresses. It's English-language friendly, from the *Herald Tribune*s in the lobby to the history of the Bastille posted in the elevator (Sb-€95, Db-€112–120, child's bed-€20, CC, 1 rue de la Bastille, Mo: Bastille, tel. 01 42 72 04 01, fax 01 42 72 56 38, www.hotel-bastille-speria.com).

Hôtel de la Place des Vosges** is so well-located—in a medieval building on a quiet street just off place des Vosges— that the staff can take or leave your business. Still, its customers leave happy (Sb-€84, Db-€120, CC, 16 rooms, 1 flight of stairs then elevator, 12 rue de Biraque, Mo: St. Paul, tel. 01 42 72 60 46, fax 01 42 72 02 64, e-mail: hotel.place.des.vosges@gofornet.com).

Hôtel des Chevaliers***, a little boutique hotel one block northwest of place des Vosges, offers small, pleasant rooms with modern comforts. Eight of its 24 rooms are off the street and quiet—worth requesting (Db-€110–130, prices depend on season, CC, 30 rue de Turenne, Mo: St. Paul, tel. 01 42 72 73 47, fax 01 42 72 54 10, e-mail: info@hoteldeschevaliers.com, Christele SE).

Hôtel St. Louis Marais** is a tiny place, well-situated on a quiet residential street between the river and rue St. Antoine, with

Marais Hotels

1. Hotel Castex
2. Hotel Bastille Speria
3. Hotel de la Place des Vosges
4. Hotel des Chevaliers
5. Hotel St. Louis Marais
6. Grand Hotel Jeanne d'Arc
7. Hotel Lyon-Mulhouse
8. Hotel Sevigne
9. Hotel Pointe Rivoli
10. Hotel de 7eme Art
11. Hotel de la Republique
12. MIJE hostels
13. Hotel Axial & Hotel Sansonnet
14. Hotel de la Bretonnerie
15. Hotel Caron de Beaumarchais
16. Hotel de Vieux Marais
17. Hotel Beaubourg
18. Hotel de Nice
19. Grand Hotel du Loiret
20. Hotel Jeu de Paume
21. Hotels Des Deux Iles & Lutece
22. BHV Department store
23. Bus #69 to Louvre, Orsay & Eiffel Tower
24. Bus #s 86 & 87 to Latin Quarter

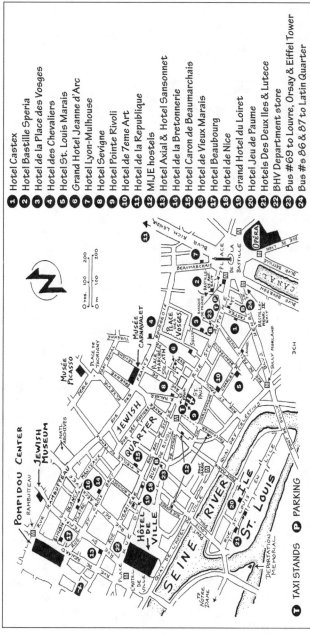

a cute lobby and 16 cozy, if pricey, rooms (Sb-€90, small Db-€105, standard Db-€120, CC, no elevator but only 2 floors, 1 rue Charles V, tel. 01 48 87 87 04, fax 01 48 87 33 26, www.saintlouismarais.com).

LOWER PRICED
Grand Hôtel Jeanne d'Arc**, a warm, welcoming place with thoughtfully appointed rooms, is ideally located for (and very popular with) connoisseurs of the Marais. Rooms on the street can be noisy until the bars close. Sixth-floor rooms have a view, and corner rooms are wonderfully bright in the City of Lights. Reserve this place way ahead (Sb-€53, Db-€73, larger twin Db-€92, Tb-€109, good Qb-€125, CC, 3 rue Jarente, Mo: St. Paul, tel. 01 48 87 62 11, fax 01 48 87 37 31, e-mail: hoteljeannedarc@wanadoo.fr, Gail SE).

Hôtel Lyon-Mulhouse**, with half of its 40 pleasant rooms on a busy street just off place de la Bastille, is a good value. Its bigger and quieter rooms on the back are worth the extra euros (Sb-€55, Db-€64, twin Db-€75, Tb-€88–92, Qb-€100, CC, 8 boulevard Beaumarchais, tel. 01 47 00 91 50, fax 01 47 00 06 31, e-mail: hotelyonmulhouse@wanadoo.fr).

Hôtel Sévigné**, less personal with dreary halls, rents 30 well-worn but sleepable rooms at fair prices, plus the cheapest breakfast in Paris at €3.50 (Sb-€56, Db-€63, Tb-€83, CC, 2 rue Malher, Mo: St. Paul, tel. 01 42 72 76 17, fax 01 42 78 68 26, www.le-sevigne.com).

Hotel Pointe Rivoli*, across from the St. Paul Métro stop, is in the thick of the Marais, with Paris' steepest stairs (no elevator) and modest, though pleasant, rooms at fair rates (Sb-€60, Db-€70, Tb-€100, CC, 125 rue St. Antoine, tel. 01 42 72 14 23, fax 01 42 72 51 11, e-mail: pointerivoli@libertysurf.fr).

Hôtel de 7ème Art**, two blocks south of rue St. Antoine toward the river, is a relaxed, Hollywood-nostalgia place, run by young, friendly Marais types, with a full-service café/bar and Charlie Chaplin murals. Its 23 rooms lack imagination, but are comfortable and a fair value. The large rooms are American-spacious (small Db-€72, standard Db-€82–92, large Db-€107–122, extra bed-€20, CC, 20 rue St. Paul, Mo: St. Paul, tel. 01 44 54 85 00, fax 01 42 77 69 10, e-mail: hotel7art@wanadoo.fr).

Hôtel de la République**, owned by the people who run the Castex (see above), is in a less appealing, out-of-the-way location than other listed Marais hotels, but often has rooms when others don't (Sb-€53, Db-€61, CC, near place de République, 31 rue Albert Thomas, 75010 Paris, Mo: République, tel. 01 42 39 19 03, fax 01 42 39 22 66, www.republiquehotel.com).

MIJE Youth Hostels: The Maison Internationale de la Jeunesse des Etudiants (MIJE) runs three classy, old residences clustered a few blocks south of rue St. Antoine. Each offers simple, clean, single-sex, one- to four-bed rooms for families and travelers under the age of 30 (exceptions are made for families). None has an elevator or double beds, each has an Internet station, and all rooms have showers. Prices are per person and favor single travelers (2 people can find a double in a simple hotel for similar rates). You can pay more to have your own room or be roomed with as many as three others (Sb-€37, Db-€27, Tb-€24, Qb-€22, no CC, includes breakfast but not towels, which you can get from a machine; required membership card-€2.50 extra/person; rooms locked 12:00–15:00 and at 1:00). The hostels are: **MIJE Fourcy** (€9 dinners available to anyone with a membership card, 6 rue de Fourcy, just south of rue Rivoli), **MIJE Fauconnier** (11 rue Fauconnier), and the best, **MIJE Maubisson** (12 rue des Barres). They all share the same contact information (tel. 01 42 74 23 45, fax 01 40 27 81 64, www.mije.com) and Métro stop (St. Paul). Reservations are accepted, though you must arrive by noon.

Sleeping near the Pompidou Center
These hotels are farther west and closer to the Pompidou Center than to place Bastille.

HIGHER PRICED
Hotel Axial Beaubourg***, a block from the Hôtel de Ville toward the Pompidou Center, has a minimalist lobby and 28 nicely decorated, plush rooms, many with wood beams (standard Db-€134–142, big Db-€165, CC, air-con, 11 rue du Temple, tel. 01 42 72 72 22, fax 02 42 72 03 53, www.axialbeaubourg.com).

MODERATELY PRICED
Hôtel de la Bretonnerie***, three blocks from Hôtel de Ville, is a fine Marais splurge. It has an on-the-ball staff, a big, welcoming lobby, elegant decor, and tastefully decorated rooms with an antique, open-beam warmth (perfectly good standard "classic" Db-€108, bigger "charming" Db-€140, Db suite-€180, Tb suite-€205, Qb suite-€230, CC, closed Aug, between rue du Vielle du Temple and rue des Archives at 22 rue Sainte Croix de la Bretonnerie, Mo: Hôtel de Ville, tel. 01 48 87 77 63, fax 01 42 77 26 78, www.bretonnerie.com).

    Hôtel Caron de Beaumarchais*** feels like a dollhouse, with a lobby cluttered with bits from an elegant 18th-century Marais house and 20 sweet little rooms. Short antique collectors love this place (small back-side Db-€130, larger Db on the front–€145, CC, air-con, 12 rue Vielle du Temple, Mo: Hôtel de Ville, tel. 01 42 72 34 12, fax 01 42 72 34 63, www.carondebeaumarchais.com).

Hôtel de Vieux Marais** is tucked away on a quiet street two blocks east of the Pompidou Center. It offers bright, spacious, well-maintained rooms, simple decor, and we-try-harder owners. Marie-Helene, the in-love-with-her-work owner, gives this place its charm. Greet Leeloo, the hotel hound (Db-€125, extra bed-€23, CC, air-con, just off rue des Archives at 8 rue du Platre, Mo: Rambuteau/Hôtel de Ville, tel. 01 42 78 47 22, fax 01 42 78 34 32, www.vieuxmarais.com).

Hôtel Beaubourg*** is a good three-star value on a quiet street in the menacing shadow of the Pompidou Center. Its 28 rooms are wood-beam comfy, and the inviting lounge is warm and pleasant (Db-€93–122 depending on the size, some with balconies-€122, twins are considerably larger than doubles, includes breakfast, CC, 11 rue Simon Lefranc, Mo: Rambuteau, tel. 01 42 74 34 24, fax 01 42 78 68 11, e-mail: htlbeaubourg@hotellerie.net).

LOWER PRICED
Hôtel de Nice**, on the Marais' busy main drag, is a turquoise-and-rose "Marie-Antoinette does tie-dye" place. Its narrow halls are littered with paintings, and its 23 rooms are filled with thoughtful touches and have tight bathrooms. Twin rooms, which cost the same as doubles, are larger, but on the street side—with effective double-paned windows (Sb-€62, Db-€97, Tb-€117, Qb-€135, CC, 42 bis rue de Rivoli, Mo: Hôtel de Ville, tel. 01 42 78 55 29, fax 01 42 78 36 07).

At **Grand Hôtel du Loiret****, you get what you pay for in an inexpensive, basic, laid-back place (S-€37, Sb-€47–62, D-€42, Db-€56–72, Tb-€72–84, CC, just north of rue de Rivoli, 8 rue des Garçons Mauvais, Mo: Hôtel de Ville, tel. 01 48 87 77 00, fax 01 48 04 96 56, e-mail: hoteloiret@aol.com).

Hotel Sansonnet**, a block from the Hôtel de Ville toward the Pompidou Center, is a homey, unassuming place with no elevator but 26 comfortable, well-maintained and good value rooms (Sb-€46–55, Db-€58–78, CC, 48 rue de la Verrerie, Mo: Hôtel de Ville, tel. 01 48 87 96 14, fax 01 48 87 30 46, www.hotel-sansonnet.com, e-mail: info@hotel-sansonnet.com).

Sleeping near the Marais on Ile St. Louis
The peaceful, residential character of this river-wrapped island, its brilliant location, and homemade ice cream have drawn Americans for decades, allowing hotels to charge top euro for their rooms. There are no budget values here, but the island's coziness and proximity to the Marais, Notre-Dame, and the Latin Quarter

compensate for higher rates. These hotels are on the island's main drag, the rue St. Louis en l'Ile, where I list several restaurants (see "Eating," below).

HIGHER PRICED
Hôtel Jeu de Paume****, located in a 17th-century tennis center, is the most expensive hotel I list in Paris. When you enter its magnificent lobby, you'll understand why. Ride the glass elevator for a half-timbered-tree-house experience and marvel at the cozy lounges. The 30 quite comfortable rooms have muted tones and feel more three-plus than four-star (you're paying for the location and public spaces). Most face a small garden and all are peaceful (Sb-€152, standard Db-€210, larger Db-€220–250, Db suite-€450, CC, 54 rue St. Louis en l'Ile, tel. 01 43 26 14 18, fax 01 40 46 02 76, www.jeudepaumehotel.com).

The following two hotels are owned by the same person. For both, if you must cancel, do so a week in advance or pay fees: **Hôtel de Lutèce***** is the best value on the island, with a sit-a-while wood-paneled lobby and fireplace and appealing air-conditioned rooms. Twin rooms are larger and the same price as double rooms (Sb-€125, Db-€149, Tb-€165, CC, 65 rue St. Louis en l'Ile, tel. 01 43 26 13 35, fax 01 43 29 60 25, www.hotel-ile-saint-louis.com). **Hôtel des Deux Iles***** is a *très* similar value, with marginally smaller rooms (Sb-€125, Db-€149, CC, air-con, 59 rue St. Louis en l'Ile, tel. 01 43 26 13 35, fax 01 43 29 60 25, www.hotel-ile-saintlouis.com).

Contrescarpe Orientation
I've patched together several areas to construct this diverse hotel neighborhood, whose strength is its central location and proximity to the Luxembourg Garden. The Latin Quarter, Luxembourg Garden, boulevard St. Germain, and Jardin des Plantes are all easily reachable by foot. Hotel listings are concentrated near the monumental Panthéon and along the more colorful rue Mouffe-tard. Perfectly Parisian place Contrescarpe ties these distinctly different areas together.

The rue Mouffetard is the spine of this area, running south from place Contrescarpe to rue Bazelles. Two thousand years ago, it was the principal Roman road south to Italy. Today, this small, meandering street has a split personality. The lower part thrives in the daytime as a pedestrian market street. The upper part sleeps during the day but comes alive after dark, teeming with bars, restaurants, and nightlife.

The flowery Jardin des Plantes park is just east, and the sublime Luxembourg Garden is just west. Both are ideal for afternoon walks, picnics, naps, and kids. The doorway at 49 rue Monge leads to a hidden **Roman arena** (Arènes de Lutèce). Today, *boules* players occupy the stage while couples cuddle on the seats. Admire the Panthéon from the outside (it's not worth paying to enter), and peek inside the exquisitely beautiful St. Etienne-du-Mont church.

The nearest **TI** is at the Louvre Museum. The **post office** (PTT) is between rue Mouffetard and rue Monge at 10 rue de l'Epée du Bois. Place Monge hosts a good **outdoor market** on Wednesday, Friday, and Sunday mornings until 13:00. The **street market** at the bottom of rue Mouffetard bustles daily except Monday (Tue–Sat 8:00–12:00 & 15:30–19:00, Sun 8:00–12:00, 5 blocks south of place Contrescarpe). Lively cafés at place Contrescarpe hop with action from the afternoon into the wee hours. **Bus** #47 runs along rue Monge north to Notre-Dame, the Pompidou Center, and Gare du Nord.

Sleeping in the Contrescarpe Neighborhood
(5th arrondissement, Mo: Place Monge, zip code: 75005)
The first six hotels here are a 10- to 15-minute walk from Notre-Dame, Ile de la Cité, and Ile St. Louis, and a five- to 10-minute walk from the Luxembourg Garden, St. Sulpice, and the grand boulevards St. Germain and St. Michel. Add 10 minutes for the last five hotels to reach the same places.

Sleeping near the Seine

MODERATELY PRICED
Hôtel des Grandes Ecoles*** is simply idyllic. A short alley leads to three buildings protecting a flower-filled garden court-yard, preserving a sense of tranquillity that is rare in a city this size. Its 51 rooms are reasonably spacious and comfortable with large beds. This romantic place is deservedly popular, so call well in advance (reservations not accepted more than 4 months ahead, Db-€95–110, a few bigger rooms-€120, extra bed-€15, parking-€25, CC, 75 rue de Cardinal Lemoine, Mo: Cardinal Lemoine, tel. 01 43 26 79 23, fax 01 43 25 28 15, www.hotel-grandes-ecoles .com, mellow Marie speaks some English, Mama does not).

LOWER PRICED
Hôtel Central* defines unpretentiousness, with a charming location, smoky reception area, steep, slippery, castle-like stair-way, so-so beds, and basic but cheery rooms (all with showers, though toilets are down the hall). It's a fine budget value (Ss-€29–37, Ds-€39–45, no CC, no elevator, 6 rue Descartes, Mo: Cardinal Lemoine, tel. 01 46 33 57 93, sweet Pilar NSE).

Contrescarpe Hotels and Restaurants

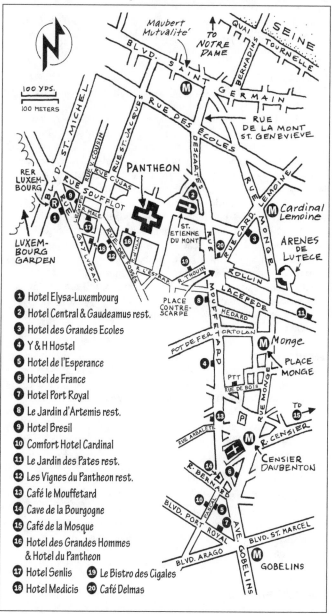

1. Hotel Elysa-Luxembourg
2. Hotel Central & Gaudeamus rest.
3. Hotel des Grandes Ecoles
4. Y & H Hostel
5. Hotel de l'Esperance
6. Hotel de France
7. Hotel Port Royal
8. Le Jardin d'Artemis rest.
9. Hotel Bresil
10. Comfort Hotel Cardinal
11. Le Jardin des Pates rest.
12. Les Vignes du Pantheon rest.
13. Café le Mouffetard
14. Cave de la Bourgogne
15. Café de la Mosque
16. Hotel des Grandes Hommes
    & Hotel du Pantheon
17. Hotel Senlis
18. Hotel Medicis
19. Le Bistro des Cigales
20. Café Delmas

Sleeping between the Panthéon and Luxembourg Garden

The following four hotels are a five-minute walk from place Contrescarpe. The RER stop Luxembourg (with direct connections to the airports) is closer than the nearest Métro stop, Maubert Mutualité.

HIGHER PRICED

Both of these hotels face the Panthéon's right transept and are owned by the same family (ask about their low-season promotional rates).

Hôtel du Panthéon*** welcomes you with a melt-in-your-chair lobby and 32 country-French-cute rooms with air-conditioning and every possible comfort. Fifth-floor rooms have skinny balconies, but sixth-floor rooms have the best views (standard Db-€188, larger Db-€218, Tb-€235, CC, 19 place du Panthéon, tel. 01 43 54 32 95, fax 01 43 26 64 65, www.hoteldupantheon.com).

Hôtel des Grandes Hommes*** was designed to look good—and it does. The lobby is to be admired but not enjoyed, and the 31 rooms are design-magazine perfect. They're generally tight but adorable, with great attention to detail and little expense spared. Fifth- and sixth-floor rooms have balconies (sixth-floor balconies, with grand views, are big enough to enjoy). For more luxury, splurge for a suite (standard Db-€218, Db suite-€250, CC, air-con, 17 place du Panthéon, tel. 01 46 34 19 60, fax 01 43 26 67 32, www.hoteldesgrandeshommes.com).

LOWER PRICED

Hôtel Senlis** hides quietly two blocks from Luxembourg Garden, with modest rooms, carpeted walls, and metal closets. Most rooms have beamed ceilings and all could use a facelift (Sb-€67, Db-€72–87, Tb-€95, Qb-€110, CC, 7 rue Malebranche, tel. 01 43 29 93 10, fax 01 43 29 00 24, www.hoteldesenlis.fr).

Hôtel Medicis is as cheap, stripped-down, and basic as it gets, with a soiled linoleum charm, a happy owner, and a great location (S-€16, D-€31, 214 rue St. Jacques, tel. 01 43 54 14 66, Denis speaks English).

Sleeping at the Bottom of Rue Mouffetard

Of my recommended accommodations in the Contrescarpe neighborhood, these are farthest from the Seine and other tourists, and lie in an appealing workaday area. They may have rooms when others don't.

HIGHER PRICED

Comfort Hôtel Cardinal*** is a well-designed hotel with less character but agreeable decor and modern comforts (ask about off-season promotional rates, Sb-€100, standard Db-€138, large Db-€185, CC, air-con, 20 rue Pascal, tel. 01 47 07 41 92, fax 01 47 07 43 80, e-mail: hotelcardinal@aol.com).

LOWER PRICED
Don't let **Hôtel Port Royal***'s lone star fool you—this 46-room place is polished bottom to top and has been well-run by the same proud family for 66 years. You could eat off the floors of its spotless, comfy rooms. Ask for a room off the street (S-€37–48, D-€64, big hall showers-€2.50, Db-€73, deluxe Db-€84, no CC, requires cash deposit, climb stairs from rue Pascal to busy boulevard de Port Royal, 8 boulevard de Port Royal, Mo: Gobelins, tel. 01 43 31 70 06, fax 01 43 31 33 67, www.portroyal.fr.st).

Hôtel de l'Esperance** is a solid two-star value. It's quiet, pink, fluffy, and comfortable, with thoughtfully appointed rooms complete with canopy beds and a flamboyant owner (Sb-€70, Db-€73–86, small Tb-€101, CC, 15 rue Pascal, Mo: Censier-Daubenton, tel. 01 47 07 10 99, fax 01 43 37 56 19, e-mail: hotel.esperance@wanadoo.fr).

Hôtel de France** is set on a busy street, with adequately comfortable rooms, fair prices, and less welcoming owners. The best and quietest rooms are *sur le cour* (on the courtyard), though streetside rooms are OK (Sb-€64, Db-€76–80, CC, requires 1 night nonrefundable deposit, 108 rue Monge, Mo: Censier-Daubenton, tel. 01 47 07 19 04, fax 01 43 36 62 34, e-mail: hotel.de.fce@wanadoo.fr).

Y&H Hostel is easygoing and English-speaking, with Internet access, kitchen facilities, and basic but acceptable hostel conditions (beds in 4-bed rooms-€22, beds in double rooms-€25, sheets-€2.50, no CC, rooms closed 11:00–16:00 but reception stays open, 2:00 curfew, reservations require deposit, 80 rue Mouffetard, Mo: Cardinal Lemoine, tel. 01 47 07 47 07, fax 01 47 07 22 24, e-mail: smile@youngandhappy.fr).

Lesser Values

MODERATELY PRICED
Hôtel Elysa-Luxembourg*** sits on a busy street at Luxembourg Garden and charges top euro for its plush, air-conditioned rooms (Db-€138, CC, 6 rue Gay Lussac, tel. 01 43 25 31 74, fax 01 46 34 56 27, www.elysa-luxembourg.fr).

LOWER PRICED
Hôtel Brésil** lies one block from Luxembourg Garden and offers little character, some smoky rooms, and reasonable rates

(Sb-€64, Db-€68–85, CC, 10 rue le Goff, tel. 01 43 54 76 11,
fax 01 46 33 45 78, e-mail: hoteldubresil@wanadoo.fr).

Sleeping near Paris, in Versailles

For a laid-back alternative to Paris within easy reach of the big city
by RER train (5/hr, 30 min), Versailles, with easy, safe parking and
reasonably priced hotels, can be a good overnight stop (see map on
page 85). Park in the château's main lot while looking for a hotel,
or leave your car there overnight (free from 19:30 to 8:00). Get a
map of Versailles at your hotel or at the TI. For restaurant recommendations, see "Eating," below.

MODERATELY PRICED

Hôtel de France*, in an 18th-century town house, offers four-
star value, with air-conditioned, appropriately royal rooms, a
pleasant courtyard, comfy public spaces, a bar, and a restaurant
(Db-€125–130, Tb-€168, CC, just off parking lot across from
château, 5 rue Colbert, tel. 01 30 83 92 23, fax 01 30 83 92 24,
www.hotelfrance-versailles.com).

LOWER PRICED

Hôtel Le Cheval Rouge**, built in 1676 as Louis XIV's stables,
now houses tourists. It's a block behind place du Marché in a
quaint corner of town on a large, quiet courtyard with free, safe
parking and sufficiently comfortable rooms (Ds-€49, Db-€58–72,
Tb-€86, Qb-€90, CC, 18 rue Andre Chenier, tel. 01 39 50 03 03,
fax 01 39 50 61 27).

Ibis Versailles** offers fair value and modern comfort, but no
air-conditioning (Db-€71, cheaper weekend rates can't be reserved
ahead, CC, across from RER station, 4 avenue du General de
Gaulle, tel. 01 39 53 03 30, fax 01 39 50 06 31).

Hôtel du Palais, facing the RER station, has clean, sharp
rooms—the cheapest I list in this area. Ask for a quiet room off the
street (Ds-€43, Db-€49, extra person-€11, CC, piles of stairs, 6
place Lyautey, tel. 01 39 50 39 29, fax 01 39 50 80 41).

Hôtel d'Angleterre**, away from the frenzy, is a tranquil old
place with comfortable and spacious rooms. Park nearby in the palace
lot (Db-€56–72, extra bed-€15, CC, just below palace to the right as
you exit, 2 rue de Fontenay, tel. 01 39 51 43 50, fax 01 39 51 45 63).

Eating in Paris

Paris is France's wine and cuisine melting pot. While it lacks a
style of its own (only French onion soup is truly Parisian), it draws
from the best of France. Paris could hold a gourmet's Olympics
and import nothing.

Picnic or go to bakeries for quick take-out lunches, or stop at a café for a lunch salad or *plat du jour*, but linger longer over dinner. Cafés are happy to serve a *plat du jour* (garnished plate of the day, about €11) or a chef-like salad (about €9) day or night, while restaurants expect you to enjoy a full dinner. Restaurants open for dinner around 19:00, and small local favorites get crowded after 21:00. Most of the restaurants listed below accept credit cards.

To save piles of euros, review the budget eating tips in this book's introduction and consider dinner picnics (great take-out dishes available at charcuteries). My recommendations are centered around the same three great neighborhoods I list accommodations for (above); you can come home exhausted after a busy day of sightseeing and have a good selection of restaurants right around the corner. And evening is a fine time to explore any of these delightful neighborhoods, even if you're sleeping elsewhere.

Restaurants

If you are traveling outside of Paris, save your splurges for the countryside, where you'll enjoy regional cooking for less money. Many Parisian department stores have huge supermarkets hiding in the basement and top-floor cafeterias offering affordable, low-risk, low-stress, what-you-see-is-what-you-get meals. The three neighborhoods highlighted in this book for sleeping in Paris are also pleasant areas to window-shop for just the right restaurant, as is the Ile St. Louis. Most restaurants we've listed in these areas have set-price *menus* between €15 and €30. In most cases, the few extra euros you pay for not choosing the least expensive option is money well spent as it opens up a variety of better choices. You decide.

Good Picnic Spots: For great people-watching, try the Pompidou Center (by the *Homage to Stravinsky* fountains), the elegant place des Vosges (closes at dusk), the gardens at the Rodin Museum, and Luxembourg Garden. The Palais Royal (across the street from the Louvre) is a good spot for a peaceful, royal picnic.

For a romantic picnic place, try the pedestrian bridge (pont des Arts) across from the Louvre, with its unmatched views and plentiful benches; the Champ de Mars park under the Eiffel Tower; and the western tip of Ile St. Louis, overlooking Ile de la Cité. Bring your own dinner feast and watch the riverboats or the Eiffel Tower light up the city for you.

Eating in the Rue Cler Neighborhood

The rue Cler neighborhood caters to its residents. Its eateries, while not destination places, have an intimate charm. My favorites are small mom-and-pop places with a love of serving good French food at good prices to a local clientele. You'll generally find great dinner *menus* for €15–23 and *plats du jour* for around €12. My first two recommendations are easygoing cafés, ideal if what you want is a light dinner (good dinner salads) or a more substantial but simple meal. Eat early with tourists or late with locals.

Café du Marché, with the best seats, coffee, and prices on rue Cler, serves hearty €7 salads and good €9 *plats du jour* for lunch or dinner to a trendy, smoky, mainly French crowd (Mon–Sat 11:00–23:00, closed Sun, at the corner of rue Cler and rue du Champ de Mars, tel. 01 47 05 51 27, well-run by Frank, Jack, and Bruno). Arrive before 19:30. It's packed at 21:00. A chalkboard lists the plates of the day—each a meal. You'll find the same dishes and prices with better (but smoky) indoor seating at their other restaurant, **Le Comptoir du Septième**, two blocks away at the Ecole Militaire Métro stop (39 avenue de la Motte Piquet, tel. 01 45 55 90 20).

Café le Bosquet is a vintage Parisian brasserie with dressy waiters and classic indoor or sidewalk tables on a busy street. Come here for a bowl of French onion soup, a salad, or a three-course set *menu* for €16 (closed Sun, many choices from a fun menu, the house red wine is plenty good, corner of rue du Champs de Mars and avenue Bosquet, tel. 01 45 51 38 13).

Leo le Lion, a warm, charming souvenir of old Paris, is popular with locals. Expect to spend €23 per person for fine à la carte choices (closed Sun, 23 rue Duvivier, tel. 01 45 51 41 77).

L'Ami de Jean celebrates the rustic joys of Basque living—and that includes good peasant-pleasing food. Beginners should trust the €15 *menu Basque*. And for a full red wine, try the Spanish Rioja. Stepping into the jumbled little room is like leaving Paris. Wear your beret (closed Sun, 27 rue Malar, tel. 01 47 05 86 89).

At **L'Affriole,** you'll compete with young professionals for a table. This small and trendy place is well-deserving of its rave reviews. Item selections change daily and the wine list is extensive, with some good bargains (€32 *menu*, closed Sun, 17 rue Malar, tel. 01 44 18 31 33).

Au Petit Tonneau is a purely Parisian experience. Fun-loving owner-chef Madame Boyer prepares everything herself, wearing her tall chef's hat like a crown as she rules from her family-style kitchen. The small dining room is plain and a bit smoky (allow €30/person with wine, open daily, 20 rue Surcouf, tel. 01 47 05 09 01).

Thoumieux, the neighborhood's classy, traditional Parisian brasserie, is a local institution and deservedly popular. It's big and dressy with formal but good-natured waiters (daily, €14 lunch *menu*, 3-course with wine dinner *menu* for €31, really good *crème brûlée*, 79 rue St. Dominique, tel. 01 47 05 49 75).

Le P'tit Troquet is a petite place, taking you back to Paris

Rue Cler Restaurants

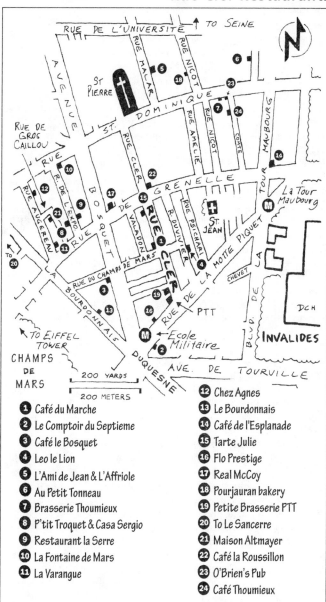

1 Café du Marche
2 Le Comptoir du Septieme
3 Café le Bosquet
4 Leo le Lion
5 L'Ami de Jean & L'Affriole
6 Au Petit Tonneau
7 Brasserie Thoumieux
8 P'tit Troquet & Casa Sergio
9 Restaurant la Serre
10 La Fontaine de Mars
11 La Varangue
12 Chez Agnes
13 Le Bourdonnais
14 Café de l'Esplanade
15 Tarte Julie
16 Flo Prestige
17 Real McCoy
18 Pourjauran bakery
19 Petite Brasserie PTT
20 To Le Sancerre
21 Maison Altmayer
22 Café la Roussillon
23 O'Brien's Pub
24 Café Thoumieux

in the 1920s, gracefully and earnestly run by Dominique. The delicious three-course €27 *menu* comes with fun traditional choices (closed Sun, 28 rue de l'Exposition, tel. 01 47 05 80 39). **Restaurant la Serre**, across the street at #29, is also worth considering (*plats du jour* €11–15, daily, good onion soup and duck specialties, tel. 01 45 55 20 96, Margot).

La Casa di Sergio is *the* place for gourmet Italian cuisine served family-style. Only Sergio could make me enthusiastic about Italian food in Paris. Sergio, a people-loving Sicilian, says he's waited his entire life to open a restaurant like this. Eating here involves a little trust . . . just sit down and let Sergio spoil you (€26–34 *menus*, closed Wed, 20 rue de l'Exposition, tel. 01 45 51 37 71).

La Fontaine de Mars is a longtime favorite for locals, charmingly situated on a classic, tiny Parisian street and jumbled square. It's a happening scene with tables jammed together for the serious business of good eating. Reserve in advance or risk eating upstairs without the fun street-level ambience (allow €40/ person with wine, nightly, where rue de l'Exposition and rue St. Dominique meet, tel. 01 47 05 46 44).

La Varangue is an entertaining one-man show featuring English-speaking Phillipe, who ran a French catering shop in Pennsylvania for three years, then returned to Paris to open his own place. He lives upstairs, and clearly has found his niche serving a Franco-American clientele who are all on a first-name basis. The food is cheap and good (try his snails and chocolate cake, but not together), the tables are few, and he opens at 18:00. Norman Rockwell would dig his tiny dining room (€9–10 *plats* and a €13.50 *menu*, always a veggie option, 27 rue Augereau, tel. 01 47 05 51 22).

Chez Agnes is the smallest restaurant listed in this book. Eccentric and flowery, it's truly a family-style place, where engaging Agnes (with dog Gypsy at her side) does it all—working wonders in her minuscule kitchen, and serving, too, without a word of English. Don't come for a quick dinner; she expects to get to know you (€23 *menu*, closed Mon, 1 rue Augereau, tel. 01 45 51 06 04).

Le Bourdonnais, boasting one Michelin star, is the neighborhood's intimate gourmet splurge. You'll find friendly but formal service in a plush and very subdued 10-table room. Micheline Coat, your hostess, will take good care of you (€42 lunch *menu*, €64 dinner *menu*, 113 avenue de la Bourdonnais, tel. 01 47 05 47 96).

Café de l'Esplanade, the latest buzz, is your opportunity to be surrounded by chic, yet older and sophisticated, Parisians enjoying top-notch traditional cuisine as foreplay. There's not a tourist in sight. It's a long, sprawling place—half its tables with well-stuffed chairs fill a plush, living room–like interior, and the other half are lined up outside under its elegant awning facing the street, valet boys, and park. Dress competitively, as this is *the* place to be seen in the 7th *arrondissement* (€20 *plats du jour*, plan on €40 plus wine for dinner, open daily, reserve—especially if you want curb-side table, smoke-free room in the back, bordering Les Invalides at 52 rue Fabert, tel. 01 47 05 38 80).

Picnicking: The rue Cler is a moveable feast that gives "fast food" a good name. The entire street is clogged with connoisseurs of good eating. Only the health-food store goes unnoticed. A festival of food, the street is lined with people whose lives seem to be devoted to their specialty: polished produce, rotisserie chicken, crêpes, or cheese.

For a magical picnic dinner at the Eiffel Tower, assemble it in no fewer than five shops on rue Cler and lounge on the best grass in Paris (the police don't mind after dusk), with the dogs, Frisbees, a floodlit tower, and a cool breeze in the Parc du Champ de Mars.

The **crêpe stand** next to Café du Marché does a wonderful top-end dinner crêpe for €4. **Asian delis** (generically called *Traiteur Asie*) provide tasty, low-stress, low-price, take-out treats (€6 dinner plates, 2 delis have tables on the rue Cler—one across from Hôtel Leveque, and the other near the rue du Champ de Mars). For a variety of savory quiches or a tasty pear-and-chocolate tart, try **Tarte Julie** (take-out or stools, 28 rue Cler). The elegant **Flo Prestige** charcu-terie is open until 23:00 and offers mouthwatering meals to go (at the Ecole Militaire Métro stop). **Real McCoy** is a little shop selling American food and sandwiches (194 rue de Grenelle). A good, small, **late-night grocery** is at 197 rue de Grenelle.

The **bakery** *(boulangerie)* on the corner of rue Cler and rue de Grenelle is the place for sandwiches, *pain au chocolat*, or almond croissants. And the **Pourjauran** bakery, offering great baguettes, hasn't changed in 70 years (20 rue Jean Nicot). The **bakery** at 112 rue St. Dominique is worth the detour, with classic decor and tables where you to enjoy your café au lait and croissant.

Cafés and Bars: If you want to linger over coffee or a drink at a sidewalk café, try **Café du Marché** (see above), **Petite Brasserie PTT** (local workers eat here, opposite 53 rue Cler), or **Café le Bos-quet** (46 avenue Bosquet, tel. 01 45 51 38 13). **Le Sancerre** wine bar/café is wood-beam warm and ideal for a light lunch or dinner, or just a glass of wine after a long day of sightseeing. The owner's cheeks are the same color as his wine (open until 21:30, great ome-lettes, 22 avenue Rapp, tel. 01 45 51 75 91). **Maison Altmayer** is a hole-in-the-wall place good for a quiet drink (9:00–19:30, next to Hôtel Eiffel Rive Gauche, 6 rue du Gros Caillou). Cafés like this originated (and this one still functions) as a place where locals en-joyed a drink while their heating wood, coal, or gas was prepared for delivery.

Nightlife: This sleepy neighborhood is not the place for night owls, but there are a few notable exceptions. **Café du Marché** and its brother, **Le Comptoir du Septième** (both listed above), hop with a Franco-American crowd until about midnight, as does the flashier **Café la Roussillon** (at corner of rue de Grenelle and rue Cler). **O'Brien's Pub** is a relaxed, Parisian rendition of an Irish pub (77 avenue St. Dominique). **Café Thoumieux** (younger brother of the brasserie listed above) has big-screen sports and a trendy young crowd (4 rue de la Comète, Mo: La Tour Maubourg).

Eating in the Marais Neighborhood

The trendy Marais is filled with locals enjoying good food in colorful and atmospheric eateries. The scene is competitive and changes all the time. Here is an assortment of places—all handy to recommended hotels that offer good food at reasonable prices, plus a memorable experience.

Eating at place du Marché Ste. Catherine: This tiny square just off rue St. Antoine is an international food festival cloaked in extremely Parisian, leafy square ambience. On a balmy evening, this is clearly a neighborhood favorite, with five popular restaurants offering €20–25 meals. Survey the square and find two French-style bistros (**Le Marché** and **Au Bistrot de la Place**), a fun Italian place, a popular Japanese/Korean restaurant, and a Russian eatery with an easy but adventurous menu. You'll eat under the trees surrounded by a futuristic-in-1800 planned residential quarter. Just around the corner with none of the ambience is **L'Auberge de Jarente**, a reliable rainy-day budget option, where a hardworking father and son team serve good Basque food (€18 3-course *menu* with wine, closed Sun–Mon, just off the square at 7 rue de Jarente, tel. 01 42 77 49 35).

Eating at place des Vosges: This elegant square, built by King Henry IV in 1605, put the Marais on the aristocratic map. And today, the posh ambience survives, with several good places offering romantic meals under its venerable arches, overlooking one of Paris' most elegant little parks. And prices are reasonable. The mod and pastel **Nectarine** at #16 is a teahouse serving healthy salads, quiches, and inexpensive *plats du jour* both day and night. Its fun menu lets you mix and match omelettes and crêpes (tel. 01 42 77 23 78). **Café Hugo**, next door (named for the square's most famous resident), is a typical bistro serving good traditional favorites such as onion soup (€5) and crêpes (€4). **Ma Bourgogne** has the snob appeal—bigger, darker, and more traditional. You'll sit under arcades in a whirlpool of Frenchness as bow-tied and black-aproned waiters serve traditional Burgundian specialties: steak, coq au vin, lots of French fries, escargot, and great red wine.

Marais Restaurants

1. Le Marche & de la Place
2. Auberge de Jarente
3. Nectarine
4. Ma Bourgogne
5. L'Impasse (Chez Robert)
6. Chez Janou
7. Bofinger
8. L'Excuse
9. L'Enoteca
10. Picolo Teatro
11. L'As du Falafel
12. Au Bourguignon du Marais
13. Les Sans Culottes
14. Studio
15. Camille
16. Au Petit Fer a Cheval
17. Café de la Poste
18. Petite Gavroche
19. Au Temps des Cerises
20. Flo Prestige
21. Le Vieux Comptoir
22. La Perla
23. The Quiet Man

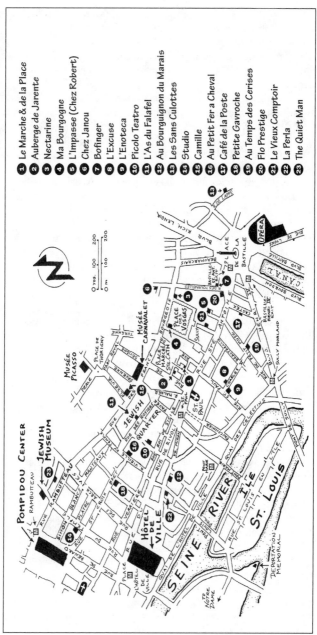

Service at this institution comes with food but no smiles (allow €38/person with wine, open daily, dinner reservations smart, no CC, at northwest corner, tel. 01 42 78 44 64).

Eating elsewhere in the Marais: The streets beyond the Ste. Catherine and des Vosges squares offer plenty more appealing choices.

L'Impasse, a cozy neighborhood bistro on a quiet alley, serves an enthusiastically French €24 three-course *menu* (very good escargot). Françoise, a former dancer and artist, runs the place *con brio* and, judging by the clientele, she's a fixture in the neighborhood. It's a spacious place with great ambience indoors and out (closed Sun, 4 impasse Guéménée, tel. 01 42 72 08 45). Françoise promises anyone with this book a free glass of *byrrh*—a French port-like drink (pron: beer). It's next to a self-serve launderette (open nightly until 21:30—clean your clothes while you dine).

Chez Janou, a Provençal bistro, tumbles out of its corner building, filling its broad sidewalk with keen eaters. At first glance, you know this is a find. It's relaxed and charming, yet youthful and busting with energy. The style is French Mediterranean with an emphasis on vegetables (€13 *plats du jour* and a €26 3-course *menu* that changes by season, a block beyond place des Vosges at 2 rue Roger-Verlomme, tel. 01 42 72 28 41).

Brasserie Bofinger is an institution in this corner of Paris. For over 100 years, it's been famous for fish and traditional cuisine with an Alsatian flair. You'll be surrounded by brisk black-and-white attired waiters in plush rooms that are reminiscent of the Roaring Twenties. The non-smoking room is best—under the grand 1919 *coupole*. Watch the boys shucking and stacking seafood platters out front before going in. Their €31 three-course with wine *menu* is a good value (daily and nightly, reservations smart, 5 rue de la Bastille, don't be confused by the lesser "Petite" Bofinger across the street, tel. 01 42 72 87 82).

L'Excuse is one of the neighborhood's top restaurants. It's a good splurge for a romantic and dressy evening in a hushed atmosphere, with lounge lizard music, elegant Mediterranean nouveau cuisine, and ambience to match. The plates are petite, but creative and presented with panache (€36 *menu*, closed Sun, reserve ahead, request downstairs—ideally by the window, 14 rue Charles V, tel. 01 42 77 98 97).

L'Enoteca is a high-energy, half-timbered Italian wine bar restaurant serving reasonable Italian cuisine (no pizza) with a tempting antipasti bar. It's a relaxed, open setting with busy, blue-aproned waiters serving two floors of local eaters (€25 meals with wine, daily, across from L'Excuse at rue St. Paul and rue Charles V, tel. 01 42 78 91 44).

Vegetarians will appreciate the excellent cuisine at the popular **Picolo Teatro** (closed Mon, near rue des Rosiers, 6 rue des Ecouffes, tel. 01 42 72 17 79) or **L'As du Falafel**, which serves the best falafel on rue des Rosiers (at #34).

Au Bourguignon du Marais, a small wine bar on the other side of rue de Rivoli, is a place that wine-lovers shouldn't miss. The excellent Burgundy wines blend well with a fine, though limited, selection of *plats du jour* (closed Sat–Sun, call by 19:00 to reserve, 52 rue Francois Miron, tel. 01 48 87 15 40).

Lively rue de Lappe is what the Latin Quarter wants to be. This street, just beyond the more stately place de la Bastille, is currently one of the wildest nightspots in Paris. You'll walk past a dizzying array of wacky eateries, bars, and dance halls. Then, sitting there like a van Gogh painting, is the popular, zinc-bar classic **Bistrot les Sans Culottes**—a time-warp bistro serving traditional French cuisine with a proper respect for fine wine (€20 3-course *menu*, 27 rue de Lappe, tel. 01 48 05 42 92). Plan on staying out past your normal bedtime. Eat here. Then join the rue de Lappe party.

Le Studio is wonderfully located close to the Pompidou Center on a 17th-century courtyard below a dance school. It's best when you can sit outside, but the salads, €12 *plats du jour*, and Tex-Mex meals are good day or night (daily, 41 rue de Temple, tel. 01 42 74 10 38).

Eating at the east end of the Marais: **Camille,** a traditional corner brasserie, is a neighborhood favorite with great indoor and sidewalk seating. White-aproned waiters serve €9 salads and very French *plats du jour* for €15 to a down-to-earth but sophisticated clientele (daily, 24 rue des Francs-Bourgeois at corner of rue Elzévir, tel. 01 42 72 29 50). **Au Petit Fer à Cheval,** named for its horseshoe-shaped bar, is an authentic gem with mirrored walls and tiled floors. The tight woody interior takes you back to the 1930s—and you'll sit on old wooden Métro seats. The sidewalk tables put you in the front row at the neighborhood's trendy and gay promenade (€10 salads, €15 *plats du jour*, explore the fun chalkboard menu, reasonable wines by the glass, daily until 24:00, 30 rue Vieille du Temple, tel. 01 42 72 47 47).

Cheap eating in the Marais: **Chinese fast food** is cheap and easy at several places along rue St. Antoine. These hardworking little places are great for a €5 meal or a quick late-night snack. **Café de la Poste** is a very tight little place serving very good €11 *plats du jour* from a small but reliable menu (closed Sun, near place de la Bastille at 13 rue Castex, tel. 01 42 72 95 35). For dirt-cheap French cooking, try €8 *plats du jour* at the charmingly basic **Petite Gavroche** (15 rue Sainte Croix de la Bretonnerie, tel. 01 48 87 74 26). **Au Temps des Cerises,** a *très* local wine bar, is relaxed and amiably run by the incredibly mustachioed Monsieur Vimard. This place is great for a colorful lunch or a very light dinner of cheese or cold meats with good wine (Mon–Fri until 20:00, closed Sat–Sun, at rue du Petit Musc and rue de la Cerisaie).

Picnicking: Picnic at the peaceful place des Vosges (closes at dusk) or on the Ile St. Louis quai (described below). Hobos stretch their euros at the supermarket in the basement of the **Monoprix** department store (near place des Vosges on rue St. Antoine). A couple of small grocery shops are open until 23:00 on rue St. Antoine (near intersection with rue Castex). For a cheap breakfast, try the tiny *boulangerie/pâtisserie* where the hotels buy their croissants (coffee machine-€0.70, baby quiche-€1.50, *pain au chocolat*-€1, 1 block off place de la Bastille, corner of rue St. Antoine and rue de Lesdiguières). Pick up something good to go at the elegant **Flo Prestige** charcuterie (open until 23:00, 10 rue Saint Antoine, tel. 01 53 01 91 91).

Nightlife: The best scene is the bars and dance halls of rue de Lappe (beyond the place de la Bastille, see above). Trendy cafés and bars also cluster on rue Vielle du Temple, rue des Archives, and rue Ste. Croix de la Bretonnerie (open generally until 2:00 in the morning), and are popular with gay men. **Le Vieux Comptoir** is tiny, lively, and just hip enough (just off place des Vosges at 8 rue de Biraque). **La Perla** is trendy and full of Parisian yuppies in search of the perfect margarita (26 rue François Miron). **The Quiet Man** is a traditional Irish pub with happy hour from 16:00 to 20:00 (5 rue des Haudriettes).

Eating on Ile St. Louis

The Ile St. Louis is a romantic and peaceful place to window-shop for plenty of promising dinner possibilities. Cruise the island's main street for a variety of options, from cozy *crêperies* to Italian (intimate pizzeria and upscale) to typical brasseries (several with fine outdoor seating face the bridge to Ile de la Cité). After dinner, sample Paris' best sorbet. Then stroll across to the Ile de la Cité to see an illuminated Notre-Dame. All listings below line the island's main drag, the rue St. Louis en l'Ile. Consider skipping dessert at a restaurant to enjoy a stroll licking the best ice cream in Paris. Read on.

These two little family-run places serve top-notch traditional French cuisine with white-tablecloth, candlelit elegance in small, 10-table rooms under heavy wooden beams. Their *menus* start with three courses at €26 and offer plenty of classic choices that change with the season for freshness. **Le Tastevin** at #46, run by Madame Puisieux, is a little more intimate (daily, tel. 01 43 54 17 31). **Auberge de la Reine Blanche** is a bit more touristy—but in the best sense, with friendly Françoise and her crew working hard to please in a characteristic little place with dollhouse furniture on the walls and a two-dove welcoming committee at the door (at #30 daily, tel. 01 46 33 07 87). Reservations are smart for each.

Café Med, closest to Notre-Dame at #77, is best for inexpensive salads, crêpes, and lighter *menus* in a tight but cheery setting (daily, 30 rue de St. Louis en l'Ile, tel. 01 43 29 73 17, charming Eva SE). Very limited wine list.

Two side-by-side places are famous for their rowdy medieval cellar atmosphere, serving all-you-can-eat buffets with straw baskets of raw veggies (cut whatever you like with your dagger), massive plates of pâté, a meat course, and all the wine you can stomach for €34. The food is just food; burping is encouraged. If you want to eat a lot, drink a lot of wine, and holler at your friends while receiving smart-aleck buccaneer service, these food fests can be fun. **Nos Ancêtres les Gaulois** ("Our Ancestors the Gauls," daily from 19:00, tel. 01 46 33 66 07) has bigger tables and seems made-to-order for local stag parties. If you'd rather be surrounded by drunk tourists than locals, pick **La Taverne du Sergeant Recruteur**. The "Sergeant Recruteur" used to get young Parisians drunk and stuffed here, then sign them into the army (daily from 19:00, #41, tel. 01 43 54 75 42).

Riverside picnic: On sunny lunchtimes and balmy evenings, the quai on the Left Bank side of Ile St. Louis is lined with locals—who have more class than money—spreading out tablecloths and even lighting candles for elegant picnics. The grocery store on the main drag at #67 is open daily until midnight if you'd like to join them. Otherwise, it's a great stroll.

Ice cream dessert: Half the people strolling Ile St. Louis are licking an ice cream cone because this is the home of "*les glaces Berthillon.*" The original Berthillon shop, at 31 rue St. Louis en l'Ile, is marked by the line of salivating customers. It's so popular that the wealthy people who can afford to live on this fancy island complain about the congestion it causes. For a less famous but at least as tasty treat, try the homemade Italian gelato a block away at **Amorino Gelati**. It's giving Berthillon competition (no line, bigger portions, easier to see what you want, and they offer little tastes—whereas Berthillon doesn't need to, 47 rue Saint Louis en l'Ile). Having some of each is a fine option.

Eating in the Contrescarpe Neighborhood
There are a few diamonds for fine dining in this otherwise rough area. Most come here for the lively and cheap eateries that line rues Mouffetard and du Pot-de-Fer. Study the many menus, compare crowds, then dive in and have fun (see map on page 113).

Near the Panthéon, **Les Vignes du Panthéon** is a homey,

traditional place with a zinc bar and original flooring. It serves a mostly local clientele and makes you feel you're truly in Paris (allow €23 for à la carte, closed Sat–Sun, 4 rue des Fossés St. Jacques, tel. 01 43 54 80 81). **Le Bistro des Cigales,** between the Panthéon and place de la Contrescarpe, offers an escape to Provence, with deep yellow and blue decor, a purely Provençal menu, helpful staff, and air-conditioned rooms (€17–22 *menus,* daily, 12 rue Thouin, tel. 01 40 46 03 76). **Gaudeamus**, with a low-profile café on one side and a pleasant bistro on the other, has friendly owners and cheap, €15 *menus* (daily, behind the Panthéon, 47 rue de la Montagne Ste. Geneviève, tel. 01 40 46 93 40). **L'Ecurie**, almost next door, is for those who prefer ambience and setting over top cuisine, with inexpensive and acceptable meals served on small, wood tables around a zinc bar in an unpretentious setting with a few outdoor tables (daily, *menus* from €15, 58 rue de la Montagne Ste. Genevieve, tel. 01 46 33 68 49).

Right on place de la Contrescarpe, sprawling **Café Delmas** is the place to see and be seen with a broad outdoor terrace, tasty salads, and good *plats du jour* from €12 (open daily). **Le Jardin d'Artemis** is one of the better values on rue Mouffetard, at #34 (€15–23 *menus,* closed Tue). **Le Jardin des Pates** is popular with less strict vegetarians, serving pastas and salads at fair prices (daily, near Jardin des Plantes, 4 rue Lacépède, tel. 01 43 31 50 71).

Cafés: The cafés on place de la Contrescarpe are popular until late (see Café Delmas, above). Both indoors and outdoors provide good people-watching. **Café le Mouffetard** is in the thick of the street-market hustle and bustle (at corner of rue Mouffetard and rue de l'Arbalète). The outdoor tables at **Cave de la Bourgogne** are picture-perfect (at the bottom of rue Mouffetard on rue de Bazeilles). At **Café de la Mosque,** you'll feel like you've been beamed to Morocco. In this purely Arab café, order a mint tea, pour in the sugar, and enjoy the authentic interior and peaceful outdoor terrace (behind mosque, 2 rue Daubenton).

Eating on Montmartre

The Montmartre is extremely touristy, with all the mindless mobs following guides to cancan shows. But the ambience is undeniable and an evening up here overlooking Paris is a quintessential experience in the City of Lights. To avoid the crowds and enjoy a classic neighborhood corner, hike from the Sacré-Coeur church away from the tourist zone down the stairs to **L'Eté en Pente Douce,** with fine indoor and outdoor seating, €9 *plats du jour* and salads, veggie options, and good wines (23 rue Muller, tel. 01 42 64 02 67). Just off the jam-packed place du Tertre, **Restaurant Chez Plumeau** is a touristy yet cheery, reasonably priced place with great seating on a tiny characteristic square (€18 *menu*, place du Calvaire, tel. 01 46 06 26 29). Along the touristy main drag and just off, several fun piano bars serve reasonable crêpes with great people-watching.

Eating in Versailles

In the pleasant town center, around place du Marché Notre-Dame, you'll find a variety of reasonable restaurants, cafés, and a few cobbled lanes (market days Sun, Tue, and Fri until 13:00; see map on page 85). The square is a 15-minute walk from the château (veer left when you leave château). From the place du Marché consider shortcutting to Versailles' gardens by walking 10 minutes west down rue de la Paroisse. The château will be to your left after entering; the main gardens, Trianon palaces, and Hameau straight ahead. The quickest way to the château's front door is along avenue de St. Cloud and rue Colbert.

These places are on or near place du Marché Notre-Dame, and all are good for lunch or dinner. **La Boeuf à la Mode** is a bistro with traditional cuisine right on the square (€23 *menu*, open daily, 4 rue au Pain, tel. 01 39 50 31 99). **Fenêtres sur Cour** is the romantic's choice, where you dine in a glass gazebo surrounded by antique shops, just below the square in "the antique village," on place de la Geôle (closed all day Mon and Tue–Wed eves, tel. 01 39 51 97 77). **A la Côte Bretonne** is the place to go for crêpes in a cozy setting (daily, a few steps off the square on traffic-free rue des Deux Ponts, at #12).

Rue Satory is another pedestrian-friendly street lined with restaurants on the south side of the château near the Hôtel d'Angleterre (10-min walk, angle right out of the château). **Le Limousin** is a warm, traditional restaurant sitting at the corner nearest the château with mostly meat dishes (lamb is a specialty, allow €30 with wine, 4 rue de Satory, tel. 01 39 50 21 50).

Transportation Connections—Paris

Paris is Europe's rail hub, with six major train stations, each serving different regions: Gare de l'Est (eastbound trains), Gare du Nord (northern France and Europe), Gare St. Lazare (northwestern France), Gare d'Austerlitz (southwest France and Europe), Gare de Lyon (southeastern France and Italy), and Gare Montparnasse (northwestern France and TGV service to France's southwest). Any train station can give you schedules, make reservations, and sell tickets for any destination. Buying tickets is handier from an SNCF neighborhood office (e.g., Louvre, Invalides, Orsay, Versailles, airports) or at your neighborhood travel agency—worth their small fee (SNCF signs in window indicate they sell train tickets). For schedules, call 08 36 35 35 35 (€0.50/min, English sometimes available).

All six train stations have Métro, bus, and taxi service. All have banks or change offices, ATMs, information desks, telephones, cafés, baggage storage *(consigne automatique)*, newsstands, and clever pick-pockets. Each station offers two types of rail service: long distance to other cities, called *Grandes Lignes* (major lines); and suburban service to outlying areas, called *banlieue* or RER. Both *banlieue* and RER trains serve outlying areas and the airports; the only difference is that *banlieue* lines are operated by SNCF (France's train system) and RER lines are operated by RATP (Paris' Métro and bus system). Paris train stations can be intimidating, but if you slow down, take a deep breath, and ask for help, you'll find them manageable and efficient. Bring a pad of paper for clear communication at ticket/info windows. All stations have helpful *accueil* (information) booths; the bigger stations have roving helpers, usually in red vests.

Station Overview

Here's an overview of Paris' major train stations. Métro, RER, buses, and taxis are well-signposted at every station. When arriving by Métro, follow signs for *Grandes Lignes*-SNCF to find the main tracks.

Gare du Nord: This vast station serves cities in northern France and international destinations to the north of Paris, including Copenhagen, Amsterdam (via pricey Thalys Train) and the Euro-star to London (see "The Eurostar Train to London," below) as well as two of the day trips described in this book (Auvers-sur-Oise and Chantilly). Arrive early to allow time to navigate this huge station. From the Métro, follow *Grandes Lignes* signs (main lines) and keep going up and up until you reach the tracks at street level. *Grandes Lignes* depart from tracks 3–21, suburban *(banlieue)* lines from tracks 30–36, and RER trains depart from tracks 37–44 (tracks 41–44 are 1 floor below). Glass train information booths *(accueil)* are scattered throughout the station and information staff circulate to help (all rail staff are required to speak English). Information booths for the **Thalys Train** (high-speed trains to Brussels and Amsterdam) are opposite track 8. All non-Eurostar ticket sales are opposite tracks 3–8. Passengers departing on the **Eurostar** (London via Chunnel) must buy tickets and check in on the second level, opposite track 6. (Note: Britain's time zone is 1 hour earlier than the Continent's; times listed on Eurostar tickets are local times.) A peaceful café/bar hides on the upper level past the Eurostar ticket windows. Storage lockers, baggage check, taxis, and rental cars are at the far end, just opposite track 3 and down the steps.

Key destinations served by Gare du Nord *Grandes Lignes:* **Brussels** (21/day, 1.5 hrs, via pricey Thalys Train), **Bruges** (18/day, 2 hrs, change in Brussels, 1 direct), **Amsterdam** (10/day,

4 hrs; see "Thalys Train" under "Gare du Nord," above), **Copen-hagen** (1/day, 16 hrs, 2 night trains), **Koblenz** (6/day, 5 hrs, change in Köln), **London** Eurostar via Chunnel (17/day, 3 hrs, tel. 08 36 35 35 39; see "The Eurostar Train to London," below). By *Banlieue/RER* lines to: **Chantilly-Gouvieux** (hrly, fewer on weekends, 35 min), **Charles de Gaulle** airport (2/hr, 30 min, runs 5:30–23:00, track 4), **Auvers-sur-Oise** (2/hr, 1hr, transfer at Pontoise).

Gare Montparnasse: This big and modern station covers three floors, serves Lower Normandy and Brittany, and offers TGV service to the Loire Valley and southwestern France and suburban service to Chartres. At street level, you'll find a bank, *banlieue* trains (serving Chartres; you can also reach the *banlieue* trains from the second level), and ticket windows in the center, just past the escalators. Lockers *(consigne automatique)* are on the mezzanine level between levels 1 and 2. Most services are provided on the second level, where the *Grandes Lignes* arrive and depart (ticket windows to the far left with your back to glass exterior). *Banlieue* trains depart from tracks 10 through 19. The main rail information office is opposite track 15. Taxis are to the far left as you leave the tracks.

    Key destinations served by Gare Montparnasse: Chartres (20/day, 1 hr, *banlieue* lines), **Pontorson-Mont St. Michel** (5/day, 4.5 hrs, via Rennes, then take bus; or take train to Pontorson via Caen, then bus from Pontorson), **Dinan** (7/day, 4 hrs, change in Rennes and Dol), **Bordeaux** (14/day, 3.5 hrs), **Sarlat** (5/day, 6 hrs, change in Bordeaux, Libourne, or Souillac), **Toulouse** (11/day, 5 hrs, most require change, usually in Bordeaux), **Albi** (7/day, 6–7.5 hrs, change in Toulouse, also night train), **Carcassonne** (8/day, 6.5 hrs, most require changes in Toulouse and Bordeaux, direct trains take 10 hrs), **Tours** (14/day, 1 hr).

Gare de Lyon: This huge station offers TGV and regular service to southeastern France, Italy, and other international destinations (for trains to Italy, see also "Gare de Bercy," below). Frequent *banlieue* trains serve Melun (near Vaux-le-Vicomte) and Fontaine-bleau (some depart from main *Grandes Lignes* level, more frequent departures one level down, follow RER-D signs, and ask at any *accueil* or ticket window where next departure leaves from).

    Grande Ligne trains arrive and depart from one level but are divided into two areas (tracks A–N and 5–23). They are connected by the long platform along tracks A and 5, and by the hallway adjacent to track A and opposite track 9. This hallway has all the services, ticket windows, ticket information, banks, shops, and access to car rental. *banlieue* ticket windows are just inside the hall adjacent to track A *(billets Ile de France)*. *Grandes Lignes* and *banlieue* lines share the same tracks. A Paris TI (Mon–Sat 8:00–20:00, closed Sun) and a train information office are opposite track L. From the RER or Métro, follow signs for *Grandes Lignes Arrivées* and take the escalator up to reach the platforms. Train information booths *(accueil)* are opposite tracks G and 11. Taxis stands are well-marked in front of the station and one floor below.

Key destinations served by Gare de Lyon: Vaux-le-Vicomte (train to Melun, hrly, 30 min), **Fontainebleau** (nearly hrly, 45 min), **Beaune** (12/day, 2.5 hrs, most require change in Dijon), **Dijon** (15/day, 1.5 hrs), **Chamonix** (9/day, 9 hrs, change in Lyon and St. Gervais, direct night train), **Annecy** (8/day, 4–7 hrs), Lyon (16/day, 2.5 hrs), **Avignon** (9/day in 2.5 hrs, 6/day in 4 hrs with change), **Arles** (14/day, 5 hrs, most with change in Marseille, Avignon, or Nîmes), **Nice** (14/day, 5.5–7 hrs, many with change in Marseille), **Venice** (3/day, 3/night, 11–15 hrs, most require changes), **Rome** (2/day, 5/night, 15–18 hrs, most require changes), **Bern** (9/day, 5–11 hrs, most require changes, night train).

Gare de Bercy: This smaller station handles some rail service to Italy during renovation work at the Gare de Lyon, Mo: Bercy, 1 stop east of Gare de Lyon on line 14).

Gare de l'Est: This single-floor station (with underground Métro) serves eastern France and European points to the east of Paris. Train information booths are at tracks 1 and 26; ticket windows and the main exit to buses and Paris are opposite track 8; luggage storage is opposite track 12.

Key destinations served by the **Gare de l'Est: Colmar** (12/day, 5.5 hrs, change in Strasbourg, Dijon, or Mulhouse), **Strasbourg** (14/day, 4.5 hrs, many require changes), **Reims** (12/day, 1.5 hrs), **Verdun** (5/day, 3 hrs, change in Metz or Chalon), **Munich** (5/day, 9 hrs, some require changes, night train), **Vienna** (7/day, 13–18 hrs, most require changes, night train), **Zurich** (10/day, 7 hrs, most require changes, night train), **Prague** (2/day, 14 hrs, night train).

Gare St. Lazare: This relatively small station serves Upper Normandy, including Rouen and Giverny. All trains arrive and depart one floor above street level. Follow signs to *Grandes Lignes* from the Métro to reach the tracks. You'll pass a mini-mall. Ticket windows and a Thomas Cook exchange are in the first hall on the second floor. The tracks are through the small hallways (lined with storage lockers). *Grandes Lignes* (main lines) depart from tracks 17–27; *banlieue* (suburban) trains depart from 1–16. The train information office *(accueil)* is opposite track 15; the reservation office is opposite track 16.

Baggage consignment and the post office are along track 27, and WCs are opposite track 19.

Key destinations served by the **Gare St. Lazare: Giverny** (train to Vernon, 5/day, 45 min; then bus or taxi 10 min to Giverny), **Rouen** (15/day, 75 min), **Honfleur** (6/day, 3 hrs, via Lisieux, then bus), **Bayeux** (9/day, 2.5 hrs, some with change in Caen), **Caen** (12/day, 2 hrs).

Gare d'Austerlitz: This small station provides non-TGV service to the Loire Valley, southwestern France, and Spain. All tracks are at street level. The information booth is opposite track 17, and a Thomas Cook exchange and all ticket sales are in the hall opposite track 10. Baggage consignment and car rental are near Porte 27 (along the side, opposite track 21).

Key destinations served by the **Gare d'Austerlitz: Amboise** (8/day in 2 hrs, 12/day in 1.5 hrs with change in St. Pierre des Corps), **Cahors** (7/day, 5–7 hrs, most with changes), **Barcelona** (1/day, 9 hrs, change in Montpellier, night trains), **Madrid** (2 night trains only, 13–16 hrs), **Lisbon** (1/day, 24 hrs).

Buses

The main bus station is Gare Routière du Paris-Gallieni (28 avenue du General de Gaulle, in suburb of Bagnolet, Mo: Gallieni, tel. 01 49 72 51 51). Buses provide cheaper—if less comfortable and more time-consuming—transportation to major European cities. Euro- lines' buses depart from here (tel. 08 36 69 52 52, www.eurolines .com). Eurolines has a couple of neighborhood offices: in the Latin Quarter (55 rue Saint-Jacques, tel. 01 43 54 11 99) and in Versailles (4 avenue de Sceaux, tel. 01 39 02 03 73).

The Eurostar Train to London
Crossing the Channel by Eurostar Train

The fastest and most convenient way to London is by rail. Eurostar is the speedy passenger train that zips you from downtown Paris to London (17/day, 3 hrs) faster and easier than flying. The train goes 190 mph in France but a doddering 80 mph in England. (When the English segment gets up to speed, the journey time will shrink to 2 hours.) The actual tunnel crossing is a 20-minute, black, silent, 100-mile-per-hour nonevent. Your ears won't even pop. Eurostar trains also run to London from Charles de Gaulle airport (requires change in Lille) and Disneyland Paris (direct).

Channel fares are reasonable but complicated. As with air- fares, the most expensive and flexible option is a full-fare ticket with no restrictions on refunds. Cheaper tickets come with more restrictions—and sell out more quickly.

Prices vary depending on when you travel; whether you can live with restrictions; and whether you're eligible for any discounts (youth, seniors, and railpass holders all qualify). The various second-class Leisure Tickets are a good deal, but many require a round-trip purchase. Compare one-way fares with cheap round-trip fares (you can forget to return).

You can check and book fares by phone or online:

U.S.: 800/EUROSTAR, www.raileurope.com (prices listed in dollars).

France: Tel. 08 36 35 35 39, www.voyages-sncf.com (prices listed in euros). In France, you also can buy tickets at any of the train stations, neighborhood SNCF offices, and most travel agencies (expect a booking fee).

Depending on whom you book with, you'll find different prices and discount deals on similar tickets (see below)—if you order from the United States, check out both. It can be a better deal to buy your ticket from a French company instead of a U.S. company—or vice-versa. If you buy from a U.S. company, you'll pay a FedEx charge for ticket delivery in the United States. If you order over the phone or online in Europe, you'll pick up your tickets at the train station—be sure to read the fine print to find out how long you have to pick up the tickets. You can purchase a Eurostar ticket in person at most European train stations, but passholder discounts are only available at Eurostar stations (such as Gare du Nord, Lille, and Calais in France).

Note that France's time zone is one hour later than Britain's. Times listed on tickets are local times.

Here are typical fares available in 2002. For 2003 fares, check the Eurostar and SNCF phone numbers and Web sites listed above.

Eurostar Full-Fare Tickets

Full-fare tickets are fully refundable even after the departure date. As with plane tickets, you'll pay more to have fewer restrictions. In 2002, one-way Business First (*Affaires* in French) cost €315 in France/$279 in the United States and included a meal (a dinner departure nets you more grub than breakfast). Full-fare second-class tickets (Standard Flexi or *Seconde Affaires* in French) cost €255/$199.

Cheaper Tickets

Since full-fare, no-restrictions tickets are so expensive, most travelers sacrifice flexibility for a cheaper ticket with more restrictions. Second class is plenty comfortable, making first class an unnecessary expense for most; prices listed below are for second class unless otherwise noted. Some of these tickets are available only in France, others only in the United States. They are listed roughly from most expensive to cheapest (with more restrictions as you move down the list).

Leisure Flexi (Loisir Flexi): €215 round-trip (round-trip purchase required, partially refundable before departure date, not available in U.S.).

U.S. Leisure: $139 one-way (partially refundable before departure date, not available in France).

Leisure (Loisir): €145 round-trip (round-trip purchase required, nonrefundable, not available in U.S.).

Leisure 7 (Loisir 7): €115 round-trip (round-trip purchase required, nonrefundable, purchase at least 7 days in advance, not available in U.S.).

Leisure 14 (Loisir 14): €95/$178 round-trip (round-trip purchase required, nonrefundable, purchase at least 14 days in advance, stay 2 nights or over a Sat, available in U.S. and France).

Weekend Day Return (Loisir Journée): €85 for same-day round-trip on a Saturday or Sunday (round-trip purchase required, nonrefundable, not available in U.S.). Note that this round-trip ticket is cheaper than many one-way tickets.

Eurostar Discounts

For Railpass Holders: Discounts are available in the United States or France to travelers holding railpasses that include France or Britain ($75 one-way for second class, $155 one-way for first class).

For Youth and Seniors: Discounts are available in the United States and France for children under 12 (€45/$69 one-way for second class) and youths under 26 (€75/$79 one-way for second class). Only in the United States can seniors over 60 get discounts ($189 one-way for first class).

Airports

Charles de Gaulle Airport

Paris' primary airport has three main terminals: T-1, T-2, and T-9. British Air, SAS, United, US Air, KLM, Northwest, and Lufthansa all normally use T-1. Air France dominates T-2, though you'll also find Delta, Continental, American, and Air Canada. Charter flights leave from T-9. Airlines sometimes switch terminals, so verify your terminal before flying. Terminals are connected every few minutes by a free *navette* (shuttle bus, line #1). The RER (Paris subway) stops near the T-1 and T-2 terminals, and the TGV (*train à grande vitesse;* pron. tay-zhay-vay) station is at T-2. There is no bag storage at the airport.

Those flying to or from the United States will almost certainly use T-1 or T-2. Below is information for each terminal. For flight information, call 01 48 62 22 80.

Terminal 1: This round terminal covers three floors—arrival (top floor), departure (one floor down) and shops (basement level). The ADP (quasi–tourist office) provides helpful tourist information on the arrival level at gate 36 (look for Meeting Point signs). They have museum passes and free maps and hotel information (daily 7:00–22:00). A nearby Relay store sells phone cards. A bank (with lousy rates) is near gate 16. An American Express cash machine and an ATM are near gate 32. Car-rental offices are on the arrival level from gates 10 to 24; the SNCF (train) office is at gate 22.

Shuttle buses to the RER and to terminal 2 (and the TGV station) leave from outside gate 36—take the elevator down to level *(niveau)* 2, walk outside to find the buses (line #1 serves T-2 including the TGV station, line #2 goes directly to the RER station). **Air France bus** departs outside gate 34. **Roissy Bus** leaves outside gate 30 (buy tickets inside at gate 30). **Taxis** wait outside gate 20 and the **Disneyland Express** bus departs from gate 32 (see below under "Transportation between Charles de Gaulle airport and Paris").

Those departing from terminal 1 will find restaurants, a PTT (post office), a pharmacy, boutiques, and a handy grocery store one floor below the ticketing desks (level 2 on the elevator).

Terminal 2: This long, horseshoe-shaped terminal is divided into several sub-terminals (or halls), each identified by a letter. Halls are connected with each other, the RER, the TGV station, and T-1 every five minutes with free *navettes* (shuttle buses, line #1 runs to Terminal 1). Here is where you should find these key carriers: in Hall A—Air France, Air Canada, and American Airlines; in Hall C—Delta, Continental, and more Air France. The RER and TGV stations are below the Sheraton Hotel (access by *navette* buses or on foot). Stops for *navette* buses, Air France buses, and Roissy Buses are all well signed and near each hall (see below under "Transportation between Charles de Gaulle airport and Paris"). ADP information desks are located near gate 5 in each hall. Car-rental offices, post offices, pharmacies, and ATM machines *(Point Argent)* are also well signed.

Transportation between Charles de Gaulle airport and Paris: Three efficient public-transportation routes, taxis, and airport shuttle vans link the airport's terminals with central Paris. All are marked with good signage and their stops are centrally located at all terminals. The **RER,** with stops near T-1 and at T-2 (€8), runs every 15 minutes and stops at Gare du Nord, Chatelet, St. Michel, and Luxembourg Garden in central Paris. When coming from Paris to the airport, T-1 is the first RER stop at Charles de Gaulle; T-2 is the second stop.

Roissy Buses run every 15 minutes to Paris' Opéra Garnier (€8, 40 min); the Opéra stop is on rue Scribe at the American Express office). Three **Air France bus** routes serve central Paris about every 15 minutes (Arc de Triomphe and Porte Maillot-€11, 40 min; Montparnasse Tower/train station-€12, 60 min; or the Gare de Lyon station-€12, 40 min).

Taxis with luggage will run from €40 to €55. If taking a cab to the airport, ask your hotel to call for you (the night before if you must leave early) and specify that you want a real taxi *(un taxi normal)* and not a limo service that costs €20 more.

Airport **shuttles** offer a stress-free trip between either of Paris' airports and downtown, ideal for single travelers or families of four or more (taxis are limited to three). Reserve from home and they'll meet you at the airport (€23 for 1 person, €27 for 2, €41 for 3, €55 for 4, plan on a 30-min wait if you ask them to pick you up at the airport). Choose between **Airport Connection** (tel. 01 44 18 36 02, fax 01 45 55 85 19, www.airport-connection.com) and **Paris Airport Services** (tel. 01 55 98 10 80, fax 01 55 98 10 89, www.parisairportservice.com).

Sleeping at or near Charles de Gaulle airport: Hôtel Ibis**, outside the RER Roissy rail station for T-1 (the first RER stop coming from Paris), offers standard and predictable accom-modations (Db-€85, CC, near *navette* bus stop, free shuttle bus to either terminal, tel. 01 49 19 19 19, fax 01 49 19 19 21, e-mail: h1404sb@accor-hotels.com). **Novotel***** is next door and the next step up (Db-€130–145, CC, tel. 01 49 19 27 27, fax 01 49 19 27 99, e-mail: h1014@accor-hotels.com).

Drivers wanting to avoid rush-hour traffic may consider sleeping north of Paris in the pleasant, medieval town of **Senlis** (15 min north of airport) at **Hostellerie de la Porte Bellon** (Db-€70, CC, in the center at 51 rue Bellon, near rue de la République, tel. 03 44 53 03 05, fax 03 44 53 29 94).

Orly Airport

This airport feels small. Orly has two terminals: Sud and Ouest. International flights arrive at Sud. After exiting Sud's baggage claim (near gate H), you'll see signs directing you to city trans-portation, car rental, and so on. Turn left to enter the main termi-nal area, and you'll find exchange offices with bad rates, an ATM, the ADP (a quasi–tourist office that offers free city maps and basic sightseeing information, open until 23:00), and an SNCF French rail desk (closes at 18:00, sells train tickets and even Eurailpasses, next to the ADP). Downstairs are a sandwich bar, WCs, a bank (same bad rates), a newsstand (buy a phone card), and a post office (great rates for cash or American Express traveler's checks). Car-rental offices are located in the parking lot in front of the terminal. For flight info on any airline serving Orly, call 01 49 75 15 15.

Transportation between Paris and Orly airport: Several efficient public-transportation routes, taxis, and a couple of air-port shuttle services link Orly and central Paris. The gate loca-tions listed below apply to Orly Sud, but the same transportation services are available from both terminals.

Bus services to central Paris: The **Air France bus** (outside gate K) runs to Paris' Invalides Métro stop (€8, 4/hr, 30 min) and is handy for those staying in or near the rue Cler neighborhood (from Invalidesbus stop, take the Métro 2 stops to Ecole Militaire to reach recommended hotels, see also under RER access below). The **Jetbus #285** (outside gate H, €5, 4/hr) is the quickest way to the Paris subway and the best way to the Marais and Contre-scarpe neighborhoods (take Jetbus to Villejuif Métro stop, buy a *carnet* of 10 Métro tickets, then take the Métro to the Sully Morland stop for the Marais area, or the Censier-Daubenton or Monge stops for the Contrescarpe area. If going to the airport, make sure your train serves Villejuif, as the route splits at the end of the line). The **Orlybus** (outside gate H, €6, 4/hr) takes you to the Denfert-Rochereau RER-B line and the Métro, offering subway access to central Paris.

These routes provide access to Paris via **RER trains:** an ADP shuttle bus takes you to RER line C, with connections to Austerlitz, St. Michel, Musée d'Orsay, Invalides, and Pont de l'Alma stations (outside gate G, 4/hr, €5.5). The **Orlyval trains** are overpriced (€9) and require a transfer at the Antony stop to reach RER line B (serving Luxembourg, Chatelet, St. Michel, and Gare du Nord stations in central Paris).

Taxis are to the far right as you leave the terminal, at gate M. Allow €26–35 for a taxi into central Paris.

Airport shuttle minivans are ideal for single travelers or families of four or more (see "Charles de Gaulle Airport," above, for the companies to contact; from Orly, figure about €18 for 1 person, €12/person for 2, less for larger groups and kids).

Sleeping near Orly Airport: Hôtel Ibis** is reasonable, basic, and close by (Db-€60, CC, tel. 01 56 70 50 60, fax 01 56 70 50 70, e-mail: h1413@accor-hotels.com). **Hôtel Mercure***** provides more comfort for a price (Db-€120–135, tel. 01 49 75 15 50, fax 01 49 75 15 51, e-mail: h1246@accor-hotels.com). Both have free shuttles to the terminal.

NORMANDY

Apple orchards, dramatic coastlines, half-timbered towns, and thatched roofs punctuate the green, rolling hills of Normandy. Parisians call Normandy "the 21st *arrondissement*." It's their escape—the nearest beach. Brits call this area close enough for a weekend away.

Normandy's history is full of war. It was founded by Viking Norsemen, who invaded from the north, settled here in the ninth century, and gave Normandy its name. A few hundred years later, William the Conqueror invaded England from Normandy. His victory is commemorated in a remarkable tapestry at Bayeux. A few hundred years after that, France's greatest cheerleader, Jeanne d'Arc (Joan of Arc), was convicted of heresy in Rouen and burned at the stake by the English, against whom she rallied France during the Hundred Years' War. Most recently, Normandy hosted a WWII battle that changed the course of history.

The rugged, rainy coast of Normandy harbors charming fishing villages, such as little Honfleur. And, on the border of Brittany, the almost surreal island abbey of Mont St. Michel rises serene and majestic, oblivious to the tides of tourists.

Planning Your Time

Rouen, Honfleur, the D-Day beaches, and Mont St. Michel all merit overnight visits. If you're driving between Paris and Honfleur, Giverny (see Paris chapter) or Rouen (sights closed Tue) are easy stops; by train, they're best as day trips from Paris. The WWII museum in Caen works well as a stop between Honfleur and Bayeux (and the D-Day beaches). Mont St. Michel is best seen early or late to avoid the masses of midday tourists. Dinan, only 40 minutes from Mont St. Michel (1 hr by train), offers an

Normandy

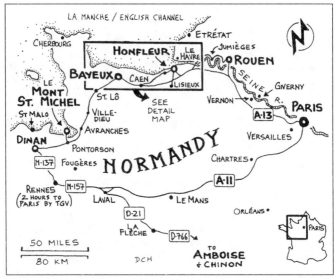

enchanting introduction to Brittany. Some enjoy Mont St. Michel as a day trip from Dinan.

Getting around Normandy

The region is great by car. Trains from Paris serve Rouen, Caen, Bayeux, Mont St. Michel (via Pontorson), and Dinan. But service between these sights can be frustrating. Plan ahead. Buses make Giverny, Honfleur, Arromanches, and Mont St. Michel accessible to train stations in nearby towns, though Sundays have little if any bus service. Mont St. Michel is a headache by train except from Paris.

Cuisine Scene—Normandy

Known as the land of the four Cs (Calvados, Camembert, cider, and *crème*), Normandy specializes in cream sauces, organ meats (sweetbreads, tripe, and kidneys—"the gizzard salads" are great), and seafood *(fruits de mer)*. Dairy products are big here. Local cheeses are Camembert (mild to very strong), Brillat-Savarin (buttery), Livarot (spicy and pungent), Pavé d'Auge (spicy and tangy), and Pont l'Evêque (earthy flavor). Normandy is famous for its powerful Calvados apple brandy, Benedictine brandy (made by local monks), and three kinds of alcoholic apple ciders (*cidre* can be *doux*—sweet, *brut*—dry, or *bouche*—sparkling and the strongest). Also look for *poiret*, a tasty pear cider.

Remember, restaurants serve only during lunch (11:30–14:00) and dinner (19:00–21:00, later in bigger cities); cafés serve food throughout the day.

ROUEN

This 2,000-year-old city of 100,000 people mixes dazzling Gothic architecture, charming half-timbered houses, and contemporary bustle like no other in France. Rouen (pron. roo-ohn) is nothing new. It was a regional capital during Roman times, and France's second largest city (with 40,000 residents—only Paris had more) in medieval times. In the ninth century, the Normans made the town their capital. William the Conqueror called it home before moving to England. The city walked a political tightrope between England and France for centuries. An English base during the Hundred Years' War, it was the place where Joan of Arc was burned in 1431. Rouen's historic wealth was based on its wool industry and trade—for centuries, it was the last bridge across the Seine before the Atlantic. In April 1944, as America and Britain weakened German control of Normandy before the D-Day landings, Allied bombers destroyed 50 percent of Rouen. While the industrial suburbs were devastated, most of the historic core survived. Today, Rouen is France's fifth-largest port and Europe's biggest food exporter (mostly wheat and grain). Rouen is also a pedestrian's delight. And on Thursday evenings—thanks to a new mayor who's big on tourism—the city comes to life with live music.

Planning Your Time

Rouen, with convenient connections to Paris (hrly, 75-min trains from Gare St. Lazare), makes an easy day trip if you want a dose of a much smaller—yet lively—French city. Considering the easy Paris connection and Rouen's ideal location in Normandy, drivers can save money and headaches by seeing Paris, then taking the train to Rouen to pick up their car (see "Helpful Hints: Car Rental," below).

Orientation

While Paris embraces the Seine, Rouen ignores it. The area we're most interested in is bounded by the river to the south, the Museum of Fine Arts (rue Jean Lacaunet) to the north, rue de la République to the east, and the place du Vieux Marché to the west. It's a 20-minute walk from the train station to the river. Everything of interest is within a 10-minute walk from the cathedral.

Tourist Information: The TI faces the cathedral. Pick up their good English walking tour flier, map with information on

Rouen's museums, and a brochure on the Route of the Ancient Abbeys—described below (May–Sept Mon–Sat 9:00–19:00, Sun 9:30–12:30 & 14:00–18:00; Oct–April Mon–Sat 9:00–18:00, Sun 10:00–13:00, tel. 02 32 08 32 40, www.rouen.fr). A small American Express office in the TI changes money.

Arrival in Rouen

By Train: Rue Jeanne d'Arc cuts down from Rouen's station (baggage check available) through the town center to the Seine River. Walk from the station down rue Jeanne d'Arc to rue du Gros Horloge. This pedestrian mall in the medieval center connects the open-air market and Jeanne d'Arc church (to your right) with the cathedral (to your left, starting point of my self-guided "Walking Tour of Rouen," below). Rouen's new subway whisks you from the train station to the Palais de la Justice in one stop (€1.25), one block above rue du Gros Horloge.

By Car: Follow signs to *Centre-ville* (city center) and the *Rive Droite* (right bank). You can park free overor along the river (metered until 19:00), or in one of many underground lots. *Parking la Vieille Tour*, just below the cathedral, is handy (€9/day). If you get turned around (likely because of all the narrow, one-way streets), aim for the cathedral spires.

Helpful Hints

Internet Access: Consider **Place Net** (37 rue de la République).

Laundry: Try **Lav-pratic Laverie** (daily 8:00–20:00, no attendant and no English—completely coin-operated and automated from central control box, 43 rue de la République, near recommended hotels and next to Internet café).

English Bookstore: **ABC Books** has nothing but American and British books (Mon–Sat 10:00–19:00, closed Sun, south of Eglise St. Ouen at 11 rue Faulx).

Market Days: The best market is on place St. Marc, a few blocks east of St. Maclou Church (Tue, Fri–Sun); the next best is on place du Vieux Marché (by Jeanne d'Arc church; daily except Mon). Markets are open roughly 8:00 to 13:00.

Taxi: Call 02 35 88 50 50.

Car Rental: Hertz is across from the train station (Mon–Fri 8:00–9:00, Sat 8:00–12:00 & 14:00–18:00, closed Sun, 130 rue Jeanne d'Arc, tel. 02 35 70 70 71). **Europcar** is on the river below the cathedral (Mon–Sat 8:00–12:00 & 14:00–19:00, closed Sun, 17 quai Pierre Corneille, tel. 02 32 08 39 09, fax 02 32 08 39 00). Figure about €70 for one day with 250 kilometers/155 miles included (that's plenty), or two days for €130 with 500 kilometers/310 miles included.

Rouen

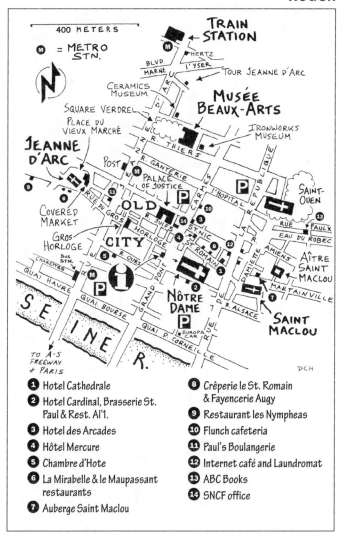

1. Hotel Cathedrale
2. Hotel Cardinal, Brasserie St. Paul & Rest. Al'1.
3. Hotel des Arcades
4. Hôtel Mercure
5. Chambre d'Hote
6. La Mirabelle & le Maupassant restaurants
7. Auberge Saint Maclou
8. Crêperie le St. Romain & Fayencerie Augy
9. Restaurant les Nympheas
10. Flunch cafeteria
11. Paul's Boulangerie
12. Internet café and Laundromat
13. ABC Books
14. SNCF office

Walking Tour of Rouen

To see the essential Rouen sights, take the short historic walk described below (note that many sights are closed 12:00–14:00). You'll start at the cathedral square (and TI), walk four blocks west to the plague cemetery, and return by walking six blocks east of the cathedral to the Jeanne d'Arc church, where you'll find several good recommended restaurants. To begin, stand in front of the cathedral.

▲▲**Cathédrale Notre-Dame**—You're seeing essentially what Monet saw (from an apartment he rented here in the early 1890s) as he painted 20 different studies of this cathedral's frilly Gothic facade at various times of day. Using the physical building only as a rack upon which to hang light, mist, dusk, and shadows, he was capturing "impressions." (One of the paintings is here in Rouen's Museum of Fine Arts, and four others are at Orsay Museum in Paris.)

Enter the cathedral (daily 8:00–18:00) and stand at the back, looking down the nave. This is a classic Gothic **nave**—four stories of pointed arch arcades, the top one filled with windows to help light the interior. Today—with the original colored glass (destroyed mostly in World War II) replaced by clear glass—the interior is lighter than intended. Why such a big cathedral in a small town? Until the 1700s, Rouen was the second city of France—rich from its wool trade and its booming port.

Next, circle counterclockwise three-quarters of the way around the church along the ambulatory (the side aisle that leads behind the high altar) before exiting via the left transept. The side chapels and windows (which come from an assortment of centuries and styles—bold blues and reds are generally from the 13th century) are described in English. Photos halfway down on the right show WWII bomb damage.

Passing an iron gate near the high altar (closed during Mass—but often open on the opposite side even during Mass), you come to several important **tombs**. Rouen was the Norman capital. The first tomb is of Rollo—the first duke of Normandy in 933 (and great-great-great-great grandfather of William the Conqueror, seventh duke of Normandy, c. 1035). That means he was chief of the first gang of Vikings (the original "Normans") who decided to actually settle here. Called "the father of Normandy," he died at the age of 80 but is portrayed on his tomb looking 33 (as was the fashion, because Jesus died at that age). Because of some later pillage and plunder, only Rollo's femur is inside the tomb. And, speaking of body part, the next tomb contains only the heart of Richard the Lionhearted (the rest of his body lies in the Abbey of Fontevraud, described in the Loire Valley chapter). A descendant of the duke who conquered the English, this Norman was both a king of the English and the 12th duke of Normandy.

Circle behind the altar. Look back above the entry to see a rare black-and-white rose window (its colored medieval glass is long gone).

A photo on the wall across the nave from Rollo's tomb shows the mess caused when a violent 1999 storm blew the spire off the

roof, sending it crashing to the cathedral floor. Looking directly above Rollo's femur, you can see the patchwork in the ceiling.
Perhaps this might be a good time to exit. Pass through the
small iron gate, turn right, and leave through the side door
(north transept).

Stepping outside, look back at the **facade.** The fine carved
tympanum (the area over the door) shows a graphic Last Judgment. Jesus stands between the saved (on the left) and the damned
(on the right). Notice the devil grasping the miser, who clutches
a bag of coins. Look for the hellish hot tub, where even a bishop
(pointy hat) is eternally in hot water.

Most of the facade has been cleaned—blasted with jets of
water—but the fine limestone carving is still black. It's too delicate to survive the hosing, and instead awaits a more expensive
laser cleaning.

From this courtyard, a gate deposits you on a charming
street, rue St. Romain. Turn right and walk downhill on...

Rue St. Romain—This street has half-timbered buildings and
lanes worth a look. Peek into the flowery pastel shop run by
Rouen's last hatmaker. Nearby, you can look through an arch back
at the cathedral's spire. Made of cast iron in the late 1800s—about
the same time Eiffel was building his tower in Paris—the spire is,
at 150 meters/490 feet, the tallest in France. You can also see the
former location of the missing smaller (green) spire—downed in
that 1999 storm. Farther down the street, just past the Mormon
church (read the French), a skinny and very picturesque half-
timbered side lane (rue des Chanoines) leads left. And beyond
that, a shop shows off a traditional art form in action...

Fayencerie Augy—Monsieur Augy welcomes potential shoppers
to browse his studio/gallery/shop and see Rouen's clay "china"
being made the traditional way. (When you enter the shop, say,
"Bonjour, Monsieur Augy" pron. oh-zhee). First, the clay is molded
and fired. Then it's dipped in white enamel, dried, lovingly hand-
painted, and fired a second time. Rouen was the first city in France
to make faience. In the 1700s, the town had 18 factories churning
out the popular product (Mon–Sat 9:00–19:00, closed Sun, 29 rue
St. Romain, VAT tax refunds nearly pay for the shipping.) For
much more faience, visit the local ceramic museum (see "More
Sights—Rouen," below). Rue St. Romain leads to the very fancy...

St. Maclou Church—This church's unique bowed facade is textbook Flamboyant Gothic. Notice the flame-like tracery decorating
its gable. Since this was built at the very end of the Gothic age—
and construction took many years—the doors are from the next
age: Renaissance (c. 1550). The interior is of no great importance
(daily 10:00–18:00).

Leaving the church, turn right, then take another right (giving the boys on the corner a wide berth) and wander past a fine wall of half-timbered buildings fronting rue Martainville to the end of St. Maclou Church.

Half-Timbered Buildings—Because the local stone—a chalky limestone from the cliffs of the Seine River—was of poor quality (your thumbnail is stronger), and local oak was plentiful, half-timbered buildings from the 14th to the 19th centuries are a Rouen forte. Cantilevered floors were standard until the early 1500s. These top-heavy designs made sense because city land was limited and property taxes were based on ground-floor square footage, and the cantilevering minimized unsupported spans on upper floors. The oak beams provided the structural skeleton of the building, which was then filled in with a mix of clay, straw, pebbles...or whatever was available.

A block farther down, at 186 rue Martainville, a covered lane leads to the...

Plague Cemetery (Aître St. Maclou)—During the great plagues of the Middle Ages, as many as two-thirds of the people in this parish died. Just taking care of the corpses was an overwhelming task for the decimated community. This half-timbered courtyard (c. 1520, free, daily 8:00–20:00) was a mass grave and ossuary where the bodies were "processed." Bodies would be dumped into a mass grave (where the well is now) and drenched in liquid lime to speed decomposition. Later, the bones would be stacked in alcoves above the colonnades that line this courtyard. Notice the ghoulish carvings (c. 1560s)—gravediggers' tools, skulls, crossbones, and characters doing the "dance of death." In this *danse macabre*, Death, the great equalizer, grabs people of all social classes. The place is now an art school. Peek in on the young artists. As you leave, find the dried black cat (died c. 1520, in tiny glass case on left). To overcome evil, it was buried during the building's construction.

Farther down rue Martainville, at place St. Marc, a colorful produce market blooms Tuesdays, Fridays, Saturdays, and Sundays until 13:00. Otherwise, leaving the boneyard, turn right and hike back up to the cathedral. Passing the cathedral, rue du Gros Horloge—the town's main shopping street since Roman times—leads to Rouen's big old clock, the...

Gros Horloge—This impressive Renaissance public clock, le Gros Horloge (pron. groh oar-lohzh, 1528), decorates the former city hall. In the 16th century, an hour hand offered ample precision; minute hands only became necessary in a later, faster-paced age. The lamb at the end of the hour hand is a reminder that wool rules (and is the source of Rouen's wealth). The town medallion features the sacrificial lamb (with both religious and business significance). But the artistic highlight fills the underside of the arch (walk under and stretch your back), with the good shepherd and lots of sheep.

Continue walking downhill and cross the busy rue Jeanne d'Arc. (The train station is on your right, the bridge over the Seine River is on your left, and the new Métro line is under your feet.) Fifty meters past the medieval McDonald's, Les Larmes de Jeanne d'Arc de Rouen (a chocolate shop at #163) would love to tempt you with its chocolate-covered almond "tears *(larmes)* of Jeanne d'Arc." While you must resist touching the chocolate fountain, you are welcome to taste a tear. One is free. A small bag costs €7. The street continues to...

Place du Vieux-Marché—The old market square, surrounded by fine, old, half-timbered buildings and plenty of good eateries, has a modern covered produce market, a park marking the site of Jeanne d'Arc's burning, and a modern church. The market leads to the garden, where a tall aluminum cross marks the spot where Rouen publicly punished and executed people. The pillories stood here. During the Revolution, the guillotine here made 800 people "a foot shorter at the top." And, in 1431, 19-year-old Jeanne d'Arc was burned here. As the flames engulfed her, an English soldier said, "Oh, my God, we've killed a saint." (Nearly 500 years later, Joan was sainted, and the soldier was proven right.) A waxy **Joan of Arc Museum** on the square tells the story of this inspirational teenager of supreme faith who, after hearing voices for several years, won the confidence of her countrymen, was given an army, and rallied the French against their English invaders. Those touched by her story will enjoy this humble museum (€4, English descriptions, daily 9:30–19:00, 33 place du Vieux-Marché).

▲**Eglise Jeanne d'Arc**—This modern church is a tribute to Jeanne d'Arc, who was canonized in 1920 and went on to become the patron saint of France. The church, completed in 1979, feels Scandinavian inside and out—reminding us again of Normandy's Nordic roots. With sumptuous 16th-century windows (salvaged from a church lost in World War II) worked into the soft architectural lines and ship's hull vaulting, it's a delightful place—reminiscent of the churches of Le Corbusier (English pamphlet describes church, closed 12:30–14:00, public WC 30 meters/100 feet from church doors).

More Sights—Rouen

These three museums are within a block of each other, closed on Tuesdays, never crowded, and can all be visited with a €5.40 combo-ticket.

▲**Museum of Fine Arts (Musée des Beaux Arts)**—This museum beautifully displays paintings from many periods, including works by

Caravaggio, Rubens, Veronese, Steen, Géricault, Ingres, Delacroix, and the Impressionists. Don't miss Monet's painting of Rouen's cathedral and the room dedicated to Géricault. Pick up the museum plan at the ticket desk. Key rooms have excellent English descriptions on small, portable boards and even have clever foldaway stools. The €2.30 audioguide is good, but spotty in its coverage (€3, Wed–Mon 10:00–18:00, 17th-century rooms close 13:00–14:00, closed Tue, 26 bis rue Jean Lecanuet, 3 blocks below station).

Museum of Ironworks (Musée le Seq des Tournelles)— This defunct Gothic church houses iron objects, many of them more than 1,500 years old. Locks, keys, tools, coffee grinders— virtually anything made out of iron is on display (€2.30, Wed–Mon 10:00–13:00 & 14:00–18:00, closed Tue, no English explanations, behind Musée des Beaux Arts, 2 rue Jacques Villon).

Museum of Ceramics—This fine old mansion is filled with Rouen's famous earthenware dating from the 16th to the 18th centuries. Unfortunately, there is not a word of English to make things meaningful to Americans (same hours and cost as Museum of Ironworks, above; 1 rue Faucon).

Sights—Near Rouen

The Route of Ancient Abbeys (La Route des Anciennes Abbayes)—This route is punctuated with abbeys, apples, Seine River views, and pastoral scenery. Drivers follow the D-982 west of Rouen. By bus, take #30, which follows the route and has two convenient morning trips to visit the Abbey of Jumièges (4/day, none Sun, 45 min one-way to Jumièges, depart from Rouen's bus station at 9 rue Jeanne d'Arc, tel. 08 25 07 60 27, see map).

Drivers can stop to admire the Romanesque church at the **Abbey of St. Georges de Boscherville** (but skip the abbey grounds). The romantically ruined abbey of **Jumièges** is *the* sight to visit on this route (follow the river on D-65 from Duclair for a more scenic approach). Founded in 654, it was destroyed by Vikings, only to be rebuilt by William the Conqueror, only to be torn down again by French revolutionaries (4, daily mid-April– mid-Sept 9:30–19:00, mid-Sept–mid-April 9:30–13:00 & 14:30– 17:30, helpful English handout). The **Auberge des Ruines,** across the street, makes a good lunch stop. Cross the Seine between Jumièges and Honfleur on the €1.50 car ferry at Duclair, or on one of three suspension bridges.

Sleeping in Rouen
(€1 = about $1, country code: 33, zip code: 75000)
Sleep Code: **S** = Single, **D** = Double/Twin, **T** = Triple, **Q** = Quad, **b** = bathroom, **s** = shower only, **CC** = Credit Cards accepted,

no CC = Credit Cards not accepted, **SE** = Speaks English,
NSE = No English, * = French hotel rating system (0–4 stars).

To help you sort easily through these listings, I've divided
the rooms into three categories based on the price for a standard
double room with bath:

Higher Priced—Most rooms more than €100.
Moderately Priced—Most rooms €100 or less.
Lower Priced—Most rooms €50 or less.

All of these hotels are perfectly central, within two blocks of
the cathedral; directions are given from the cathedral. Because the
town is busy with business travelers on workdays and quiet on
weekends, the TI offers a "*bon weekend*" plan, where participating
hotels offer two weekend nights (Fri, Sat, or Sun) for the price of
one. While this sounds good, in practice it's hard to cash in on.
Free rooms must be claimed at the time of reservation. If you walk
into the TI without hotel reservations, ask for the *bon weekend*
deal at that time. If you book ahead with a hotel, request the deal
directly from the hotel. Don't get your hopes up.

HIGHER PRICED
Hôtel Mercure***, a block north of the cathedral, is an ideally
situated, sprawling business hotel with professional staff, a vast
lobby, a bar, and rooms loaded with modern comforts (Db-€99–
105, CC, elevator, parking garage-€10/day, 7 rue Croix de Fer,
tel. 02 35 52 69 52, fax 02 35 89 41 46, e-mail: h1301@accor-hotels
.com, SE).

MODERATELY PRICED
The following two hotels are equally good.

Hôtel Cardinal**, warmly run by Madame Picard and her
English-speaking daughter Sandrine, is a great value. Nearly
all of its spotless and comfortable rooms look right onto the
cathedral; some have private balconies, and a few are ideal for
families (Sb-€42–57, small Db-€49, big Db-€66, Tb-€76,
Qb-€83, extra bed-€10, good breakfast buffet-€6.50, CC,
elevator, 1 place de la Cathédrale, tel. 02 35 70 24 42, fax 02
35 89 75 14, e-mail: hotelcardinal.rouen@wanadoo.fr).

Hôtel de la Cathédrale** welcomes you with a flowery,
umbrella-filled courtyard; a cozy, wood-beamed breakfast room;
and characteristic rooms, some with hardwood floors (Sb-€45–
56, Db-€53–64, Tb-€69–79, extra bed-€10, breakfast buffet-
€7.50, CC, elevator, overnight parking-€5, 24-hr parking-€10,
12 rue St. Romain, a block from St. Maclou Church, tel. 02 35 71
57 95, fax 02 35 70 15 54, www.hotel-de-la-cathedrale.fr, e-mail:
contact@hotel-de-la-cathedrale.fr, friendly Nathalie SE).

LOWER PRICED

Hôtel des Arcades*, two short blocks north of the cathedral, is a safe, central budget option with sufficiently spacious and comfortable rooms and a friendly, French-only welcome (D-€26, D with toilet only-€31, Db-€42, CC, 52 rue des Carmes, tel. 02 35 70 10 30, fax 02 35 70 08 91, www.hotel-des-arcades.fr).

Chambre d'Hote: Monsieur Philippe Aunay rents two rooms in his 17th-century half-timbered home, which feels like a cross between a museum and a rummage sale. It's like sleeping at your eccentric grandma's house. One room comes with a piano, a bathtub, and a shower. The other is a three-room mini-apartment, complete with a small kitchen and two bathrooms (Sb-€35, Db-€50, Tb-€80, Qb-€100, 5b-€125, includes breakfast, no CC, 45 rue des Ours, no sign, push buzzer, tel. 02 35 70 99 68).

Eating in Rouen

Restaurant Al'1, on a leafy square under the facade of the cathedral, is *the* place for a hearty salad (€9 salads are big enough for 2, Mon–Fri 12:00–15:30 & 19:00–22:00, closed Sat–Sun, indoor/outdoor seating, slick and efficient service, 3 place de la Cathédrale). **Brasserie St. Paul**, two doors down, is also good.

Two of Rouen's best moderately priced restaurants face place du Vieux Marché across from the Jeanne d'Arc church: **La Mirabelle** is best for seafood (*menus* from €17, daily, 3 place du Vieux Marché, tel. 02 35 71 58 21). **Le Maupassant**—a jolly place with an outdoor terrace and three lively floors filled with red velvet booths and appreciative locals—is famous for its *moelleux au chocolate*, melted chocolate over ice cream and cake (regional *menus* from €16, daily, 39 place du Vieux Marché, tel. 02 35 07 56 90).

Crêperie le St. Romain, between the cathedral and St. Maclou Church, is a good budget option. It's a welcoming place, run by an eager-to-please owner who serves filling €7 crêpes with small green salads (closed Sun–Tue, 52 rue St. Romain, tel. 02 35 88 90 36).

L'Auberge St. Maclou, which occupies a red-timbered building next to St. Maclou Church, is quiet and intimate, offering reasonable regional *menus* from €13 (closed Sun–Mon, 222 rue St. Martainville, tel. 02 35 71 06 67).

Restaurant les Nympheas is your chance to dress up for white-tablecloth elegance and extremely attentive service, yet still not go broke. Named for Monet's water lilies, the restaurant carries an ambience more modern than ye olde, but it does offer the option of women's menus (without prices), a throwback to an earlier time when ladies weren't supposed to know what their dates were paying. The €32 *menu* offers four fine courses with plenty of choices. Expect to pay €20 for half a bottle of wine (dinner from 19:30, closed Sun–Mon, reservations smart, a block beyond old market square at 7 rue de la Pie, tel. 02 35 89 26 69). The lack of English in this formal setting adds a touch of adventure to the experience.

Flunch hangs at the other end of the extreme—not a tablecloth or candle in sight. Here, you'll find family-friendly, dirt-cheap, point-and-shoot cafeteria food in a fast-food setting (€4 salad bar; €8 *menu* with salad bar, main course, and drink; good kids' menu, open until 22:00, a block from cathedral at 66 rue des Carmes).

For **picnics**, try the morning open-air markets (daily except Monday, mentioned in "Helpful Hints," above) or any small grocery store. Several late-night mini-markets are on rue de la République between rue St. Romain and rue de l'Hôpital (open until 24:00).

Rouen's **best bakery** is Paul's. It's always jammed, and it's a delight even if you're only looking (corner of rue Jeanne d'Arc and rue Rollon, a block above rue du Gros Horloge).

Transportation Connections—Rouen

Rouen is well-served by trains from Paris, through Amiens to other points north, and through Caen to other destinations west and south.

By train to: Paris' Gare St. Lazare (15/day, 75 min), **Bayeux** (3/day, 3.5 hrs, change in Caen), **Pontorson-Mont St. Michel** (5/day, 7 hrs, via Paris, change train stations from St. Lazare to Montparnasse, then TGV to Rennes, then 1.75-hr bus to Mont St. Michel; see "Getting to Mont St. Michel," below).

By train and bus to: Honfleur (5/day, 1.5 hrs, train to Le Havre, then bus over pont de Normandie to Honfleur—Le Havre's bus station is 1 block from train station, turn left out of station and cross big boulevard; or in 2.5 hrs via Caen, 3/day—train from Rouen to Caen, then bus to Honfleur).

HONFLEUR

Honfleur (pron. ohn-flur) escaped the bombs of World War II, and feels as picturesque as it looks. Gazing at its cozy harbor, lined with skinny, soaring houses, it's easy to overlook the historic importance of this port. For over a thousand years, sailors have enjoyed Honfleur's ideal location, where the Seine meets the English Channel. William the Conqueror received supplies shipped from Honfleur. And Samuel de Champlain sailed from here in 1608, discovering the St. Lawrence Waterway and founding Quebec City. Honfleur was also a favorite of 19th-century Impressionists: Boudin (pron. boo-dan) lived and painted here, attracting Monet and others from Paris. In some ways, modern art was born in the fine light of idyllic Honfleur.

Today's Honfleur, long eclipsed by the gargantuan port of Le Havre just across the Seine, happily uses its past as a bar stool and sits on it.

Orientation

All of Honfleur's appealing streets and activities are within a short stroll of its old port (Vieux Bassin). The Seine River flows just east of the center, the hills of the Côte de Grace form its western limit, and rue de la République slices north-south through the center to the port.

Tourist Information: The TI is in the left end of the flashy glass public library *(Mediathéque)* on quai le Paulmier, two blocks from the Vieux Bassin toward Le Havre. Their town map is useless. The €8.50 **museum pass** saves money only if you visit at least three museums (Easter–Oct Mon–Sat 9:30–12:30 & 14:00–18:30, Sun 10:00–17:00, no midday closing in summer; Nov–Easter Mon–Sat 9:00–12:00 & 14:00–18:00, closed Sun, tel. 02 31 89 23 30, www.ot-honfleur.fr).

Arrival in Honfleur

By Bus: Get off at the small *gare routière* near the TI (useful information counter, confirm your departure, see "Transportation Connections," below). To reach the TI, old town, and port, walk five minutes up quai le Palmier (with Hôtel Moderne on your left).

By Car: Follow *Centre-ville* signs and park as close to the port (Vieux Bassin) as possible to unload your bags. Parking is tight in Honfleur, especially on summer and holiday weekends. The vast *Parking du Bassin* is close (across from TI), but charges €10/day (€1.50/hr). For an extra five-minute walk, you can park all day for 2 at the metered *Parking Priviligié* (follow parking signs at roundabout near river, park at far end, and cross gray swivel bridge on foot for quick access to port). Street meters are free from 19:00 to 9:00, and your hotel may have helpful parking suggestions. If driving into town and on a budget, note that there are free alternatives to the impressive but expensive (€6) toll bridge, pont de Normandie, connecting Rouen and Honfleur. The bridges a few kilometers east of pont de Normandie are toll-free.

Helpful Hints

Laundry: A good launderette *(Lavomatique)* is a block behind and toward the port from the TI (daily 7:00–20:00, 4 rue Notre-Dame).
Saturday Morning Farmers' Market: The area around Eglise Ste. Catherine is a colorful market every Saturday (9:00–12:30).

Honfleur

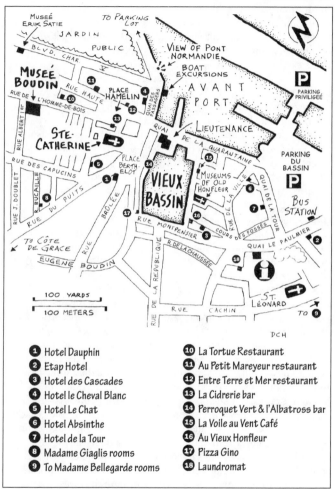

1 Hotel Dauphin	**10** La Tortue Restaurant
2 Etap Hotel	**11** Au Petit Mareyeur restaurant
3 Hotel des Cascades	**12** Entre Terre et Mer restaurant
4 Hotel le Cheval Blanc	**13** La Cidrerie bar
5 Hotel Le Chat	**14** Perroquet Vert & l'Albatross bar
6 Hotel Absinthe	**15** La Voile au Vent Café
7 Hotel de la Tour	**16** Au Vieux Honfleur
8 Madame Giaglis rooms	**17** Pizza Gino
9 To Madame Bellegarde rooms	**18** Laundromat

Sights—Honfleur

The Old Basin (Vieux Bassin)—Stand at the river side of
Honfleur's square harbor (with your back to the river) and survey
the town. The word Honfleur is Scandinavian, meaning the shelter
(*fleur*) of Hon (a Norseman who settled here). Eventually, the harbor was fortified with a wall with two gates (the 1 surviving gate is
on your right) and a narrow boat passage protected by a chain. Just
in front of the barrel-vaulted old entry to the town, you can see a

bronze bust of Champlain—the explorer who sailed from here with an Honfleur crew to make his discoveries in Canada. The basin, once filled with fishing boats, is now home to local yachts. Turn around to see various tour and fishing boats and the sleek suspension bridge, pont de Normandie (described below), in the distance. Boats catch flatfish, scallops, and tiny shrimps.

On the left, you may see a fisherman's wife—like Linda—selling *crevettes* (shrimp). You can buy them *cuites* (cooked) or *vivantes* (alive and wiggly). Linda is happy to let you sample one (rip off the cute little head and tail and pop the middle into your mouth—*delicieux!*) or buy a cupful to go (€1.50, daily in season).

Walk around the basin (to the left) past the old-time carousel, where you're likely to see an artist sitting at an easel (as Boudin and Monet did). Many consider this spot the birthplace of Impressionism. Artists still set up on this side of the basin to catch the light playing on the line of buildings, slate, timbers, geraniums, clouds, and reflections in the water. Claude Monet came here to visit the artist Boudin, a hometown boy, and the battle cry of the Impressionists—"Out of the studio and into the light!"—was born.

▲▲**Eglise Ste. Catherine**—It seems that if you could turn this church over, it would float. That's because it was built by a community of sailors and fishermen in a region with plenty of boatbuilders and no cathedral architects. Sit down inside. When the first nave was built in 1466, it was immediately apparent that more space was needed—so the second was built in 1497. Because it felt too much like a market hall, side aisles were added. Notice the oak pillars. Since each had to be the same thickness, and trees come in different sizes, some are full length and others are supported by stone bases. In the last months of World War II, a bomb fell through the roof—but didn't explode. The pipe organ is popular for concerts. The modern pews are designed to flip so you can face the music. Take a close look at the many medieval instruments carved into the railing below the organ—a 16th-century combo in wood.

The church's bell tower was built not atop the church, but across the square—to lighten the load on the roof of the wooden church and to minimize fire hazards. The church is free. The tower—a tiny museum with a few church artifacts—is not worth the 1.50 (tower and church open daily 9:00–18:30 in summer, otherwise 9:00–12:00 & 14:00–18:00).

▲**Eugène Boudin Museum**—This pleasant, airy museum houses three interesting floors of exhibits: first floor—Norman costumes; second floor—the Boudin collection; and third floor—the Hambourg and Rachet collection.

First floor: Monsieur and Madame Louveau—see their photo in costume as you enter—gave their town this fine collection of local traditional costumes. The hats, blouses, and shoes are supported by paintings that place them in an understandable historical and cultural context. Of special interest are the lace bonnets typical of 19th-century Normandy. You could tell a woman's village by her bonnet. The dolls are not toys for tots, but marketing tools for traveling clothing merchants—designed to show off the latest fashions.

Second floor: After walking through a temporary exhibition hall, you come to a fine gallery of 19th-century paintings arranged chronologically, from Romanticism through Realism to Impressionism. Normandy artists showing their work in Paris—such as Eugène Boudin—created enough of a stir that Normandy became in vogue, and many Parisian artists (such as Claude Monet and other early Impressionists) traveled here to tune in to the action. Boudin (1824–1898) made a big impression on the father of Impressionism. This collection of his paintings—which he gave to his hometown— provides a good study of the evolution from realistic portrayals of subjects (outlines colored in—like a coloring book) to masses of colors catching light (Impressionism). Boudin's beach scenes, showing aristocrats taking a healthy saltwater dip, helped fuel that trend. His skies were good enough to earn him the nickname "king of skies."

Third floor: In 1988, Andre Hambourg and his wife, Nicole Rachet, donated their art—enjoyably Impressionistic but from the mid-20th century—to this museum,

Cost and Hours: €5, mid-March–Sept Wed–Mon 10:00–12:00 & 14:00–18:00, Oct–mid-March 10:00–12:00 & 14:30–17:00, closed Tue year-round, elevator, no photos, rue de l'Homme de Bois, tel. 02 31 89 54 00.

▲**Maisons Satie**—The museum, housed in composer Erik Satie's birthplace, presents his music in a creative and enjoyable way. Upon entry, you get a headset. As you wander from room to room, infrared signals transmit bits of Satie's music, along with a first-person story, to your headset. As if living as an artist in Paris in the 1920s, you'll drift past winged pears, strangers in the window, and small girls with green eyes. (If you like what you hear . . . don't move. The infrared transmission is sensitive, and the soundtrack switches every few feet.) The finale—performed by you—is the Laboratory of Emotions. For a relaxing sit, enjoy the 12-minute movie (4/hr, time of next showing marked on door) showing modern dance springing from Satie's collaboration with Picasso types (€5, daily May–Sept 10:00–19:00, Oct–April 11:00–18:00, free English audioguide, 5-min walk from harbor at 67 boulevard Charles V).

Museums of Old Honfleur—Two side-by-side museums combine to paint a picture of daily life in Honfleur since the Middle Ages. The curator creatively supports the artifacts with paintings, making the cultural context clearer. The **Musée de la Marine**

fills a small 15th-century church (facing Vieux Bassin) with an interesting collection of ship models and marine paraphernalia. The **Musée d'Ethnographie et d'Art Populaire**, located in the old prison and courthouse on a very quaint old lane, re-creates typical rooms, cramming them with objects of daily life from various eras (€3 for both or €2 each, both open Tue–Sun 10:00–12:00 & 14:00–18:00, closed Mon, ask for English explanation pages).

Boat Excursions—Boats to pont de Normandie (see below) depart from in front of Hôtel Cheval Blanc (€6-adult,€ 4.60-child, run Easter–Nov, 50 min, tel. 02 31 89 41 80). Any trip like this away from town includes two boring stops through the locks. The tour boat *Calypso* gives 40-minute trips around Honfleur's harbor (€3.80, no stops for locks).

Côte de Grace Walk—For good exercise and a bird's-eye view of Honfleur and pont de Normandie, take the steep, 15-minute walk up to the Côte de Grace viewpoint (from Eglise Ste. Catherine, walk past Hôtel Dauphin and up rue Brûlée, turn right on rue Eugène Boudin, then turn left at the top and climb la Rampe de Mont Joli; best early in the morning or at sunset).

▲**Normandie Bridge (Pont de Normandie)**—The 2-kilometer-long (1.25 miles) pont de Normandie is the longest cable-stayed bridge in the Western world. This is a key piece of a super-freeway that links the Atlantic ports from Belgium to Spain (€6–11). View the bridge from Honfleur (better from an excursion boat or above the town on Côte de Grace viewpoint; best when floodlit) and consider visiting the free Exhibition Hall (under tollbooth on Le Havre side, daily 8:00–19:00). The Seine finishes its winding 800-kilometer/500-mile journey here. From its source, it drops only 450 meters/1,500 feet. It flows so slowly that in certain places, a stiff breeze can send it flowing upstream.

Sleeping in Honfleur
(€1 = about $1, country code: 33, zip code: 14600)

Honfleur is busy on weekends and holidays and in the summer. English is widely spoken. The lower room rates listed below are for off-season (generally Oct–May).

HIGHER PRICED

Hôtel le Cheval Blanc*** is a waterfront splurge in an old, half-timbered building with port views from every pleasant room, many with queen-size beds, and a rare (in this town) elevator (Sb-€67–78, Db-€70–198, most Db-about €122, includes good buffet breakfast and taxes, must cancel with at least 1 week's notice or lose deposit, 2 quai de Passagers, tel. 02 31 81 65 00, fax 02 31 89 52 80, e-mail: lecheval.blanc@wanadoo.fr).

Hôtel Absinthe*** is a tastefully restored place with seven cushy rooms behind the restaurant Le Bistro du Port. Whirlpool tubs, wood-beamed decor, and a cozy lounge with a fireplace make this a good splurge (Db-€126, Db suite-€220, extra bed-€24, CC, 1 rue de la Ville; if no receptionist, keys available in restaurant Absinthe across alley, tel. 02 31 89 23 23, fax 02 31 89 53 60, www.absinthe.fr).

MODERATELY PRICED

Hôtel Dauphin** is Honfleur's best midrange bet, with a family feel, a homey lounge/breakfast room, many stairs, and an Escher-esque floor plan. The rooms—some with open-beam ceilings, some with street noise—are all comfortable (Db-€46–61, Tb-€70–104, pay-as-you-go breakfast upgrades include cereal, yogurt, or fruit-€1 each, and freshly squeezed juice-€2, CC, a stone's throw from church at 10 place Berthelot, tel. 02 31 89 15 53, fax 02 31 89 92 06, www.hotel-du-dauphin.com, e-mail: hotel.dudauphin @wanadoo.fr, friendly Valerie SE).

Hôtel le Chat*** offers wood-beamed, quasi-classy rooms in a historic, ivy-covered stone building across from the Ste. Catherine church. The six *chambres mansardées* (rooms under the roof) are coziest, but—with sloping ceilings and small windows—they're hot in summer (Db-€82–90, CC, restaurant, place Ste. Catherine, tel. 02 31 14 49 49, fax 02 31 89 28 61, e-mail: hotel.lechat@honfleur.com).

Hôtel de la Tour*** is a basic hotel near the parking lots, offering efficient rooms and little personality (Sb-€56–66, Db-€68–78, loft family rooms-€94–120, CC, elevator, 3 quai de la Tour, near bus terminal and TI, tel. 02 31 89 21 22, fax 02 31 89 53 51, www.hoteldelatourhonfleur.com).

LOWER PRICED

Hôtel des Cascades* is well-located above a restaurant and across from the TI. While it's a bit musty and the beds are squishy, it's still a good budget option (Db-€31–46, third person-€8 more, room 17 is best, dinner may be required on weekends and in summer, CC, facing rue Montpensier at 17 place Thiers, tel. 02 31 89 05 83, fax 02 31 89 32 13, Melanie SE).

Etap Hôtel is modern, efficient, and tight, with dirt-cheap, antiseptically clean rooms (Sb-€29, Db-€37, Tb-€45, elevator, CC, across from bus station and main parking lot on rue des Vases, tel. 02 31 89 71 70, fax 02 31 89 77 88).

Chambres d'Hôte

Honfleur has many *chambres d'hôte* (the TI has a long list), but most are too far from the town center. The following two, each a short walk from the center, are fine values.

MODERATELY PRICED
Gregarious **Madame Giaglis** (Lilliane) is stage director for an utterly delightful bed-and-breakfast with six rooms surrounding a perfectly Norman courtyard, small terrace, and garden. The rooms—as cheery as the owner—are big, with a separate sitting area and firm beds (Db-€60, no CC, 200 meters/650 feet up rue Brulée from Hôtel du Dauphin at 74 rue Brulée, tel. 06 22 34 78 94, e-mail: giaglis@wanadoo.fr).

LOWER PRICED
Gentle **Madame Bellegarde** offers comfortable rooms in her traditional home (Db-€30–34, family-friendly Tb with kitchenette and great bathroom view-€53, 54 rue St. Leonard, 10-min uphill walk from TI, 3 blocks up from St. Leonard church in nontouristy part of Honfleur, look for sign in window, tel. 02 31 89 06 52).

Eating in Honfleur

Eat seafood here, but be careful. Honfleur's many restaurants serve primarily a tourist clientele, so quality varies wildly. Trust our suggestions and consider your hotelier's opinion. It's a tough choice between the hard-to-resist waterfront tables of the many lookalike places lining Vieux Bassin, and those with more solid reputations on small side streets. To enjoy the ambience at a smaller price, consider a portside breakfast. If it's even close to sunny, skip your hotel breakfast and eat on the port, where several cafés offer *petit dejeuner* for about €6 (**L'Albatross** is good). Views are best from the lower side of the port (towards Le Havre). **La Voile au Vent**, with great views, is the only all-day café on this side.

A few doors separate two of Honfleur's best moderately priced restaurants (reserve ahead): **Au Petit Mareyeur** is warm, intimate, and all about seafood (€19 *menu*, try the *bouillabaisse Honfleuraise*, closed Mon–Tue, 4 place Hamelin, tel. 02 31 98 84 23); **Entre Terre et Mer** has some outdoor seating and a brighter interior with a good range of regional dishes (*menus* from €20, daily, 12 place Hamelin, tel. 02 31 89 70 60). Near the bottom of the street, **La Cidrerie** is a cozy cider bar with fresh crêpes, Calvados, and great ambience (closed Tue–Wed, set back on cathedral side of place Hamelin at #26). Simple little **La Tortue,** between the port and Boudin Museum, serves good €16 and €22 *menus* (closed Tue off-season, 36 rue de l'Homme de Bois, tel. 02 31 89 04 93).

On the port, **Pizza Gino**—with waterfront tables—hides in the corner, on the side of the port with taller buildings (€10 for decent pizza, daily, tel. 02 31 89 99 86). **Au Vieux Honfleur** sits elegantly across the port with cozy indoor dining and outdoor tables with views, and a locally respected cuisine (*menus* from €28, daily, 13 quai St. Etienne, tel. 02 31 89 15 31).

Nightlife in Honfleur centers on the old port. Two bar/cafés sit 50 meters/165 feet apart on the side of the port with taller buildings, dividing Honfleur's after-hours clientele by age: the **Perroquet Vert** entertains a 40-something crowd, while **L'Albatross** is clearly Generation X.

Transportation Connections—Honfleur

Buses connect Honfleur with Le Havre, Caen, Deauville, and Lisieux, where you'll catch a train to other points. While train and bus service are usually coordinated, ask at Honfleur's bus station for the best connection for your trip (info desk open Mon–Fri 9:00–12:15 & 14:30–17:30, Sat 9:15–12:15, open Sun 9:15–12:15 only in summer, tel. 02 31 89 28 41). Railpass holders will save money by connecting through the nearest city, as bus fares increase with distance.

By bus and/or train to: Caen (hrly buses on line #20, 2 hrs), **Bayeux** (5/day, 3 hrs, 1-hr bus to Lisieux then 1-hr train, or via more frequent 2-hr buses to Caen, then 30-min train), **Rouen** (3/day, 2 hrs, #20 or #50 bus over pont de Normandie to Le Havre, then train to Rouen; or in 3 hrs via Caen), **Paris'** Gare St. Lazare (5/day, 3 hrs; 1-hr bus to Lisieux or Deauville, then 2-hr train to Paris; buses from Honfleur meet most Paris trains).

BAYEUX

Only 10 kilometers/6 miles from the D-Day beaches, Bayeux was the first city liberated after the landing. Incredibly, the town was spared the bombs of World War II. After a local convent chaplain made sure London knew that this was not a German headquarters and of no strategic importance, a scheduled bombing raid was canceled—making Bayeux the closest city to the D-Day landing site not destroyed. Even without its famous tapestry and proximity to the D-Day beaches, Bayeux would be worth a visit for its pleasant *centre-ville* and awe-inspiring cathedral (beautifully illuminated at night). Bayeux makes a good home base for visiting the area's sights, particularly if you lack a car.

Orientation

Tourist Information: The TI is two blocks north of the cathedral on the street that connects place St. Patrice and the tapestry (on the small bridge, pont St. Jean). Pick up a town map, the excellent *D-Day Landings and the Battle of Normandy* brochure, bus schedules to the beaches, and regional information (June–Aug Mon–Sat 9:00–19:00, Sun 9:00–12:00 & 13:00–18:00; Sept–May Mon–Sat

9:30–12:30 & 14:00–17:30, Sun 10:00–12:30 & 14:00–17:30, Internet access, on pont St. Jean leading to pedestrian street rue St. Jean, tel. 02 31 51 28 28, www.bayeux-tourism.com).

Arrival in Bayeux

Navigating Bayeux is a breeze. By car, look for the cathedral spires and follow the signs to *Centre-ville*, then *Tapisserie*. On foot, it's a 20-minute walk from the train station to the tapestry and 15 minutes from the tapestry to place St. Patrice (recommended hotels and Sat market). Allow €5 for a taxi from the train station to any recommended hotel or sight in Bayeux.

Helpful Hints

Internet Access: Get online at the TI (see above for hours and location).

Laundry: There are two launderettes, both near place St. Patrice: one at 4 rue St. Patrice, the other at 69 rue des Bouchers (both open daily 7:00–21:00).

Walking Tour: Tours in English of old Bayeux are offered daily at 14:30 and 16:30 in July and August (€4, 90 min, meet at Hôtel du Doyen near cathedral, call to ask about off-season tours, tel. 02 31 92 14 21).

Market Days: The Saturday market (on place St. Patrice) is much larger than the Wednesday market (on pedestrian rue St. Jean). Both markets end by 13:00.

Car Rental: Bayeux offers few choices (you'll do better in the bigger city of Caen). **Hertz** is at the Shell Station on the ring road at the town's eastern limit (boulevard du 6 Juin, tel. 02 31 92 25 33, fax 02 31 22 88 27). **Scauto** is handier, just below the train station at the BP gas station (tel. 02 31 92 23 25, fax 02 31 51 18 30).

Bike Rental: Try **Cycles 14** (€15/day, on ring road at boulevard W. Churchill at eastern corner of town, tel. 02 31 92 27 75) or ask at the TI.

Sights—Bayeux

▲▲▲**Bayeux Tapestry**—Actually made of wool embroidered onto linen cloth, this document—precious to historians—is a 70-meter/230-foot cartoon telling the story of William the Conqueror's rise from duke of Normandy to king of England and his victory over Harold at the Battle of Hastings. Long and skinny, it was designed to hang from the nave of Bayeux's cathedral.

Your tapestry visit has three parts, explaining the basic story of the battle three times—which was about right for me: First (after noting the time of the next movie showing at the top of the steps), you'll walk through a room full of mood-setting images into a

Bayeux

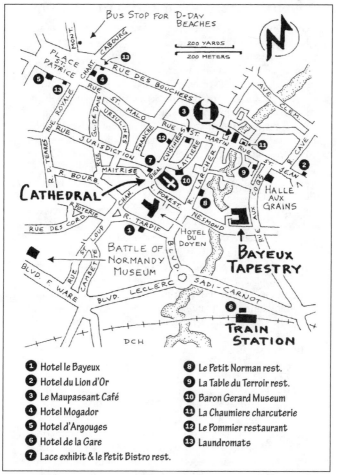

BUS STOP FOR D-DAY BEACHES

200 YARDS
200 METERS

CATHEDRAL

BATTLE OF NORMANDY MUSEUM

BAYEUX TAPESTRY

HALLE AUX GRAINS

HOTEL DU DOYEN

TRAIN STATION

BLVD. LECLERC
SADI-CARNOT

PLACE ST. PATRICE

RUE DES BOUCHERS

RUE DES CORD.

① Hotel le Bayeux
② Hotel du Lion d'Or
③ Le Maupassant Café
④ Hotel Mogador
⑤ Hotel d'Argouges
⑥ Hotel de la Gare
⑦ Lace exhibit & le Petit Bistro rest.
⑧ Le Petit Norman rest.
⑨ La Table du Terroir rest.
⑩ Baron Gerard Museum
⑪ La Chaumiere charcuterie
⑫ Le Pommier restaurant
⑬ Laundromats

room that contains a replica of the tapestry, with extensive explanations. You'll then continue to a room designed to show Norman culture and the impact it ultimately had on England. Next, a 15-minute AV show in the cinema (up one flight) gives a relaxing dramatization of the event. Finally, you'll see the real McCoy. Before entering, pick up the headphones (worth the wait and €1), which give a top-notch, fast-moving, 20-minute scene-by-scene narration complete with period music. If you lose your place, you'll find subtitles in Latin.

Bayeux History—The Battle of Hastings

Because of this pivotal battle, the most memorable date of the Middle Ages is 1066. England's King Edward was about to die without an heir. The big question: Who would succeed him—Harold, an English nobleman and the king's brother-in-law, or William, duke of Normandy and the king's cousin? Edward chose William and sent Harold to Normandy to give William the news. On the journey, Harold was captured. To win his release, he promised he would not contest the decision and be loyal to William. To test his loyalty, William sent Harold to battle for him in Brittany. Harold was successful, and William knighted him. To further test his loyalty, William had Harold swear on the relics of the Bayeux cathedral that when Edward died, he would allow William to ascend the throne. Harold returned to England, Edward died, and Harold grabbed the throne. William, known as William the Bastard, invaded England to claim the throne he reasoned was rightfully his. Harold met him in southern England at the town of Hastings, where their forces fought a fierce 14-hour battle. Harold was killed and his Saxon forces were routed. William—now "the Conqueror"—marched to London and claimed his throne, becoming king of England as well as duke of Normandy.

The advent of a Norman king of England muddied the political waters, setting in motion 400 years of conflict between England and France—not to be resolved until the end of the Hundred Years' War (around 1450).

The Norman conquest of England brought England into the European mainstream (but still no euros). The Normans established a strong central English government. They brought with them the Romanesque style of architecture (e.g., the Tower of London and Durham Cathedral) that the English call "Norman." Historians speculate that had William not succeeded, England would have remained on the fringe of Europe (like Scandinavia), and French culture (and language) would have prevailed in the New World. Hmmm.

Remember, this is Norman propaganda—the English (the bad guys, referred to as *les goddamns*, after a phrase the French kept hearing them say) are shown with mustaches and long hair; the French (*les* good guys) are clean-cut and clean shaven—with even the backs of their heads shaved for a better helmet fit.

Cost and Hours: €6.40, mid-March–mid-Oct daily 9:00–18:30, until 19:00 May–Aug; mid-Oct–mid-March daily 9:30–12:30 & 14:00–18:00, tel. 02 31 51 25 50). Arrive by 9:00 or late in the day to avoid crowds. When buying your ticket, find out the English film times. To minimize congestion in the actual tapestry hall, try to see the 14-minute film first, exit the way you entered, and backtrack to see the replica before the original tapestry (cinema-goers pile into the original tapestry room after each film). Because of the exhibit's generous English descriptions, the €2 English guide booklet is worthwhile only as a souvenir.

▲▲**Bayeux Cathedral**—This massive building towers over Bayeux. As you approach, notice its two towers—originally Romanesque, capped later with tall Gothic spires. The little rectangular stone house atop one tower was the watchman's home, from which he'd keep an eye out for incoming English troops during the Hundred Years' War . . . and then again for the same purpose five centuries later, this time for Germans. Bayeux was liberated on D-Day plus one, June 7. About the only casualty was the German lookout—shot while doing just that from the window of this house. The west facade is structurally Romanesque, but with a decorative Gothic "curtain" added.

Walk inside. The view of the **nave** from the top of the steps shows a fun mix of Romanesque and Gothic. Historians believe the tapestry originally hung here. Imagine it proudly circling the Norman congregation, draped around the nave from the arches. The nave's huge, round lower arches are Romanesque (11th century) and decorated with the same zigzag pattern that characterizes this "Norman" art in England. The nave is so bright because of the huge windows above, in the Gothic half of the nave. The glass was originally richly colored (like the rare surviving 13th-century bits in the high central window above the altar). The finest example of 13th-century "Norman" Gothic is in the choir (the fancy area behind the central altar). Each of the columns is decorated with Romanesque carvings. But those carvings lie under a Gothic-style stone exterior (with characteristic tall, thin lines adding a graceful verticality to the overall feel of the interior).

For maximum 1066 atmosphere, step into the crypt (below central altar)—an area used originally as a safe spot for the cathedral relics. The crypt shows two interesting columns with fine Romanesque carving. During a reinforcement of the nave, these two columns were replaced. Workers removed the Gothic veneer and discovered their true inner Romanesque beauty (free, daily 9:00–18:00, July–Aug until 19:00). The cathedral is beautifully illuminated after dark.

Lace Conservatory (Conservatoire de la Dantelle)—The Adam and Eve house (notable for its carved 15th-century facade—find Adam, Eve, and the snake) offers a free chance to watch lace workers design and weave intricate lace as they did in the 1600s, and see examples of their finest works over the years (free, Mon–Sat 9:30–12:30 & 14:00–18:00, closed Sun, across from cathedral entrance).

Baron Gerard Museum—This museum, located in Hôtel du Doyen outside the cathedral's south transept, houses a collection of porcelain and lace and a modest painting gallery (free with ticket to tapestry, daily 10:00–12:30 & 14:00–18:00, in summer until 19:00 with no midday closing).

▲**Bayeux Memorial Museum/Battle of Normandy**—This museum, providing a good overview of the Battle of Normandy, features tanks, jeeps, uniforms, and countless informative displays, plus a good 30-minute film (€5.50, daily 9:30–18:30, mid-Sept–April closes 12:30–14:00, on Bayeux's ring road, 20 min on foot from center, tel. 02 31 51 46 90).

Sleeping in Bayeux
(€1 = about $1, country code: 33, zip code: 14400)
Hotels are a good value here. Drivers should also see "Sleeping in and near Arromanches," page 172.

Sleeping near the Tapestry

HIGHER PRICED
Hôtel le Lion d'Or*** is Bayeux's close-to-classy Old World hotel, with a palm tree–lined courtyard, easy parking, professional service, and an elegant restaurant (small Db-€83, Db-€111–130, Tb-€135–160, prices include buffet breakfast, CC, 71 rue St. Jean, tel. 02 31 92 06 90, fax 02 31 22 15 64, www.liondor-bayeux.fr).

MODERATELY PRICED
Le Maupassant Café has clean and well-furnished rooms over a café, and it's particularly good deal if you get a room without a bathroom (new owners might upgrade rooms and prices, S-€27, D-€35, Db-€57, Tb-€61, 19 rue St. Martin, tel. 02 31 92 28 53, fax 02 31 02 35 40).

LOWER PRICED
Hôtel le Bayeux**, run by amiable Monsieur Lamontagne, has long halls, bright colors, and clean, comfortable rooms at great rates (Db-€43–53, Tb-€56–66, Qb-€72, CC, a block from cathedral's right transept at 9 rue Tardif, CC, easy parking, tel. 02 31 92 70 08, fax 02 31 21 15 74).

Sleeping near place St. Patrice

These hotels, both an excellent value, are a 10-minute walk up rue St. Martin from the TI. Both are just off the big place St. Patrice (easy parking).

MODERATELY PRICED

Hôtel d'Argouges** greets travelers with a flowery courtyard and three-plus-star comfort at two-star prices. Every room is warmly decorated and meticulously cared for by the formal owners, M. and Mme. Ropartz. Named for its builder, Lord d'Argouges, this tranquil retreat has a château-like feel, with classy public lounges and a lovely private garden (Sb-€50, Db-€64–76, fine family suites-€90–125, deluxe megasuite-€190, extra bed-€15, CC, free parking, just off the huge place St. Patrice at 21 rue St. Patrice, tel. 02 31 92 88 86, fax 02 31 92 69 16, e-mail: dargouges@aol.com).

LOWER PRICED

Hôtel Mogador** is a sure two-star bet, with welcoming Monsieur Mencaroni at the helm. Choose between cozy wood-beamed rooms on the busy square or quiet, more modern rooms off the street (Sb-€37, Db-€42–47, Tb-€55, CC, good breakfast, 20 rue Alain Chartier/place St. Patrice, tel. 02 31 92 24 58, fax 02 31 92 24 85, SE).

Sleeping near the Station

LOWER PRICED

Desperate train travelers can bed down in the basic, simple rooms of the unpredictable **Hôtel de la Gare*** (D-€23, Db-€39, no CC, 26 place de la Gare, tel. 02 31 92 10 70, fax 02 31 51 95 99).

Eating in Bayeux

It's easy to dine inexpensively in Bayeux. The pedestrian rue St. Jean is lined with *crêperies*, simple restaurants, and the best charcuterie in town, **La Chaumière** (salads and quiches to go, across from Hôtel Churchill, open until 19:30). A short block off rue St. Jean, **La Table du Terroir** is run by a butcher, so meat is tops in this fun, traditional place where clients share monastic plank-tables (€11 lunch *menu*—no choice, dinner *menus* from €16, closed Sun–Mon, 42 rue St. Jean, tel. 02 31 92 05 53). A block farther up the rue St. Jean, the recommended **Hôtel le Lion d'Or** is where locals go for a special meal. Its big dining room is hunting-lodge elegant and accustomed to foreigners (*menus* at €21 and €31, closed Mon; see "Sleeping in Bayeux," above).

Several good places cluster near the cathedral. **Le Petit Bistro** is aptly named, with six intimate tables opposite the cathedral entry at 2 rue Bienvenue (*menus* from €19, closed Sun, tel. 02 31 51 85 40). **Le Pommier,** a block away, is an easygoing place with a good variety of reasonable choices served with ambience, inside or out (€9 *plats du jour, menus* from €12, closed Tue–Wed, 38 rue des Cuisiniers, tel. 02 31 21 52 10). Just below the cathedral, locals enjoy the *très* reasonable **Le Petit Normand** (*menus* from €14, daily, 21 rue Larcher, tel. 02 31 22 88 86).

Transportation Connections—Bayeux

By train to: Paris' St. Lazare (9/day, 2.5 hrs, 3 require change in Caen), **Amboise** (4/day, 5 hrs, change in Caen and Tours, or Paris Montparnasse and Tours-St. Pierre des Corps), **Rouen** (3/day, 3 hrs, change in Caen), **Caen** (10/day, 15 min), **Honfleur** (5/day, 2.5 hrs; train to Lisieux or Caen, then bus to Honfleur; trip is quicker via Caen; for bus information call 02 31 89 28 41), **Pontorson-Mont St. Michel** (2/day, 1 at about 7:45, the other at about 17:00, 2 hrs to Pontorson with bus to Mont St. Michel; see "Getting to Mont St. Michel," below).

By bus to the D-Day beaches: Bus Verts serves the area (TI has schedules, tel. 08 10 21 42 14), with stops in Bayeux at place St. Patrice and at the train station. Line #75 runs to Arromanches (3/day, 20 min), and line #70 serves the American Cemetery (2–4/day, 35 min). Bus Verts also runs a summer line.

D-DAY BEACHES

Along the 120 kilometers/75 miles of Atlantic coast north of Bayeux, stretching from Sainte Marie du Mont to Ouistreham, you'll find WWII museums, monuments, cemeteries, and battle remains left in tribute to the courage of the British, Canadian, and American armies who successfully carried out the largest military operation in history. It was on these beautiful beaches, at the crack of dawn, June 6, 1944, that the Allies finally gained a foothold in France and Nazi Europe began to crumble.

> *"The first 24 hours of the invasion will be decisive . . . the fate of Germany depends on the outcome . . . for the Allies, as well as Germany, it will be the longest day."*
> —Field Marshal Erwin Rommel to his aide,
> April 22, 1944. From *The Longest Day*.

Getting around the D-Day Beaches

On Your Own: A car is ideal, particularly for three or more people. If you have a railpass and an avid interest in World War II, consider stowing your railpass and renting a car for a day or two to do this area efficiently and properly (see Bayeux "Helpful Hints," above, for car and bike rental; the Bayeux TI has more information). Park in well-surveyed locations at the sights, as break-ins have been a problem, particularly at the American Cemetery. To mix in some exercise, you can also bike between the sights. Buses connect Bayeux, the coastal town of Arromanches, and the most impressive D-Day (*Jour J* in French) sights (see "Transportation Connections—Bayeux," above).

By Taxi: Taxi minivans shuttle up to seven people between the key sights at surprisingly fair rates. Prices per taxi (not per person) are: €16 from Bayeux to Arromanches, €32 round-trip with one-hour wait time; €27 from Bayeux to the American Cemetery, €45 round-trip with one-hour wait time; and €65 round-trip for the American Cemetery and Pointe du Hoc with two hours total wait time at the sights (other combinations possible, taxi tel. 02 31 92 92 40).

By Tour: Several companies offer excursions to the D-Day beaches from Bayeux or Caen (€31–35/4 hrs, €60–70/full day). These companies cover pretty much the same sights, though only the first two cover all the key sights I list: The **Caen Battle of Normandy Museum** offers tours of the D-Day beaches in combination with a visit to their museum (see "Sights—Caen," below). **D-Day Tours** has "licensed guides" and uses minivans and, if needed, €50-person buses for its tours (half-day departures from Bayeux daily at 8:30 and 13:30, tel. 02 31 51 70 52, fax 02 31 51 74 74, e-mail: francois.gauthron@wanadoo.fr). **Victory Tours** is Dutch-run, less formal and a bit cheaper, and uses minivans only (departs from Bayeux only, tel. 02 31 51 98 14, cellular 06 75 12 88 28, fax 02 31 51 07 01, www.lignerolles.homestead.com). **Salient Tours** advertises "expert British guides" and offers 9:00 departures from Caen and 14:30 departures from Bayeux (each lasts 3.5 hrs); the Caen departures cover only the British sector (including Arromanches), while Bayeux departures cover only the American sector (tel. 06 76 38 96 89).

60th Anniversary: In June 2004, the region will celebrate the 60th anniversary of the landings. The celebration will bring, along with more festivities, more congestion. If you're planning a visit then, book a hotel well in advance.

Sights—Caen

▲▲▲**Caen's Battle of Normandy Museum (Le Memorial)**— Caen (pron. kah), the modern capital of lower Normandy, has the best WWII museum in France. Officially named the Memorial for Peace (le Memorial), it effectively puts the Battle of Normandy in a broader context. Your visit has five parts: the lead-up to World War II, the actual Battle of Normandy, two video presentations,

D-Day Beaches

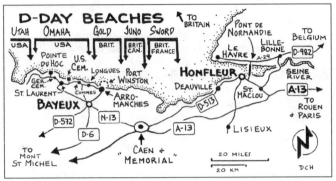

the Cold War, and the ongoing fight for peace (Nobel Prize Gallery and Peace Gardens).

The museum is brilliant. Begin with a downward spiral stroll, tracing (almost psychoanalyzing) the path Europe followed from the end of World War I to the rise of fascism to World War II.

The lower level gives a thorough look at how World War II was fought—from General de Gaulle's London radio broadcasts to Hitler's early missiles to wartime fashion to the D-Day landings.

The new Cold War wing gives a fine overview of the bipolar world that followed World War II, with fascinating insights into the battle waged by the USSR and the United States for the hearts and minds of their people until the fall of Communism.

You then see two powerful movies. *Jour J (D-Day)* is a 30-minute film showing the build-up to D-Day, the day itself, and the successful campaign from there to Berlin (every 40 min from 10:00 to 19:00, works in any language, pick up schedule as you enter). While snippets of the footage come from the movie *The Longest Day*, most of it consists of actual battle scenes. The second movie, *Esperance (Hope)*, is a thrilling sweep through the pains and triumphs of the 20th century (plays on the half-hour, 20 min, also good in all languages).

The memorial then takes you beyond World War II, where the Gallery of Nobel Peace Prizes celebrates the irrepressible human spirit. It honors the courageous and too-often-inconspicuous work of people like Andrei Sakharov, Elie Wiesel, and Desmond Tutu, who understand that peace is more than an absence of war.

The finale is a walk through the U.S. Armed Forces Memorial Garden. I was bothered by the mindless laughing of lighthearted children unable to appreciate their blessings. Then I read on the pavement: "From the heart of our land flows the blood of our youth, given to you in the name of freedom." And their laughter made me happy.

Cost and Hours: €16 (free for all veterans and kids under 10). The museum is open daily from 9:00 to 19:00 (until 20:00 mid-July–Aug, closes at 18:00 Nov–Feb, ticket office closes 75 min before museum, tel. 02 31 06 06 44—as in June 6, 1944, fax 02 31 06 01 66, www.memorial-caen.fr).

Allow a minimum of 2.5 hours for your visit, including an hour for videos; no guided tours are available. Free supervised babysitting is offered for children under 10 (for whom the exhibits are too graphic).

Tours: The museum runs seven-person minivan guided tours of the D-Day beaches. Tours include entry to Caen's Battle of Normandy Museum and four-hour tours of the D-Day beaches, including Longues-sur-Mer, Arromanches, Omaha Beach, American Cemetery, and Pointe du Hoc (€55 for morning departure, €67 for afternoon departure, both cover same sights, afternoon tour is a bit longer, daily departures April–Sept at 9:00 and 14:00, Oct–March at 13:00 only, contact Caen Museum for details and to reserve and pay in advance, CC, www.memorial-caen.fr/circuits).

Getting to Museum: Finding the memorial is quick and easy for drivers. It's just off the ring-road freeway *(périphérique nord)* in Caen *(sortie* #7, look for signs to Memorial). By train, Caen is two hours from Paris (€14/day) and 15 minutes from Bayeux (€10/day). To get to the memorial from Caen's train station, take bus #17-Memorial (exit right out of station, second shelter, buses every 20 min, or taxi-€9 one-way).

The City of Caen: WWII bombs destroyed most of the city. But today's Caen (population 115,000) bristles with confidence, students, and a well-restored old city. The **TI** is on place St. Pierre, 10 blocks across the canal from the train station (June–Sept Mon–Sat 9:00–19:00, Sun 9:00–17:00; Oct–May Mon–Sat 9:00–13:00 & 14:00–19:00, Sun 9:00–13:00 & 14:00–17:00, from the station, walk up avenue du 6 Juin, tel. 02 31 27 14 14). The looming château and pedestrian streets are within a few blocks of the TI. **Hôtel de France****, a three-minute walk from the station, has plain but sleepable rooms (Db-€42–50, CC, 10 rue de la Gare, turn right out of station, right on first main street, and you'll see signs, tel. 02 31 52 16 99, fax 02 31 83 23 16).

ARROMANCHES

This small town was ground zero for the D-Day invasion. Almost overnight, it sprouted the immense Port Winston, enabling the Allies to establish a foothold in Normandy from which to begin their victorious push to Berlin to end World War II. Today, you'll find a fine museum, an evocative beach and bluff, and a delightful little town offering a pleasant cocktail of war memories, cotton candy, and beachfront trinket shops. The **TI** is across the parking lot from the museum on rue Colonel Rene Michel (daily 10:00–12:00 & 14:00–18:00, longer hours in summer, tel. 02 31 21 47 56, www.arromanches.com). The population of tiny Arromanches just reached 500 people (about the same as on June 6, 1944). There's a supermarket (above the town by the parking lot), a post office, and an ATM (near the museum). Arromanches and Bayeux are connected by five buses a day in the summer, two a day off-season (30-min ride). To get a taxi, you'll need to call one in Bayeux (tel. 02 31 92 92 40). For accommodations, see "Sleeping in Arromanches," below.

Sights—Arromanches

▲▲**Port Winston and the D-Day Landing Museum (Musée du Débarquement)**—The first-ever prefab harbor was created by the British in Arromanches. Since it was Churchill's brainchild, it was named Port Winston. Walk along the seafront promenade and imagine the building of this port. Seventeen old ships, which crossed the English Channel under their own steam and were sunk by their crews bow to stern, formed the first shelter. Then 115 football-field–size cement blocks (called Mulberries) were towed across the channel and sunk. This created a four-mile-long break-water 1.5 miles off shore—a port the size of Dover. Then, seven floating steel "pierheads" with extendable legs were set up and linked to shore by four mile-long floating roads made of concrete pontoons. Antiaircraft guns were set up on the pontoons. Within six days, 54,000 vehicles, 326,000 troops, and 110,000 tons of goods had been delivered. An Allied toehold on Normandy was secure. Eleven months later, Hitler was dead and the war was over.

The D-Day Landing Museum, which faces the still-visible remains of the temporary harbor, provides an instructive hour to those interested. With models, maps, mementos, and two short audiovisual shows, this low-tech exhibit tells the story of this incredible undertaking. One video (7 min, ground floor) recalls D-Day. The other (13 min, upstairs) features the construction of the temporary port—ask for English times (€6, pick up English flier at door, daily May–Aug 9:00–19:00, April and Sept 9:00–18:00, Oct–Dec and Feb–March 9:30–12:30 & 13:30–17:00, closed Jan, tel. 02 31 22 34 31).

Hike 10 minutes to the top of the bluff behind the museum for the view (€1.50 to park if you came by car) and ponder how, from this makeshift harbor, the liberation of Europe commenced. *The Price of Freedom* offers D-Day footage in a noisy montage of videos on its 360-degree screen (€3.75, 2 showings/hr, last at 18:40, 20 min).

But the most thought-provoking experience in town is simply to wander the beach among the concrete and rusted litter of the battle, and be thankful that all you hear are birds and surf.

Sights—Near Arromanches

Longues-sur-Mer—Several German bunkers, guns intact, are left guarding against seaborne attacks on the city of Arromanches (€5 booklet is helpful, skip the €4 tour). Walk to the observation post for a great view over the channel (located between Arromanches and Port en Bessin; turn right at signal in Longues-sur-Mer). You can drive right down to the water by continuing down the small road past the parking lot.

▲▲▲**American Cemetery at St. Laurent**—Crowning a bluff just above Omaha Beach and the eye of the D-Day storm, nearly 10,000 brilliant white-marble crosses and Stars of David glow in memory of Americans who gave their lives to free Europe on the beaches below.

First, stop by the Visitors' Office to pick up an English information sheet. Read the 1956 letter from the French president (on the wall above the fireplace), which eloquently expresses the feeling of gratitude the French still have for the United States. The attendant at the computer terminal has a database providing ready access to the story of any serviceman who died in Normandy.

Walk past the memorial and cemetery to the bluff overlooking the piece of Normandy beach called "that embattled shore—portal of freedom." It's quiet and peaceful today, but imagine the horrific carnage of June 6, 1944.

Walk back to the memorial, where you'll see giant reliefs of the Battle for Normandy and the Battle for Europe etched on the walls. Behind that is the semicircular Garden of the Missing, with the names of 1,557 soldiers who were never found.

Finally, wander among the peaceful and poignant sea of crosses. Notice the names, home states, and dates of death inscribed on each. Immediately after the war, all the dead were buried in temporary cemeteries. In the mid-1950s, the families of the soldiers decided if they should remain with their comrades or be brought home. Officers are disproportionately left here. Their families knew they'd want to be buried with the men they fought and died with.

France has given the United States permanent free use of this 172-acre site. It is immaculately maintained by the American Battle Monuments Commission (free, open daily 9:00–17:00, park carefully, break-ins have been a problem here).

German Military Cemetery—To ponder German losses, drop by this somber, thought-provoking resting place of 21,000 German soldiers. While the American Cemetery is the focus of American visitors, visitors here speak in hushed German. The site is glum, with two graves per simple marker and dark crosses that huddle together in groups of five. It's just south of Pointe du Hoc (right off N-13 in village of La Cambe, 22 km/13.5 miles west of Bayeux; follow signs to *Cimetiére Allemand*).

▲▲**Pointe du Hoc**—During the D-Day invasion, 225 U.S. rangers attempted a castle-style assault of the German-occupied cliffs by using grappling hooks and ladders borrowed from London fire departments. Only 90 survived. German bunkers and bomb craters remain as they were found (20 min by car west of American Cemetery in St. Laurent, just past Vierville-sur-Mer). A museum dedicated to the rangers is in nearby Grandcamp-Maisy.

Sleeping in and near Arromanches, near the D-Day Beaches
(€1 = about $1, country code: 33)

Sleeping in Arromanches
Arromanches, with its pinwheels and seagulls, has a salty beach-town ambience that makes it a good overnight stop. For evening fun, try the cheery bar at **Pappagall Hôtel d'Arromanches** or, for a more nightclub scene, have a drink at the **Pub Marie Celeste**, around the corner on rue de la Poste.

MODERATELY PRICED
Friendly **Pappagall Hôtel d'Arromanches**** is a good value, with nine smartly appointed rooms, tight stairways and halls, a fun bar, and a cheery restaurant (Db-€57, Tb-€78–85, 10 percent more July–Aug—Db-€64, includes breakfast, 2 rue Colonel Rene Michel, 14117 Arromanches, tel. 02 31 22 36 26, fax 02 31 22 23 29, e-mail: hoteldarromanche@ifrance.com).

Hôtel de la Marine** is less welcoming but offers beach views from most of its 28 comfy rooms and from its elegant restaurant (Db-€71, Tb-€76, Qb-€118, €10 less without a sea view, family rooms-€85–116, CC, restaurant *menus* from €15, quai du Canada, tel. 02 31 22 34 19, fax 02 31 22 98 80, e-mail: hotel.de.la.marine@wanadoo.fr).

Sleeping near Arromanches
Chambres d'hôte litter the coast (the TIs in Bayeux and Arromanches have long lists).

HIGHER PRICED

For a refined yet still rural experience, find la **Ferme de la Ranconnière****, a well-restored, 13th-century fortified manor home five kilometers/three miles southeast of Arromanches near the hamlet of Crepon. You'll find 35 rooms and oodles of character, wood beams, and stone. Half pension is required, but the meal is fine and you're in the middle of nowhere anyway (half pension €54–84 per person, price range corresponds to the size of the room, CC, Route d'Arromanches, tel. 02 31 22 21 73, fax 02 31 22 98 39, www.ranconniere.com).

MODERATELY PRICED

Consider the almost mystical **Château du Bosq** in Commes. Seven kilometers/four miles from Bayeux, this *très* rustic, 700-year-old château comes with turrets, a water-filled moat, a peaceful restaurant, and minimally decorated rooms. It's quiet: no TV, no phones, no noise, no kidding (Db-€46–76, extra bed-€11, between Arromanches and American Cemetery, 14520 Commes, tel. 02 31 92 52 77, fax 02 31 92 26 71).

LOWER PRICED

It's worth the effort to track down **Andre and Madeleine Sebires'** working farmhouse, with four homey and cheap rooms and a pleasant garden. It's in tiny Ryes (between Bayeux and Arromanches) at the Ferme du Clos Neuf—and tough to find. Try these directions from Arromanches: Take D-87, enter Ryes and pass the church on the left; then, at first junction, turn right onto rue de la Forge (look for the faded *Chambres* signs) and continue until you cross a tiny bridge. Turn right just after the bridge onto rue de la Triangle and follow small sign on right to Le Clos Neuf. If the Sebires prove too elusive, call from Ryes, and they'll come get you (Sb-€26, Db-€32, Tb-€40, includes breakfast, zip code: 14400, tel. 02 31 22 32 34, NSE).

MONT ST. MICHEL

For over a thousand years, the distant silhouette of this island-abbey sent pilgrims' spirits soaring. Today, it does the same for tourists. Mont St. Michel, which through the ages has been among the top four pilgrimage sites in Christendom, floats like a mirage on the horizon, though it does show up on film. Today, 2.5 million visitors—far more tourists than pilgrims—flood the single street of the tiny island each year.

Orientation

Mont St. Michel is connected by a three-kilometer/two-mile causeway to the mainland and surrounded by a vast mudflat. Your visit

Mont St. Michel Area

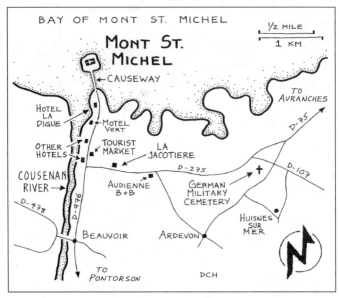

features a one-street village that winds up to the fortified abbey. Between 10:00 and 16:00, tourists trample the dreamscape (as earnest pilgrims did 800 years ago). A ramble on the ramparts offers mudflat views and an escape from the tourist zone. While four tacky history-in-wax museums tempt hiking visitors, the only worthwhile entry is the abbey itself, at the summit of the island.

Daytime Mont St. Michel is a touristy gauntlet—worth a stop, but a short one will do. The tourist tide recedes late each afternoon. On nights from autumn through spring, the island stands serene—its floodlit abbey towering above a sleepy village.

Arrive late and depart early if you can. The abbey interior should be open until midnight from May through September (off-season until 22:00). To avoid the human traffic jam on the main drag, follow the detour path up or down the mount described below under "The Village below the Abbey."

Tourist Information: The overwhelmed TI (and WC) is to your left as you enter Mont St. Michel's gates. They have *chambres d'hôte* (B&Bs on the nearby mainland) listings, English tour times for the abbey, bus schedules, and the tide table *(Horaires des Marées)*, which is essential if you plan to explore the mudflats outside Mont St. Michel (daily July–Aug 9:00–19:00, Sept–Oct and April–June 9:00–12:30 & 14:00–18:30, Nov–March until 17:30, tel. 02 33 60 14 30, www.manchetourisme.com). A post office (PTT) and ATM are 50 meters/165 feet beyond the TI.

Tides: The tides here rise over 15 meters/50 feet—the largest and most dangerous in Europe. During a flood tide, the ocean rushes in at 12 miles per hour. High tides *(grandes marées)* lap against the tourist-office door (where you'll find tide hours posted).

Parking: Park in the pay parking lot near the base of the island. Very high tides rise to the edge of the causeway—leaving the causeway open, but any cars parked below it underwater. Safe parking is available at the foot of Mont St. Michel (€3); you will be instructed where to park under high-tide conditions. There's plenty of parking, except midday in high season. Jot down your parking sector and plan on a 10-minute walk to the island from your car.

Sights—Mont St. Michel

These sights are listed in the order you approach them from the mainland.

The Bay of Mont St. Michel—The vast Bay of Mont St. Michel, which turns into a mudflat at low tide, has long played a key role here. Since the sixth century, hermit monks in search of solitude lived here. The word "hermit" comes from an ancient Greek word meaning "desert." The next best thing to a desert in this part of Europe was the sea. Imagine the "desert" this bay provided as the first monk climbed the rock to get close to God. Add to that the mythic tide—sending the surf speeding eight miles in and out with each tide cycle. Long before the causeway was built, when le Mont was an island, pilgrims would approach across the mudflat aware that the tide swept in "at the speed of a galloping horse" (well, maybe a slow horse . . . 12 miles/hr, or about 2 feet/second).

Quicksand was another peril. But the real danger for adventurers today is the thoroughly disorienting fog and the fact that the sea can encircle unwary hikers. (Bring a cell phone.) Braving these devilish risks, for centuries pilgrims kept their eyes on the spire crowned by their protector, St. Michael, and eventually reached their spiritual goal.

The Causeway—In 1878, a causeway was built, letting pilgrims come and go without hip boots, regardless of the tide. While this increased the flow of visitors, it stopped the flow of water around the island. The result: This part of the bay has silted up, and Mont St. Michel is no longer an island. A new bridge will be built in the next few years, allowing the water to circulate—so Mont St. Michel will once again be an island (with a shuttle bus or train to zip visitors between the island and a distant car park).

The Village below the Abbey—Mont St. Michel's main street

(Grand rue)—lined with shops and hotels leading to the abbey—
is grotesquely touristy. It is some consolation to remember that,
even in the Middle Ages, this was a commercial gauntlet, with
stalls selling souvenir medallions, candles, and fast food. With
only 30 full-time residents, the village lives solely for tourists.
After the TI, check the tide warnings posted on the wall and pass
through the imposing doors. Before the drawbridge, on your left,
peek through the door of Restaurant le Mère Poulard. The original Madame Poulard (the maid of an abbey architect who married
the village baker) made quick and tasty omelettes here. They were
popular for pilgrims who needed to beat the tide to get out in pre-
causeway days and—even at the rip-off price of €23—they're a hit
with tourists today. Pop in for a minute, just to enjoy the show as
old-time-costumed cooks beat omelettes, daddy, eight to the bar.

As you pass through the old drawbridge, you hit the main
(and only) street and begin your trudge through the crowds uphill past several gimmicky museums to the abbey (all island hotel
receptions are located on this street). Or, if the abbey's your goal,
you can miss the crowds by climbing the first steps on your right
after the drawbridge and following the ramparts in either direction up and up to the abbey (quieter if you go right). Public WCs
are next to the TI, halfway up, and at the abbey entrance. You
can attend Mass at the tiny St. Pierre church (Thu and Sun at
11:00, opposite Hôtel la Vielle Auberge).

▲▲**Abbey of Mont St. Michel**—Mont St. Michel has been an
important pilgrimage center since A.D. 708, when the bishop of
Avranches heard the voice of Archangel Michael saying, "build
here and build high." With brilliant foresight, Michael reassured
the bishop, "If you build it . . . they will come." Today's abbey is
built on the remains of a Romanesque church, which was built on
the remains of a Carolingian church. Saint Michael, whose gilded
statue decorates the top of the spire, was the patron saint of many
French kings, making this a favored sight for French royalty
through the ages. St. Michael was particularly popular in Counter-
Reformation times, as the Church employed his warlike image in
the fight against Protestant heresy.

While this abbey has 1,200 years of history, much of its
story was lost when its archives were taken to St. Lo for safety
during World War II—only to be destroyed during the D-Day
fighting. As you climb the stairs, imagine the pilgrims and
monks who for centuries have worn down the edges of these
same stone steps.

Tour the abbey following a one-way route. Keep climbing to
the ticket booths and turnstile. Then climb some more, passing a
public WC and a room with interesting models of the abbey

Mont St. Michel

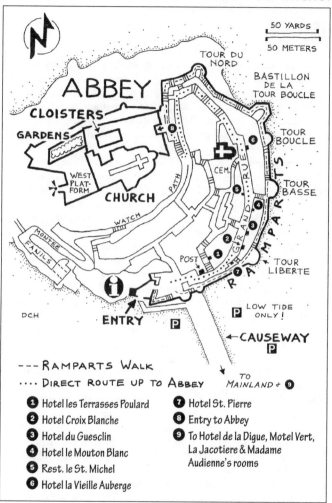

50 YARDS
50 METERS

TOUR DU NORD

BASTILLON DE LA TOUR BOUCLE

ABBEY

CLOISTERS

GARDENS

TOUR BOUCLE

WEST PLAT-FORM

CHURCH

CEM

TOUR BASSE

WATCH PATH

MONTÉE FANILS

GRAND RUE

POST

RAMPARTS

TOUR LIBERTE

ENTRY

DCH

LOW TIDE ONLY!

CAUSEWAY

TO MAINLAND & ⑨

- - - RAMPARTS WALK
..... DIRECT ROUTE UP TO ABBEY

① Hotel les Terrasses Poulard
② Hotel Croix Blanche
③ Hotel du Guesclin
④ Hotel le Mouton Blanc
⑤ Rest. le St. Michel
⑥ Hotel la Vieille Auberge

⑦ Hotel St. Pierre
⑧ Entry to Abbey
⑨ To Hotel de la Digue, Motel Vert, La Jacotiere & Madame Audienne's rooms

through the ages and a guides' desk (posting the time of the next tour), and finally to the...

West Terrace: A fire destroyed the west end of the church in 1776, leaving this fine view terrace. The original extent of the church can be seen in the pavement stones (as well as the stonecutter numbers, generally not exposed like this—a reminder that they were paid by the piece). The buildings of Mont St. Michel are made of granite stones quarried from the Isles of Chausey (visible on a clear day, 32 kilometers/20 miles away). Tidal power was ingeniously harnessed to load, unload, and even transport the stones as barges hitched a ride with each incoming tide.

As you survey the Bay of Mont St. Michel, notice the polder land—farmland reclaimed by Normans in the 19th century with the help of Dutch engineers. The lines of trees mark strips of land used in the process. Today, this reclaimed land is covered by salt-loving plants and grazed by sheep whose salty meat is considered a local treat. You're standing 73 meters/240 feet above sea level at the summit of what was an island called "the big tomb." The small island just farther out is "the little tomb."

Survey the bay stretching from Normandy to Brittany. The river below marks the historic border between the two lands. Brittany and Normandy have long vied for Mont St. Michel. In fact, the river used to pass Mont St. Michel on the other side, making the abbey part of Brittany. Today, it's just barely—but thoroughly—part of Normandy. Now head back into the...

Abbey Church: Sit on a pew near the front of the church, under the little statue of the archangel St. Michael (with the spear to defeat dragons and evil, and the scales to evaluate your soul). Monks built as close to heaven as possible, on the tip of this rock. The downside: not enough level ground to support a sizable abbey and church. The solution: Four immense crypts were built under the church to create a platform supporting each of its wings. While most of the church is Romanesque (round arches, 11th century), the apse behind the altar was built later and is Gothic (and, therefore, is filled with much more light). In 1421, the crypt that supported the apse collapsed, taking its end of the church with it. Almost none of the original windows survive (victims of fires, storms, lightning, and the Revolution). Just outside the church, you'll find the...

Cloisters: A standard feature of an abbey, this was the peaceful zone connecting various rooms where monks could tend their gardens (food and herbs for medicine), meditate, and read the Bible. The great view window is enjoyable today (what's the tide doing?), but it was of no use to the monks. The more secluded a monk could be, the closer he was to God. (A cloister, by definition, is an enclosed place.) Notice the carved frieze featuring various plants, heightening the Garden-of-Eden ambience the cloister offered the monks. The statues of various saints carved among the columns were defaced—literally—by French Revolutionary troops. Continue on the tour to the...

Refectory: This was the dining hall where the monks consumed both food and the word of God in silence, as one read in a monotone voice from the Bible (pulpit on the right near the far end). The monks gathered as a family here in one undivided space under one big arch—an impressive engineering feat in its day. The abbot ate at the head table. Guests sat at the table in the middle. The clever columns are thin but very deep, offering maximum support while allowing in maximum light. From 966 until 2001, this was a Benedictine abbey. In 2001, the last three Benedictine monks checked out and a new order of monks from Paris took over. Stairs lead down to the...

Guests' Hall: St. Benedict wrote that guests should be welcomed according to their status. That meant that when the king (or other VIPs) visited, they were wined and dined without a hint of monastic austerity. This room was once brilliantly painted, with gold stars on a blue sky across the ceiling and a floor of glazed red and green tiles—all bathed in glorious sunlight made divine as it passed through a filter of stained glass. The painting of this room was said to be the model for Sainte-Chapelle in Paris. The big double fireplace served as a kitchen—kept out of sight by hanging tapestries. Hike the stairs to the...

Hall of the Grand Pillars: As the huge abbey was perched on a pointy rock, four sturdy crypts like this were built to prop it up. You're standing under the Gothic portion of the abbey church. This was the crypt that collapsed in 1421. Notice the immensity of the columns (4.5 meters/15 feet around) in the new crypt—rebuilt with a determination not to fall again. To see what kind of crypt collapsed, walk on to the...

Crypt of St. Martin: This simple, 11th-century, Romanesque vault has only a tiny window for light, since the walls needed to be solid and fat to support the buildings above. Next, you'll find the...

Ossuary (identifiable by its big tread-wheel): The monks celebrated death as well as life. This part of the abbey housed the hospital, morgue, and ossuary. Because the abbey graveyard was small, it was routinely emptied, and the bones were stacked here.

During the Revolution, monasticism was abolished and the church property was taken by the atheistic government. From 1793 to 1863, Mont St. Michel was used as an Alcatraz-type prison—its first inmates were 300 priests who refused to renounce their vows. (Victor Hugo complained that using such a place as a prison was like keeping a toad in a reliquary.) The big tread-wheel—the kind that did heavy lifting for big building projects throughout the Middle Ages—is from the decades when the abbey was a prison. Teams of six prisoners marched two abreast—hamster-style—in the wheel, powering two-ton loads of stone and supplies up Mont St. Michel. Spin the rollers of the sled next to the wheel. Look down the steep ramp. While you're here, notice the parking lot and crowds below. When the tide is very high, careless drivers can become carless drivers. A few years ago, a Scottish bus driver (oblivious to the time and tide but very busy in a hotel room) lost his bus...destroyed by a salty bath. Local police tethered it to the lot so it wouldn't float away. Finish your visit walking through the Promenade of the Monks, under more Gothic vaults, through the shop, past an impressive model of the spire-crowning statue of St. Michael, and down into the garden. From here, look up at the marvel of medieval engineering.

The "Merveille": This was an immense building project—a marvel back in 1220. Three levels of buildings were created—one for security, one for feasting, and one for serenity. It was a medieval skyscraper, built to support the cloisters at church level. (Remember looking out of those top windows earlier?) The vision was even grander. The place where you're standing was to be built up in similar fashion to support a further expansion of the church. But the money ran out, and the project was abandoned. Stairs lead from here back into the village. But to avoid the human traffic jam, once you hit the stairs you climbed on your way up, scale a few stairs on your left (marked *Chemin des Ramparts*), turn right, and hike down via the...

Ramparts: Mont St. Michel is ringed by a fine example of 15th-century fortifications. They were built to defend against a new weapon—the cannon. Rather than tall, they were low—to make a smaller target—and connected by protected passageways, enabling soldiers to zip quickly to whichever zone was under attack. The five-sided Boucle Tower (1481) is designed with no blind angles, so defenders can protect it and the nearby walls in all directions. While the English took all of Normandy, they never took this well-fortified island. Mont St. Michel, for its stubborn success against the English in the Hundred Years' War, became a symbol of French national identity.

Cost and Hours: €7 entry (mid-May–mid-Sept daily 9:00–18:30, spring and fall 9:30–17:00, closes at 16:00 in winter, ticket office closes 60 min earlier, abbey may be open summer eves—see "Evening Visits," below, tel. 02 33 89 80 00). Buy your ticket to the abbey and keep climbing. Allow 20 minutes to climb at a steady pace from the TI. You'll find no English explanations in the abbey. You can rent an **audioguide** (€4, €5.50 for two) or take the 75-minute English-language **tour** (free, tip requested, 4–6 tours/day, first tour usually at 10:00, last at 17:00, confirm tour times at TI, meet at top terrace in front of church, groups can be large).

Evening Visits: These might not be continued in 2003. If they are offered, the abbey will be open on summer evenings (except Sun): Specifically, the gardens are open 19:00 to 21:00, and the abbey interior is open from 21:00 to 24:00. With lasers, mood music, and videos, it's like a self-guided sound-and-light show. The €9 entry includes the garden and abbey; arrive at about 20:30 and do both (Mon–Sat in July–Aug, Fri–Sat only in Sept).

After dark, the island is magically floodlit. Views from the ramparts are sublime. For the best view, exit the island and walk out on the causeway a few hundred meters.

▲▲**Stroll around Mont St. Michel**—To resurrect that Mont St. Michel dreamscape and evade all those tacky tourist stalls, you can walk out on the mudflats around the island. At low tide, it's reasonably dry and a great memory. This can be extremely dangerous, so be sure to double-check the tides. Remember the scene from the Bayeux tapestry where Harold rescues Normans from the quicksand? It happened somewhere in this bay. You may notice groups hiking in from the muddy horizon. The tourist office advises against going out at all. Attempting this without a local guide is reckless.

Sights—Near Mont St. Michel

German Military Cemetery (Cimetière Militaire Allemand)— Located five kilometers/three miles from Mont St. Michel near tiny Huisnes-sur-Mer, this somber but thoughtfully presented cemetery/mortuary houses the remains of 12,000 German soldiers and offers insight into their lives with letters they sent home (English translations). From the lookout, there are sensational views over Mont St. Michel.

Sleeping on or near Mont St. Michel
(€1 = about $1, country code: 33, zip code: 50116)

Sleeping on the island, inside the walls, is the best way to experience Mont St. Michel, though drivers should also consider the *chambres d'hôtes* listed below. There are eight small hotels on the island, three of which are family-run with a greater interest in your stay. Many hotels feel tired, and their staffs seem burned out. While some pad their profits by *requesting* guests to buy dinner from their restaurant, requiring it is illegal. Several are closed from November until Easter. Because most visitors only day-trip here, finding a room is generally no problem.

Hotels on Mont St. Michel

When a price range is given for rooms, the higher-priced rooms generally have bay views.

HIGHER PRICED

Hôtel les Terrasses Poulard***, 50 meters/165 feet after the TI, rents the most polished and overpriced rooms on the island (Db-€105–170, CC, tel. 02 33 60 14 09, fax 02 33 60 37 31).

MODERATELY PRICED

The following hotels are listed in order of altitude (the first are lowest on the island and closest to parking).

Hôtels St. Pierre and Croix Blanche***, owned by the same company, sit side by side, each with comfortable rooms, some with good views. St. Pierre is more polished, with a good breakfast buffet; Croix Blanche has an Internet station (Db€-84–105, Tb-€120, Qb-€120–150, CC, tel. 02 33 60 14 03, fax 02 33 48 59 82).

Hôtel du Guesclin** is family-run and *très* traditional, with a well-respected restaurant and good, clean rooms at competitive rates, but comes with a thoroughly disagreeable owner whose retirement is overdue (Db-€43–72, Tb-€84, CC, tel. 02 33 60 14 10, fax 02 33 60 45 81).

Hôtel le Mouton Blanc** is company-owned, but has decent, generally cozy rooms and a young, helpful staff (Db-€66, Tb/Qb-€82–98, CC, tel. 02 33 60 14 08, fax 02 33 60 05 62).

Restaurant le St. Michel, across from Hôtel le Mouton Blanc, rents six rooms in a nearby annex and is the best budget value on the island. It's run by lighthearted Patricia, Philippe, and Freddo, all of whom speak English (Db-€47–57, CC, no dinner requirements but a good restaurant, tel. & fax 02 33 60 14 37, www.lesaintmichelridel.com).

Vieille Auberge** is family-run by entrepreneurial Nadine (SE) and her Old World mother-in-law, Madame. Their rooms are among the best for the price, and the four rooms with large view terraces are my pick for the island—but don't let Madame talk you into more room than you need (Db-€55, Db with view-€65, my favorite Db with view and terrace-€100, extra bed-€16, CC, tel. 02 33 60 14 34, fax 02 33 70 87 04).

Sleeping on the Mainland

Modern hotels gather at the mainland end of the causeway, offering soulless but cheaper rooms with easy parking and many tour groups. The Motel Vert (see below) rents bikes, offering easy access to the island.

MODERATELY PRICED

The friendly **Hôtel de la Digue***** is the best and most convenient place to stay. Most rooms are spacious and well-equipped (ask for a room with private terrace on the riverside: *chambre avec petit balcon sur la Couesnon*). You can dine with a partial view of Mont St. Michel at their restaurant (small Db-€61–66, spacious Db-€72–80, Tb-€84, Qb-€95, CC, good breakfast-€8.50, tel. 02 33 60 14 02, fax 02 33 60 37 59, www.ladigue.fr). From here, it's a wonderful 20-minute walk to Mont St. Michel.

Motel Vert is close, huge (112 rooms), and cheap (Db-€40–78, CC, bike rental, tel. 02 33 60 09 33, fax 02 33 60 20 02).

Chambres d'Hôte
Simply great values, these converted farmhouses are near the village of Ardevon, a few minutes' drive from the island toward Avranches.

LOWER PRICED
Charming Madame Brault's stone farmhouse, **La Jacotière**, is closest (walkable to the causeway), with six immaculate, modern rooms and great views of Mont St. Michel from her picnic-perfect garden (Db-€38, studio with view-€42, extra bed-€10, CC, tel. 02 33 60 22 94, fax 02 33 60 20 48, e-mail: la.jacotiere@wanadoo.fr, SE).

About 1.5 kilometers/1 mile farther away from Mont St. Michel, you'll find equally charming **Madame Audienne**'s stone farmhouse, with two wings (each with five rooms). Like Mama, the older wing feels a wee bit tired, but has more character; and like daughter Estelle (SE), the modern wing is young and bright (spacious, tiled rooms with modern facilities). Most rooms have good views of Mont St. Michel, better from Estelle's wing (Sb-€25, Db-€35, Tb/Qb-€45, includes breakfast, no CC, tel. & fax 02 33 48 28 89).

Sleeping in Pontorson
(€1 = about $1, country code: 33, zip code: 51170)
Train travelers could sleep in dismal Pontorson, a 15-minute drive from Mont St. Michel.

LOWER PRICED
Hôtel Vauban**, across from the train station, is quiet and comfortable (D-€31, Db-€38–49, Tb-€52, 2 boulevard Clemenceau, tel. 02 33 60 03 84, fax 02 33 60 35 48).

Eating on Mont St. Michel
Puffy omelettes *(omelette Montoise)* are the island's specialty. Also look for mussels (best with *crème fraîche*) and seafood platters, locally raised lamb (a saltwater-grass diet gives the meat a unique taste), and Muscadet wine (dry, cheap, and white).

Patricia and Phillipe run the lighthearted and reasonable **Le St. Michel** (good omelettes and mussels, tel. 02 33 60 14 37), across from Hôtel le Mouton Blanc. The recommended **Hôtel du Guesclin**'s upstairs restaurant is understandably popular. For lunch, try the *moules à la crème fraîche* (mussels with cream) at the recommended **Hôtel la Vieille Auberge** (closes at 19:00). The tourist *supermarché*, on the mainland near Hôtel de la Digue, has what you need for a romantic picnic (daily 8:30–20:00), though you can buy sandwiches, salads, and drinks to go on the island. Picnic in the small park below the abbey (to the left as you look up at the abbey).

Transportation Connections— Mont St. Michel

The nearest train station is in **Pontorson** (called Pontorson-Mont St. Michel), with an easy bus connection to Mont St. Michel (6 buses/day, 16/day in summer, 15 min). Most trains that arrive in Pontorson are met by a bus waiting to take passengers on to Mont St. Michel (winter evening trains may not have a bus connection; call Couriers Bretons for all bus information in this region—tel. 02 99 19 70 70). Taxis from Pontorson to Mont St. Michel (or vice versa) cost about €14 (€20 after 19:00 and on weekends/holidays, try to share a cab, taxi tel. 02 33 60 26 89).

Four daily buses also run directly between Mont St. Michel and **Rennes** (1.75 hrs), with connections to many destinations.

By bus and train via Rennes to: Paris (catch bus to Rennes—see above, then train to Paris—4/day, 4 hrs, TGV), **Dinan** (catch bus to Rennes, then train to **Dinan**—2/day, 4 hrs, transfer in Dol).

By bus and train via Pontorson to: Paris (catch bus to Pontorson—see above, then train to Paris—2/day, 5 hrs, transfer in Caen or Rennes), **Bayeux** (2 trains/day, 2.5 hrs), **Dinan** (3 trains/day, 2 hrs, transfer in Dol), **St. Malo** (3/day, 1.5 hrs, transfer in Dol), **Amboise** (4/day, 7 hrs, transfers in Caen and Tours' main station).

By bus from Mont St. Michel to: St. Malo (2–3/day, 75 min direct).

BRITTANY

The Couesnon River, just west of Mont St. Michel, marks the border between Normandy and Brittany. The peninsula of Brittany is rugged, with an isolated interior, a well-discovered coast, strong Celtic ties, and a passion for crêpes (which they call *galettes*) and *cidre* (alcoholic apple cider served in bowls). This region of independent-minded locals is linguistically and culturally quite different from Normandy and, for that matter, the rest of France.

In 1491, Brittany's Duchess Anne was forced to marry the French king, and Brittany became part of France—allowing France to overcome the independence of this feisty province. Brittany lost its freedom but, with Anne as queen, gained certain rights (such as free roads—even today, 500 years later, Brittany highways come with no tolls...unique in France).

As you wander, notice the pride locals take in their Breton culture. For instance, music stores sell more Celtic music than anything else. It's hard to imagine that this music was forbidden as recently as the 1980s. During a more repressive time, many of today's big pop stars were underground artists. In fact, in the recent past, a child would lose her French citizenship if christened with a Celtic name.

But the freckled locals are now free to wave their flag, sing their songs, and speak their language (there's a Breton TV station and radio station). Like their Irish counterparts, Bretons—many with red hair and freckles—are chatty, their bars are alive with music of struggles against an oppressor, and the sea forms much of their identity. The coastal route from Mont St. Michel through the town of Cancale (famous for oysters; good lunch stop), Pointe du Grouin (good hiking), and the historic walled city of St. Malo gives a good introduction to this province.

Cuisine Scene—Brittany

While the endless coastline suggests otherwise, there is more than seafood to this rugged, Celtic land. Crêpes are to Bretons what pasta is to Italians: a basic, reasonably priced, daily necessity. *Galettes* are savory buckwheat crêpes, commonly filled with ham, cheese, eggs, mushrooms, spinach, seafood, or a combination.

Oysters are the second food of Brittany and are now available all year. Mussels, clams, and scallops are often served as main courses. Look for *moules marinières* (mussels steamed in white wine, parsley, and shallots) and crêpes with scallops.

Farmers compete with fishermen for the hearts of locals, growing fresh vegetables such as peas, beans, and cauliflower.

For dessert, look for *far Breton*, a traditional custard dessert often served with prunes. Dessert crêpes, made with white flour, are served with a variety of toppings.

Cider is the locally produced drink. Order *un bol de cidre* (a traditional bowl of cider) with your crêpes.

Remember, restaurants serve only during lunch (11:30–14:00) and dinner (19:00–21:00, later in bigger cities); cafés serve food throughout the day.

DINAN

If you have time for only one stop in Brittany, do Dinan. Its hefty ramparts bundle its half-timbered and cobbled quaintness into Brittany's best medieval town center. While it has a touristic icing—plenty of *crêperies*, shops selling Brittany kitsch, and colorful flags—it is clearly a workaday Breton town filled with people who understand what a beautiful place they call home. This delightfully preserved ancient city (which escaped the bombs of World War II) is conveniently located (1 hour from Mont St. Michel) and peaceful. You'll awaken to the sound of roosters.

Orientation

Dinan's old city is contained within its medieval ramparts, climbing steeply uphill east to west from the river Rance and its small port to huge place du Guesclin, where you'll find lots of parking and the TI. Place des Merciers is ground zero for most activities in Dinan.

Tourist Information: Pick up a map and bus and train schedules, and ask about walking tours of Dinan and boat trips on the Rance river, but skip their overpriced tourist magazine (mid-June–mid-Sept Mon–Sat 9:00–19:00, Sun 10:00–12:20 & 14:30–18:00; Oct–May Mon–Sat 9:00–12:30 & 14:00–18:00, closed Sun; just off place du Guesclin near Château de Dinan on 9 rue du Château, tel. 02 96 87 69 76).

Arrival in Dinan

By Train: To get to the center from Dinan's Old World train station (no lockers or bag check), either call a taxi (see "Helpful Hints," below) or walk 20 minutes (left out of station, right at Hôtel Europa up rue Carnot, right on rue Thiers, then left across big place Duclos-Pinot, passing Café de la Mairie to reach the old center).

By Bus: Dinan's bus stop is in front of the post office on place Duclos-Pinot, five minutes to the center (for directions, see "By Train," above).

By Car: Dinan is confusing for drivers; follow *Centre-ville* signs to *la gare* (train station). From there, follow the walking route described above ("By Train") to reach the massive place du Guesclin (free parking except July–Sept and on market day—Thu).

Helpful Hints

Internet Access: Try **Aerospace Cyber Café** (near place du Guesclin at 9 rue de la Chaux, tel. 02 96 87 04 87).

Laundry: Pressing-Laverie's charming owner does your laundry in a few hours (Mon 14:00–19:00, Tue–Sat 8:30–12:00 & 13:45–19:00, closed Sun, about 4 blocks from train station at 19 rue de Brest, tel. 02 96 39 71 35).

Walking Tours: The TI offers 90-minute walking tours of old Dinan in French and English (€5, daily in summer, Sat only April–Sept, get details at TI).

Picnic-Perfect Park: A lovely park hides behind the big church of St. Ouen.

Market Days: Thursday is the big market day on place du Guesclin (8:00–13:00). Wednesday is flea-market day on place St. Sauveur.

Taxi: Call tel. 02 96 39 74 16, cellular 06 07 49 95 31 or 06 08 00 80 90 (8-seat minivans available).

Car Rental: Consider **Europcar** (48 rue de Brest, tel. 02 96 85 07 51) or the less-central **Hertz** (Garage Galivel, Z. A. Bel Air, tel. 02 96 39 44 20).

Bike Rental: Peugeot Cycles Scardin is a block from the train station at 30 rue Carnot (tel. 02 96 39 21 94).

Sights—Dinan

Dinan Self-Guided Walking Tour—Frankly, I wouldn't go through a turnstile in Dinan. The attraction here is the town itself. Enjoy the old town center, ramble the ramparts, and check out the old riverfront harbor. Here are some ideas, laced together as a quick walk starting at the place du Guesclin (pron. gek-lahn). As you wander, notice the pride locals take in their Breton culture.

Dinan

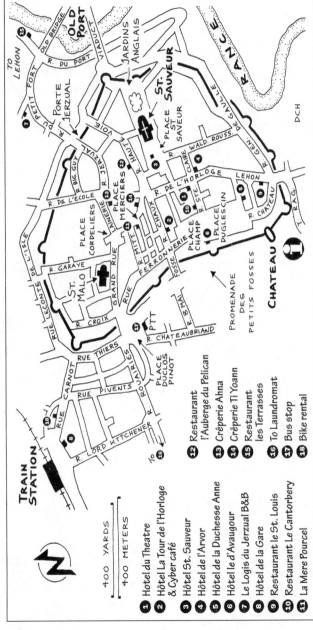

1 Hôtel du Theatre
2 Hôtel La Tour de l'Horloge & Cyber café
3 Hôtel St. Sauveur
4 Hôtel de l'Arvor
5 Hôtel de la Duchesse Anne
6 Hôtel d'Avaugour
7 Le Logis du Jerzual B&B
8 Hôtel de la Gare
9 Restaurant le St. Louis
10 Restaurant Le Cantorbery
11 La Mere Pourcel
12 Restaurant l'Auberge du Pelican
13 Crêperie Ahna
14 Crêperie Ti Yoann
15 Restaurant les Terrasses
16 To Laundromat
17 Bus stop
18 Bike rental

Place du Guesclin: This sprawling town square is named after the 14th-century local knight who became a great French military leader (famed for victories over England). For 700 years, merchants have filled the square selling their produce and crafts (in modern times, every Thu 8:00–13:00). The TI and some impressive fortifications are just beyond the square. The *donjon* (keep) and nearby walls are all that's left of Dinan's once-massive castle. The museum (no English) and the view from the top are both disappointing. From the statue of Guesclin, rue Ste. Claire leads to the...

Théâtre des Jacobins: This theater fronts a pleasant little square. The theater was once one of the many convents that dominated the town. In fact, in medieval times, one-third of Dinan consisted of convents—not uncommon in Brittany, which remains the most Catholic part of France. As you walk down Rue de l'Horloge toward the clock tower, you'll see on your left...

Nobody's Tombstone: The tombstone without a head is a town mascot. It's actually a prefab tombstone, made during the Hundred Years' War, when there was more death than money in France. A portrait bust would be attached to this generic body for a proper yet economic burial. Continue to the...

Clock Tower: The old town spins around this clock tower, which long symbolized the power of the town's merchants. The tower comes with a mediocre little museum and 160 steps to a fine city view (€2.50, daily 10:00–18:30). Across from the tower, a bakery sells *ker-y-pom* (€1.50): traditional Breton shortbread biscuits with butter, honey, and an apple-pie filling. When warm, they're the best taste treat in town. Past the tower, take the first left into Dinan's historic commercial center, the place des Merciers.

Characteristic Old Town Center: These half-timbered, arcaded buildings are Dinan's oldest and most picturesque. They date from the time when property taxes were based on the square footage of your ground floor. To provide shelter from both the taxes and the rain, buildings started with small ground floors, then expanded outward into upper floors. In medieval times, shopkeepers would sell their goods in front of their homes under the shelter of their leaning walls. Picturesque rue de la Cordonnerie is a fine example of a medieval lane with overhanging buildings whose roofs nearly touch. After a disastrous 18th-century fire, a law required that the traditional thatch be replaced by safer slate.

Best Town View: Walk past Dinan's basilica (of little sightseeing importance), through a pleasant English garden, and to St. Catherine's tower for a great view of the river valley below the town. From here, you enjoy a commanding view of the old port and the Rance River (described below). A short walk from here along rue du Rempart leads to the best stretch of the...

Ramparts: For the best look at Dinan's impressive fortified wall, hike from the Jerzual gate past the Governor's tower to St. Malo's gate (where rue de l'Ecole leads back into town).

While the old port town was destroyed repeatedly, these ramparts were never taken by force. (They were taken, however, by siege.) If an attacker got by the *contrescarpe* (second outer wall) and through the moat, he could be pummeled by nasty things dropped through the holes lining the ramparts. Venture out on the Governor's tower to see how the cannon slots enabled defenders to shoot in all directions. Today, the ramparts seem only to guard the town's residential charm—gardens, wells, and homey backyards.

When you're done exploring the ramparts, you can follow the steep and scenic rue Jerzual from the old town center under the medieval gate (Porte Jerzual) and down to the...

Old Port: This was the birthplace of Dinan a thousand years ago. It was once an export and fishing port, connected to the sea, 15 miles away, by the Rance River. By taxing river traffic, the town grew. The tiny Old Bridge *(Vieux Pont)* dates to the 15th century. But because this location was so exposed, the townsfolk later retreated to the bluff behind its current fortifications. Notice the viaduct—built by Monsieur Eiffel in around 1850 to send traffic around the town and alleviate congestion. Until then, the main road crossed the tiny Old Bridge and went up the steep rue Jerzual through Dinan—which is where you can head, now that our walk is finished, unless you want to spend more time exploring the...

Rance River: The river, now canalized with locks stopping any current and an embankment towpath, is great for lazy walks, boat rides, and bike rides (see "Sights—Near Dinan," below). **Musée du Rail**—Train buffs can wax nostalgic at this 1:87-scale railroad model with trains from many periods (€2.50, June–mid-Sept daily 14:00–18:00, closed mid-Sept–May, at train station, tel. 02 96 39 81 33).

Sights—Near Dinan

▲**Rance River Valley**—The best thing about Dinan's port is the access it provides to dreamy riverside paths that meander along the gentle Rance Valley. You can walk, bike, or boat in either interesting direction.

On Foot: For a breath of fresh Brittany air, cross the Old Bridge in Dinan's port, turn right, and walk the river trail 30 level minutes to the pristine little village of Lehon. A proud ninth-century abbey, flowery cobbled lanes, and **La Marmite de l'Abbaye** café/restaurant greet visitors (lunch salads, wood-fire-grilled meats for lunch and dinner, and drinks in between, closed Mon, tel. 02 96 86 77 39).

By Bike: For bike rental, see "Helpful Hints," above. Cyclists can follow the "On Foot" route, above, then cross Lehon's bridge and continue along the canal for as far as their legs will take them, passing Breton cows, cute little lock houses, sublime scenery, and other nature-lovers. The villages of Evran and Treverien are both within reach (allow 45 min from Dinan to Evran, 25 min more to Treverien). By turning left rather than right at Dinan's port (and staying on the Dinan side of the river), bikers can join the parade of ocean-bound boats. It's a breezy and level 30-minute ride past rock faces, cornfields, and slate-roofed homes to the picturesque Port de Lyet (cross small dam to reach village, trail ends a short distance beyond). **Le Ty-Corentin** café/restaurant is perfectly positioned in the port (open daily for lunch and dinner or a refreshing drink, except non-summer Wed, tel. 02 96 83 21 10).

By Boat: Boats depart from Dinan's port at the bottom of rue Jerzual 15 meters/50 feet to the left of the Old Bridge on the Dinan side (schedules depend on tides, get details at TI). The one-hour cruise comes with a live English-speaking guide, plenty of scenery, and a chance to go through a lock. A longer cruise (a slow and very scenic 2.5 hrs) goes to St. Malo (€16 one-way, €21 round-trip, enjoy St. Malo, then take the bus back).

▲**Half-Day Loop Drives**—Dinan is ideally situated for a quick taste-of-Brittany driving route that samples a bit of the rugged peninsula's coast and interior. If you're connecting Dinan and Mont St. Michel and are pressed for time, link the two with a worthwhile little detour (these directions from Dinan to Mont St. Michel): Make a brief stop in cute little St. Suliac, on the Rance estuary north of Dinan. From there, it's a short skip up to St. Malo (good lunch stop, see below). Then take the scenic drive east on D-201 to Pointe du Gouin and Cancale, continuing on the D-155 to Mont St. Michel.

With a full half-day to explore the diverse region around Dinan, drive to Cap Frehel on the D-794. Circumnavigate Cap Frehel counterclockwise and consider touring the more-impressive-from-the-outside Fort la Latte (great views and setting over crashing waves). The most scenic road segment links Cap Frehel and Sables d'Or. Continue your coastal explorations at the fishing village of Erquy (good beaches).

▲**St. Malo**—Come here to experience *the* Breton beach resort. Stroll high up on the impressive ramparts that circle the old city, eat seafood, walk as far out on the beaches as the tides allow, then return to Dinan for the night. St. Malo is an easy 45-minute drive or a one-hour bus or train ride from Mont St. Michel or Dinan— a great day trip. The bus stop and **TI** are at Esplanade St. Vincent, across from the old city gate (TI tel. 02 99 56 64 48).

▲**Dinard**—This upscale old beach resort comes with a kid-friendly beach and plenty of old-time, Coney Island beach-promenade ambience (2 buses/day from Dinan, 16 km/10 miles). The small passenger-only ferry to St. Malo provides the most scenic arrival in St. Malo (departs from below Promenade de Clair de Lune at Embarcadere).

▲**Fougères**—This very Breton city is a memorable stop for drivers traveling between the Loire châteaux and Mont St. Michel. Fougères has one of Europe's largest medieval castles, a fine city center, and a panoramic park viewpoint (from St. Leonard church in Jardin Public). Try one of the café/*crêperies* near the castle, such as the tempting Crêperie des Remparts, one block uphill from the castle. Pick up a city map and castle description in English at the castle entrance. The interior is grass and walls.

Sleeping in Dinan
(€1 = $1, country code: 33, zip code: 22100)
Sleep Code: **S** = Single, **D** = Double/Twin, **T** = Triple, **Q** = Quad, **b** = bathroom, **s** = shower only, **CC** = Credit Cards accepted, **no CC** = Credit Cards not accepted, **SE** = Speaks English, **NSE** = No English, * = French hotel rating system (0–4 stars).

To help you sort easily through these listings, I've divided the rooms into three categories based on the price for a standard double room with bath:

Higher Priced—Most rooms more than €100.
Moderately Priced—Most rooms €100 or less.
Lower Priced—Most rooms €50 or less.

Weekends and summers are busy. Dinan likes its nightlife, so be careful of loud rooms over bars, particularly on weekends.

Sleeping in the Old Center

MODERATELY PRICED
Hôtel de l'Arvor**, ideally located a block off place du Guesclin, is a good midrange value with 30 modern, adequately maintained rooms (with so-so beds) wrapped in an old stone facade (standard Db-€47, larger Db-€62, Tb-€64–70, CC, 5 rue Pavie, tel. 02 96 39 21 22, fax 02 96 39 83 09).

LOWER PRICED
Hôtel Du Théâtre, with the cheapest rooms in this book, sits across from Hôtel de l'Arvor above a small café. Its six no-star rooms are clean and cheery, though some can be smoky (S-€15, D-€21, Db-€27, Tb-€36, no CC, 2 rue Ste. Claire, tel. 02 96 39 06 91, reserved but friendly Michel NSE).

    Hôtel La Tour de l'Horloge**, an 18th-century manor

house burrowed deep in the center, rents 12 modern rooms with little personality but fair rates (rooms fronting the bar-lined rue de Chaux can be noisy, Db-€47, Tb-€66, Qb-€79, CC, 5 rue de la Chaux, tel. 02 96 39 96 92, fax 02 96 85 06 99, e-mail: hiliotel@wanadoo.fr, SE).

Hôtel St. Sauveur rents six sharp rooms in a 15th-century home over a fun pub (with pool table), on a characteristic square by the basilica (Db-€43, Tb-€57, CC, 19 place St. Sauveur, tel. 02 96 85 30 20, fax 02 96 87 91 66).

Chambres d'Hôtes Le Logis du Jerzual is a haven of calm. It's in an old building with terraced gardens, just up from the port off a characteristic street (a long, steep climb below the main town). The rooms, wonderfully furnished with antiques, fine carpets, and canopied beds, are an excellent value (Sb-€30, Db-€50–70, extra bed-€15, includes breakfast, CC, tel. 02 96 85 46 54, fax 02 96 39 46 94, e-mail: sry.logis@9online.fr, delightful Sylvie SE). Drive up rue du Petit Port from the port (it's well-signed) and drop your bags. Parking is close.

Sleeping on Place du Guesclin

These hotels offer the easiest, closest parking on place du Guesclin (except on Wed night, since Thu is market day).

HIGHER PRICED

Hôtel le d'Avaugour***, facing a busy street, is Dinan's best and priciest hotel, with an efficient staff (SE) and a backyard garden oasis over the town's medieval wall. The wood-furnished rooms have all the comforts and great beds. All bathrooms have bath-showers and speakers for the TV so you can hear the BBC while soaking (prices vary greatly by season, rooms over garden are best, Db-€100, Tb-€130, CC, elevator, big buffet breakfast, 1 place du Champ, tel. 02 96 39 07 49, fax 02 96 85 43 04, e-mail: avaugour.hotel@wanadoo.fr).

LOWER PRICED

Hôtel de la Duchesse Anne*, run by friendly Giles, offers reasonable comfort, a small bar, and a *crêperie* (Db-€43–46, Tb-€56, Qb-€70, includes breakfast, CC, 10 place du Guesclin, tel. 02 96 39 09 43, fax 02 96 87 57 26).

Sleeping near the Station

LOWER PRICED

Hôtel de la Gare* faces the station and offers the complete Breton experience, with *charmant* Laurence and Claude (who both love

Americans), a local café hangout, and surprisingly quiet, polished, and comfortable rooms for a bargain (Ds-€24, Db or Tb-€38–40, CC, place de la Gare, tel. 02 96 39 04 57, fax 02 96 39 02 29).

Eating in Dinan

Dinan has good restaurants for every budget. Since *galettes* (crêpes) are the specialty, *crêperies* are a good and inexpensive choice (and are on every corner). **Crêperie Ahna** is one of the best (crêpes with ham are too salty—I prefer the crêpes with scallops and cream). It's also a cozy place with more than just crêpes: try the *pierrades*—meat dishes grilled on hot stones (7 rue de la Poissonnerie, tel. 02 96 39 09 13). **Crêperie Ti Yoann** ("Chef Johann" in Breton) is also good and cheap (€7 for 3 courses and cider, 17 rue de l'Apport, tel. 02 96 87 56 75).

If you're not in the mood for crêpes, try **Le St. Louis**, where flames from the fireplace flicker on wood beams and white tablecloths (€16 *menu*, great salad bar and dessert buffet, closed Wed except in summer, hidden 2 blocks behind place du Guesclin at 9 rue de Lehon, tel. 02 96 39 89 50, charming Marie-Claire SE).

Le Cantorbery is a warm place, where meats are grilled in the dining room's fireplace *à la tradition* and the seafood is *très* tasty (*menus* from €20, just off place du Guesclin at 6 rue Ste. Claire, tel. 02 96 39 02 52, closed Mon except in summer).

And if you want the best, **La Mère Pourcel**, with dressy service and refined cuisine under medieval yet elegant beams, is my Dinan splurge (*menus* from €27, 3 place des Merciers, tel. 02 96 39 03 80).

If fine seafood at reasonable prices appeals, try **L'Auberge du Pelican** (indoor and outdoor tables, just off place St. Sauveur at 3 rue Haute-Voie, tel. 02 96 39 47 05).

You'll find several cozy restaurants in the old port (long, steep walk down rue Jerzual); **Les Terrasses** sits right on the river and has a good €16 *menu* (also good just for a drink on its riverfront terrace, tel. 02 96 39 09 60).

Transportation Connections—Dinan

By train to: Paris' Montparnasse (6/day, 4 hrs, change in Dol and Rennes), **Pontorson-Mont St. Michel** (3/day, 1–2 hrs, change in Dol, then bus or taxi from Pontorson, best connection is 12:45 departure from Dinan), **St. Malo** (3/day, 1 hr, change in Dol, bus is better, see below), **Amboise** (6/day, 5–6 hrs, via Rennes, then TGV to Paris with no station change needed in Paris; or cross-country via Rennes, Le Mans, and Tours (2/day, 5–6 hrs).

By bus to: St. Malo (3–4/day, 50 min, faster and better than trains, as bus stops in both cities are more central), **Mont St. Michel** (3/day, 2 hrs, change in St. Malo).

THE LOIRE

The Loire River, which glides gently east to west across France and separates north from south, gave its name to this popular tourist region. The Loire Valley is carpeted with fertile fields, crisscrossed by rivers and streams, and studded with hundreds of castles and palaces in all shapes and sizes. The medieval castles explain the area's strategic value during the Hundred Years' War. Renaissance palaces replaced medieval castles when a "valley address" became a must among the hunt-crazy rich and royalty. Today, the Loire Valley has a split personality: It's one of France's most important agricultural regions, and a burgeoning bedroom community of Paris, thanks to the TGV *(train à grand vitesse)* bullet trains that link France's capital with this pastoral area in an hour.

In the Loire region, you'll pass many little vegetable gardens along the rivers. These are community gardens, given to residents by the French government after World War II, when food was scarce and land was plentiful (and cheap). It took years for the food supply system to be reorganized, given the structural damage to railways, roads, and farms. While community gardens were the policy throughout France, they are more numerous and more visible in this region.

Planning Your Time

Many travelers find the Loire a good first or last stop on their French odyssey (5 TGV trains/day connect Paris' Charles de Gaulle airport in 1 hour with the city of Tours, which has car rental agencies at the station).

Use Amboise (good for Eurailers or drivers) or Chenonceaux (good for drivers) as a home base for touring the famous châteaux east of Tours: Chenonceau, Blois, Chambord, Chaumont-sur-Loire, and Cheverny. Use Chinon or Azay le Rideau as your home base to visit the châteaux west of Tours: Chinon, Azay le Rideau, Langeais, and Villandry.

A day and a half is sufficient to sample the best châteaux. (Many find the Loire manageable as a day trip from Paris; see "By Minibus Tours," below.) Drivers with only a day could consider this plan: Visit Chenonceau (in town of Chenonceaux) early when crowds are smaller, spend midday at Chambord, and enjoy Cheverny late (the hunting dogs are fed at 17:00).

If arriving by car, try to see one château on your way in (e.g., Chambord if arriving from the north, Langeais or Villandry from the west, or Azay le Rideau from the south). If arriving by train from Paris, consider a stop in Blois and the bus excursion to Chambord and Cheverny (see "Getting around the Loire Valley," below), or go directly to Amboise and try to visit Le Clos Lucé that afternoon.

Don't go overboard on château-hopping. Two châteaux, possibly three (if you're a big person), make up the recommended daily dosage. Famous châteaux are least crowded early and late. Most open around 9:00 and close between 18:00 and 19:00. During the off-season, many close from 12:00 to 14:00 and at 17:00.

A good one-day plan for those with no car and no money for a minivan tour is to catch the once-per-day bus from Amboise to Chenonceaux (see "Getting around the Loire Valley," below), tour Chenonceau, then spend the afternoon enjoying Amboise, its château, and Leonardo's last home, Le Clos Lucé.

If you're driving to the Dordogne from the Loire, the A-20 autoroute via Limoges (and Oradour-sur-Glane) is fastest and toll-free.

Getting around the Loire Valley

By Train: With easy access from Amboise, Tours is the transport hub for train travelers. It has two important train stations and a bus station with service to several châteaux. The main train station is called "Tours SNCF," and the smaller TGV station is "St. Pierre des Corps." Check the schedules carefully, as service is sparse on some lines. The châteaux of Chenonceau, Langeais, Chinon, and Azay le Rideau have some train and/or bus service from Tours' main station (although Chenonceau is better by bus or bike from Amboise).

By Bus: There's one bus per day from **Amboise to Chenonceaux** (departs Amboise about 10:50, 15-min trip, returns from Chenonceaux at 12:40, allowing you about 80 min at the château; in summer, there's also an afternoon departure at about 14:20 with a return from Chenonceaux at about 16:45).

The Loire Valley

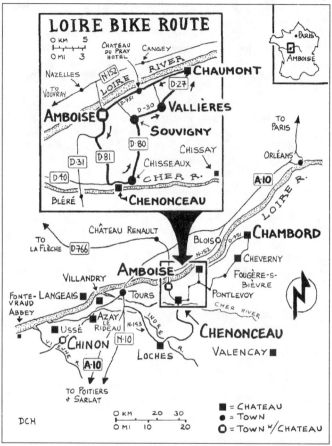

From mid-May until early September, a handy **excursion bus from the Blois** train station (20 min by train from Amboise) serves Chambord and Cheverny, giving you 90 minutes at each château (€10 includes bus fare and discounts on château entries; departs Blois station at 9:10, returns at 13:10; or departs Blois at 13:20, returns at 18:00). When combined with a visit to the château in Blois, this makes a good and full day. For details, call the Blois TI at 02 54 90 41 41 (also see "Blois" under "More Châteaux East of Tours," below).

By Minibus Tour: Pascal Accolay runs **Acco-Dispo**, a small, personal minibus company with good all-day château tours from Amboise and Tours. Costs vary with the itinerary (€16–28/half-day, €37–43/day). English is the primary language. While you'll get a fun and enthusiastic running commentary on the road, covering each château's background as well as the region's contemporary scene, you're on your own at each château (and you pay the admission fee). All-day tours depart about 8:30, afternoon tours depart about 12:50. Both return to Amboise around 18:30. Several itinerary options are available; most include Chenonceau. Reserve two to three days ahead if possible; groups are small, ranging from two to eight château-hoppers. (Day trippers from Paris find this service convenient; after a one-hour ride on the TGV to Tours, they're met near the central station and delivered there at the end of the day.) Ask about Acco-Dispo's multiday tours of the Loire and Brittany (daily, free hotel pickups, 18 rue des Vallées in Amboise, tel. 06 82 00 64 51, fax 02 47 23 15 73, www.accodispo-tours.com).

Excursions SNCF also provides daily minibus and big bus tours from Tours' SNCF station to a variety of châteaux with information headphones on the bus ride (half-day trips: €15 for 1 château, departs at 9:00; €25 for 2–3 châteaux, departs at 13:15; entry fees not included, leave from bus platform 6, tel. 02 47 05 46 09, fax 02 47 58 71 73, or reserve through Ligeris TI, e-mail: info@ligeris.com).

By Taxi: A taxi from Amboise to Chenonceaux costs about €16. Your hotel can call one for you. The meter doesn't start until you do (see "Amboise—Helpful Hints," below).

By Rental Car: You can rent cars at either of Tours' train stations and in Amboise (see "Amboise—Helpful Hints").

By Bike: Cycling options are endless in this region where the elevation gain is generally manageable (still, many find even the shortest rides exhausting and too time-consuming). Amboise, Blois, and Chinon make the best bike bases. From Amboise, allow an hour to Chenonceaux (warning: the first 3 km/2 miles are uphill). Serious bikers can ride to Chaumont in 90 minutes and connect Amboise, Chenonceaux, and Chaumont with an all-day 60-kilometer/37-mile pedal (see Loire Valley map in this chapter for details). The TI in Amboise promises signed bike routes to several châteaux in 2003. From Blois by bike to Chambord is a manageable 75-minute, one-way ride, but adding Cheverny makes a grueling, full-day, 50-kilometer/30-mile round-trip. Most can do the pleasant bike ride from Chinon to Ussé (big hill when leaving Chinon), and some will find the energy to continue to Langeais. Only those in top shape will enjoy continuing on to Villandry (see "Chinon," below). Call the Blois TI for bike-rental information (tel. 02 54 90 41 41).

Cuisine Scene—Loire Valley

Here in "the garden of France," anything from the earth is bound to be good. Loire Valley rivers produce fresh trout *(truite)*, salmon *(saumon)*, and smelt *(éperlau)*, which are often served fried *(friture)*. Rillettes, a stringy pile of cooked then whipped pork, makes for a cheap, mouthwatering sandwich spread (use lots of mustard and add a baby pickle, called a *cornichon*). The area's fine goat cheeses include Crottin de Chavignol *(crottin* means horse dung, which is what this cheese, when aged, resembles), Saint-Maure Fermier (soft and creamy), and Selles-sur-Cher (mild). For dessert, try a delicious *tarte Tatin* (upside-down caramel-apple tart). The best and most expensive white wines are the Sancerres, which are made in the less-touristed, western edge of this region. Less expensive but still tasty are Tourraine Sauvignons and the sweeter Vouvrays, whose grapes are grown near Amboise. Vouvray is also famous for its light and refreshing sparkling wines. The better reds come from Chinon and Bourgeuil.

Remember, restaurants serve only during lunch (11:30–14:00) and dinner (19:00–21:00, later in bigger cities); cafés serve food throughout the day.

AMBOISE

Straddling the widest part of the Loire, the town of Amboise slumbers in the shadow of its hilltop château. A castle has overlooked the Loire from Amboise since Roman times. Leonardo da Vinci retired here...just one more fine idea.

As the royal residence of François I (ruled 1515–1547), Amboise wielded far more importance than you'd imagine from a lazy walk down the pleasant pedestrian-only commercial zone at the base of the palace. In fact, its 14,000 residents are quite conservative, giving the town "an attitude"—as if no one told them they're no longer the second capital of France. The locals are the kind who keep their wealth to themselves; consequently many fine mansions hide behind nondescript facades. There's even a royalist element here (and the duke of Paris, the guy who'd be king if there was one, lives here).

The one-kilometer-long (0.6 mile) "Golden Island" is the only island in the Loire substantial enough to be flood-proof and have permanent buildings (including a soccer stadium and a 13th-century church). This was important historically as a place where north and south France, divided by the longest river in the country, came together. Truces were made here. The Loire marked the farthest north the Moors conquered as they pushed through Europe from Morocco. Today, it still divides the country (for example, weather reports say "north of the Loire...and south of the Loire").

With or without a car, Amboise is an ideal small-town home base for exploring the best of château country.

Orientation

Amboise (pop. 11,000) covers both sides of the Loire and an island in the middle. The train station is on the north side of the river, but nearly everything else is on the south (château) side, including the TI.

Pedestrian-friendly rue National leads from the base of the château through the center past the clock tower—once part of the town wall—to the striking Romanesque Church of St. Denis.

Tourist Information: The information-packed TI is in the round building on the riverbank at quai du Général de Gaulle (April–Sept Mon–Sat 9:30–13:00 & 14:00–18:30, July–Aug 9:00–20:00, Oct–March Mon–Sat 10:00–12:30 & 14:00–18:30, Sun all year 10:00–13:00 & 15:00–18:30, tel. 02 47 57 09 28, www.amboise-valdeloire.com). Their city map shows restaurants, hotels, and château information, including the time and place of English-language sound-and-light shows. They can reserve a room for you in a hotel or *chambre d'hôte*, but first peruse the photo album of regional *chambres d'hôte*. Ask for information on bike routes and their brochure that outlines a self-guided walking tour of Amboise.

Arrival in Amboise

By Train: Amboise's train station, with a post office and taxi stand, is birds-chirping peaceful (tel. 02 47 23 18 23). Turn left out of the station, make a quick right, and walk down rue de Nazelles five minutes to the bridge that leads you over the Loire and into town. Within three blocks of the station, you'll find a recommended hotel, B&B, and bike-rental shop.

By Car: Drivers set their sights on the flag-festooned château capping the hill. Most recommended accommodations and restaurants cluster just downriver of the château. Warning: When driving through Amboise with the river on your left, some streets on your right have the right-of-way when merging. Park on the street near your hotel or near the TI.

Helpful Hints

Bike Rental: Rent a bike for about €11 per half day and €14 per full day (leave your passport or a photocopy of it). Two reliable places are **Locacycle** (daily 9:00–19:00, near TI at 2 rue Jean-Jacques Rousseau, tel. 02 47 57 00 28, English spoken) and **Cycles Richard** (Mon–Sat, closed 12:00–14:00 and all day Sun, located on train-station side of river, just past bridge at 2 rue de Nazelles, tel. 02 47 57 01 79, NSE).

Car Rental: Avis is expensive (approx. €82/day with 150 kilometers/90 miles free, across from Amboise TI, tel. 02 47 23 21 11); **Garage Jourdain** costs about half that price (approx. €40/day with 100 kilometers/60 miles free, downriver from TI at 105 route de Tours, tel. 02 47 57 17 92, fax 02 47 57 77 50). Both close Monday through Friday from 12:00 to 14:00 and at 18:00 weekdays, 17:00 on Saturdays, and all day Sunday.

Taxi: Call 02 47 57 17 92 (allow €16 to Chenonceaux).

Market Days: Open-air markets are held on Friday (smaller) and Sunday (bigger) in the parking lot behind the TI on the river.

Chocolate Fantasy: An essential and historic stop for chocoholics is **Bigot Patisserie & Chocolatier** (1 block off river, where place Michel Debré meets rue Nationale).

Laundry: The handy coin-op Lav'centre is a block from rue Chaptal toward the château on 9 allée du Sergent Turpin (daily 7:00–21:00, Oct–May until 20:00). The door locks at closing time; leave beforehand or you'll trigger the alarm system.

Bookstore: Maison de la Presse has a small selection of English novels and a good selection of maps and English guidebooks such as Michelin's *Châteaux of the Loire* Green Guide (English versions cost about €12, 40 percent off U.S. price; across from TI at 7 quai du General de Gaulle).

Private Château Guide: Those staying in or around Amboise with a rental car may want to hire Brian Whitmarsh, an English expat who's lived here for 12 years. He loves the local history and culture and enjoys showing travelers through the often confusing and stingy-with-English-information châteaux. He does two castles in a half day and four castles (or 3 and a wine-tasting) in a full day, and can tailor the day to your interests (€80/4.5 hrs, €150/very full day, prices per group up to seven, with a little luck you can hire Brian on short notice, tel. & fax 02 47 35 46 14).

Sights—Amboise

▲▲**Le Clos Lucé**—In 1516, Leonardo da Vinci packed his bags (and several of his favorite paintings, including the *Mona Lisa*) and left an imploding Rome for better working conditions in the Loire Valley. He accepted the position of engineer, architect, and painter to the French king. This "House of Light" is the plush palace where he spent his last three years. France's Renaissance king François I set Leonardo up here just so he could enjoy his intellectual company. François was 22 when his 65-year-old mentor moved in. There's a touching sketch in Leonardo's bedroom of François comforting his genius pal on his deathbed. The house was built in 1450—just within the protective walls of the town— as a guest house to the château. While it housed VIPs before and

Amboise

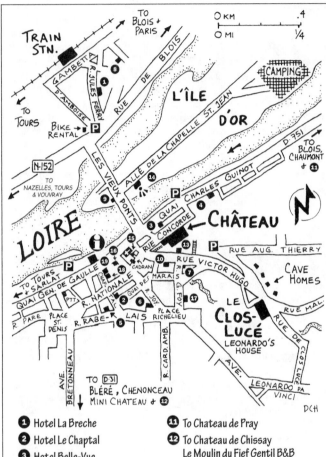

1 Hotel La Breche

2 Hotel Le Chaptal

3 Hotel Belle-Vue

4 Le Manoir des Minimes

5 Le Vieux Manoir

6 Hotel Le Blason

7 Café des Arts

8 Le Petit Clos B&B

9 Le St. Vincent restaurant

10 L'Epicerie & La Florentine rest.

11 To Chateau de Pray

12 To Chateau de Chissay
    Le Moulin du Fief Gentil B&B
    La Chevalerie B&B

13 L'Amboiserie rest.

14 Le Shaker bar

15 Bigot Patisserie

16 Creperie L'Ecu

17 La Maison Enchantee

18 Laundromat

19 Maison de la Presse

after Leonardo, today it thoughtfully re-creates (with adequate English information) the everyday atmosphere Leonardo enjoyed as he lived here—pursuing his passions to the very end. The ground floor is filled with sketches recording the storm patterns of Leonardo's brain and models of his remarkable inventions (inspired by designs occurring in nature, built according to his notes). It's hard to imagine that this Roman candle of creativity died nearly 500 years ago. In the model room, notice the entry to the long tunnel connecting this house with the château. The garden café is reasonable and appropriately meditative; above it is a French-only video about Leonardo (€6.50 entry, Sept–June daily 9:00–19:00, July–Aug 9:00–20:00, shorter hours off-season, follow the free and fine English handout, tel. 02 47 57 62 88). It's a 15-minute walk from the TI, up past troglodyte homes (unsafe parking lot at Le Clos Lucé).

Château d'Amboise—This royal residence was built over the reign of three kings. And part of it was designed by Leonardo da Vinci. The king who did most of the building (Charles VIII) is famous for accidentally killing himself by walking into a doorjamb on his way to a tennis match (seriously). Later occupants were more careful. François I brought the Renaissance here in 1516 (through Leonardo da Vinci). While the English handout helps, no room stands out as exceptionally furnished or compelling, and this place pales when compared to other area châteaux. But the grand views over Amboise and the river almost merit the entry fee. After climbing the flower-lined ramp, your first stop is the lacy, petite chapel where Leonardo da Vinci is supposedly buried. This flamboyant little Gothic chapel comes with two fireplaces "to comfort the king" and a plaque "evoking the final resting place" of Leonardo. Where he's actually buried, no one seems to know. Views of rooftops and the Loire River follow you through red-brick rooms lined with high-backed chairs and massive stone fireplaces. At stop #2 ("the Sentry Walk"), plans show the château's original size. The bulky horsemen's tower climbs 40 meters/130 feet in five spirals—designed for a mounted soldier in a hurry. As you leave the tower, stay left and walk on the outside passage around the same tower, minding the gargoyle's big mouths above. Best château views are from the garden terraces farther upriver past the royal croquet set (€6.50, March–Oct daily 9:00–18:00, until 19:00 in summer, off-season closes 12:00–14:00 and at 17:00, tel. 02 47 57 00 98).

Caveau des Vignerons—This small cave offers free tastings of regional wines, cheeses, and foie gras (April–Sept 10:00–19:00, under Amboise's château across from recommended l'Epicerie restaurant).

▲**La Maison Enchantée**—It's a small world after all in this musical world of dolls. Push the buttons and watch 300 dolls dance or act in 25 different settings. Themes range from the Wild West to *Dr. Jekyll and Mr. Hyde* to the *Hunchback of Notre-Dame* (adult-€5.40, child-€4.30, April–Oct Tue–Sun 10:00–12:00 & 14:00–18:00, summers 10:00–19:00, Nov–March Tue–Sun 14:00–17:00, walk down rue de la Tour from château to 7 rue du General Foy, tel. 02 47 23 24 50).

Mini-Château—This five-acre park on the edge of Amboise (on the route to Chenonceaux) shows all the Loire châteaux in 1:25-scale models, forested with 600 bonsai trees and laced together by a model TGV train. For kids, it's a great introduction to the real châteaux you'll be visiting. The English brochure is essential (adult-€10, kids ages 4–16-€6, April–Sept daily 10:00–18:00, 9:00–19:00 in summer, off-season closes at 17:00, tel. 02 47 23 44 44). You'll find other kid-oriented attractions at Mini-Château; skip the donkey show, but consider playing a round of mini-golf and feeding the fish in the moat (a great way to get rid of that old baguette).

▲**Château d'Amboise Sound-and-Light Show**—If you're into S&L, this is considered one of the best shows of its kind in the area. While it's entirely in French, you can buy the English translation for €5. Volunteer locals from toddlers to pensioners recreate the life of François I with costumes, jugglers, impressive light displays, and fireworks. Dress warmly and be prepared for a long show (adults-€16, kids ages 6–14-€6, 10 nights a month through July and Aug 22:30–24:00, details at TI). The ticket window is on the ramp to the château and opens at 20:30. While you may feel locked in, you're welcome to leave at any time.

Vouvray Wine-Tasting—Jean-Pierre Laisement, a local vintner, welcomes visitors to his Caves Laisement winery with a fun wine-tasting and a look around his place. His elderly mother serves while his truffle dog, Razor, looks on. Telephone before dropping in to be sure Monsieur Laisement is at home (15 km/9 miles toward Tours from Amboise off RN 152 near Les Patys, 15 rue de la Vallee Coquette, Vouvray, tel. 02 47 52 74 47).

Sleeping in Amboise
(€1 = about $1, country code: 33, zip code: 37400)
Sleep Code: **S** = Single, **D** = Double/Twin, **T** = Triple, **Q** = Quad, **b** = bathroom, **s** = shower only, **CC** = Credit Cards accepted, **no CC** = Credit Cards not accepted, **SE** = Speaks English, **NSE** = No English, * = French hotel rating system (0–4 stars).

   To help you sort easily through these listings, I've divided the rooms into three categories based on the price for a standard double room with bath:

Higher Priced—Most rooms more than €90.
Moderately Priced—Most rooms €90 or less.
Lower Priced—Most rooms €60 or less.

Amboise is busy in the summer, but there are lots of hotels and *chambres d'hôte* (CH) in and around the city; the TI can help with reservations.

Hotels near the Station

LOWER PRICED

Hôtel La Brèche** is a good little refuge run by a we-try-harder family, with modest yet spotlessly comfortable rooms (smallish bathrooms) and a peaceful garden with table tennis and a few ducks. It's a 15-minute walk from the city center and a two-minute walk from the train station. Many rooms overlook the garden; those on the street are generally larger. Half pension, required in the summer, gets you a prizewinning dinner that includes a good salad bar and dessert buffet for an extra €13 per person. Box lunches are also available for €8 (S/D-€28, Sb/Db-€50, Tb-€49–55, Qb-€60, a few good family rooms-€72, CC, 26 rue Jules Ferry, tel. 02 47 57 00 79, fax 02 47 57 65 49, www.labreche-amboise.com, charming Christian SE and Annick does her best).

Le Petit Clos *chambre d'hôte* is nearby and has three cheery, cottage-type, ground-floor rooms on a quiet, picnic-perfect private garden. Sweet Madame Roullet and her just-as-sweet husband, Dominique, speak a leetle English. This place is immaculate, as Madame was a nurse in her other life (Db-€54, family room for up to 5 people-€110, no CC, includes big, farm-fresh breakfast with homemade everything, easy parking in garden, turn left out of station and follow tracks 200 meters/650 feet to rue Balzac and turn right, it's at #7, tel. 02 47 57 43 52).

Hotels in the Center

HIGHER PRICED

Le Manoir les Minimes****, a renovated 17th-century mansion, feels over the top with precious furniture, but works for those seeking luxury in Amboise. Rooms are modern and large (standard Db-€80–105, larger Db-€100–120, deluxe Db-€125–160, 3–4 person suites-€195–230, extra bed-€20, CC, 34 quai Charles Guinot, 3 blocks upriver from bridge, tel. 02 47 30 40 40, fax 02 47 30 40 77, www.manoirlesminimes.com).

Le Vieux Manoir is a better high-end splurge. American expats Gloria and Bob Bellnap, a wealth of information, have lovingly restored this secluded but central one-time convent with an attention to detail that Martha Stewart would envy. The atrium-like breakfast room opens to manicured gardens, the public spaces are American-cozy, and the six bedrooms would make an antique collector drool (2-night minimum €125–165/night, includes hearty breakfast; ask about the too-perfect, 2-room apartment; easy parking, no CC; pay in euros, U.S. dollars, British sterling, or personal check; 13 rue Rabelais, tel. & fax 02 47 30 41 27, www.le-vieux-manoir.com).

MODERATELY PRICED
Hôtel Belle-Vue*** overlooks the river where the bridge hits the town and is a good, central, midrange value (prices and comfort are more 2-star than 3). This hotel has spacious public rooms, dark halls, and effective double-paned windows. Half of its traditional rooms overlook the château; four come with huge, shared terraces (prices include a buffet breakfast, Db-€60–69, Tb-€75–84, Qb-€98, CC, elevator, 12 quai Charles-Guinot, tel. 02 47 57 02 26, fax 02 47 30 51 23).

LOWER PRICED
Hôtel Le Blason**, with friendly staff and a good restaurant, is a half-timbered, old building five blocks from the river on a noisy street. Rooms are small, bright, and modern with fans and good rates (Sb-€45, Db-€50, Tb-€55, CC, quieter rooms in back and on top floor, close parking, 11 place Richelieu, tel. 02 47 23 22 41, fax 02 47 57 56 18, e-mail: leblason@wanadoo.fr, Danielle SE).

Hôtel Le Chaptal** offers one-star comfort and prices. It's basic, cheap, and *très* frumpy. The rooms need attention (marginal beds, old carpets), but the price is fair (Db-€33–39, Tb-€43, Qb-€49, CC, 13 rue de Chaptal, tel. 02 47 57 14 46, fax 02 47 57 67 83, NSE). In summer they request that you dine in their cheery, inexpensive dining room.

Café des Arts is an artsy, welcoming café offering seven spic-and-span, linoleum-floored, and modern bunk-bedded rooms for a good price (S-€16, D-€29, T-€43, Q-€54, up to 6 possible, across from château exit at 32 rue Victor Hugo, tel. & fax 02 47 57 25 04).

Sleeping near Amboise
The area around Amboise is replete with good value accommodations in every shape, size, and price range. A listing follows of those that justify the detour. (For more listings, drivers could also check out "Sleeping in Chenonceaux," below.)

HIGHER PRICED

You'll feel a hint of the original medieval fortified castle behind the Renaissance elegance of the 750-year-old **Château de Pray**********. The dining room is splendid and the chef is talented (€39–62 *menus*, reservations required). The pool lies below the château (Db in modern annex–€100, smaller Db in main building–€115, larger Db–€145–165, extra bed–€32, CC, 5-min drive upriver from Amboise, toward Chaumont on D-751, tel. 02 47 57 23 67, fax 02 47 57 32 50, e-mail: chateau.depray@wanadoo.fr).

Château de Chissay*********, a five-minute drive east of Chenonceaux, offers a noble experience and a royal splurge. Perched above a valley in a private park, this storybook 15th-century château was home to two French kings. Now it's home to a large swimming pool, regal rooms, and professional service (standard but beautiful Db–€121–145, big Db–€180–206, suites–€230–260, rooms with valley views more costly but great, ask about weekend deals, optional dinner from €32, CC, no elevator, 41400 Chissay, tel. 02 54 32 32 01, fax 02 54 32 43 80, e-mail: chateau-chissay@wanadoo.fr).

Le Fleuray is a lovingly restored French farmhouse wrapped in a peaceful country setting about 15 minutes northeast of Amboise in Cangey. It's warmly operated by owners Hazel and Peter Newington. She runs the kitchen, while he handles the hotel details. The rooms are floral-print-bright pretty; those in the outbuildings are a bit larger and family-friendly, with gardens at the doorstep. The restaurant is worth staying home for (Db–€70–106, menus from €27, CC, tel. 02 47 56 09 25, fax 02 47 56 93 97, www.lefleurayhotel.com, e-mail: lefleurayhotel@wanadoo.fr).

MODERATELY PRICED

Château de Nazelles *chambre d'hôte* is for those who want a château hotel experience *sans* pretension. Young, friendly, and English-speaking Monsieur and Madame Fructus have tastefully restored this four-room, 16th-century hillside castle, once home to the original builder of Chenonceau. Trails to the forest above, a cliff-sculpted pool, and lush gardens with views over Amboise are all included (Db–€85–90, includes breakfast, CC, tel. & fax 02 47 30 53 79, www.chateau-nazelles.com). From Amboise, take N-152 toward Tours, turn right on D-5, then left in Nazelles-Negron on D-1 and quickly veer right above the post office (PTT) to 16 rue Tue la Soif; look for small *Gîtes* sign.

For a "Peter Mayle does the Loire" experience 15 minutes from Amboise and Chenonceaux, sleep at Roger and Ann's beautifully renovated 16th-century mill house, **Le Moulin du Fief Gentil**, where you get four acres and a backyard pond (fishing possible), smartly decorated rooms, and a splendid common living room. Ask about their cooking courses, and if Ann is cooking, splurge for dinner (Db-€74–120, dinner-€30/person, no CC, 37150 Bléré, tel. 02 47 30 32 51, fax 02 47 30 22 38, www.fiefgentil.fr.fm, e-mail: fiefgentil@wanadoo.fr). It's located on the edge of Bléré (from Bléré, follow signs toward Luzille).

LOWER PRICED
Closer to Amboise, the bargain *chambres* at **La Chevalerie** are family-friendly in every way—total seclusion in a farm setting, a swing set, a tiny fishing pond, common kitchens, and connecting rooms wrapped in a warm reception (Db-€37, Tb-€49, Qb-€61, no CC, 37150 La Croix en Touraine, from Amboise take D-31 toward Bléré and look for sign on your left after about 4 km/ 2.5 miles, tel. 02 47 57 83 64).

Eating in Amboise

Amboise is filled with inexpensive and forgettable restaurants. Those nearest the château are busy with tourists, but offer good enough value. **L'Amboiserie** is reasonable, with a large selection of basic dishes (crêpes, salads, meats) and a pleasant, umbrella-dotted upstairs terrace (daily, 7 rue Victor Hugo, tel. 02 47 39 50 40). **L'Epicerie** is the romantic's choice at 46 place Michel Debré (good €18 *menu*, tel. 02 47 57 08 94). Next door at #50, **La Florentine** is kid-friendly, with good pizza and pasta (daily, tel. 02 47 57 49 49). Near the pedestrian street rue Nationale, **Crêperie L'Ecu** is good and quiet (closed Mon, indoor/outdoor seating, 7 rue Corneille).

In any weather, **La Brèche**'s cozy restaurant with outdoor terrace is a good value, with a salad bar and dessert buffet (daily, see "Hotels near the Station," above); the walk home includes a floodlit château.

On the island, across from the château, **Le St. Vincent** is where local hoteliers send their discerning clients. The cheery interior is Provençal yellow and blue, with a van Gogh motif. Even more important, the food is tasty, fresh, and beautifully presented, with a four-course *menu* for €24 and a fine discounted lunch menu (daily, 7 rue Commire, reservations smart, especially for a view window table for 2, tel. 02 47 30 49 49). Across the street, **Le Bar Shaker** offers scenic cocktails and outdoor tables with late-night château views.

Eating near Amboise: Drivers should consider making the 15-minute drive to Cangey for dinner with Peter and Hazel at **Le Fleuray** (see above under "Sleeping near Amboise"), and those willing to pay for the best can drive five minutes to **Château**

de Pray for a royal experience (reserve ahead, see "Sleeping near Amboise," above).

Transportation Connections—Amboise

Twelve 15-minute trains per day link Amboise to the regional train hub of St. Pierre des Corps (suburban Tours). From there, you'll find reasonable connections to distant points (including the TGV to Paris Montparnasse). Transferring in Paris can be the fastest way to reach many French destinations, even in the south.

By train to: Paris (20/day, 1.5 hrs, 8/day direct to Paris Auster-litz and 12/day to Paris Montparnasse with change at St. Pierre de Corps), **Sarlat** (4/day, 5–6 hrs, change at St. Pierre des Corps then TGV to Libourne or Bordeaux St. Jean, then train through Bordeaux vineyards to Sarlat), **Limoges** (near Oradour-sur-Glane, 9/day, 4 hrs, change at St. Pierre des Corps and Vierzon or at Les Aubrais-Orleans and Vierzon, then tricky bus connection from Limoges to Oradour-sur-Glane), **Pontorson/Mont St. Michel** (4/day, 7 hrs, changes at Tours main station, Caen, then bus from Pontorson; or via Paris TGV with changes at St. Pierre des Corps, Paris Montparnasse, then bus from Rennes, 4/day, 7 hrs), **Bayeux** (9/day, 5–6 hrs, changes in Caen and Tours, or at Paris Mont-parnasse and St. Pierre des Corps).

By bus to: Chenonceaux (1/day, 15 min, departs Amboise about 10:50 from bus stop across from post office on route de Montrichard, returns from Chenonceaux at 12:40, plus in sum-mer an afternoon departure at about 14:20 with a return from Chenonceaux about 16:45).

CHENONCEAUX

This quiet, sleepy village—with a knockout château—makes a good home base for drivers. Note that Chenonceaux is the name of the town and Chenonceau (no "x") is the name of the château, but they're pronounced the same: shuh-non-so.

The **TI** is on the main road from Amboise as you enter the village (tel. 02 47 23 94 45). You can taste the wine from Chenon-ceaux's vineyards for €1.50; look for signs in the TI's parking lot.

▲▲▲**Chenonceau**—The toast of the Loire, this 16th-century Renaissance palace arches gracefully over the Cher River. Under-standably popular, Chenonceau is the third most-visited château in France (after Versailles and Fontainebleau). To beat the crowds, arrive at 8:45 or after 17:30, and plan on a 15-minute walk from the parking lot to the château.

While earlier châteaux were built for defensive purposes, Chenonceau was the first great pleasure palace. Nicknamed "**the château of the ladies**," it housed many famous women over the centuries. The original builder's wife oversaw the construction of the main part of the château. In 1547, King Henry II gave the château to his mistress, Diane de Poitiers. She added an arched bridge across the river to access the hunting grounds. She enjoyed her lovely retreat until Henry died (pierced in a jousting tournament in Paris) and his vengeful wife, Catherine de' Medici, unceremoniously kicked her out (and into the château of Chaumont). Catherine added the three-story structure on Diane's bridge. She died before completing her vision of a matching château on the far side of the river, but not before turning Chenonceau into the local aristocracy's place to see and be seen. (Note that whenever you see a split coat of arms, it belongs to a lady—half her husband's and half her father's.)

Approaching Chenonceau, you'll cross three moats and two drawbridges and pass an old round tower, which predates the main building. Notice the tower's fine limestone veneer, added so the top would better fit the new château.

The main château's original oak door greets you with F's, for François I (ruled 1515–1547), his fire-breathing salamander emblem, and coats of arms. The knocker is high enough to be used by visitors on horseback. The smaller door within the big door could be for two purposes: To enter after curfew, or to open the door in winter without letting out all the heat.

The interior is fascinating—but only if you take full advantage of the excellent 20-page booklet given out at the door. Follow that, but notice the few details described below as well:

In the **guard room**, the fine original tiles survive best near the walls. While the tapestries kept the room cozy, they also functioned to tell news or recent history (to the king's liking, of course).

The finely detailed **chapel** survived the vandalism of the Revolution because the fast-thinking lady of the palace filled it with firewood. Angry masses were supplied with mallets and instructions to smash everything royal and religious. While this room was both, all they saw was wood. The hatch door provided a quick path to the kitchen and an escape boat downstairs. The windows—blown out during World War II, are replacements from the 1950s.

The centerpiece of the **bedroom of Diane de Poitiers** is a portrait of Catherine de' Medici. After the queen booted out the mistress, she placed her own portrait over the fireplace, but she never used the bedroom of her husband's mistress. The 16th-century tapestries here are among the finest in France. Each one took an average of 60 worker years to make. Study the complex compositions of the *Triumph of Charity* and the violent *Triumph of Force*.

The **gallery,** at 60 meters/200 feet long, spanned the river with three stories—the upper stories house double-decker ball-rooms and guest rooms. Notice how differently the slate and limestone of the checkered floor wear after 500 years. Imagine grand banquets here. Catherine, a contemporary of Queen Elizabeth I of England, wanted to rule with style. She threw wild parties, employing her ladies to circulate and soak up all the political gossip possible from the well-lubricated Kennedys and Rockefellers of her realm. Parties included mock naval battles in the river and grand fireworks displays out the windows. For a quick walk outside (and more good palace views), cross the bridge, pick up a reentry ticket, take your stroll (you're across the river from the château), then show your reentry ticket when you return. Chenonceau, which marked the border between free and Nazi France in World War II, was the scene of dramatic prisoner swaps.

The staircase leading **upstairs** wowed royal guests. It was the first non-spiral staircase they'd seen . . . quite a treat in the 16th century. The upper gallery usually contains a temporary modern art exhibit. Small side rooms on the upper floor show fascinating old architectural sketches of the château. The walls, 6 meters/ 20 feet thick, were honeycombed with the flues of 224 fireplaces and passages for servants to do their pleasure-providing work unseen. There was no need for plumbing. Servants fetched, car-ried, and dumped everything pipes do today. The balcony here provides fine views of the gardens—originally functional with vegetables and herbs. The estate is still full of wild boar and deer—the primary dishes of past centuries.

The state-of-the-art (in the 16th century) **kitchen** is not to be missed. It was in the basement because heat rises (helping heat the palace), and it was near water (to fight the inevitable kitchen fires). Beyond the fine servants' dining room, there's a landing bay for goods to be ferried in and out. In 1916, the château was a hospital for France's countless wounded soldiers—with a hundred beds lining its gallery. The slick kitchen is from that time.

Chenonceau's crowds are the worst in the Loire—arrive early or late (château entry-€7.75, mid-March–mid-Sept daily 9:00–19:00, early closing off-season, tel. 02 47 23 90 07). Rentable rowboats offer an idyllic way to savor graceful château views (€2/30 min, 10:00–19:00, 4 people per boat).

The château stables (in front of the grand entry) house the **Musée de Cires**, which puts a waxy face on the juicy history of the château. It's well-described in English and offers a good intro before you actually tour the place (€3). Next door is a fine modern cafeteria. Fancy meals are served in the orangery behind the stables.

Sleeping in Chenonceaux
(€1 = about $1, country code: 33, zip code: 37150)

MODERATELY PRICED
Hôtel la Roseraie*** is a lovely place. While English-speaking
Laurent and Sophie will spoil you, their delightfully decorated,
country-classy rooms will enchant you (Db-€44–90, a few grand
family rooms-€72–120, CC, free parking, heated pool, rental
bikes, and a wood-beamed dining room where I dress up and
splurge for dinner—€16/€22/€30 *menus*, located dead center
on main drag at 7 rue Dr. Bretonneau, hard-to-read sign, tel.
02 47 23 90 09, fax 02 47 23 91 59, www.charminghotel.com).

Relais Chenonceaux***, across from Hôtel La Roseraie, has
modern, wood-finished rooms and a flowery patio (Db-€46–64,
Tb-€63–72, Qb-€76, CC, tel. 02 47 23 98 11, fax 02 47 23 84 07,
www.chenonceaux.com).

LOWER PRICED
Hostel du Roy**, a good but basic value, has simple rooms, a quiet
garden courtyard, and an average restaurant (Db-€38–42, Tb-€45–
51, Qb-€50–70, CC, 9 rue Dr. Bretonneau, 5-min walk to château,
tel. 02 47 23 90 17, fax 02 47 23 89 81, www.hostelduroy.com,
Nathalie SE).

Eating in Chenonceaux
For a splurge, try **Hôtel la Roseraie** (see "Sleeping," above).
Au Gateau de Breton is a friendly, reasonable, and good restaurant for lunch or dinner (closed Tue–Wed, 16 rue Dr. Bretonneau,
tel. 02 47 23 90 14).

Transportation Connections—Chenonceaux
By train to: Tours (3/day, 30 min).
By bus to: Amboise (1/day, 15 min, departs Chenonceaux
at 12:40, and in summer also at 16:45).

MORE CHÂTEAUX EAST OF TOURS
To explore the following châteaux, use either Amboise (above) or
Chenonceaux (above) as your home base.

The region between the Loire and Paris is the breadbasket
of France, with fertile soil and a temperate climate. (It has almost
no snow or need for summer air-conditioning.) Because this rich
land was vulnerable from attacks from the west (those pesky dukes
of Anjou), the first châteaux were defensive. Later, when the country was more established and the kings lived in the neighborhood,
these were the palaces of France's rich and powerful.

▲▲**Blois** (pron. blwah)—With quick access to Chambord (bus or car, see "Getting around the Loire Valley," above), a fresh coat of paint, dolled-up pedestrian areas, and a dynamite château, Blois is a good urban stop in this mostly rural region. The **Château Royal** is in the city center, with no nearby forest, river, or lake. It's an easy walk from the train station, near ample underground parking, and just above the TI. Pick up an English brochure and read the English displays at this well-presented castle. This château was home to Louis XII and François I, and is where Catherine de' Medici spent her last night. Begin in the courtyard, where four different wings, ranging from Gothic to neoclassical, surround you and underscore the importance of this château over many centuries. Your visit to the château's interior begins in the dazzling Hall of the Estates General and continues to a great display of gargoyles and models in a small lapidary museum, up through several gorgeously tiled and decorated royal rooms, and ends in a fine arts museum with a 16th-century who's who portrait gallery and interesting ironworks room (château entry-€6, combo-ticket with sound-and-light show-€11, April–Sept daily 9:00–18:00, until 19:30 July–Aug, Oct–March 9:00–12:30 & 14:00–17:30, occasional tours in English, sound-and-light show many evenings April–Sept).

If stopping here around lunchtime, plan on eating at **Le Marignan** on a breezy, traffic-free square in front of the château (good salads, fast service, 5 place du Château, tel. 02 54 74 73 15). At the top of the hour, you can watch the stately mansion opposite the château become "the dragon house" as monsters crane their long necks out its many windows. The House of Magic, home of Robert Houdin, the illusionist whose name Houdini took, offers an interesting but overpriced history of illusion and magic (€7.50, daily 10:00–18:00, often with a lunch break).

The **TI** is just below the château (April–Sept daily 9:00–19:00, Oct–March Mon–Sat 9:00–12:30 & 14:00–18:00, Sun 9:30–12:30, 3 avenue Jean Laigret, tel. 02 54 90 41 41). Save time to explore the city center using the TI's handy walking-tour brochure; the brown and purple routes are best.

▲▲▲**Chambord** (pron. shahm-bor)—With 440 rooms and 365 fireplaces, this place is big. It's surrounded by Europe's largest enclosed forest park—a game preserve defined by a 30-kilometer-long (20 miles) wall, teeming with wild deer and boar. Chambord, which began as a simple hunting lodge for bored Blois counts, became a monument to the royal sport and duty of hunting. (Apparently, hunting was considered important to keep the animal population under control and the vital forests healthy.) Starting in 1518, François I, using 1,800 workmen over 15 years, created this "weekend retreat" (leaving his signature salamander everywhere).

François was an absolute monarch—with an emphasis on absolute. In 32 years of rule (1515–1547), he never called the estates general (a rudimentary parliament in old regime France). This grand hunting palace was another way to show off his power. Charles V—the Holy Roman Emperor and most powerful man of the age—was invited here and thoroughly wowed.

The château, six times the size of most, consists of a Greek cross–shaped keep with four towers and two wings surrounded by stables. It has three floors: first floor—reception rooms; second floor—royal apartments; third floor—now a hunting museum; and rooftop—for viewing the hunt. Because hunting is best in the winter, when the leaves are gone and visibility is best, Chambord was a winter palace, so it has lots of fireplaces. Only 80 of Chambord's rooms are open to the public—and that's plenty. Here are the highlights:

From the ground floor (reception rooms, nothing much to see), climb the monumental **double-spiral staircase** (likely inspired by Leonardo da Vinci, who died just as construction was starting). Allowing people to go up and down without passing each other (look up the center from the ground floor), it's a masterpiece of the French Renaissance.

On the second floor, with its marvelously decorated vaulted ceilings, are the royal apartments in the **king's wing**, including François I and Louis XIV's bedrooms. The rooms devoted to the **Count of Chambord**—the final owner of the château—are interesting. This 19th-century, last of the French Bourbons was next in line to be the king when France decided it didn't need one. He was raring to rule. You'll see his coronation outfits and even souvenirs from the coronation that never happened. Notice his boyhood collection of little guns, including a working mini-cannon.

The third floor, a series of ballrooms that once hosted post-hunt parties, is now a museum with finely crafted **hunting weapons and exhibits**—myths and legends, traditions and techniques from the 16th, 17th, and 18th centuries.

The **rooftop**, a pincushion of spires and chimneys, was a viewing terrace for the ladies to enjoy the spectacle of their ego-pumping hunters. On hunt day, a line of beaters would fan out and work in from the distant walls, flushing animals to the center where the king and his buddies waited. To see what happens when you put 365 fireplaces in your house, just count the chimneys (used to heat the place in winter even today—notice all the firewood laying around). Notice the lantern tower of the tallest spire, which glowed with a torch at night when the king was in. From the rooftop, view the fine king's wing—marked by FRF (François Roi de France) and bristling with fleurs-de-lis.

This château requires good information to make it come alive. The brochure is useless. Better options are the free 90-minute **tour** (daily at 12:30-€4) or the **audioguide** (€4, second earphone-€1.50).

Admission to the château costs €7 (April–Sept daily 9:00–18:15, off-season closes at 17:15, tel. 02 54 50 40 00). From July through September, the château is open evenings (21:30–24:00 but not on Sun) with music and mood lighting (€12, or €14 for a day-and-night ticket). Also look for horse-riding demonstrations (€7.50, June–Sept daily at 11:45 and 17:00, tel. 02 54 20 31 01).

Chambord's **TI**, next to the souvenir shops, has information on bike rentals and *chambres d'hôte* (tel. 02 54 20 34 86). One daily 40-minute bus connects Chambord with Blois' train station on weekdays, but the Blois excursion bus is better (€10, departs Blois at 9:10 and 13:20; for more info, see "Getting around the Loire Valley," above).

Sleeping in Chambord: To wake up with Chambord out your window, try **Hôtel du Grand St-Michel****. It comes with Old World hunting-lodge charm, an elegant dining room (€16 and €21 *menus*), and a chance to roam the château grounds after the peasants are run out (Db-€59, big Db with view of château-€75—worth the extra cost, extra person-€13, CC, 41250 Chambord, tel. 02 54 20 31 31, fax 02 54 20 36 40).

▲▲▲**Cheverny** (pron. shuh-vayr-nee)—The most lavish furnishings of all the Loire châteaux decorate this stately hunting palace. Those who complain that the Loire châteaux have stark and barren interiors missed Cheverny. Because the palace was built and decorated from 1604 to 1634 and is immaculately preserved, it offers a unique architectural harmony and unity of style. From the start, this château has been in the Hurault family, and Hurault pride shows in its flawless preservation and intimate feel. The viscount's family still lives on the third floor—you'll see some family photos. Cheverny was spared by the French Revolution; the owners were popular then, as today, even among the village farmers.

Walking across the finely manicured grounds, you approach the gleaming château with its row of Roman emperors—Julius Caesar in the center. The fine English flier at the door describes the interior beautifully. The private apartments upstairs were occupied until 1985 and show the French art of living. In the bedroom—literally fit for a king—study the fun ceiling art, especially the "boys will be boys" cupids. You'll find a Raphael painting, a grandfather clock with a second hand that's been ticking for 250 years, a family tree going back to 1490, and a letter of thanks from George Washington to this family for their help in booting out the English. The attic of the orangery out back was filled with treasures from the Louvre during World War II, including the *Mona Lisa*.

Barking dogs remind visitors that the viscount still loves to hunt. The **kennel** (200 meters/650 feet in front of the château, signs to *Chenil*) is especially interesting at dinnertime, when the 70 hounds are fed (April–Nov at 17:00, Dec–March at 15:00). The dogs—half English foxhound and half French *Poitou*—are bred to have big feet and lots of stamina. They're fed once a day. The feeding is a spectacle demonstrating their strict training. Before chow time, the hungry dogs are let out. They fill the little kennel rooftop to watch the trainer bring in troughs stacked with delectable raw meat. He opens the gate and they gather enthusiastically around the food, yelping hysterically. Only when the trainer says to eat do these finely trained hounds dig in. You can see the dogs at any time, but the feeding show is worth planning for. The adjacent trophy room bristles with over a thousand antlers and the heads of five wild boars.

Admission to the château is €6 (April–Sept daily 9:15–18:45, Oct–March daily 9:30–12:00 & 14:15–17:00, pick up English self-guided tour brochure at château, not where you buy your ticket, tel. 02 54 79 96 29).

Cheverny village has a small grocery and several cafés. The town is easy to reach from Blois by excursion bus (see "Getting around the Loire Valley," above).

Fougères sur Bièvre (pron. foo-zher soor bee-eh-vruh)—This feudal castle is worth a look even if you don't go inside. Located a few minutes from Cheverny on the way to Chenonceaux and Amboise, it's right in the village (constructed for defense, not hunting) and was built over the small river (unlimited water supply during sieges). It has been completely renovated, and, while there are no furnishings, you'll see models of castle-construction techniques. Contemplate the impressive roof structure, gaze through loopholes, stand over drop holes in the main tower (hot oil, anyone?), and ponder two medieval latrines demonstrating how little toilet technology has changed in 800 years. Posters throughout (French only) describe modern renovation techniques (€4, April–Sept daily 9:30–12:00 & 14:00–18:00, Oct–March closes at 16:30, helpful English handout).

▲▲**Chaumont-sur-Loire** (pron. show-mon-soor-lwahr)—Chaumont's first priority was defense; a castle has been here since the 11th century (you'll appreciate its strategic location on the long climb up from the village below). Built mostly in the 15th and 16th centuries, this place was force-swapped by Catherine de' Medici for Diane de Poitiers' Chenonceau; you'll see tidbits about both women inside. Louis XVI, Marie-Antoinette, Voltaire, and Benjamin Franklin all spent time here.

Today's château offers a good look at the best defense design in 1500 (on a cliff with a dry moat, big and small drawbridges with classic ramparts, loopholes for arrows, and machicolations—holes for rocks and hot oil against attackers). The entry is littered with various coats of arms. As you enter, take a close look at the two drawbridges.

Inside, the heavy defensive feel is replaced with a luxurious palace feel. Around 1700, a more stable age, the fourth wing was taken down to give the terrace a fine river valley view. The 50-meter-deep well (165 feet) is fun for echoes. Study the fun spouts and decor on the courtyard walls.

Your walk through the palace—mostly restored in the 19th century—is poorly described in the flier you'll pick up as you enter. Here's more helpful information on what you'll see.

The case of **ceramic portrait busts** date from 1770, when the lord of the house had a tradition of welcoming guests by having their portrait sketched, then giving them a ceramic bust made from this sketch when they departed. Find Ben Franklin's medallion.

The **dining room**'s fanciful limestone fireplace is finely carved. Find the food (frog legs, snails, goats for cheese), the maid with the billows, and even the sculptor with a hammer and chisel at the top.

The treasury box in the **guard room** upstairs is a fine example of 1600 locksmithing. The lord's wealth could be locked up here as safely as possible in those days—false keyhole, no handles, even an extra box inside for diamonds.

The **bedroom** has a private balcony overlooking the chapel—handy when the lord wants to go to church on a bad hair day. The sentimental glass, from 1880, shows scenes from the castle's history. The tiny balcony window has an original etching of Catherine de' Medici's favorite nephew. Gaze at him and imagine the elegance of 16th-century court life. Catherine de' Medici, who missed her native Florence, brought a touch of Italy to all her châteaux. As you leave, appreciate the nifty central handrail on the spiral staircase.

The **stables** were entirely rebuilt in the 1880s. The medallion above the door reads "*pour l'avenir*" (for the future), showing off a real commitment to horse technology. Inside, circle clockwise. Notice the deluxe horse stalls—padded with bins and bowls for hay, oats, and water, and complete with strategically placed drainage ditch. The horses were named for Greek gods and great châteaux. The horse gear was rigorously maintained for the safety of carriage passengers. The covered alcove is where the horse and carriage were prepared for the prince. And the former kiln was redesigned to be a room for training the horses.

The estate is a **tree garden** set off by a fine lawn. Trees were imported from throughout the Mediterranean world to be enjoyed and to fend off any erosion on this strategic bluff.

The château entry fee of €5.50 includes the stables (daily May–mid-Sept 9:30–18:30, spring and fall 10:30–17:30, winter 10:00–17:00, English handout available, tel. 02 54 51 26 26). Drivers can save a 10-minute uphill hike by driving up and around to park (free) at the higher "Annex du Château" entrance.

Loches and Valancay (pron. lohsh, vah-lahn-say)—Overlooked Loches, located about 30 minutes south of Amboise, would be my choice for the best Loire home base, were it more central. This pretty town sits on the region's loveliest river, the Indre, and offers an appealing mix of medieval monuments, stroll-worthy streets, and fewer tourists. The castle dominates the skyline and is worth a short visit. The Wednesday street market is small but lively. **Hôtel George Sand*** is right on the river, with a well-respected restaurant, an idyllic terrace, and rustically comfortable rooms (Db-€47–70, a few large Db-€110, CC, no elevator, 300 meters/985 feet south of TI at 39 rue Quintefol, tel. 02 47 59 39 74, fax 02 47 91 55 75).

The nearby Renaissance château of **Valancay** is a massive, lavishly furnished structure with echoes of Talleyrand (Napoleon's prime minister), lovely gardens, and many kid-friendly summer events such as fencing demonstrations (€6, March–Nov daily 9:30–18:00, until 19:30 in summer, closed Dec–Feb, audioguide available, tel. 02 54 00 10 66).

CHINON

This pleasing town straddles the Vienne River and hides its ancient cobbles under a historic castle. Chinon (pron. shee-non) is best known today for its popular red wines (tasting opportunities abound), but for me, it makes the best home base for seeing the sights west of Tours: Azay le Rideau, Villandry, Langeais, Ussè, and the Abbey of Fontevraud.

Everything of interest to travelers is between the château and the river. The **TI** has bike rentals, *chambres d'hôte* listings, wine-tasting details, and a handy, English-language, self-guided tour of the town (May–Sept daily 9:00–19:00, Oct–April Mon–Sat 10:00–12:00 & 14:00–18:00, in village center on place Hofhein, tel. 02 47 93 17 85).

Bike Rental: Rent bikes at Agnes Sorel Hôtel (helpful owners suggest routes, 4 quai Pasteur, tel. 02 47 93 04 37).

Sights—Chinon

▲▲**Château de Chinon**—Don't underestimate this crumbled castle, especially if you're looking for a stark medieval comparison

Chinon

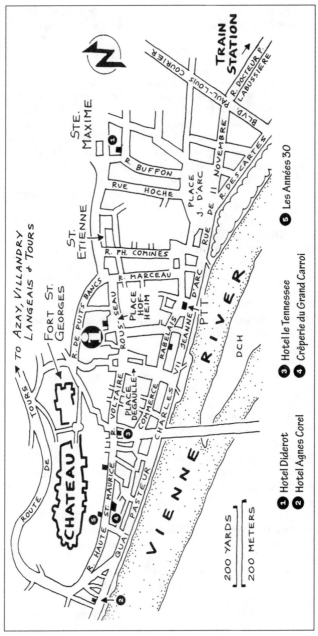

TRAIN STATION

STE. MAXIME

R. BUFFON

RUE HOCHE

ST. ETIENNE

R. PH. COMINES

R. MARCEAU

FORT ST. GEORGES

TO AZAY, VILLANDRY LANGEAIS & TOURS

R. DE PUITS BANCS

PLACE HOF-HEIM

ROUSSEAU

CHATEAU

ROUTE DE TOURS

R. HAUTE ST. MAURICE

QUAI PASTEUR

VOLTAIRE

PLACE DEGAULLE

COMMERCE

RABELAIS

VII

CHARLES

JEANNE D'ARC

R. PAUL-LOUIS COURIER

R. DE II NOVEMBRE

PLACE J. D'ARC

RUE D'ARC

R. DESCARTES

BLVD. DOCTEUR P. LABUSSIERE

PTT

VIENNE RIVER

DCH

200 YARDS

200 METERS

❶ Hotel Diderot
❷ Hotel Agnes Corel
❸ Hotel le Tennessee
❹ Crêperie du Grand Carroi
❺ Les Années 30

to châteaux of the lavish hunting-lodge variety. Henry II and Eleanor of Aquitaine loved this place, and it was here that Joan of Arc first encouraged Charles VII to take the throne. It's a steep walk up from the town of Chinon, but the views are sensational. What remains of this 12th-century castle is well-presented in English by tour-on-your-own pamphlets or, better, on unusually good live tours (6/day in summer, 4/day in winter, free with ticket, call for hours). Start in the "exposition room" with a short, automated history of the château (every other show presented in English), and end at the impressive *donjon* (keep) housing a three-floor museum about Joan of Arc. For information broadcast on a loudspeaker in English, press the English button by the door at the exit of each room. Enjoy the stunning views from the top (€4.50, mid-March–Oct daily 9:00–19:00, Nov–mid-March 9:00–12:00 & 14:00–17:30, tel. 02 47 93 13 45).

Sleeping in Chinon
(€1 = about $1, country code: 33, zip code: 37500)
Hotels are a good value in Chinon. If you sleep here, walk out to the river after dark for a floodlit view of the castle walls.

MODERATELY PRICED
Hôtel Diderot**, an appealing 18th-century manor house on the eastern edge of town, offers comfortable rooms surrounding a peaceful courtyard. Ground-floor rooms on the courtyard are a bit dark but have private patios. There are a few good family rooms (Sb-€41–52, Db-€49–64, extra bed-€13, CC, 4 rue Buffon, tel. 02 47 93 18 87, fax 02 47 93 37 10, www.hoteldiderot.com, friendly Rachel and Laurent speak enough English).

    Hôtel Agnes Sorel, a 10-minute walk west of the TI, is intimate and cozy with welcoming owners (Stephane and Catherine) and 10 traditionally furnished rooms, a few with river views, and four rooms in an annex surrounding a flowery courtyard (Db-€46–72, Db suite-€93, T/Qb suite-€112, CC, rental bikes, 4 quai Pasteur, tel. 02 47 93 04 37, fax 02 47 93 06 37).

LOWER PRICED
Le Tennessee, with clean linoleum rooms above a café in the town center, is this town's best budget value, with no stars, no fluff, lots of stairs, and an owner with an attitude (Db-€31, CC, 11 rue Voltaire, tel. 02 47 93 02 85, fax 02 47 98 43 72).

Eating in Chinon
Crêperie du Grand Carroi makes great crêpes at reasonable prices (closed Tue, just off pedestrian rue Voltaire at 30 rue du

Grand Carroi). **Les Années 30** is my favorite restaurant in town
(€24 *menus*, 78 rue Voltaire, tel. 02 47 93 37 18). For an incredible
experience and a meal you won't soon forget, drive 15 minutes to
Villandry and dine at the farmhouse **Etape Gourmande**. Have
your hotel reserve for you (€13–25 *menus*, daily 12:00–15:00
& 19:30–21:00, closed mid-Nov–mid-March, Domaine de la
Giraudière, 1 km from château toward Druye, tel. 02 47 50 08 60).

MORE CHÂTEAUX WEST OF TOURS

▲**Azay le Rideau** (pron. ah-zay luh ree-doh)—Most famous for
its romantic, reflecting-pond setting, serene Azay le Rideau sits in a
beautiful park. Its interior is far more interesting if you rent the
€4.50 audioguide (€6 entry, April–Sept daily 9:30–18:00, until 19:00
in summer, Oct–March 9:00–12:30 & 14:00–17:30, imaginative
€10 sound-and-light show May to mid-Sept, tel. 02 47 45 42 04).

Azay's **TI** is behind Hôtel Le Grand Monarque on place
l'Europe (April–Oct daily 9:00–13:00 & 14:00–18:00, Nov–March
Tue–Sat 14:00–18:00, tel. 02 57 45 44 40).

The town's appealing center may convince you to set up here.
If you do, **Hôtel Biencourt**** is ideal, near the château and a very
good value with light, airy rooms in a restored convent (Db-€35–
52, CC, 7 rue de Balzac, 37190 Azay le Rideau, tel. 02 47 45 20 75,
fax 02 47 45 91 73, e-mail: biencourt@infonie.fr).

▲▲**Langeais** (pron. lahn-zhay)—This epitome of medieval
castles, complete with a moat, drawbridge, lavish defenses, and
turrets, is elegantly furnished and has basic English descriptions
in each room. Langeais, which provides a good feudal contrast
to the other more playful châteaux, is the area's fourth-most-
interesting castle after Chenonceau, Chambord, and Cheverny
(€7, daily mid-March–mid-Oct 9:30–18:30, until 20:00 in
summer, mid-Oct–mid-March 10:00–17:00, tel. 02 47 96 72 60,
frequent train service from Tours).

▲**Villandry** (pron. vee-lahn-dree)—This unremarkable château,
a ▲▲▲ sight for gardeners, has the region's best gardens, immaculately maintained and arranged in elaborate geometric patterns.
The garden overlook behind the château is terrific. The 10-acre,
Italian Renaissance–style garden (designed c. 1530) is full of symbolism that's explained in the flier you pick up as you enter. Even
the herb and vegetable sections are artistic. This was the home
France's minister of finance built in 1536—politicians.... The
château interior is forgettable, but the château ticket gives you a
10-minute *Four Seasons of Villandry* slide show (with period music)
that offers a look at the gardens throughout the year (€7.50, €5
for gardens only, Easter–Sept daily 9:00–19:00, Oct–Easter closes
at 17:30, tel. 02 47 50 02 09).

Ussè (pron. oos-seh)—This château, famous as the "*Sleeping Beauty* castle," is worth a quick photo stop for its fairy-tale turrets and gardens, but don't bother touring it. The best view, with reflections and a golden-slipper picnic spot, is from just across the bridge.

▲**Abbaye de Fontevraud** (pron. fohn-tuh-vroh)—Located a 15-minute drive west of Chinon, this well-presented 12th-century abbey housed nuns and monks and was run by powerful women. The tombs of Henry II, Eleanor of Aquitaine, and Richard the Lionhearted are in the beautifully austere church. Don't miss the one-of-a-kind medieval kitchen (€5.50, June–mid-Sept daily 9:00–18:15, mid-Sept–May 9:30–12:00 & 14:00–18:00, closes at 17:00 Nov–Mar, 4 tours/day in English, or tour it alone using the informative handout, tel. 02 41 51 71 41, www.abbaye-fontevraud.com).

DORDOGNE

The Dordogne River Valley is a dreamy blend of natural and man-made beauty. Walnut orchards, tobacco, and corn fields carpet the valley, while stone fortresses stand guard on cliffs above. During much of the on-again, off-again Hundred Years' War, this lazy river separated Britain and France. Today's Dordogne carries more tourists than goods, and struggles to manage its popularity.

The joys of the region include rock-sculpted villages, fertile farms surrounding I-could-retire-here cottages, film-gobbling vistas, relaxed canoe rides, and a local cuisine worth loosening your belt for. The Dordogne's most thrilling sights are its caves, decorated with prehistoric artwork. The caves of Font-de-Gaume and Peche Merle have the greatest ancient cave paintings (15,000 years old) still open to the public.

To explore this beautiful river valley, sleep near or in Beynac or Sarlat. Sarlat works best for train travelers. If you're visiting in summer, consider splurging for a rare air-conditioned room.

Planning Your Time

You'll want two days to explore this magnificent region. Your sight-seeing obligations are prehistoric cave art, the Dordogne River Valley, the town of Sarlat, and, if you have a bit more time, the Lot River Valley (best done when heading to or from the south)—or, if wine matters, St. Emilion, two hours to the west. You'll need a full roll of film for the riverfront villages and medieval castles, a water-proof camera for your canoe trip, and a bib to drool on as you gaze at 15,000-year-old art. Call well in advance to reserve a ticket to the cave art at Grotte de Font-de-Gaume (easier at Peche Merle caves) or ask your hotel for help when you reserve your room (see below under "Cro-Magnon Caves in the Dordogne Region"). This area is inundated with tourists in August.

A good way to organize your first day would be a morning in Sarlat (ideally during market day), and an afternoon canoe trip, with time at the end to explore Beynac and/or Castelnaud. If it's not market day in Sarlat, do the canoe trip first thing (9:00ish) and you'll have the river to yourself.

For part or most of a second day, drivers can begin with a tour of a Cro-Magnon cave (several listed below), then explore the less-traveled Vézère River connecting Les Eyzies, La Roque St. Christophe, and the Lascaux II cave at Montignac (canoes also available on the Vézère). Train travelers with a second day should take one of the minivan or taxi excursions described below.

With a third day and a car, head upriver to explore Roca-madour, Gouffre de Padirac, and storybook villages such as Carennac, Autoire, and Loubressac. With good preparation, train travelers can fit in more stops (see "Transportation Connections—Sarlat," below).

As you drive in or out the day before or after (connecting the Dordogne with the Loire and Carcassonne), break the long drives with stops in Oradour-sur-Glane and Collonges la Rouge to the north (the A-20 autoroute from Souillac is currently free and provides quick access to Oradour and the Loire Valley), and by all means cruise the Lot Valley on your way south (from Cahors to Cajarc). If you're heading west, take time to sample the Bordeaux wine region's prettiest town, St. Emilion.

Getting around the Dordogne

This region is a joy with a car, but tough without. You could rent a car or a bike (in Sarlat or Les Eyzies), take a minivan excursion (see below), or get to Beynac and toss your itinerary into the Dordogne.

By Bike or Moped: Bikers find the Dordogne beautiful but darn hilly, with busy main roads. Consider a moped, if you dare. Rent bikes and mopeds in Sarlat (see "Helpful Hints," under Sarlat, below). A scenic Dordogne Valley loop ride is described in "Sights—Along the Dordogne River," below.

By Train: Train service is sparse. Trains run from Sarlat to the Font-de-Gaume caves in Les Eyzies (transfer in Le Buisson, 30-min walk from station to caves), but leave you in Les Eyzies all day.

By Car: Roads are small, slow, and scenic. There is no autoroute near Sarlat, so you'll need more time than usual to get in to, out of, and around this relatively remote region. You can rent a car in Sarlat (see "Helpful Hints," under Sarlat, below), though bigger cites such as Bordeaux and Brive-la-Gaillarde offer more choices and better deals.

Heart of the Dordogne

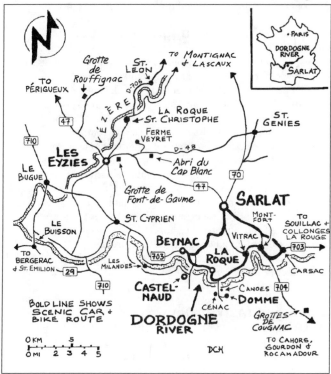

By Custom Taxi/Minivan Excursions: Decouverte et Loisirs offers four different minivan tours in French and English for one to eight people (depart at 11:00, return at 18:00), though none visit the Font-de-Gaume cave (€29–44 per person, tel. 05 65 37 19 00). A better option, which allows you to include Font-de-Gaume, is to go with friendly Philippe, owner of **Allo-Taxi Philippe.** He likes Americans, speaks English, and has a new vehicle with leather interior and raised seats for better viewing. Philippe will custom-design your tour, help with cave reservations, and give running commentary on his region during your excursion. Many pickup locations are possible, including Bordeaux's airport and remote train stations (€25/hour for up to 7 people, tel. 05 53 59 39 65, cellular 06 08 57 30 10, e-mail: allophilippetaxi @orange.fr). **Allo Sarlat Taxi** is another taxi service that does excursions (tel. 05 53 59 02 43, cellular 06 80 08 65 05).

For taxi service from Sarlat to Beynac or La Roque-Gageac,

allow €10–12 (€20 at night); from Sarlat to Les Eyzies, allow €25 one-way (€38 at night and on Sun) or €45 round-trip.

Cuisine Scene—Dordogne River Valley

Gourmets flock to this area for its geese, ducks, and wild mushrooms. The geese produce (involuntarily) the region's famous foie gras (they're force-fed, denied exercise, and slaughtered for their livers). Foie gras tastes like butter and costs like gold. The duck specialty is *confit de canard* (duck meat preserved in its own fat—sounds terrible but tastes great). *Pommes Sarladaise* are mouthwatering, thinly sliced potatoes fried in duck fat and commonly served with *confit de canard*. Wild truffles are dirty black mushrooms that farmers traditionally locate with sniffing pigs and then charge a fortune for (€457 per kilo, $190 per pound). Native cheeses are Cabécou (a silver-dollar-sized, pungent, nutty-flavored goat cheese) and Echourgnac (made by local Trappist monks). You'll find walnuts *(noix)* in salads, cakes, and liqueurs. Wines to sample are Bergerac (red and white) and Cahors (a full-bodied red). The *vin de noix* (sweet walnut liqueur) is perfect before dinner.

Remember, restaurants serve only during lunch (11:30–14:00) and dinner (19:00–21:00, later in bigger cities); cafés serve food throughout the day.

Dordogne Market Days

Market days are a big deal in rural France, and nowhere more than in the Dordogne. I've listed good market days below for every day of the week, so there's no excuse for drivers not to experience a market in the Dordogne. Here's what to look for.

Strawberries *(fraises):* Everyone in France knows the best strawberries come from this region. Available from April to November, they're gorgeous, and they smell even better than they look. Buy *un barquette* (small basket) and keep the leftovers for breakfast tomorrow. Look also for *fraises des bois*, tiny, sweet, and less visually appealing strawberries found in nearby forests.

Cheese *(fromages):* The region is famous for its Cabécou cheese (see above), though you'll often find Auvergne cheeses (St. Nectaire and Cantal are the most common) from just east of the Dordogne as well (usually in big rounds).

Truffles: Often only the bigger markets will have these ugly jet-black mushrooms on display. Their season is our off-season (Nov–Feb), when you'll find them at every market. Those you see displayed at other times are sterilized. On Sarlat market days, there's usually a guy in the center of la place de la Liberté with a photo of his grandfather and his truffle-hunting dog.

Anything with walnuts *(aux noix): Pain aux noix* are

thick-as-a-brick bread loafs chock full of walnuts. *Moutarde de noix* is walnut mustard. *Confiture de noix* is a walnut spread for hors d'oeuvres. *Gateaux de noix* are tasty cakes laced with walnuts. *Liqueur de noix* is a marvelous creamy liquor, great over ice or blended with a local white wine.

Goose liver pâté (foie gras): This spread is made from geese (better) and ducks (still good), or from a mix of the two. You'll see two basic forms: *entier* and *bloc*. Both are 100 percent foie gras; *entier* is a piece cut right from the product, *bloc* has been whipped to make it easier to spread. Foie gras is best accompanied by a sweet white wine (like a Sauterne). You can bring the tins back into the United States, *pas de problème*.

Dried sausages *(saucissons sec):* Long tables piled high with dried sausages covered in herbs or stuffed with local goodies are a common sight in French markets. You'll always be offered a mouthwatering sample. Those made in the Dordogne come stuffed with walnuts.

Olive oil *(Huile d'olive):* You'll find stylish bottles of oil flavored with walnuts, chestnuts *(chataignes)*, and hazelnuts *(noisettes)*—good for cooking, ideal on salads, and great as gifts.

Olives and nuts *(olives et noix):* These interlopers from Provence find their way to every market in France.

Liquors *(liqueurs):* While they're not made in this region, Armagnac, Cognac, and other southwest fruit–flavored liquors are often available from a seller or two. Philippe makes it to many of the markets; look for his stand in Sarlat on Wednesday and Saturday, and try his *liqueur de pomme verte* and his *crème de Myrtilles*. His family has been distilling these creations for over 200 years.

Dordogne Market Schedule

Sunday: St. Cyprien (lively market, 10 min west of Beynac), Montignac (near Lascaux), and St. Genies (halfway between Sarlat and Montignac, a tiny, intimate market in a lovely village with few tourists)
Monday: Les Eyzies (Font-de-Gaume caves are here)
Tuesday: Cénac (canoe float begins here), Le Bugue (great market, 20 min west of Beynac)
Wednesday: Sarlat (bustling market)
Thursday: Domme
Friday: Souillac (transfer point to Cahors, Carcassonne)
Saturday: Sarlat, Cahors (both are excellent)

SARLAT

Sarlat (pron. sar-lah) is a pedestrian-filled banquet of a town, scenically set amid forested hills. There are no blockbuster sights here, just a seductive tangle of golden cobblestone alleys that are off-limits to cars, and peppered with beautiful buildings and foie gras stores (geese hate Sarlat). The town is warmly lit at night and perfect for after-dinner strolls. Sarlat is just the right size—large enough to have a theater with four screens and small enough so that everything is an easy stroll from the town center. Sarlat has been a haven for writers and artists throughout the centuries and remains so today.

Orientation

Rue de la République slices like an arrow through the circular old town. Sarlat's smaller half has few shops and many quiet lanes; all of the action lies east of rue de la République. Get lost.

Tourist Information: The English-speaking TI is on rue Tourny, 50 meters/165 feet to the right of the cathedral as you face it. Ask for a free map of the city, *chambres d'hôte* listings, brochures on most regional sights, and the useful *Guide Pratique* booklet, which has car, bike, and canoe rental information (April–Nov Mon–Sat 9:00–19:00, Sun and Dec–March 10:00–12:00 & 14:00–18:00, tel. 05 53 31 45 45, www.sarlat-tourisme.com). Ask about occasional English walking tours (€4, 90 min, meet at TI).

Arrival in Sarlat

By Car: Sarlat's limited access funnels cars to narrow streets, creating long backups at busy times. Parking can be a headache, particularly on market days. Try along avenue Gambetta in the north end of town or in one of the signed lots along the ring road. Be careful not to park on a market street on Tuesday or Friday nights.

By Train: Train travelers have a mostly downhill 20-minute walk to the center (consider a taxi, about €6, see "Helpful Hints," below). To walk into town, turn left out of the station and follow avenue de la Gare as it curves downhill, then turn right at the bottom on avenue Thiers to reach the center.

Helpful Hints

Internet Access: Of Sarlat's three Internet cafés, the most central is Cyber Café (19 rue de la République, tel. 05 53 31 67 04).

Laundry: The town launderette (daily 9:00–22:00) is across from the recommended Hôtel la Couleuvrine (self-serve or leave and pick up).

Car Rental: Try **Europcar** (le Pontet, place de la Lattre de Tassigny, tel. 05 53 30 30 40, fax 05 53 31 10 39) or **Budget** (Centre Commercial du Pontet, tel. 05 53 28 10 21, fax 05 53 28 10 92).

Bike Rental: Rent bicycles at **Peugeot-Cycles Sarladais** (36 avenue Thiers, tel. 05 53 28 51 87, fax 05 53 28 50 08) or at **Budget** car rental (listed above).

Taxi: Call Philippe of **Allo-Taxi Philippe** at tel. 05 53 59 39 65, cellular 06 08 57 30 10.

Sights—Sarlat

▲▲**Strolling Sarlat**—You can use the TI's free map (with a microscopic-print walking tour), or buy the informative three-panel *City of Sarlat* brochure (€4.60 on sale at many shops), as you follow this walking tour.

Place du Peyrou: Start in front of the cathedral on **place du Peyrou**. An eighth-century Benedictine abbey stood where the cathedral does today and provided the stability for Sarlat to grow into an important trading city in the Middle Ages (see "Medieval Monasteries," page 420). Unlike other castle-protected villages you'll visit in this area, this abbey town grew up without natural or man-made defenses. The building to your right is the old Bishop's Palace, built right into the cathedral, providing a short commute for the bishop and looking *molto* Italian with the top-floor loggia (notice the building on the opposite side of the square with a similar loggia). Sarlat saw its zenith after the Hundred Years' War (about 1450–1550), when Renaissance style was the fashion and Italian architects were in high demand. Many of Sarlat's most impressive buildings date from this prosperous era. That beautiful house on your left dates from this period. It was the home of Etienne de La Boétie (pron. lah bow-ess-ee), a 16th-century radical who spoke and wrote against the rule of tyrants, and who remains a local favorite. Notice how the nearby house arches over the small street, a common practice to maximize buildable space in the Middle Ages. The **cathedral** began as an abbey church and today shows an eclectic mix of styles with almost no exterior decoration. It was dedicated to St. Sacerdos, a bishop from nearby Limoges whose claim to fame was curing leprosy. Walk inside. The interior is freshly cleaned. A column on the right shows a long list of hometown boys who gave their life for their country in World War I.

Lantern of the Dead (Lanterne des Morts): Exit the cathedral via the right transept into what were once the abbey's cloisters. Snoop through two quiet courtyards and then turn left, making your way toward the rear of the cathedral. Climb the steps to that medieval space capsule, the Lantern of the Dead. Tradition has it that a flame glowed from this tower, identifying the location of a cemetery where big shots were buried in the Middle Ages. It looks more like a medieval spaceship to me.

Notice the stone roofs on many buildings. Called *lauzes* in French, these flat limestone rocks are common in this area and made cheap, durable roofing material. They last about 200 years and weigh about 1,000 pounds per square meter. The steep pitch of the roofs common in this region helped disperse the weight over a greater area.

Exit right (with your back to the lantern). Cross one street then turn left on impasse de la Vielle Poste, then make a quick right on rue d'Albusse, then left on rue de la Salamandre (street of the salamander). Peer in that Gothic framed doorway just below on your right. Spiral stairways like these were replaced with grand Renaissance stairways when income and space permitted. Locals like to say that Sarlat is a Renaissance city built on medieval foundations. Continue downhill until you reach...

Place de la Liberté: This has been Sarlat's main market square since the Middle Ages. The café in front of you is the best place to people-watch. Sarlat's pretty town hall stands behind you. The tallest building to the right, with that clear glass Gothic framed window, was the church of Sainte Marie; it's now a daily indoor market (open to the public). Those huge gray doors would make Boeing envious—they weigh seven tons, and are opened with big hand cranks. Walk toward the church, taking the steps just to its right. The tan boy has the best view over place de la Liberté. Veer left behind him, down the ramp into a postcard-perfect square...

Place des Oies (Square of the Geese): Feathers fly when geese are traded here on market days (on Sat Nov–March). It's serious business that's been happening here since the Middle Ages. Trophy homes surround this cute little square on all sides. On the right lived the wealthy merchant—his tower was a sign of prestige; the bigger the better. Walk to the building with the Gothic window frame opposite the tower home. Enter the wooden doorway a few doors to the right and admire the massive Renaissance stairway. These stairways were huge consumers of space, requiring a big house and a bigger income. Spiral stairs were far more space-efficient even back then. Continue working your way down the rue de Consuls and enter the straight-as-an-arrow rue de la République.

Rue de la République: This awful thoroughfare dates from the mid-1800s, when blasting big roads through medieval cities was the fashion. It wasn't until 1963 that Sarlat's other streets would become off-limits to cars, thanks to France's minister of culture at the time, André Malraux, whose *Loi de Malraux* served to preserve and restore important monuments and neighborhoods throughout France. Eager to preserve France's architectural heritage, private investors, cities, and regions worked together to create traffic-free zones and rebuild crumbled buildings. Without this law, Sarlat might well have traffic throughout its old center, and other such "efficient" roads like this crisscrossing it.

▲▲**Open-Air Markets**—Sarlat has been an important market town since the Middle Ages. Outdoor markets still thrive on Wednesday morning and all day Saturday (see "Dordogne Market Days," above). Saturday's market is best in the morning (produce and food vendors leave at noon) and seems to swallow the entire town. The best markets after Sarlat's are in St. Cyprien on Sunday and in Le Bugue on Tuesday.

Sleeping in Sarlat
(€1= about $1, country code: 33, zip code: 24200)
Sleep Code: **S** = Single, **D** = Double/Twin, **T** = Triple, **Q** = Quad, **b** = bathroom, **s** = shower only, **CC** = Credit Cards accepted, **no CC** = Credit Cards not accepted, **SE** = Speaks English, **NSE** = No English, * = French hotel rating system (0–4 stars).

To help you sort easily through these listings, I've divided the rooms into three categories based on the price for a standard double room with bath:

Higher Priced—Most rooms more than €75.

Moderately Priced—Most rooms €75 or less.

Lower Priced—Most rooms €50 or less.

Even with summer crowds, Sarlat is the train traveler's best home base. In July and August several hotels require half pension.

The hotels in the town center are Hôtel de la Madeleine, Hôtel des Recollets, Hôtel la Couleuvrine, and Hôtel de la Mairie. Of the *chambres d'hôte* listed, Toulemon and Le Manoir d'Aillac are central.

HIGHER PRICED
Hôtel de Selves*, a 10-minute walk down avenue Gambetta from place de la Petite Rigaudie, is sleek and modern, with good beds and pastel decor surrounding a swimming pool and pretty garden (Sb-€60–84, Db-€70–88, Db with balcony-€96, extra bed-€22, CC, air-con, sauna, elevator, garage-€8, 93 avenue de Selves, tel. 05 53 31 50 00, fax 05 53 31 23 52, www.selves-sarlat.com).

Hôtel de la Madeleine* is a grand place with formal service, elegant lounges, and cavernous, air-conditioned rooms (higher prices are for larger rooms, usually with bathtubs, Sb-€60–72, Db-€68–83, Tb-€95, Qb-€110, garage parking-€5.50, CC, elevator, Internet access, at north end of ring road at 1 place de la Petite Rigaudie, tel. 05 53 59 10 41, fax 05 53 31 03 62, www.hoteldelamadeleine-sarlat.com, SE).

MODERATELY PRICED
Hôtel des Recollets is popular and offers modern comfort under heavy stone arches, with smartly decorated rooms, big beds,

Sarlat

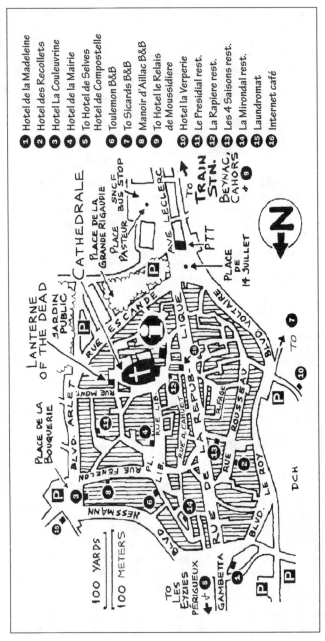

1. Hotel de la Madeleine
2. Hotel des Recollets
3. Hotel La Couleuvrine
4. Hotel de la Mairie
5. To Hotel de Selves
   Hotel de Compostelle
6. Toulemon B&B
7. To Sicards B&B
8. Manoir d'Aillac B&B
9. To Hotel le Relais
   de Moussidiere
10. Hotel la Verperie
11. Le Presidial rest.
12. La Rapiere rest.
13. Les 4 Saisons rest.
14. La Mirondal rest.
15. Laundromat
16. Internet café

and a mellow courtyard on Sarlat's quiet side (Db-€50–60, Tb-€56–68, Qb-€75, no restaurant, CC, 4 rue Jean-Jacques Rousseau, 3 blocks down rue de la République from Hôtel de la Madeleine, tel. 05 53 31 36 00, fax 05 53 30 32 62, www .hotel-recollets-sarlat.com, Christophe SE).

LOWER PRICED
Hôtel la Couleuvrine** has plenty of medieval character and mostly cozy rooms, many of which need new carpeting. Families enjoy *les châmbres familles*, and a few rooms have private terraces (Db-€43–52, Tb-€58, CC, elevator, on ring road at 1 place de la Bouquerie, tel. 05 53 59 27 80, fax 05 53 31 26 83, www.la-couleuvrine.com). Half pension is encouraged at busy periods and in summer (figure €53 per person for room, breakfast, and dinner, with fine cuisine in an elegant restaurant).

Hôtel de la Mairie** plays second fiddle to its café. It's young and basic, with big rooms right on the main square. Rooms #3 and #6 have the best views (Db-€45, Tb-€55, Qb-€65–75, CC, place de la Liberté, check in at café, tel. 05 53 59 05 71, fax 05 53 59 59 95).

Hôtel de Compostelle**, a 10-minute walk down avenue Gambetta from Hôtel de la Madeleine, has little character, but it does have modern rooms and a few good family suites (Db-€48–52, Tb-€70, Qb-€72–80, €6–8 more in July and Aug, CC, elevator, 64 avenue de Selves, tel. 05 53 59 08 53, fax 05 53 30 31 65, e-mail: hotel.compostelle@wanadoo.fr).

Chambres d'Hôte: These three *chambres d'hôte* are all good values, central, and compare well with the hotels listed.

Friendly, English-speaking Pierre-Henri **Toulemon** and French-speaking Diane have three large, great-value rooms with independent entry in a 17th-century home a few steps from the main square (Db-€35–43, €6 per extra person up to 5, no CC, no deposit required, simply call 1–2 days ahead to confirm your approximate arrival time, 4 rue Magnanat, look for big steps from northeast corner of place de la Liberté, tel. 05 53 31 26 60, cellular 06 08 67 76 90, www.toulemon.com).

Le Manoir d'Aillac is a grand mansion owned by the Paulsens, German refugees (who lived in New Jersey for 9 years) with three stone-and-wood furnished rooms with a separate entry (Db-€42–50, CC, open mid-May–mid-Sept, walk through courtyard next to Rossignol restaurant at 13 rue Fenelon, tel. 05 53 59 02 63, e-mail: josef.paulsen@wanadoo.fr, SE).

The old-fashioned **Sicards** rent three fine rooms in a newer home just off the ring road on the southeastern edge of the old town, a five-minute walk from the TI (Sb-€28, Db-€29–33, Tb-€36, no CC, Le Pignol, rue Louis Arlet, tel. 05 53 59 14 28, NSE).

Sleeping near Sarlat

Many golden stone hotels (with easy parking) surround Sarlat for those who prefer to be close, yet semirural.

HIGHER PRICED
Hôtel le Relais de Moussidière***, a five-minute drive below Sarlat off the road to Domme/Beynac, offers affordable luxury in a lovely setting, with a huge pool, private terraces, and an almost tropical feel (fine "standard" Db-€92–100, bigger Db-€130, CC, in Moussidière Basse, just south of Sarlat on road to Bergerac, tel. 05 53 28 28 74, fax 05 53 28 25 11).

MODERATELY PRICED
Hôtel La Verperie** (Green Fields), sits barely above Sarlat and is aptly named. Ideal for budget-minded families, the hotel has affordable rates, pool, table tennis, swings, major grass, a restaurant, and adequate comfort in the bungalow-like rooms, each with a simple terrace (Db-€53–60, Tb-€69, Qb-€75–94, an easy 15-min walk west of the city off Cahors/Perigueux road, look for brown Allée des Acacias signs, tel. 05 53 59 00 20, fax 05 53 28 58 94, e-mail: hotelaverperie@wanadoo.fr, British Michelle SE).

Eating in Sarlat

Sarlat is packed with restaurants, all of which serve local specialties, some of which are good.

Les 4 Saisons offers a fresh €18 *menu* that changes at least monthly (on Sarlat's quieter side, just off rue de la République June–Sept daily, closed Wed off-season, 2 Côte de Toulouse, tel. 05 53 29 48 59).

At **Le Presidial,** dine inside or out in this historic building and enjoy a memorable meal (*menus* from €25, closed Mon, rue Landry, tel. 05 53 28 92 47).

La Rapière, opposite the cathedral, provides wood-beam coziness and outdoor tables (*menus* from €19, June–Sept daily, closed Sun off-season, place de la Cathédrale, tel. 05 53 59 03 13).

La Mirondal is good for a quicker meal, with reasonable salads, *plats du jour*, and *menus* (daily, a block off rue de la République at 7 rue des Consuls, tel. 05 53 29 53 89). Drivers can go to Beynac or La Roque-Gageac for a beautiful setting and excellent value (see "Eating in Beynac," below).

Transportation Connections—Sarlat

Sarlat's TI has schedules. Souillac and Perigueux are the train hubs for points within the greater region. For all destinations below, you can go west via the Libourne/Bordeaux line (transferring in either city depending on your connection), or east via SNCF bus to Souillac (covered by railpass). I've listed the fastest path in each case. Sarlat train info: tel. 05 53 59 00 21.

By train to: Paris (7/day, allow 6 hrs; 3/day with change in Libourne or Bordeaux St. Jean, then TGV; and 4/day via bus to Souillac then train with possible change in Brive-la-Gaillarde), **Amboise** (3/day, 5 hrs, via Libourne or Bordeaux St. Jean, then TGV to St. Pierre des Corps, then local train to Amboise), **Limoges/Oradour-sur-Glane** (difficult trip, 5/day, 3–4 hrs; 3/day via bus to Souillac and train to Limoges, then bus to Oradour; 2/day with change in Le Buisson and Perigueux), **Cahors** (5/day, 2–3 hrs, bus to Souillac, then train to Cahors), **Albi** and **Carcassonne** (2/day in 4.5 hrs with changes in Le Buisson, Agen, and Toulouse; 3/day in 6–7 hrs via bus to Souillac then train with changes possible in Brive-la-Gaillarde and Toulouse).

To Beynac: Beynac is accessible only by taxi (about €15) or bike (best rented in Sarlat).

BEYNAC-CAZENAC

The feudal village of Beynac (pron. bay-nak) tumbles down a steep hill from its massive castle to the river far below and sees fewer tourists than its big brother, Sarlat. You'll have the Dordogne River at your doorstep and a perfectly preserved medieval village winding like a sepia film set from the beach to the castle above. The floodlit village is always open for evening strollers. Some of the film *Chocolat* was filmed here, adding to its popularity with tourists (for another *Chocolat* setting, see also "Sights—Near Semur-en-Auxois" in Burgundy chapter).

Orientation

A too-busy road separates Beynac from its river. The village climbs steeply uphill from there to the château. Pay to park at lots on the river, way up at the castle (follow signs to Château de Beynac), or halfway between. A trail follows the river toward Castelnaud (begins across from Hôtel Bonnet), with great views back toward Beynac (ideal at night) and, for able route finders, a healthy hike to Castelnaud (1 hr).

Tourist Information: The TI is at the village riverside parking lot (daily 10:00–12:00 & 14:00–18:00, closed Sun Oct–March, tel. & fax 05 53 29 43 08, www.perigord.tm.fr, Corinne and Fleurance SE). Pick up the *Plan de Beynac* (in English) for a simple, self-guided walking tour. The post office (with ATM) is across the street.

Sights—Beynac

▲**Château de Beynac**—This brooding, cliff-clinging castle soars 150 meters/500 feet above the Dordogne River. During the Hundred Years' War, the castle of Beynac housed the French, while the British set up across the river at Castelnaud. From the condition of the castles, it looks like France won. The sparsely furnished castle is most interesting for the valley views. Tour it on your own from 12:15 to 13:45; otherwise you must go with a free French-speaking guide. Pick up the English translation (€6.60, March–Oct 10:00–18:00, Nov 10:00–17:00, Dec–April 12:00–16:00, last tour departs 45 min before closing, tel. 05 53 29 50 40).

River Cruise Trips—Boats leave from Beynac's riverside parking lot and give a mildly interesting, relaxing 50-minute cruise of the Dordogne with English explanations (€6, about every 30 min 10:00–18:00, Easter–Oct, tel. 05 53 28 51 15).

Foie Gras in the Making—You can witness (evenings only) the force-feeding of geese *(la gavage)* at many places. Look for *Gavage* signs, but beware: You are expected to buy, and locals know that Americans are squeamish. Friendly Madame Gauthier's farm offers a peek at the *gavage* and is down the road behind Château de Beynac (park there or walk 10 min from château through parking lot and away from river—you'll see signs, demonstrations 18:00–19:30, tel. 05 53 29 51 45).

Sleeping in Beynac
(€1 = about $1, country code: 33, zip code: 24220)

Those with a car should sleep in or near Beynac. With hotel pickup services and taxis, even those without a car may find Beynac worth the trouble. The tiny Beynac TI posts a listing on its door of all accommodations with prices and current availability. You must pay to park in the riverfront lot between 10:00 and 19:00. Leave nothing in your car at night as theft is a problem.

LOWER PRICED

Hôtel Bonnet**, on the eastern edge of town, offers reasonable comfort, river views from many rooms (some noise, though windows are double-paned), a peaceful backyard garden, and a well-respected restaurant that feels like a hunting lodge (Db-€48–55, Tb-€58, free parking or €3 in their garage, CC, tel. 05 53 29 50 01, fax 05 53 29 83 74, e-mail: hbonnet@free.fr).

   Hostellerie Maleville, with a riverfront reception near Beynac's main intersection, offers 12 clean and quiet rooms in an annex up the street at their **Hôtel Pontet**** (Db-€46, Tb-€56, Qb-€62, CC, includes use of pool at their other hotel in nearby

Vézac, check in at Hostellerie Maleville, tel. 05 53 29 50 06, fax 05 53 28 28 52, www.hostellerie-maleville.com).

Le Café de la Rivière, just next door to Hostellerie Maleville, has two airy and pleasant rooms and even more pleasant owners, Hamish and Xanthe (British expats). The rooms are next to a garden café and have river views and some road noise through the double-paned windows (Db-€48–55, no CC, tel. 05 53 28 35 49, e-mail: cafe-de-la-riviere@wanadoo.fr).

Chambres Residence Versailles does its name justice, with five immaculate rooms that Louis would have appreciated, laundry facilities, a quiet terrace and garden, and, best of all, the welcoming Fleurys, who speak just enough English (Db-€48, 3 rooms have fine views, includes English breakfast, no CC, route du Château, tel. & fax 05 53 29 35 06). With the river on your right, take the small road—wedged between the hill and Hôtel Bonnet—800 meters/0.5 mile up, turn right at the sign that points left to le Château, and continue 100 meters/330 feet.

Sleeping near Beynac, in Vézac

LOWER PRICED

For motel-like comfort, drive 2 kilometers/1.25 miles east from Beynac to Vézac and try either the more polished **Relais des 5 Châteaux**** (Db-€44–50, CC, good restaurant, nice pool, tel. 05 53 30 30 72, fax 05 53 30 30 08, e-mail: 5chateaux@perigord .com), or the quieter and more family-friendly **l'Oustal**, with a pool, table tennis, and volleyball (Sb-€47, Db-€52, Tb-€55–60, Qb-€64–69, higher-priced rooms face pool, families should ask for their loft rooms—*chambres mezzanine*, CC, 24220 Vézac, tel. 05 53 29 54 21, fax 05 53 29 45 65, www.hostellerie-maleville.com).

Eating in Beynac

You'll dine well in air-conditioned comfort at **Hôtel du Château** (at main intersection on river, CC, tel. 05 53 29 50 13), and for the same price under wood beams at **Hôtel Bonnet** (see "Sleeping," above, each with *menus* from €15). **Taverne des Remparts** is a good value high above the town; I can't imagine leaving Beynac without relaxing at their view-perfect café—best at night (closed Mon, CC, call to reserve, tel. 05 53 29 57 76, across from castle, Jerome and Sophie SE). Next door to Hostellerie Maleville at **Le Café de la Rivière,** Hamish and Xanthe serve low-stress, less traditional food (even hamburgers) on a beautiful terrace with valley views (tel. 05 53 28 35 49). **La Petite Tonnelle** is intimate, welcoming, and reasonable (100 meters/330 feet from river on road to castle, *menus* from €14, tel. 05 53 29 95 18).

Beynac also offers a dreamy dinner-picnic site. Walk up the hill (easier said . . .), pass the château, continue out of the village, and turn right at the cemetery and walk about 50 meters/165 feet.

Sights—Along the Dordogne River

▲▲▲**Dordogne Valley Scenic Loop Ride or Drive**—The most scenic stretch of the Dordogne lies between Carsac and Beynac. From Sarlat, follow signs toward Cahors and Carsac, then veer right to Eglise de Carsac (visit this tiny Romanesque church if it's open). From Carsac, follow the river via Montfort, La Roque-Gageac, and Beynac. Bikers, note that the round-trip from Sarlat totals about 45 kilometers/28 miles. Less ambitious bikers will find the 30-kilometer/18-mile loop ride from Sarlat to La Roque-Gageac to Beynac and back to Sarlat sufficient. This trip works just as well from Beynac.

▲▲**Castelnaud**—Château de Beynac's crumbling rival looks a little less mighty, but the inside packs a medieval punch. Several rooms display weaponry and artifacts from the Hundred Years' War. The courtyard comes with a well 46 meters/150 feet deep (drop a pebble) and an entertaining video showing catapults, which litter the grounds, in action. The rampart views are as unbeatable as the siege tools outside the walls are formidable. Borrow the English explanations from the ticket seller for the room-by-room story (€6.50, 3 English tours/day in summer, May–Sept daily 10:00–19:00, July–Aug 9:00–20:00, Oct–April 10:00–18:00, Dec–Feb closes for lunch and at 17:00, last entry 1 hr before closing, from the river it's a steep, 20-minute hike through a pleasant peasant village, the €2 car park is an over-the-hills drive but gets you closer, tel. 05 53 31 30 00). There's a view café just below and a fun medieval gift shop at the entrance.

You can stop at Castelnaud halfway through your canoe trip, or take a one-hour hike from Beynac along a difficult-to-follow riverside path (it hugs the river as it passes through campgrounds and farms).

▲**La Roque-Gageac**—A few minutes upriver from Beynac, La Roque (the rock), as the locals call this village, hangs between the river and the cliffs. This place can be busy, as road traffic and pedestrians are funneled to the riverfront road. Get off the road and find the back alleys, and for views and calm, wander up the narrow tangle of lanes that seem to disappear into the cliffs. La Roque was once a thriving port, exporting Limousin oak to Bordeaux for wine barrels. Find the old ramp leading down to the river. Look for markers showing the water levels of three floods and ask someone about the occasional rock avalanches from above. The sky-high **Fort Troglodyte** is a good energy-burner, but

The Dordogne Region

offers little more than views (€4, get English explanation, daily 10:00–19:00). The small **TI** is in a parking lot at the east end of town (Easter–Sept only, daily 10:00–12:00 & 14:00–18:00, tel. 05 53 29 17 01).

Sleeping in La Roque: For a small splurge, enjoy a romantic dinner and, better yet, stay overnight at the reasonable **Hôtel Belle Etoile****. It has classic decor, a cozy bar, river views from most rooms (best rooms on main floor), and a restaurant worth the detour (closed Mon). The hotel is closed from October through March (non-riverside Db-€49, riverview rooms-€77, CC, no half pension requirement, reserve private parking ahead, 24250 La Roque-Gageac, tel. 05 53 29 51 44, fax 05 53 29 45 63, e-mail: hotel.belle-etoile@wanadoo.fr, friendly Danielle SE). At the eastern edge of the village, **Hôtel Gardette**** has well-kept rooms (5 with river views), good rates, a terrace café, and easy parking (Db-€32–46, CC, at main parking lot, 24250 La Roque-Gageac, tel. 05 53 29 51 58, fax 05 53 28 38 73, e-mail: egardette@aol.com).

Domme—The only reason to climb the hill to this over-boutiqued, soulless town is for the truly magnificent valley view. Turn your back on the trinkets and have a sensational view drink or lunch at the **Belvedere Café** (dinners also served), or, better, stay at the splendid **Hôtel l'Esplanade*****, with the best view rooms in the Dordogne and an excellent, though pricey, restaurant (Db with view-€75, Db with view and balcony-€130, extra person-€16, CC, air-con, reserve early for a dinner terrace table with commanding view, *menus* €30–80, 24250 Domme, tel. 05 53 28 31 41, fax 05 53 28 49 92, e-mail: esplanade.domme@wanadoo.fr). Just below, in unassuming little Cénac, **La Touille Chambres** are in a newer home and owned by a charming couple (Serge and Myreille, NSE) who take great pride in their very comfortable and great-value rooms, each with independent entry (D-€28, Db-€31, Tb-€39, no CC, 24250 Cénac St. Julien, 200 meters/650 feet on right after crossing the bridge to Cénac, follow green signs, tel. 05 53 28 35 25, cellular 06 08 60 91 58, e-mail: sbarry.latouille@wanadoo.fr).

▲▲▲Dordogne Canoe Trips—For a refreshing break from the car or train, explore the riverside castles and villages of the Dordogne by canoe. Several outfits rent plastic two-person canoes (and 1-person kayaks) and will pick you up at an agreed-upon spot (even in Sarlat if your group is large enough or business is slow). If Beynac is your home base, make sure the outfit allows you to get out in Beynac. For €20, two can paddle the best two-hour stretch from Cénac to Beynac (includes shuttle, call ahead to arrange if you don't have a car, in summer the usual pickup time in Beynac is 9:00). In Cénac, look for **Dordogne Randonées** (coming from Sarlat or Beynac, take the first left after crossing the bridge to Cénac, tel. 05 53 28 22 01, e-mail: randodordogne@wanadoo.fr). In La Roque-Gageac, **Canoe-Dordogne** rents canoes for the pleasant two-hour float to Château Milandes (€20, tel. 05 53 29 58 50). While you need to be in decent shape for the longer trips, it's OK if you're a complete novice—the only white water you'll encounter will be your partner frothing at the views. You'll get a life vest and, for a few extra euros, a watertight bucket. Beach your boat wherever you want to take a break. The best stops are the villages of La Roque-Gageac, Castelnaud, and Beynac.

Cro-Magnon Caves in the Dordogne Region

There are four caves in this region with original cave paintings that tourists can still admire: the top-quality Grotte de Font-de-Gaume (tours in English offered only in summer); the deep

Grotte de Rouffignac; the smaller yet interesting Grotte de Cougnac (some tours in English, fewer crowds); and the well-organized and impressive Grotte du Pech Merle (some English tours; listed under "Sights—Southeast of the Dordogne," below). Dress warmly for any cave visit, even if it's hot outside.

The first four cave sights—Grotte de Font-de-Gaume, Grotte de Rouffignac, Roque St. Cristophe, and Abri du Cap-Blanc—are within a 20-minute drive of Les Eyzies. The last two sights—Lascaux and Grotte de Cougnac—are a 30-minute drive from Sarlat (in opposite directions).

Les Eyzies-de-Tayac—This town is the overrun touristy hub of this cluster of historic caves, castles, and rivers and only merits a stop for its museum (see below). The **TI** rents bikes (July–Aug Mon–Sat 9:00–19:00, Sun 10:00–12:00 & 14:00–18:00, otherwise Mon–Sat 9:00–12:00 & 14:00–18:00, Sun 10:00–12:00 & 14:00–17:00, tel. 05 53 06 97 05, fax 05 53 06 90 79). The train station is a level 500 meters from the center (turn right out of the station).

National Museum of Prehistory—This museum makes a good first stop in your prehistory lesson. Appropriately located on a cliff ledge (across from Les Eyzies' TI), it has four small rooms with good English explanations. Among its many prehistoric artifacts are everyday tools, impressively sculpted clay bison, and a variety of human and animal skeletons dating from 50,000 B.C. (€4.50, July–Aug daily 9:30–19:00, mid-March–June and Sept–mid-Nov Wed–Mon 9:30–12:00 & 14:00–18:00, closes Tue except July–Aug and at 17:00 mid-Nov–mid-March).

Sleeping near Les Eyzies: Just 10 minutes by car from Les Eyzies, the remote hilltop farm at **Ferme Veyret** is as real as it gets. Mama greets you with a huge smile and nary a word of English, son cooks, and daughter does everything else. The rooms are spotless and furnished like grandma's, but with modern conveniences like hair dryers. You'll be expected to dine here, and you'd be a fool not to, as dinner includes everything from aperitif to *digestif*, with five courses in between and wine throughout (Db-€42 per person, includes breakfast and dinner, big pool, cows, pigs, en route to Abri du Cap-Blanc, look for yellow signs, 24620 Les Eyzies de Tayac, tel. 05 53 29 68 44, fax 05 53 31 58 28, www.perigord.com/auberge-veyret).

Caves near Les Eyzies-de-Tayac

▲▲▲**Grotte de Font-de-Gaume**—Even if you're not a connoisseur of Cro-Magnon art, you'll dig this cave. It's the last cave in Europe with prehistoric (polychrome) painting still open to the public, and its turnstile days are numbered. On a carefully guided and controlled 100-meter/330-foot walk, you'll see about 20 red-and-black bison—often in elegant motion—painted with a moving sensitivity. Your guide—with a laser pointer and great reverence—will trace the faded outline of the bison and explain how 15,000 years ago, cave dwellers used local minerals and the rock's natural contour to give the paintings dimension. The paintings were discovered by the village schoolteacher in 1901. Tickets are now limited to 200 a day, since heavy-breathing tourist hordes damage the art by raising and lowering the temperature and humidity levels.

Visits are by appointment only. Reserve in advance by phone; your hotel can make the call. Summertime spots are booked a month in advance. Even off-season, it's smart to call ahead and get a time. Request an English tour (usually summers only) and arrive 30 minutes early or lose your spot. You'll find it interesting even in French, but ask for the English brochure and read through the books in the gift shop before you go (€5.50, April–Sept 9:00–12:00 & 14:00–18:00, Oct–March 9:30–12:00 & 14:00–17:30, closed Wed, no photography or large bags, tel. 05 53 06 86 00, fax 05 53 35 26 18). Drivers who can't get a spot here (or who want to see completely different caves) should try the caves at Rouffignac (see below) or aim for the more remote Grotte du Pech Merle, an hour east of Cahors (see "Sights—Southeast of the Dordogne," below).

▲**Abri du Cap-Blanc**—In this prehistoric cave (just up the road from Font-de-Gaume), early artists used the rock's natural contours to add dimension to their sculpture. The small museum, with English explanations, will prepare you, and the useful English handout will guide you. Look for places where the artists smoothed or roughened the surfaces to add depth. In this single stone room, your French-speaking guide will spend 30 minutes explaining 14,000-year-old carvings. Impressive as these carvings are, their subtle majesty bypasses some. Free 45-minute tours leave on the half hour (€5.50, April–Nov 2, 10:00–12:00 & 14:00–19:00, no midday closing July and Aug, closed Nov 3–Feb, tel. 05 53 29 21 74). The sight is well-signed, three kilometers/two miles after Grotte de Font-de-Gaume on the road to Sarlat.

▲▲**Grotte de Rouffignac**—This is the second-best cave in the area after Font-de-Gaume. Dress warmly; the visit lasts 70 minutes and extends one kilometer into the hillside. In this extensive cave, a French-speaking guide escorts you on a small train, stopping to point out engravings of mammoths (done with wood sticks—many of those vertical lines are prehistoric bear-claw scratches) and brilliant black paintings of rhinos, bison, horses, mammoths, and reindeer. The most interesting stop is at the end as you descend from the train into a vault of black-and-white ceiling paintings (notice the original level of the floor through the end of this cave; the artists had to crawl to this place and draw while lying on their backs). The horse is amazing. The helpful guides make time to answer questions in English but usually lead the tour in French; call ahead and ask about English tours (€5.70, daily April–Nov 10:00–11:30 & 14:00–17:00, July–Aug 9:00–12:00 & 14:00–18:00, closed Dec–March, no reservations, tours leave about every 30 min, best strategy is to arrive before opening time and take the first tour—afternoons are busier, and the summertime 14:00 lineup can be ugly, tel. 05 53 05 41 71). It's well-signed from the route between Les Eyzies and Perigueux; allow 20 minutes from Les Eyzies.

Roque St. Christophe—Like hanging gardens over the Vézère River, these extensive, cliff-hugging ledges and caves (no paintings) were inhabited from 50,000 years ago to the Middle Ages, and help paint a picture of life before written history. They'll pique your interest with their sheer size, multiple levels, and stunning setting. The €1.50 English handout is well-done and essential if you don't take the usually required 45-minute tour (€5.50, daily March–Oct 10:00–18:00, Nov–Feb 11:00–17:00, tel. 05 53 50 70 45, lots of steps, 8 km north of Les Eyzies, follow signs to Montignac, good café/snack bar). Adorable St. Leon, just north of Roque St. Christophe, makes a nice lunch or coffee stop.

▲▲**Lascaux**—The region's most famous cave paintings are at Lascaux, 22 kilometers/14 miles north of Sarlat and Les Eyzies. In the interest of preservation, these caves are closed to tourists. But the adjacent Lascaux II copy caves are impressive in everything but authenticity. At Lascaux II, the reindeer, horses, and bulls of Lascaux I are painstakingly reproduced by top artists using the same dyes, tools, and techniques their predecessors did 15,000 years ago. Anyone into caveman art will appreciate the thoughtful explanations. It's worth working your schedule around English tour times (€8, daily April–Sept 9:30–18:30, July–Aug daily 9:00–20:00, Oct–March Tue–Sun 10:00–12:00 & 14:00–17:30; call ahead for English tour times, 40 min, 5 tours/day in July–Aug, on demand in off-season; from mid-April–mid-Sept tickets are sold only at Montignac TI, caves 2.5 km/1.5 miles south of Montignac, TI tel. 05 53 51 96 23 or 05 53 35 50 10). Pleasant Montignac is worth a wander.

Sleeping near Lascaux: The **Hôtel Château de la Fleunie*** offers regal 15th-century château accommodations surrounded by pastures and mountain goats, the biggest private pool I've seen in France, tennis courts, and a restaurant with *beaucoup* ambience (modern annex with terrace Db-€58, in the château Db-€60–75, Tb-€100, tower room-€135, *menus* from €24, CC, 10-min drive north of Montignac on road to Brive,

24570 Condat sur Vézère, tel. 05 53 51 32 74, fax 05 53 50 58 98, www.lafleunie.com).

▲**Grotte de Cougnac**—Located 30 kilometers/19 miles south of Sarlat, this less-touristy cave is handy for drivers. The cave offers impressive rock formations and a more intimate look at Cro-Magnon cave art. It's five kilometers/three miles north of Gourdon, just off D-704, near the cute village of Payrignac (€5.25, July–Aug daily 9:00–18:00, otherwise 9:30–11:00 & 14:00–17:00, English book available, 70-min tours, some in English, call ahead, tel. 05 65 41 47 54).

Sights—North of the Dordogne, near Limoges

▲▲▲**Oradour-sur-Glane**—Located two hours north of Sarlat and 25 kilometers/15 miles west of Limoges, this is one of the most powerful sights in France. French schoolchildren know this town well. Most make a pilgrimage here. *La Ville Martyr*, as it is known, was machine-gunned and burned on June 10, 1944, by Nazi troops. The Nazis were either seeking revenge for the killing of one of their officers (by French Resistance fighters in a neighboring village) or simply terrorizing the populace in preparation for the upcoming Allied invasion (this was 4 days after D-Day). With cool German attention to detail, the Nazis methodically rounded up the entire population of 642 townspeople. The women and children were herded into the town church, where they were teargassed and machine-gunned. Plaques mark the place where the town's men were grouped and executed. The town was then set on fire, its victims left under a blanket of ashes. Today, the ghost town, left untouched for nearly 60 years, greets every pilgrim who enters with only one English word: Remember.

Start at the **underground museum** (*Centre de la Memoire*), which provides a good social and political context for the event (with some English explanation), including home videos of locals before the attack and disturbing footage of the actual event (€6, daily 9:00–19:00, closes at 18:00 Nov–April). Then, with hushed visitors, walk the length of Oradour's main street, past gutted, charred buildings in the shade of lush trees, to the underground memorial on the market square (rusted toys, broken crucifixes, town mementos under glass). Visit the cemetery where most lives ended on June 10, 1944, and finish at the church, with its bullet-pocked altar (entry to Oradour village is free, same hours as the museum).

Public transport here is a challenge. Four daily buses connect Limoges with Oradour in 20 minutes (10-min walk from Limoges train station to bus stop on place Winston Churchill). Consider a taxi. Limoges is a stop on an alternative train route between Amboise and Sarlat.

Mortemart—With a car and extra time, visit this nontouristy village (15-min drive northwest of Oradour on D-675). You'll find a medieval market hall, a few cafés, and a sweet château (good picnic benches behind). **Hôtel Relais**** offers five rooms over a well-respected restaurant (Db-€46, Tb-€60, CC, *menus* from €15.50, 87330 Mortemart, tel. & fax 05 55 68 12 09).

▲**Collonges la Rouge**—Connoisseurs of beautiful villages need to visit this deep red sandstone and slate-roofed village that curls down a friendly hill. Collonges is a scenic 15-minute drive east of the A-20 autoroute (exit at Noailles), just south of Brive-la-Gaillarde and about a 50-minute drive from Sarlat.

The **TI** (near the top of town, tel. 05 55 25 32 25) has a brochure with English explanations and information on other nearby worth-a-wander villages. Don't miss the church's Moorish entry, wavy floor, and holy dome. Like all adorable villages, Collonges has plenty of shops and is fairly busy at midday from June through September. **Le Relais St. Jacques**** feels cozy and is the only game in town (Db-€50, CC, tel. 05 55 25 41 02, fax 05 55 84 08 51, e-mail: relais-st-jacques@yahoo.fr).

Sights—Southeast of the Dordogne

Some find this remote, less-visited section of the Dordogne even more beautiful than the area around Sarlat. Follow the Dordogne upriver east from Souillac to connect these *charmant* villages: Martel, Carennac, Loubressac, Autoire, and the impressively situated Château de Castelnau-Bretenoux (worthwhile inside and out). Just below are the Tom Sawyer–like Gouffre de Padirac and the cliff-hanging Rocamadour.

Rocamadour (▲▲ **after dark)**—One hour east of Sarlat, the dramatic rock-face setting and medieval charm of this historic pilgrimage town can be trampled daily by hordes of tourists. Those who arrive late and spend the night enjoy fewer crowds and a floodlit fantasy. Those who come only during the day might wonder why they did, as there's little to do here except to climb the steps as pilgrims did (and some still do), or cheat and take the elevator to a few churches and stare at the view.

Rocamadour has three basic levels: the bottom-level pedestrian street with shops and restaurants, the chapel level 143 steps up (or €1 elevator, €2 round-trip) with a snazzy Museum of Sacred Art (€4.75, excellent English handout), and a private château at the very top (€2.50 elevator, €4 round-trip, skip the €2.30 château view). Eight hundred years ago, there were even more tourists climbing these steps, as this was an important stop on the famous pilgrimage route to Santiago de Compostela in Spain. In 1244, these steps attracted a Crusade-bound Saint Louis (he built Sainte-Chapelle in Paris).

There are two **TIs:** the glassy TI that you come to first in l'Hospitalet (above Rocamadour) and down in La Cité Medievale on the level pedestrian street (July–Aug daily 10:00–20:00, otherwise 10:00–12:30 & 14:00–18:00, tel. 05 65 33 22 00). Ask about occasional English tours of the chapels.

Trains (transfer in Brive-la-Gaillarde) leave you about five kilometers/three miles from the village (€8 taxi, tel. 05 65 33 63 10). Drivers can approach Rocamadour in two ways: Park at the top (then walk down a series of switchbacks or take the elevator down—€4 round-trip, follow signs to *Parking Château*), or drive to the bottom (then walk or take the elevator up—€2 round-trip).

Sleeping in and near Rocamadour: Every hotel has a restaurant where they'd like you to dine. **Hôtel des Pelerins****, near the western end of the pedestrian street in La Cité Medievale, has immaculate, comfortable rooms; the best ones have balconies and face the valley (Sb-€39–48, Db-€44, Db with view and balcony-€57, Tb-€59, CC, tel. 05 65 33 62 14, fax 05 65 33 72 10, www.terminus-des-pelerins.com). **Hôtel Sainte Marie**** has a privileged location 143 steps above the main pedestrian drag (take the elevator) and rumpled rooms, most with great views (D-€40, Db-€50, Tb-€55, Qb-€59, CC, tel. 05 65 33 63 07, fax 05 65 33 69 08, www.hotel-sainte-marie.fr).

You can sleep peacefully eight kilometers/five miles from Rocamadour in the sublime *chambre d'hôte* **Moulin de Fresquet.** Gracious Gerard has restored an ancient mill complete with antique-furnished rooms, outdoor terraces, and a duck pond—with ducks for pets, not for dinner. If Gerard is cooking, eat here (Db-€51–67, Tb-€81, Qb-€87, dinner-€19, 46500 Gramat, tel. 05 65 38 70 60, cellular 06 08 85 09 21, fax 05 65 33 60 13, www.moulindefresquet.com, SE).

▲▲**Gouffre de Padirac**—Twenty minutes from Rocamadour is a fascinating cave (lots of stalagmites but no cave art). Buy the cheapest English-language booklet on the caves, read it while you wait in line, and you'll be well-briefed to follow the 70-minute French-language tour through this huge system of caverns. You'll ride elevators, hike along a buried stream, and even take a subterranean boat ride; dress warmly (€7.80, April–Oct daily 9:00–12:00 & 14:00–18:00, long lines at 14:00; no lunch closing in July–Aug, closed Nov–March, day trips organized from Rocamadour TI, tel. 05 65 33 64 56).

▲▲▲**Lot River Valley**—Ninety minutes south of the Dordogne, the overlooked Lot River meanders under stubborn cliffs, past tempting villages, and through a stunningly beautiful valley. The fortified bridge at Cahors, prehistoric cave paintings at Grotte du Pech Merle, and breathtaking town of St. Cirq Lapopie are remarkable sights in this valley—each within a half hour of the others. These sights are worthwhile for drivers connecting the Dordogne with Albi or Carcassonne, or as a long day trip from Sarlat. With extra time, spend a night in St. Cirq Lapopie (see below), and, with more time, continue upriver to Cajarc (those going to or coming from the south can scenically connect with Albi via Villefranche de Rouergue and Cordes-sur-Ciel).

Pont Valentré at Cahors—One of Europe's finest medieval monuments, this fortified bridge was built in 1308 to keep the English out of Cahors. It worked. Learn the story of the devil on the center tower. The steep trail on the non-city side leads to great views (keep climbing, avoid branch trails, be careful if the trail is wet) and was once part of the route to Santiago de Compostela. Just past the city-side end of the bridge is Le Cèdre, a wine shop/café/souvenir stand with delightful owners; say *bonjour* to Marie-Danielle and Jean-Claude and ask to sample Cahors' black wine and foie gras (duck is cheaper than goose and just as tasty). They have reasonable salads and sandwiches and can ship wine to the United States. If you need an urban fix, stroll the pedestrian-friendly alleys between Cahors' cathedral and the river.

▲▲**Grotte du Pech Merle**—About 30 minutes east of Cahors, this cave, with prehistoric paintings of mammoths, bison, and horses, rivals the better-known ones at Grotte de Font-de-Gaume. The cave is filled with interesting stalactite and stalagmite formations. I liked the mud-preserved Cro-Magnon footprint. Call to reserve a time and ask about English tours (English spoken). Start at the museum with a film subtitled in English, then descend to the caves. If you can't join an English tour, ask for the English translation booklet. In summer, arrive by 9:30 or call to reserve a spot (€7, Easter–Oct daily 9:30–12:00 & 13:30–17:00, closes earlier off-season, tel. 05 65 31 27 05, fax 05 65 31 20 47).

▲▲**St. Cirq Lapopie**—Beg, borrow, or steal a night in St. Cirq Lapopie (pron. san seer lah-poh-pee). Clinging to a ledge 180 meters/600 feet above the Lot River, this spectacularly situated village knows only two directions—straight up and way down. And while you need to be careful of summer crowds, St. Cirq has not been blemished by boutiques and remains pin-drop peaceful after-hours. Wander the rambling footpaths and uneven lanes, find the best light for your memories, and appreciate where you are. You'll find superb picnic perches, a few galleries, and several restaurants. Views from the bottom and top (find the small parking lot) of the village justify the effort. The **TI** is located across from Auberge du

Sombral (tel. 05 65 31 29 06). St. Cirq has 18 rooms, none of which are open off-season (mid-Nov–March), 10 of which are at the cozy, central **Auberge du Sombral**** , run with panache by Madame Haldeveled (Db with shower-€64, Db with tub-€72, CC, tel. 05 65 31 26 08, fax 05 65 30 26 37, phone better than fax). **Hôtel de la Pelissaria***** , at the lower end of the village, has eight carefully tended rooms cascading down the hill amid terraced gardens and postcard views up to the main village (standard Db-€82, superior Db-€112, CC, tiny pool, no restaurant, tel. 05 65 31 25 14, fax 05 65 30 25 52, e-mail: lapelissariahotel@minitel.net).

ST. EMILION AND BORDEAUX WINE COUNTRY

Two hours due west of Sarlat and just 40 minutes from Bordeaux, St. Emilion is another pretty face just waiting to flirt with you. Carved like an amphitheater in the bowl of a limestone hill, St. Emilion's manicured streets connect picture-perfect squares and well-stocked wine shops. There's little to do here other than enjoy the setting, and, of course, sample the local product. Wine has been good to this prosperous area, which accounts for barely five percent of Bordeaux's famous red wine production (about 60 percent of the grapes you see are Merlot). From the staff of St. Emilion's well-organized TI to the surprisingly friendly wine shops, everyone here speaks English.

Park free along the wall at signed parking areas (or at your hotel). While there is a train station in St. Emilion, it's a 20-minute walk from town, with no taxis and very few trains. Get off in Libourne (5 miles away, with better train service), and take a cab from there (€15, tel. 06 07 63 62 56 or 06 09 35 78 39), or take an infrequent bus to St. Emilion from the *gare routière* next to the train station (2/day).

The **TI** is a block from the main road and has everything you need, including Internet access, bike rental (and recommended bike routes), wine-tasting excursions, good information on St. Emilion's few sights, and a long list of *chambres d'hôte* (daily June–mid-Sept 9:30–19:00, until 20:00 July–Aug, mid-Sept–May 9:30–12:30 & 13:45–18:45, Nov–March closes at 18:00, place Pioceau, tel. 05 57 24 72 90). They offer frequent and mildly interesting 45-minute tours of the unusual underground church, Trinity chapel, and catacombs (€5, tour mandatory, starts at TI, ask about English tours or get the English handout).

You can climb the **bell tower** in front of the TI for a fine view (€1, get key at TI), though the view is better from the **Tour du Donjon** several blocks below (also €1, closed 12:45–14:00).

Of course, St. Emilion's primary sightseeing is for your

palate. You can sample the tasty homemade macaroons at many
shops. And while the TI offers €8 bus excursions to the vineyards
(includes a tasting), the many **wine shops** offer the best and easiest
way to sample the array of local wines. Small shops typically greet
visitors with a central tasting table, maps of the vineyards, and several open bottles. And while it's hard to distinguish the shops from
each other, you'll be pleasantly surprised at the welcoming attitude
and passion they show for their wines (remember, everyone here
speaks English). Americans may represent only about 15 percent of
the visitors, but we buy 40 percent of their wine. While it is hoped
that you will buy (particularly if you taste many wines), and shipping is easy (except to California and Texas), there is no pressure
nor fee for the tastings. Find friendly Dominique at **Caveau
des Vins** at 8 rue de la Cadene and let his passion speak for itself
(tel. 05 57 24 63 00), or find Frederic at **Cercle des Oenophiles**
on rue Guadat (ask to visit the nearby cellars with over 400,000
stored bottles of wine, tel. 05 57 74 45 55). Both shops offer large
selections from a variety of vineyards and are open 10:00–19:00
or 20:00 in summer.

Sleeping in St. Emilion
(€1 = about $1, country code: 33, zip code: 33330)
There are no cheap accommodations in this town, with its well-
heeled following.

    L'Auberge de la Commanderie** is the best midrange
value, with welcoming owners and sharp rooms—better in
the main building, though the annex has good family rooms
(Db-€55–77, Tb-€100–120, CC, free parking, tel. 05 57 24
70 19, fax 05 57 74 44 53, www.aubergedelacommanderie.com).

    Au Logis des Remparts*** is a block away with bigger,
très snazzy rooms and a pool with a garden overlooking the
vineyards (Db-€76–97, Tb-€110–195, Qb-€195, CC, easy
parking, tel. 05 57 24 70 43, fax 05 57 74 47 44, e-mail: logis
-des-remparts@wanadoo.fr).

Eating in St. Emilion
Skip the cafés lining the street by the TI, and find the cafés on
the melt-in-your-chair place du Marché. **Amelia-Canta** is the
best spot on this square, with café fare and *menus* from €15–20
(daily, tel. 05 57 74 48 03).

    Logis de la Cadene, sitting just above the place du Marché,
is the place for a special dinner, with romantically set tables
inside or out and cuisine locals rave about (*menus* from €20,
reserve ahead, tel. 05 57 24 71 40).

BASQUE COUNTRY
(LE PAYS BASQUE)

Two hours southwest of Bordeaux and far off most Americans' radar screens lies this ancient, independent corner of Europe. In Basque country, bright white chalet-style homes with deep red-and-green shutters scatter across lush rolling hills; the Pyrenees mountains soar high above the Atlantic; and surfers and sardines share the waves. Insulated from mainstream Europe for centuries, this plucky region has for more than 7,000 years just wanted to be left alone. An easily crossed border separates the French Pays Basque from the Spanish Pais Vasco, allowing you to sample both sides from a single base. Central, cozy, and manageable Saint-Jean-de-Luz makes the ideal home base for exploring the best of French and Spanish Basque lands.

The French and Spanish Basque regions share a common language *(Euskadi)*, flag (same colors as the houses—white, red, and green), and cuisine. But they have taken different routes since the French Revolution. The Revolution "tamed" French Basque ideas of independence 130 years before Spain's Generalissimo Franco did the same to his separatist-minded Basques. Language is the key to this unique culture; locals say it dates back to Neolithic times. Still spoken by 70 percent of the locals in some French villages, *Euskadi* is understood far less in the Pais Vasco, where Franco effectively blunted any expression of Basque individualism for 40 years. The bombed city of Guernica, halfway between San Sebastián and Bilbao, survives as a tragic example of Franco's efforts to suppress Basque independence.

Today, Basque lands are undergoing a 21st-century renaissance with the brilliant revitalization of long ignored cities like Bayonne, dazzling new architecture replacing rusted industries in Bilbao, and enthusiastic visitors rejuvenating the once trendy resorts of San Sebastián and Biarritz.

Basque Country

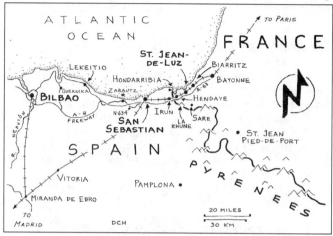

There's also a renewed awareness of the importance of the Basque language (absolutely unrelated to any other). Look for street signs, menus, and signs in shops. Basque, with its seemingly impossible-to-pronounce words filled with k's and z's (rest rooms in Basque are *gizonak* for men and *emakumeak* for women), makes speaking French suddenly seem easy.

The Basque terrorist organization, ETA (which stands for Basque, country, and freedom), is primarily active on the Spanish side of the border and supported by a tiny minority of the population. They focus their anger on political targets and go largely unnoticed by tourists.

Cuisine Scene—Basque Country

Mixing influences from mountain, sea, Spain, and France, Basque food is reason enough to visit the region. Unusual in France, the local cuisine—dominated by seafood, tomatoes, and red peppers—offers some spicy dishes. The red peppers hanging from homes in small villages end up in *piperade*, a dish combining peppers, tomatoes, garlic, ham, and eggs. Don't leave without trying *ttoro* (pron. t-oro), Basque's answer to bouillabaisse and cioppino. Look for anything *Basquaise* (cooked with tomato, eggplant, red pepper, and garlic), such as *thon* (tuna) or *poulet* (chicken). Local cheeses come from Pyrenean sheep's milk *(pur brebis)*. And the local ham *(jambón de Bayonne)* is famous throughout France. Hard apple cider is the locally made beverage. The region's wine, Irouleguy, isn't worth its price.

Remember, French restaurants serve only during lunch (11:30–14:00) and dinner (19:00–21:00, later in bigger cities); cafés serve food throughout the day.

Planning Your Time

Allow two full days to sample French and Spanish Basque country. Most of your sightseeing will be cultural and scenic, as only two sights merit the entry fee (the Museum of Basque Culture in Bayonne and the Guggenheim modern art museum in Bilbao).

On the French side, you'll want time for the easygoing beach resort of Saint-Jean-de-Luz, the striking capital city of Bayonne, and the villages that curl up in the protective arms of the Pyrenees foothills, such as Ainhoa, Sare, and Saint-Jean-Pied-de-Port.

Barely across the border, little Hondarribia offers a quick peek into Spain. Just 30 minutes deeper is the glittering resort of San Sebastián, and an hour beyond that, Bilbao.

Getting around the Basque Country

Just 130 kilometers/80 miles separates the two Basque capitals, Spanish Bilbao and French Bayonne. Freeways, trains, and buses provide convenient connections between Bayonne, Saint-Jean-de-Luz, San Sebastián, and to a lesser extent, Bilbao.

By Bus and Train from Saint-Jean-de-Luz: Trains link Saint-Jean-de-Luz with Bayonne (25 min), Saint-Jean-Pied-de-Port (90 min, transfer in Bayonne), San Sebastián (1 hr, transfer in Hendaye), and Hondarribia (1 hr, transfer to bus in Hendaye). Excursion tours provide the easiest public transport access to Bilbao's Guggenheim. Buses serve many pretty Basque villages.

By Car: From Saint-Jean-de-Luz, drivers can zip on the autoroute to San Sebastián (30 min) and Bilbao (90 min). The curving coastal route from San Sebastián to Bilbao takes you through Zarautz, Getaria, Ondarroa, Lekeitio, and Guernica. Scenic local roads connect the villages. For a good sampling of traditional Basque villages, from Saint-Jean-de-Luz connect Ascain, Sare, Ainhoa, Cambo-les-Bains, and Saint-Jean-Pied-de-Port.

SAINT-JEAN-DE-LUZ (Donibane Lohizune in Basque)

Saint-Jean-de-Luz (pron. san-zhahn-duh-looz) sits happily off the beaten path, cradled between its small port and gentle bay. Pastry shops serving Basque specialties and shops selling berets greet ice-cream lickers on the traffic-free streets, while soft, sandy beaches tempt travelers to toss their speedy itineraries into the bay. Mont Rhune towers above the happy scene.

Orientation

Saint-Jean-de-Luz's old city lies between the train tracks to the south and the Atlantic to the north. La Nivelle river feeds its port to the west, and rue Thiers forms the center city's eastern limit. The main traffic-free street, rue Gambetta, channels walkers through the center halfway between the train tracks and the ocean. The small town of Ciboure across the river holds nothing of interest to us. The **TI** is in a small red-roofed building a block off the port and three blocks north of the train station on place du Marechal Foch (Sept–June Mon–Sat 9:00–12:30 & 14:30–18:30, Sun 10:00–13:00, July–Aug 9:00–19:30, Sun 10:00–13:00 & 15:00–19:00, tel. 05 59 26 79 63, www.saint-jean-de-luz.com).

Arrival in Saint-Jean-de-Luz

By Train: From the station, follow the walkway under the tracks and under the road, then up the second set of steps to boulevard Commandant Passicot. Walk left along this street past Hôtel Centrale, stay straight around the traffic circle, and carry on along avenue de Verdun to the TI, just across the second traffic circle.

By Bus: The bus station is in the green gazebo-like structure next to the train station. To reach the TI, walk past the Hôtel Centrale and follow the directions under "By Train," above.

By Car: Follow signs for *Centre-ville*, then *Gare*, and *Office de Tourisme*. Parking (except for some peak summer days) is relatively easy. Hotels can advise you.

Helpful Hints

Laundry: The cleanest launderette in France is **Laverie du Port**, across from the TI at 5 place Marechal Foch (daily 7:00–21:00). As you do your clothes, notice how the Renault garage across the road is dressed in Basque colors.

Car Rental: Avis is handiest, at the train station (Mon–Sat 8:00–12:00 & 14:00–18:00, closed Sun, tel. 05 59 26 76 66, fax 05 59 26 76 62).

Sights—Saint-Jean-de-Luz

Remember, you're using Saint-Jean-de-Luz as a base for Basque day-tripping, not as a must-see destination. The only sight worth entering is the church where Louis XIV and Marie-Thérèse tied the royal knot (described below). Skip the homes where each stayed prior to the big day; both are best from the outside. Otherwise, Saint-Jean-de-Luz is best appreciated along its pedestrian streets, lively squares (don't miss place Louis XIV), and golden sandy beaches. The park at the far eastern end of the beachfront promenade at Pointe Sainte-Barbe makes a good walking destination,

Saint-Jean-de-Luz

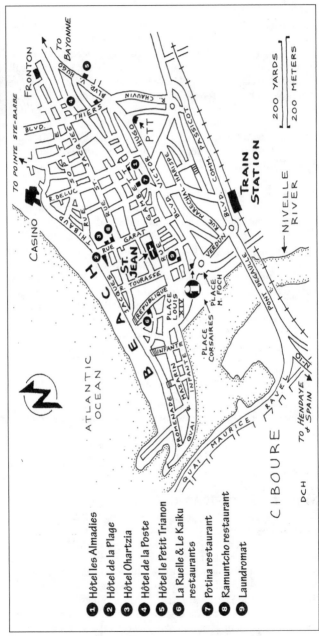

1. Hôtel les Almadies
2. Hôtel de la Plage
3. Hôtel Ohartzia
4. Hôtel de la Poste
5. Hôtel le Petit Trianon
6. La Ruelle & Le Kaiku restaurants
7. Potina restaurant
8. Ramuntcho restaurant
9. Laundromat

with views and walking trails. Fishing boats take tourists for short cruises into the Atlantic (inquire at the TI).

Church (Eglise St-Jean Baptiste)—The marriage of Louis XIV and Marie-Thérèse put Saint-Jean-de-Luz on the map to stay, and this church is where it all took place. The ultimate in political marriages, the knot tied between Louis and Marie also cinched a reconciliation deal between Europe's two most powerful countries in 1660. The king of Spain, Philip IV (who bankrupted his country by building El Escorial Palace), gave his daughter in marriage to the king of France (who, of course, built Versailles). This marriage united Europe's two largest palaces and helped wrap up a hundred years of hostility, forging an alliance that enabled both to focus attention on other matters (like England). Little Saint-Jean-de-Luz was selected for its 15 minutes of fame because it was roughly halfway from Madrid to Paris, and virtually on the France–Spain border. The wedding cleared out both Versailles and El Escorial palaces, as anyone who was anyone attended this glamorous event.

The church, centered on the pedestrian street rue Gambetta, seems modest enough from the outside. The ceiling could be the hull of a ship turned upside down. The dark wood balconies running along the nave and at the rear—segregating the men from the women and children—are typical of Basque churches. Only men could sit in these privileged seats until the early 1960s. The number of levels depended on the importance of the church, and this church, with three levels, is the largest Basque church in France. The small paddle-wheel ship hanging in the center was a gift from Napoleon III's wife, Eugenie. It's a one-meter-long (3 feet) model of a ship she was on that almost sank just offshore. The Baroque altar, which feels Spanish, doesn't seem to go with the rest of the church. Drop €1 in the box to see it brilliantly lit. As you leave the church, turn left, then notice the sealed doorway, the church's original entrance. It was sealed after the royal marriage to symbolize a permanent closing of the door on troubles between France and Spain.

***Pelota* Matches**—There are over 20 versions of the Basque-invented game that Americans know as jai alai. In the traditional version, called *pelota*, players in white pants and red scarves or shirts use a long, hook-shaped racket (called a *txistera*) to whip a ball (smaller and far bouncier than a baseball) back and forth off walls at more than 150 miles per hour. The men's-only game can also be played bare-handed (ouch) or with a glove, and with a wall at one or both ends of the court. You'll see fronton (courts) in every town, looking like handball courts. The players are not professional, but betting on them is common. The TI in Saint-Jean-de-Luz sells tickets and has a schedule of matches throughout the area; you're more likely to find a match in summer.

Sleeping in Saint-Jean-de-Luz
(€1 = about $1, country code: 33, zip code: 37400)
Sleep Code: **S** = Single, **D** = Double/Twin, **T** = Triple, **Q** = Quad, **b** = bathroom, **s** = shower only, **CC** = Credit Cards accepted, **no CC** = Credit Cards not accepted, **SE** = Speaks English, **NSE** = No English, * = French hotel rating system (0–4 stars).

To help you sort easily through these listings, I've divided the rooms into three categories based on the price for a standard double room with bath:
Higher Priced—Most rooms €85 or more.
Moderately Priced—Most rooms less than €85.
Lower Priced—Most rooms €65 or less.

Hotels are a good value. All of them charge a hefty 20 percent more from July through September. Most hoteliers speak English.

HIGHER PRICED
Hôtel les Almadies*, on the main pedestrian street, is a new boutique hotel with seven flawless rooms, comfy public spaces with clever modern touches, and an owner who cares (Db-€86–105, CC, 58 rue Gambetta, tel. 05 59 85 34 48, fax 05 59 26 12 42, e-mail: hotel.lesalmadies@wanadoo.fr, charming Madame Hargous speaks a little English).

MODERATELY PRICED
Hôtel de la Plage* has the best location right on the ocean; many rooms have ocean views. All of the rooms will be entirely renovated for 2003, so these prices are estimates (Db-€65–85, ocean view Db-€85–100, Tb-€80–95, view Tb-€100–120, CC, air-con, garage-€8, 33 rue Garrat, tel. 05 59 51 03 44, fax 05 59 51 03 48, www.hoteldelaplage.com).

LOWER PRICED
Hôtel Ohartzia* one block off the beach, is comfortable, clean, and homey, with well-cared-for rooms and a bird-chirping, flower-petaled garden (Db-€56–62, CC, 28 rue Garrat, tel. 05 59 26 00 06, fax 05 59 26 74 75, www.hotel-ohartzia.com).

Hôtel de la Poste*, a cross between a haunted house and a hunting lodge, has a massive stairway and truly Old World, wood-beamed character everywhere. Rooms are spacious, priced to sell, and decorated for a time that's long since passed (Db-€44–68, Tb-€77, Qb-€84, CC, garage-€6.10, a few blocks east of traffic-free area, 83 rue Gambetta, tel. 05 59 26 04 53, fax 05 59 26 42 14,

e-mail: hotelposte@clubinternet.fr, friendly Nathalie SE like
an American).

Hôtel le Petit Trianon**, on a major street, is well-run,
simple, spotless, and traditional, with louder rooms on the street
side (and no double-paned windows). To get a room over the
courtyard, ask for *coté cours* (pron. coat-ay coor; Db–€50–65,
CC, 56 boulevard Victor Hugo, tel. 05 59 26 11 90, fax 05 59
26 14 10, e-mail: lepetittrianon@wanadoo.fr).

Eating in Saint-Jean-de-Luz

Saint-Jean-de-Luz restaurants are known for offering good-value,
high-quality cuisine. Every restaurant listed below specializes in
Basque cuisine. Most hungry visitors explore the traffic-free rue
de la République, running from place Louis XIV and the Ocean
promenade. Banners fly overhead while cheek-to-jowl restaurants
hustle to keep pace with demand. On this street, **La Ruelle** at
#19 is popular, relaxed, and inexpensive (*menus* from €16, CC,
tel. 05 59 26 37 80). **Le Kaiku,** next door at #17, is a step up in
decor and cuisine (*menus* from €34, CC, tel. 05 59 26 13 20). A
few blocks away, just off rue Gambetta, **Potina** won't win awards
for ambience, but the cuisine might, and the price is right (*menus*
from €22, good daily specials from €14, closed Mon, CC, place
du Midi, tel. 05 59 26 02 76). **Ramuntcho** is a fun-loving, banner-
draped place with easygoing service and good food (*menus* from
€17, next to recommended Hôtel Ohartzia at 24 rue Garat, closed
Mon, tel. 05 59 26 038 90).

Transportation Connections—
Saint-Jean-de-Luz

The train station in Saint-Jean-de-Luz is called Saint-Jean-de-
Luz-Ciboure. Bus and rail service are reduced on Sundays.

By train to: Bayonne (12/day, 25 min), **Saint-Jean-Pied-
de-Port** (8/day, 90 min, transfer in Bayonne), **Paris** (7/day,
5.5 hrs, possible transfer in Bordeaux), **Bordeaux** (12/day, 2 hrs),
Sarlat (4/day, 4 hrs, transfer in Bordeaux or Libourne), **Carcassonne** (5/day, 6 hrs, transfers likely in Bayonne and Toulouse)
San Sebastián (10/day, 1 hr, take 12-min train to French border
town of Hendaye/Gare SNCF stop, where Topo trains depart
to San Sebastián every 30 min at :03 and :33 after the hour from
7:00 to 22:00).

By bus to: San Sebastián (15/day, 25 min).

By excursion bus to: Guggenheim Bilbao (4 days/week,
departs 13:00 from bus terminal next to train station, returns 19:30,
€28 round-trip, includes admission, ask at TI), **Pamplona** (during
Running of the Bulls, 4/day, 1 hr, ATCRB buses, tel. 05 59 26 06 99).

Villages in the French Basque Country

Use Saint-Jean-de-Luz as your base to visit the Basque sights described below. Plan your stay with the help of "Transportation Connections—Saint-Jean-de-Luz," above.

Traditional villages among the green hills with buildings colored like the Basque flag offer the best glimpse at Basque culture. Cheese, hard cider, and *pelota* players are the primary products of these villages, which attract few foreigners but many French summer visitors. Most of these villages have welcomed pilgrims bound for Santiago de Compostela since the Middle Ages. Today's hikers lace together local villages or head into the Pyrenees (TIs have details). The most appealing villages lie in the foothills of the Pyrenees, spared from beach-scene development.

Sare, sitting at the base of towering Mont Rhune, is among the most picturesque—and touristed. It's easily reached from Saint-Jean-de-Luz by bus or car. A small tourist train takes tourists from the town to the top of Mont Rhune for fantastic views (great only if it's clear, crowded on weekends and in the summer).

Ainhoa, farther up, is a smaller town that sees fewer tourists. Its chunks of fortified walls and gates mingle with red-and-white half-timbered buildings. The 14th-century church and fronton court share center-stage. Find the Chapelle de Notre-Dame d'Aranazau for a fine village view.

Saint-Jean-Pied-de-Port is the most popular of all (1 hr from Bayonne by scenic train, 70 min by car from Saint-Jean-de-Luz, and just 10 min to Spain). This walled town is famous as the final stopover in France for Santiago-bound pilgrims, who gathered here to cross the Pyrenees together and continue their march through Spain. You'll find scallop shells—the symbol of St. Jacques (French for James)—etched on walls throughout the town. This place is packed in the summer (come early or late). Find the main drag, rue de la Citadelle, with its pastel-pink buildings, and stroll it as pilgrims have for over 1,000 years. Climb to la Citadelle for views, but skip the €2 Bishop's Prison (Prison des Eveques).

BAYONNE (Baiona)

To really feel the pulse of French Basque country, visit Bayonne. This forgotten capital of the French Basque lands, just 25 minutes by train northeast of Saint-Jean-de-Luz, is a fun, easy, half-day trip. Come here to taste its lively old town and to admire its impressive Museum of Basque Culture. Known for establishing Europe's first whaling industry and for inventing the bayonet, today's Bayonne is more famous for its ham (*jambón de Bayonne*) and chocolate. Bayonne is just the right size—alive with opportunities, yet wholly manageable.

Bayonne's two rivers, Adour and Nive, divide the city into three parts: St. Esprit, with the train station, and the more interesting Grand and Petit Bayonne, which make up the old town.

In pretty Grand Bayonne, tall, slender buildings climb above cobbled streets and are decorated, as usual, with green and red shutters, but lacking the white facades of those in Saint-Jean-de-Luz. Make sure to stroll the streets around the cathedral and along banks of the smaller Nive river, where you'll find the Market Hall (Les Halles).

Tourist Information: The TI is a block off the mighty Adour river, on the northeastern edge of Grand Bayonne (Mon–Sat 9:00–18:00, closed Sun except in July–Aug open 10:00–13:00, place des Basques, tel. 05 59 46 01 46). Pick up a copy of the self-guided walking tour in English.

Arrival in Bayonne: To reach the TI and Grand Bayonne from the train station, walk straight out, cross the first street and traffic circle, then make a right on the next street that leads across the broad river. Cross a second smaller bridge, then drop down to Grand Bayonne, where you'll want to focus your time. Drivers should aim for the Office de Tourisme and park there.

Sights—Bayonne

Cathédrale Ste. Marie, bankrolled by the whaling community, sits dead center in Grand Bayonne and is worth a peek. With no more whales to catch, Bayonne turned to producing mouth-watering chocolates and marzipan—look for shops on the arcaded **rue du pont Neuf**.

The ramparts, while open for walking, do not allow access to either of Bayonne's castles—both are closed to the public.

The superb **Museum of Basque Culture** (Musée Basque, located on the smaller, less visited side in Petit Bayonne) explains every aspect of French Basque culture from cradle to grave. While English explanations are not yet available (but are planned), the 2,000 exhibits are sufficiently self-explanatory to allow determined, non-French-speaking visitors to appreciate the marvelous collection (€5.50, Tue–Sun May–Oct Tue–Sun 10:00–18:30, Tue–Sat Nov–April 10:00–12:30 & 14:00–18:00, closed Sun).

Transportation Connections—Bayonne

By train to: Saint-Jean-de-Luz (12/day, 25 min).

Day Trip to Spanish Basque Country (Pais Vasco)

A short dash into Spain is now a breeze, thanks to the euro currency and lack of border checks.

Key Spanish Phrases

Good day.   *Buenos días.*   bway-nohs dee-ahs
Mr./Mrs.   *Señor/Señora*   sayn-yor/sayn-yor-ah
Please.   *Por favor.*   por fah-bor
Thank you.   *Muchas gracias.*   moo-chahs grah-thee-ahs
coffee with milk   *café con leche*   kah-feh kohn lay-chay
sandwich   *bocadillo*   boh-kah-dee-yoh
Where is...?   *¿Donde está...?*   dohn-day ay-stah
Tourist office   *Turismo*   too-rees-moh
City center   *Centro ciudad*   thehn-troh thee-oo-dahd

Phones: Spain's telephone country code is 34. Remember that French phone cards and stamps will not work in Spain.

Hours: Most Spanish sights and stores close from about 13:00 to 16:00, and dinner doesn't begin until 21:00 (though tapas appetizers are always available).

SAN SEBASTIÁN (Donostia)

Shimmering above the breathtaking bay of La Concha, elegant and prosperous San Sebastián (Donostia in Basque) has a favored location with golden beaches lining its perfectly round bay, capped with twin peaks at either end and a cute little island in the center. A pedestrian-friendly beachfront promenade runs the length of the bay, with an intriguing old town at one end and a smart shopping district in the center. It's a big city with about 180,000 residents and almost that many tourists in high season (July–Sept). With a romantic setting, the soaring statue of Christ gazing over the city, and the late-night lively old town, San Sebastián has a distinct Rio de Janeiro aura. While there's no compelling museum to visit, the scenic city provides a pleasant sampling of Spain.

Planning Your Time

San Sebastián is worth a day. Start your morning at the hill of Monte Igueldo (described below; consider a taxi to the funicular). Then stroll the waterfront walkway to and through the old town and port (taking time to explore). Then head up to the hill of Monte Urgull. Everything is within walking distance; skip the double-decker hop-on, hop-off bus tours.

Orientation

The San Sebastián we're interested in surrounds the Bay of Concha (Bahia de la Concha), and can be divided into three

San Sebastián

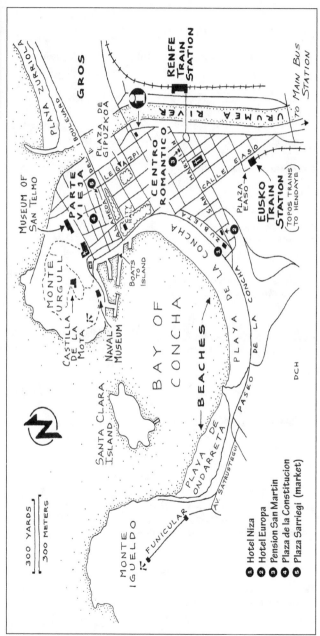

300 YARDS
300 METERS

GROS

RENFE TRAIN STATION

PLAYA ZURRIOLA

BOULEVARD

PLAZA DE GIPUZKOA

MUSEUM OF SAN TELMO

CENTRO ROMANTICO

PARTE VIEJA

CALLE IGENTIA 2PI

CALLE MAYOR

CITY HALL

CALLE MARLIN

CALLE EASO

PLAZA EASO

EUSKO TRAIN STATION
(TOPOS TRAINS TO HENDAYE)

URUMEA RIVER

TO MAIN BUS STATION

CASTILLA DE LA MOTA

MONTE URGULL

NAVAL MUSEUM

BOATS TO ISLAND

CALLE ZUBIETA

SANTA CLARA ISLAND

BAY OF CONCHA

BEACHES

PLAYA DE LA CONCHA

PASEO DE LA CONCHA

PLAYA DE ONDARRETA

AV. SATRUSTEGUI

MONTE IGUELDO

FUNICULAR

DCH

1 Hotel Niza
2 Hotel Europa
3 Pension San Martin
4 Plaza de la Constitucion
5 Plaza Sarriegi (market)

areas: Playa de la Concha (best beaches), the shopping district (called *centro romantico*, just east of Playa de la Concha), and the skinny, straight streets of the old town (called *parte vieja*, to the north of the shopping district). It's all bookended by mini-mountains: Monte Urgull to the north and east, Monte Igueldo to the south and west. The River (Rio) Urumea divides central San Sebastián from the beachfront extension called Gros (of no interest unless you want to see Spanish surfers).

Tourist Information: The main TI, which lies between the shopping area and old city a block from the river, has complete information on city and regional sights. Pick up the excellent booklet in English (called Donostia/San Sebastián); of its three well-described walking tours, the Old Quarter/Monte Urgull walk is the best. The TI also has bus and train schedules (June–Sept Mon–Sat 8:00–20:00, Sun 10:00–14:00; Oct–May Mon–Sat 9:00–14:00 & 15:30–19:00, Sun 10:00–14:00, Calle Reina Regente 3, tel. 943-481-166).

Useful Phone Numbers: For a taxi, call 943-464-646. For the police, dial 943-467-766. For flight information, call San Sebastián's airport (in Hondarribia, 19 km/12 miles away) at tel. 943-668-500.

Arrival in San Sebastián

By Train: If you're coming on a Topo train from Hendaye on the French border, get off at the Eusko Tren station. It's a level 15-minute walk to the center. Exit the station and walk across the long plaza, then walk eight blocks down Calle Easo to reach the beach. The old town will be to your right, Playa de la Concha to your left.

By Bus: If you're arriving by bus from Hondarribia, hop off at pretty Plaza de Gipuzkoa (first stop after crossing the river, in shopping area, near TI). To reach the TI, walk down Legazpi and turn right on the parkway boulevard, Alameda del Boulevard.

By Car: Coming from France, it's best to park at the station in Hendaye and take the frequent, cheap Topo trains, since navigating San Sebastián is tricky. If you do drive into San Sebastián, follow *Centro Ciudad* signs into San Sebastián's center and park in a pay lot (many are well-signed).

Sights—San Sebastián

Old City (Parte Vieja)—Huddling securely in the shadow of its once-protective Monte Urgull, the old town is where San Sebastián was born about a thousand years ago. Lively tapas (*pintxos*, pron. PEEN-chohs) bars, heavy Baroque churches, and surprise plazas entertain locals and tourists 24 hours a day. Note that the raucous nightlife and street noise in this part of town means that many hotels in this area are not for light sleepers.

Plaza de la Constitución—This striking square, where bullfights used to be held (notice the seat numbering on the balconies), is a fine place to sample a plate of *pintxos* with a glass of *txacoli* (pron. tax-OH-lee), the local light, sparkling white wine that is often theatrically poured from high above the glass.

Museum of San Telmo—Formerly a Dominican monastery, this museum proudly displays paintings by Basque artists (free, Tue–Sat 10:30–13:00 & 16:00–20:00, Sun 10:30–14:00, closed Mon, Plaza Zuloaga 1, tel. 943-424-970).

Cruise—Small boats cruise from the old town's port to the island in the bay (Isla Santa Clara), where you can hike the trails and have lunch at the lone café (€2.50 round-trip, every 30 min, 10:00–19:00, until 20:00 June–Sept).

Naval Museum—Located at the port, this museum shows the seafaring city's history and provides a link between the Basque culture and the sea (€2, Tue–Sat 9:00–13:30 & 16:00–19:30, Sun 11:00–14:00, closed Mon).

Monte Urgull—The once-mighty castle (Castilla de la Mota) atop the hill deterred most attackers, allowing the city to prosper in the Middle Ages. The museum of San Sebastián history located within the castle is mildly interesting. The best views from the hill are not from the statue of Christ, but from the ramparts on the left side as you face the hill, just above the port's aquarium.

Monte Igueldo—For the best views, ride the funicular up the hill of Monte Igueldo, a mirror image of Monte Urgull. The views into the distant green mountains, along the coast, and over San Sebastián are sensational day or night. The entrance to the funicular is behind the tennis club on the far western end of Playa de Ondarreta, which extends from Playa de la Concha to the west (€1.50, daily 8:00–18:00, until 20:00 June–Aug).

Sleeping in San Sebastián
(€1 = about $1, country code: 34)
Sleep Code: **S** = Single, **D** = Double/Twin, **T** = Triple, **Q** = Quad, **b** = bathroom, **s** = shower only, **CC** = Credit Cards accepted, **no CC** = Credit Cards not accepted, **SE** = Speaks English, **NSE** = No English.

HIGHER PRICED
Best Western's **Hotel Europa**, a block from the beach, is pricey but central, and it offers all of the comforts (Db-€116–140, CC, San Martin 52, tel. 943-470-880, fax 943-471-730, www.hotel -europa.com).

Hotel Niza, with its waterfront setting on the western edge of Playa de la Concha, offers the best overall value. Half of its rooms (some with balconies) overlook the bay. All of its rooms are comfortable and pleasantly decorated, and share the same million-euro view breakfast room/café (Db-€90–115, CC, Zubieta 56, tel. 943-426-663, fax 943-441-251, www.hotelniza.com, SE).

LOWER PRICED

Pension San Martin, in the shopping area a few blocks from beaches and the old town, has a forgettable entry with comfortable and well-cared-for rooms (Db-€35–55, CC, San Martin 10, tel. 943-428-714).

If you want to stay in the lively old town above a tapas bar, and if you can stand nonstop noise, **Pension Amaiur** is the place for you (S-€30, D-€50, T-€75, family room-€85, kitchen facilities, Internet access-€1/18 min, excursions available, next to Santa Maria church, Calle 31 de Agosto 44, tel. 943-429-654, www.pensionamaiur.com, e-mail: reservas@pensionamaiur.com).

Eating in San Sebastián

On menus, you'll see *bacalao* (salted cod), best when cooked *à la bizkaina* (with tomatoes, onions, and roasted peppers); *merluza* (hake), a light white fish prepared in a variety of ways; and *chipirones en su tinta* (squid served in their own black ink). Carnivores will find plenty of lamb (try *chuletas de buey*, massive lamb chops). Local brews include *sidra* (hard apple cider), *txacoli* (light white wine), and *Izarra* (herbal-flavored brandy).

San Sebastián's old town provides the ideal backdrop for tapas hopping. The selection of tapas is amazing. Every other shop seems to be a tapas bar, especially on these streets: Calles Fermin Calebeton, San Jeronimo, and 31 de Agosto.

For reasonably priced meals in an appealing setting, try **Bodégon Alejandro** (closed Wed, in the thick of the old town on Calle Fermin Calebeton 4, tel. 943-477-737). **Casa Urola**, a few steps away, is also good and a bit more traditional (Calle Fermin Calebeton 22, tel. 943-421-175).

For picnics, try the public market at Plaza Sarriegi near the TI.

Transportation Connections—San Sebastián

All Barcelona, Madrid, and Paris trains require reservations.

By train to: Barcelona (2/day, 8.5–9.5 hrs, plus 10-hr night train except on Sat), **Madrid** (Sun–Fri: 4/day, Sat: 2/day, 6–8.5 hrs, plus daily 10.5-hr night train), **Hendaye/French border** (2/hr, 30 min, departs Eusko Tren station at :15 and :45 after the hour

7:00–22:00), **Paris** (get to Hendaye—see above, then 4/day, 5.5 hrs, or 8.5-hr night train).

By bus to: Bilbao (2/hr from 6:00 to 22:30, 70 min, departs San Sebastián's main bus station on Plaza Pio XII, on the river 2 blocks below Euska Tren station, bus tel. 902-101-210; once in Bilbao, buses leave you a 30-minute walk to the museum), **Hondarribia** (5/hr, 45 min, many bus stops, most central is on Plaza de Gipuzkoa in shopping area).

BILBAO AND THE GUGGENHEIM MUSEUM

In the last five years, the cultural and economic capital of the Pais Vasco, Bilbao (pop. 1 million), has seen a transformation like no other Spanish city. Entire sectors of the industrial city's long-depressed port have been cleared away to allow construction of a new opera house, convention center, and the stunning Guggenheim museum of modern art.

Tourist Information: Bilbao's main TI is across the river from the train station (on Paseo del Arenal 1), though the office across from the Guggenheim is more convenient for most (Mon–Fri 9:00–14:00 & 16:00–19:30, Sat–Sun 10:00–14:00, tel. 944-795-760).

Arrival in Bilbao

Finding the museum is easy: Pink signs guide drivers and walkers to this city's most famous sight. Still, it's handy to be able to ask: *¿Donde está el museo Guggenheim?* (pron. dohn-day ay-stah el moo-say-oo "Guggenheim").

By Train: Bilbao's Renfe station is on the river in central Bilbao, a pleasant 20-minute walk through the downtown to the museum; ask for a map of Bilbao at the train information office (or pay €4 for a taxi).

By Bus: Buses stop at the Termibus station on the eastern edge of downtown, about 1.5 kilometers/1 mile southwest of the museum, leaving you with a less-than-appealing 30-minute walk. Your best bet is a taxi (€4.50).

By Car: The museum is signed from the freeway; look for the pink signs to the Guggenheim and follow them to the museum parking.

Sights—Bilbao

▲▲▲**Guggenheim Bilbao**—Frank Gehry's remarkable building opened in 1998, reinvigorating the modern art and architectural world. Most travelers concede that this titanium tile–clad building, looking like a huge, silvery, Cubist fish, overwhelms the art within it. Take some time to admire the outside of the museum before you plunge in.

Guarding the main entrance is artist Jeff Koons' dog (13 meters/42 feet tall) made of flowers, who answers to "Puppy." Inside, you'll find an impressive atrium from which the other galleries branch off. Pick up a map and plan your attack. Thanks to the fact that this museum is part of the Guggenheim "family" of museums, the permanent collection of modern paintings is strong—but it perpetually rotates and isn't as impressive as collections in Madrid, London, and Paris. You might see a Miró, a Modigliani, and a Picasso or two. Although many Basques would love to see it here, one painting you won't find is Picasso's famous *Guernica*, named after the nearby Basque town bombed to smithereens by Hitler's Luftwaffe (at Franco's request) in 1936.

The best approach to your visit is simply to immerse yourself in a modern art happening, rather than count on seeing a particular piece or a specific artist's works.

The building's walls can be moved to best display the ever-changing special exhibits and installments *del día*, often consisting of huge, post-WWII minimalist works that you may struggle to "get."

The museum offers free audioguides and guided tours in English; call 944-359-090 for the schedule (entry: €8.50, July–Aug daily 9:00–21:00; Sept–June Tue–Sun 10:00–20:00, closed Mon; café, no photos, Metro: Moyua, Abandoibarra Et. 2, tel. 944-359-080, www.guggenheim-bilbao.es).

Transportation Connections—Bilbao

By bus to: San Sebastián (2/hr from 6:00 to 22:30, 70 min, departs Bilbao's Termibus station, arrives in San Sebastián at Plaza Pio XII).

HONDARRIBIA

For a taste of small-town Pais Vasco, dip into this enchanting, seldom-visited town. Much smaller and easier to manage than San Sebastián, and also closer to France (across the Bay of Txingudi from Hendaye), Hondarribia allows travelers a stress-free opportunity to enjoy Basque culture.

The town comes in two parts: the lower port town and the historic, balcony-lined streets of the hilly upper town. The **TI** is located between the two, two blocks up from the port on Jabier Ugarte Kalea 6 (Mon–Fri 9:30–14:00 & 16:00–18:30, Sat 10:00–14:00, closed Sun, tel. 943-645-458). You can follow their self-guided tour of the old town (English brochure available) or just lose yourself within the walls. Explore the wrought-iron railings and plazas of the upper city. Today, Today Charles V's odd, squat castle is a parador (Db-€140, CC, Plaza de Armas 14, tel. 943-645-500, e-mail: hondarribia@parador.es). Tourists are allowed to have a sangria in the *muy* cool bar, though the terraces are for guests only. In the modern, lower town, straight shopping streets serve a local clientele and a pleasant walkway takes strollers along the beach.

Transportation Connections—Hondarribia
By bus to: San Sebastián (3/hr, 45 min to go 19 km/12 miles), **Hendaye/French border** (3/hr, 20 min). The bus stop in Hondarribia is across from the post office, one block below the TI.

    By boat to: Hendaye (2/hr, 10 min, runs about 11:00–19:00).

LANGUEDOC

From the 10th to the 13th centuries, this powerful and independent region ruled most of southern France between the Rhône River and the Pyrenees mountains. The brutal Albigensian (Cathar) Crusades began here in 1208 and ultimately led to Languedoc's demise and eventual incorporation into the state of France.

The name *languedoc* comes from the *langue* (language) its people spoke: *Langue d'oc* ("language of Oc," *Oc* for the way they said "yes") was the dialect of southern France; *langue d'oil* was the dialect of northern France (where *oil*, later to become *oui*, was the way of saying "yes"). As Languedoc's power faded, so did its language.

The Moors, Charlemagne, and the Spanish have all called this area home. You'll see, hear, and feel the strong Spanish influence. I'm lumping Albi in with the Languedoc region, though locals don't think of it as true Languedoc.

While sharing many of the same attributes as Provence (climate, wind, grapes, and sea), this sunny, intoxicating, southwesternmost region of France is allocated little time by most travelers. Pay homage to Toulouse-Lautrec in Albi; spend a night in Europe's greatest fortress city, Carcassonne; scamper up a remote Cathar castle; and sift the sand in Collioure.

Planning Your Time

Key sights in Languedoc are Albi, Carcassonne, Minerve, the Cathar castle ruins, and Collioure. Albi makes a good day or overnight stop between the Dordogne region and Carcassonne. Plan your arrival at Carcassonne carefully: Arrive late in the afternoon, spend the night, and leave by noon the next day, and you'll miss the day-trippers. Collioure is your Mediterranean beach town vacation from your

Languedoc

vacation. To find the Cathar castle ruins and Minerve, you'll need wheels of your own and a good map. If you're driving, the most exciting Cathar castles—Peyrepertuse and Queribus—work well as stops between Carcassonne and Collioure.

No matter what kind of transportation you use, Languedoc is a logical stop between the Dordogne and Provence or on the way to Barcelona, which is just over the border.

Getting around Languedoc

Albi, Carcassonne, and Collioure are accessible by train (though connections to Albi can be awkward), but a car is essential for seeing the remote sights. Pick up your rental car in Albi or Carcassonne, and buy the local Michelin map #83. Roads can be pencil-thin, and traffic slow. East of Montauban, the D-115 from Bruniquel (along l'Averyon River then south to Cordes) is dreamy, and D-964 south of Bruniquel to Gaillac gives a scenic route to Albi (see "Route of the Bastides," below).

Drivers continuing north should consider the beautiful but slow drive through the Lot River Valley via Villefranche de Rouergue and Cajarc (see "Sights—Southeast of the Dordogne," in previous chapter).

Cuisine Scene—Languedoc

Hearty peasant cooking and full-bodied red wines are Languedoc's tasty trademarks. Be adventurous. Cassoulet, an old Roman concoction of goose, duck, pork, mutton, sausage, and white beans, is the main-course specialty. You'll also see *cargolade*, a satisfying stew of snail, lamb, and sausage. Local cheeses are Roquefort and Pelardon (a nutty-tasting goat cheese). Corbières, Minervois, and Côtes du Roussillon are the area's good-value red wines. The locals distill a fine brandy, Armagnac, which tastes just like cognac and costs less.

Remember, restaurants serve only during lunch (11:30–14:00) and dinner (19:00–21:00, later in bigger cities); cafés serve food throughout the day.

ALBI

Those coming to see the basilica and the Toulouse-Lautrec Museum will be pleasantly surprised by Albi's sienna-toned bricks and the half-timbered buildings lining the town's many traffic-free streets. Lost in the Dordogne-to-Carcassonne shuffle and overshadowed by its big brother Toulouse, unpretentious Albi awaits your visit with minimal tourist trappings. Train travelers with limited time may find the detour to Albi too time-consuming.

Orientation: Albi's sights, pedestrian streets, and hotels cluster within a 10-minute walk of the basilica. The **TI** is between the basilica and Toulouse-Lautrec Museum (July–Aug Mon–Sat 9:00–19:30, Sept–June Mon–Sat 9:00–12:30 & 14:00–18:00, Sun all year 10:30–12:30 & 14:00–17:30, tel. 05 63 49 48 80).

Arrival in Albi

By Train: There are two stations in Albi; you want *Albi-Ville*. From the station, take a left onto avenue Marechal Joffre, walking past Hôtel Regina, and then another left on avenue General de Gaulle; cross place Laperouse, keeping left of the gardens, then follow the signs to *Cathédrale* and to Albi's old town. Lockers are available at the station.

By Car: Follow signs to *Centre-ville* and *Cathédrale*, and park in front of the basilica.

The Cathars

The Cathars were a heretical group of Christians who grew in numbers under a tolerant rule in Languedoc from the 11th through the 13th centuries. They saw life as a battle between good (the spiritual) and bad (the material) and considered material things evil and of the devil. While others called them "Cathars" (from the Greek word for "pure") or "Albigenses" (for their main city, Albi), they called themselves simply "friends of God." Cathars focused on the teachings of St. John and recognized only baptism as a sacrament. Because they believed in reincarnation, they were vegetarians.

Travelers encounter the Cathars in their Languedoc sightseeing because of the Albigensian Crusades (1209–1240s). The king of France wanted to consolidate his grip on southern France. The pope needed to make a strong point that the only acceptable Christianity was Roman style. Both found self-serving reasons to wage a genocidal war against these people, who never amounted to more than 10 percent of the local population and who coexisted happily with their non-Cathar neighbors. After a terrible generation of torture and mass burnings, the Cathars were wiped out. The last Cathar was burned in 1321.

Today, tourists find haunting castle ruins (once Cathar strongholds) high in the Pyrenees and eat hearty *salade Cathar*.

Sights—Albi

Pick up a map of the city center at the TI (get the purple *circuit poupre* walking tour in English), and follow its suggested walking tour, reading the English information posted at key points along the way. On this walk, you'll see...

▲▲▲**Basilique Ste. Cécile**—This 13th-century fortress/basilica was the nail in the Albigensian coffin. Both the imposing exterior and the stunning interior of this cathedral drive home the message of the Catholic (read "universal") Church. The extravagant porch looks like the afterthought it was. The interior is an explosion of colors and geometric shapes framing a vivid *Last Judgment*. Even with the gaping hole that was cut from it to make room for a newer pipe organ, the *Last Judgment* makes its point in a way that would stick with any medieval worshiper (daily June–Sept 8:30–18:45, Oct–May closes 12:00–14:30 and at 18:30, €3 headsets provide an excellent 1-hr, self-guided tour). The choir is worth the small admission, and the sound-and-light show—*Son et Lumière Spectacle*, offered in summer—is worth staying up for (€4.75, 22:00, ask at TI).

Albi

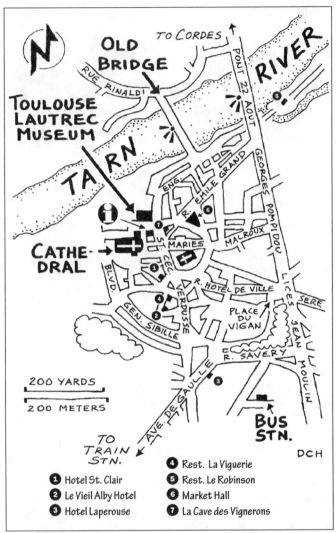

OLD BRIDGE

TO CORDES

RIVER

RUE RINALDI

PONT 22 AOÛT

TOULOUSE LAUTREC MUSEUM

TA RN

ENG.

R. ÉMILE GRAND

GEORGES POMPIDOU

CATHE-DRAL

MARIES

MALROUX

BLVD.

ST.

CEC

R. HÔTEL DE VILLE

LICES

SÈRE

GEN. SIBILLE

VERDUSSE

PLACE DU VIGAN

JEAN MOULIN

R. SAVERY

200 YARDS

200 METERS

AVE. DE GAULLE

BUS STN.

TO TRAIN STN.

DCH

❶ Hotel St. Clair
❷ Le Vieil Alby Hotel
❸ Hotel Laperouse
❹ Rest. La Viguerie
❺ Rest. Le Robinson
❻ Market Hall
❼ La Cave des Vignerons

▲▲**Musée Toulouse-Lautrec**—The Palais de la Berbie (once the fortified home of the archbishop) has the world's best collection of Lautrec's paintings, posters, and sketches. The artist, crippled from youth and therefore on the fringe of society, had an affinity for people who didn't quite fit in. He painted the dregs of Parisian society because they were his world. His famous Parisian nightlife posters are here. The top floor houses a skippable collection of contemporary art (€4, audioguide-€3, April–May daily 10:00–12:00 & 14:00–18:00; June and Sept daily 9:00–12:00 & 14:00–18:00; July–Aug daily 9:00–18:00; Oct–March Wed–Mon 10:00–12:00 & 14:00–17:00, closed Tue, tel. 05 63 49 48 70). The gardens below have fine views.

Eglise St. Salvy and Cloître—This is an OK church with fine cloisters. Delicate arches surround an enclosed courtyard, providing a peaceful interlude from the shoppers that fill the pedestrian streets (open all day).

La Cave des Vignerons—This wine cave presents regional wines in an appealing setting (across from basilica, where rue des Fargues meets the square).

Market Hall—The quiet Art Nouveau market is good for picnic-gathering and people-watching (Tue–Sun until 13:00, closed Mon, 2 blocks from basilica).

City Views—For great views of Albi and the Tarn River, walk or drive past the basilica down to either of these bridges: the pont Vieux or the newer and higher pont 22 Aout 1944.

Sights—Near Albi

▲**Route of the Bastides**—The hilly terrain north of Albi was tailor-made for medieval villages to organize around for defensive purposes. Here, fortified villages *(bastides)* spill over hilltops, above rivers, and between wheat fields and forests, creating a worthwhile detour for drivers. Connect these *bastides:* Castelnau de Montmiral (wonderful main square, 10 min from Albi), adorable little Bruniquel (my favorite), vertical Penne, too-popular Cordes-sur-Ciel, and, if you really want to get off the beaten path, the ridge-top village of Najac.

Cordes-sur-Ciel—Hill town–lovers can't resist this brilliantly situated, well-preserved medieval marvel just 25 kilometers/ 15 miles north of Albi. Cordes, once an important Cathar base, is now filled with boutiques and too many tourists on weekends and in the summer. It's a steep, 30-minute walk up to the town from the lower parking lots (€2.50, first hour is free); take the shuttle bus (€2 round-trip, 4/hr, buy ticket at parking meter or from driver, departs from place Jeanne Ramel-Cals, next to TI). Trains get you as far as Cordes-Vindrac, where a taxi-bus will shuttle you 5 kilometers/3 miles to Cordes (Mon–Sat-€4, Sun-€6, tel. 05 63 56 14 80). Cordes has two **TIs**, one at the base of the hill town and another in the center (daily Sept–June 10:30–12:30 & 14:00–18:00, July–Aug 10:00–19:00, tel. 05 63 56 00 52).

The rustic **Hostellerie de Vieux Cordes***** at the top is the place to stay; some rooms have valley views (Db-€45–64, CC, 21 rue St. Michel, 81170 Cordes, tel. 05 63 53 79 20, fax 05 63 56 02 47, www.thuries.fr).

Najac—This is Cordes *sans* crowds and appropriate only for hill-town nuts, as it requires a serious detour. This narrow *bastide* caps a high ridge and lies beneath a ruined castle.

At the welcoming **Hôtel du Barry****, all rooms have great views, and the restaurant justifies the detour (Db-€54–63, prices are per person and include breakfast and dinner, CC, free parking, 12270 Najac, tel. 05 65 29 74 32, fax 05 65 29 75 32, www.oustal-del-barry.com).

Gorges du Tarn—Adventure-lovers can canoe, hike, or drive the stunning Tarn River gorge by heading east from Albi to Millau, then following the gorge all the way to St. Enimie. Roads are slow but spectacular. The best base for canoeing is from tiny La Malene (40 km/25 miles northeast of Millau).

Stay in the simple but comfortable **Auberge de l'Emar-cadere** (Db-€44, Tb-€48, CC, tel. 04 66 48 51 03, fax 04 66 48 58 94) or in the country-luxurious **Manoir de Montesquiou** (Db-€68–103, big Db-€134, extra bed-€16, you'll be expected to dine at its great restaurant-€28, CC, tel. 04 66 48 51 12, fax 04 66 48 50 47, www.manoir-montesquiou.com).

Sleeping in Albi
(€1 = about $1, country code: 33, zip code: 81000)
Sleep Code: **S** = Single, **D** = Double/Twin, **T** = Triple, **Q** = Quad, **b** = bathroom, **s** = shower only, **CC** = Credit Cards accepted, **no CC** = Credit Cards not accepted, **SE** = Speaks English, **NSE** = No English, * = French hotel rating system (0–4 stars).

To help you sort easily through these listings, I've divided the rooms into three categories based on the price for a standard double room with bath:

Higher Priced—Most rooms more than €90.
Moderately Priced—Most rooms €90 or less.
Lower Priced—Most rooms less than €60.

LOWER PRICED
Hôtel St. Clair**, offering steep stairs, a small courtyard, and good rooms, is decorated with a loving touch and run by friendly, English-speaking Michelle (Db-€41–55, Tb-€57–67, CC, 2 blocks from basilica in pedestrian zone on rue St. Clair, tel. 05 63 54 25 66, fax 05 63 47 27 58, e-mail: micheleandrieu@hotmail.com).

Le Vieil Alby Hôtel**, located in the heart of Albi's pedestrian area, has modern, well-maintained rooms, and is run by helpful, English-speaking Monsieur Sicard (Sb/Db-€41–56, Tb-€59, garage-€7, CC, 25 rue Toulouse-Lautrec, tel. 05 63 54 14 69, fax 05 63 54 96 75).

Hôtel Laperouse**, run by gentle Monsieur Chartrou, is a simple place one block from the old town and a 10-minute walk to the train station. It has easy parking, a quiet garden, and a big pool, and is a good value—spring for a room with balcony over the pool (Sb/Db-€35–58, CC, 21 place Laperouse, tel. 05 63 54 69 22, fax 05 63 38 03 69).

Eating in Albi
Albi is filled with inexpensive restaurants serving a rich local cuisine (be careful of the popular organ meat dishes). Several good places line the rue Toulouse-Lautrec (2 blocks from Hôtel St. Clair). **La Viguiere** at #7 stands above the rest in price, quality, and ambience (€21 *menu*, tel. 05 63 54 76 44). At #25, the recommended **Le Vieil Alby Hôtel** restaurant is traditional and reliable (*menus* from €14.50). For a fun experience, find **Le Robinson**, where Lices Georges Pompidou meets the river. A path leads down to the river to this vine-strewn paradise (reasonable *menus*, 142 rue Eurand Branly, tel. 03 63 46 15 69). For more happening café action, head to the grand place du Vigan.

Transportation Connections—Albi
You'll connect to just about any destination through Toulouse.

By train to: Toulouse (11/day, 70 min), **Carcassonne** (9/day, 2.5 hrs, change in Toulouse), **Sarlat** (2/day in 4.5 hrs with changes in Toulouse, Agen, and Le Buisson; or 3/day in 6–7 hrs via Souillac with changes possible in Brive-la-Gaillarde and Toulouse, then bus from Souillac), **Paris** (7/day, 6–7.5 hrs, change in Toulouse, then TGV, night train).

CARCASSONNE
Medieval Carcassonne is a 13th-century world of towers, turrets, and cobblestone alleys. It's a walled city and Camelot's castle rolled into one, frosted with too many tourists. At 10:00, the salespeople stand at the doors of their main-street shops, their gauntlet of tacky temptations poised and ready for their daily ration of customers. A quieter Carcassonne rattles in the early morning breeze, so spend the night.

If you're sensitive to crowds, consider sleeping in nearby Caunes-Minervois (see "Sleeping near Carcassonne," below), or rent a bike and cruise the Canal du Midi's level towpath (see "Sights—Carcassonne," below).

Locals like to believe that Carcassonne got its name this way:

Carcassonne Overview

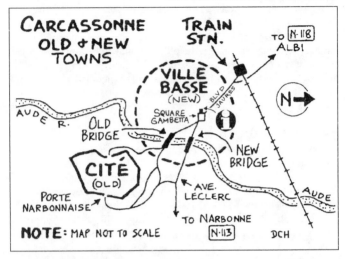

1,200 years ago, Charlemagne and his troops besieged this fortress/town (then called La Cité) for several years. A cunning townsperson named Madame Carcas saved the town. Just as food was running out, she fed the last bits of grain to the last pig and tossed him over the wall. Splat. Charlemagne's bored and frustrated forces, amazed that the town still had enough food to throw fat party pigs over the wall, decided they would never succeed in starving the people out. They ended the siege and the city was saved. Madame Carcas *sonne*-d (sounded) the long-awaited victory bells, and La Cité had a new name: Carcas-sonne. Historians, however, suspect that Carcassonne is a Frenchified version of the town's original name (Carcas).

From Rick's journal on his first visit to Carcassonne: "Before me lives Carcassonne, the perfect medieval city. Like a fish that everyone thought was extinct, somehow Europe's greatest Romanesque fortress city has survived the centuries. I was supposed to be gone yesterday, but here I sit imprisoned by choice—curled in a cranny on top of the wall. The wind blows away the sounds of today, and my imagination 'medievals' me. The moat is one foot over and 100 feet down. Small plants and moss upholster my throne."

Orientation

Contemporary Carcassonne is neatly divided into two cities: The magnificent La Cité (fortified city) and the lively *ville basse* (modern, lower city). Two bridges connect the two parts, the busy pont Neuf and the pedestrian-only pont Vieux, both with great views.

Tourist Information: Carcassonne has three TIs: one at the train station, one in La Cité, and one in the *ville basse*. The handy **La Cité TI** is just to your right as you enter the main gate called Narbonnaise (daily 9:00–18:00, until 19:00 July–Aug). The TIs at the train station and in the *ville basse* (on place Gambetta, near huge French flags at 15 boulevard Camille Pelletan) share the same hours (Mon–Sat 9:00–12:15 & 14:00–18:30, closed Sun, tel. 04 68 10 24 30). Pick up the map of La Cité and the one-page history in English, get English tour times for Château Comtal, and ask about festivals and minivan excursions. The tower opposite the TI has information on walking tours of the walls and a fine wood model of La Cité. Notice that no house rises above the fortified walls.

Arrival in Carcassonne

By Train: The train station is located in the *ville basse*, a 30-minute walk from La Cité. Ask at the station TI about the free *navette* shuttle signed La Cité (daily June–Sept only, no service 12:00–14:00, walk 5 blocks straight out of train station to rue Verdun, or walk 1 block straight out of the station and find bus #2 across from McDonald's, about every 45 min, €0.80, pay driver). At €7, the taxi works for me. Walkers can continue on foot past McDonald's, up the pedestrian street, to the heart of the *ville basse*. From there, a left on rue de Verdun takes you to place Gambetta and across pont Vieux to La Cité. Check bags across from the train station at Hôtel Terminus (€2 per bag).

By Car: Following signs to La Cité, you'll come to a large parking lot (€3.50) and a drawbridge (Porte Narbonnaise) at the walled city's entrance. If staying inside the walls, show your reservation (verbal assurances won't do) and park free in the outside lot, then drive into the city after 18:00. Theft is common—leave nothing in your car at night.

Sights—Carcassonne

▲▲▲**Medieval Wall Walk**—You'll enter La Cité via the Porte Narbonnaise (TI is just inside to the right). The drawbridge was made crooked to slow attackers' rush to the main gate (and is just as effective with tourists today). Avoid the circus on the main street that leads up from Porte Narbonnaise, and enter the walls with me— through the back door. After crossing the drawbridge (or visiting the TI), walk the cobbled path between the walls *(les lices)* in the uphill direction. Climb to the outer wall walk and find a seat.

La Cité was Europe's greatest medieval fortress, with three kilometers of massive walls and 52 menacing towers. Strategically located near the intersection of the north-south, east-west trade routes, people have occupied this site since

Carcassonne's La Cité

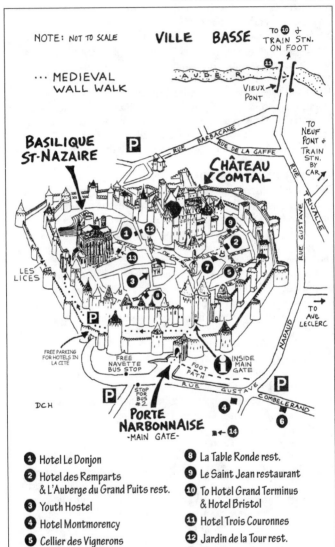

NOTE: NOT TO SCALE

VILLE   BASSE

... MEDIEVAL
WALL WALK

BASILIQUE
ST-NAZAIRE

CHÂTEAU
COMTAL

LES
LICES

FREE PARKING
FOR HOTELS IN
LA CITÉ

FREE
NAVETTE
BUS STOP

STOP
FOR
BUS
#2

DCH

PORTE
NARBONNAISE
-MAIN GATE-

INSIDE
MAIN
GATE

FOOT
PATH

RUE   GUSTAVE

COMBELERAND

TO ⑩ &
TRAIN STN.
ON FOOT

VIEUX
PONT

A U B E R.

TO
NEUF
PONT &
TRAIN
STN.
BY CAR

RUE BARBACANE

RUE DE LA GAFFE

RUE GUSTAVE

NAPAUD

TO
AVE
LECLERC

① Hotel Le Donjon

② Hotel des Remparts
& L'Auberge du Grand Puits rest.

③ Youth Hostel

④ Hotel Montmorency

⑤ Cellier des Vignerons

⑥ Hotel Espace Cité

⑦ Chambre d'hote

⑧ La Table Ronde rest.

⑨ Le Saint Jean restaurant

⑩ To Hotel Grand Terminus
& Hotel Bristol

⑪ Hotel Trois Couronnes

⑫ Jardin de la Tour rest.

⑬ Hotel de la Cité

⑭ Hotel Mercure

Neolithic times. The Romans built here first; the mostly medieval inner wall was constructed on top of the Roman wall. Look for big blocks of stone or smaller rocks mixed with red bricks for evidence of the Romans. The outer wall was not built until the 1200s. Look over the wall and be impressed with how high you are above the moat below. There never was any water in that moat, nor for that matter was there water in most medieval defensive moats—too much trouble. A good ditch sufficed, except when attackers were able to tunnel underneath the wall. The area between the two walls was used for jousting practice and other knightly games.

La Cité's golden age was during the 1100s, when independent rulers with open minds allowed Jews and Cathars to live and prosper within the walls, and troubadours wrote poems of ideal love. This liberal attitude made for a rich intellectual life, but also proved to be La Cité's downfall. The Crusades to rid France of the dangerous Cathar movement caused Carcassonne's defeat and eventual incorporation into the kingdom of France. The walls of this majestic fortress were partially reconstructed in 1844 as part of a program to restore France's important monuments.

Keep working your way around the walls and enter La Cité at the first entrance possible, near the Basilique St. Nazaire (see description below). If the tower to your right is open, climb it. It's the only section of the inner wall you can climb without a tour, and the tower-top *librarie* (bookstore) is good. The best guidebook to Carcassonne is the skinny *City of Carcassonne* by Editions du Patrimoine (€6). From here, you can meander the streets of La Cité, or return to the *lices* and continue circumnavigating the fortress. Several sections of the outer wall walk are closed, but enough is open to give you a good sample. Savor every step and view.

▲**Summer Festivals**—Carcassonne erupts into a medieval frenzy of events during much of July and August. Get details at the TI, and ask about the *spectacle équestre* (jousting matches). July 14 fireworks will knock your socks off.

▲▲▲**Walk to Pont Vieux**—For the best view back onto the floodlit city, hike down to the old bridge. As you exit the Narbonnaise Gate, go left on rue Nadaud to rue Gustave, then turn left onto rue Trivalle. Return via the back-door entry to La Cité near Basilique St. Nazaire.

Basilique St. Nazaire—Enter this church and slowly walk down the center. Notice the Romanesque arches supporting the aisle and the delicately vaulted Gothic arches over the altar. Enjoy the explosion of color of the 14th-century stained glass. This is one of the best examples of Gothic architecture in southern France.

Château Comtal—Carcassonne's third layer of defense was originally built in 1125, but was completely redesigned in later reconstructions. Peek into the inner courtyard, ask about the free English tours (generally 2–4/day May–Sept), and admire the towers (€5.50, daily June–Sept 9:30–19:30, April, May, and Oct 9:30–18:00, Nov–March 9:30–17:00).

Cellier des Vignerons—Duck into this snappy wine bar to sample from a vast selection of local wines and enjoy the peaceful outdoor terrace. You are expected to buy a bottle if you taste, but prices are reasonable (13 rue du Grand Puits).

Canal du Midi—Completed in 1681, this sleepy, 250-kilometer/155-mile canal connects France's Mediterranean and Atlantic coasts. Before railways, Canal du Midi was jammed with commercial traffic. Today, it's busy with pleasure craft. Look for the slow-moving hotel barges strewn with tanned and well-fed vacationers. The towpath that spans the length of the canal makes for relaxed, level biking. The canal runs right in front of the train station in Carcassonne (ask TI about bike rental).

Sleeping in Carcassonne

Sleeping in Carcassonne's La Cité

Sleep in or near the old walls. In the summer, when La Cité is jammed with tourists, consider sleeping in quieter Caunes-Minervois (see "Sleeping near Carcassonne," below). Several places, including a hostel, offer rooms inside the walls. Except for the mid-July–mid-August peak, there are plenty of rooms.

HIGHER PRICED

Best Western's **Hôtel Le Donjon***** offers tight but well-appointed rooms, a mood-setting lobby, and a great location inside the walls (Sb-€64–80, Db-€78–105, Tb-€80–130, breakfast buffet-€10, parking-€5, CC, air-con, elevator, tel. 04 68 11 23 00, fax 04 68 25 06 60, e-mail: info@bestwestern-donjon.com). They have an annex (Hôtel des Remparts) that's closer to the castle and is reserved only through the main hotel.

Hôtel de la Cité**** offers deluxe everything wrapped in an old stone building next to Basilique St. Nazaire. Peaceful gardens, a swimming pool, fine public spaces, an elegant restaurant, and reliable luxury are yours—for a price (Db-€250–360, suites-€415–525, extra bed-€55, garage-€15, CC, place de l'Eglise, tel. 04 68 71 98 71, fax 04 68 71 50 15, www.hoteldelacite.com).

LOWER PRICED

Madame Cordonnier's *chambre d'hôte*, across from Hôtel des Remparts (inquire in small boutique), has one double room and two huge, apartment-like rooms that could sleep five and have a kitchenette and private terrace (Db-€52, Tb-€56, Qb-€68, family deals, stocked fridge and self-serve breakfast included, no CC, tel. & fax 04 68 25 16 67).

The **Auberge de Jeunesse** (youth hostel) is clean and well-run, with an outdoor garden courtyard, self-service kitchen, TV room, bar, Internet station, and a welcoming ambience. If you ever wanted to bunk down in a hostel, do it here—all ages welcome. Only summer is tight—reserve ahead. Nonmembers pay €3 extra (dorm bed-€13, sheets-€2.80, 2 doubles, a few quads, otherwise 6 to a room, includes breakfast, CC, open all day, rue de Vicomte Trencavel, tel. 04 68 25 23 16, fax 04 68 71 14 84, www.hostelbooking.com). They also offer their guests (not the public) reasonably priced minivan excursions to otherwise inaccessible sights.

Sleeping near La Cité

HIGHER PRICED
Hôtel Trois Couronnes*** offers the only view rooms of La Cité I could find, just across the pont Vieux, if you can get a view room and get by the awful exterior (Db with view-€107, CC, elevator, 2 rue des Couronnes, 15-min walk from train station, tel. 04 68 25 36 10, fax 04 68 25 92 92).

Hotel Mercure***, hiding behind the parking lots and Hôtel Montmorency, and a five-minute walk to La Cité, has 61 tight but comfortable rooms, a refreshing garden, a generously sized pool, big elevators, a bar/lounge, and a restaurant (small Db-€92, moderate Db-€95, Tb-€145, CC, free parking, 18 rue Camille Saint Saëns, tel. 04 68 11 92 82, fax 04 68 71 11 45, e-mail: h1622@accor-hotels.com).

MODERATELY PRICED
At **Hôtel Montmorency****, Cecile, Stephane, and dog Opus are perfect hosts, having created the best value in Carcassonne with comfortable rooms knocking at the door of La Cité's drawbridge. Gaze at the walls from the cool of the pool or from terrace tables. Rooms in the annex building are very sharp, with warm colors, air-conditioning, and firm beds. Five of the rooms have a small terrace; those in the main building are more traditional, without air-conditioning (Db annex-€62–70, Db main building-€40–56, Tb annex-€70–84, CC, free parking, 2 rue Camille Saint-Saëns, tel. 04 68 11 96 70, fax 04 68 11 96 79, www.lemontmorency.com, e-mail: le.montmorency@wanadoo.fr).

Near the train station: Grand Hôtel Terminus***, while a bit faded, is friendly, turn-of-the-century grand, and worth ducking into for its lobby alone. Just across from the station, the rooms are sufficiently comfortable, with high ceilings (standard Db-€73–80, superior Db-€97, CC, elevator, 2 avenue Marechal Joffre, tel. 04 68 25 25 00, fax 04 68 72 53 09). **Hôtel Bristol****, on the canal facing the station, has adequate rooms at fair rates (Sb-€50–67, Db-€54–72, Tb-€78, garage-€8, CC, elevator, 7 avenue Foch, tel. 04 68 25 07 24, fax 04 68 25 71 89).

LOWER PRICED

Hôtel Espace Cité**, two blocks downhill from Hôtel Montmorency, is sterile and shiny with small rooms, but it's handy for drivers (Db-€50–55, Tb-€60–65, Qb-€70–75, CC, air-con, 132 rue Trivalle, tel. 04 68 25 24 24, fax 04 68 25 17 17, www .hotelespacecite.fr).

Sleeping near Carcassonne

MODERATELY PRICED

To experience unspoiled, tranquil Languedoc, sleep surrounded by vineyards, a 15-minute drive from Carcassonne, in the unspoiled village of Caunes-Minervois (zip code: 11600). Comfortably nestled in the foothills of the Montaigne Noire, Caunes-Minervois offers an eighth-century abbey, two cafés, a good pizzeria, a few wineries, and very few tourists. My two hotel recommendations sit side by side in the heart of the village, with owners eager to help you explore their region.

Americans Terry and Lois Link take good care of you at **L'Ancienne Boulangerie**, where rooms are designed with care, the beds are tops, and the breakfast terrace will slow your pulse. Ask Terry about his how-to book on living in France (S-€25, Sb-€40, D-€40, Db-€60, a lofty family room-€15 per extra person, includes breakfast, rue St. Genes, tel. 04 68 78 01 32, e-mail: ancienneboulangerie@compuserve.com).

Hôtel d'Alibert**, a wonderfully Old World place with traditionally French rooms, is run by Frederic with relaxed panache (large Db-€46–61, extra person-€10, CC, place de la Mairie, tel. 04 68 78 00 54, e-mail: frederic.dalibert@wanadoo.fr). Don't skip a meal in his terrific restaurant (closed Sun–Mon).

Closer to Carcassonne, British Diana and Chris of **La Ferme de la Sauzette** warmly welcome travelers in their cottage-like farmhouse with five antiqued rooms and the possibility of a home-cooked dinner (Sb-€51–60, Db-€58–67, Tb-€78, dinner with wine-€26, no CC, take D-42, then D-142 south from Carcassonne 5 km/3 miles to Cazilhac, Sauzette is on the left, 3 km/1.9 miles from Cazilhac town hall, or *mairie*, along D56 in direction of Villefloure, 11570 Cazilhac, tel. 04 68 79 81 32, fax 04 68 79 65 99, www.lasauzette.com).

Eating in La Cité

Skip the touristy joints lining the main drag.

Le Jardin de la Tour is where the locals go for reliable cuisine and friendly service. The tranquil rear garden tables look up to the château, the interior rooms are medieval-cozy (ask your hotel to reserve when you arrive, earlier the better, *menus* from €19, great cassoulet, try the tomato *tarte Tatin*, entrance is easy to miss, next to L'Ecu d'Or restaurant, daily, tel. 04 68 25 71 24).

At **Le St. Jean**, dine peacefully and well enough with exceptional views of the château (*menus* from €16, behind Hôtel des Remparts).

Inexpensive meals and a lighthearted staff make **L'Auberge du Grand Puits** a low-risk option (hearty cassoulet, place des Grands Puits, daily, tel. 04 68 71 27 88).

La Table Ronde is also inexpensive (€11 *menu*, daily, 30 rue du Plô, tel. 04 68 47 38 21).

Picnics can be gathered at the small *alimentation* (grocery) on the main drag (generally open until 19:30). For your beggar's banquet, picnic on the city walls. For fast, cheap, hot food, look for places on the main drag with quiche and pizza to go.

In the lower city, the canalfront **La Maison** is *le* place to go. Mouthwatering cuisine like grandma made, a funky decor, and friendly owners await (*menus* from €20, turn right out of train station and follow the canal to 48 route de Minervoise, closed Sun and Mon, tel. 04 68 72 52 20).

Transportation Connections—Carcassonne

By train to: Sarlat (2/day in 4.5 hrs with changes in Toulouse, Agen, and Le Buisson; or 3/day in 6–7 hrs via Souillac with changes possible in Brive-la-Gaillarde and Toulouse, then bus from Souillac), **Arles** (6/day, 3 hrs, 3 require changes in Narbonne and Nîmes or Avignon), **Nice** (6/day, 6–9 hrs, fastest via change in Marseille), **Paris**' Gare Montparnasse (8/day, a few direct in 10 hrs or in 6.5 hrs by TGV with changes in Toulouse and possibly Bordeaux), **Toulouse** (hrly, 1 hr), **Barcelona** (3/day, 5 hrs, change in Narbonne and Port Bou, the border town).

Sights—Languedoc

The land around Carcassonne is littered with romantically ruined castles, lost abbeys, and photogenic hill towns. The ruined castles of Peyrepertuse and Queribus make good stops between Carcassonne and Collioure (allow 2 hours from Carcassonne on narrow, winding roads), and the Abbey of Fontfroide and gorge-village of Minerve work well for Provence-bound travelers. While public transportation is hopeless, taxis capable of seating six cost €165 for a day excursion (taxi tel. 04 58 71 50 50). Ask at the Carcassonne TI about the possibility of minivan excursions (planned for 2003).

▲▲▲Châteaux of Hautes Corbières—Two hours south of Carcassonne, in the scenic foothills of the Pyrenees, lies a series of surreal, mountain-capping castle ruins. The Maginot Line of the 13th century, these sky-high castles were strategically located between France and the Spanish kingdom of Roussillon. As you can see by flipping through the picture books in Carcassonne tourist shops, these castles' crumpled ruins are an impressive contrast to the restored walls of Carcassonne. Bring a good map (lots of tiny roads) and sturdy walking shoes—prepare for a climb and be wary of slick stones.

The most spectacular is the château of **Peyrepertuse**. The ruins seem to grow right out of a narrow splinter of cliff. The views are so sensational you feel you can reach out and touch Spain. Let your imagination soar, but watch your step as you try to reconstruct this eagle's nest (€4, April–Oct 9:00–19:00, until 20:30 June–Sept, Nov–March 10:00–17:00, tel. 04 68 45 40 55). Canyon-lovers will enjoy the detour to the nearby and narrow **Gorges de Galamus**, just north of St. Paul de Fenouillet. Closer to D-117, **Queribus** towers above (steep hike) and is famous as the last Cathar castle to fall. It was left useless when the border between France and Spain was moved (in 1659) farther south into the high Pyrenees (€4, get English pamphlet, April–Oct daily 9:00–sunset, Nov–March weekends only 10:00–sunset).

Châteaux of Lastours—Sixteen kilometers/10 miles north of Carcassonne, these four ruined castles cap a barren hilltop and offer drivers a handy, if less impressive, look at the region's Cathar castles. From Carcassonne, follow signs to Mazamet, then Conques sur Orbiel, then Lastours. In Lastours, park at the lot as you enter the village, then walk to the old factory (look for *accueil* signs) to the slick new ticket office (get the English information on the castles). It's a 20-minute uphill walk to the castles that were the inheritance of sons from a ruler who wanted to treat each fairly. Drive high to the belvedere for a panorama overlooking the castles (€4 for access to castles and belvedere viewpoint, daily April–Sept 10:00–18:00, Oct 10:00–17:00, closed Nov–March).

▲Abbaye de Fontfroide—Hidden in the Corbières mountains, this beautiful abbey is a worthwhile detour just 10 kilometers/6 miles south of Narbonne (exit 38 from A-9 autoroute). Founded in 1093, this once-powerful Cistercian abbey worked the front lines against the spread of Catharism. The assassination of one of its monks unleashed the terrible Albigensian Crusades. Today's abbey is privately owned and well-restored, with 3,000 roses, sublime cloisters, a massive church, and a monk's dormitory amid total isolation.

Call ahead for English tours or visit on a French-only tour with printed English explanations (€6.50, daily April–Oct 10:00–12:15 & 13:45–17:30, July–Aug 9:30–18:00, Nov–March 10:00–12:00 & 14:00–16:00, hourly tours, tel. 04 68 45 18 31).

▲**Minerve**—A one-time Cathar hideout, spectacular Minerve is sculpted out of a deep canyon that provided a natural defense. But strong as it was, it didn't keep out the pope's army. The village was razed during the vicious Albigensian Crusades. The view from the small parking lot alone (€2) justifies the detour. Cross the bridge on foot, then wander into the village to its upper end and a ruined tower. A path leads down to the river from here (watch your step as you descend); you can reenter the village from the riverbed at its lower end.

Minerve has two pleasant cafés, one hotel, an intriguing museum of prehistory, a few wine shops—and not much more. Stay here and melt into southern France (literally, if it's summer); you won't regret it. Sleep and eat at the friendly and cozy **Relais Chantovent** (Sb-€37, Db-€39–47, Tb-€44, Qb-€50, CC, Minerve 34210, tel. 04 68 91 14 18, fax 04 68 91 81 99). People travel great distances to dine here (*menus* from €15, closed Sun–Mon), so reserve early. The **Café de la Place** provides the perfect break and has a pool for anyone's use (€3, tel. 05 68 91 22 94).

Minerve is between Carcassonne and Beziers, 15 kilometers/ 9 miles northeast of Olonzac and 40 minutes by car from Carcassonne. It's a good stop between Provence and Carcassonne. In the mood for wine-tasting? The **Trois Blasons Cave des Vignerons** in Azillanet (just south of Minerve) has a fine selection of regional wines. For a more personal experience, say *bonjour* to my friends Monsieur and Madame Remaury, who offer a good selection and an exquisite setting from which to sample the local product (coming from Minerve, it's just past Azillanet, look for signs to **Domaine de Pech d'Andre** on your left, tel. 04 68 91 22 66; a leetle Engleesh spoken).

COLLIOURE

Surrounded by less appealing resorts, lovely Collioure is blessed with a privileged climate and a romantic setting. By Mediterranean standards, this seaside village should be overrun—it has everything. Like an ice-cream shop, Collioure offers 31 flavors of pastel houses and six petite, scooped-out, and pebbled beaches sprinkled lightly with beachgoers. This sweet scene, capped by a winking lighthouse, sits under a once-mighty castle in the shade of the Pyrenees. Evenings are best in Collioure—as the sky darkens, yellow lamps reflect warm pastels and deep blues.

Just 25 kilometers/15 miles from the Spanish border, Collioure shares a common history and independent attitude with its Catalan siblings on the other side of the border. Happily French yet proudly Catalan, it sports the yellow and red flag, street names in French and Catalan, and business names with *el* and *las* rather than *le* and *les*. Sixty years ago, most villagers spoke Catalan, and today the language is enjoying a resurgence as Collioure rediscovers its roots.

Come here to unwind and regroup. Even with its crowds of French vacationers in peak season (July and August are jammed), Collioure is what many are looking for when heading to the Riviera—a sunny, relaxing splash in the Mediterranean.

Check your ambition at the station. Enjoy a slow coffee on *le* Med, lose yourself in the old town's streets, comparison-shop the gelati shops on rue Vauban, and snuggle into a pebble-sand beach (waterproof shoes are so helpful).

Orientation

Most of Collioure's shopping, sights, and hotels are in the old town, across the drainage channel from Château Royal. There are good views of the old town from across the bay near the recommended Hôtel Boramar, and brilliant views from the hills above.

Tourist Information: The TI is behind the main beachfront cafés at 5 place du 18 Juin (open all year Mon–Sat 9:00–12:00 & 14:00–18:00, closed Sun except July–Aug, tel. 04 68 82 15 47, www.collioure.com).

Market Days: Markets are held on Wednesday and Saturday mornings on place Marechal Leclerc, across from Hôtel Fregate.

Laundry: Laverie 3L will do your laundry while you do your relaxing (daily July–Aug 9:00–19:00, otherwise daily 9:00–12:00 & 15:00–18:00, 1 block up from post office at 28 rue de la République, tel. 04 68 98 04 17).

Car Rental: National Car rental is located in the Garage Renault, opposite the launderette on rue de la République (tel. 04 68 82 08 34).

Taxi: Call 04 68 82 27 80 or 04 68 82 09 30.

Arrival in Collioure

By Train: Walk out of the station, turn right, and follow the road downhill for about 10 minutes until you see Hôtel Fregate (hotels are listed from this point).

By Car: Parking is tricky here, and almost impossible in summer, when day-trippers occupy the available spaces. Arrive early or late for easiest parking. Follow Collioure *Centre-ville* signs. Look for a parking spot on the street or, if you have no luck, follow *Gare SNCF* signs (use pay lot at the train station until you find better). Ask your hotel for parking suggestions and take everything out of the car.

Collioure

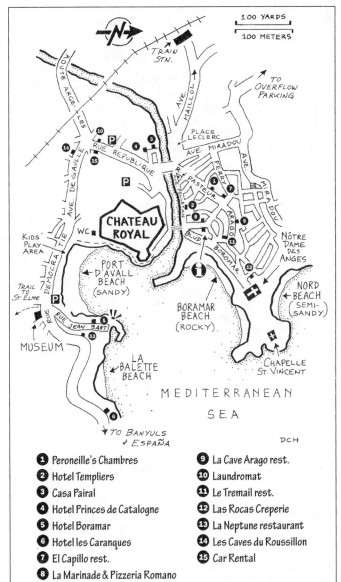

1. Peroneille's Chambres
2. Hotel Templiers
3. Casa Pairal
4. Hotel Princes de Catalogne
5. Hotel Boramar
6. Hotel les Caranques
7. El Capillo rest.
8. La Marinade & Pizzeria Romano
9. La Cave Arago rest.
10. Laundromat
11. Le Tremail rest.
12. Las Rocas Creperie
13. La Neptune restaurant
14. Les Caves du Roussillon
15. Car Rental

Sights—Collioure

Beaches—You'll find the best sand-to-stone ratio at plages St. Vincent and at Port d'Avall; (paddleboat/kayak rental–€11/hr). The tiny plage de la Balette is quietest, with views of Collioure.

Château Royal—This 800-year-old château comes with great rampart walks, views, and mildly interesting exhibits on local history and contemporary art (€3, daily June–Sept 10:00–17:15, Oct–May 9:00–16:15).

Notre-Dame des Anges—The waterfront church, with its one-of-a-kind lighthouse-bell tower and over-the-top altar, is worth a gander (daily 9:00–12:00 & 14:00–18:00). Explore past the church and find beastly good views from the jetty wall at plage St. Vincent (best at sunset and after dinner).

Path of Fauvism (Chemin de Fauvism)—As you stroll Collioure's waterfront, notice the prints hanging on the walls. You're on the "Chemin de Fauvism," where you'll find copies of Derain's and Matisse's works inspired by their stays in Collioure in 1905. But as in Arles and van Gogh, there are no original paintings of theirs left here for us to enjoy (the museum in Ceret has a good collection; see "Sights Near Collioure," below).

Wine-Tasting—Collioure produces well-respected wines, and many shops offer relaxed tastings of the sweet Banyuls and Collioure reds and rosés. Try **Les Caves du Roussillon,** with a great selection from many wineries and good prices (daily 9:30–12:30 & 15:00–19:30, 9 avenue General de Gaulle).

Cruise—Consider a **Promenade sur Mer** boat excursion (€6, 1-hr Mediterranean cruise toward Spain and back, 5/day Easter–Sept weather permitting, leaves from breakwater near château, great views but commentary in French only, tel. 04 68 81 43 88).

Hike to Fort St. Elme—This vertical hike (1 hour, one-way) is best done early or late and is worth the sweat even if you don't make it to the top. You can't miss the square castle lurking high above Collioure. Catch the trail from Collioure's museum, behind Hôtel Triton. Stone steps lead up from behind the museum to a windmill (a good low-energy destination), then farther up to the castle. The path, marked with yellow dashes, is easy to follow. The view from the top is sensational. The privately owned castle is not open to the public. Cheaters can drive here by driving to Port Vendres, then following the small road from its train station. The TI has information on other hikes in the area.

Sights—Near Collioure

Day Trip to Spain—The 25-kilometer/15-mile, 40-minute coastal drive via the Col de Banyuls into Spain is beautiful and well worth the countless curves, even if you don't venture past the border.

Train travelers can day-trip to Spain, either to Barcelona (3 hrs one-way, 4/day) or, closer, Figueres and its Salvador Dalí museum (€9, daily July–Sept 9:00–19:45, Oct–June 10:30–17:45, tel. 972-677-500). Get train schedules at the station. **Ceret**—This enchanting town awaits 40 windy kilometers/ 25 miles inland, with fountains and mountains at its front door, and an excellent modern art museum with works by some of Collioure's more famous visitors, including Picasso, Miró, Chagall, and Matisse (€6, daily mid-June–mid-Sept 10:00–19:00, otherwise 10:00–18:00, tel. 04 68 87 27 76). This makes a fine day trip from Collioure (allow 50 min to Ceret by car, or train to nearby Perpignan and bus from there, get details at TI).

Sleeping in Collioure
(€1 = about $1, country code: 33, zip code: 66190)
You have two good choices for hotel location: tucked behind the château in the old town (closer to train station), or in a quieter area across the bay, with views of the old town (10-min walk from château).

Sleeping in the Old Town
Directions to the following places are given from the big Hôtel Fregate, at the entrance to the old town.

HIGHER PRICED
Mediterranean-elegant **Casa Pairal*****, opposite Hôtel Fregate, is Collioure's best-value splurge. Enter to sounds of a fountain gurgling in the flowery courtyard; recline in lounges in the garden or by the pool. Rooms are Old World comfortable, with air-conditioning (small Db-€69–75, pleasant Db-€79–93, big Db-€88–123, Tb-€131–152, extra bed-€20, garage-€8, CC, impasse Palmiers, tel. 04 68 82 05 81, fax 04 68 82 52 10, www.roussillhotel.com, charming Chantal SE, reserve ahead for room and parking).

MODERATELY PRICED
The art-happy **Hôtel Templiers****, one block down the drainage road from Hôtel Fregate, rents delightfully decorated rooms, some with views. Air-conditioning and an elevator are planned for 2003 (Db-€55–70, ask about connecting family rooms, CC, 12 avenue l'Amiraute, tel. 04 68 98 31 10, fax 04 68 98 01 24, e-mail: info@hotel-templiers.com).

For American style and efficiency, try **Princes de Catalogne***** for spacious, comfortable, and air-conditioned rooms; ask for a room on the mountain side—pron. *coat-ay mon-tan-yah* (Db-€56–69, extra person-€11, CC, next to Casa

Pairal, rue des Palmiers, tel. 04 68 98 30 00, fax 04 68 98 30 31, www.hotel-princescatalogne.com).

LOWER PRICED
The cheapest rooms in the old town are the simple, spotless, and mostly spacious rooms at Monsieur and Madame **Peroneille's Chambres,** on the pedestrian street two blocks past Hôtel Fregate. The more serious Monsieur (speaks Catalan) and bubbly Madame have rented these rooms for over 30 years and haven't yet learned a word of English; the ball is in your court (Ds-€40, Db-€43, Tb-€60, Qb-€68, no CC, 20 rue Pasteur, tel. 04 68 82 15 31, fax 04 68 82 35 94). The rooms in the main building *(la maison principale)* are infinitely better than those in the annex. Ask to see the rooftop terrace.

Sleeping across the Bay

MODERATELY PRICED
On the view side of the bay, the low-key but well-maintained **Hôtel Boramar**** is a solid value. Get a room with a terrace facing the sea, or sleep elsewhere (Db without view-€47, Db with view-€56, Tb with view-€62, CC, rue Jean Bart, tel. 04 68 82 07 06, no fax, no e-mail, but good place).

The idyllic **Hôtel les Caranques**,** 100 meters/330 feet farther down the coast, tumbles down the cliffs, offering sea views and balconies from every one of its linoleum-floor, simple-but-spotless rooms. Enjoy the several view terraces and the four-star breakfast room panorama (D-€39, Db-€62–70, CC, 5-min walk from Hôtel Triton, route de Port Vendres, tel. 04 68 82 06 68, fax 04 68 82 00 92, www.les-caranques.com).

Eating in Collioure
Collioure is famous for its Catalan cuisine, featuring anchovies, seafood, and local wines. Restaurants are open daily unless noted.

In the old town, **Le Tremail** serves fine seafood and Catalan specialties to contented clients one block from the bay, where rues F. Arago and Mailly meet (closed Mon–Tue, tel. 04 68 82 16 10).

La Marinade is good for seafood (€18 *menu*, near TI at 14 place du 18 Juin, tel. 04 68 82 09 76). **El Capillo** is also a good value, but has no outdoor tables (2 rue Pasteur, tel. 04 68 82 48 23).

Pizzeria Romana, across from the TI, is cheap, fun, and lighthearted (6 place du 18 Juin).

Las Rocas Pizzeria/Crêperie, snuggled in a corner by the church, is more peaceful, with views of the fort and mountains and good enough pizza.

For a lively, local, and smoky tapas-bar experience, find **La Cave Arago** (closed Mon–Wed, 18 rue F. Arago, tourists tolerated).

But if you want the best, reserve ahead, then cross the bay to **La Neptune** for sumptuous seafood and views of Collioure (*menus* from €30, 9 route de Port Vendres, tel. 04 68 82 02 27).

I love buying something to go (*à emporter*; pron. ah em-pohr-tay) and finding a romantic spot to eat along the water.

Transportation Connections—Collioure

By train to: Carcassonne (9/day, 2 hrs, 6 require change in Narbonne), **Paris** (5/day, 6 hrs with changes in Perpignan or Montpellier and Lyon then TGV to Gare Montparnasse, 1 direct train to Gare d'Austerlitz in 10 hrs and a handy night train), **Barcelona** (4/day, 3 hrs, change in Cerbère), **Avignon/Arles** (7/day, 3.5 hrs, many transfer points possible). Consider handy night trains to Paris, key Italy destinations, and Geneva. The train station ticket office closes at 17:45 (tel. 04 68 82 05 89).

PROVENCE

This magnificent region is shaped like a giant wedge of quiche. From its sunburned crust, fanning out along the Mediterranean coast from Nîmes to Nice, it stretches north along the Rhône Valley to Orange. The Romans were here in force and left many ruins—some of the best anywhere. Seven popes; great artists, such as van Gogh, Cézanne, and Picasso; and author Peter Mayle all enjoyed their years in Provence. The region offers a splendid recipe of arid climate (except for occasional vicious winds known as the mistral), captivating cities, exciting hill towns, dramatic scenery, and oceans of vineyards.

Explore the ghost town that is ancient Les Baux and see France's greatest Roman ruin, Pont du Gard. Spend your starry, starry nights where van Gogh did, in Arles. Uncover its Roman past, then find the linger-longer squares and café corners that inspired Vincent. Youthful but classy Avignon bustles in the shadow of its brooding pope's palace. It's a short hop from Arles or Avignon into the splendid scenery and villages of the Côtes du Rhône and Luberon regions that make Provence so popular today. And if you need a Provençal beach fix, consider Cassis, barely east of Marseille.

Planning Your Time

Make Arles or Avignon your sightseeing base, particularly if you have no car. Arles has an undeniably scruffy quality and good-value hotels, while Avignon (three times larger than Arles) feels sophisticated and offers more nightlife and shopping. Italophiles prefer smaller Arles, while poodles pick urban Avignon.

To measure the pulse of Provence, spend at least one night in a smaller town. Vaison la Romaine is ideal for those heading

Provence

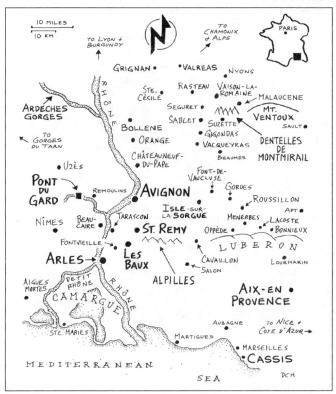

to/from the north, and Isle sur la Sorgue is centrally located between Avignon, the wine route, and the Luberon (all described below). The small port town of Cassis is a worthwhile Mediterranean meander between Provence and the Riviera (and more appealing than the resorts of the Riviera). Most destinations are accessible by public transit.

You'll want a full day for sightseeing in Arles (best on Wed or Sat, when the morning market rages), a half day for Avignon, and a day or two for the villages and sights in the countryside.

Getting around Provence

By Car: The yellow Michelin map of this region is essential for drivers. Avignon (population 100,000) is a headache for drivers; Arles (population 35,000) is easier, though it still requires go-cart driving skills. Park only in well-watched spaces and leave nothing

in your car. For some of Provence's most scenic drives, follow my
day trip routes (see "Villages of the Côtes du Rhône" and "The
Hill Towns of Luberon," below). If you're heading north from
Provence, consider a three-hour detour through the spectacular
Ardèche Gorges (see Côtes du Rhône loop trip, below).

By Bus or Train: Public transit is good between cities and
marginal at best to small towns. Frequent trains link Avignon,
Arles, and Nîmes (about 30 min between each), and buses connect
smaller towns. Les Baux is accessible by bus from Arles. Pont du
Gard and St. Rémy—and to a lesser extent, Vaison la Romaine
and some Côtes du Rhône villages—are accessible by bus from
Avignon. While a tour of the villages of Luberon is possible only
by car or bus excursion from Avignon, nearby Isle sur la Sorgue is
an easy hop by train or bus from Avignon. The TIs in Arles and
Avignon have information on bus excursions to regional sights
that are hard to reach *sans* car (€18/half day, €30/full day).
Cassis has train service via Marseille or Toulon.

Cuisine Scene—Provence

The almost extravagant use of garlic, olive oil, herbs, and tomatoes
makes Provence's cuisine France's liveliest. To sample it, order
anything *à la Provençale*. Among the area's spicy specialties are
ratatouille (a thick mixture of vegetables in an herb-flavored tomato
sauce), *brandade* (a salt cod, garlic, and cream mousse), aioli (a gar-
licky mayonnaise often served atop fresh vegetables), tapenade
(a paste of pureed olives, capers, anchovies, herbs, and sometimes
tuna), *soupe au pistou* (vegetable soup with basil, garlic, and cheese),
and *soupe à l'ail* (garlic soup). Look also for *riz Camarguaise* (rice
from the Camargue) and *taureau* (bull meat). Banon (wrapped in
chestnut leaves) and Picodon (nutty taste) are the native cheeses.
The region's sheep's milk cheese, Brousse, is creamy and fresh.
Provence also produces some of France's great wines at relatively
reasonable prices. Look for Gigondas, Sablet, Côtes du Rhône,
and Côte de Provence. If you like rosé, try the Tavel. This is the
place to splurge for a bottle of Châteauneuf-du-Pape.

Remember, restaurants serve only during lunch (11:30–14:00)
and dinner (19:00–21:00, later in bigger cities); cafés serve food
throughout the day.

Provence Market Days

Provençal market days offer France's most colorful and tantalizing
outdoor shopping. The best markets are on Monday in Cavaillon,
Tuesday in Vaison la Romaine, Wednesday in St. Rémy, Thursday
in Nyons, Friday in Lourmarin, Saturday in Arles, Uzès, and Apt,
and, best of all, Sunday in Isle sur la Sorgue. Crowds and parking

problems abound at these popular events—arrive by 9:00, or, even
better, sleep in the town the night before.

Monday:	Cavaillon, Cadenet (near Vaison la Romaine)
Tuesday:	Vaison la Romaine, Tarascon, and Gordes
Wednesday:	St. Rémy, Arles, and Violes (near Vaison la Romaine)
Thursday:	Nyons, Beaucaire, Vacqueyras, and Isle sur la Sorgue
Friday:	Lourmarin (a good one), Remoulins (near Pont du Gard), Bonnieux (smaller but fun), and Châteauneuf-du-Pape
Saturday:	Arles, Uzès, Valreas, and Apt (near Luberon hill towns)
Sunday:	Isle sur la Sorgue, Mausanne (near Les Baux), and Beaucaire

ARLES

By helping Julius Caesar defeat Marseille, Arles (pron. arl) earned
the imperial nod and was made an important port city. With the
first bridge over the Rhône River, Arles was a key stop on the
Roman road from Italy to Spain, the Via Domitia. After reigning
as a political hot spot of the early Christian Church (the seat of an
archbishopric for centuries) and thriving as a trading city on and
off until the 18th century, Arles all but disappeared from the map.
Van Gogh settled here a hundred years ago, but left only memories. American bombers destroyed much of Arles in World War
II. Today, Arles thrives again with one of France's few commun-
ist mayors. This compact city is alive with great Roman ruins, an
eclectic assortment of museums, made-for-ice-cream pedestrian
zones, and squares that play hide-and-seek with visitors.

Orientation

Arles faces the Mediterranean and turns its back to Paris. Its
spaghetti street plan disorients the first-time visitor. Landmarks
hide in the medieval tangle of narrow, winding streets. Everything
is deceptively close. While Arles sits on the Rhône, it completely
ignores the river (the part of Arles most damaged by Allied bombers
in World War II). The elevated riverside walk provides a direct
route to the excellent Ancient History Museum, an easy return to
the station, and fertile ground for poorly trained dogs. Hotels have
good, free city maps, but Arles works best if you simply follow
street-corner signs pointing you toward the sights and hotels of the
town center. Racing cars enjoy Arles' medieval lanes, turning sidewalks into tightropes and pedestrians into leaping targets. The free
"Starlette" minibus-shuttle circles the town's major sights every

15 minutes, but does not serve the Ancient History Museum, so it isn't very helpful (just wave at the driver and hop in; Mon–Sat 7:30–19:30, never on Sun). It does serve the train station, the only stop you pay for (€0.80).

Tourist Information: The main TI is on the ring road, esplanade Charles de Gaulle (April–Sept daily 9:00–18:45, Oct–March Mon–Sat 9:00–17:45, Sun 10:30–14:30, tel. 04 90 18 41 20). There's also a TI at the train station (all year, Mon–Sat 9:00–13:00, closed Sun). Both TIs can reserve a hotel room (€1 fee). Pick up the good city map and information on the Camargue wildlife area. Ask about bullfights and bus excursions to regional sights.

Arrival in Arles

By Train and Bus: Both stations are next to each other on the river and a 10-minute walk from the center. Lockers are not available. Pick up a city map at the train station TI and get the bus schedule to Les Baux at the bus station (tel. 04 90 49 38 01). To reach the old town, turn left out of the station.

By Car: Follow signs to *Centre-ville*, then follow signs toward *gare SNCF* (train station). You'll come to a huge roundabout (place Lamartine) with a Monoprix department store to the right. Park along the city wall or in nearby lots; pay attention to No Parking signs on Wednesday and Saturday until 13:00, and note that some hotels have limited parking. Leave nothing in your car as theft is a big problem. From place Lamartine, walk into the city through the two stumpy towers or take bus #1 (€0.80, 2/hr).

Helpful Hints

Launderettes: One is at 12 rue Portagnel; another is nearby at 6 rue Cavalarie, near place Voltaire (both daily 7:00–21:00, later once you're in, look for English directions for machines).

Public Pools: Arles has two public pools (one indoor and one outdoor). Ask at the TI or your hotel.

Taxis: Arles' taxis charge a minimum fee (about €10). Nothing in town is worth a taxi ride (figure €35–45 to Les Baux or St. Rémy, tel. 04 90 96 90 03).

Bike Rental: Try the Peugeot store (15 rue du Pont, tel. 04 90 96 03 77). While Vaison la Romaine and Isle sur la Sorgue make better biking bases (see below), rides to Les Baux (very steep climb) or into the Camargue work from Arles, provided you're in great shape (forget it in the wind).

Car Rental: Avis is at the train station (tel. 04 90 96 82 42), Europcar is downtown (2 bis avenue Victor Hugo, tel. 04 90 93 23 24), National is just off place Lamartine toward the station (4 avenue Paulin Talabot, tel. 04 90 93 02 17).

Local Guide: Jacqueline Neujean, an excellent guide, knows Arles like the back of her hand (€90/2 hrs, tel. 04 90 98 47 51).

Sights—Roman Arles

The worthwhile **monument pass** *(le pass monuments)* covers Arles' many sights and is valid for one week (€12, €10 under 18, sold at each sight). Otherwise, it's €3–4 per sight and €5.50 for the Ancient History Museum. While any sight is worth a few minutes, many aren't worth the individual admission. Many sights begin closing rooms 30 minutes early. Start at the Ancient History Museum for a helpful overview, then dive into the sights (ideally in the order described below).

▲▲▲**Ancient History Museum (Musée de L'Arles Antique)**— Begin your visit of Arles in this superb, air-conditioned museum. Models and original sculpture (with the help of the free English handout) re-create the Roman city of Arles, making workaday life and culture easier to imagine. Notice what a radical improvement the Roman buildings were over the simple mud-brick homes of the pre-Roman inhabitants. Models of Arles' arena even illustrate the moveable stadium cover, good for shade and rain. While virtually nothing is left of Arles' chariot racecourse, the model shows that it must have rivaled Rome's Circus Maximus. Jewelry, fine metal and glass artifacts, and well-crafted mosaic floors make it clear that Roman Arles was a city of art and culture. The finale is an impressive row of pagan and early Christian sarcophagi (second through fifth centuries). In the early days of the Church, Jesus was often portrayed beardless and as the good shepherd—with a lamb over his shoulder.

Built at the site of the chariot racecourse, this museum is a 20-minute walk from Arles along the river. Turn left at the river and take the riverside path to the big modern building just past the new bridge—or take bus #1 (€0.80) from boulevard des Lices and the TI (€5.50, March–Oct daily 9:00–19:00, Nov–Feb 10:00–17:00, tel. 04 90 18 88 88).

▲▲**Roman Forum (Place du Forum)**—After seeing the Ancient History Museum, start your explorations here, at the political and religious center of Roman Arles. Named for the Roman Forum that once stood here, this café-crammed square is always lively and best at night. The bistros on the square, while no place for a fine dinner, put together a good salad—and when you sprinkle in the ambience, that's €10 well spent.

Stand at the corner of the Hôtel Nord Pinus and find the information plaque. The illustration shows the two parts of the forum—the upper part dating from the first century B.C., where public meetings were held and temples were tended, and the lower

Arles

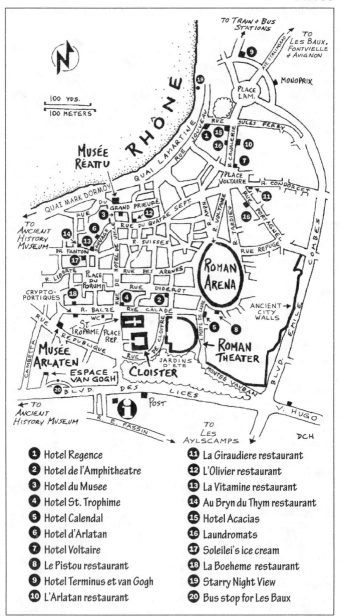

1 Hotel Regence
2 Hotel de l'Amphitheatre
3 Hotel du Musee
4 Hotel St. Trophime
5 Hotel Calendal
6 Hotel d'Arlatan
7 Hotel Voltaire
8 Le Pistou restaurant
9 Hotel Terminus et van Gogh
10 L'Arlatan restaurant

11 La Giraudiere restaurant
12 L'Olivier restaurant
13 La Vitamine restaurant
14 Au Bryn du Thym restaurant
15 Hotel Acacias
16 Laundromats
17 Soleilei's ice cream
18 La Boeheme restaurant
19 Starry Night View
20 Bus stop for Les Baux

part dating from the fourth century A.D., which served primarily as a marketplace. The blue lines show the underground support system required to support the southern end of the forum, which was built on lower ground (we'll visit the forum shortly). The area downhill from the forum was devoted mostly to public baths. You're standing at the entry of a temple. Look up to see the only two columns that survive; the steps that led to the temple are buried below (the Roman city level was 6 meters/20 feet below you). Van Gogh lounged near these same columns—his *Le Café de Nuit* was painted from this square (see "Sights—Van Gogh in Arles," below).

The guy on the pedestal is Frédéric Mistral; he received the Nobel Prize for literature in 1904. He used his prize money to preserve and display the folk identity of Provence—by founding the Arlaten Folk Museum—at a time when France was rapidly centralizing.

To see the Cryptoportiques, the key to appreciating place du Forum, leave the square with Hôtel Nord Pinus on your right and turn right on the first street (rue Balze).

Cryptoportiques du Forum—The only Baroque church in Arles (admire the wood ceiling) provides a dramatic entry to this underground system of arches and vaults that supported the southern end of the Roman Forum (and hid resistance fighters during World War II). The galleries of arches demonstrate the extent to which Roman engineers would go to follow standard city plans—if the land didn't suit the blueprint, change the land (€3.50, daily May–Sept 9:00–11:30 & 14:00–18:30, Oct and April 9:00–11:30 & 14:00–17:30, Nov–March 10:00–11:30 & 14:00–16:30).

The next stop is place de la République and St. Trophime. As you exit, turn right, walk two blocks, and turn right up the steps to Arles' city hall. Cross through the open room and inspect the unusual ceiling above—constructed without mortar (this still stymies engineers today). On the other side, step out to the square.

▲▲**St. Trophime Cloisters and Church (Cloître St. Trophime)**—This church, named after a third-century bishop of Arles, sports the finest Romanesque west portal (main doorway) I've seen anywhere. But first enjoy place de la République (a happening place for young Arlesians at night). Sit on the steps opposite the church. The **Egyptian obelisk** used to be the centerpiece of Arles' Roman Circus. Watch the peasants—pilgrims, locals, and street musicians. There's nothing new about this scene.

Like a Roman triumphal arch, the church trumpets the promise of Judgment Day. The tympanum (the semicircular area above the door) is filled with Christian symbolism. Christ sits in majesty, surrounded by symbols of the four evangelists (Matthew—the winged man, Mark—the winged lion, Luke—the ox, and John—the eagle). The 12 apostles are lined up below Jesus. Move closer. This is it. Some are saved and others aren't. Notice the condemned—a chain gang on the right bunny-hopping over the fires of hell. For them, the tune trumpeted by the three angels on the very top is not a happy one. Ride the exquisite detail back to a simpler age. In an illiterate medieval world, long before the vivid images of our Technicolor time, this message was a neon billboard over the town's square. A chart just inside the church (on the right) helps explain the carvings.

On the right side of the nave, a fourth-century, early-Christian sarcophagus is used as an altar. The adjacent **cloisters** are the best in Provence (enter from square, 20 meters/65 feet to right of church). Enjoy the sculpted capitals of the rounded Romanesque columns (12th century) and the pointed Gothic columns (14th century). The second floor offers only a view of the cloisters from above (€4, daily May–Sept 9:00–18:30, Oct, March, and April 9:00–17:30, and Nov–Feb 10:00–16:30).

To get to the next stop, the Classical Theater, face the church, walk left, then take the first right on rue de la Calade.
Classical Theater (Théâtre Antique)—Precious little survives from this Roman theater, which served as a handy town quarry throughout the Middle Ages. Walk to a center aisle and pull up a stone seat. Built in the first century B.C., it was capable of seating 10,000 eager-to-be-entertained Arlesians (they preferred comedy to tragedy). To appreciate the original size of the theater, look left to the upper left side of the tower and find the protrusion that supported the highest seating level (there were 3 levels). Today, 3,000 can attend events in this still well-used, restored facility. Two lonely Corinthian columns look out from the stage over the audience. The orchestra section is defined by a semicircular pattern in the stone. Walk to the left side of the stage, step up, then look down to the narrow channel that allowed the stage curtain to disappear below. Take a stroll backstage through broken bits of Rome, and loop back to the entry behind the grass (€3, you can see much of the theater by peeking through the fence for free, daily May–Sept 9:00–11:30 & 14:00–18:30, Oct and April 9:00–11:30 & 14:00–17:30, Nov–March 10:00–11:30 & 14:00–16:30). To best understand this monument, turn left as you exit, left again on the first street (rue du Cloitre) and follow signs left again to **Jardins d'Eté**. You'll find an information plaque with an illustration of the theater and have a good view of the supporting arches.

For the next stop, the Roman Arena, return to the theater entrance, pass the theater on your right and walk uphill a block.
▲▲▲**Roman Arena (Amphithéâtre)**—Enter and sit somewhere

in the shade. Nearly 2,000 years ago, gladiators fought wild animals here to the delight of 20,000 screaming fans—cruel. Today,
matadors fight wild bulls to the delight of local fans—still cruel.
In the Roman era, games were free (sponsored by city bigwigs),
and fans were seated by social class (the closer to the action you sat,
the higher your standing). Notice the many exits around the arena
as you scan the facility. These allowed for rapid dispersal after the
games (a necessity, as fans would be whipped into a frenzy after the
games, and fights would break out if they couldn't exit quickly).
In the halls below your seat, gladiators and animals would prepare
for battle. They fought no lions here, as revered lions were kept
for Rome's Colosseum. While the top row of arches is long gone,
three towers survive from medieval times, when the arena was used
as a fortress. The view is exceptional from the tower you can climb.
Until the early 1800s, this stadium corralled 200 humble homes
and functioned as a town within a town. The exterior arches of the
arena were sealed—anything for security. To see two still-sealed
arches, turn right on exiting the arena and walk to Andaluz restaurant, then look back (€4, daily May–Sept 9:00–18:30, Oct, March,
and April 9:00–17:30, and Nov–Feb 10:00–16:30).

Sights—Van Gogh in Arles

"The whole future of art is to be found in the south of France."
—Vincent van Gogh, 1888

Vincent was 35 years old when he arrived in Arles in 1888,
and it was here he discovered the light that would forever change
him. Coming from the gray skies and flatlands of Holland and
Paris, he was bowled over by everything Provençal—jagged peaks,
gnarled olive trees, brilliant sunflowers, and the furious wind. Van
Gogh painted in a flurry in Arles, producing more paintings than
at any other period of his too-brief career, over 200 in just a few
months. Sadly, none of his paintings remain in Arles, though we
can visit the sights from which he painted. Below are several places
where the spirit of Vincent can still be found.

Espace Van Gogh (Mediathèque)—The hospital where Vincent
was sent to treat his self-inflicted ear wound is today a cultural
center. It surrounds a garden that the artist would have loved (free,
only the courtyard is open to public, near Musée Arlaten on rue
President Wilson). He was sent from here to the mental institution in nearby St. Rémy (see "Sights—St. Rémy," below) before
Dr. Gachet invited him to Auvers-sur-Oise, outside of Paris.

Fondation Van Gogh—A ▲▲ sight for his fans, this small, pricey
gallery features works by several well-known contemporary artists
paying homage to Vincent through their thought-provoking interpretations of his art (€7, not covered by monument pass, great

collection of van Gogh prints and postcards in free entry area, April–mid-Oct daily 10:00–19:00, mid-Oct–March Tue–Sun 9:30–12:00 & 14:00–17:30, closed Mon, facing Roman Arena at 24 bis Rond Point des Arènes).

Café de Nuit—Across from Hôtel Nord Pinus on place du Forum, this café was the subject of one of Vincent's first paintings in Arles. While his painting showed the café a brilliant yellow due to the glow of light when he painted it, the facade was bare limestone, just like those of the other cafés on this square. The current owners of the café had it painted neon yellow to match van Gogh's famous painting.

Starry Night—From place Lamartine, walk to the river, then look toward Arles to find where Vincent set his easel for this famous painting where stars boil above the skyline of Arles. Riverfront cafés that once stood here were destroyed by bridge-seeking bombs in World War II, as was the bridge whose remains you see on your right. As you gaze over the river, be impressed (one more time) with Roman engineering—somehow, they managed to build a bridge over this powerful river 2,000 years ago.

More Sights—Arles

▲▲**Wednesday and Saturday Markets**—On these days until noon, Arles' ring road erupts into an outdoor market of fish, flowers, produce, and you-name-it (boulevard Emile Combes on Wed, boulevard Lices on Sat). Join in, buy flowers, try the olives, sample some wine, and swat a pickpocket. On the first Wednesday of the month, it's a grand flea market.

Musée Arlaten—This cluttered folklore museum, given to Arles by Nobel Prize–winner Frédéric Mistral (see "Roman Forum" listing, above), overflows with interesting odds and ends of life in Provence. It's like a failed 19th-century garage sale: shoes, hats, wigs, old photos, bread cupboards, and a model of a beetle-dragon monster, all crammed too close together to really be appreciated. If you're fond of folklore, this museum is for you; if you're not, duck in just to see the southern limit of the Roman Forum in the entry courtyard (€4, pick up excellent English brochure, April–Sept daily 9:00–12:30 & 14:00–18:00, Oct–March until 17:00, 29 rue de la République, tel. 04 90 96 08 23).

Musée Réattu—Housed in a beautiful, 15th-century mansion, this mildly interesting, mostly modern art collection includes 57 Picasso drawings (some two-sided and all done in a flurry of creativity—I liked the bullfights best), a room of Henri Rousseau's Camargue watercolors, and an unfinished painting by the neoclassical artist Réattu, none with English explanations (€3, plus €1.50 for special exhibits, daily April–Sept 9:00–12:00

& 14:00–18:30, Oct and March until 17:00, Nov–Feb until 16:00, 10 rue de Grand Prieuré, tel. 04 90 96 37 68).

▲▲**Bullfights (Courses Camarguaise)**—Occupy the same seats fans have used for nearly 2,000 years, and take in one of Arles' most memorable experiences—a bullfight *à la Provençale* in an ancient arena. Three classes of bullfights take place here. The *course protection* is for aspiring matadors; it's a daring dodge-bull game of scraping hair off the angry bull's nose for prize money offered by local businesses (no blood). The *trophée de l'avenir* is the next class, with amateur matadors. The *trophée des as excellence* is the real thing à la Spain: outfits, swords, spikes, and the whole gory shebang (tickets €5–10; Easter–Oct Sat, Sun, and holidays; skip the "rodeo" spectacle, ask at TI). There are nearby village bullfights in small wooden bullrings nearly every weekend (TI has schedule).

The Camargue—Knocking on Arles' doorstep, this is one of the few truly "wild" areas of France, where pink flamingos, wild bulls, and the famous white horses wander freely amid rice fields, lagoons, and mosquitoes. It's a ▲▲▲ sight for nature-lovers, but boring for others. The D-37 that skirts the Etang de Vaccarès lagoon has some of the best views. The **Musée Camarguais** describes the natural features and traditions of the Camargue (some English information) and has a 3.5-kilometer/two-mile nature trail. It's 12 kilometers/7.5 miles from Arles on D-570 toward Ste. Marie de la Mer; at the *Mas du Pont de Rousty* farmhouse, look for signs (€5, May–Sept daily 9:15–17:45, Oct–March Wed–Mon 10:15–16:45, closed Tue, tel. 04 90 97 10 82). Buses serve the Camargue (and the museum) from Arles' train station (tel. 04 90 96 36 25).

Sleeping in Arles
(€1 = about $1, country code: 33, zip code: 13200)
Sleep Code: **S** = Single, **D** = Double/Twin, **T** = Triple, **Q** = Quad, **b** = bathroom, **s** = shower only, **CC** = Credit Cards accepted, **no CC** = Credit Cards not accepted, **SE** = Speaks English, **NSE** = No English, ***** = French hotel rating system (0–4 stars).

To help you sort easily through these listings, I've divided the rooms into three categories based on the price for a standard double room with bath:

Higher Priced—Most rooms more than €90.
Moderately Priced—Most rooms €90 or less.
Lower Priced—Most rooms €60 or less.

Hotels are a great value here; many are air-conditioned, though few have elevators.

HIGHER PRICED

Hôtel d'Arlatan***, built over the site of a Roman basilica, is classy in every sense of the word. It has sumptuous public spaces, a tranquil terrace, designer pool, and antique-filled rooms, most with high, wood-beamed ceilings and stone walls. In the lobby of this 15th-century building, a glass floor looks down into Roman ruins (Db-€90–160, Db/Qb suites-€180–250, CC, great buffet breakfast-€10, parking-€11, air-con, elevator, 26 rue du Sauvage, 1 block off place du Forum, tel. 04 90 93 56 66, fax 04 90 49 68 45, www.hotel-arlatan.fr, e-mail: hotel-arlatan@provnet.fr).

MODERATELY PRICED

These hotels are worthy of three stars; each offers exceptional value.

Hôtel de l'Amphithéâtre**, a carefully decorated, boutique hotel, is just off the Roman Arena. Public spaces are very sharp and the owners pay attention to every detail of your stay. All rooms have air-conditioning, the Belvedere room has the best view over Arles I've seen, and the suite rooms have four-star comfort (Db-€44–64, Tb-€84, CC, parking-€4, 5 rue Diderot, 1 block from arena, tel. 04 90 96 10 30, fax 04 90 93 98 69, www .hotelamphitheatre.fr, SE).

Hôtel du Musée** is a quiet, delightful, manor-home hide-away with 20 comfortable, air-conditioned rooms, a flowery two-tiered courtyard, and a snazzy art-gallery lounge. The rooms in the new section are worth the few extra euros and steps. Charm-ing Laurence speaks some English (Sb-€41–48, Db-€48–63, Tb-€60–72, Qb-€80, CC, buffet breakfast-€7, parking-€7, 11 rue du Grande Prieuré, follow signs to Musée Réattu, tel. 04 90 93 88 88, fax 04 90 49 98 15, www.hoteldumusee.com.fr, e-mail: contact@hoteldumusee.com.fr).

Hôtel Calendal**, located between the Roman Arena and Classical Theater, has Provençal chic and a large outdoor courtyard, smartly decorated rooms, Internet access, and seductive ambience (Db facing street-€45–65, Db facing garden-€65–75, Db with balcony-€80, Tb-€85, Qb-€90, CC, lunch-€12, air-con, reserve ahead for parking-€10, 5 rue Porte de Laure, just above arena, tel. 04 90 96 11 89, fax 04 90 96 05 84, www.lecalendal.com, SE).

LOWER PRICED

The first three are closest to the train station:

Hôtel Régence** sits on the river, with immaculate and comfortable rooms, good beds, safe parking, and easy access to the train station (new owners may modify these prices, Db-€30–48, Tb-€40–57, Qb-€60, choose riverview or quiet, air-con courtyard rooms, CC, 5 rue Marius Jouveau, from place Lamartine turn right immediately after passing through towers, tel. 04 90 96 39 85, fax 04 90 96 67 64).

Hôtel Acacias**, just off place Lamartine and inside the old city walls, is a modern new hotel. It's a pastel paradise, with rooms that are a smidge too small but have all the comforts, including cable TV, hair dryers, and air-conditioning (Db-€46–51, Tb-€61–75, Qb-€78–83, CC, buffet breakfast-€5.50, elevator, 1 rue Marius Jouveau, tel. 04 90 96 37 88, fax 04 90 96 32 51, www.hotel-acacias.com, e-mail: contact@hotel-acacias.com, gentle Sylvie SE).

Hôtel Terminus et van Gogh* has bright, basic rooms in van Gogh colors, facing a busy roundabout at the gate of the old town, a long block from the train station. This building appears in the painting of van Gogh's house; the artist's house was bombed in World War II (Db-€37–44, Tb-€46, Qb-€54, CC, 5 place Lamartine, tel. & fax 04 90 96 12 32).

Hôtel St. Trophime** is another fine old mansion converted to a hotel, with a grand entry, charming courtyard, broad halls, large rooms, and (rare in Arles) an elevator, but no air-conditioning (new owners may change these prices, standard Db-€48, larger, off-street Db-€57, Tb-€65, huge Qb-€73, CC, garage-€7, 16 rue de la Calade, near place de la République, tel. 04 90 96 88 38, fax 04 90 96 92 19).

Perfect for starving artists, the clean, spartan, and friendly **Hôtel Voltaire*** rents 12 small rooms with ceiling fans and great balconies overlooking a caffeine-stained square, a block below the arena (D-€25, Ds-€28, Db-€36, third or fourth person-€8 each, CC, 1 place Voltaire, tel. 04 90 96 49 18, fax 04 90 96 45 49).

Sleeping near Arles, in Fontvieille
(See also "Sleeping in and near Les Baux," below.) Many drivers, particularly those with families, prefer staying in the peaceful countryside with good access to the area's sights. Just 10 minutes from Arles and Les Baux, and 20 minutes from Avignon, little Fontvieille slumbers in the shadows of its big-city cousins (though it has its share of restaurants and boutiques).

HIGHER PRICED
Le Peiriero*** is a pooped parent's dream come true, with a grassy garden, massive pool, table tennis, badminton, and (believe it or not) three miniature golf holes. The spacious family loft rooms, capable of sleeping up to five, have full bathrooms on both levels. This complete retreat also comes with a terrace café and restaurant (the higher prices in the doubles category are for rooms over the garden, Db-€80–100, Tb-€88, Tb loft-€140, CC, breakfast buffet-€9, air-con, free parking, 34 avenue de Les Baux, just east of

Fontvieille on road to Les Baux, tel. 04 90 54 76 10, fax 04 90 54 62 60, www.hotel-peiriero.com).

Le Domaine de la Forest is a restored farmhouse with modern apartments for five to six people (kitchen, 2 bedrooms, private terrace). Surrounded by vineyards and rice fields, this rural refuge offers a pool, swings, and a volleyball court. While most spend a full week, shorter stays are possible off-season (nightly-€92, weekly rental required in summer-€534, from Arles take D-17 toward Fontvieille and look for *Gîtes Ruraux* signs, route de L'Aqueduc Romain, just off D-82, 13990 Fontvieille, tel. 04 90 54 70 25, fax 04 90 54 60 50, www.domaine-laforest.com).

Eating in Arles

All restaurants listed have outdoor seating except L'Olivier and La Boeheme.

Eating on or near place du Forum: Great atmosphere and mediocre food at fair prices await on place du Forum; **L'Estaminet** probably does the best dinner (I like the salade Estaminet). **La Vitamine** has decent salads and pastas—show this book and enjoy a free *kir* (closed Sun, just below place du Forum on 16 rue Dr. Fanton, tel. 04 90 93 77 36). Almost next door, **Au Bryn du Thym** is popular and specializes in traditional Provençal cuisine (€18 *menu*, closed Tue, 22 rue Dr. Fanton, tel. 04 90 49 95 96). A block above the forum, **La Boeheme** is a good and friendly budget option with a €13 vegetarian *menu* and a €15 Provençal *menu* (6 rue Balze, tel. 04 90 18 58 92). A few blocks below place du Forum, near the recommended Hôtel du Musée, **L'Olivier** is my Arles splurge, offering exquisite Provençal cuisine (€28 *menu*, 1 bis rue Réattu, reserve ahead, tel. 04 90 49 64 88).

Eating near the Roman Arena: For about the same price as on place du Forum, you can enjoy reliable cuisine with a point-blank view of the arena at the welcoming **Le Pistou** (*menus* from €15, open daily, at the top of the arena, 30 rond point des Arenes). **La Giraudière**, a few blocks below the arena on place Voltaire, offers good regional cooking and air-conditioning (€20 *menu*, closed Tue, tel. 04 90 93 27 52). The friendly, unpretentious **L'Arlatan,** across from the recommended Hôtel Acacias, serves fine meals and great desserts (€16 *menu*, closed Wed, opposite launderette at 7 rue Cavalarie, tel. 04 90 96 24 85).

For the best ice cream in Arles, find **Soleilei's**; all ingredients are natural, with unusual flavors such as *fadoli*, an olive-oil ice cream (across from recommended La Vitamine restaurant at 9 rue Dr. Fanton).

Picnics: A big, handy Monoprix supermarket/department store is on place Lamartine (Mon–Sat 8:30–19:25, closed Sun).

Transportation Connections—Arles

By bus to: Les Baux (4/day, 30 min, none on Sun, fewer Nov–March, first departure 8:30, last at 14:30, ideal departure is 8:30 with a return from Les Baux about 11:20 or 12:40), **Camargue/ Ste. Marie de la Mer** (8/day Mon–Sat, less on Sun, 1 hr). There are two stops in Arles: the *Centre Ville* stop is on 16 boulevard Clemenceau (2 blocks below main TI, next to Café le Wilson); the other is at the train station (tel. 04 90 49 38 01).

By train to: Paris (17/day, 2 direct TGVs in 4 hrs, 15 with change in Avignon in 5 hrs), **Avignon** (14/day, 20 min, check for afternoon gaps), **Carcassonne** (6/day, 3 hrs, 3 with change in Narbonne), **Beaune** (10/day, 4.5 hrs, 9 with change in Nîmes or Avignon and Lyon), **Nice** (11/day, 4 hrs, 10 with change in Marseille), **Barcelona** (2/day, 6 hrs, change in Montpellier), **Italy** (3/day, change in Marseille and Nice; from Arles, it's 4.5 hrs to Ventimiglia on the border, 9.5 hrs to the Cinque Terre, 8 hrs to Milan, 11 hrs to Florence, or 13 hrs to Venice or Rome).

AVIGNON

Famous for its nursery rhyme, medieval bridge, and brooding Palace of the Popes, contemporary Avignon (pron. ah-veen-yohn) bustles and prospers behind its mighty walls. During the 68 years (1309–1377) that Avignon starred as the *Franco Vaticano*, it grew from a quiet village to the thriving city it remains. With its large student population and fashionable shops, today's Avignon is an intriguing blend of youthful spirit and urban sophistication. Street mimes play to international crowds enjoying Avignon's ubiquitous cafés and trendy boutiques. If you're here in July, be prepared for the rollicking theater festival and reserve your hotel months early. Clean, sharp, and very popular Avignon is more impressive for its outdoor ambience than its museums and monuments. See the pope's palace, then explore its thriving streets and beautiful vistas from the Parc de Rochers des Doms.

Orientation

The cours Jean Jaurés (which turns into rue de la République) runs straight from the train station to place de l'Horloge and the Palace of the Popes, splitting Avignon in two. The larger right (eastern) half is where the action is. Climb to the parc de Rochers des Doms for a fine view, enjoy the people scene on place de l'Horloge, meander the backstreets (see "Sights—Discovering Avignon's Backstreets," below), and lose yourself in a quiet square. Avignon's shopping district fills the traffic-free streets where rue de la République meets place de l'Horloge. Walk or drive across pont Daladier (bridge) for a great view of Avignon and the Rhône River.

Tourist Information: The main TI is between the train station and the old town at 41 cours Jean Jaurés (April–Oct Mon–Sat 9:00–18:00, Sun 9:00–17:00, Nov–March Mon–Fri 9:00–18:00, Sat 9:00–17:00, Sun 10:00–12:00, longer hours during July festival, tel. 04 32 74 32 74, www.avignon-tourisme.com). A branch TI is inside the city wall at the entrance to pont St. Bénezet (April–Oct only, daily 9:00–19:00). Get the better tear-off map and pick up the free, handy *Guide Pratique* (info on car and bike rental, hotels, and museums) as well as their Avignon discovery guide, which includes several good (but tricky to follow) walking tours. Make sure to get the **free "Avignon Passion" discount card** if you plan to visit more than one sight. You pay full price at first sight, get your card stamped, then get good reductions at others (e.g., €2 less at Palace of the Popes, €3 less at Petit Palais). The TI offers informative English-language **walking tours** of Avignon (€8, €5 with discount card, Tue, Thu, and Sat at 10:00, Sat only Nov–March, depart from the main TI). They also have information on bus excursions to popular regional sights (including the wine route, Luberon, and Camargue). Many of Avignon's sights are closed on Tuesdays.

Arrival in Avignon

By Train: TGV passengers take the €1 shuttle bus (*navette*, 4/hr, 10 min) from the space-age new TGV station to the central station in downtown Avignon (car rental at TGV station; nothing within walking distance). All other trains serve the central station (*gare centrale*, baggage check available). From the central station, walk through the city walls onto the cours Jean Jaurés (TI 3 blocks down at #41). The bus station (*gare routière*) is 100 meters to the right of the central train station (just beyond Ibis hotel).

By Car: Drivers enter Avignon following *Centre-ville* signs. Park close to pont St. Bénezet, either outside the wall or in the big structure just inside the walls and use that TI. Figure €1.50/hour and €8/day for pay lots. Hotels have advice for smart overnight parking. Leave nothing in your car.

Helpful Hints

Reduced Prices for Sights: Get an "Avignon Passion" discount card; see "Tourist Information," above.

Book Ahead for July: During the July theater festival, rooms are rare—reserve very early or stay in Arles or St. Rémy (see "Sleeping in Arles," above, or "Sleeping in St. Rémy," below).

Laundry: Handy to most hotels is the launderette at 66 place St. Corps, where rue Agricol Perdiguier ends (daily 7:00–20:00).

Internet Access: Webzone, on place Pie, is right behind the medieval tower (daily 14:00–midnight).

English Bookstore: Try Shakespeare Bookshop (Tue–Sat 9:30–12:30 & 14:00–18:30, closed Mon, 155 rue Carreterie, in Avignon's northeast corner, tel. 04 90 27 38 50).

Car Rental: All the agencies are at the TGV station with long hours, seven days/week.

Sights—Avignon

I've listed sights in the best order to visit, and have added a short walking tour of Avignon's backstreets to get you beyond the surface. Entries are listed at full price and with discount card. Remember to pick up your discount card at the TI—you pay full price at the first sight.

Start your tour where the Romans did, on place de l'Horloge, and find a seat on a stone bench in front of city hall (Hôtel de Ville). **Place de l'Horloge**—This square was Avignon's forum during Roman rule. In those days, Avignon played second fiddle to the important city of Arles. In the Middle Ages, this square served as the main market square, and today, it is Avignon's main café square (lively ambience, high prices, low food quality). Named for a medieval clock tower that city hall now hides, this square's present popularity arrived with the trains in 1854. Walk a few steps to the center, and look down the main drag, rue de la République. When trains arrived in Avignon, proud city fathers wanted a direct, impressive way to link the new station to the heart of the city (just like in Paris)—so they plowed over homes to create the rue de République and widened the place de l'Horloge. Today's new, suburban TGV train station is no less contentious. According to locals, it benefits only rich Parisians, as Provence is now within easy weekend striking distance, allowing rural homes to be gobbled at inflated prices that locals can't afford (adding insult to injury, Avignon residents must now take a bus from the city center to the train station).

To get to the next listing, Palace Square, walk past the merry-go-round, then past the Hotel des Papes into the square. **Palace Square (Place du Palais)**—Sit on a stump in front of the Conservatoire National de Danse et Musique. In the 1300s, this was ground zero for the church. When the church bought Avignon, they gave it a complete facelift, turning the city into Europe's largest construction zone and clearing out vast spaces like this. The pope's palace alone demanded three acres of building; add nearly five kilometers of protective wall and 39 towers circling the city, the need for "appropriate" cardinal housing (read: mansions), and residences for other hangers-on from Rome, and you have a bonanza of a building contract. Avignon's population grew from 6,000 to 25,000 in short order (today, 16,000 people

Avignon

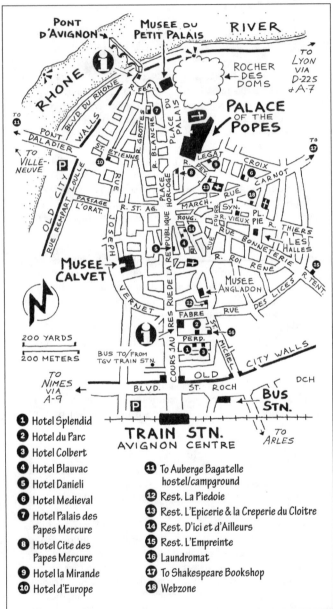

1. Hotel Splendid
2. Hotel du Parc
3. Hotel Colbert
4. Hotel Blauvac
5. Hotel Danieli
6. Hotel Medieval
7. Hotel Palais des Papes Mercure
8. Hotel Cite des Papes Mercure
9. Hotel la Mirande
10. Hotel d'Europe
11. To Auberge Bagatelle hostel/campground
12. Rest. La Piedoie
13. Rest. L'Epicerie & la Creperie du Cloitre
14. Rest. D'ici et d'Ailleurs
15. Rest. L'Empreinte
16. Laundromat
17. To Shakespeare Bookshop
18. Webzone

live within the walls). You can see the limit of the pre-pope city by looking at your map. Rues Joseph Vernet, Henri Fabre, des Lices, and Philonarde follow the route of the defensive wall before the pope's arrival.

The Petit Palais (little palace) seals the left end of the end of the square and was built for a cardinal; today, it houses medieval paintings (see description below). The church to the left of the Palace of the Popes is Avignon's cathedral. It predates the Church's purchase of Avignon by 200 years; its modest size reflects Avignon's modest, pre-pope population. Golden Mary wasn't up on the rooftop until 1859 (part of the city's beautification project). Behind you was the pope's mint, conveniently located as money was a perpetual concern among popes. Today, it's a school for dance and music.

Musée du Petit Palais—This palace superbly displays medieval Italian painting and sculpture. Since the Catholic Church was the patron of the arts, all 350 paintings deal with Christian themes. Visiting this museum before going to the Palace of the Popes gives you a sense of art and life during the Avignon papacy (€6, €3 with discount card, Wed–Mon 9:30–13:00 & 14:00–17:30, closed Tue, at north end of place du Palais).

▲**Parc de Rochers des Doms and Pont St. Bénezet**—For a panoramic view over Avignon and the Rhône Valley, hike above the Palace of the Popes to the rock top—Parc de Rochers des Doms—where Avignon was first settled. At the far end of this lookout, drop down a few steps for a good view of pont St. Bénezet.

This bridge, whose construction and location were inspired by a shepherd's religious vision, is the "pont d'Avignon" of nursery-rhyme fame upon which everyone is dancing. Imagine a 22-arch, 1,000-meter-long (3,000 feet) bridge extending across two rivers to the lonely Tower of Philip the Fair, the bridge's former toll-gate, on the distant side (equally great view from that tower back over Avignon; see below). The island the bridge spanned is now filled with campgrounds. You can pay €3 to walk along a section of the ramparts and do your own jig on pont St. Bénezet (nice view, otherwise nothing special). The castle on the right, St. André Fortress, was once another island in the Rhône. Cross Daladier Bridge for the best view of the old bridge and Avignon's skyline.

▲**Palace of the Popes (Palais des Papes)**—In 1309, a French pope was elected (Pope Clement V). At the urging of the French king, His Holiness decided he'd had enough of unholy Italy. So he loaded his carts and moved north to peaceful Avignon for a steady rule under a supportive king. The Catholic Church literally bought Avignon (then a two-bit town), and popes resided here until 1403. From 1378 on, there were twin popes, one in Rome and one in

Avignon, causing a schism in the Catholic Church that wasn't fully resolved until 1417.

The pope's palace is two distinct buildings: one old and one older. Along with lots of big, barren rooms, you'll see frescoes, tapestries, and some beautiful floor tiles. The audioguide tour does a decent job of overcoming the lack of furnishings and gives a thorough history lesson while allowing you to tour this largely empty palace at your own pace. Enjoy the view and windswept café at the tower. You'll exit to the rear of the palace, where my walking tour begins (see below). To return to the palace square, make two rights after exiting (€9.50, €7.50 with discount card, daily mid-March–Oct 9:00–19:00, July–Aug until 20:00, Nov–mid-March 9:00–17:45, ticket office closes 1 hr earlier, tours in English twice daily March–Oct, tel. 04 90 27 50 74).

Discovering Avignon's Backstreets—Use the map in this book and the TI's barely adequate, single-sheet-of-paper city map to help navigate this easy 30-minute level walk. This tour begins in the small square behind the pope's palace, where visitors exit. (If you skipped the palace interior, walk down the Palace Square—with the palace to your left—and take the first left down a narrow cobbled lane—rue Peyrolerie; you'll pop out in a small square behind the pope's palace. Veer left and you're ready to go.)

Hôtel la Mirande, Avignon's finest hotel, faces the pope's palace and is, amazingly, a welcoming place. You're invited to explore. Find the atrium lounge and consider a coffee break amid the understated luxury (afternoon tea with all the pastries is served 15:00–18:00). Inspect the royal lounge and dining room (recommended in "Eating in Avignon," below); cooking courses are offered in the basement below. Rooms start at €300.

Turn left out of the hotel and left again on rue Peyrolerie (street of the Coppersmiths), then take your first right on rue des Oiseaux d'Or and enter the tranquillity surrounding the **Church of St. Pierre**. Admire the original chestnut doors (the interior is generally closed), then take the alley to the left under and into what was the cloister of St. Pierre's (place des Chataignes, see "Eating in Avignon" for good places to eat on both sides of the church). Leave the square with the church on your right, cross busy rue Carnot and look back to the church that now seems far larger.

Walk to the **Banque de Chaix**. The building opposite, with its beam support showing, is a rare leftover from the Middle Ages. Notice how the building widens the higher it gets. A medieval loophole based taxes on ground floor area—everything above was tax-free. Walk down the rue des Fourbisseurs (street of animal furs) and notice how the top floors almost meet. Fire was a constant danger in the Middle Ages, as flames leapt easily from one home to the next. In fact, the lookout guard's primary responsibility was alerting locals to fires, not the enemy. Virtually all of Avignon's medieval homes have been replaced by safer structures.

Turn left on the traffic-free street rue du Vieux Sextier (street of the balance, for weighing items); another left under the first arch leads to **Avignon's Synagogue**. The popes' toleration allowed the Jews a place to relocate after being kicked out of Spain. More than 500 Jewish families took advantage of this opportunity. To visit the synagogue, press the buzzer and the friendly local rabbi will be your guide (Mon–Fri 10:00–12:00 & 15:00–17:00, closed Sat–Sun).

From here, double back to rue du Vieux Sextier and turn right to return to place de l'Horloge via Avignon's shopping streets. To dive really deep into Avignon's backstreets (allow another 20 min), leave the synagogue the way you came, cross rue du Vieux Sextier and turn left on the next street, rue de la Bonneterie (street of bonnets, or hats). Follow this all the way to **rue des Tenturiers**, head-quarters in Avignon for all that's hip. Earthy cafés, galleries, and a small stream (a branch of the Sorgue river) with waterwheels line this tie-dyed street that served as the cloth industry's dyeing and textile center in the 1800s. Those stylish Provençal fabrics and patterns you see for sale everywhere started here. Go as far as the second waterwheel before doubling back, then turn left on the rue des Lices (where the first medieval wall stood). This will lead you back to the rue de la République, Avignon's main drag.

More Sights—Avignon

Fondation Anglandon-Dubrujeaud—This museum mixes a small but enjoyable collection of art from Post-Impressionists (including Cézanne, van Gogh, Daumier, Degas, and Picasso) with re-created art studios and furnishings from many periods. It's a quiet place with a few superb paintings (€5, €3 with discount card, Tue–Sun 13:00–18:00, closed Mon, 5 rue Laboureur).

Musée Calvet—This fine-arts museum impressively displays its good collection without a word of English explanation (€6, €3 with discount card, Wed–Mon 10:00–12:00 & 14:00–18:00, closed Tue, on quieter west half of town at 65 Joseph Vernet; its antiquities collection is a few blocks away at 27 rue de la République, same hours and ticket).

Sights near Avignon, in Villeneuve-lès-Avignon

▲**Tower of Philip the Fair (Tour Phillipe-le-Bel)**—Built to protect access to the pont St. Bénezet in 1307, this massive tower offers the best view over Avignon and the Rhône basin. It's best late in the day (€1.60, €0.90 with discount card, April–Sept daily 10:00–12:00 & 15:00–19:00, Oct–March Tue–Sun 10:00–12:00 & 15:00–17:30, closed Mon). To reach the tower from Avignon, it's a five-minute drive (cross pont Daladier bridge, follow signs to Villeneuve-lès-Avignon); boat ride (Bâteau-Bus departs from Mireio Embarcadere near pont Daladier); or a bus ride on #11 (2/hr, catch bus across from train station inside city wall, in front of post office, on cours President Kennedy).

Sleeping in Avignon
(€1 = about $1, country code: 33, zip code: 84000)
Hotel values are generally better in Arles, though the range of choices here is impressive. These are all solid values.

HIGHER PRICED

Cité des Papes Mercure***, a modern hotel chain within spitting distance of the Palace of the Popes, has 73 smartly designed, small-ish rooms, musty halls, unbeatable views from the breakfast room, air-conditioning, elevators, and all the comforts (Db-€107, extra bed-€13, CC, many rooms have views over place de l'Horloge, 1 rue Jean Vilar, tel. 04 90 80 93 00, fax 04 90 80 93 01, e-mail: h1952@accor-hotels.com). The **Palais des Papes Mercure***** (same chain, same price) is nearby, just inside the walls, near pont St. Bénezet (87 rooms, CC, rue Ferruce, tel. 04 90 80 93 93, fax 04 90 80 93 94, e-mail: h0549@accor-hotels.com).

At **Hôtel d'Europe******, be a gypsy in the palace at Avignon's most prestigious address—if you get one of the 17 surprisingly reasonable standard rooms (standard Db-€125–155, first class-€215, deluxe Db-€298, CC, breakfast-€20, garage-€14, elevator, every comfort, 12 place Crillon, near pont Daladier, tel. 04 90 14 76 76, fax 04 90 14 76 71, www.hotel-d-europe.fr).

MODERATELY PRICED

Hôtel Blauvac** offers 16 mostly spacious, high-ceilinged rooms (most with an upstairs loft) and a sky-high atrium in a grand old manor home near the pedestrian zone (Sb-€54–61, Db-€55, Db loft-€63, Tb/Qb-€77–85, CC, 11 rue de La Bancasse, 1 block off rue de la République, tel. 04 90 86 34 11, fax 04 90 86 27 41, www.hotel-blauvac.com, friendly Nathalie SE like an American).

Hôtel Danieli** is a Hello-Dolly fluffball of a place, renting 29 generally large rooms on the main drag with air-conditioning and many tour groups (Sb-€60–65, Db-€70–85, Tb-€80–100, Qb-€92–110, CC, elevator, 17 rue de la République, tel. 04 90 86 46 82, fax 04 90 27 09 24, www.hotel-danieli-avignon.com).

Hôtel Medieval** is burrowed deep with unimaginative, big, and comfortable rooms in a massive stone mansion (Db-€50–68, extra bed-€8, kitchenettes available but require 3-day minimum stay, CC, 15 rue Petite Saunerie, 5 blocks east of place de l'Horloge, behind Eglise St. Pierre, tel. 04 90 86 11 06, fax 04 90 82 08 64, e-mail: hotel.medieval@wanadoo.fr).

LOWER PRICED
The next three listings are a 10-minute walk from the station; turn right off cours Jean Jaurés on rue Agricol Perdiguier.

At **Hôtel Splendid***, the friendly Pre-Lemoines rent 17 cheery rooms with firm beds, air-conditioning, and small bathrooms for a fair price (Sb-€39, Db-€49, CC, 17 rue Agricol Perdiguier, tel. 04 90 86 14 46, fax 04 90 85 38 55, www.avignon-et-provence.com/hotels/le-splendid/).

Hôtel du Parc*, across the street, is a similar value without air-conditioning, but with Avignon native Madame Rous in charge (D-€34, Ds-€42, Db-€46, CC, get a room over the park, tel. 04 90 82 71 55, fax 04 90 85 64 86, e-mail: hotelsurparc@aol.com).

Hôtel Colbert** is a fine midrange bet. Parisian refugees Patrice (SE) and Sylvie (NSE) are your hosts, and their care for this hotel shows in the attention to detail, from the peaceful patio to the warm room decor (Sb-€38–44, Db-€44–58, Tb-€58–79, CC, air-con, 7 rue Agricol Perdiguier, tel. 04 90 86 20 20, fax 04 90 85 97 00, e-mail: colbert.hotel@wanadoo.fr).

Auberge Bagatelle's hostel/campground offers dirt-cheap beds, a lively atmosphere, busy pool, café, grocery store, launderette, great views of Avignon, and campers for neighbors (D-€24, dorm bed-€11, CC, across pont Daladier on the Island—Ile de la—Barthelasse, bus #10 from main post office, tel. 04 90 86 30 39, fax 04 90 27 16 23).

Eating in Avignon
Skip the overpriced places on the place de l'Horloge and find a more intimate location for your dinner (many to choose from).

Eating near the Church of St. Pierre
L'Epicerie, charmingly located and popular, on a tiny square a few blocks east of place de l'Horloge, offers a good selection of à la carte items (daily, 10 place St. Pierre, tel. 04 90 82 74 22).

Crêperie du Cloitre, on the other side of the Church of St. Pierre (under the arch from L'Epicerie restaurant), has more ambience and inexpensive meals (big salad and main course crêpe for about €12, closed Sun–Mon, on place des Chataignes).

Eating Elsewhere in Avignon

At intimate **La Piedoie,** a few blocks northeast of the TI, eager-to-please owner Thierry Piedoie serves fine Provençal dishes (€27 *menu,* 26 rue des Trois Faucons, tel. 04 90 86 51 52).

D'Ici et d'Ailleurs (meaning "from here and elsewhere"), one block from place de l'Horloge, is a good budget value for discerning diners, with decor as soothing as the prices (*menu* from €14, Mon–Sat, closed Sun, 4 rue Galande, tel. 04 90 14 63 65).

L'Empreinte is good for North African cuisine in a trendy location (copious couscous for €10–15, daily, 33 rue des Tenturiers, tel. 04 32 76 36 35).

Hotel la Mirande is the perfect splurge. Reserve ahead here for understated elegance and Avignon's top cuisine (€40–50 *menus,* 4 place de la Mirande, tel. 04 90 86 93 93, fax 04 90 86 26 85, www .la-mirande.fr).

Transportation Connections—Avignon

Trains

Remember, there are two train stations in Avignon, the new suburban TGV station and the main station in the city center (€1 shuttle buses connect both stations, 4/hr, 10 min). Both have baggage checks; car rental is available at the TGV station. Some cities are served by slower local trains from the main station and by faster TGV trains from the TGV station; I've listed the most convenient stations for each trip.

By train from Avignon's main station to: Arles (12/day, 20 min), **Orange** (16/day, 20 min), **Nîmes** (14/day, 30 min), **Isle sur la Sorgue** (6/day, 30 min), **Lyon** (10/day, 2 hrs, also from TGV station—see below), **Carcassonne** (8/day, 3 hrs, 7 with change in Narbonne), **Barcelona** (2/day, 6 hrs, change in Montpellier).

By train from Avignon's TGV station to: Nice (10/day, 4 hrs, a few direct, most require transfer in Marseille), **Lyon** (12/day, 1.5 hrs), **Paris'** Gare du Lyon (14 TGVs/day, 2.5 hrs, 3 with change in Lyon), **Paris'** Charles de Gaulle airport (7/day, 3 hrs).

Buses

The bus station (*halte routière,* tel. 04 90 82 07 35) is just past and below the Ibis hotel to the right as you exit the train station (information desk open Mon–Fri 8:00–18:00, Sat 8:00–12:00, closed Sun). Nearly all buses leave from this station. The main exception is the SNCF bus service that runs from the TGV station to Arles (10/day, 30 min). The Avignon TI should have schedules. Service is reduced or nonexistent on Sunday and holidays.

By bus to: **Pont du Gard** (5/day in summer, 4/day off-season, 40 min, see details under "Pont du Gard," below). Consider visiting Pont du Gard, continuing on to Nîmes or Uzès (see "Sights near Pont du Gard—Uzès," below) and returning to Avignon from there (use the same Pont du Gard bus stop you arrived at to continue on to Nîmes and Uzès). Try these plans: Take the 12:05 bus from Avignon, arriving at Pont du Gard at 12:50. Then take either the 14:45 bus from there to Nîmes, where trains run hourly back to Avignon, or a 16:00 bus (Mon–Fri) on to Uzès, arriving at 16:30, with a return bus to Avignon at 18:30.

By bus to other regional destinations: **St. Rémy** (7/day, 45 min, handy way to visit its Wed market), **Isle sur la Sorgue** (5/day, 45 min), **Vaison la Romaine**, **Sablet**, and **Seguret** (3/day during school year, called *période scolaire*, 1/day otherwise and 1/day from TGV station, 75 min), **Gordes** (via Cavaillon, 1/day, very early, 2 hrs, spend the night or taxi back to Cavaillon), **Nyons** (2/day, 2 hrs).

More Sights in Provence

A car is a dream come true here. Below I've described key sights and two full-day excursions deep into the countryside (see "Villages of the Côtes du Rhône" and "The Hill Towns of Luberon," below), both better done as overnights. Les Baux and St. Rémy work well by car with the Luberon excursion. The town of Orange ties in tidily with a trip to the Côtes du Rhône villages. The Pont du Gard is a short hop west of Avignon and on the way to/from Languedoc for drivers. Travelers relying on public transportation will find their choices very limited. St. Rémy and Isle sur la Sorgue are the most accessible small-town experiences. However you tour this magnificent area, notice the wind buffeting rows of bamboo and cypress and how buildings are oriented south, with few or no windows facing north.

LES BAUX

Crowning the rugged Alpilles mountains, this rock-top castle and tourist village is a ▲▲▲ sight, worth visiting for the lunar landscape alone. Arrive by 9:00 or after 17:00 to avoid ugly crowds. Sunsets are sacrosanct, and nights in Les Baux are pin-drop peaceful; the castle is beautifully illuminated (though closed after dark). There's no free parking; get as close to the top as you can (€4 up top, €3 on road far below).

In the tourist-trampled live city (see definition below), you'll find the **TI** (daily April–Sept 9:00–19:00, Oct–March 9:00–18:00, in Hôtel de Ville, tel. 04 90 54 34 39), too many shops, great viewpoints, and an appealing exhibit of paintings by Yves Brayer, who spent his final years here (€3, daily 10:00–12:00 & 14:00–18:30, in Hôtel des Porcelets).

A 12th-century regional powerhouse, Les Baux was razed in 1632 by a paranoid Louis XIII, who was afraid of these trouble-making upstarts. What remains is the reconstructed "live city" of tourist shops and snack stands and, the reason you came, the "dead city" (Ville Morte or Citadelle des Baux) ruins carved into, out of, and on top of a rock 200 meters/650 feet high. Climb through the "modern village" to the sun-bleached top where la Citadelle awaits (best early in the morning or early-evening light). Find the perfect view from the highest perch and try to imagine 6,000 people living within these stone walls. Survey the small museum as you enter la Citadelle (good exhibits, pick up the English explanations) and don't miss the slide show on van Gogh, Gauguin, and Cézanne in the little chapel across from the museum (€6.50 entry to la Citadelle, includes a free and helpful audioguide, and entry to all the town's sights, daily Easter–Oct 9:00–19:00, until 20:00 July–Aug, Nov–Easter 9:30–17:00).

The best view of Les Baux day or night is one kilometer north on D-27 near **Caves de Sarragnan**, where you can sample wines in a very cool rock quarry that dates from the Middle Ages (daily April–Sept 10:00–12:00 & 14:00–19:00, Oct–March closes at 18:00, tel. 04 90 54 33 58). On the way, you'll pass **Cathédrale d'Images**, a mesmerizing sound-and-slide show that immerses visitors in regional themes by projecting 3,000 images inside a rock quarry (€7, daily 10:00–18:00, just above Les Baux on D-27).

Four daily buses serve Les Baux from the Arles bus station (30 min, see "Transportation Connections—Arles," above).

Sights between Les Baux and Arles

Abbey de Montmajour—You can't miss this brooding structure, just a few minutes from Arles toward Les Baux. A once-thriving abbey and a convenient papal retreat, it dates from 948. The vast, vacant abbey church is a massive example of Romanesque architecture, though for me, it's another big empty space (€6, April–Sept daily 9:00–19:00, Oct–March 10:00–13:00 & 14:00–17:00, tel. 04 90 54 64 17).

▲**Roman Aqueduct**—I love lost Roman ruins, and there's no better example than these 2,000-year-old crumbled arches from the principal aqueduct that served Arles (entering the city at the Roman Arena). Coming from Arles, take D-17 toward Fontvieille, then follow signs on the right to *L'Aqueduc Romain* just before Fontvieille. Follow that road for three kilometers/two miles to the romantically ruined remains (no sign, just after *Los Pozos Blancos* sign, look for stone walls on both sides of the road). Follow the dirt path to the right along the ruins for about 130 meters/425 feet where you enter the water canal, then come to a cliff over the farmland below. Now, imagine the Pont du Gard in front of you.

Sleeping in and near Les Baux
(€1 = about $1, country code: 33)
For more accommodations, see also "Sleeping near Arles," above, and "Sleeping in St. Rémy," below.

HIGHER PRICED

The appealing **Le Mas d'Aigret***** crouches just past Les Baux on the road to St. Rémy. Lie on your back and stare up at the castle walls rising beyond your swimming pool in this Provençal oasis. Many of the smartly designed rooms have private terraces and views over the valley, and the restaurant is troglodyte-chic. Some road noise is noticeable during the day (smaller Db-€100, larger Db with terrace-€130, Tb-€175–200, CC, air-con, tel. 04 90 54 20 00, fax 04 90 54 44 00, www.masdaigret.com).

LOWER PRICED

Hôtel Reine Jeanne** is 50 meters/165 feet to your right after the main entry to the live city (standard Db-€51, Db with deck-€63, great family suite-€90, CC, most air-con, ask for *chambre avec terasse*, good *menus* from €20, 13520 Les Baux, tel. 04 90 54 32 06, fax 04 90 54 32 33, www.la-reinejeanne.com).

Le Mas de L'Esparou *chambre d'hôte*, a few minutes below Les Baux, is welcoming (Jacqueline loves her job, and her lack of English only makes her more animated) and kid-friendly, with spacious rooms, a swimming pool, table tennis, and distant views of Les Baux. Monsieur Roux painted the paintings in your room and has a gallery in Les Baux (Db-€60, extra person-€16, no CC, a few kilometers north of Mausanne on D-5, look for sign, 13520 Les Baux de Provence, tel. & fax 04 90 54 41 32, NSE).

Le Mazet des Alpilles, a small home with three tidy rooms with air-conditioning just outside the unspoiled village of Paradou, five minutes below Les Baux, may have space when others don't (Db-€52, ask for her largest room, child's bed available, no CC, follow signs from the D-17, in Paradou look for route de Brunelly, 13520 Paradou, tel. 04 90 54 45 89, fax 04 90 54 44 66, e-mail: lemazet@wanadoo.fr, Annick NSE).

ST. RÉMY DE PROVENCE
This sophisticated town is famous for its Wednesday market (until 12:30), the ruins of a once-thriving Roman city (Glanum), and the mental ward where van Gogh was sent after slicing off his ear.

St. Rémy is a scenic 10-minute drive (or a 2-hour walk) over the hills and through the woods from Les Baux. Almost too close to Avignon for its own good (though very accessible by bus), St. Rémy's pleasant old city is ringed by a busy road. The small streets within the ring road are *très* strollable.

Sights—St. Rémy

▲Glanum—These crumbled stones are the foundations of a Roman market town, located at the crossroads of two ancient trade routes between Italy and Spain. A massive Roman arch and tower stand proud and lonely near the ruins' parking lot. The arch marked the entry into Glanum, and the tower is a memorial to the grandsons of Emperor Caesar Augustus. The setting is stunning, though shadeless, and the small museum at the entry sets the stage well. While the ruins are, well, ruined, they remind us of the range and prosperity of the Roman Empire. Along with other Roman monuments in Provence, they allow us to paint a more complete picture of Roman life. The English handout is helpful, but consider buying one of the two English booklets (one has better photos, the other provides much better background). Inside the ruins, signs give basic English explanations at key locations, and the view from the belvedere justifies the effort (€6, daily April–Sept 9:00–12:00 & 14:00–19:00, Oct–March 9:30–12:00 & 14:00–17:00).

Cloître St. Paul de Mausole—Just below Glanum is the still-functioning mental hospital (Clinique St. Paul) that treated Vincent van Gogh from 1889 to 1890. The €3 entry fee buys a four-minute video (English and French) and entry into the small chapel, intimate cloisters, and a re-creation of his room. You'll find limited information in English about Vincent's life. Amazingly, he painted 150 works in his 53 weeks here—none of which remain anywhere close today. The contrast between the utter simplicity of his room (and his life) and the multimillion-dollar value of his paintings today is jarring. The site is managed by VALETUDO, a center specializing in art therapy (daily April–Oct 9:30–19:00, Nov–March 10:30–13:00 & 13:30–17:00). Outside the complex, dirt paths lead to Vincent's favorite footpaths with (sometimes vandalized) copies of his paintings from where he painted them.

Sleeping in St. Rémy
(€1 = about $1, country code: 33)

HIGHER PRICED

Mas de Carassins*, a 15-minute walk from the center, is impeccably run by friendly Michel and Pierre (Paris refugees). Luxury is made affordable here, and care is given to every aspect of the hotel, from the generously sized pool and gardens to the muted room decor and the optional €25 dinner (standard Db-€92–105, deluxe Db-€115, large Tb-€145, extra bed-€13, CC, air-con, table tennis, bike rental, 1 Chemin Gaulois, look for signs 180 meters/590 feet toward Les Baux from TI, tel. 04 90 92 15 48, fax 04 90 92 63 47, e-mail: carassin@pacwan.fr).

MODERATELY PRICED
Hotel Villa Glanum**, right across from the Glanum ruins, is a modern, good midrange bet with 27 rooms and a pool (Ds-€58, Db-€76, Tb-€91, Qb-€106, CC, 46 avenue Van Gogh, 13210 Saint Rémy, tel. 04 90 92 03 59, fax 04 90 92 00 08, e-mail: villa.glanum@wanadoo.fr).

LOWER PRICED
Auberge de la Reine Jeanne** is central, cozy, and typical of many French hotels in that the rooms take a backseat to the restaurant. The 11 traditionally decorated rooms overlook a courtyard jammed with tables and umbrellas, and are clean and spacious, with big beds (Db-€59, Tb-€68, Qb-€75, CC, fine restaurant-€24 *menu*, on ring road at 12 boulevard Mirabeau, tel. 04 90 92 15 33, fax 04 90 92 49 65).

Eating in St. Rémy
The town is packed with fine restaurants. To dine well, try **Auberge de la Reine Jeanne** (see above). **Crêperie Lou Planet** is cheap and peaceful, on pleasant place Favier (open until 20:00).

PONT DU GARD
One of Europe's great ▲▲▲ treats, this perfectly preserved Roman aqueduct was built as the critical link of a 56-kilometer/35-mile canal that, by dropping one foot for every 300, supplied 44 million gallons of water daily to Nîmes, one of western Europe's largest cities. After years of work, the new **Grande Expo** does this sight justice with a phenomenal museum, a 23-minute movie, and a kid's space (called *Ludo*), all designed to improve your appreciation of this remarkable sight.

Start at the *rive gauche* (left bank of the Pont du Gard). You'll be greeted by the Grande Expo's linear new structure, housing the three exhibits. Begin with the informative but silly movie, if the English times are convenient; otherwise, skip it. Spend most of your time in the museum. The multimedia approach will draw you into daily Roman life: You'll learn about the many uses of water in Roman times; see examples of lead pipes, faucets, and siphons; marvel at the many models; walk through a rock quarry; and learn how they moved those huge rocks into place and how those massive arches were made. English video screens and information displays help make things as clear as spring water. The *Ludo* kid's space does the same for kids (English displays), giving them a scratch-and-sniff experience of various aspects of Roman life and the importance of water (€13, €43 for family of 2 adults and up to 4 kids, daily Easter–Nov 9:30–19:00, mid-June–Aug until 21:30, Dec–Easter until 18:00, tel. 04 66 37 50 99). The high-priced entry fees include all three exhibits and parking (which costs €4.60 otherwise).

The actual Pont du Gard **aqueduct** is free and open until midnight (the illumination is beautiful after dark). It's a level, 300-meter/985-foot walk to the aqueduct from the Grande Expo. Inspect the bridge closely and imagine getting those stones to the top. The entire structure relies on perfect stone placement; there's no mortar holding this together. Signs direct you to "panoramas" above the bridge on either side, but you'll get better views by walking along the riverbank below—either upstream or downstream—or, more refreshing, by floating flat on your back; bring a swimsuit and sandals for the rocks (always open and free).

Consider **renting a canoe** from the town of Collias to Pont du Gard (€27 per 2-person canoe; they pick you up at Pont du Gard—or elsewhere, if prearranged—and shuttle you to Collias, where you float down the river to nearby town of Remoulins, can be shuttled back to Pont du Gard; 2-hr trip, though you can take as long as you like, Collias Canoes, tel. 04 66 22 85 54, SE).

Transportation Connections—Pont du Gard

By car: Pont du Gard is an easy 25-minute drive due west of Avignon (follow signs to Nîmes) and 45 minutes northwest of Arles (via Tarascon). The *rive gauche* parking is off D-981 that leads from Remoulins to Uzès. (Parking is also available on the *rive droite* side but is farther away from the museum.)

By bus: Buses run to Pont du Gard *(rive gauche)* from Nîmes, Uzès, and Avignon. Combine Uzès (see below) and Pont du Gard for a good day excursion from Avignon (5/day in summer, 3/day off-season, 40 min to Pont du Gard; see info on "Transportation Connections—Avignon," above). The bus stop at Pont du Gard is in the new parking lot near the Grande Expo on the left bank *(rive gauche)*. The return stop to Avignon is to your left before crossing the traffic circle. Make sure you're waiting for the bus on the correct side of the traffic circle.

Sights near Pont du Gard

Uzès—An intriguing, less trampled town, Uzès (pron. oo-zehs) is best seen slowly on foot, with a long coffee break in its beautifully arcaded and mellow main square, the place aux Herbes (not so mellow during the colorful Wed and bigger Sat-morning market). The city is the sight; there are no important museums. Most of the center city is traffic-free and tastefully restored. (Uzès is officially in Languedoc, not Provence.)

At the **TI**, pick up the English walking tour brochure (May–Sept Mon–Fri 9:00–18:00, Sat–Sun 10:00–13:00 & 14:00–17:00; Oct–April Mon–Fri 9:00–12:00 & 13:30–18:00, Sat 10:00–13:00, closed Sun, on ring road on place Albert 1er, tel. 04 66 22 68 88). Skip the dull and overpriced palace of the Duché de Uzès (€9, French-only tour). You can enjoy the unusual Tour Fenestrelle—all that remains of a 12th-century cathedral—from the outside only.

Uzès is a short hop west (by bus) of Pont du Gard and is well-served by bus from Nîmes (9/day, 60 min) and Avignon (3/day, 60 min).

VILLAGES OF THE CÔTES DU RHÔNE: A LOOP TRIP FOR WINE-AND-VILLAGE-LOVERS

If you have a car and a fondness for wine or beautiful countryside, take this loop through Provence's Côtes du Rhône wine country (1–3 buses/day from Avignon—75 min, and Orange—30 min—follow a similar route to Vaison la Romaine). Endless vineyards, rugged mountains, and stone villages fill your windshield. While this trip is doable as a day trip by car from Arles or Avignon (allow an entire day for this 130-kilometer/80-mile round trip from Avignon), you won't regret a night or two in one of the villages listed below. Vaison la Romaine makes the best base and is ideal if you're heading to, or coming from, the north.

Here's our route: From Avignon, follow the N-7 toward Orange, then follow signs to Châteauneuf-du-Pape (short stop here). From there, track signs to Courthézon, where you'll cross the freeway and follow signs to Vaison la Romaine, then Gigondas (longer stop here). From Gigondas, follow Sablet, then Seguret (short stop), then Vaison la Romaine (longer stop). From Vaison, loop back on the other side of the Dentelles de Montmiral by driving to Malaucene, then find the D-90 turn-off to Suzette (café stop required), then follow signs to Carpentras and Beaumes de Venise, and enjoy some of Provence's most amazing scenery as you head over these hills.

This route is peppered with tasting opportunities, perfect picnic spots, and recommended lunch cafés. The Côtes du Rhône is hospitable and offers relaxed wine-tasting at its best, and most villages have a *Caveau des Vignerons* (wine-making cooperative),

Provence Wine Country

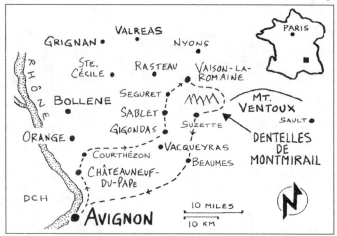

which are easy places to sample a variety of wines. I've listed places to sleep, eat, and taste throughout this route in the description below.

Those with more time should drive to the top of Mont Ventoux and visit the village of Sault, the lavender capital (this is a must if you're here anytime from late June to late July, when the lavender blooms). To add the Roman theater in Orange to this day trip, visit Orange after Châteauneuf-du-Pape.

The less traveled Dromme region just north of Vaison la Romaine is worthwhile if you're continuing to the Alps or if you're here in July when lavender blooms. It's laced with vineyards (producing less expensive yet good wines), lavender fields, and still more postcard-perfect villages. From Vaison, take the loop north to Visan, Valreas, Taulignan, and Nyons, and then back to Vaison. Pleasant Nyons is France's olive capital and hosts a dynamite Thursday-morning market. Each village is a detour waiting to happen.

Sights—The Wine Villages

Here's a review of the wine villages you'll pass on our Côtes du Rhône drive.

Châteauneuf-du-Pape—Châteauneuf-du-Pape means "new castle of the pope"; the old one was the Palace of the Popes in Avignon. This one was built as a summer retreat, and it's now a ruin capping the beautiful-to-see, little-to-do hill town. Wine-loving popes also planted the first vines here in the 1300s. Signs let you know that "here start the vineyards of Châteauneuf-du-Pape." Pull over and stroll into a vineyard with a view of the hill town. Notice the sea of stones beneath your feet. This rocky soil is perfect for making a lean and mean grape. You'll pass the welcoming **Musée du Vin** just before entering the village. It's a good way to begin your Côtes du Rhône exploration with a self-guided tour of the wine-making process (English explanations in the notebooks). You also get three free wines for tasting, with a helpful explanation (free, daily 9:00–12:00 & 14:00–18:00, route d'Avignon, tel. 04 90 83 70 07). The wine boutique–lined village of Châteauneuf is a pretty face with little personality; skip it unless you're serious about tasting. The helpful TI is at the base of the pedestrian street on place Portail (tel. 04 90 83 71 08).

▲**Gigondas**—Nestled enviably at the base of the Dentelles de Montmiral mountains, this prosperous village produces some of the region's best wines and is ideally situated for hiking, mountain biking, and driving into these spectacular mountains. Stop to take a village stroll (see below) and sample exquisite wines. Several good tasting opportunities await on the main square. **Le Caveau de Gigondas** is best, with a vast selection, nifty micro-bottle samples, and a donation-if-you-don't-buy system (daily 10:00–12:00 & 14:00–18:30, 2 doors down from TI).

The info-packed **TI** has a list of welcoming wineries, *chambres d'hôte*, and good hikes or drives into the mountains (closed 12:00–14:00, tel. 04 90 65 85 46). The €2.50 map *Chemins et Sentiers du Massif des Dentelles* is helpful, though not critical, since routes are well-signed. Route #1 is an ideal one-hour walk above Gigondas to great views from the Belvedere du Rocher du Midi (route #2 extends this hike into a 3-hour loop).

Drivers can bump their way into incredible scenery by following the dirt road to the Col du Cayron (drive past recommended Hôtel les Florets and park where the road turns bad, good day hikes from here).

If you're not in a hurry, seriously consider lunch on the terrace of Hôtel les Florets (listed below).

Sleeping and Eating in Gigondas: The peaceful and traditional **Hôtel les Florets****, one kilometer above the village, is a complete refuge and a good value. It's huddled at the foot of the Dentelles de Montmiral peaks (great hiking from here), with a huge terrace van Gogh would have loved, thoughtfully designed rooms, and an exceptional restaurant (Db-€85, Tb-€100, annex rooms are best, CC, *menus* from €23, 84190 Gigondas, tel. 04 90 65 85 01, fax 04 90 65 83 80).

Sablet—This perfectly circular wine village, while impressive from a distance, has little of interest except scads of *chambres d'hôte*, well-signed from the road. Sablet wines are reasonable and tasty (the TI and wine cooperative share space in the town center).

Seguret—Almost too perfect, little Seguret is etched into the side of a hill and has a smattering of shops, two cafés, made-to-stroll lanes, and a natural spring. Come here for compelling vistas and a quiet lunch.

Sitting on the road to Sablet, just below town, **La Bastide Bleue** is blue-shutter Provençal, with seven rooms at fair prices and a charming restaurant (Sb-€40, Db-€47–56, includes breakfast, *menus* from €19, CC, just below Seguret, route de Sablet, tel. & fax 04 90 46 83 43).

VAISON LA ROMAINE

With quick access to adorable villages and Mont Ventoux, and vineyards knocking at its door, this thriving little town (pop. 6,000) makes a great base for exploring the Côtes du Rhône region by car or bike. You get two villages for the price of one: Vaison's "modern" lower city is like a mini-Arles, with worthwhile Roman ruins, a lone pedestrian street, and too many cars. The medieval hill town looms above and is car-free, with meandering cobbled lanes, a dash of art galleries and cafés, and a ruined castle (good view from its base).

Orientation

The city is split in two by the Ouveze River. The newer city (*ville-basse*) lies on its right bank; the medieval city (*ville-haute*) is above on the left bank. The impressive pont Roman (Roman bridge) connects the two, and was the only bridge to survive a terrible flood that killed 30 persons in 1992.

Tourist Information: The superb TI is in the newer city, between the two Roman ruin sites, at place de Chanoine Sautel. Get English tour times for the Roman ruins, ask about festivals and bike rental, pick up the excellent *Fiches d'Itineraries* (a detailed guide to walks and bike rides from Vaison, ask for English version), and say *bonjour* to charming Valerie, who has worked here for 17 years (May–Sept Mon–Sat 9:00–12:30 & 14:00–18:45, Sun 9:00–12:00; Oct–April Mon–Sat 9:00–12:30 & 14:00–17:45, closed Sun, tel. 04 90 36 02 11, www.vaison-la-romaine.com).

Helpful Hints

The **launderette** (Laverie la Lavandiere) is on Cours Taulignan near avenue Victor Hugo (Mon–Sat 9:00–12:00 & 15:00–18:45, closed Sun). You can rent **bikes** at Lacombe on avenue Jules Ferry (tel. 04 90 36 03 29). Consider hiring the superb **local guide** Anne-Marie Melard to bring the Roman ruins to life (reserve ahead through TI).

Arrival in Vaison la Romaine

By Bus: The stop is in front of Cave la Romaine winery; walk five minutes down avenue de Gaulle to reach the TI.

By Car: Follow signs to *Centre-ville*, then *Office de Tourisme;* park free across from the TI.

Sights—Vaison la Romaine

▲**Market Day**—The amazing Tuesday market (until 12:30) is worth organizing your trip and parking plans around. Sleep here Monday night.

Roman Ruins—If you've seen Pompeii, this will seem like small potatoes, but the remains of Vaison's two Roman sights—La Villasse and Puymin—are well-presented and give a good picture of life during the Roman Empire. Both ancient sites, separated by a modern road, show the foundations of the same Roman town that once stood here. The worthwhile museum inside the Puymin ruins has English explanations (€7, includes both sets of ruins as well as the cloister at the cathedral Notre-Dame de Nazareth; daily June–Sept 9:30–18:00, Oct–March 10:00–12:30 & 14:00–18:00, Nov–Feb closes at 16:00; English tours of ruins available April–Sept, several days/week, usually at 11:00, check with TI; or get informative English handout and do tour on your own; even better, call ahead to the TI and reserve local guide Anne-Marie Melard, see above).

In summer, ask about night visits to the ruins. After the fall of the Roman Empire, Vaison's residents headed for the hills and established the Ville-Haute just above. It must have been strange to have peered over the walls to the onetime great civilization that La Villasse and Puymin ruins represented.

Hiking—The TI has good information on relatively easy hikes into the hills above Vaison. Hikers shouldn't leave Vaison without the free *Fiches d'Itineraries* (in English). It's about 90 minutes to the tiny hill town of Crestet, though the views begin immediately. To find this trail, drive or walk up past the *ville-haute* with the castle on your left, find the Chemin des Fontaines, and stay the course. You'll soon come to an orientation table and fine views; stay on this road to reach Crestet.

Biking—Connect these villages for a great 18-kilometer/11-mile loop ride: Vaison la Romaine, St. Romain en Viennois, Puymeras, Faucon, and St. Marcellin les Vaison (TI has details).

Wine-Tasting—Cave la Romaine, a five-minute walk up avenue General de Gaulle from the TI, offers a variety of great-value wines from nearby villages in a pleasant, well-organized tasting room (daily 8:30–13:00 & 14:00–19:00, avenue St. Quenin, tel. 04 90 36 55 90). To truly enjoy the region's bounty, drive a

Vaison la Romaine

P PARKING
B BUS STOP

① Hôtel Le Beffroi
② Hôtel Burrhus
③ Hôtel des Lis
④ La Fête en Provence B&B
⑤ La Bartavelle restaurant

⑥ Le Bateleur restaurant
⑦ Le Tournesol restaurant
⑧ Pascal Boulangerie/Café
⑨ View Crêperie and Pizzeria
⑩ Bike rental
⑪ Laundromat

few minutes south to **Le Domaine des Girasols**, where friendly Françoise or John (SE) will take your palate on a tour of some of the area's best wine (well, that's my opinion). It's well-marked and worth a stop in Rasteau.

Sleeping in or near Vaison la Romaine
(€1 = about $1, country code: 33, zip code: 84110)
Hotels here are a good value, though none have elevators. Those in the medieval town *(ville-haute)* are quieter, cozier, cooler, and a 15-minute walk uphill from the TI (parking available nearby).

HIGHER PRICED
Hôtel Le Beffroi*** in the *ville-haute* is red-tile-and-wood-beamed classy, with mostly spacious rooms (some with views), a good restaurant, pleasing public spaces, a garden, and a small pool with views. The rooms are split between two buildings a few doors apart—I prefer the main building (Db-€73–107, CC, *menus* from €24, parking is tight, rue de l'Eveche, tel. 04 90 36 04 71, fax 04 90 36 24 78, www.le-beffroi.com).

MODERATELY PRICED
Hôtel Burrhus**, with *moderniste* decor, is easily the best value in the lower city. It's right in the thick of things, with a large, shady terrace over the raucous place Montfort (Db-€46–61, extra bed-€11, some rooms have air-con, request a room off the square if you want to sleep, tel. 04 90 36 00 11, fax 04 90 36 39 05, CC, e-mail: info@burrhus.com). Ask about their adjacent and cushier **Hôtel des Lis***** (Db-€49–74, CC, contact Hôtel Burrhus for reservations and reception).

    La Fête en Provence's *chambres* sit above a good restaurant in the *ville-haute* (*menu*-€24) and overlook a stone courtyard (Db-€50–75, huge duplex sleeps up to 5 people-€107, CC, place du Vieux Marche, tel. 04 90 36 36 43, fax 04 90 36 21 49, e-mail: fete-en-provence@wanadoo.fr).

Sleeping near Vaison la Romaine

MODERATELY PRICED
Château Taulignan's *chambres d'hôte*, with six large rooms (and large beds), offers a kid-friendly, dreamy setting from which to contemplate this beautiful region. This small country château is guarded by vineyards and pine trees and comes with a big pool, table tennis, and wonderful strolling (Db-€85–100, CC, fees apply to any room cancellation—no matter how far ahead, 84110 St. Marcellin, tel. 04 90 28 71 16, fax 04 90 28 75 04, www.taulignan.com, Irish-born Helen SE). It's just five minutes from Vaison's TI; follow *Carpentras* signs and look for brown *Chambres d'hôte* signs just as you leave Vaison.

    A few kilometers away, below spectacularly situated Crestet (follow Carpentras from Vaison), **l'Ermitage Chambres** is well-run by British expat Nick and native Nicole, who were born for this business. Their renovated, rustic farmhouse comes with three big, simple rooms; firm beds; and a pool with magnificent views. They also rent a two-bedroom apartment on a weekly basis (Db-€65, Tb-€80, apartment-€600/week, no CC, turn right off D-938 at Loupiotte restaurant, 84110 Crestet, tel. 04 90 28 88 29, fax 04 90 28 72 97, www.lermitage.net, e-mail: nick.jones@wanadoo.fr).

La Treille *chambres* lies on D-90 between Malaucene and Beaumes de Venise in the tiny hamlet of Suzette. Welcoming Madame Garrigou runs this perfectly situated stone home with views to live for and rooms to stretch out in. Each room comes with a private terrace and a cavernous bathroom; many have small kitchens (Db-€62–78, Tb-€73–93, Qb-€84–93, 84190 Suzette, tel. 04 90 65 03 77, cellular 06 13 89 59 00).

LOWER PRICED

L'Ecole Buissonnière *chambres* are run by another charming Anglo-French team, Monique and John, who have found complete isolation just 10 minutes from Vaison la Romaine in a tastefully restored farmhouse with three well-appointed rooms, each with very different personalities. I liked the Camargue loft room best (Db-€51, Tb-€62, Qb-€73, no CC, between Villedieu and Buisson on D-75, tel. 04 90 28 95 19, e-mail: ecole.buissonniere@wanadoo.fr).

Eating in and near Vaison la Romaine

La Bartavelle is the place to savor traditional French cuisine in the lower city (€22 *menu*, closed Mon, 12 place Sus-Auze, reserve ahead, tel. 04 90 36 02 16).

Le Bateleur is small, simply decorated, and good (€23 *menu*, closed Mon, near Roman bridge at 1 place Theodore Aubanel, tel. 04 90 36 28 04). Closed

~~Le Tournesol offers the~~ best midrange dinner value in town (€16 *menu*, 34 cours Taulignan, tel. 04 90 36 09 18).

Of the many cafés on place Montfort, **Pascal Boulangerie/ Café** (at the far end) is the best value, though it's not open for dinner.

The atmospheric *ville-haute* has a view *crêperie* and a pizzeria with fair prices.

Drivers could seek out the relaxed, roadside **Restaurant Loupiote**, where the locals go (below Crestet on D-938, a 5-min drive from Vaison la Romaine, tel. 04 90 36 29 50). Closed Monday

Les Coquelicots café is a most scenic 20-minute drive away in adorable little Suzette and is best "in season," when you can dine outside. The food is simple and cheap, the setting is why you came (closed Tue–Wed, tel. 04 90 65 06 04). From Vaison, drive to Malaucene, then follow D-90 to Suzette.

Transportation Connections— Vaison la Romaine

The most central bus stop is at Cave Vinicole. **By bus to: Avignon** (2/day, 75 min), **Orange** (3/day, 50 min). Bus info tel. 04 90 36 09 90.

Other Highlights of the Côtes du Rhône

▲▲**Orange**—This most northern town in Provence is notable for its Roman arch and theater. The 18-meter-tall (60 feet) Roman Arc de Triomphe (from 25 B.C., north of city center on avenue Arc de Triomphe) honors Julius Caesar's defeat of the Gauls in 49 B.C., but is lightweight compared to the best-preserved Roman Theater *(Théâtre Antique)* in existence. Information panels in English describe many aspects of the theater. Find a seat up high to appreciate the acoustics and contemplate the idea that, 2,000 years ago, Orange residents enjoyed grand spectacles with high-tech sound and light effects, such as thunder, lightning, and rain. A huge awning could be unfurled from that awesome 40-meter-high (130 feet) stage wall to provide shade that you might appreciate now. It still seats 10,000 (€4.60, daily April–Sept 9:00–18:30, Oct–March 9:00–12:00 & 13:30–17:00). Your ticket includes entrance to the city museum across the street, which has a few interesting renderings of the theater but no English explanations.

Orange has two helpful **TIs**, one that drivers will park near, and another across from the Roman Theater (tel. 04 90 34 70 88). Drivers simply follow *Centre-ville* signs, then *Théâtre Antique* signs, and park in the big lot near the TI. Trains run hourly between Avignon and Orange (15 min). From Orange's train station, it's a 15-minute walk to the theater (follow signs to *Centre-ville*, then *Théâtre Antique*, and if you can't find it, ask a local, *"Où est la Théâtre Antique?"*, pron. oo-ay lah tay-ah-truh ahn-teek).

Buses to Vaison la Romaine and other wine villages depart from the big square, place Pourtoules (turn right out of the Roman Theater and right again on rue Pourtoules).

▲**Mont Ventoux and Lavender**—This sight is worth ▲▲ from late June to early August, when the lavender blooms. Go only if it's clear and you can see the top of this 1,800-meter/6,000-foot, barren, wind-blown mountain; prepare for much cooler temperatures. Mont Ventoux is Provence's rooftop. You're above the tree line amid wildflowers, butterflies, and views extending from the lower Alps across what seems like all of southern France. Near the old observatory and Air Force control tower, **Le Vendran** restaurant offers jaw-dropping views. Thirty minutes east, lavender fields forever surround the village of Sault (pron. so), which produces 40 percent of France's lavender essence. To reach Mont Ventoux, go to Malaucene, then take the twisty D-974. If continuing to Sault (also worthwhile only when the lavender blooms), take D-974, then D-164. Pick up a "Les routes de la Lavande" brochure at Sault's TI for driving and walking routes in the area (TI tel. 04 90 64 01 21). Route maps can also be downloaded at www.routes-lavande.com.

▲**Ardèche Gorges**—A 45-minute drive west of Vaison la Romaine, abrupt chalky-white cliffs follow the Ardèche River through immense canyons and thick forests. From Vaison, go to Bollene then follow the villages of Pont St. Esprit to Vallon Pont d'Arc (which offers all-day canoe-kayak floats through the gorge). If continuing north, connect Privas and Aubenas, then head back to the autoroute. Adorable Balazuc, a village north of the gorges, makes a fine stop.

NOT QUITE A YEAR IN PROVENCE: THE HILL TOWNS OF LUBERON

The Luberon region, stretching 50 kilometers along a ridge of rugged hills east of Avignon, hides some of France's most appealing and popular hill towns (including Bonnieux, Lacoste, Oppède le Vieux, Roussillon, Joucas, and Gordes).

Those intrigued by Peter Mayle's *A Year in Provence* will enjoy a day joyriding through the region. Mayle's best-selling book describes the ruddy local culture from an Englishman's perspective, as he buys a stone farmhouse, fixes it up, and adopts the region as his new home. This is a great read while you're here.

The Luberon terrain in general (much of which is a French regional natural park) is as appealing as its hill towns. Gnarled vineyards and wind-sculpted trees separate tidy stone structures from abandoned buildings—little more than rock piles—that seem to challenge city slickers to fix them up.

The wind is an integral part of life here. The infamous mistral, finishing its long ride in from Siberia, hits like a hammer—hard enough, it's said, to blow the ears off a donkey. Throughout the region you'll see houses designed with windowless walls facing the mistral.

Planning Your Time

To enjoy the windblown ambience of the Luberon, plan a leisurely day trip visiting three or four of the characteristic towns (impossible *sans* car). Isle sur la Sorgue, located halfway between Avignon and the Luberon, has train service from Avignon (easy day trip) and Nice (via Marseille) and makes a good biking base.

Luberon

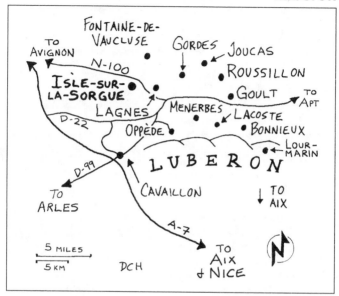

For the ultimate Luberon experience, hill-town connoisseurs with cars should bypass Isle sur la Sorgue and sleep in one of the villages described below. The famous villages are beautiful, but attract tourists like flypaper. For a quieter overnight, sleep in Oppède le Vieux, Joucas, or Lacoste. You'll pass *Chambres d'hôte* everywhere (TIs have long lists)—many are pricey and lovingly restored by foreigners.

Getting around the Luberon

By Bus: To reach the hill towns such as Roussillon, go to Cavaillon or Apt, then taxi (1 bus/day from Avignon to Gordes, 2 buses/day from Cavaillon to Gordes, bus tel. 04 90 71 03 00).

By Train: Trains get you as far as Isle sur la Sorgue from Avignon (6/day, 30 min) or from Nice (4/day, 4 hrs, transfer in Marseille). Isle sur la Sorgue's train station is called L'Isle Fontaine de Vaucluse.

By Car: Town-hop for a day, side-tripping from your home base, or visit these villages as a detour en route to the French Riviera. Of course, tumbling in for an hour from the parking lot, you'll be just another flash-in-the-pan, camera-toting Provence fan. Spend a night, and you'll feel more a part of the scene. You need Michelin #246 to follow this scenic loop: Take the N-100

east of Avignon toward Apt and find little Lagnes just after Isle
sur la Sorgue. Go through Lagnes, then Cabrieres d'Avignon,
Gordes, Goult, and Roussillon. From Roussillon, follow Bonnieux
and cross the Roman pont Julien, then find Lacoste, Menerbes,
and, to complete the loop, Oppède le Vieux. I've listed places to
sleep and eat in several of these villages (see below).

ISLE SUR LA SORGUE

This sturdy market town, literally, "Island on the Sorgue River,"
sits within a split in its crisp, happy little river and makes a good
base for exploring the Luberon and Avignon. Do not confuse it
with the nearby plain town of Sorgue. And don't underestimate
the importance of this river to the region's economy. The fresh
spring water of the many branches of the Sorgue (that divide in
Isle sur la Sorgue) have for a long time provided nourishment for
crops and power for key industries. While Isle sur la Sorgue is
renowned for its market days, it is otherwise a pleasantly average
town with no important sights and a steady trickle of tourism.
It's calm at night and downright dead on Mondays.

Isle sur la Sorgue has crystal-clear water babbling under
pedestrian bridges lined with flower boxes, and its old-time carousel is always spinning. The town erupts into a market frenzy each
Sunday and Thursday, with hardy crafts and local produce (Sun
market is astounding and famous for its antiques; Thu market
is more intimate).

Navigate the town by its mossy waterwheels, which, while
still turning, power only memories of the town's wool and silk
industries. The 12th-century church with a festive Baroque
interior seems too big for the town.

Tourist Information: The **TI**, next door to the church,
has a line on rooms in private homes, all of which are outside
the town (Tue–Sat 9:00–12:30 & 14:00–18:00, Sun 9:00–12:30,
closed Mon, tel. 04 90 38 04 78). Ask where you can rent a bike.
These places make good biking destinations: Velleron (8 km/5
miles away, flat, a tiny version of Isle sur la Sorgue, with waterwheels, fountains, and an evening farmer's market held Mon–
Sat 18:00–20:00), Lagnes (5 km away, mostly flat, a pretty,
well-restored hill town with views from its ruined château), and
Fontaine de Vaucluse (11 km away, uphill, see "More Luberon
Towns," below). A launderette is on l'Impasse de la République
(open 8:00–20:00).

Sleeping in and near Isle sur la Sorgue
(€1 = about $1, country code: 33, zip code: 84800)
Arrive the night before market day to best experience the town.

MODERATELY PRICED
Hôtel les Nevons**, two blocks from the center (behind the PTT—post office), is motel-modern outside. Inside, however, it seems to do everything right, with comfortable, air-conditioned rooms (a few family suites), small rooftop pool, Internet access, and eager-to-please owners, Mireille and Jean-Philipe (Db-€60, exrta person-€16, includes breakfast, CC, easy and secure parking-€7.75, 205 Chemin des Nevons, tel. 04 90 20 72 00, fax 04 90 20 56 20, www.hotel-les-nevons.com).

Loy Soloy Restaurant/Hôtel is the prow of the ship at the split of the river, with the best view rooms in town (rooms 1, 2, 3, and 7 have the views, reasonable comfort, and road noise, Db-€63, CC, 2 avenue Charles de Gaulle, tel. & fax 04 90 38 03 16).

LOWER PRICED
The bargain beds in town are sufficiently clean and almost quiet, above a local bar at **Hôtel Le Cours de l'Eau** (D-€21, Db-€33, CC, on ring road opposite Café de la Sorgue at place Gambetta, tel. 04 90 38 01 18, no fax, NSE).

Eating in and near Isle sur la Sorgue

Begin your dinner with a glass of wine at the cozy **Le Caveau de la Tour de l'Isle** (part wine bar, part wine shop, open until about 20:00, 12 rue de la République). **L'Oustau de l'Isle** is well-suited for a fine dinner (*menus* from €21, closed Wed–Thu off-season, 21 avenue des 4 Otages, near post office, tel. 04 90 38 54 83). The riverfront cafés, **Café de la Sorgue** and the better **Café de Bellevue**, offer credible cuisine with riverside ambience. The **Fromenterie** bakery next to the PTT sells really rich quiches.

ROUSSILLON

With all the trendy charm of Santa Fe on a hilltop, this town will cost you at least a roll of film (and €2 for parking). Climb a few minutes from either parking lot, past the picture-perfect square and under the church to the summit of the town (follow signs to *Castum*), where a dramatic view, complete with a howling mistral and a helpful *table d'orientation*, awaits. Then, back under the church, see how local (or artsy) you can look in what must be the most scenic village square in the Luberon. On the south end of town, beyond the upper parking lot, a brilliant ochre canyon—formerly a quarry—is busy with walkers and explains the color of this village (€1.50). You could paint the entire town without ever leaving the red and orange corner of your palette. Many do. While Roussillon receives its share of day-trippers, evenings are romantically peaceful. Thursday

is Roussillon's market day. Every day is Christmas for thieves—
take everything out of your car.

Sleeping in Roussillon
(€1 = about $1, country code: 33, zip code: 84220)
The **TI**, across from the David restaurant, posts a list of hotels
and *chambres d'hôte* (April–Oct Mon–Sat 9:30–12:00 & 13:30–
18:30, Sun 14:00–18:30, Nov–March Mon–Sat 13:30–17:30,
closed Sun, tel. 04 90 05 60 25). For additional hotel and restaurant listings, see "More Luberon Towns," below.

MODERATELY PRICED
Hôtel Reves d'Ocres**, the only hotel in the town center, is run
by charming Sandrine and laid-back Web, with reasonably comfortable, spacious rooms—the best have view terraces (Db-€61,
Tb-€76, balcony room about €8 extra, CC, air-con turned on at
the desk, route de Gordes, tel. 04 90 05 60 50, fax 04 90 05 79 74).

LOWER PRICED
Madame Cherel rents simple but clean rooms with firm mattresses and a common view terrace (D-€32–35, no CC, 3 blocks
from upper parking lot, between gas station and school, La Bur-
lière, tel. 04 90 05 68 47). Cherel speaks English, is a wealth of
regional travel tips, and rents mountain bikes to guests only
(€15/day).

Sleeping near Roussillon
For drivers only, the next three listings are most easily found by
turning north off N-100 at the Roussillon/Les Huguets sign:

MODERATELY PRICED
Les Puches *chambre d'hôte* offers smart rooms with terraces and
a pool that glissades over the edge (Db-€61–69, no CC, 2 km/
1.25 miles below Roussillon toward Bonnieux on D-104, just past
Hôtel Les Sables d'Ocre, tel. & fax 04 90 05 66 02).

LOWER PRICED
Les Passiflores *chambre d'hôte*, on D-108 between Roussillon and
Bonnieux in Les Huguets, is everything a *chambre d'hôte* should
be: rustic, charming, comfortable, and owned by the delightful
Chantal (Db-€46–50, includes breakfast, ask if she'll cook you
dinner-€18 for the works, no CC, tel. & fax 04 90 05 69 61, NSE).
   Hôtel Les Sables d'Ocre** is modern and kid-friendly, with
good rooms, a big pool, lots of grass, and fair rates (Db-€53,
Db with garden balcony-€60–69, extra bed-€10, CC, 1 km after

leaving Roussillon toward Apt at intersection of D-108 and D-104, tel. 04 90 05 55 55, fax 04 90 05 55 50, e-mail: sablesdocre@free.fr).

Eating in Roussillon

Le Piquebaure hangs on a cliff and is the best bet in town for a fine meal (€20 *menus*, €12 garnished *plats du jour*, below Hôtel Reves d'Ocres, route du Gordes, closed Mon off-season, tel. 04 90 05 79 65).

Inside the village, **Le Bistrot de Roussillon** is center-stage on the square with view tables in the rear (€23 *menu*, closed Thu, tel. 04 90 05 74 45). **Aux Agapes,** just off the main square, does a good wood-fired pizza for €8 (if you like peppers, try their *salade Agapes*).

More Luberon Towns

Fontaine de Vaucluse—You'll read and hear a lot about this sublimely located village at the source of the river Sorgue, where the medieval Italian poet Petrarch mourned for his love, Laura. This beautiful river seems to magically appear from nowhere (the actual source is a murky green water hole) and flows through Fontaine de Vaucluse, past a lineup of cafés, souvenir shops, and enough tourists to make Disney envious. Arrive by 9:00 or after 19:00, or skip it.

Gordes—This is the most touristy and trendy town in the Luberon. Parisian big shots love it. Once a virtual ghost town of derelict buildings, it's now completely fixed up and filled by people who live in a world without calluses. The view as you approach is incredible and merits a detour, though the village has little of interest. The nearby and still-functioning 12th-century **Abbey de Senanque** can be crowded but is splendidly situated and worth a visit. When the lavender blooms (late June–July) this is a ▲▲▲ sight (€4.60, Mon–Sat 10:00–12:00 & 14:00–18:00, Sun 14:00–18:00, arrive early to beat crowds).

Joucas—This village is everything Gordes is not: understated, quiet, and overlooked. Tiny cobbled lanes and well-restored homes play host to artists and a smattering of locals.

At **La Maison de Mistral**, gregarious Marie-Lucie Mistral (they named the wind after her) has five oh-so-cozy rooms in her *chambre d'hôte*, with a breakfast terrace to linger over and access to a nearby pool (Db-€53, extra person-€15.25, includes breakfast, no CC, rue de l'Eglise, tel. 04 90 05 74 01, cellular 06 62 08 15 03, fax 04 90 05 67 04, e-mail: pmistral@free.fr).

Lacoste—Slumbering under its ruined castle, tiny, steep, and quiet-at-night Lacoste has great views of the picturesque town of Bonnieux (listed below). Tuesday is market day here.

Café de Sade is spotless, with six rooms above a little restaurant (D-€32, Db-€46, family room-€61, dorm beds-€11.50, no CC, for dorm only, bring your own sheet or pay €3.80 to rent one, tel. 04 90 75 82 29, fax 04 90 75 95 68). For a country-elegant dinner, **Le Relais du Procureur** is worth the detour (€20 *menu*, closed Tue, tel. 04 90 75 84 78).

Bonnieux—Spectacular from a distance, this town disappoints up close. It lacks a pedestrian center, though the Friday morning market briefly creates one.

Oppède le Vieux—This is a windy barnacle of a town, with a few boutiques and a dusty main square at the base of a short, ankle-twisting climb to a ruined church and castle. The Luberon views justify the effort. This way-off-the-beaten-path fixer-upper of a village must be how Gordes looked before it became chic. It's ideal for those looking to perish in Provence.

Goult—Bigger than its sister hill towns, this surprisingly quiet town seems content away from the tourist path. Wander up the hill to the panorama and windmill, and review its restaurants, where you won't compete with tourists for a table.

CASSIS

Cowering in the shadow of impossibly high cliffs, Cassis (pron. kah-see) is an unpretentious beach town offering travelers a sunny time-out from their busy vacation. Two hours away from the fray of the Côtes d'Azur, Cassis is a poor man's St. Tropez. Outdoor cafés line the small port on three sides, where boaters chat up café clients while cleaning their boats. Cassis is popular with the French and close enough to Marseille to be busy on weekends and all summer. Come to Cassis for true bouillabaisse, to swim in crystal-clear water, and to scour its fjord-like *calanques*. Cassis is too far from Nice for day-tripping.

Orientation

The Massif du Puget encloses Cassis on three of its four sides. The Cap Canaille cliff with the castle (property of the Michelin family) rises from the southeast. All roads spill into the port, and drivers should park at one of the well-signed pay lots above the port to avoid parking purgatory. The train station is three kilometers/ two miles from Cassis, buses connect with most trains, and taxis cost about €9 with bags.

Tourist Information: The **TI** is on the port and can answer your every question from scuba diving to kayak rental, and help you find a room (May–Sept daily 9:00–18:00, Oct–April Mon–Sat 9:00–12:30 & 13:30–17:30, Sun 10:00–12:30, quai des Moulins, tel. 04 42 01 71 17, www.cassis.enprovence.com).

Helpful Hints

The **shops** drop in price the farther you get from the port.

A terrific **launderette/Internet café** is up rue Victor Hugo at 9 rue Authemann (daily 9:00–21:00). Here, you can do your laundry (or they'll do it for you while you sightsee), check your e-mail, and buy phone cards.

Sights—Cassis

Beaches—Cassis' beaches are a sand/pebble mix. You can walk 15 minutes to plage du Bestouan and rent cushy mats, or find a sandy spot at the beach just south of the port.

▲▲*Calanques*—Cassis is all about *les Calanques* (pron. luh cah-lahnk). That's why most come here—but until you see them, it's hard to understand what all the excitement is about. The splintered, pasty-white rocks create fjord-like inlets, with translucent blue water and intimate beaches. Most *calanques* are prickly extensions of cliffs that border the shore, but some rise directly out of the Mediterranean. You can cruise by boat, kayak, or hike to several *calanques*.

Boats will take you to any combination of 10 *calanques*, providing a water-based perspective (3 *calanques*-€10.50, 2/hr, 45 min; 5 *calanques*-€12.50, 2/day, 65 min; 10 *calanques*-€20, 1/day, 2 hrs). The three-*calanques* tour seems best. Buy tickets at the small booth on the south side of the port where boats depart.

Trails allow hiking/riding to three of the *calanques*. If you plan to spend time at a *calanque*, do so at Calanque d'En Vau; a boat provides direct round-trip service (2/hr, €11.50, one-way tickets available). Boats can drop you on a cliff if the sea is calm (short jump), but it's a steep, treacherous hike down to the beach for inexperienced climbers, and an even more difficult hike back up (you'll pay a surcharge to get off unless you buy a one-way ticket, and boats are often reluctant to let you off, so make sure they understand you want to get off at Calanque d'En Vau before buying your ticket). Hiking from Cassis to Calanque d'En Vau is a safer option, though you must get a map from the TI to follow the correct route. Avoid the shoreline route that requires rappelling skills; take the inland route and you'll do fine (some enjoy taking the boat there and hiking back). The TI has complete information on hiking and boating to the *calanques*. Bring water, sunscreen, and everything you need for the day, as there are no shops.

▲**La Route des Cretes**—Those with cars or a willingness to hire a taxi (€25 for a good 45-min trip, 4 people per taxi) can consider this amazing drive, straight up to the top of Cap Canaille to the industrial town of La Ciotat. Acrophobics should skip this narrow, twisty road that provides numbingly high views over Cassis and the

Cassis

100 YARDS
100 METERS

TO P

ST. MICHEL

TO BESTOUAN (SMALL) BEACH + CALANQUES

TO BUS STOP, D:1 + AUTOROUTE

P

CASINO

POST

TO CALANQUES

KAYAK RENTAL

P O R T

(BIG) B E A C H

DCH

PLACE MONTMORIN

TO CLOS STE MAGDALEINE WINERY + CAP CANAILLE

RUE DE L'ARENE

❶ Hotel le Cassitel
❷ Hotel le Liautaud
❸ Hotel le Golfe
❹ Hotel la Rade
❺ Hotel Laurence
❻ Rest. la Paillote
❼ Rest. L'Ousteau de la Mer
❽ Bar Canaille
❾ Rest. Bonaparte
❿ Laundromat and Internet

Mediterranean at every turn. From Cassis, follow signs to La Ciotat/Toulon, then *la Route des Cretes*. Drive as far as you like; it's about 45 minutes all the way to La Ciotat.

Sleeping in Cassis
(€1 = about $1, country code: 33, zip code: 13260)
Hotels are a bargain compared with those on the Côte d'Azur. Note that many close from November to March, and most come with late-night noise on weekends and in summer.

HIGHER PRICED
La Rade***, on the quieter northwest corner of the port, has great views from its teak poolside chairs. It offers small but adequate rooms with air-conditioning and a busy road below (Db-€105–115, apartments-€160–170, CC, route des Calanques,

tel. 04 42 01 02 97, fax 04 42 01 01 32, www.hotel-cassis.com, e-mail: larade@hotel-cassis.com).

MODERATELY PRICED
Le Cassitel**, near the TI, is cute, cozy, and located on the harbor over a sprawling café. The rooms with water views have nightlife noise (Db-€53–63, extra bed-€16, garage-€11, CC, place Clemenceau, tel. 04 42 01 83 44, fax 04 42 01 96 31, e-mail: cassitel@hotel-cassis.com).

Le Liautaud**, while perfectly located on the port near the TI, has uninspired rooms that are bare-bones modern. Noise can be a problem (Db-€60–70, CC, 2 rue Victor Hugo, tel. 04 42 01 75 37, fax 04 42 01 12 08, SE).

Hôtel le Golfe**, a two-minute walk below La Rade, is over a lunch-only café. Half of its comfortable, long, and narrow rooms come with memorable views and small balconies; the others come with memorable air-conditioning (Db with view-€73, Db without view-€58, extra bed-€16, 2 extra beds-€24, CC, 3 grand Carnot, tel. 04 42 01 00 21, fax 04 42 01 92 08, friendly Michele SE).

LOWER PRICED
Hôtel Laurence**, two blocks off the port beyond Hôtel Cassitel, offers the best budget beds I found, in bland, tight, but clean rooms, some with decks and views (Db-€34–52, Db with terrace-€62, no CC, 8 rue de l'Arene, tel. 04 42 01 88 78, fax 04 42 01 81 04).

Eating in Cassis
L'Oustau de la Mer has generally tasty cuisine and friendly service (closed Thu, 20 quai de Baux, tel. 04 42 01 78 22).

La Paillote sits on the harbor, with fair prices given its location and generally good food (stick to seafood dishes, closed Sun–Mon, quai J-J Barthelemy, tel. 04 42 01 72 14).

Bar Canaille is a casual, lunch-only place that has fabulously fresh seafood. It's tucked away in the corner of the port; look for the bright yellow awning (22 quai des Baux, tel. 04 42 01 72 36).

Bonaparte is off the harbor and cheaper (14 rue du General Bonaparte, closed Sun–Mon, tel. 04 42 01 80 84).

Transportation Connections—Cassis
While the station is three kilometers/two miles from the port, shuttle buses meet most trains, and taxis are reasonable.

By train to: Arles (7/day, 2 hrs, change in Marseille), **Avignon** (7/day, 2 hrs, change in Marseille), **Nice** (7/day, 3 hrs, change in Toulon or Marseille), **Paris** (7/day, 4 hrs, change in Marseille).

THE FRENCH RIVIERA

A hundred years ago, celebrities from London to Moscow flocked here to socialize, gamble, and escape the dreary weather at home. The belle époque is today's tourist craze, as this most sought-after, fun-in-the-sun destination now caters to budget travelers as well. Some of the Continent's most stunning scenery and intriguing museums lie along this strip of land—as do millions of heat-seeking tourists. Nice has world-class museums, a grand beachfront prome-nade, a seductive old town, and all the drawbacks of a major city (traffic, crime, pollution, etc.). But the day trips possible from Nice are easy and brilliant: Monte Carlo welcomes everyone with cash registers open, Antibes has a romantic port and silky-sandy beaches, and the hill towns present a breezy and photogenic alternative to the beach scene. Evenings on the Riviera, a.k.a. the Côte d'Azur, were made for a promenade and outdoor dining.

Choose a Home Base

I've focused my accommodations listings on three different places: Nice, Antibes, and Villefranche-sur-Mer. **Nice** is the region's capital and France's fifth-largest city. With excellent public transportation to most regional sights, this is the Riviera's most practical base for train travelers. Urban Nice also has a full palette of museums and rock-hard beaches, the best selection of hotels in all price ranges, and a thriving nightlife. A car is a headache in Nice. Nearby **Antibes** is smaller, with fewer hotels but fine sandy beaches, good hiking, and the Picasso Museum. It has frequent train service to Nice and Monaco, and is easier for drivers. **Villefranche-sur-Mer** is the romantic's choice, with a serene setting and small-town warmth. It has finely ground pebble beaches, good public transportation (particularly to Nice and Monaco), and easy parking. Its few hotels leap from simple to sublime, letting Nice handle the middle ground.

Planning Your Time

Most should plan a full day for Nice and at least a half day each for Monaco and Antibes. Monaco is best at night (sights are closed but crowds are few; consider dinner here), and Antibes during the day (good beaches and Picasso Museum). The hill towns of St. Paul-de-Vence, Vence, and Eze Village are lower priorities, particularly if you don't have a car. The Riviera is infamous for staging major events—it's best to avoid the craziness and room shortage if you can (unless, of course, you're a fan). Here are the three biggies in 2003: Nice Carnival (Feb 21–March 5); Grand Prix of Monaco (May 23–26); Cannes Film Festival (May 21–26).

Getting around the Riviera

Getting around the Côte d'Azur by train or bus is easy (park your car and leave the driving to others). Drivers who want to see some of the Riviera's best scenery should follow the coast road between Cannes and Fréjus (when arriving in or leaving the Côte d'Azur), take the short drive along *Moyenne Corniche* from Nice to Eze Village, and take my recommended hill-town drive to the Gorges du Loup.

Nice is perfectly located for exploring the region. Monaco, Eze Village, Villefranche, Antibes, St. Paul, and Cannes are all a 15- to 60-minute bus or train ride apart from each other. The TI (and probably your hotel) has information on minivan excursions from Nice (half day–about €60, full day–€76–107; Tour Azur is one of many, tel. 04 93 44 88 77, www.tourazur.com).

Bus service can be cheaper and more frequent than rail service, depending on the destination. At Nice's efficient bus station (*gare routière*) on boulevard J. Jaures (see map of Nice in this chapter), you'll find a baggage check (called *messagerie*, available Mon–Sat 7:30–18:00), clean WCs for €0.50, and several bus companies offering free return trips to some destinations (keep your ticket). Get schedules and prices from the helpful English-speaking clerk at the information desk in the bus station (tel. 04 93 85 61 61). Buy tickets in the station or on the bus.

Here's an overview of public transport options to key Riviera destinations from Nice (rt = round-trip, ow = one-way):

Destination	Bus	Train
Monaco	4/hr, 40 min, €3.80, r/t	2/hr, 20 min, €3.40, o/w
Villefranche	4/hr, 15 min, €1.70, r/t	2/hr, 10 min, €1.50, o/w
Antibes	3/hr, 50 min, €4.20, o/w	2/hr, 25 min, €3.80, o/w

The French Riviera

Destination	Bus	Train
Cannes	way too long	2/hr, 30 min, €4.90, o/w
St. Paul	2/hr, 45 min, €3, o/w	none
Vence	2/hr, 45 min, €4.60, o/w	none
Eze Village	every 2 hrs, 25 min, €2.50, r/t	none
La Turbie	5/day, 45 min, €2.90, r/t	none

    Two bus companies, RCA and Cars Broch, provide service on the same route between Nice, Villefranche, and Monaco; RCA's buses run more frequently.

Cuisine Scene—Côte d'Azur

The Côte d'Azur (technically a part of Provence) gives Provence's cuisine a Mediterranean flair. Local specialties are bouillabaisse (the spicy seafood stew-soup that seems worth the cost only for those with a seafood fetish), *bourride* (a creamy fish soup thickened with aioli, a garlic sauce), and *salade niçoise* (pron. nee-swaz; a tomato, potato, olive, anchovy, and tuna salad). You'll also find these tasty bread treats: *pissaladière* (bread dough topped with onions, olives, and anchovies), *fougasse* (a spindly, lace-like bread), *socca* (a thin chickpea crêpe), and *pan bagnat* (like a *salade niçoise* stuffed into a huge hamburger bun). Italian cuisine is native (ravioli was first made in Nice), easy to find, and generally a good value (*pâtes fraîches* means fresh pasta). White and rosé Bellet and the rich reds and rosés of Bandol are the local wines.

This is the most difficult region in France in which to find distinctive restaurants. Because most visitors come more for the sun than the cuisine, and because the clientele is predominantly international, most restaurants aim for the middle and are hard to distinguish from each other. Look for views and ambience, and lower your expectations.

Remember, restaurants serve only during lunch (11:30–14:00) and dinner (19:00–21:00, later in bigger cities); cafés serve food throughout the day.

Art Scene—Côte d'Azur

The list of artists who have painted the Riviera reads like a Who's Who of 20th-Century Art: Renoir, Matisse, Chagall, Braque, Dufy, Léger, and Picasso all lived and worked here. Their simple, semiabstract, and, above all, colorful works reflect the Riviera. You'll experience the same landscapes they painted in this bright, sun-drenched region punctuated with views of the "azure sea." Try to imagine the Riviera with a fraction of the people and development you see today.

But the artists were mostly drawn to the simple lifestyle of fishermen and farmers that has reigned here since time began. These *très* serious artists, as they grew older, retired in the sun and turned their backs on modern art's "isms", instead painting with the wide-eyed wonder of children, using bright primary colors, simple outlines, and simple subjects.

A terrific concentration of well-organized contemporary art museums (many described below) litter the Riviera, allowing art-lovers to appreciate these artists' works while immersed in the same sun and culture that inspired them. Many of the museums were designed to blend the art with surrounding views, gardens, and fountains, highlighting that modern art is not only stimulating, but sometimes simply beautiful.

NICE

Nice (pron. neece) is the ultimate tourist melting pot. You'll share its international beaches with the chicest of the chic, the cheapest of the cheap, and everyone else in this scramble to be where the mountains meet the water. Nice's spectacular Alps-to-Mediterranean surroundings, eternally entertaining seafront promenade, and fine museums make settling into this big city relatively painless. And in Nice's traffic-free old city, Italian and French flavors mix to create a spicy Mediterranean dressing. Nice may be nice, but it's hot and jammed in July and August (reserve ahead). Get a room with air-conditioning *(une chambre avec climatization)*. Everything you'll want in Nice is walkable or a short bus ride away.

Orientation

Most sights and hotels recommended in this book are located near the avenue Jean Médecin, between the train station and the beach. It's a 20-minute walk from the train station to the beach (or a €9 taxi ride), and a 20-minute walk along the promenade from the fancy Hôtel Negresco to the heart of Old Nice.

Tourist Information: Nice has four helpful TIs: at terminal 1 at the airport (Mon–Sat 8:00–22:00, Sun 8:00–20:00); next to the train station (Mon–Sat 8:00–20:00, Sun 9:00–18:00); on RN-7 after the airport on the right (summers only, 8:00–20:00); and across from the beach at 5 promenade des Anglais (Mon–Sat 8:00–20:00, Sun 9:00–18:00). All can book rooms for a small fee, tel. 08 92 70 74 07, www.nicetourisme.com). Pick up the excellent, free Nice map (which lists all the sights and hours), the extensive *Practical Guide to Nice*, information on regional day trips (such as maps to Antibes), and the museums booklet.

Consider buying the **museum pass**. The regional *Carte Musées* is a great value for those planning to visit more than one museum in a day or several museums over a few days (€8/1 day, €15/3 consecutive days, €24/7 consecutive days, valid at all museums described in this chapter except Foundation Maeght, sold at any TI or participating museum).

Arrival in Nice

By Train: Nice has one main station (*Nice-Ville*, lockers available) where all trains stop and you get off. Avoid the suburban stations, and never leave your bags unattended. The TI is next door to the left as you exit the train station; car rental and taxis are to the right. To reach most of my recommended hotels, turn left out of the station, then right on avenue Jean Médecin. To get to the beach and the promenade des Anglais from the station, continue on foot for 20 minutes down avenue Jean Médecin or take bus #12 (stop on Jean Médecin). To get to the old city and the bus station *(gare routière)*, catch bus #5 from avenue Jean Médecin.

By Car: Follow Nice Centre/Promenade des Anglais whether arriving from east, west, or north and try to avoid arriving at rush hour, when the promenade des Anglais grinds to a halt (Mon–Fri 17:00–19:30). Ask your hotel for advice on where to park (allow €9–14/day). The parking garage at the Nice Etoile shopping center on avenue Jean Médecin is handy to many of my hotel listings (ticket booth on third floor, about €14/day, €8 20:00–8:00). All on-street parking is metered.

By Plane: Nice's mellow, user-friendly airport is on the Mediterranean, about 20 minutes west of the city center. The TI and international flights use terminal 1; domestic flights use terminal 2 (airport tel. 04 93 21 30 30). At terminal 1, you'll find the TI, banks (so-so rates), ATM, and car rental just outside customs. Taxis wait immediately outside the terminal (allow €25–30 to Nice hotels, €45 to Villefranche). Turn left after passing customs and exit the doors at the far end to find the bus information office (taxi vouchers to Villefranche and other non-Nice destinations sold here). Three bus lines run from the airport to Nice: #99 runs nonstop to the main train station (stall #1, €3.50, 2/hr until 21:00, 20 min, drops you within a 10-min walk of many of my hotel listings), local bus #23 (stall #6, €1.40, 4/hr, 40 min, direction: St. Maurice, serves stops between the airport and SNCF station), and the yellow "NICE" bus to the bus station (*gare routière*, stall #1, €3.50, 3/hr, 25 min). Buy tickets in the office or from the driver. To get to Villefranche from the airport, take the yellow "NICE" bus to the bus station (*gare routière)* and transfer to the Villefranche bus (€1.40, 4/hr). Buses also run from the airport to Antibes (1/hr, 20 min, €7), and to Monaco (1/hr, 50 min, €14).

Helpful Hints

Theft Alert: Nice is notorious for pickpockets. Have nothing important on or around your waist, unless it's in a money belt tucked out of sight (no fanny packs, please); don't leave anything visible in your car; be wary of scooters when standing at intersections; don't leave things unattended on the beach while swimming; and stick to main streets in Old Nice after dark.

Museums: Most Nice museums are closed Tuesdays, and free the first Sunday of the month. For information on the museum pass, see "Tourist Information," above.

U.S. Consulate: If you lose your passport, this is the place to go (7 avenue Gustave V, tel. 04 93 88 89 55, fax 04 93 87 07 38).

Medical Help: Riviera Medical Services has a list of English-speaking physicians. They can help you make an appointment or call an ambulance (tel. 04 93 26 12 70).

Rocky Beaches: To make life tolerable on the rocks, swimmers should buy a pair of the cheap plastic beach shoes (flip-flops fall off in the water) sold at many shops.

American Express: AmEx faces the beach at 11 promenade des Anglais (tel. 04 93 16 53 53).

English Bookstore: Try **The Cat's Whiskers** (closed Sun, 26 rue Lamartine, near Hôtel Star).

Laundry: Self-serve launderettes abound in Nice; ask your hotelier for suggestions and guard your load.

Internet Access: It's easy in Nice. Ask your hotelier for the nearest Internet café.

English Radio: Tune into Riviera-Radio at FM 106.5 for English radio.

Getting around Nice

Bus fare is €1.40 and an all-day pass is €4, though walking gets you to most places.

Taxis allow four passengers in Nice and are handy to Chagall and Matisse museums. They normally only pick up at taxi stands (*tête de station*) or by a telephoned request. You'll pay €1 per bag and supplements for service on Sunday and after 19:00 any day (tel. 04 93 13 78 78).

Sights—Nice

▲▲**Promenade des Anglais**—Welcome to the Riviera. There's something for everyone along this seven-kilometer-long (4 miles) seafront circus. Watch the Europeans at play, admire the azure Mediterranean, anchor yourself in a blue chair, and prop your feet up on the made-to-order guardrail. Join the evening parade of tans along the promenade. Start at the pink-domed Hôtel Negresco and, like the belle époque (late-19th-century) English aristocrats for whom the promenade was built, stroll to the old town and Castle Hill (20-min walk).

Hôtel Negresco, Nice's finest hotel and a historic monument, offers the city's most costly beds and a free "museum" interior (reasonable attire is necessary to enter). March straight through the lobby into the exquisite Salon Royal. The czar's chandelier hangs from an Eiffel-built dome. Read the explanation, check out the room photos, and stroll the circle. On your way out, pop into the Salon Louis XIV (more explanations).

The next block to your left as you exit has a lush park and the Masséna Museum (closed until 2004). The TI is beyond that. Cross over to the seaside promenade.

Pull up a chair and admire the scene. *La Baie des Anges* (Bay of Angels) is named for the arrival of Nice's patron saint, Répararte, who supposedly was escorted into this bay by angels in the fourth century. To your right is the airport, built on a landfill, and, on that tip of land way out there, Cap d'Antibes. Until 1860, Antibes and Nice were in different countries; the Italians (of Savoy-Piedmont) gave Nice to the French as thanks for their

Nice

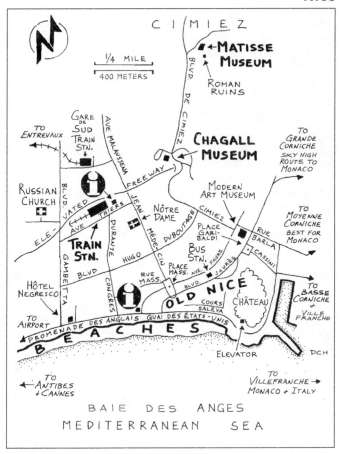

help during the reunification of Italy in 1860. To the far left lies Villefranche-sur-Mer (beyond that tower at land's end), Monaco, then Italy. Behind you are the pre-Alps (les Alpes Maritimes), which gather threatening clouds and leave the Côte d'Azur to enjoy the sunshine more than 300 days a year. The broad sidewalks of the promenade des Anglais (literally, Walkway of the English) were financed by wealthy English tourists who wanted a "safe" place to stroll and admire the view. By 1787, there was already sufficient tourism in Nice to justify its first casino (a leisure activity imported from Venice). In fact, an elegant casino stood on pilings in the sea until the Germans destroyed it during World War II.

Turn around. To the right of Hôtel Negresco sit two other belle époque establishments: the West End and Westminster hotels. These hotels represent Nice's arrival as a tourist mecca 100 years ago, when the combination of leisure time and a stable economy allowed tourists to find the sun even in winter. Tourism as we know it today took off after World War II (blame planes, trains, and automobiles), allowing even budget travelers to appreciate this once-exclusive resort. Now get down to that beach.

Beaches—Nice is where the jet set relax *à la plage*. After settling into the smooth pebbles, you can play beach volleyball, table tennis, or *boules*; rent paddleboats, personal watercraft, or windsurfing equipment; explore ways to use your zoom lens as a telescope; or snooze on comfy beach beds with end tables (mattress-€9, mattress and chaise lounge-€11, umbrella-€4.60). Have lunch in your bathing suit (€9 salads and pizzas). Before heading off in search of sandy beaches, try it on the rocks. As you stroll the promenade, look for the *Plage Publique* signs explaining the 15 beach no-nos (translated in English).

Nice in the Buff: A Walk through Old Nice (Vieux Nice)

This walk, worth ▲▲, is best done early in the morning. Allow an hour, with a stop for coffee and *socca* (chickpea crêpe), and use the free city map, focusing on the enlargement of Vieux Nice. We'll begin our tour on place Massena, at the end of avenue Jean Médecin nearest the sea.

   1. Place Massena: Walk to the fountains and face them. You're standing on Nice's most important river, the Paillon (it was covered in the 1800s). Turn around. You can track the river's route under the green parkway as it makes its way to the sea at the Meridien hotel. For centuries, this river was Nice's border, and natural defense. A fortified wall ran along its length to the sea. It wasn't until the arrival of tourism in the 1800s that Nice expanded over and beyond the river. The rich red coloring of the buildings around you was the preference of Nice's Italian rulers.

   Cross the square and drop into old Nice by following the steps that lead to rue de l'Opera between the curved buildings. Turn left on rue St. François de Paule.

   2. Rue St. François de Paule: You've entered old Nice. Peer into the Alziari olive oil shop at #14. Dating from 1868, it produces what many claim is the world's best olive oil. Wander in and fill your own container from the vats. A block down on the left (#7), Patisserie Auer's belle époque storefront has changed little since the pastry shop opened in 1820. The writing on the window says "For over 170 years from father to son." Ask about the tastings and demonstrations in the *degustatión* room. Behind you is Nice's just-renovated grand opera house, from the same era.

Sift your way through souvenirs to the cours Saleya (pron. sah-lay-yuh).

3. Cours Saleya: Named for its broad exposure to the sun (*soleil*, pron. soh-lay), this cacophony of color, sights, smells, and people is the belly of old Nice and has been its main market square since the Middle Ages. Today, it collects people, produce, and flowers as if it's a trough between city and sea (produce market held daily except Mon until 13:00, an antique market takes over the square on Mon). Amazingly, cars could be parked here until 1980, when the mayor of Nice had an underground parking garage built and returned this square to walkers and shoppers. Thread the needle through the center. The first section is devoted to freshly cut flowers that seem to grow effortlessly and everywhere in this ideal climate. Continue to the first produce stand (Le Grand Bleu restaurant should be on your right). Facing you is Thérèse (pron. tear-ehz), self-proclaimed Queen of the Market. Listen for her sing-song sales pitch, buy some berries, and say, "*Bonjour, Madame la Reine du Marché.*"

You can climb the steps past trash sacks above the Grand Bleu restaurant for a good market view, or position yourself in front of the steps. From your perch, look up to the hill that dominates to the east. The city of Nice was first settled there by Greeks in about 500 B.C. In the Middle Ages, a massive castle stood up there, with turrets, high walls, and soldiers at the ready. With the river guarding one side and the sea the other, this mountain fortress was invincible—at least until Louis XIV leveled it in 1706. Nice's medieval seawall ran along the lineup of two-story buildings you're standing along. Now, look across cours Saleya to the large "palace." This was the Ducal Palace (called La Prefecture today), where the kings of Savoy-Piedmont (Nice's Italian rulers in the 1700s and 1800s) would reside when in Nice. Resume your stroll down the center of cours Saleya and stop when you see La Cambuse restaurant on your left. Hovering over the black barrel with the paella-like pan on top is another Theresa. She's cooking *socca*, Nice's chickpea crêpe specialty. Spring for a paper wad of *socca* (careful, it's hot, but good).

Continue down cours Saleya. That fine golden building at the end of the cours is where Henri Matisse lived for 17 years (on the second floor). Turn left at the Civette du Cours café, and find rue de la Poissonerie.

4. Rue de la Poissonerie: Stop at #4. Look up. Adam and Eve are squaring off, each holding a zucchini-like gourd. This scene represents the annual rapprochement in Nice to make up for the sins of a too-much-fun Carnival (Mardi Gras). Nice residents have partied hard during Carnival for over 700 years. The iron grill above the door allows cooling air to enter the building, but keeps out uninvited guests. You'll see lots of these open grills in old Nice. They were part of an ingenious system of sucking cool air in from the sea up, through the homes and out roof vents. Across the street, check out the small church dedicated to St. Rita, the patron saint of desperate causes. She holds a special place in locals' hearts, and this church is Nice's most popular. Baroque was the fashion (thank the Italians).

Turn right on the next street, then left on "Right" Street (rue Droite).

5. Rue Droite: In the Middle Ages, this straight, skinny street provided the most direct route from wall to wall, or river to sea, and today makes me feel like I've been beamed to Naples. Stop at Esipuno's bakery (#38). Thirty years ago, this baker was voted the best in France, and his son now runs the place. Notice the firewood stacked by the oven. Farther along at #28, the *socca*-seller's husband makes the *socca* in the wood-fired oven, then carts it to her barrel on cours Saleya. The balconies of the mansion in the next block announce the Palais Lascaris (1647), a rare souvenir from one of Nice's most prestigious families (not worth touring, but you can admire the entry).

Turn left on the rue des Loges, then left again on rue Centrale to reach our next stop, on place Rossetti.

6. Place Rossetti: The most Italian of Nice's piazzas, place Rossetti feels more like Rome than Nice. This square comes alive after dark. Don't miss the gelato at Fennochio's, but skip the lousy restaurants. Walk to the fountain and stare back at the church. This is Nice's cathedral of St. Répararte, an unassuming building for a major city's cathedral. The cathedral was relocated here in the 1500s, when Castle Hill (see below) was temporarily converted to a military-only function. The name comes from Nice's patron saint, a teenage virgin named Répararte whose martyred body was floated to Nice in the fourth century, accompanied by angels. Enter and you'll find a Baroque bonanza as wide as it is deep. Back outside the cathedral, the steps leading up rue Rossetti are the most direct path from here to Castle Hill (15 min straight up, consider the elevator on quai des Etats Unis).

7. Castle Hill (Colline du Château)—Climb or, better yet, take the elevator up this saddle horn in the otherwise flat city center for the view (elevator is next to Hôtel Suisse where bayfront road curves right, €0.70 one-way, €1 round-trip). The views over Nice, the port (to the east), the Alps foothills, and the Mediterranean make a good reward, better if you took the elevator, best at sunset or whenever it is really clear (park closes at 20:00 in summer, earlier off-season). Until the 1100s, the city of Nice was crammed on this hill-top, as it was too risky to live in the flatlands below. Today, you'll find a waterfall, a playground, two cafés (fair prices), and a cemetery, but no castle on Castle Hill. To walk down to the old town, follow signs from just below the upper café to *Vielle Ville* (not *le Port*), and turn right at the cemetery, then look for the walkway down on your left.

Museums—Nice

▲▲**Musée National Marc Chagall**—Even if you're suspicious of modern art, this museum—with the largest collection of Chagall's work anywhere—might appeal to you. After World War II, Chagall returned from the United States to settle in nearby Vence. Between 1954 and 1967, he painted a cycle of 17 large murals designed for, and donated to, this museum. These paintings, inspired by the books of Genesis, Exodus, and the Song of Songs, make up the "nave," or core, of what Chagall called the "House of Brotherhood."

Each painting is a lighter-than-air collage of images drawing from Chagall's Russian-folk-village youth, his Jewish heritage, bib-lical themes, and his feeling that he existed somewhere between heaven and earth. He felt the Bible was a synonym for nature, and color and biblical themes were key ingredients for understanding God's love for his creation. Chagall's brilliant blues and reds cele-brate nature, as do his spiritual and folk themes. Notice the focus on couples. To Chagall, humans loving each other mirrored God's love of creation.

Don't miss the stained-glass windows of the auditorium (enter through the garden), early family photos of the artist, and a room full of Chagall lithographs. The small €3 guidebook begins with an introduction by Chagall (€5.50, Wed–Mon 10:00–17:00, until 18:00 July–Aug, closed Tue, ask about English tours, tel. 04 93 53 87 31). An idyllic café awaits in the garden.

Getting to Chagall and Matisse Museums: The Chagall Museum is a confusing but manageable 15-minute walk from the top of avenue Jean Médecin and the train station; the Matisse Muse-um (described below) is a 30-minute uphill walk from the Chagall Museum, though free bus service between the two is provided on line #15 (buses stop a block from Chagall on boulevard de Cimiez heading uphill). Buses #15 and #17 serve Chagall and Matisse from the eastern, Italy side of avenue Jean Médecin (both run 6/hr, €1.40). Consider walking to Chagall and taking the free bus to Matisse.

To walk to the Chagall Museum, go to the train-station end of avenue Jean Médecin and turn right onto rue Raimbaldi along the overpasses, then turn left under the overpasses onto avenue Comboul. Once under the overpass, angle to the right up rue

Olivetto to the alley with the big wall on your right. A pedestrian path soon emerges, leading up and up to signs for Chagall and Matisse. The bus to Matisse is on avenue Cimiez, two blocks up from Chagall.

▲**Musée Matisse** (▲▲▲ for his fans)—The art is beautifully displayed in this elegant (but unfortunately not air-conditioned) orange mansion and represents the single largest collection of Matisse paintings. While many don't get Matisse, this museum offers a painless introduction to this influential artist whose style was shaped by the southern light and by fellow Côte d'Azur artists, Picasso and Renoir. Watch as his style becomes simpler with time. A room on the top floor has models of his famous Chapelle du Rosaire in nearby Vence and illustrates the beauty of his simple design (€3.80, April–Sept Wed–Mon 10:00–18:00, Oct–March 10:00–17:00, closed Tue, ask about English tours, take bus #15 or #17 to Arènes stop, see directions under Chagall Museum listing above, tel. 04 93 81 08 08).

Modern Art Museum (Musée d'Art Moderne et d'Art Contemporain)—This ultramodern museum features an enjoyable collection of art from the 1960s and 1970s, including works by Andy Warhol and Roy Lichtenstein, and offers frequent special exhibits (€3.80, Wed–Mon 10:00–18:00, closed Tue, on promenade des Arts near bus station, tel. 04 93 62 61 62).

Other Nice Museums—These museums offer decent rainy-day options (generally open Tue–Sun 10:00–12:00 & 14:00–18:00, closed Mon). The **Fine Arts Museum** (Musée des Beaux Arts), with 6,000 works from the 17th to 20th centuries, will satisfy your need for a fine-arts fix (€3.80, 3 avenue des Baumettes, in western end of Nice, tel. 04 92 15 28 28). The **Naval Museum** (Musée de la Marine) is interesting and relevant (closed Mon–Tue, €2.50, in Tour Bellanda, halfway up Castle Hill, tel. 04 93 80 47 61). Nice's city museum, **Museum Masséna** (Musée Masséna), is closed until 2004. The **Archaeological Museum** (Musée Archeologique) displays Roman ruins and various objects from the Romans' occupation of this region (€3.80, near Matisse Museum at 160 avenue des Arenes, tel. 04 93 81 59 57).

▲**Russian Cathedral (Cathedrale Russe)**—Even if you've been to Russia, this Russian Orthodox church—which claims to be the finest outside Russia—is interesting. Its one-room interior is filled with icons and candles. In 1912, Czar Nicholas II gave this church to his aristocratic country folk, who wintered on the Riviera. (A few years later, Russian comrades who didn't winter on the Riviera shot him.) Here in the land of olives and anchovies, these proud onion domes seem odd. But, I imagine, so did those old Russians (€1.85, daily 9:00–12:00 & 14:30–18:00, services Sat at 18:00,

Sun at 10:00, no shorts, 10-min walk behind station at 17 boulevard du Tsarevitch, tel. 04 93 96 88 02).

Nightlife
Nice's bars play host to the Riviera's most happening late-night scene, full of jazz and rock 'n' roll. Most activity focuses on old Nice, near place Rossetti. Plan on a cover charge or expensive drinks. If you're out very late, avoid walking alone.

Between Nice and Monaco
▲▲▲**The Three Cornices**—Nice and Monaco are linked with three coast-hugging routes, all offering sensational views and a different perspective on this billion-dollar slice of real estate. The *Basse Corniche* (the Lower Cornice, often called *Corniche Inférieure*) strings ports, beaches, and villages together for a traffic-filled ground-floor view. The *Moyenne Corniche* (Middle Cornice) is higher, quieter, and far more impressive. It runs through Eze Village and provides great views over the Mediterranean with several scenic pullouts (the pullout above Villefranche-sur-Mer is best). Napoleon's crowning road-construction achievement, the *Grande Corniche* (Great Cornice), caps the cliffs with staggering views from almost 480 meters/1,600 feet above the sea. For the best of all worlds, take the *Moyenne Corniche* from Nice to Eze Village, find the *Grande Corniche/La Turbie* from there, and drop down to Monaco after La Turbie (see "Sights near Villefranche-sur-Mer," below). Buses travel each route; the higher the cornice, the less frequent the buses (get details at Nice's bus station).

Sleeping in Nice
(€1 = about $1, country code: 33, zip code: 06000)
Sleep Code: **S** = Single, **D** = Double/Twin, **T** = Triple, **Q** = Quad, **b** = bathroom, **s** = shower only, **CC** = Credit Cards accepted, **no CC** = Credit Cards not accepted, **SE** = Speaks English, **NSE** = No English, * = French hotel rating (0–4 stars). Hotels have elevators unless otherwise noted.

To help you sort easily through these listings, I've divided the rooms into three categories based on the price for a standard double room with bath:

Higher Priced—Most rooms more than €100.
Moderately Priced—Most rooms €100 or less.
Lower Priced—Most rooms €65 or less.

Don't look for charm in Nice. Go for modern and clean with a central location and, in summer, air-conditioning. Reserve early for summer visits. Prices generally drop €5–10 from October to April (the rates listed are for May–Sept) and increase during

Nice Hotels and Restaurants

1/4 MILE
400 METERS

|||| = PEDESTRIAN ZONE

TO MATISSE MUSEUM

N

GARE DU SUD

CHAGALL MUSEUM

TRAIN STATION

TO MATISSE MUSEUM

DCH

1 Hotel du Petit Louvre
2 Hotel Clemenceau
3 Hotel St. Georges
4 Hotel Star
5 Hotel Vendome
6 Hotel Lorrain
7 Hotel les Camelias
8 Hotel Massena
9 Hotel Lafayette
10 Hotel Oasis

11 Hotel Windsor
12 Hotel Excelsior
13 Hotel Suisse
14 Hotel Mercure
15 Hotel Trianon
16 Nissa Socca café
17 Acchiardo's rest.
18 Lulu's Cantine
19 L'Authentic, Le Vin sur Vin, & Le Cenac rest.

20 Le Cote Grill
21 Les Viviers rest.
22 Charcuterie Julien deli, Le Safari & La Cambuse restaurants
23 La Part des Anges rest.
24 Hotels Splendid & Gounod
25 L'Univers restaurant
26 Lou Mourleco Rest.

Carnival (Feb 21–March 5) and the Monaco Grand Prix (May 23–26). Most hotels near the station are overrun, overpriced, and loud. I sleep halfway between old Nice (*vieux* Nice) and the train station, near avenues Jean Médecin and Victor Hugo. Drivers can park under the Nice Etoile shopping center (on avenue Jean Médecin and boulevard Dubouchage).

HIGHER PRICED

Hôtel Masséna****, a few blocks from place Masséna in an elegant building, is a consummate business hotel offering 100 four-star rooms with all the comforts at reasonable rates (Db-€100–145, larger Db-€175, extra bed-€30, CC, reserve a parking space ahead-€16, Internet access in lobby, 58 rue Giofreddo, tel. 04 92 49 88 88, fax 04 92 49 88 89, www.hotel-massena-nice.com).

MODERATELY PRICED

Hôtel Excelsior***, one block below the station, is a diamond in the rough, with 19th-century decor, a lush garden courtyard with a fountain, pleasant rooms with real wood furnishings, and an elegant dining room (*menus* from €22). Rooms on the garden are best in the summer; those streetside have balconies and get winter sun (Db-€72–100, CC, 19 avenue Durante, tel. 04 93 88 18 05, fax 04 93 88 38 69, www.excelsiornice.com, e-mail: excelsior.hotel @wanadoo.fr).

Hôtel Vendome***, a mansion set off the street, gives you a whiff of *la belle époque*, with pink pastels, high ceilings, and grand staircases. Rooms are small but adequate; the best have balconies—request a *chambre avec balcon*. The best rooms are on the fifth floor (Sb-€85–92, Db-€100–110, Tb-€113–122, Qb-€132, CC, air-con, limited off-street parking-€8, 26 rue Pastorelli, tel. 04 93 62 00 77, fax 04 93 13 40 78, e-mail: contact@vendome-hotel-nice.com).

Hôtel Lafayette*** looks big and average from the outside, but inside it's a cozy, good value offering 18 sharp, spacious, three-star rooms at two-star rates, all one floor up from the street. Sweet Sandrine will take good care of you (Sb-€62–79, Db standard-€70–79, Db spacious-€84–98, extra bed-€18, CC, no elevator, meek air-con, 32 rue de l'Hôtel des Postes, tel. 04 93 85 17 84, fax 04 93 80 47 56, e-mail: lafayette@nouvel-hotel.com).

Hôtel Mercure***, on the water behind cours Saleya, offers predictable, modern rooms at good rates, considering the location (Sb-€84, Db-€94, CC, air-con, some balconies and views, 91 quai des Etats Unis, tel. 04 93 85 74 19, fax 04 93 13 90 94, e-mail: h0962@accor-hotels.com).

Hôtel Suisse*** has Nice's best ocean views for the money, with many balconied rooms. Rooms are comfortable, with air-conditioning and modern conveniences, and are surprisingly quiet given the busy street below (skip Db without view-€74, take Db with great view-€95–115, extra bed-€20, CC, 15 quai Rauba-Capeu, tel. 04 92 17 39 00, fax 04 93 85 30 70, e-mail: hotelsuisse.nice@wanadoo.fr).

LOWER PRICED
Hôtel Trianon**, with formal owners, is a small, big-city refuge with good rates and bright, spotless rooms, half of which overlook a small park (Db-€45–60, CC, 15 avenue Auber, tel. 04 93 88 30 69, fax 04 93 88 11 35).

Hôtel du Petit Louvre* is basic, but a solid budget bet, with playful owners (the Vilas), art-festooned walls, and adequate rooms (Ds-€37, Db-€41, Tb-€43–50, CC, payment due on arrival, 10 rue Emma Tiranty, tel. 04 93 80 15 54, fax 04 93 62 45 08, e-mail: petilouvr@aol.com).

Hôtel Clemenceau** is a good value with a homey, family feel and mostly spacious, traditional, and well-cared-for rooms, some with balconies, some without closets, all air-conditioned (S-€31, Sb-€43, D-€43, Db-€46, Tb-€69, Qb-€84, kitchenette-€8 extra and for long stays only, CC, no elevator, 3 avenue Clemenceau, 1 block west of avenue Jean Médecin, tel. 04 93 88 61 19, fax 04 93 16 88 96, e-mail: hotel-clemenceau@wanadoo.fr, Marianne SE).

Hôtel St. Georges**, a block away, is big and bright, with air-conditioning, a backyard garden, reasonably clean and comfortable rooms, and happy Jacques at the reception (Sb-€55, Db-€65, 3-bed Tb-€82, extra bed-€16, CC, 7 avenue Clemenceau, tel. 04 93 88 79 21, fax 04 93 16 22 85, e-mail: nicefrance.hotelstgeorges @wanadoo.fr).

Hôtel Star**, a few blocks east of avenue Jean Médecin, is immaculate, air-conditioned, comfortable, and a truly great value. It's run by intense Françoise, who expects you to respect her high standards (Sb-€35–45, Db-€45–60, Tb-€60–75, CC, fine beds, beach towels, no elevator, 14 rue Biscarra, reserve by fax or e-mail rather than by phone, tel. 04 93 85 19 03, fax 04 93 13 04 23, www.hotel-star.com, e-mail: star-hotel@wanadoo.fr).

Hôtel les Camelias** reminds me of the Old World places I stayed in as a kid traveling with my parents. A well-located, dark, creaky, and floral place burrowed behind a small parking lot and garden, it has linoleum halls, simple rooms, lumpy beds, and a loyal clientele who give the TV lounge a retirement-home-after-dinner feeling. Some rooms have balconies—request a *chambre avec balcon* (Ss-€41, Ds-€48, Db-€63, includes breakfast, parking-€5, CC, 3 rue Spitaleri, tel. 04 93 62 15 54, fax 04 93 80 42 96, formal Madame Vimont and her son Jean Claude SE). The €11 four-course dinner is simple, hearty, and stress-free.

Hôtel Lorrain** offers kitchenettes in all of its modern, linoleum-floored, and spacious rooms and is conveniently located one block from the bus station and old Nice (Db-€42–46, Tb-€68–78, Qb-€78–111, CC, 6 rue Gubernatis, push top buzzer to release door, tel. 04 93 85 42 90, fax 04 93 85 55 54, e-mail: hotellorrain@aol.com).

Hotels near Boulevard Victor Hugo
The next four hotels are on or very near this tree-lined boulevard, several blocks west of avenue Jean Médecin and about five blocks from the beach.

HIGHER PRICED
Hôtel Windsor***, a snazzy, airy, garden retreat with contemporary rooms designed by modern artists, has a swimming pool, free gym, and €10 sauna (Db-€100–130, extra bed-€20, rooms over garden worth the higher price, CC, 11 rue Dalpozzo, 10 blocks west of Jean Médecin and 5 blocks from sea, tel. 04 93 88 59 35, fax 04 93 88 94 57, www.hotelwindsornice.com).

Hôtel Splendid**** is a worthwhile splurge if you miss your Hilton. The rooftop pool, Jacuzzi, and panoramic breakfast room alone almost justify the cost—throw in luxurious rooms, a free gym, Internet access, and air-conditioning, and you're as good as home (Db-€195, deluxe Db with terrace-€240, suites-€320, limited parking-€16, CC, 50 boulevard Victor Hugo, tel. 04 93 16 41 00, fax 04 93 16 42 70, www.splendid-nice.com).

Hôtel Gounod***, behind Hôtel Splendid, shares the same owners, allowing its clients free access to Hôtel Splendid's pool, Jacuzzi, and other amenities. Don't let the lackluster lobby fool you. Its fine rooms are spacious, air-conditioned, and richly decorated, with high ceilings (Db-€90–130, palatial 4-person suites-€190, parking €11–16, CC, 3 rue Gounod, tel. 04 93 16 42 00, fax 04 93 88 23 84, www.gounod-nice.com).

MODERATELY PRICED
Hôtel l'Oasis*** is just that, a surprising oasis of calm, set back from the street surrounding a large courtyard. Rooms are also calming, with air-conditioning, earth tones, pleasing fabrics, sharp bathrooms, and reasonable rates. Madame Le Cam and her dog, Fever, manage this well-run hotel with style (Sb-€64, Db-€74–86, Tb-€86–106, CC, 23 rue Gounod, tel. 04 93 88 12 29, fax 04 93 16 14 40, www.hotel-oasis-nice.com.fr).

Eating in Nice

My recommended restaurants are concentrated in the same neighborhoods as my recommended hotels. The promenade des Anglais is ideal for picnic dinners on warm, languid evenings, and the old town is perfect for restaurant-shopping. Wherever you dine, save room for gelato at Fenocchio's on place Rossetti in old Nice (86 flavors from tomato to lavender), and don't miss the evening parade along the Mediterranean (best view at night is from the east end of the quai des Etats Unis on the tip below Castle Hill).

Nice's dinner scene focuses on cours Saleya, which is as entertaining as the food is average. It's a fun, festive place to compare tans and mussels. Comparison-shopping is half the fun. **La Cambuse** is the lone exception, offering a more refined setting and fine cuisine for a bit more (allow €40, 5 cours Saleya, tel. 04 93 80 82 40), though **Le Safari** is the best of the rest and less (at the Castle Hill end, 1 cours Saleya, tel. 04 93 80 18 44).

Charcuterie Julien is a good deli that sells an impressive array of dishes by weight. Buy 200 grams of your choice, plopped into a plastic carton to go (*pour emporter*, pron. poor ahn-por-tay) or eat there (Thu–Tue 11:00–19:30, closed Wed, on cours Saleya at rue de la Poissonnerie).

Nissa Socca offers good, cheap Italian cuisine a few blocks from cours Saleya in a lively atmosphere (opens at 19:00, closed Sun, arrive early, a block off place Rossetti on rue Ste. Répararte, tel. 04 93 80 18 35).

Deeper in the old city, **Acchiardo's** is a budget traveler's best friend, with simple, hearty food at bargain prices and no fluff (closed Sat–Sun, 38 rue Droite, tel. 04 93 85 51 16).

The simple wood benches of **Lou Pilha Leva** offer a fun, *très* cheap dinner option with Niçoise specialties; order your food on one side and drinks from the other (located where rue des Loges and Centrale meet in old Nice).

The extreme opposite, **L'Univers** is the proud owner of a Michelin star. This Riviera-elegant place is as relaxed as a "top" restaurant can be, from its casual decor to the tasteful dinnerware (*menus* from €35, 53 boulevard Jean Juares, tel. 04 93 62 32 22, e-mail: plumailunivers@aol.com).

These restaurants lie closer to most of the recommended hotels. For the most authentic Niçoise cuisine in this book, reserve a table at the *charmant* and well-run **Bistrot Les Viviers** (allow €35 for dinner, closed Sun, 22 rue Alphonse Karr, 5-min walk west of avenue Jean Médecin, tel. 04 93 16 00 48, make sure to reserve for the *bistrot*, not their classier restaurant next door). **Lulu's Cantine** is a fine value, wonderfully small, charming, and

Czech-owned, with homemade recipes from Nice to Prague (26 rue Alberti, tel. 04 93 62 15 33). Wine-lovers will swoon for a table at **La Part des Anges**, a wine shop with a few tables in the rear serving a limited, mouthwatering menu with a large selection of wines (open daily for lunch, Fri–Sat only for dinner, reserve ahead, 17 rue Gubernatis, tel. 04 93 62 69 80).

Several relaxed cafés line the broad sidewalk on rue Biscarra, just east of avenue Jean Médecin behind Nice Etoile. **L'Authentic**, **Le Vin sur Vin**, and **Le Cenac** are all reasonable, though L'Authentic is best. One block away, friendly **Lou Mourleco** insists on serving only what's fresh, so the menu changes constantly at this more traditional Niçoise establishment (15 rue Biscarra, tel. 04 93 80 80 11). On the other side of avenue Jean Médecin, **Le Côte Grill** is bright, cool, and easy, with a salad bar, air-conditioned rooms, a large selection at reasonable prices, and a friendly staff (1 avenue Georges Clemenceau, tel. 04 93 82 45 53).

Transportation Connections—Nice

By train to: Arles (11/day, 3.5 hrs, 10 with change in Marseille), **Paris'** Gare de Lyon (14/day, 5.5–7 hrs, 6 with change in Marseille), **Venice** (3/day, 3/night, 11–15 hrs, 5 require changes), **Chamonix** (4/day, 11 hrs, 2–3 changes), **Beaune** (7/day, 7 hrs, change in Lyon), **Digne/Grenoble** (consider the scenic little trains that run from Nice to Digne, then on to Grenoble; see "Travel Notes on Connecting Nice and the Alps" at end of this chapter), **Munich** (2/day, 12 hrs with 2 changes, 1 night train with a change in Verona), **Interlaken** (1/day, 12 hrs), **Florence** (4/day, 7 hrs, changes in Pisa and/or Genoa, night train), **Milan** (4/day, 5–6 hrs, 3 with changes), **Venice** (4/day, 8 hrs, 2 changes required or a direct night train), **Barcelona** (3/day, 11 hrs, long change in Montpellier, or a direct night train).

By plane to: Paris (hrly, 1 hr, about same price as train ticket).

VILLEFRANCHE-SUR-MER

Come here for upscale, small-town Mediterranean atmosphere. Villefranche (between Nice and Monte Carlo, with frequent 15-min buses and trains to both) is quieter and more exotic than Nice. Narrow cobbled streets stumble into the mellow waterfront, a scenic walkway below the castle leads to the hidden port, and luxury yachts glisten in the harbor. Almost-sandy beaches, a handful of interesting sights, and quick access to Cap Ferrat keep visitors just busy enough.

The **TI** is in the park François Binon, just below the main bus stop (July–Aug daily 9:00–19:00, Sept–June Mon–Sat 9:00–12:00 & 14:00–18:30, closed Sun, a 20-min walk or €8 taxi from

Villefranche-sur-Mer

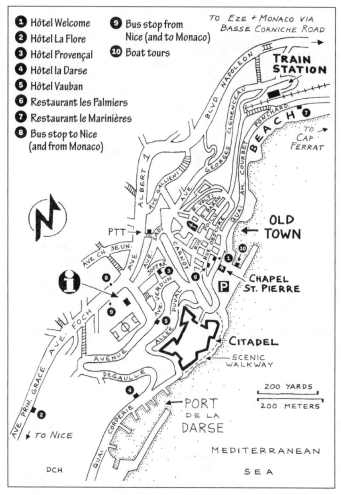

1 Hôtel Welcome
2 Hôtel La Flore
3 Hôtel Provençal
4 Hôtel la Darse
5 Hôtel Vauban
6 Restaurant les Palmiers
7 Restaurant le Marinières
8 Bus stop to Nice (and from Monaco)
9 Bus stop from Nice (and to Monaco)
10 Boat tours

TO EZE + MONACO VIA BASSE CORNICHE ROAD

TRAIN STATION

BEACH

TO CAP FERRAT

OLD TOWN

PTT

CHAPEL ST. PIERRE

CITADEL

SCENIC WALKWAY

200 YARDS
200 METERS

PORT DE LA DARSE

TO NICE

MEDITERRANEAN SEA

DCH

train station, tel. 04 93 01 73 68). Pick up the brochure detailing a self-guided walking tour of Villefranche and information on boat rides and the Rothschild Villa Ephrussi's gardens (see "Sights near Villefranche-sur-Mer," below).

The dramatic interior of **Chapel of St. Pierre**, decorated by Jean Cocteau, is the town's cultural highlight, but at €2 it's not worth it for many (daily 10:00–12:00 & 15:00–19:00, below Hôtel Welcome). **Boat rides** *(promenades en mer)* are offered several days a week (June–mid-Sept, €12, 2 hrs, across from Hôtel Welcome, tel. 04 93 76 65 65). Lively *boules* action takes place each evening just below the TI and the huge soccer field. Walk beyond the train station for views back to Villefranche and a quieter beach.

Even if you're sleeping elsewhere, consider an ice cream–licking village stroll. The last bus leaves Nice for Villefranche at about 19:45; the last bus from Villefranche to Nice leaves at about 21:00; and one train runs later (24:00). Beware of taxi drivers who overcharge—the normal weekday, daytime rate to central Nice is about €28; to the airport, figure about €45 (tel. 06 09 33 36 12).

Sleeping in Villefranche-sur-Mer
(€1 = about $1, country code: 33, zip code: 06230)
There's precious little middle ground here. Hotels tend to be either linoleum-floor cheap or million-dollar-view expensive.

HIGHER PRICED
Hôtel Welcome*** is buried in the heart of the old city, right on the water, with most of the 32 rooms overlooking the harbor. You'll pay top price for all the comforts in a very sharp, professional hotel that seems to do everything right and couldn't be better located—ask about the new wine bar ("comfort" Db with balcony-€135–155, superior Db with view and balcony-€155–175, extra person-€35, CC, air-con, garage parking €16, 1 quai Courbet, tel. 04 93 76 27 62, fax 04 93 76 27 66, www.welcomehotel.com).

MODERATELY PRICED
The rooms at both Hôtel La Flore and Hôtel Welcome, while different in cost, are about the same in comfort. La Flore has a pool and free parking, Welcome is on the harbor. If your idea of sightseeing is to enjoy the view from your bedroom deck, the dining room, or the pool, stay at **Hôtel La Flore*****, where most rooms have unbeatable views. These prices drop about 10 to 15 percent from October through March (Db no view-€84, Db view-€116, Db view and deck-€130, extra person-€32, Qb loft with huge terrace-€190, CC, air-con, free parking, fine restaurant, elevator, just off main road high above harbor, 5 boulevard Princess Grace de Monaco, 2 blocks from TI toward Nice, tel. 04 93 76 30 30, fax 04 93 76 99 99, www.hotel-la-flore.fr, e-mail: hotel-la-flore@wanadoo.fr, SE).

Hôtel Provençal** needs a facelift, but offers air-conditioning, fine views, and nifty balconies from well-worn rooms with awful furniture (Db-€63–92, Tb-€73–85, extra bed-€9, 10 percent off with this book and a 2-night stay, CC, skip cheaper no-view rooms, a block from TI at 4 avenue Maréchal Joffre, tel. 04 93 76 53 53, fax 04 93 76 96 00, e-mail: provencal@riviera.fr).

LOWER PRICED
Hôtel la Darse**, an appealing and unassuming little hotel sitting in the shadow of its highbrow brothers, offers a low-key alternative right on the water in Villefranche's old port. The rooms are quiet and simple, though the owners have big plans to renovate the hotel and add an elevator. Rooms facing the sea have great view balconies (Db-€47–55, Db view-€58–68, extra person-€10, CC, from TI walk or drive down avenue General de Gaulle to the old Port de la Darse, tel. 04 93 01 72 54, fax 04 93 01 84 37, e-mail: hoteldeladarse@wanadoo.fr, friendly Paola SE).

Hôtel Vauban*, two blocks down from the TI, is a curious and basic place with homey, red-velvet decor, and a few cheery, simple rooms (Db-€45, Db with view-€65, no CC, 11 avenue General De Gaulle, tel. 04 93 76 62 18, no fax, e-what?, NSE).

Eating in Villefranche-sur-Mer

Pickings are slim in this land of high rollers. The places lining the port are expensive and vary in quality; less expensive places are off the port. For a relaxed dinner (pizza, crêpes, and salads), try **Les Palmiers**, just above Hôtel Welcome. To eat well, spring for dinner at **Hôtel La Flore** (allow €28–46, see "Sleeping in Villefranche-sur-Mer," above). For a cool view and good-enough food at reasonable prices, consider **Restaurant les Marinières,** on the beach below the train station (salads and à la carte, open daily, tel. 04 93 01 76 06).

Sights near Villefranche-sur-Mer

Cap Ferrat—This is the peninsula you're staring at across the bay from Villefranche. An exclusive, largely residential community, it's just off the Nice–Monaco route and receives less traffic than other towns. Drive, bus, or walk here from Villefranche to visit the extravagant gardens of **Rothschild Villa Ephrussi**, offering stunning views east to Villefranche and west toward Monaco. You will see seven lush, varied gardens and several lavishly decorated rooms (€8, €2.50 for English tours generally between 11:00 and 14:00, Feb–Oct daily 10:00–18:00, until 19:00 in July–Aug, Nov–Jan Mon–Fri 14:00–18:00, Sat–Sun 10:00–18:00, tel. 04 93 01 45 90). From Villefranche, it's a scenic 50-minute walk around the bay past the train station or 10 minutes by bus #111. A few kilometers beyond sits the sophisticated port-village of St. Jean Cap Ferrat, offering more yachts, boardwalks, views, and boutiques in a less frenzied atmosphere.

▲**Eze Village**—Floating high above the sea, flowery Eze Village (don't confuse it with the seafront town of Eze Bord de la Mer) mixes perfume outlets, upscale boutiques, steep cobbled lanes, and magnificent views. About 15 minutes east of Villefranche on the *Moyenne Corniche* (6 buses/day from Nice, 25 min), this medieval hill town makes a handy stop between Nice and Monaco. Drop in on the Fragonard or Gallimard perfume outlets to learn about the interesting fabrication process and shop the fragrant collections (both daily 8:30–18:00, Gallimard breaks for lunch 12:00–14:00). Pull up a pew in Eze's charming church (Eglise Paroissial), but skip the Jardins Exotiques (exotic gardens). For a panoramic view and ideal picnic perch (they say on a clear day, you can see Corsica), walk up to the hill town from the parking lot, take a left at the top of the first hill, following the sign to Eze Bord de la Mer, and walk 30 steps down a dirt path. Come for sunset and stay for dinner to enjoy a more peaceful Eze. You'll dine well at the stone-cozy **Le Troubador** (€30 *menu*, closed Sun–Mon, 4 rue de Brec, tel. 04 93 41 19 03), and for less at the more basic **Nid de L'Aigle** (Eagle's Nest, tel. 04 93 41 19 08), which offers better views.

▲**La Turbie**—High above Monaco lies one of this region's most dramatic panoramas. Take a bus from Nice or Monaco, or drive the *Grande Corniche* to La Turbie (10 min east above Eze Village). Turn right at La Regence Café in La Turbie to find the viewpoint. It costs €4 to enter the grounds and climb *La Trophée des Alpes*, the massive Roman monument erected to guard the Roman road and commemorate Caesar Augustus' conquering of the Alps. It's not worth the effort nor the money for most to enter the sight, since the free viewpoint at the parking turnaround is virtually as good. (If you do enter the sight, follow signs to Panorama for the best views and picnic-perfect benches.) The village of La Turbie is worth a wander and has plenty of cafés and restaurants. The view over Monaco is even greater after dark.

ANTIBES

Antibes may be busier than Villefranche, but it's infinitely more manageable than Nice. The old town's cluster of red-tiled roofs and twin medieval lookout towers rising above the blue Mediterranean is postcard-perfect. Come here for yachts, sandy beaches, an enjoyable old town, excellent hiking, and a great Picasso collection. Twenty-five minutes west of Nice by train (skip the 50-min bus), Antibes' glamorous port anchors Europe's most sumptuous yachts—boat-lovers are welcome to browse. The festive old town is charming in a sandy-sophisticated way and sits atop the ruins of the fourth-century B.C. Greek city of Antipolis. Unfortunately, hotels aren't a very good value here, so I prefer Antibes as a day trip.

Orientation

The old town lies between the port and boulevards Albert 1er and Robert Soleau. Place Nationale is the hub of activity in the old town. Lively rue Auberon connects the port and the old town. Stroll along the sea between the Picasso Museum and place Albert 1er (where boulevard Albert 1er meets the sea); the best beaches lie just beyond place Albert 1er, and the path is beautiful. Good play areas for children are on place des Martyrs de la Resistance (close to recommended Hôtel Relais du Postillon). Near the port in the old town, you'll find **Heidi's English Bookshop** (great selection, daily 10:00–19:00, 24 rue Auberon) and a **launderette** (14 rue Thuret).

Tourist Information: There are two TIs. The most convenient is located in the old town, just inside the walls from the port at 21 boulevard D'Aguilllons (Sept–May Mon–Fri only 10:00–18:00, June–Aug daily 8:30–21:00, tel. 04 93 34 65 65). The main *Maison de Tourisme* is in the newer city (July–Aug Mon–Sat 9:00–19:00, Sun 9:00–13:00, Sept–June Mon–Sat 9:00–12:30 & 14:00–18:30, closed Sun, located just east of the old town where boulevard Albert 1er and rue de République meet at 11 place de Gaulle, tel. 04 92 90 53 00). At either TI, pick up the excellent city map, the interesting walking tour of old Antibes brochure (in English), and get details on the hikes described below. The Nice TI has Antibes maps; plan ahead.

Arrival in Antibes

By Train: To get to the port (5-min walk), cross the street right in front of the station and follow avenue de la Liberatión downhill. To reach the main TI in the modern city (15-min walk), exit right from the station on avenue Soleau; follow *Maison du Tourisme* signs to place de Gaulle. A free minibus *(Minibus Gratuit)* circulates around Antibes from the train station and serves place Albert 1er, the old town, and the port (4/hr), or you can call a taxi (tel. 04 93 67 67 67).

By Bus: The bus station is on the edge of the old town on place Guynemer, a block below the TI.

By Car: Follow *Centre-ville*, *Vieux Port* signs and park near the old town walls, as close to the beach as you can (first half-hour is free, €3.70/3 hrs, or about €8/day). Enter the old town through the last arch on the right.

Sights—Antibes

Market Hall (Marché Provençal)—The daily market bustles under a 19th-century canopy and features flowers, produce, Provençal products, and beach accessories (in old town behind

Picasso Museum on cours Masséna, daily until 13:00, closed
Mon off-season). You'll also find antique/flea markets on place
Nationale and place Audiberti (next to the port) on Thursdays
and Saturdays (7:00–18:00).

▲▲**Musée Picasso (Château Grimaldi)**—Sitting serenely
where the old town meets the sea, this museum offers a remarkable collection of Picasso's work: paintings, sketches, and ceramics. Picasso, who lived and worked here in 1946, said if you
want to see work from his Antibes period, you'll have to do it in
Antibes. You'll understand why Picasso liked working here. Several photos of the artist make this already intimate museum more
so. In his famous *Joie de Vivre* (the museum's highlight), there's
a new love in Picasso's life, and he's feelin' groovy (€4.60, June–
Sept Tue–Sun 10:00–18:00, July–Aug until 20:00 on Wed and
Fri; Oct–May 10:00–12:00 & 14:00–18:00, closed Mon, tel.
04 92 90 54 20).

Musée d'Histoire et d'Archéologie—Featuring Greek, Roman,
and Etruscan odds and ends, this is the only place to get a sense
of this city's ancient roots. I liked the 2,000-year-old lead anchors
(€3, no English explanations, June–Sept 10:00–18:00, Oct–May
10:00–12:00 & 14:00–18:00, closed Mon, on the water between
Picasso Museum and place Albert 1er).

Fort Carré—This impressively situated citadel dates from 1487
and was the coast's last fortification before Italy. More importantly,
it protected Antibes from its two key rivals, Nice and Corsica,
until the late 1800s. You can tour the unusual four-pointed fort
that at its height held 200 soldiers. There's precious little to see
inside the fort, though the views from the top walkways are sensational, and for me, justify the time. Tours in English and French
depart every 30 minutes (€3 entry, includes tour, daily June–Sept
10:15–17:30, Oct–May closes at 16:00). Scenic footpaths link the
fort to the port along the sea. It's a 35-minute portside walk from
the old town to the fort (consider taking a taxi there and walking
back). By foot or car, follow avenue 11 Novembre around the port,
stay on the main road (walkers can follow path by sports fields),
then park on the beach just after the soccer field. A signed dirt
path leads to Le Fort Carré. Keep following green-lettered signs
to *Le Fort/Sens de la Visite*.

Beaches (Plages)—The best beaches stretch between Antibes'
port and Cap d'Antibes, and the very best (plages Salis and Ponteil)
are just south of Place Albert 1er. All are golden and sandy. Plage
Salis is busy in summer, but it's manageable, with snack stands
every 100 meters/330 feet and views to the old town. The closest
beach to the old town is at the port (plage de la Gravette) and
remains relatively calm in any season.

Antibes

- 1 Hotel Le Cameo
- 2 Auberge Provençale
- 3 Hotel Relais du Postillon
- 4 Hotel Mas Djoliba
- 5 Hotel Beau Site
- 6 Rest. Chez Juliette
- 7 Heidi's English Bookshop
- 8 Laundromat & Au Pied Dans le Plat rest.
- 9 Market Hall
- 10 Les Vieux Murs restaurant

Hikes and Day Trips from Antibes

From place Albert 1er (where boulevard Albert 1er meets the beach), there's a great view of plage Salis and Cap d'Antibes. That tower on the hill is your destination for the first walk described below. The longer hike along Cap d'Antibes begins on the next beach, just over that hill (see below).

▲**Chapelle et Phare de la Garoupe**—The chapel and lighthouse, a 20-minute uphill climb from the far end of plage Salis (follow Chemin du Calvaire up to lighthouse tower), offer magnificent views (best at sunset) over Juan les Pins, Antibes, the pre-Alps, and Nice. Roads allow car access.

Cap d'Antibes Hike (Sentier Touristique de Tirepoll/Sentier Littoral)—At the end of the mattress-ridden plage de la Garoupe (over the hill from lighthouse) is a well-maintained trail around Cap d'Antibes. The beautiful trail follows the rocky coast for about three kilometers/two miles, then heads inland. Take bus #2A from the bus station (2/hr, get return times) to the closest stop to the plage de la Garoupe, or drive to Hôtel Beau Site and walk 10 minutes down to plage de la Garoupe (parking available). The trail begins at the far right end of the beach. Allow two hours for the loop that ends at the recommended Hôtel Beau Site, or just walk as far as you'd like and then double back (use your Antibes map).

Day Trips from Antibes—Antibes is halfway between Nice and Cannes (easy train service to both), and close to the artsy pottery and glassblowing village of Biot, home of the Fernand Léger Museum (frequent buses, ask at TI). And while Cannes has much in common with its sister city, Beverly Hills, and little of interest for me, its beaches and the beachfront promenade are beautiful.

Sleeping in Antibes
(€1 = about $1, country code: 33, zip code: 06600)
Central pickings are slim here; most hotel owners seem more interested in their restaurants.

HIGHER PRICED
Mas Djoliba*** is a good splurge but best for drivers, since it's a 15-minute walk from the beach and old Antibes, and a 25-minute walk to the station. Reserve early for this tranquil, bird-chirping, flower-filled manor house where no two rooms are the same. Dinner (by the pool) is required from May to September (Db with breakfast and dinner-€67–85 per person, off-season Db-€76–107 for 2 people—room only; several good family rooms, breakfast-€8.50, CC, 29 avenue de Provence, from boulevard Albert 1er, turn right up avenue Gaston Bourgeois, tel. 04 93 34 02 48, fax 04 93 34 05 81, www.hotel-djoliba.com, e-mail: hotel.djoliba@wanadoo.fr).

MODERATELY PRICED
Auberge Provençale*, on charming place Nationale, has a popular restaurant and seven reasonably nice rooms (those on the square get all the noise, day and night), but nonexistent, couldn't-care-less management (Db-€63–85, Tb-€72–94, Qb-€108, CC, reception in restaurant, 61 place Nationale, tel. 04 93 34 13 24, fax 04 93 34 89 88). Their huge loft room, named "Celine," faces the back,

comes with a royal canopy bed and a dramatic open-timbered ceiling, and costs no more than the other rooms.

Hôtel Relais du Postillon**, on a thriving square, offers 15 small, tastefully designed rooms, accordion bathrooms, and helpful owners who take more pride in their well-respected restaurant (Db-€44–82, CC, *menus* from €32, 8 rue Championnet, tel. 04 93 34 20 77, fax 04 93 34 61 24, www.relais-postillon.com, SE).

Hôtel Beau Site***, my only listing on Cap d'Antibes and a 10-minute drive from the old town, is a good value if you want to get away, but not *too* far away. The friendly owners, nice pool, outdoor terrace, easy parking, and 30 pleasant rooms make it worthwhile (Db-€52–107, CC, 141 boulevard Kennedy, tel. 04 93 61 53 43, fax 04 93 67 78 16, www.hotelbeausite.net). From the hotel, it's a 10-minute walk down to the crowded plage de la Garoupe and a nearby hiking trail.

LOWER PRICED
Hôtel Le Cameo** is a rambling, refreshingly unaggressive old place above a bustling bar (what reception there is, you'll find in the bar). The public areas are dark, but its nine, very simple, linoleum-lined rooms are almost huggable. All open onto the charming place Nationale, which means you don't sleep until the restaurants close (Ds-€47, Db-€58, Ts-€55, Tb-€66, CC, 5 place Nationale, tel. 04 93 34 24 17, fax 04 93 34 35 80, NSE).

Eating in Antibes
Les Vieux Murs is the place to sample regional specialties (€40 *menu*, along ramparts beyond Picasso Museum at 25 promenade Admiral de Grasse, tel. 04 93 34 66 73).

Au Pied dans le Plat serves reliably good meals at fair prices in a pleasant setting (*menus* from €23, closed Mon, 6 rue Thuret, tel. 04 93 34 37 23).

The recommended hotels **Relais du Postillon** and **Auberge Provençale** offer well-respected cuisine (listed above).

Lively place Nationale is filled with tables and tourists (great ambience), while locals seem to prefer the restaurants along the market hall. Just off place Nationale, **Chez Juliette** offers budget meals (*menus* from €14, rue Sade).

Romantics and those on a budget should buy a picnic dinner and head for the beach.

MONACO
Still impressive despite overdevelopment, high prices, and wall-to-wall daytime tourists, Monaco will disappoint anyone looking for something below the surface. This glittering, two-square-

kilometer (.7 square miles) country is a tax haven for its minuscule full-time population (30,000, 83 percent foreigners), who pay no income tax, and is the kind of place you visit once and probably don't need to see again. France surrounds Monaco on all sides but the Mediterranean and provides Monaco's telephones (French phone cards work here), electricity, and water. About the only thing you'll use that's made locally is a stamp. Try to come at night, when the real Monaco steps out.

Orientation

Monaco (the principality) is best understood when separated into its three tourist areas: Monaco-Ville, Monte Carlo, and La Condamine (a fourth area, Fontvieille, is of no interest to tourists). Monaco-Ville, dangling on the rock high above, is the oldest section and houses Prince Rainier's palace and all sights except the casino; Monte Carlo is the area around the casino; and La Condamine (the port) divides the two. A bus ride on routes #1 or #2 links all areas (10/hr, €1.40, or €3.50 for 4 tickets). It's a 15-minute uphill walk from the port (and train station) to Prince Rainier's palace, 20 minutes to the casino, and a 40-minute down-and-up walk between the palace and the casino.

Tourist Information: There are several TIs. The main TI is near the casino (2 boulevard des Moulins), but the handiest one for most is in the train station; pick up a city map (daily 9:00–19:00, tel. 00-377/92 16 61 66). From June to September, you'll find information kiosks in the Monaco-Ville parking garage and on the port.

Telephone Tip: To call Monaco from France, dial 00, then 377 (Monaco's country code), and the eight-digit number. Within Monaco, simply dial the eight-digit number.

Arrival in Monaco

By Bus from Nice and Villefranche: Keep your receipt for the return ride (RCA buses run twice as often as Cars Broch). There are three stops in Monaco, in order from Nice: in front of a tunnel at the base of Monaco-Ville (place d'Armes), on the port, and below the casino (on avenue d'Ostende). The first stop is the best starting point. From there, you can walk up to Monaco-Ville and the palace (10 min straight up), or catch a local bus (lines #1 or #2); cross the street right in front of the tunnel and walk with the rock on your right—the bus stop and steps up to Monaco-Ville are 70 meters/230 feet away. The bus stop back to Nice is across the major road from your arrival point at the light. The last bus leaves Monaco for Nice at about 19:00 (the last train leaves about 23:30).

By Train from Nice: A dazzling but confusing new train station provides central access to Monaco. The TI, baggage check, and ticket windows are up the escalator at the end of the tracks.

Monaco

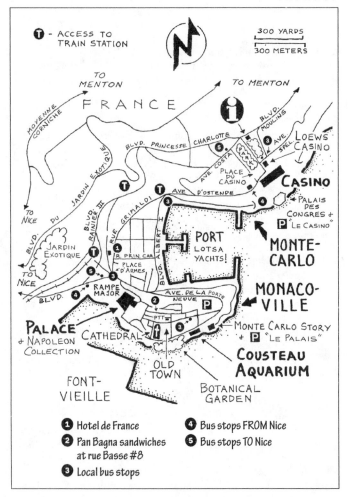

T - ACCESS TO TRAIN STATION

300 YARDS
300 METERS

TO MENTON

FRANCE

TO MENTON

MOYENNE CORNICHE

BLVD. PRINCESSE CHARLOTTE

BLVD. MOULINS

AVE. SPEL

LOEWS CASINO

AVE. COSTA

PLACE DU CASINO

CASINO

JARDIN EXOTIQUE

BLVD. RAINIER II

RUE GRIMALDI

AVE. D'OSTENDE

PALAIS DES CONGRES & P "LE CASINO"

TO NICE

BLVD. DU

BLVD. ALBERT I

PORT LOTSA YACHTS!

MONTE-CARLO

JARDIN EXOTIQUE

R. PRIN. CAR.

PLACE D'ARMES

MONACO-VILLE

TO NICE

RAMPE MAJOR

AVE. DE LA PORTE NEUVE

P

BLVD.

PTT

Monte Carlo Story & P "Le Palais"

PALACE & Napoleon Collection

CATHEDRAL

OLD TOWN

COUSTEAU AQUARIUM

FONT-VIEILLE

BOTANICAL GARDEN

❶ Hotel de France
❷ Pan Bagna sandwiches at rue Basse #8
❸ Local bus stops
❹ Bus stops FROM Nice
❺ Bus stops TO Nice

To reach Monaco-Ville, walk along the platform toward Nice following *Sortie la Condamine*, then *Access Port* signs. The stop for local buses is in front of the station exit. The port is a few blocks downhill, the casino is uphill along the left side of the port, and Monaco-Ville is uphill to the right of the port. The most direct route to the casino from the station is up the escalator from the platform, left past the TI, and up the elevator. Exit the station and turn left on boulevard Princesse Charlotte.

By Car: Driving here actually works, though you'll feel like you've completed your own Grand Prix by the time you park. Follow *Centre-ville* signs into Monaco, then be ready to follow the red-letter signs to *Le Casino* or *Le Palais*, which guide you to parking structures near the casino or under Monaco-Ville. You need to be a quick, agile driver to navigate the many curves. The first hour of parking is free; the next costs €2.80.

Sights—Monaco-Ville

Start with a look at Monaco-Ville from the square in front of the palace. To reach the palace square, you can catch bus #1 or #2 to place de la Visitatión, a five-minute walk away. Turn right when you exit the bus and continue straight down either of the streets that run from the end of the *place* (the street leaving the square on the left goes by the post office). If you're walking up from the port, you'll end up at the palace square. Now, find a seat overlooking the port for a *magnifique* view (particularly at night).

This little, pastel Hong Kong lookalike was born on this rock in 1215 and has managed to remain an independent country for most of its almost 800 years. A medieval castle sat where the palace is today, its strategic setting having a lot to do with Monaco's ability to resist attackers. They still **change guards** the old-fashioned way (11:55 daily, fun to watch but jam-packed). As you look back over the glitzy port, notice the faded green roof above and to the right—it's the casino that made Monaco famous (and rich). Since 1929, cars have raced around the port and in front of the casino in one of the world's most famous races, the Grand Prix of Monaco (May 23–26 in 2003).

Now walk to the statue of the monk grasping a sword near the palace. Meet François Grimaldi, a renegade Italian who captured Monaco dressed as a monk in 1297, and began the dynasty that still rules the principality. Prince Rainier is his great, great, great...grandson, making Monaco Europe's longest-lasting monarchy, and the only country where the ruler is not elected. Walk to the opposite side of the square and Louis XIV cannonballs. Down below is Monaco's newest area, Fontvieille, where much of its post–WWII growth has been. Prince Rainier has continued (some say, been obsessed with) Monaco's economic growth, creating landfills (such as Fontvieille), flashy ports, new beaches, and the new rail station. Today, thanks to Prince Rainier's efforts, tiny Monaco is a member of the United Nations. The current buzz is about how soon he'll hand over the reigns of the principality to his son, Albert.

Hungry? You'll find good *pan bagnat* and other sandwiches at 8 rue Basse, on the street leaving the square to the left. You can buy stamps (mail from here!) at the PTT, located a few blocks down rue Comte F. Gastaldi.

Palace—Automated and uninspired tours (in English) take you through part of the prince's lavish palace in 30 merciful minutes and yet still manage to describe every painting. The rooms are well-furnished and impressive, but interesting only if you haven't seen a château lately (€6 June–Sept daily 9:30–18:20, Oct 10:00–17:00, closed off-season).

Napoleon Collection—Napoleon occupied Monaco after the French Revolution. This is the prince's private collection of what Napoleon left behind: military medals, swords, guns, letters, and, most interesting, his hat. I found this collection more appealing than the palace (€4, June–Sept daily 9:30–18:30, Oct–May 10:00–17:00, next to palace entry).

Cathédrale de Monaco—This somber cathedral, built in 1878, is where Princess Grace is buried (near the left transept).

Jardins Botanique—Take in sensational views as you meander back to the bus stop through these immaculately maintained gardens (or pick up a *pan bagnat* sandwich in the old town and picnic here).

Cousteau Aquarium (Musée de l'Océanographique)— Inaugurated in 1910, this monumental building overhangs the Mediterranean. Its hugeness testifies to the oceanographic zeal of Prince Albert I. It can be jammed and sometimes disappoints, though kids love it (€11, ages 6–18-€5.35, April–Sept daily 9:00–19:00, until 20:00 July–Aug, March and Oct 9:30–19:00, Nov–Feb 10:00–18:00, CC, at opposite end of Monaco-Ville from palace, down the steps from Monaco-Ville bus stop).

Monte Carlo Story—This informative 35-minute film gives a helpful account (English headphones) of Monaco's history and offers a comfortable soft-chair break from all that walking (€6, usually on the hour 11:00–17:00 March–Oct, until 18:00 July–Aug, 14:00–17:00 only Nov–Feb, frequent extra showings for groups that you can join; from the Monte Carlo side of the aquarium, take the escalator into the parking garage, then take the elevator down and follow the signs, it's just past the café).

Leave Monaco-Ville and ride the shuttle bus (the stop is up the steps across from the aquarium) or stroll down through the pedestrian-pleasant port and up to Monte Carlo.

Sights—Monte Carlo

▲**Casino**—Stand in the park, above the traffic circle in front of the casino (opens at noon). In the mid-1800s, Prince Charles began an aggressive economic development plan to bail out Europe's poorest country. He built spas and a casino to lure a growing aristocratic class with leisure time. It worked. Today, Monaco has the world's highest per-capita income. The name Monte Carlo means "Charles' Hill" in Spanish (the Spanish were traditional protectors of Monaco and have 200 guards present today). The casino is designed to make the wealthy feel comfortable while losing money. Architect? Charles Garnier agreed to design this Casino/Opera House in 1878, in part to thank the prince for his financial help in completing the Paris Opéra, which he also designed. The central doors provide access to slot machines, private gaming rooms, and the Opera House. The private gaming rooms take up much of the left wing of the building.

Count the counts and Rolls-Royces in front of Hôtel de Paris (built at the same time), then strut inside past the slots and find the sumptuous atrium. This is the lobby for the Opera House; doors open only during performances. There's a model of the opera at the end of the room and marble WCs on the right. Anyone over 21 (even in shorts, if before 20:00) can get as far as the one-armed bandits (open at 12:00, push the button on the slot machines to claim your winnings), though you'll need decent attire to go any farther; and after 20:00, shorts are off-limits anywhere.

Cost and Hours: The first rooms, Salons Européens, open at 12:00 and cost €10 to enter. The glamorous private game rooms where you can rub elbows with high rollers open at 16:00, others not until 21:00, and cost an additional €10.

A tie and jacket are not necessary until evening, and can be rented at the bag check for €30 plus a €40 deposit. Dress standards for women are far more relaxed (only tennis shoes are a definite no-no). The scene is great at night and downright James Bond–like in the private rooms. The park behind the casino offers a peaceful café and a good view of the casino's rear facade and of Monaco-Ville. Entrance is free to all games in the new, plebeian, American-style Loews Casino, adjacent to the old casino.

The return bus stop to Nice is at the top of the park above the casino on avenue de la Costa. To return to the train station from the casino, walk up the parkway in front of the casino, turn left on boulevard des Moulins, right on impasse de la Fontaine, climb the steps, and turn left on boulevard Princesse Charlotte (the entrance to the train station is next to Parking de la Gare).

Near Monte Carlo: Menton

Grand, beautiful, and overlooked Menton is a peaceful and relaxing spa/beach town with a fine beachfront promenade and a sandy-cobbled old town (TI tel. 04 93 57 57 00). It's just a few minutes by train (8/day) from Monte Carlo or 40 minutes from Nice.

Sleeping and Eating in Monaco
(€1 = about $1, country code: 377)
Since Monaco is by far best after dark, consider sleeping here. The perfectly pleasant **Hôtel de France**** is reasonable (Sb-€67, Db-€85, includes breakfast, CC, 6 rue de la Turbie, near west exit from train station, tel. 00-377/93 30 24 64, fax 00-377/92 16 13 34, e-mail: hotel-france@monte-carlo.mc). Several cafés serve basic fare at reasonable prices (day and night) on the port, along the traffic-free rue Princesse Caroline.

INLAND HILL TOWNS OF THE RIVIERA
Some of France's most dramatic hill towns are ignored in this region more famous for its beaches and casinos. A short ride away from the Mediterranean reaps huge rewards: lush forests, spectacular canyons, and of course, hilltop villages to lose yourself in.
▲**Hill-Town Drive to the Gorges du Loup**—To lose the maddening crowds, connect these lost treasures: Start in Vence (if you're really early, you could try St. Paul-de-Vence), then drive to Tourrettes sur Loup, Pont du Loup, then follow signs leading into Gorges du Loup. Drive as far into the Gorges as you like, ideally go all the way to the pont de Bramafen, then loop back on the other side via the sky-high village of Gourdon, then on to adorable Le Bar sur Loup before returning to Nice. Allow all day for this loop with time to wander the villages. The round-trip drive from Nice without stops would take about two hours. Buses serve Vence and St. Paul-de-Vence from Nice, and Tourrettes sur Loup from Vence.
St. Paul (-de-Vence)—This most famous of Riviera hill towns has lost its appeal and is now an overrun and over-restored artist-shopping-mall. Wall-to-wall upscale galleries and ice cream shops compete for the attention of the hordes of day-trippers. Avoid visiting between 11:00 and 18:00 (I avoid it completely). If you must go, meander deep into St. Paul's quieter streets and wander far to enjoy the panoramic views (TI tel. 04 93 32 86 95).

The best reason by far to visit St. Paul is for the nearby, prestigious, and far-out Fondation Maeght's modern art collection. It's a steep (uphill) 15-minute walk from St. Paul (ask the bus driver for best stop). This engaging museum provides a good introduction to modern art. Its world-class contemporary art collection (with works by Léger, Miró, Calder, and Braque, among others) is beautifully arranged between pleasant gardens and well-lit rooms. Don't miss the chapel, designed by Georges Braque, or the frequent special exhibits (€8.50, daily July–Sept 10:00–19:00, Oct–June 10:00–12:30 & 14:30–18:00, tel. 04 93 32 81 63).
Vence—Vence disperses St. Paul's crowds over a larger and more

engaging city. The mountains are close and the breeze is fresh in this town that bubbles with work-a-day life and tourist activity (no boutique shortage here). Stroll the narrow lanes of the old town *(Cité Historique)*, look for informative wall plaques in English, enjoy a drink on a quiet square, and find the small cathedral with its Chagall mosaic. Outdoor markets thrive in the old town on Tuesdays and Fridays until 12:30, and daily on the massive place du Grand Jardin. Vence's **TI** is at 8 place du Grand Jardin (Mon–Sat 9:00–12:30 & 14:00–18:00, closed Sun, July–Aug Mon–Sat 9:00–19:00, Sun 9:00–13:00, tel. 04 93 58 06 38). The bus stop for Nice and St. Paul is next to the TI (schedules are posted in the window). If arriving by car, follow *Cité Historique* signs and park on place de Grand Jardin.

Matisse's much-raved-about **Chapelle du Rosaire** may disappoint all but his fans, for whom this is a rich and rewarding pilgrimage (an easy 20-min walk from Vence TI, turn right out of TI and walk down avenue Henri Isnare, then right on avenue de Provence, following signs to St. Jeannet). The yellow, blue, and green-filtered sunlight does a cheery dance across the simple tile sketches (€2.50, Tue and Thu 10:00–11:30 & 14:00–17:30, Mon and Wed 14:00–17:30; Mass is Sun at 10:00 followed by tour of chapel, closed Nov, tel. 04 93 58 03 26).

Sleeping and Eating in Vence (zip code: 06140): If Vence tempts you to stay, consider the little **Auberge des Seigneurs****, a short walk from the bus stop and TI (turn left out of TI then left again after a block); it's filled with character (spacious Db-€60–67, CC, no elevator, place du Frene, tel. 04 93 58 04 24, fax 04 93 24 08 01). **Hôtel la Villa Roseraie*****, an oasis with a pool, lovely garden, and carefully decorated rooms, is on the fringe of the city on the road to Col de Vence (Db-€67–133, CC, parking, easy walk to Matisse's chapel and a 15-min walk to TI, 128 avenue Henri Giraud, tel. 04 93 58 02 20, fax 04 93 58 99 31, e-mail: rvilla5536@aol.fr). **La Pecheur de Soleil Pizzeria** offers inexpensive meals on a quiet square (1 place Godeau, tel. 04 93 58 32 56). **Auberge des Seigneurs** is a cozy place for a good dinner *(menus* from €27, recommended above, closed Mon).

Tourrettes sur Loup—This impressively situated hill town is hemmed in by forests and looks ready to slide down its steep hill. Here, you'll find more arts and crafts, but fewer tourists. Known as the "Village Violette," Tourrettes produces more violets than anywhere else in France. You'll find great views of Tourrettes as you drive to Pont du Loup.

Le Bar sur Loup—The most peaceful and least invaded of these inland hill towns, medieval Bar huddles around its castle and Gothic church. Here, you can relax and truly smell the flowers.

Travel Notes on Connecting Nice and the Alps—La Route Napoléon

After getting bored in his toy Elba empire, Napoleon gathered his entourage, landed on the Riviera, bared his breast, and told his fellow Frenchmen, "Strike me down or follow me." France followed. But just in case, he took the high road, returning to Paris along the route known today as La Route Napoléon. (Waterloo followed shortly afterward.)

By Car: The route between the Riviera and the Alps is beautiful (from south to north, follow Digne, Sisteron, and Grenoble). An assortment of pleasant villages with inexpensive hotels lies on this route, making an overnight easy. Little Entrevaux feels forgotten and still stuck in its medieval shell. Cross the bridge, meet someone friendly, and consider the steep hike up to the citadel (€1.50). Sisteron's Romanesque church and view from the citadel above make this town worth a quick leg stretch. If a night in this area appeals, stay farther north, surrounded by mountains. **Hôtel Ferrat****, near the tiny hamlet of Clelles, is a simple, family-run mountain hacienda at the base of Mont Aiguille (after which Gibraltar was modeled) and is a good place to break this long drive. Enjoy your own *boules* court, swimming pool, and good restaurant (Db-€43–58, CC, 38930 Clelles, tel. 04 76 34 42 70, fax 04 76 34 47 47).

By Train: Leave the tourists behind and take the scenic train-bus-train combination that runs between Nice, Digne, and Grenoble through canyons, along white-water rivers, between snow-capped peaks, and through many tempting villages. Start with a 9:00 departure from Nice on the little *Chemins de Fer de Provence* train to Digne (€17, 25 percent discount with railpass, 4/day, 3 hrs, departs from Gare du Sud station, about 10 blocks behind Nice's main station, 4 rue Alfred Binet, tel. 04 97 03 80 80). In Digne, you can catch a main-line train (covered by railpasses) to other destinations; or, better, catch the bus (quick transfer, free with railpass) to Veynes (6/day, 90 min) where you can then catch the most scenic two-car train to Grenoble (5/day, 2 hrs). From Grenoble, connections are available to many destinations. To do the entire trip from Nice to Grenoble in one day, you must start with the 9:00 departure from Nice (arrives Grenoble about 18:00), but I'd spend the night in one of the tiny villages en route. Clelles has the best hotel, but Sisteron and Entrevaux are also interesting (see "By Car," above).

THE FRENCH ALPS
(ALPES-SAVOIE)

Savoie, home to Europe's highest mountains, is the top floor of the
French Alps (the lower Alpes-Dauphiné lie to the south). More than
just a pretty face, stubborn Savoie maintained its independence from
France until 1860, when peaks became targets, rather than obstacles
for tourists. Its borders once extended down to the Riviera and across
the Rhône Valley. Home to skier Jean-Claude Killy and the first
winter Olympics, today's Savoie is France's mountain-sports capital,
with 15,771-foot Mont Blanc as its centerpiece. Savoie feels more
Swiss than French.

The scenery is simply spectacular. Serenely self-confident
Annecy is a picture-perfect blend of natural and man-made beauty.
In Chamonix, it's just you and Madame Nature—there's not a
museum or important building in sight. If the weather's right, take
Europe's ultimate cable-car ride to the 3,780-meter/12,600-foot
Aiguille du Midi in Chamonix.

Planning Your Time
Surrounded by mountains, lakefront Annecy has boats, bikes,
hikes, arcaded walking streets, and good transportation connections (most trains to Chamonix pass through Annecy, making it
a convenient stopover). But if you're pressed for time and antsy
for Alps, go straight to Chamonix. Here, you can skip along alpine
ridges, stroll tranquil river paths, zip down the mountain on a
wheeled bobsled, or rent a mountain bike. Plan a minimum of
two nights and one day in Chamonix, and try to work in a night
or two in Annecy. Since weather is everything, get the forecast
by calling ahead (tel. 08 92 68 02 74) and, if it looks good, get
thee to Chamonix; if it's gloomy, Annecy offers more to do. Both
Chamonix and Annecy are overwhelmed with tourists in summer.

The French Alps

(If you're driving or training from here to the Riviera, see "La Route Napoléon" tips at the end of the previous chapter.)

Getting around the Alps

Annecy and Chamonix are well-connected by trains. Buses run from Chamonix to nearby villages, and the Aiguille du Midi lift takes travelers from Chamonix to Italy over Europe's most scenic border crossing.

Cuisine Scene—Savoie

Savoie cuisine is mountain-hearty. Its Swiss-similar specialties include *fondue savoyarde* (melted Beaufort and Comté cheeses and local white wine, sometimes with a dash of cognac), raclette (chunks of semi-melted cheese served with potatoes, pickles, sausage, and bread), *tartiflettes* (hearty scalloped potatoes with melted cheese), *poulet de Bresse* (the best chicken in France), *morteau* (smoked pork sausage), *gratin savoyarde* (a potato dish with cream, cheese, and garlic), and fresh fish. Local cheeses are Morbier (look for a charcoal streak down the middle), Comté (like Gruyère), Beaufort (aged for 2 years, hard and strong), Reblochon (mild and creamy), and Tomme de Savoie (mild and semi-hard). Evian water comes from Savoie, as does Chartreuse liqueur. Aprémont and Crépy are two of the area's surprisingly good white wines. The local beer, Baton de Feu, is more robust than other French beers.

Remember, restaurants serve only during lunch (11:30–14:00) and dinner (19:00–21:00, later in bigger cities); cafés serve food throughout the day.

ANNECY

There's something for everyone in this lakefront resort city that knows how to be popular: mountain views, flowery cobbled lanes and canals, a château, and swimming in—or boating on—the crystal-clear lake. Sophisticated Annecy (pron. ahn-see) is France's answer to Switzerland's Lucerne, and, while you may not have glaciers knocking at your door as in nearby Chamonix, the distant peaks make a beautiful picture with Annecy's lakefront setting. Annecy has a few museums, but don't kid yourself—you're here for its lovely setting and strollable streets.

Orientation

Modern Annecy sprawls for kilometers, but we're interested only in its compact old town tucked back in the southwest corner of the lake. The old town is bounded by the château to the south, the TI and rue Royale to the north, rue de la Gare to the west, and, above all, the lake to the east.

Tourist Information: The TI is a few blocks from the old town across from the big grass field in the brown-and-glass Bonlieu shopping center (daily in summer 9:00–18:30, off-season 9:00–12:30 & 13:45–18:00, 1 rue Jean Jaures, tel. 04 50 45 00 33, www.lakeannecy.com). Get a city map, the *Vieil Annecy* walking tour brochure, the map of the lake showing the bike trail, and, if you're spending a few days, the helpful *Annecy Guide* has everything a traveler needs to know. You'll also find TIs in virtually every village on the lake: Talloires, Menthon-St. Bernard, Veyrier du Lac, Bout du Lac, St. Jorioz, and Sevrier.

Arrival in Annecy

By Train: To reach the old town and TI, leave the station (baggage check available), veering left at street level, and walk by Hôtel des Alpes along rue de la Poste. Turn left on rue Royale, which leads to the TI.

By Car: Annecy is a traffic mess. Avoid most of the snarls by taking the Annecy Sud exit from the autoroute and following Albertville signs. Upon entering Annecy, either turn left at the roundabout below the hospital for the city center and TI (free parking lot across from hospital or use Hôtel de Ville's parking structure—€1.50/hr—after the roundabout) or follow *Château* signs to park free above the old town at Annecy's château (but this lot is often full). Don't follow signs for Annecy-le-Vieux; it's another town entirely.

Helpful Hints

Launderette: It's at the western edge of the old town where rue de la Gare meets rue Faubourg des Balmettes (daily 7:00–21:00, 4 rue Faubourg des Balmettes).

Internet Access: L'Emailerie serves drinks and has American keyboards, high-speed connections, and a digital camera you can use for free (daily 10:00–20:00, across from recommended Vivaldi restaurant on faubourg des Annociades).

Sights—Annecy

Strolling—The canals and arcaded streets of this handsome old town are made for ambling. The TI's *Vieil Annecy* brochure describes a good walking tour with worthwhile historic informa-tion (you'll pass the next 2 sights described below). Wander deep past luscious ice-cream shops and waterfront cafés. A thriving outdoor market occupies most of the old-town center on Tues-day, Friday, and Sunday mornings.

Museum of Annecy (Palais de l'Ile)—Once a prison, this museum cuts like the prow of a ship through the canal, but is not worth your time or money.

Château Museum (Musée-Château d'Annecy)—This mildly interesting museum mixes local folklore, anthropology, natural history, and modern and fine arts with great views over the lake and city (€4.60, June–Sept Wed–Mon 10:30–18:00, closed Tue; Oct–May Wed–Mon 10:00–12:00 & 14:00–18:00, closed Tue).

▲**Boating**—Rent a paddleboat equipped with a slide (€8/30 min, €12/hr) or a motorboat (€22/30 min, €37/hr) and tool around the lake. It's incredibly clear and warmer than you'd think.

You can also let a one-hour cruise do the work for you (€10–12, 7 departures/day April–Sept, 18/day in summer, Compagnie des Bateaux du Lac Annecy, on lake behind Hôtel de Ville, tel. 04 50 51 08 40, www.annecy-croisieres.com). Get schedules and prices at the TI or at the boat dock right on the lake where the canal meets the old town. Their *Omnibus* boat connects villages along the lake with Annecy, but only three times a day.

Annecy

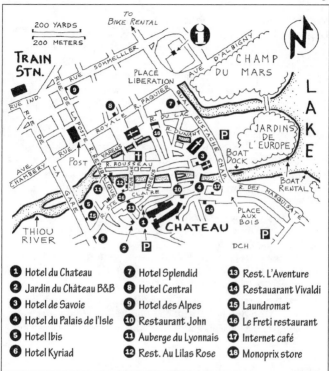

1 Hotel du Chateau
2 Jardin du Château B&B
3 Hotel de Savoie
4 Hotel du Palais de l'Isle
5 Hotel Ibis
6 Hotel Kyriad
7 Hotel Splendid
8 Hotel Central
9 Hotel des Alpes
10 Restaurant John
11 Auberge du Lyonnais
12 Rest. Au Lilas Rose
13 Rest. L'Aventure
14 Restauarant Vivaldi
15 Laundromat
16 Le Freti restaurant
17 Internet café
18 Monoprix store

For a rewarding full-day excursion, take the 10:30 boat to **Menthon-St. Bernard**, hike 2.5 hours to lovely **Talloires,** then catch the boat back to Annecy. From the boat dock in Menthon-St. Bernard, walk to the right along the shore toward the large palace and follow the signposts for Roc de Chère. The path leads over the Roc, passing the Golf de Talloires. Wear good shoes—the stretch into Talloires drops steeply. Cross Talloires to the port and beach (swim and lunch there) and catch the 15:00 boat back to Annecy to arrive about 16:15.

▲**Biking and In-Line Skating**—A bike trail *(piste cyclable)* runs along the entire west side of the lake (TI has free map and list of bike rental shops; Little Big Shop rents bikes and in-line skates, 80 rue Carnot, tel. & fax 04 50 67 42 13). The small village of Duingt is 12 level kilometers/7 miles away and makes a good destination. Consider riding to Duingt and taking the *Omnibus* boat back (€5, 3 departures/day, 45 min, bikes allowed). Leave Annecy on main road N508 (busy road, but there is a bike lane); after entering the town of Sevrier, you'll see a sign for the *Piste Cyclable* to the left. Follow it along the lake to Duingt.

Driving—For the best car-accessible views overlooking Annecy, drive 20 kilometers/12.5 miles to Col de la Forclaz (1,100 meters/ 3,600 feet, restaurants with view terraces). Take D-508 south along the lake past Duingt and turn left on D-42 a few minutes after leaving the lake (allow 45 min one-way with traffic). This also ties in easily with the scenic route to Chamonix via N-508.

Sleeping in Annecy
(€1 = about $1, country code: 33, zip code: 74000)

Sleep Code: **S** = Single, **D** = Double/Twin, **T** = Triple, **Q** = Quad, **b** = bathroom, **s** = shower only, **CC** = Credit Cards accepted, **no CC** = Credit Cards not accepted, **SE** = Speaks English, **NSE** = No English, * = French hotel rating system (0–4 stars).

To help you sort easily through these listings, I've divided the rooms into three categories based on the price for a standard double room with bath:

Higher Priced—Most rooms more than €100.
Moderately Priced—Most rooms €100 or less.
Lower Priced—Most rooms €65 or less.

Reserve ahead, particularly in summer and during holiday weekends. Most hotels can help you find free overnight parking.

Hôtel du Château and Jardin du Château Bed & Breakfast lie just below the château (free parking at château) up rampe du Château from the old town. The rest of my listings are in the pedestrian-friendly center and tend to be noisier (ask about parking deals).

HIGHER PRICED

Hôtel Splendid*** offers all the comforts, though little personality, on Annecy's busiest street, across from the TI. It makes a striking impression, with its almost-lakefront location and grand facade (Sb-€85–95, Db-€95–105, breakfast buffet-€12, CC, air-con, big beds, some non-smoking rooms, 4 quai Eustache Chappuis, tel. 04 50 45 20 00, fax 04 50 45 52 23, www.splendidhotel.fr).

MODERATELY PRICED

At **Jardin du Château Bed & Breakfast**, friendly Anne-Marie and Jean-Paul have created the ultimate urban refuge at their chalet *chambre d'hôte*, with a small garden and eight modern yet cozy rooms, all with kitchenettes and some with views and balconies (Db-€60–85, great family rooms-€85–105, no CC, bike rental, open May–Oct, closed Nov–April, 1 place du Château, tel. & fax 04 50 45 72 28, e-mail: jardinduchateau@wanadoo.fr, SE).

Hôtel Ibis** is a good if sterile option, with tight and tidy rooms and easy parking underneath. It's well-situated on a modern square in the old town, a few blocks from the train station (Db-€55–74, breakfast-€5.50, CC, elevator, 12 rue de la Gare, tel. 04 50 45 43 21, fax 04 50 52 81 08, e-mail: hO538@accor-hotels.com).

Hôtel du Palais de l'Isle*** is romantically located in the thick of the old town, with comfortable, ultramodern rooms (Db-€69–91, extra bed-€10, breakfast-€8.30, CC, air-con in some rooms, elevator, 13 rue Perriere, tel. 04 50 45 86 87, fax 04 50 51 87 15, www .hoteldupalaisdelisle.com, e-mail: palisle@wanadoo.fr).

LOWER PRICED

Hôtel du Château**, just below the Jardin du Château, has bright, spotless rooms, some with views; sharp bathrooms, all with showers; precious few parking spots (free, first come); and a cool view terrace (Sb-€45, Db-€51–57, Tb-€58, Qb-€71, CC, no elevator, 16 rampe du Château, tel. 04 50 45 27 66, fax 04 50 52 75 26, e-mail: hotelduchateau@fnac.net, SE).

Hôtel de Savoie**, located on the canal a block from the lake and run by charming Madame Lavorel, has character and a few view rooms (Db without view-€51–61, Db with canal view-€61–80, extra person-€8, CC, no elevator, place St. François, tel. 04 50 45 15 45, fax 04 50 45 11 99).

Hôtel Kyriad**, a few doors down from Hôtel Ibis, is a good hotel-chain option. It's surprisingly cozy, with comfortable and well-designed rooms (Db-€58, CC, air-con, no elevator, 1 faubourg des Balmettes, tel. 04 50 45 04 12, fax 04 50 45 90 92, www.annecy-hotel-kyriad.com).

Hôtel Central* is just that, and also simple, homey, and welcoming. It's on a quieter courtyard off a big pedestrian street (Ds-€35, Db-€40, extra person-€6, CC, no elevator, 6 bis rue Royale, tel. 04 50 45 05 37, fax 04 50 51 80 19, informal owner Stefan SE, e-mail: stefanpicollet@hotmail.com).

Hôtel des Alpes**, with a serious owner and immaculate, comfortable, and bright rooms, is to the left across from the train station at a busy intersection (Sb-€42, Db-€50–60, Tb-€57, Qb-€64, CC, no elevator, 12 rue de la Poste, tel. 04 50 45 04 56, fax 04 50 45 12 38).

Eating in Annecy

All of these places are in the old town. **Restaurant John** specializes in tasty regional cuisine at fair prices (€17.50 *menu*, closed Tue and Thu, at the foot of rampe du Château, 10 rue Perriere, tel. 04 50 51 36 15). Locals flock to **Le Freti** for mouthwatering fondue, raclette, or anything with cheese in it (walk through door at 12 rue Ste. Claire, it's on first floor, tel. 04 50 51 29 52). **Auberge du Lyonnais,** which sprawls along the canal with scenic outdoor tables, is a well-respected and classy place for Savoyard fare (*menus* from €27.50, daily, 9 rue de la République). **Au Lilas Rose** is a funky, fine little place for inexpensive fondue (daily, on canal at passage de l'Evêché, tel. 04 50 45 37 08). If the local food seems too cheesy, **L'Aventure** specializes in excellent southwestern French cuisine (closed Wed, 33 rue Ste. Claire, tel. 04 50 45 45 05, friendly Bannes SE).

Picnics: Look for the **Monoprix** department store at the corner of rue du Lac and rue Notre-Dame (Mon–Sat 8:30–19:30, closed Sun, food on first floor).

Transportation Connections—Annecy
By train to: Chamonix (8/day, 2.5 hrs, change in St. Gervais), **Beaune** (9/day, 5 hrs, change in Lyon), **Nice** (8/day, 7–9 hrs, change in Lyon or Valence), **Paris'** Gare de Lyon (11/day, 4–5 hrs, many with change in Lyon, night train).

CHAMONIX
Hemmed in by snow-capped peaks, churning with mountain lifts, and crisscrossed with hiking trails, the resort of Chamonix (pron. shah-moh-nee) is France's best base for alpine exploration. Officially called Chamonix-Mt. Blanc, it's the largest of five villages at the base of Mont Blanc. Chamonix's purpose in life has always been to accommodate visitors with some of Europe's top alpine thrills—it's super-busy in the summer and on winter holidays, but peaceful at other times. Chamonix's sister city is Aspen.

Planning Your Time
Ride the lifts early (crowds and clouds roll in later in the morning) and save your afternoons for lower altitudes. If you have one sunny day, spend it this way: Start with the Aiguille du Midi lift (go as early as you can, reservations possible), take it all the way to Hellbronner (hang around the needle longer if you can't get to Hellbronner), double back to Plan de l'Aiguille, hike to Montenvers and the Mer de Glace (snow level permitting), and train down from there. If the weather disappoints or the snow line's too low, hike the Petit Balcon Sud trail.

Orientation
Eternally white Mont Blanc is Chamonix's southeastern limit; the Aiguilles Rouges mountains form the northwestern limit. The frothy Arve River splits Chamonix in two. The small pedestrian zone, just west of the river, and rues du Docteur Paccard

Chamonix Valley Overview

① GRAND BALCON NORD - BEST HIKE!
② GRAND BALCON SUD - GREAT HIKE
③ PETIT BALCON SUD - GOOD HIKE
④ LAC BLANC - GREAT HIKE
⑤ ARVE RIVERBANK STROLL

and Joseph Vallot make up Chamonix's core. The TI is west of the river, just above the pedestrian zone, while the train station is east of the river.

Tourist Information: Pick up the town and valley map and consider the €4 hiking map called *Carte des Sentiers* (see "Chamonix Area Hikes," below). Ask for hours of lifts (important), biking information, and help with hotel reservations. Weather forecasts are posted near the door (July–Aug daily 8:30–19:00, Sept–June daily 9:00–12:30 & 14:00–18:30, on place du Triangle de l'Amitié, next to Hôtel Mont Blanc, 1 block above pedestrian zone, tel. 04 50 53 00 24, fax 04 50 53 58 90, www.chamonix.com).

Chamonix Quick History

1786—Messieurs Balmot and Paccard are the first to climb Mont Blanc

1818—First ascent of Aiguille du Midi

1860—After a visit by Louis Napoleon, the trickle of nature-loving visitors to Chamonix turns to a gush

1924—First winter Olympics held in Chamonix
1955—Aiguille du Midi *téléphérique* opens to tourists
2003—Your visit

Arrival in Chamonix

By Train: Walk straight out of the station (bag check available) and up avenue Michel Croz. In three blocks, you'll hit the center; turn left at the big clock, then right for the TI.

By Car: For most of my hotels and the TI, take the Chamonix Nord turnoff (second exit coming from Annecy) and park in the lot adjacent to the large traffic circle near Hôtel Alpina or at your hotel. To reach the hotels I list for drivers, take Chamonix Sud exit (first exit). Most parking is metered, though your hotel can direct you to free parking.

The Mont Blanc tunnel that connects Chamonix with Italy is finally open after a devastating fire in 1999 (€26 one-way, €32 round-trip).

Getting around the Valley

Note that lifts and cogwheel trains are named for their highest destination (e.g., Aiguille du Midi, Montenvers, and Le Brévent).

By Lifts: Gondolas *(téléphériques)* climb mountains all along the valley, but the best one leaves from Chamonix (see "Sights— Chamonix," below). Sightseeing is optimal from the Aiguille du Midi gondola, but hiking is generally better from the Le Brévent gondola (less snow and plenty of views to Mont Blanc). Kids ages 4 to 11 *(enfants)* ride for 30 percent less, and kids 12 to 15 *(juniors)* ride for 15 percent less. While the lift to Aiguille du Midi stays open year-round, the *télécabines* on the Panoramic du Mont Blanc to Hellbronner (Italy) are open only from May or June to early October and in good weather (call the TI to confirm). Other area lifts are open from January to mid-April and from July to late October.

By Foot: See "Chamonix Area Hikes," below.

By Bike: The TI has a brochure proposing the best bike rides and where to rent. The peaceful river-valley trail is ideal for bikes and pedestrians.

By Bus or Train: One road and one rail line lace together the towns and lifts of the valley. Local buses run twice an hour from in front of the TI for local destinations.

Helpful Hints

Laundry: Laverie Alpina is in the Galerie Alpina shopping center (daily 8:00–19:00 in high season, closed Sun and midday in off-season, tel. 04 50 53 30 67); if they have time, they will do your laundry for you (leave a tip). You'll also find a Laverie near the Aiguille du Midi lift at 174 avenue du Aiguille du Midi (daily 9:00–20:00).

Internet Access: Cybar is exactly that, a cybercafé-bar, so it's open late (rue des Moulins). I-guest has a coin-operated *automat*, with instructions in English allowing entry when the shop is closed (daily 16:00–20:00, 22 galerie Blanc Neige, behind the recommended restaurant Le Bivouac).

Sights—Chamonix

▲▲▲**Aiguille du Midi** (pron. ay-gwee doo mee-dee)—This is easily the valley's (and arguably, Europe's) most spectacular and popular lift. If the weather's clear, the price doesn't matter. Pile into the *téléphérique* (gondola) and soar to the tip of a rock needle 3,780 meters/12,600 feet above sea level. Chamonix shrinks as trees fly by, soon replaced by whizzing rocks, ice, and snow until you reach the top. No matter how sunny it is, it's cold. The air is thin. People are giddy. Fun things can happen at Aiguille du Midi if you're not too winded to join the locals in the halfway-to-heaven tango.

From the top of the lift, cross the bridge and ride the elevator through the rock to the summit of this pinnacle (€3 in high season, free off-season). Missing the elevator is a kind of Alpus-Interruptus I'd rather not experience. The Alps spread out before you. In the distance is the bent little Matterhorn, the tall, shady pyramid behind a broader mountain, listed on the observation table in French as "Cervin—4,505 meters"/14,775 feet. And looming just over there is **Mont Blanc,** the Alps' highest point at 4,807 meters/15,771 feet. Use the free telescope to spot mountain climbers; over 2,000 climb this mountain each year. Dial English and let the info box take you on a visual tour. Check the temperature next to the elevator. Plan on 32 degrees Fahrenheit even on a sunny day. Sunglasses are essential.

Explore Europe's tallest lift station. More than 150 meters/490 feet of tunnels lead to a cafeteria, a restaurant, a gift shop, and the icicle-covered gateway to the glacial world. This "ice tunnel" is where summer skiers and mountain climbers depart. Just observing is exhilarating. Peek down the icy cliff and ponder the value of an ice axe.

Next, for your own private glacial dream world, get into the little red *télécabine* (called Panoramic du Mont Blanc) and head south to **Hellbronner Point,** the Italian border station. This line stretches 5 kilometers/3 miles with no solid pylon. (It's propped by a "suspended pylon," a line stretched between two peaks 400 meters/1,300 feet from the Italian end.) In a gondola for four, you'll dangle silently for 40 minutes as you glide over the glacier to Italy. Hang your head out the window; explore every corner of

Over the Alps—France to Italy

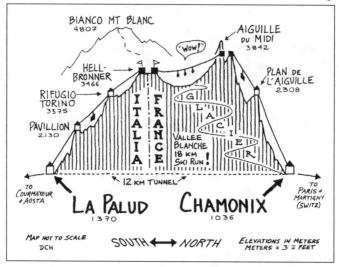

BIANCO MT BLANC
4807

HELL-
BRONNER
3466

AIGUILLE
DU MIDI
3842

"Wow!"

RIFUGIO
TORINO
3375

PLAN DE
L'AIGUILLE
2308

PAVILLION
2130

ITALIA   FRANCE

G L A C I E R

VALLEE
BLANCHE
18 KM
SKI RUN!

12 KM TUNNEL

TO
COURMAYEUR
& AOSTA

TO
PARIS &
MARTIGNY
(SWITZ)

LA PALUD
1370

CHAMONIX
1036

MAP NOT TO SCALE
DCH

SOUTH ←→ NORTH

ELEVATIONS IN METERS
METERS × 3 ≅ FEET

your view. From Hellbronner Point, you can continue down into Italy (see "Transportation Connections," below), but there's really no point unless you're traveling that way.

From Aiguille du Midi, you can ride all the way back to Chamonix or, far better, get off halfway down at **Plan de l'Aiguille** and take a hike plus a train ride down to Chamonix. From Plan de l'Aiguille, hike 20 minutes down to the refuge with great views and reasonable lunches. From the refuge, hike the spectacularly scenic, undulating two- to three-hour trail to Montenvers (overlooking the Mer de Glace glacier; see "Mer de Glace" and "Chamonix Area Hikes, Hike #1," below). From Montenvers, ride the train (€10) into Chamonix. Don't hike all the way down to Chamonix from Plan de l'Aiguille or Montenvers (Mer de Glace); it's a long, steep walk through thick forests with few views.

To beat the hordes and clouds, ride the **lifts** (up and down) as early as you can. To beat major delays in August, leave by 7:00. If the weather has been bad and turns good, expect crowds in any season (worse on weekends). If it's clear, don't dillydally. Lift hours are weather-dependent, but generally run daily from 7:00 to 17:00 in summer; 8:00 to 16:45 in May, June, and September; and 8:00 to 15:45 in winter. The last *télécabine* (called Panoramic du Mont Blanc) departure to Hellbronner is about 14:00.

In peak season, smart travelers reserve the Aiguille du Midi lift in advance either at the information booth next to the lift (open mid-June to mid-Sept) or by telephone in any season (toll-free tel. 08 92 68 00 67, English spoken). For €2, you can reserve up to 10 days in advance and must pick up your reservation at the lift station at least 30 minutes before your departure. Note that you can't reserve the *télécabines* to Hellbronner.

Costs: These are approximate ticket costs for summer (slightly less off-season, ask about the special family rates). From Chamonix to: Plan de l'Aiguille—€14 round-trip (€12 one-way); Aiguille du Midi—€33 round-trip (€28 one-way, not including parachute); the Panoramic du Mont Blanc *télécabine* to Hellbronner—€50 round-trip (€38 one-way). If you are planning to stop at Plan de l'Aiguille on the way back down and hike to Montenvers (see hike #1), ask about a "special randonée" ticket for €31.

Tickets from Aiguille du Midi to Hellbronner are sold at the base or on top (€17 round-trip, €10 one-way). It's €22 to drop down into Italy (sold at Hellbronner, other currencies also accepted, maybe credit cards by 2003). *Si*, you can bring your luggage.

Time to allow: Chamonix to Aiguille du Midi—20 minutes one-way, two hours round-trip, three to four hours in peak season; Chamonix to Hellbronner—90 minutes one-way, three to four hours round-trip, longer in peak season. On busy days, minimize delays by making a reservation for your return lift time upon arrival at the top (tel. 04 50 53 30 80).

▲**Mer de Glace (Montenvers)**—From Gare de Montenvers (the little station over the tracks from Chamonix's main train station), the cogwheel Train du Montenvers toots you up to tiny Montenvers (pron. mohn-ton-vare) and a rapidly moving and dirty glacier called the Mer de Glace (Sea of Ice, pron. mayr duh glahs) and a fantastic view up the white valley (Vallée Blanche) of splintered, snow-capped peaks (€13 round-trip, €10 one-way). The glacier—France's largest, at 10 kilometers/6 miles long—is impressive from above and below. The **ice caves** are funky and filled with ice sculptures (take the small gondola down, €6 round-trip to the caves, includes entry, or hike down 20 min and pay €3 to enter). If you've already seen a glacier up close, you might skip this one. For lunch with great views at Montenvers, consider Bar Panoramique's sandwiches, or Refuge-Hôtel Montenvers (big salads and pasta dishes; also has cool rooms—see "Sleeping in Chamonix," below).

From Montenvers, you can hike uphill three to four hours to Plan de l'Aiguille (though it's easier the other way), then catch the Aiguille du Midi lift from there. Or just hike toward Plan de l'Aiguille as far as you feel—the views get better and better.

▲**Luge (Luge d'été)**—Here's something for thrill-seekers. Ride a chairlift up the mountain and scream down a twisty, banked, concrete slalom course on a wheeled sled. Chamonix has two roughly parallel luge courses. While each course is a kilometer long and about the same speed, one is marked for slower bobsledders, the other for the speed demons. Young or old, hare or tortoise, any fit person can manage a luge. Don't take your hands off your stick; the course is fast and slippery. The luges are set in a grassy park with kids' play areas (€5/1 ride, €21.50/5 rides, €38/10 rides, rides can be split with companions, July–Aug daily 10:00–19:30, June 15–30 and Sept 1–15 daily 13:30–18:00, otherwise weekends only, call for spring and fall hours and ask about night luging in summer, closed in winter, 15-min walk from center, over the tracks from train station, follow signs to *Planards*, tel. 04 50 53 08 97).

Parasail (Parapente)—For €77, you too can jump off a mountain and sail over Chamonix in a tandem parasail with a trained, experienced pilot (Summits Parapente, reserve ahead, tel. 04 50 53 50 14, fax 04 50 55 94 16, www.summits.fr).

▲▲▲*Téléphériques* **to Le Brévent and La Flégère**—While Aiguille du Midi gives a more spectacular ride, the Le Brévent and La Flégère lifts offer distinctly different hiking and viewing options, as you get unobstructed panoramas across to the Mont Blanc range from this opposite side of the valley. The Le Brévent (pron. luh bray-vahn) lift is in Chamonix; the La Flégère (pron. lah flay-zhair) lift is in nearby Les Praz (pron. lay prah). They are connected by a scenic hike or by bus along the valley floor (see "Chamonix Area Hikes, Hike #2," below), and both have sensational view-cafés for non-hikers.

The **Le Brévent lift** is a 10-minute walk up the road above Chamonix's TI. This *téléphérique* stops halfway up at Planpraz station (€10 round-trip, €8 one-way, nice restaurant, great views and hiking) and continues to the top (Brévent station) with more views and hikes, though Planpraz offers plenty for me (€15 round-trip, €12 one-way from Chamonix, daily 9:00–16:30, 8:00–17:30 July–Aug, closed May–mid-June and Oct).

The **La Flégère lift** runs from the neighboring village of Les Praz with just one stop at La Flégère station (€8 one-way, €10 round-trip, daily 9:00–16:30, 7:40–17:30 in summer, closed May–mid-June and Oct). Hikes to Planpraz and Lac Blanc leave from the top of this station.

Chamonix Area Hikes

Your first stop should be at the full-service Maison de la Montagne, across from the TI. You can hire a guide to help you scale Mont Blanc at the Compagnie des Guides on the ground floor (Tue–Sat 9:00–12:00 & 15:30–19:00, closed Sun–Mon). Do-it-yourselfers can visit the Office de la Haute Montagne on the third floor (Office of the High Mountains, daily 9:00–12:00 & 15:00–18:00, closed Sun except summer, tel. 04 50 53 22 08). Here, you can pore over trail maps, get up-to-date trail and weather conditions from the English-speaking staff, and study their English guidebooks (and photocopy key pages). Ask to look at the trail guidebook (€12.50, sold in many stores, includes good *Carte des Sentiers* trail map) and photocopy the pages of the hikes you're planning. The region's hiking map *(Carte des Sentiers)* is extremely helpful; pick it up at the TI (€4). For your hike, wear warm clothes and good shoes. Pack sunglasses, sunscreen, rain gear, water, and snacks.

I've described three big hikes and two easier walks below (see map on page 394). These hikes give nature-lovers of almost any ability a good opportunity to enjoy the valley in just about any weather. Start early, when the weather's generally best. This is critical in summer; if you don't get in the lifts by 8:30, you'll join a conveyor belt of hikers. If starting later or walking longer, confirm lift closing hours, or you'll end up with a long, steep hike down. Trails are rocky and uneven. Take your time, watch your footing, don't take shortcuts, and make sure to say *bonjour* to your fellow hikers.

▲▲▲**Hike #1: Plan de l'Aiguille to Montenvers/Mer de Glace (Grand Balcon Nord)**—This is the easiest way to incorporate a two- to three-hour high-country walk into your ride down from the valley's greatest lift, and check out a glacier to boot. The well-used trail undulates (dropping 450 meters/1,500 feet) and is moderately easy, provided the snow is melted (get trail details at the Office de la Haute Montagne, above). From the Aiguille du Midi lift, get off halfway down (Plan de l'Aiguille) and follow signs down to the refuge (reasonable food and drinks). From there, follow Montenvers signs for about an hour. When the trail splits, follow signs to *Signal Montenvers*, rather than Montenvers, as it's more scenic and easier. At this point, you'll climb to the best views of the trail. It's a long, incredibly scenic drop to Montenvers and the Mer de Glace (€10 train back to Chamonix at the small gondolas, don't walk it). Snow covers this trail generally until June.

▲▲▲**Hike #2: La Flégère to Planpraz (Grand Balcon Sud)**—This glorious hike undulates above Chamonix valley, offering staggering views of Mont Blanc and countless other peaks, glaciers, and wildflowers. With just 113 meters/370 feet difference in elevation between La Flégère and Planpraz lift stations, this hike, while it has its ups and downs, is *relatively* easy. From Chamonix, you can drive five minutes; walk 40 minutes along the Arve River (see Hike #5, below); or take the Chamonix bus (10-min ride, every 30 min) to the tiny village of Les Praz and La Flégère lift station. Ride the lift up to La Flégère (€8) and walk down to the Refuge-Hôtel. Find the signs to Planpraz (you don't want Les Praz-Chamonix—that's

Chamonix Valley Hikes and Lifts

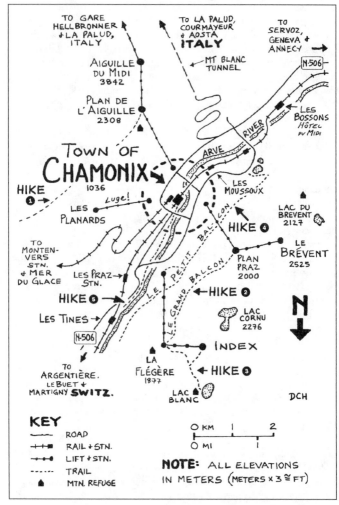

TO GARE
HELLBRONNER
& LA PALUD,
ITALY

TO LA PALUD,
COURMAYEUR
& AOSTA
ITALY

TO
SERVOZ,
GENEVA &
ANNECY

MT BLANC
TUNNEL

N·506

AIGUILLE
DU MIDI
3842

PLAN DE
L'AIGUILLE
2308

LES
BOSSONS
*HÔTEL
DU MIDI*

ARVE   RIVER

TOWN OF
CHAMONIX
1036

LES
MOUSSOUX

HIKE ❶

Luge!

LES
PLANARDS

HIKE ❹

LAC DU
BRÉVENT
2127

PETIT BALCON

LE GRAND BALCON

TO
MONTEN-
VERS
STN.
& MER
DU GLACE

LES PRAZ
STN.

PLAN
PRAZ
2000

LE
BRÉVENT
2525

HIKE ❺

LES TINES

HIKE ❷

LAC
CORNU
2276

N

N·506

INDEX

TO
ARGENTIÈRE.
LEBUET &
MARTIGNY **SWITZ.**

LA
FLÉGÈRE
1877

HIKE ❸

LAC
BLANC

DCH

KEY

——— ROAD

+++■ RAIL & STN.

•—•—● LIFT & STN.

------- TRAIL

▲ MTN. REFUGE

0 KM   1   2

0 MI   1

NOTE: ALL ELEVATIONS
IN METERS (METERS × 3 ≅ FT)

straight down), then hike the undulating Grand Balcon Sud to Planpraz station, the midway stop on the Le Brévent lift line (allow 2.5 hrs). Take the Planpraz lift down to Chamonix (€8); skip the steep hike down (of course, this route can be done in reverse, but you have to walk backwards). Ask for the round-trip rate between La Flégère and Planpraz (Le Brévent) lifts, available at either lift (saves €6).

▲▲▲**Hike #3: La Flégère to Lac Blanc** (pron. lock blah)—This is the most demanding trail of those I list, climbing steeply and steadily over a rough, boulder-strewn trail for 90 minutes to snowy Lac Blanc (some footing is tricky and good shoes or boots are essential). I like this trail, as it gets you away from the valley edge and opens views to peaks you don't see from other hikes. The destination is a frigid, snow-white lake surrounded by peaks and a nifty chalet-refuge offering good lunches (and dinners with accommodations). The views on the return trip are breathtaking. Check for snow conditions on the trail and go early (particularly in summer), as there is no shade and this trail is popular. Follow directions from Hike #2 to La Flégère station (above), then walk out the station's rear doorway past the orientation table/view area and follow signs to Lac Blanc. The trail is well-signed and improves in surface quality as you climb. While you can eliminate much of the uphill hiking by riding the lift up to Index from La Flégère, the trail from Index to Lac Blanc generally requires serious skill and equipment due to snow—ask.

▲**Hike #4: Petit Balcon Sud**—This two-hour hike parallels the Grand Balcon Sud at a lower elevation and is ideal when snow or poor weather make other hikes problematic. No lifts are required—just firm thighs to climb to the trail. From Chamonix, walk up to Le Brévent lift station. Follow the asphalt road to the left of the lift leading uphill; it turns into a dirt road that signs mark as the Petit Balcon Sud trail. After about an hour, look for signs down to Les Praz (not La Flégère!). When you reach the asphalt road, turn left to explore the village of Les Praz, or turn right for the bus stop and river trail back to Chamonix. Return via Chamonix bus or by walking the level Arve River trail (40 min). This hike works just as well in reverse.

Hike #5: Arve Riverbank Stroll—For an easy forested-valley stroll, follow the Arve River toward Les Praz. Cross the river from Chamonix's Hôtel Alpina, turn left, and walk until you pass the tennis courts. Cross two bridges to the left and turn right along the rushing Arve River, or keep right after the tennis courts and enter the Le Bouchet woods. Both trails can be linked for a loop, and both will get you to Les Praz—a pleasant destination with several cafés and a charming village green.

Sleeping in Chamonix
(€1 = about $1, country code: 33, zip code: 74400)
Reasonable hotels and dorm-like chalets abound. With the helpful TI, you can find budget accommodations anytime. Mid-July to mid-August is most difficult, when some hotels have five-day minimum-stay requirements. Prices tumble off-season. If you want a view of Mont Blanc, ask for *côté Mont Blanc* (pron. coat-ay

mohn blah). Summertime travelers should seriously consider a
night in a refuge-hotel high above. All hoteliers speak English.

Hotels in the City Center

HIGHER PRICED

Hôtel la Savoyarde***, a steep but rewarding walk above
Chamonix, has views from the outdoor café tables, smart chalet
ambience, and a good restaurant. Rooms are pleasant and all have
tubs, not showers (Db-€135, Tb-€173, Qb-€209, CC, includes
breakfast, add €14/person for dinner, next to Le Brévent lift, 28
rue des Moussoux, tel. 04 50 53 00 77, fax 04 50 55 86 82,
www.lasavoyarde.com).

MODERATELY PRICED

Hôtel de l'Arve** has a slick, modern, alpine feel, with sharp view
rooms right on the Arve River overlooking Mont Blanc, or smaller,
cheaper rooms without the view. The fireplace lounge, pleasant garden, sauna, and climbing wall add to this place's appeal, though I'd
skip their dinner (standard Db-€52–74, larger room or with views
Db-€60–98, extra person-€12, good buffet breakfast-€7.60, CC,
elevator, behind huge Hôtel Alpina, 60 impasse des Anémones, tel.
04 50 53 02 31, fax 04 50 53 56 92, www.hotelarve-chamonix.com,
e-mail: contact@hotelarve-chamonix.com, Isabelle and Beatrice SE).

    Richemond Hôtel**, with an almost retirement-home feel
in its alpine-elegant public spaces, is dead center. The rooms
are traditional, comfortable, and generally spacious. There's also
an outdoor terrace and a game room with a pool table and table
tennis (Sb-€44–51, Db-€65–78, Tb-€77–96, Qb-€82–102, buffet
breakfast-€8, CC, 228 rue du Docteur Paccard, tel. 04 50 53 08
85, fax 04 50 55 91 69, www.richemond.fr).

    Chalet Beauregard, Chamonix's most classy *chambre d'hôte*,
is a short but steep walk above the TI. It's a relaxed and peaceful
place with a private garden. Five of its seven cushy rooms have balconies with grand views (Sb-€46–77, Db-€61–92, Tb-€86–107,
no CC though personal checks in U.S. dollars accepted, includes
breakfast, free parking, may require 5-day minimum in summer, on
road to Le Brévent lift, 182 montée La Mollard, tel. & fax 04 50 55
86 30, www.chalet-beauregard.com, Manuel and Laurence SE).

    Hôtel Gourmets et Italy***, with cozy public spaces, a cool
riverfront terrace, and balcony views from many of its tastefully decorated rooms, is a fair value (Db-€67–100, Tb-€82–102, Qb-€88–
108, CC, elevator, 2 blocks from casino on Mont Blanc side of river
at 96 rue du Lyret, tel. 04 50 53 01 38, fax 04 50 53 46 74, www
.hotelgourmets-chamonix.com, e-mail: hgicham@aol.com).

Chamonix Town

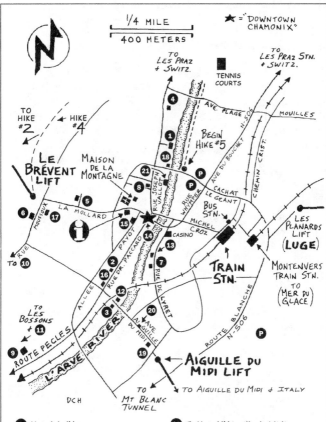

1 Hotel de l'Arve
2 Richemond Hotel
3 Hotel Au Bon Coin
4 Hotel Boule de Neige
5 Chalet Beauregard B&B
6 Hotel Savoyarde
7 Hotel Gourmets et Italy
8 Hotel Touring & Super U grocery
9 Chalet Chantel Hotel
10 Auberge du Bois Prin & La Girandole B&B
11 To Hotel l'Aiguille du Midi
12 La Boccalatte restaurant
13 Chez Nous restaurant
14 L'Atmosphere rest.
15 La Calèche restaurant
16 Le Bivouac rest. & Internet café
17 La Cabolée restaurant
18 Casino grocery & laundromat
19 Laundromat
20 Creperie Fleur de Sel
21 Internet café

LOWER PRICED

Hôtel Au Bon Coin**, a few blocks toward the town center from
the Aiguille du Midi lift, is a modest, wood-paneled place with
great views, private balconies, and thinnish walls in most of its
spotless, well-cared-for rooms. The cheaper rooms lack views and
private bathrooms (D-€38, Ds-€44, Db with view and balcony-
€60, Tb-€62, Qb-€78, CC, usually closed mid-April–June, 80
avenue L'Aiguille du Midi, tel. 04 50 53 15 67, fax 04 50 53 51 51,
e-mail: hotel.auboncoin@wanadoo.fr, Dermot and Julie SE).

Boule de Neige* (Snowball) hotel is a small, simple, and
central budget option run by a friendly owner who was born in
Chamonix. Two rooms share a huge view terrace (D-€31–39,
Db-€40–57, T-€43–51, Tb-€53–63, breakfast-€6, CC, 362 rue
Joseph Vallot, tel. 04 50 53 04 48, fax 04 50 55 91 09, e-mail:
laboule@claranet.fr).

Hôtel Touring**, with basic but cavernous rooms (many
with 4 beds), some saggy beds, and a friendly British staff, is good
for families (Ds-€38–49, Db-€46–60, third person-€10, fourth
person-€16, CC, 95 rue Joseph Vallot, tel. 04 50 53 59 18, fax
04 50 53 97 71, e-mail: hoteltouring@aol.com).

Hotels for Drivers
A few minutes above Chamonix, these places are practical only by car.

HIGHER PRICED

Auberge du Bois Prin****, my only four-star listing, has the best
views I found, cozy ambience, and a melt-in-your-chair restaurant.
Five of the 11 rooms in this flowery chalet come with a balcony
facing Mont Blanc (Db-€173–196, extra person-€44, CC, includes
breakfast, sauna, Jacuzzi, elevator, *menus* from €27.50 for guests;
follow Les Moussoux from Chamonix Sud exit, tel. 04 50 53 33 51,
fax 04 50 53 48 75, www.boisprin.com).

MODERATELY PRICED

Chalet Chantel**, which feels more like a bed-and-breakfast
inn, is meticulously kept by friendly Peter (British) and Françoise
(French). The place is small, homey, and reasonable, with afternoon tea served during non-summer months. Balcony rooms
facing Mont Blanc are worth reserving (Db-€69–76, includes
breakfast, CC, take Chamonix Sud exit and look for red signs,
391 route des Pecles, tel. 04 50 53 02 54, fax 04 50 53 54 52,
e-mail: chantel@chamonixleguide.com).

LOWER PRICED

Chambre d'Hôte la Girandole, just above Auberge du Bois Prin, may be the highest home in Chamonix, with three ground-floor rooms, three good bathrooms in the hall, and immense views from the flowery garden (Sb-€50, Db-€58, includes breakfast, no CC, 46 Chemin de la Perserverance, tel. 04 50 53 37 58, fax 04 50 55 81 77).

Sleeping near Chamonix

If Chamonix overwhelms you, spend the night in one of the valley's overlooked, lower-profile villages.

MODERATELY PRICED

Three kilometers from Chamonix, in the village of Les Bossons (toward Annecy), lies the best two-star hotel in the valley, **Hôtel l'Aiguille du Midi****. The ultimate hostess, Martine Farini (SE), runs this mountain retreat in a park-like setting, with a swimming pool, tennis court, Jacuzzi, table tennis, and a laundry room to boot. The alpine-comfortable rooms aren't big and you won't care. Chamonix locals come here for their big meal (Db-€65–75, add 30 percent each for third and fourth person, CC, elevator, half pension preferred in summer, €27 *menu* or à la carte, easy by train, get off at Les Bossons, tel. 04 50 53 00 65, fax 04 50 55 93 69, www.hotel-aiguilledumidi.com).

Refuges and Refuge-Hotels near Chamonix

Chamonix has the answer for hikers who want to sleep high above, but don't want to pack tents, sleeping bags, stoves, or food: refuges and refuge-hotels (open mid-June–mid-Sept, depending on snow levels). Refuges have fewer amenities and require a longer walk to reach than refuge-hotels. Refuges generally have bunks only (about €11–14), no hot water, and hearty meals (dinner-€12–23, breakfast-€6). Refuge-hotels usually have some private rooms (and dorm rooms), hot showers down the hall, and more full-service restaurants. You must reserve in advance (a few days are generally enough), then pack your small bag for a memorable night among new international friends. The Office de la Haute Montagne in Chamonix can explain your options (see "Chamonix Area Hikes," above).

Refuges: Chalet-Refuge Lac Blanc requires a 90-minute uphill hike but is a fun, cozy, and sharp place with five bed "cubbies," a friendly caretaker who loves meeting foreigners, and an English-speaking staff (half pension-€45/person, kids under 14-€25, no CC, tel. 04 50 53 49 14, for more information, see "Chamonix Area Hikes, Hike #3," above).

Refuge-Hotels: Refuge-Hôtel Montenvers, right at the Montenvers train stop, is wood-everywhere rustic (about €46/person for half pension in a double room, CC, good showers down the hall, tel. 04 50 53 12 54, fax 04 50 53 98 72; for directions see "Sights—Chamonix, Mer de Glace," above). **Refuge-Hôtel La Flégère** hangs on the edge. It's simpler, but ideally located for hiking to Lac Blanc or Planpraz (3 private rooms with 5 beds, many dorm beds, €29/person half pension, CC, fireplace, cozy bar/café, right at La Flégère lift, tel. 04 50 53 06 13, fax 04 50 53 22 65). For directions, see "Chamonix Area Hikes, Hike #2," above.

Eating in Chamonix

La Boccalatte is a simple, good value with a lively atmosphere and a large selection of local specialties. It's run by a friendly Alsatian, English-speaking Thierry (daily until 22:00, across from Hôtel au Bon Coin, 59 avenue de l'Aiguille du Midi, tel. 04 50 53 52 14).

Chez Nous serves Savoyard specialties with a wood-bench-warm ambience and fair prices (€15 *menu*, great fondue comes with a green salad and potatoes, turn right at casino, 78 rue du Lyret, tel. 04 50 53 91 29).

La Calèche serves delectable Savoyard specialties in a warm, alpine setting (€17 *menus*, the €23 *menu* is much better, 18 rue Paccard, tel. 04 50 55 94 68).

Aptly named **L'Atmosphere** is where locals go when the mood matters (€19 *menu*, better at €24.50, open daily, snooty service, next to post office at 123 place Balmat, tel. 04 50 55 97 97).

Le Bivouac is cute and unpretentious, with good local and Italian specialties served without a smile (€13 *menu*, 266 rue Paccard, tel. 04 50 53 34 08).

Friendly **Fleur de Sel** (Anne SE) serves good and cheap crêpes. It's near the Aiguille du Midi lift and is good for lunch or dinner (daily, 199 avenue de l'Aiguille du Midi, tel. 04 50 53 16 04).

La Cabolée, next to the Brévent *téléphérique*, is a hip eatery with great omelettes and a wonderful view from its outdoor tables.

Grocery Stores: The best grocery is Casino, in the shopping center below Hôtel Alpina. The more central Super U is next to Hôtel Touring at 117 rue Joseph Vallot (Mon–Sat 8:30–19:30, Sun 8:30–12:00, closed Sun off-season).

Transportation Connections—Chamonix

Bus and train service to Chamonix is surprisingly good. You'll find helpful bus and train information desks at the train station.

By train to: Annecy (6/day, 2.5 hrs, change in St. Gervais), **Beaune** and **Dijon** (7/day, 7 hrs, changes in St. Gervais and Lyon, sometimes more changes), **Nice** (4/day, 10 hrs, change in St. Gervais and Lyon), **Arles** (8/day, 8.5 hrs, change in St. Gervais and Lyon), **Paris'** Gare de Lyon (8/day, 7 hrs, change in Martigny and Geneva or Lausanne, handy night train), **Martigny, Switzerland** (11/day, 1.5 hrs, scenic trip), **Geneva** (3/day, 3.5 hrs, changes in St. Gervais, La Roche-sur-Foron, and Annemasse).

By bus: Buses provide service to destinations not served by train and also to some cities that are served by train—but at a lower cost and higher speed. Get information at the TI or bus station (*gare routière*); the information office is outside Chamonix's SNCF train station (tel. 04 50 53 01 15). Long distance buses depart from the train station, not from local bus stops.

To Italy: See "Itinerary Options," below.

Itinerary Options from Chamonix

A Day in French-Speaking Switzerland—There are plenty of tempting alpine and cultural thrills just an hour or two away in Switzerland. A road-and-train line sneaks you scenically from Chamonix to the Swiss town of Martigny. While train travelers cross without formalities, drivers are charged a one-time 40-SF fee (€30) for a permit to use Swiss autobahns.

A Little Italy—The remote Valle d'Aosta and its historic capital city of Aosta are a spectacular gondola ride over the Mont Blanc range. The side-trip is worthwhile if you'd like to taste Italy (spaghetti, gelato, and cappuccino), enjoy the town's great evening ambience, or look at the ancient ruins in Aosta, often called the "Rome of the North."

Take the spectacular lift (Chamonix–Aiguille du Midi–Hellbronner) to Italy, described in "Sights—Chamonix," above. From Hellbronner, catch the €22 lift down to La Palud and take the bus to Aosta (hrly, change in Courmayeur). Aosta's train station has connections to anywhere in Italy.

For a more down-to-earth experience, you can take the bus from Chamonix to Aosta. Get schedules at the TI or the bus station (located at train station). If buses are allowed in the newly reopened Mont Blanc tunnel, it's a 90-minute trip to Aosta; if buses aren't allowed in the tunnel, it'll take three hours via Martigny. Drivers can simply drive through the Mont Blanc tunnel (€26 one-way, €32 round-trip).

BURGUNDY AND LYON

The rolling hills of Burgundy gave birth to superior wine, fine cuisine, and sublime countryside. This deceptively peaceful region witnessed Julius Caesar's defeat of the Gauls, and then saw the Abbey of Cluny rise from the ashes of the Roman Empire to vie with Rome for religious influence in the 12th century. Burgundy's last hurrah came in the 15th century, when its powerful dukes controlled an area that extended north to Holland. Today, bucolic Burgundy stretches from about Auxerre in the north to a bit north of Lyon in the south, and is crisscrossed with canals and dotted with quiet farming villages. It's also the transportation funnel for eastern France and makes a convenient stopover for travelers (car or train), with quick access north to Paris or the Alsace, east to the Alps, and south to Provence.

Only a small part of Burgundy is covered by vineyards, but grapes are what they do best. The white cows you see everywhere are Charolais. France's best beef ends up in *boeuf Bourguignon*.

Lyon—the gateway to Burgundy, Provence, and the Alps—is easily accessible by train or car. This captivating place is France's most interesting major city after Paris. If you need a city fix, linger in Lyon.

Planning Your Time

Stay in or near Beaune. It's conveniently located for touring the vineyards and countryside. Plan on a half day in Beaune and a half day for the countryside. Ideally, sleep in Beaune Friday night and awake to the sounds of the Saturday market.

Lyon, 130 kilometers south of Beaune, is France's best-kept urban secret and merits at least one night and a full day.

Burgundy

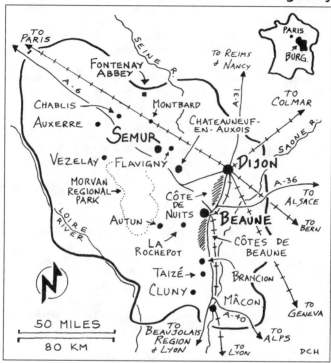

Much closer to Paris, unspoiled Semur-en-Auxois and the handful of nearby and overlooked sights appeal to those looking for something different.

Getting around Burgundy

Trains link Beaune with Dijon to the north and Lyon to the south; less-frequent buses cruise the wine route between Dijon, Beaune, and Chalon-sur-Saône. Bikes and minivan tours get nondrivers from Beaune into the countryside. Buses connect Semur-en-Auxois with Dijon and Montbard rail stations.

Cuisine Scene—Burgundy and Lyon

Arrive hungry. Considered by many to be France's best, Burgundian cuisine is peasant cooking elevated to an art, and entire lives are spent debating the best restaurants and bistros in Lyon.

Several classic dishes were born in Burgundy: *escargots Bourguignon* (snails served sizzling hot in garlic butter), *boeuf Bourguignon* (beef simmered for hours in red wine with onions and mushrooms), *coq au vin* (chicken stewed in red wine), and *oeufs en meurette* (poached eggs on a large crouton in red wine), as well as the famous Dijon mustards. Look also for *jambon persillé* (cold ham layered in a garlic-parsley gelatin), *pain d'épices* (spice bread), and *gougère* (light, puffy cheese pastries). Native cheeses are Epoisses and Langres (both mushy and great) and my favorite, Montrachet (a tasty goat cheese). *Crème de cassis* (black currant liqueur) is another Burgundian special-ty; look for it in desserts and snazzy drinks (try a *kir*).

Lyon offers *le top* in French cuisine. Surprisingly afford-able, this is an intense palate experience—try the *salade lyon-naise* (croutons, ham, and a poached egg on a bed of lettuce), *andouillettes* (pork sausages), and *quenelles* (large dumplings, sometimes flavored with fish).

Remember, restaurants serve only during lunch (11:30–14:00) and dinner (19:00–21:00, later in bigger cities); cafés serve food throughout the day.

Along with Bordeaux, Burgundy is why France is famous for wine. From Chablis to Beaujolais, you'll find it all here: great fruity reds, dry whites, and crisp rosés. The three key grapes are Chardonnay (dry, white wines), Pinot Noir (medium-bodied red wines), and Gamay (light, fruity wines such as Beaujolais). Every village produces its own distinctive wine, from Chablis to Meur-sault to Chassagne-Montrachet. Road maps read like fine wine lists. If the wine village has a hyphenated name, the latter half of its name often comes from the town's most important vine-yard (e.g., Gevery-Chamberin, Ladoix-Serrigny). Look for the *Dégustation Gratuite* (free tasting) signs and prepare for serious tasting—and steep prices, if you're not careful. For a more relaxed tasting, head for the hills: The less prestigious Hautes-Côtes (upper slopes) produce some terrific and overlooked wines. Look for village cooperatives, or try our suggestions for Beaune tastings (see "Wine-Tasting," below). The least expensive (but still tasty) wines are Bourgogne Ordinaire and Passetoutgrain (both red), and whites from the Macon and Chalon areas. If you like rosé, try Marsannay, considered one of France's best.

BEAUNE

You'll feel comfortable right away in this prosperous and popular wine capital, where life centers on the production and consumption of the prestigious, expensive Côte d'Or wines. *Côte d'Or* means "golden hillsides," and they are a spectacle to enjoy in late Octo-ber, as the leaves of the vineyards turn color.

Medieval monks and powerful dukes of Burgundy each called Beaune home for a while, both providing stability that helped establish this town's prosperity. Today, one of the world's most important wine auctions takes place here during the third week of November, when the Hospice de Beaune's wines are sold.

Orientation

Beaune is a compact little city (pop. 25,000) with a handful of interesting monuments and vineyards on its doorstep. Limit your Beaune ramblings to the town center, contained within its medieval walls and circled by a one-way ring road, and find a quiet moment to walk into the vineyards just west of the center. All roads and activities converge on the perfectly French place Carnot, as do Wednesday and Saturday markets. Beaune is quiet on Sundays and on Monday mornings.

Tourist Information: There are two TIs: one in the city center, the other on the ring road. The city center TI is across the street from Hôtel Dieu on place de la Halle (April–Nov Mon–Sat 9:30–19:00, summers until 20:00, Sun 10:00–12:30 & 14:00–17:00, Dec–March Mon–Sat 10:00–18:00, Sun 10:00–13:00 & 14:00–17:00, tel. 03 80 26 21 30). The other TI is across from the post office on the ring road's southeastern corner, handy for drivers (Mon–Sat 9:00–12:00 & 14:00–18:00, closed Sun, look for Porte Marie de Bourgogne on the red banner). Both have city maps (with a town walking tour described), a room-finding service, a list of *chambres d'hôte*, and bus schedules. Ask about guided English walking tours (€6.50, usually at noon, mid-June–mid-Sept) and pass on their museum pass.

Arrival in Beaune

By Train: To reach the city center from the train station (lockers available), walk straight out of the station up avenue du Huit (8) Septembre, cross the busy ring road, and continue up rue du Château, then rue du Tonneliers. A left on rue des Enfants leads to Beaune's pedestrian zone and place Carnot.

By Bus: Beaune has no bus station—only several stops in the center. Ask the driver for *le centre-ville*. The Jules Ferry stop is central and closest to the train station; the Clemenceau stop is best for visiting Château La Rochepot (see "Sights—Beaune Region," below).

By Car: Follow *Centre-ville* signs to the ring road. Once on the ring road, turn right at the first signal after the post office (rue d'Alsace) and park for free in place Madeleine.

Helpful Hints

Laundry: Beaune's only launderette is between the train station and place Madeleine, at 17–19 rue du Faubourg St. Jean (daily 6:30–21:00).

Bike Rental: See "Getting around the Beaune Region," below.

Best Souvenir Shopping: The **Athenaeum** has a great variety of souvenirs and some books in English, with a great children's section upstairs (daily 10:00–19:00, across from Hôtel Dieu at 7 rue de l'Hôtel Dieu).

Best Wine Stores: Dennis Perret has a good, varied selection in all price ranges and a helpful, English-speaking staff (they can chill a white for your picnic). If you've tasted a wine you like elsewhere, they can usually find a less costly bottle with similar qualities (June–Nov Mon–Sat 9:00–19:00, Dec–May closed 12:00–14:00, closed Sun, 40 place Carnot, tel. 03 80 22 35 47). I also like the wine hardware store, **Comptoir du Vin**, for wine paraphernalia (where the rue d'Alsace runs into place Carnot, Mon–Sat 8:00–12:45 & 13:45–19:00, closed Sun).

Sights—Beaune

▲▲**Hôtel Dieu**—The Hundred Years' War and the Black Death devastated Beaune, leaving more than 90 percent of its population destitute. Nicholas Rolin, chancellor of Burgundy and a peasant by birth, had to do something for "his people." So, in 1443, he paid to build this Flamboyant Flemish/Gothic charity hospital; it was completed in only eight years. Tour it on your own with the helpful English handout. In the St. Louis wing (where patients replaced the winepresses that once occupied this space), you'll find van der Weyden's dramatic *Last Judgment* polyptych, commissioned by Rolin to give the dying something to ponder. For a closer look, ask the attendant to maneuver the giant roaming monocle. Keep this painting in mind if you see the *Isenheim Altarpiece* in Colmar—they were commissioned for similar reasons, but with very different results (€5.10, April–Nov daily 9:00–18:30, Dec–March 9:00–11:30 & 14:00–17:30).

▲**Collégiale Notre-Dame**—Built in the 12th and 13th centuries, this is a good example of Cluny-style architecture (except for the front porch addition). Enter to see the 15th-century tapestries (behind the altar, drop in a coin for lights), a variety of stained glass, and what's left of frescoes depicting the life of Lazarus (daily 9:00–19:00). To find the Musée du Vin from here, walk 30 steps straight out of the cathedral, turn left down a cobbled alley (rue d'Enfer), keep left, and enter the courtyard of Hôtel des Ducs— today's Musée du Vin, located in the old residence of the dukes of Burgundy.

Musée du Vin de Bourgogne—You don't have to like wine to appreciate this folk-wine museum. The history and culture of Burgundy and wine were fermented in the same bottle. At least wander into the courtyard for a look at the duke's palace, antique

Beaune

In map:
TO N-74 DIJON, SAVIGNY. & ⑩
R. DUBOIS
R. FAUB. ST. NIC.
R. LORRAINE
BLVD. FOCH
BLVD. JOFFRE
* RING ROAD IS ONE-WAY COUNTER CLOCKWISE
TO TRAIN STN. & ⑤
R. COLLEGE
MUSÉE DU VIN
AVE 8 SEPT.
⑳ [26]
R. CHÂTEAU
TO PARC DE LA BOUZAISE
ST. MART.
NÔTRE DAME
PLACE MONGE
TONNELIERS
① ⑲
FBG ST. JEAN
BLVD. FERRY
PLACE MADELEINE
⑦
AVE DE LA REPUB.
BLVD. CLEMENCEAU
RAMPARTS WALK
PARADIS
⑲ ③ ⑰
R. THIERS
P. JOIGNEAUX
⑧ ⑮
⑨
③ ②
PLACE CARNOT
R. D'ALSACE
R. FAUB. MAD.
P
⑬
⑯ TO ⑪
JAFF.
R. MAUFOUX
R. MAUFOUX
⑭
⑳ ④ ⑱
HOTEL DIEU
⑳ ⑫
TO BLIGNY & ㉑
R. FAUB. BRET.
HÔTEL DIEU
⑳ ㉔ ㉕
BLVD. ST-JACQUES
⑥
PTT
SUPER-MARKET
TO A-6
* NOT TO SCALE - PLACE MADELEINE TO HÔTEL DIEU IS A 10 MIN. WALK

TO D-973 & N-74
DCH
///// PEDESTRIAN ZONE - RUE MONGE & RUE CARNOT
LA ROCHEPOT, POMMARD, CHAGNY & ⑫ ⑳
IIII STAIRS

① Hotel des Remparts
② Hotel Tulip Inn-Athanor
③ Abbaye de Mazieres
④ Le Gourmandin rooms
⑤ To Hotel de France
⑥ Hotel Ibis
⑦ Laundromat
⑧ Hotel Rousseau
⑨ Hotel de la Paix
⑩ To Hotels le Home & Villa Louise
⑪ To Hotel Parc
⑫ To B&B's & rest. near La Rochepot
⑬ Les Caves Madeleine & Les Tontons rest.

⑭ La Grilladine rest.
⑮ l'Auberge Bourguignone rest.
⑯ Relais de la Madeleine rest.
⑰ Bistrot Bourguignon wine bar
⑱ Café Hallebarde
⑲ Pickwicks Pub
⑳ To Le Relais de la Diligence
㉑ Au Bon Accueil
㉒ Marche aux Vins
㉓ Tourist Office
㉔ Cave des Cordeliers
㉕ Jardin des Remparts
㉖ Bike rental

winepresses (in the barn), and a concrete model of Beaune's 15th-century street plan. Inside the museum, you'll find a great model of the region, tools, costumes, and scenes of Burgundian wine history—but no tasting. English explanations are in each room (€5.10, ticket good for other Beaune museums, daily 9:30–18:00, closed Tue Dec–Jan).

Ramparts Walk, Parc de la Bouzaise, and Vineyards—Consider a stroll above Beaune on a short segment of its 13th-century wall to get a sense of its once-impressive medieval defenses, but don't skip a chance to wander into nearby vineyards. Find the ramp on the right (Remparts des Dames) where the rue Maufoux meets the ramparts. Wander north to the next street (avenue de la République), drop down and turn left, cross the ring road, then follow the same stream that runs under the Hôtel Dieu for three blocks to the park. The vineyards are behind the park, with small roads, paths, and views—best at sunset (walkers need 15 min from Beaune's center to reach the vineyards, drivers need about 2 min).

Wine-Tasting

Countless opportunities exist (for a price) for you to learn the fine points of Burgundy's wines. Shops everywhere offer free, and generally friendly and informative, tastings (with the expectation that you'll buy at least one bottle). Several large cellars (caves) charge an entry fee, allowing you to taste a variety of wines (with less expectation that you'll buy). Most of these caves offer some form of introduction or self-guided tour (see also "Minibus Tours," below). The following three places are a block from the TI and stack up conveniently next to each other.

Start or end your tour at the **Athenaeum**, which is a bookstore (with many titles in English), wine bar, and English-speaking Burgundian wine chamber of commerce, all in one (daily 10:00–19:00, across from Hôtel Dieu and next to TI at 7 rue de l'Hôtel Dieu). You'll pay by the glass (€3–6) and select from a good list.

▲▲▲**Marché aux Vins**—Across the street from the Athenaeum, this is Beaune's wine smorgasbord and the best way to sample its impressive wines. Hand the mademoiselle €9 for a wine-tasting cup (you get to keep it) and scorecard, then plunge into the labyrinth of candlelit caves dotted with 18 barrels, each offering a new tasting experience (4 Chardonnays, 14 Pinot Noirs). You're on your own. The best reds are upstairs in the chapel, at the end of the tasting. You officially have 45 minutes in the cellars, though enforcement is *très* lax. Bring some crackers to cleanse your palate and help you really taste the differences—but be discreet (mid-June–mid-Sept daily 9:30–17:30, otherwise 10:00–12:00 & 14:00–17:30, tel. 03 80 25 08 20).

Caves des Cordeliers—Better for those with less stamina, this historic cave offers self-guided tours of their "museum cellars" (English explanations), with just six wines to taste (€6, July–Sept 9:30–18:30, Oct–June 9:30–12:00 & 14:00–18:00, 6 rue de l'Hôtel Dieu, 1 block toward ring road from Marché aux Vins, tel. 03 80 25 08 85).

Wine-Tasting outside Beaune—The TI has a long list of area vintners for those who want to venture into the countryside. You're expected to buy a bottle or two unless you're with a group tour (see also "Bike Routes" under "Sights—Beaune Region" and "The Hautes-Côtes to Châteauneuf-en-Auxois," below, for more tasting ideas). The famous *Route des Grands Crus* that connects Burgundy's most prestigious wine villages is disappointing north of Aloxe Corton, as you're forced onto the unappealing N-74. Consider instead the beautiful routes connecting villages between Beaune and La Rochepot and south to Santanay (e.g., Monthelie, Nantoux, St. Romain, and St. Aubin are all off the famous path and offer ample tastings; see "Scenic Drive to La Rochepot," below).

Minibus Tours of Vineyards near Beaune—Wine Safari offers minibus wine-tasting tours in three two-hour itineraries (€34, tour #2 is best for beginners, tours depart from TI generally at 14:30 and 17:00, call TI for information and to reserve, TI tel. 03 80 26 21 30). These tours are well-run, in English, and get you into the countryside and smaller wineries. Transco buses also run from Beaune through all the great wine villages (see "Getting around the Beaune Region," below).

Sleeping in Beaune
(€1 = about $1, country code: 33, zip code: 21200)
Sleep Code: **S** = Single, **D** = Double/Twin, **T** = Triple, **Q** = Quad, **b** = bathroom, **s** = shower only, **CC** = Credit Cards accepted, **no CC** = Credit Cards not accepted, **SE** = Speaks English, **NSE** = No English, * = French hotel rating system (0–4 stars).

To help you sort easily through these listings, I've divided the rooms into three categories based on the price for a standard double room with bath:

Higher Priced—Most rooms more than €90.
Moderately Priced—Most rooms €90 or less.
Lower Priced—Most rooms €60 or less.

HIGHER PRICED
Abbaye de Mazières*** hides near the basilica deep in Beaune's center, with 12 big, colorful, Old World rooms over a restaurant in a 15th-century building (Db-€64–110, Tb-€84–117, extra bed-€15, CC, no lobby, reception at restaurant, many stairs, parking

garage-€8, 19 rue Mazières, tel. 03 80 24 74 64, fax 03 80 22 49 49, e-mail: abbayedemazieres@wanadoo.fr; if no response, contact Hôtel Tulip, below).

MODERATELY PRICED

At **Hôtel des Remparts*****, the formal Epaillys offer classy but affordable rooms in a manor house with beamed ceilings, period furniture, a quiet courtyard, and great family rooms (Db-€51–80, most at €74, Db suite-€100, Tb-€84–95, Qb-€110, CC, cozy attic rooms, parking-€7.50, 48 rue Thiers, between train station and main square, just inside ring road, tel. 03 80 24 94 94, fax 03 80 24 97 08, e-mail: hotel.des.remparts@wanadoo.fr, SE).

Hôtel de France** is ideal for train travelers and handy for drivers, with easy parking across from the train station. It's friendly and well-run, with spotless rooms, air-conditioning, and Diana the sheepdog (Sb-€38–60, Db-€50–65, Tb-€60–75, CC, 35 avenue du Huit Septembre, tel. 03 80 24 10 34, fax 03 80 24 96 78, e-mail: hotfrance.beaune@wanadoo.fr, SE).

Hôtel Tulip Inn***, with a central location, mixes modern comfort in smaller rooms with a touch of old Beaune and cozy public spaces (Db-€74–101, most about €80, extra bed-€15, CC, elevator, parking garage-€8, 9 avenue de la République, tel. 03 80 24 09 20, fax 03 80 24 09 15, e-mail: hotel.athanor@wanadoo.fr, SE).

Hôtel Ibis**, modern, efficient, and comfortable enough, with a pool and airy terrace, is located at the ring road and avenue Charles de Gaulle (Db-€53–65, CC, tel. 03 80 22 75 67, fax 03 80 22 77 17, e-mail: ibisbeaune@wanadoo.fr). There's another Ibis hotel closer to the autoroute, but it's less central.

LOWER PRICED

Le Gourmandin restaurant, right on place Carnot, rents three spacious, comfortable, and air-conditioned rooms with many stairs. It's an excellent value (Db-€55, big Db/Tb or Qb-€70, CC, 8 place Carnot, tel. 03 80 24 07 88, fax 03 80 22 27 42, e-mail: gourm01@aol.com).

Sleeping on Place Madeleine

These hotels are a few blocks from the city center and train station and offer easy parking.

MODERATELY PRICED

Hôtel de la Paix***, just off place Madeleine, is an intimate, solid value with appealing rooms. Owner Jean Paul cares, and he speaks English (Sb-€54, Db-€69, loft Tb-€92, Qb-€110, CC, 45 rue du Faubourg Madeleine, tel. 03 80 24 78 08, fax 03 80 24 10 18, SE).

LOWER PRICED
Hôtel Rousseau, on place Madeleine, is a no-frills place that turns its back on Beaune's sophistication. The cheerful, quirky, and hard-to-find owner (Madame Rousseau), her pet birds, and a charming garden will make you smile. The cheapest rooms are simple, clean, and fine. The rooms with showers are just like grandma's, with plenty of comfort, and all of the rooms are quiet (S-€27, D-€31, D with toilet–€41, Db-€51, T with toilet-€49, Tb-€56, Q-€48, Qb-€62, showers down the hall-€3, includes breakfast, no CC, free private parking, 11 place Madeleine, tel. 03 80 22 13 59, fax . . . why would I need that?).

Sleeping near Beaune
You'll find some exceptional and family-friendly values within a short drive of Beaune. Hotels in famous wine villages are generally pricey and overrated.

Hotels

HIGHER PRICED
Hôtel Villa Louise*** is a small, upscale place burrowed in the prestigious wine village of Aloxe Corton, five minutes north of Beaune. Many of its *très* cozy and tastefully decorated rooms over-look vineyards, a pool, and a rear garden made for sipping wine. The friendly wine-making owners, the Perrins (SE), are happy to show you their vaulted cellars (Db-€98–150, most about €115, CC, Jacuzzi, sauna, 21420 Aloxe Corton, tel. 03 80 26 46 70, fax 03 80 26 47 16, e-mail: hotel-villa-louise@wanadoo.fr).

MODERATELY PRICED
Hôtel Le Home** sits just off busy N-74, one kilometer north of Beaune, and is a fine value, with cushy rooms in an old mansion. The rooms in the main building are Laura Ashley–soft (Db-€56–60, Tb-€70–76; top-floor rooms are the most romantic), and those on the parking courtyard (only Db-€64) come with stone floors, small terraces, and bright colors (CC, free parking, 138 route de Dijon, tel. 03 80 22 16 43, fax 03 80 24 90 74). Call ahead—it's popular.

Hôtel Parc** is located in the flowery little village of Levernois, down in the valley away from the vines-and-wine hoopla and quick to the freeway. This enchanting, vine-covered manor house is flaw-lessly maintained, with fine rooms showing great attention to detail surrounding a large grassy garden (Db-€47–86, most about €47, Tb-€60–100, Qb-€105, CC, 5 min across autoroute from Beaune, 21200 Levernois, tel. 03 80 24 63 00, fax 03 80 24 21 19, e-mail: hotel.le.parc@wanadoo.fr).

Chambres d'Hôte

The Côte d'Or has many *chambres d'hôte*; get a list at the TI and reserve ahead in the summer. The cliff-dwelling villages of Baubigny, Orches, and Evelles, just under La Rochepot (zip code for all: 21340), make fine bases and offer many *chambres d'hôte*.

HIGHER PRICED

Château de Melin, close to Beaune just outside the wine village of Auxey Duresses, is home to Paul Dumay wines (tastings available). This beautifully restored château offers top comfort, complete with a small pond, vineyards, and gardens to stretch out in (Db-€86–105, Tb-€120, Qb-€135, includes breakfast, no CC, 21190 Auxey Duresses, tel. 03 80 21 21 19, fax 03 80 21 21 72, www.chateaudemelin.com).

LOWER PRICED

Madame Fussi, in Baubigny, has three comfortable rooms (including 1 family-ideal suite) in a modern home over a sweeping lawn (Db-€42, Tb-€50, no CC, tel. & fax 03 80 21 84 66). **Madame Lagelee,** just down the road in Evelles, has a big apartment on a private courtyard (Sb-€28, Db-€40, Tb-€46, Qb-€54, no CC, tel. 03 80 21 79 57). Charming **Isabelle Raby,** a kilometer above in Orches, has a double room, a good family room, and a third room planned, facing a grassy yard with views and a cute pool; ask to see their cellar (Db-€47, Tb-€60, Qb-€72, includes big breakfast, no CC, tel. & fax 03 80 21 78 45, e-mail: praby@wanadoo.fr).

Eating in Beaune

Eating in the Center: For a traditional Burgundian setting, step down to the wine-soaked-cellar atmosphere of the 12th-century **Abbaye de Mazières** (€15 *menu* is OK, €23 *menu* is far better, closed Tue, see "Sleeping in Beaune," above).

Consider **La Grilladine** for fine traditional Burgundian cuisine—escargot, hot goat-cheese salad, the eggy *oeufs en meurette*—at digestible prices (good €18 *menu Bourguignon*, closed Mon, 17 rue Maufoux, tel. 03 80 22 22 36).

Le Jardin des Remparts is ideal for a splurge (*menus* €30–70, closed Sun–Mon, reserve ahead, on ring road at 10 rue de l'Hôtel Dieu, tel. 03 80 24 79 41, e-mail: lejardin@club-internet.fr).

Eating on Place Madeleine: Try the relaxed ambience and friendly surroundings of **Les Caves Madeleine** and dine at large tables surrounded by shelves of wine (good wines by the glass, €14 *plats du jour* and €20 *menus*, closed Thu and Sun, 8 rue Faubourg Madeleine).

Les Tontons, a few doors down, serves fine regional cuisine in a friendly and intimate setting (*menus* from €17, 22 place Madeleine, tel. 03 80 24 19 64).

L'Auberge Bourguignonne is the most traditional of the places I list, from service to decor to *menus* (*menus* from €15, daily, air-con, 4 place Madeleine, tel. 03 80 22 23 53).

Relais de la Madeleine is Beaune's budget-minded restaurant, run by the entertaining "Monsieur Neaux-Problem" (€11.50 *menu*, closed Wed, 44 place Madeleine, tel. 03 80 22 93 30).

Picnics: **Supermarché Casino** has a great selection, deli, and fair prices (Mon–Sat 8:30–20:00, through the arch off place Madeleine). Peruse the food souvenirs at **Amuse Bouche** (7 place Carnot).

Bars

Beaune's best wine bar is the relaxed **Bistrot Bourguignon** (pricey wines by the glass and good but limited menu, on a pedestrian-only street at 8 rue Monge, closed Sun, occasional jazz concerts, tel. 03 80 22 23 24).

Drop by **Café Hallebarde** for a grand selection of draft beer (24 rue d'Alsace), and if you're tired of speaking French, pop into the late-night-lively **Pickwicks Pub** (behind church at 2 rue Notre-Dame).

Eating near Beaune

Five minutes away by car is **Le Relais de la Diligence**, where you can dine surrounded by vineyards and taste the area's best budget Burgundian cuisine with many *menu* options (*menus* from €15, daily, take N-74 toward Chagny/Chalon and turn left at L'Hôpital Meursault on D-23, tel. 03 80 21 21 32).

Le Pommard, between Beaune and La Rochepot, is traditional and reasonable (*menus* from €15, on main road from Beaune in Pommard, tel. 03 80 22 08 08).

Au Bon Accueil is relaxed and country-cozy, on a hill above Beaune, with great outdoor tables and five-course *menus* for €18 (smaller *menu* for €14, closed Mon–Wed, leave Beaune's ring road and take Bligny-sur-Ouche turnoff, you'll see signs a few minutes outside Beaune, tel. 03 80 22 08 80).

For a complete French experience, call ahead for a table at **Auberge du Vieux Pressoir,** below La Rochepot in tiny Evelles (€25 *menus*, closed Wed, tel. 03 80 21 82 16).

For exquisite French cuisine with hints of Japanese flavors at semi-splurge prices, drive five minutes north of Beaune to Pernand Vergelesses and dine facing vineyards at **Le Charlemagne** (*menus* from €35, reserve ahead, closed Mon and Wed, tel. 03 80 21 51 45).

Transportation Connections—Beaune

By train to: Dijon (17/day, 25 min), **Paris'** Gare de Lyon (12/day, 2.5 hrs, 10 require change in Dijon), **Colmar** (6/day, 4–5 hrs, changes in Dijon and in Besançon, Mulhouse, or Beflort), **Arles** (10/day, 4.5 hrs, 9 with change in Lyon and Nîmes or Avignon), **Chamonix** (7/day, 7 hrs, changes in Lyon and St. Gervais, some require additional changes), **Annecy** (9/day, 5 hrs, change in Lyon), **Amboise** (8/day, 6 hrs, most with changes in Dijon and in Paris, arrive at Paris' Gare de Lyon, then Métro to Austerlitz or Montparnasse stations).

Getting around the Beaune Region

By Bus: Transco bus #44 runs from Beaune through the vineyards and villages south to Chalon-sur-Saône, west to La Rochepot, and north to Dijon. About 10 buses per day link Beaune and Dijon via the famous wine villages; ask at the TI for schedules and stops or call for information (tel. 03 80 42 11 00).

By Bike: Well-organized, English-speaking Florent at **Bourgogne Randonnées** has good bikes, bike racks, maps, and thorough countryside itineraries (get his advice on your plan). He can deliver your bike to your hotel anywhere in France (bikes-€3/hr, €15/day, Mon–Sat 9:00–12:00 & 13:30–19:00, Sun 10:00–12:00 & 14:00–17:00, near train station at 7 avenue du Huit Septembre, tel. 03 80 22 06 03, fax 03 80 22 15 58).

Sights—Beaune Region

▲▲**Bike Routes**—Immaculate vineyards, lush countryside, and little-traveled roads make this area perfect for biking. Some routes are fairly level; others require realistic self-evaluation of your fitness. Get the local Michelin map and heed the advice from Bourgogne Randonnées (see above). You'll find small paved lanes leading into the vineyards above most villages, offering peaceful alternatives to the busier roads. Bring food and water, as you'll find few shops along these roads. For a relatively easy and rewarding ride, connect these three renowned wine villages with a 16-kilometer/10-mile, half-day loop ride: Savigny-les-Beaune, Aloxe Corton, and Pernand Vergelesses.

Start by finding Savigny-les-Beaune's center. Consider visiting the château for its motorcycle, racing car, and airplane collection (April–Sept daily 9:00–18:30), and find Henri de Villamont's tasting room, where Annie (SE) will treat your taste buds well (reasonable prices, good selection; look for signs just past their red-and-white brick building, tel. 03 80 21 52 13). From Savigny, find the small road north to Pernand Vergelesses (turn left at unsigned T-intersection to join main road to Pernand

Beaune Region

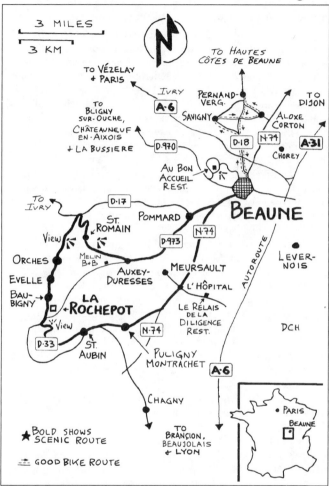

3 MILES
3 KM

TO HAUTES
CÔTES DE BEAUNE

TO VÉZELAY
& PARIS

IVRY

A-6

TO DIJON

PERNAND-
VERG.

SAVIGNY

ALOXE
CORTON

TO
BLIGNY
SUR-OUCHE,
CHÂTEAUNEUF
EN-AIXOIS
+ LA BUSSIERE

D-970

D-18

N-74

A-31

CHOREY

AU BON
ACCUEIL
REST.

TO
IVRY

D-17

ST.
ROMAIN

POMMARD

BEAUNE

View

D-973

N-74

AUTOROUTE

LE VER-
NOIS

ORCHES

MELIN
B+B

AUXEY-
DURESSES

MEURSAULT

L'HÔPITAL

EVELLE

BAU-
BIGNY

LA
ROCHEPOT

LE RELAIS
DE LA
DILIGENCE
REST.

DCH

View

D-33

ST.
AUBIN

N-74

PULIGNY
MONTRACHET

A-6

CHAGNY

★ BOLD SHOWS
SCENIC ROUTE

🚲 GOOD BIKE ROUTE

TO
BRANCION,
BEAUJOLAIS
+ LYON

PARIS

BEAUNE

Vergelesses). An immediate right off this main road leads down
a small lane to Aloxe Corton, with many tasting opportunities,
but no cafés, in the village center. The road leads uphill from
here to Pernand Vergelesses, where you can enjoy a well-deserved
drink at the cozy Café Luxembourg. Signs lead you back to Beaune
from Pernand Vergelesses. Tiny lanes ideal for biking lead into
the vineyards above the bigger road between Savigny and Pernand
Vergelesses.

For a more rigorous, all-day ride, consider biking the "Scenic Drive to La Rochepot," described below.

▲**Château La Rochepot**—This very Burgundian castle rises above the trees and its village, 12 kilometers/8 miles from Beaune. It's accessible by car, bike (hilly), or infrequent bus. Cross the drawbridge and knock three times with the ancient knocker to enter. This pint-size castle is splendid inside and out. Tour half on your own and the other half with a French guide (get the English handout, some tours in English, call ahead). The kitchen will bowl you over. Look for the 15th-century highchair in the dining room. Climb the tower and see the Chinese room, sing chants in the resonant chapel, and make ripples in the well. (Can you spit a bull's-eye? It's 72 meters/240 feet down!) Don't leave without driving, walking, or pedaling up D-33 a few hundred meters toward St. Aubin (behind Hôtel Relais du Château) for a romantic view (€5.50, Wed–Mon June–Aug 10:00–18:00, Sept–May 10:00–11:30 & 14:00–17:30, closed Tue year-round and at 16:30 Nov–March, tel. 03 80 21 71 37).

Scenic Drive to La Rochepot: From Beaune, take D-973 toward La Rochepot. Right after Auxey Duresses, follow St. Romain and climb to the upper village and find signs to *Château-Pointe de Vue* for a great picnic site and nice views. Leave St. Romain, climbing toward Ivry-en-Montagne (D-17), then turn left to Orches (spectacular view turnouts soon after turn), and continue on to La Rochepot. After visiting the château, leave La Rochepot, continuing over the hill to St. Aubin and Gamay via D-33 (it runs behind Hôtel Relais du Château in La Rochepot). Follow the tiny road to Puligny-Montrachet and Meursault, and head back to Beaune via D-973.

The Hautes-Côtes to Châteauneuf-en-Auxois

This half-day loop trip links vineyards, pastoral landscapes, the Burgundy canal, a Cistercian abbey, and a medieval village. (If you're heading to Paris, Châteauneuf-en-Auxois can be done en route or as an overnight stop.) It requires a car, the local Michelin map 243, and navigational patience. Leave Beaune's ring road toward Dijon on N-74. Soon, take the Savigny-les-Beaune turnoff, then connect Pernand Vergelesses with the Hautes-Côtes villages of Echevronne, Magny-les Villiers, Villers la Faye, and Marey-les-Fussey. **Wineries** in these villages offer stress-free tastings. (More serious tasters should consider these wineries: Henri de Villamont in Savigny-les-Beaune—see "Bike Routes," above; Lucien Jacob in Echevronne, tel. 03 80 21 52 15, SE; and Domaine Thevenot Le Brun in Marey-les-Fussey, tel. 03 80 62 91 64, NSE). Then head west over the hills to Pont d'Ouche. At Pont d'Ouche, follow the canal toward Pouilly-en-Auxois to Châteauneuf-en-Auxois.

Châteauneuf's medieval **château** towers over the valleys below. This perfectly feudal village huddles securely in the shadow of the castle and merits a stroll. Park at the lot in the upper end of the village and don't miss the panoramic viewpoint near the parking lot. Walk into the courtyard and tour the château if you have time (€4, daily 10:00–12:00 & 14:00–19:00, get English handout).

Signs behind Châteauneuf lead to La Bussière's **abbey**, which was founded in the 13th century by Cistercian monks but goes largely unnoticed by tourists today. Stroll the lovely gardens and check out the refectory (look for door in rear of main building marked *Accueil*; enter and walk upstairs). Ask for the key to the *vieux pressoir* (old press). You can dine here under Gothic arches for €15 (lunch or dinner, includes wine, must call to reserve, tel. 03 80 49 02 29).

The scenic return to Beaune is via Pont d'Ouche (toward Bligny-sur-Ouche), where you turn left, go uphill through Bouilland, and then downhill through Savigny-les-Beaune.

Sleeping in or near Châteauneuf-en-Auxois
(€1 = about $1, country code: 33, zip code: 21320)

MODERATELY PRICED
Hostellerie du Château**, in Châteauneuf, offers rooms in two locations. Its main building ("Hôtel") is a better value than its annex up the street, called "La Residence" (with larger, less cozy rooms). Many rooms in the Hôtel are half-timbered and have views of the château; the tiny top-floor doubles are adorable, and rooms with showers are small. The Hôtel's garden terrace has tables and swings and faces the château (Db-€45–70, extra bed-€9, CC, restaurant serves fine *menus* from €23, tel. 03 80 49 22 00, fax 03 80 49 21 27, www.hostellerie-chateauneuf.com).

LOWER PRICED
Charming **Annie Bagatelle** has four beautiful rooms, two with lofts (Sb-€40–50, Db-€46–58, extra person-€8, no CC, at upper end of village, second courtyard down from fountain on the left, tel. 03 80 49 21 00, fax 03 80 49 21 49, e-mail: jean-michel.bagatelle@wanadoo.fr, SE a little).

To sleep floating on a luxury hotel barge at two-star prices with views of Châteauneuf's brooding castle, find the canal-front village of Vandenesse-en-Auxois. Here, the **Lady A** barge offers tight, cozy rooms. Friendly Lisa cooks an elaborate dinner upon request for €22, including wine (Sb-€40, Db-€50, includes breakfast, call way ahead in summer, no CC, tel. 03 80 49 26 96, fax 03 80 49 27 00, SE). The *écluse* (lock house) at the bridge offers

small groceries, wine-tastings, and inexpensive *chambres* at
Chez Monique et Pascal (Sb/Db-€42, Tb-€50, no CC,
tel. 03 80 49 27 12, fax 03 80 49 26 05).

Eating in Châteauneuf-en-Auxois

Three Châteauneuf restaurants offer Burgundian cuisine at fair
prices: **La Grill du Castel** (meal-sized salads, great escargots,
boeuf Bourguignon, menus from €16, CC, tel. 03 80 49 26 82),
L'Orée du Bois Crêperie (simple, friendly, and inexpensive),
and the country-elegant **Hostellerie du Château** (see above),
where I splurge for dinner.

SEMUR-EN-AUXOIS

If you have time for one more night in Burgundy, spend it here.
This happy little town feels real. There are no important sights to
digest—just a seductive jumble of Burgundian alleys perched above
the meandering Armancon River and behind the town's four massive towers—all beautifully illuminated after dark. Use Semur-en-
Auxois (pron. suh-moor-ahn-ohx-wah) as a base to visit the handful
of interesting sights nearby, including the *Chocolat*-famous hill town
of Flavigny, the historic fields of Alesia (where Julius Caesar defeated
Gaul), and the immaculate abbey of Fontenay—all within 20 minutes
of Semur. Semur is also about 45 minutes from the famous church
in Vézelay and two hours from Paris, making it a handy first- or
last-night stop on your trip. Don't miss the smashing panorama of
Semur, best at night, from the viewpoint by the Citroën shop where
D-980 and D-954 intersect (drive or hike downhill from TI, follow
Montbard signs, and turn left at Citroën dealership).

Tourist Information: The helpful TI is across from Hôtel
Côte d'Or at Semur's medieval entry (mid-June–Sept Mon–Sat
9:00–19:00, Sun 10:00–12:00 & 15:00–18:00; Oct–mid-June Mon
14:00–18:00, Tue–Sat 9:30–12:00 & 14:00–18:00, closed Sun,
2 place Gaveau, tel. 03 80 97 05 96, www.ville-semur-en-auxois.fr).
Pick up their city walks brochure, information on the regional
sights, and bike rental information and suggested routes (hilly
terrain). There's a handy SNCF rail office in the TI where
railpass users can get free tickets for the bus to Montbard.

The town has three sights: the Church of Notre-Dame, which
dominates its small square (impressively clean after years of work,
decent English handout); the small Municipal Museum (skip it); and
the newly opened Tour de l'Orle d'Or (1 of Semur's 4 defensive towers, good views, some English information is promised on exhibits
about the Middle Ages, get update from TI). But Semur is best experienced by following the TI's walking tours. The longer, yellow route
takes you down to the river and up to good views over Semur.

Sleeping in Semur-en-Auxois
(€1 = about $1, country code: 33, zip code: 21140)
Hotels and restaurants are a good value here.

LOWER PRICED
Hôtel les Cymaises** offers three-star comfort for the price of two, with good rooms and big new beds in a manor house with a quiet courtyard (Db-€52–57, Tb-€68, 2-room Qb-€85–98, CC, 7 rue du Renaudot, private parking, tel. 03 80 97 21 44, fax 03 80 97 18 23, e-mail: hotel.cymaises@libertysurf.fr).

The simple little **Hôtel des Gourmets*** is tucked below the main pedestrian street and is good for those on a tight budget who are also seeking a good restaurant (D-€26, Db-€41, T/Q-€32, 5- to 6-person room-€58, extra bed-€5, CC, traditional *menus* from €13, 4 rue Varenne, tel. 03 80 97 09 41, fax 03 80 97 17 95).

Eating in Semur-en-Auxois
Franco-American-owned **Le Calibressan** offers zesty French cuisine with a dash of California, *menus* from €16, a cool salad bar, and wood-beam coziness; say hello to friendly Jill (closed Sun–Mon, 16 rue Fevret, tel. 03 80 97 32 40).

Tiny, reasonable **Les Minimes** is a local institution, but can be smoky (€15 *menu*, closed Sun–Mon, 39 rue des Vaux, tel. 03 80 97 26 86).

L'Entracte is where everybody goes for pizza, pasta, salads, and more in a relaxed atmosphere (open daily, 4 rue Fevret). **Les Gourmets** is also good, traditional, and reasonable (closed Mon–Tue; see "Sleeping in Semur-en-Auxois," above).

The historic charcuterie across from the church is ready to supply your dinner picnic.

Transportation Connections— Semur-en-Auxois
By bus to: Montbard (which has a train station and connects with TGV trains; 3 buses/day—early morning, noon, and evening, 20 min, railpass gets you a free ticket, get ticket at station or at TI in Semur), **Dijon** (3/day, 1 hr). Bus info: tel. 03 80 42 11 00.

Sights—Near Semur-en-Auxois
▲**Abbey of Fontenay**—This isolated Cistercian abbey—which has managed to avoid serious damage over the centuries (and is still occupied by its owners)—gives us the single best picture of medieval abbey life through its many well-preserved buildings. The abbey was founded in 1181 by St. Bernard as a back-to-basics reaction to the excesses of Benedictine abbeys, such as Cluny.

Medieval Monasteries

France is littered with medieval monasteries. Most have virtually no furnishings (they never had many), leaving the visitor with little to reconstruct what life must have been like in these cold stone buildings a thousand years ago. A little history can help breathe life into these important yet underappreciated monuments.

After the fall of the Roman Empire, monasteries arose as refuges of peace and order in a chaotic world. While the pope got rich and famous playing power politics, monasteries worked to keep the focus on simplicity and poverty. Throughout the Middle Ages, monasteries were mediators between man and God. In these peacefully remote abbeys, Europe's best minds would struggle with the interpretation of God's words. Every sentence needed to be understood and applied. Answers were debated in universities and contemplated in monasteries.

St. Benedict established the Middle Ages' most influential monastic order (Benedictine) in Montecassino, Italy, in A.D. 529. He scheduled a rigorous program of monks' duties, combining manual labor with intellectual tasks. His monastic movement spread north and took firm root in France, where the abbey of Cluny (Burgundy) eventually controlled over 2,000 dependent abbeys and vied with the pope for control of the Church. Benedictine abbeys grew dot-com rich, and with wealth came excess (such as private bedrooms with baths). Monks lost sight of their purpose and became soft and corrupt. In the late 1100s, a determined and charismatic St. Bernard rallied the Cistercian order by going back to the original rule of St. Benedict. Cistercian

It thrived as a prosperous "mini-city" for 672 years until the French Revolution, when it became property of the nation and was eventually sold.

As you enter the abbey's small gatehouse, look for the small round hole under the drawing of the abbey's layout. Dogs barked through this hole to alert the gatekeeper of the arrival of guests. Get your ticket and the good English explanation, and let the clerk explain the clockwise route you must follow. The owners occupy the buildings closest to you—so they're off-limits.

Your tour starts in a divine church with a dirt floor and ethereal light—if you listen well, you can almost hear the brothers chanting. You'll also visit a vast wood-beamed dormitory where all would sleep fully dressed on thin mats, lovely cloisters where monks could shave and wash up, a chapter house where daily meetings would take place abbeys thrived as centers of religious thought and exploration from the 13th through the 15th centuries.

Cistercian abbots ran their abbeys like little kingdoms, doling out punishment and food to the monks, and tools to peasant farmers. Abbeys were occupied by two groups: the favored monks from aristocratic families (such as St. Bernard), and a larger group of lay brothers from peasant stock who were given the heaviest labor and could only join the Sunday services.

Monks' days were broken into three activities: prayer, divine reading, and labor. Monks lived in silence and poverty with few amenities—meat was forbidden, as was cable TV. In summer, they got two daily meals; in winter, just one. Monks slept together in a single room on threadbare mats covering solid-rock floors.

With their focus on work and discipline, Cistercian abbeys became leaders of the medieval industrial revolution. Among the few literate people in Europe, monks were keepers of technological knowledge—about clocks, waterwheels, accounting, foundries, gristmills, textiles, and agricultural techniques. Abbeys became economic engines that helped drive France out of its Middle-Aged funk.

As France (and Europe) slowly got its act together in the late Middle Ages, cities reemerged as places to trade and thrive. Abbeys gradually lost their relevance in a brave new humanist world. Kings took over abbot selection, further degrading the abbeys' power, and Gutenberg's movable type made monks obsolete. The French Revolution closed the book on abbey life, occupying and destroying many, such as Cluny.

and punishments were doled out, a copying room, a bakery, a heating room, an infirmary, and an iron forge. The small exposition rooms near the exit *(sortie)* have some English information and a reproduction of the Papal Bull of Pope Alexander III in 1168, giving Fontenay its rights and privileges (€7.50, daily 10:00–12:00 & 14:00–17:00, 20-min drive from Semur via Montbard, no bus, taxi from Montbard-€12, tel. 03 80 92 15 00).

Flavigny-sur-Ozerain—Ten minutes from Semur, Flavigny is taking the excitement of its *Chocolat*-covered Hollywood image in stride. This unassuming and serenely situated village feels permanently stuck in the past, with one café, one *crêperie*, and two boutiques. There's little to do here other than appreciate the setting (best from the grassy ramparts). Pick up a map at the **TI** (daily April–Sept 10:00–12:30 & 13:00–19:30, Oct and March

10:00–12:30 & 13:00–18:00, closed Nov–Feb, down rue de l'Eglise in front of church). You can also buy the locally produced *Anis* candies and visit the ancient church of St. Genest (open 14:00–17:45; if closed, ask at the Mairie—town hall—next door).

If you do come, stay for lunch. **La Grange** (the barn) serves farm-fresh fare, including luscious quiche, salad, fresh cheeses, pâtés, and fruit pies (July–mid-Sept daily 12:30–16:00, Sun only rest of year, across from church, look for brown doors and listen for lunch sounds, tel. 03 80 35 81 78). **Le Relais de Flavigny** is an appealing little restaurant with seven bargain rooms above (S/D-€26, Ss/Ds-€31, CC, *menus* from €12, good lunch salads served when it's warm, at the bottom of rue de l'Eglise from church, 21150 Flavigny-sur-Ozerain, tel. 03 80 96 27 77, www .le-relais.fr). Next door, **l'Ange Souriant Chambre d'Hôte** offers more comfort and intimacy (Sb-€47, Db-€51, Tb-€85, tel. & fax 03 80 96 24 93).

To reach Flavigny from Semur, leave Semur following Venary les Laumes and look for the turnoff to Flavigny via Pouillenay. The approach to Flavigny from Pouillenay on D-9 is camera-ready. Park at the gate or in the lot just below. From this lot, signs lead to Alise Ste. Reine, described below (great views back to Flavigny as you leave).

Alise Ste. Reine—A five-minute drive from Flavigny, this vertical little village is allegedly where, in 52 B.C., Julius Caesar defeated the Gallic leader Vercingetorix to win Gaul for the Roman Empire and forever change France's destiny. Follow signs to *Statue de Vercingetorix* up through the village to the very top and find the park with the huge statue of the Gallic warrior overlooking his Waterloo. Stand as he did and imagine yourself trapped on this hilltop. The orientation table under the gazebo shows how the Roman camps had him surrounded; the red line marks the Roman fortifications. Today, this place is perfect for picnics. You'll pass signs to the little Musée et Fouilles (museum and excavations of the Gallo-Roman town of Alesia) on your way to the top, both of mild interest. After you leave the statue, the first left downhill leads to Flavigny.

▲▲**Vézelay**—For over seven centuries, pilgrims have overrun this hill town to get to its famous church, the Basilica of St. Madeleine. Built to honor its famous relics (the bones of Mary Magdalene, who had been possessed by the devil and then saved) and to welcome pilgrims, this is one of Europe's largest and best-preserved Romanesque churches. Its appeal lies in its simplicity and the play of light on the pleasing patterns of stones. Notice the absence of distracting decoration and bright colors. To appreciate this, compare this church to another of the same era, Notre-Dame de Paris.

The effect when you enter the basilica's interior is mesmerizing. The tympanum (semicircular area over the door) and capitals provide what decoration there is through astonishing sculptures. These tell Bible stories in much the same way stained-glass windows do in Gothic churches. Notice how unappealing the newer Gothic apse feels in comparison to the older Romanesque nave. One-hour guided tours in English depart from inside the basilica between 10:00 and 12:00 and from 14:00 to 17:00 (donation requested, tel. 03 86 33 39 50), or you can buy their fine €5 booklet inside the church (free entry to church, daily 8:00–19:30). The view from the park behind the church is sublime.

Vézelay's **TI** is near the church (rue St. Pierre, tel. 03 86 33 23 69). The **Auberge de la Coquille** is a warm, cozy place to eat, with reasonable salads, crêpes, and full-course *menus* (halfway up to the church at 81 rue St. Pierre, tel. 03 86 33 35 57).

Vézelay is about 45 minutes northwest of Semur (20 min off the autoroute to Paris). Train travelers must either go to nearby Semicelles (via Auxerre) and taxi from there (allow €14 one-way, tel. 03 86 32 31 88) or take the once-a-day bus from Avallon or Montbard (near Semur-en-Auxois) that leaves you in Vézelay for seven hours.

Sights—Between Burgundy and Lyon
▲**Brançion and Chapaize**—An hour south of Beaune by car (20 km/12.5 miles west of Tournus on D-14) are two churches that owe their existence and architectural design to the nearby and once-powerful Cluny Abbey.

Brançion's nine-building hamlet floats on a hill with the purest example of Romanesque architecture I've seen: a 12th-century church (with faint frescoes inside), a charming château (climb the tower for views), and a 15th-century market hall. **Auberge du Vieux Brançion** offers fine Burgundian cuisine at fair prices (€18 *menus*). For a peaceful break, spend a night in one of the Auberge's simple, frumpy, but cozy rooms (Ds-€36, Db-€54, good family rooms-€54–69, tel. & fax 03 85 51 03 83, www.brancion.fr).

A few kilometers closer to Beaune, **Chapaize**'s beautiful church is famous for its 11th-century belfry and its leaning-to-the-leeward interior (English brochure is available). Wander around the back for a view of the belfry and pause at the friendly café across the street.

To connect these towns scenically from Beaune, follow N-74 south to Chagny (Burgundy's ugliest town), find Remigny and follow D-109 to Aluze, then follow D-978 east and D-981 south through Givry, Buxy, and on to Chapaize.

Cluny and Taizé—Twenty kilometers/12.5 miles southwest of Brançion lies the historic town of Cluny. The center of a rich and powerful monastic movement in the Middle Ages is today a pleasant town with the very sparse and crumbled remains of its once-powerful abbey. To see a new trend in monasticism, consider visiting the booming Christian community of Taizé (pron. teh-zay), just north of Cluny. Brother Roger and his community welcome visitors who'd like to spend a few days getting close to God through meditation, singing, and simple living. Call or write first if you plan to stay overnight. There are dorm beds only (Taizé Community, 71250 Cluny, tel. 03 85 50 14 14).

Beaujolais Wine Country—Just south of Cluny and north of Lyon, the beautiful vineyards and villages of the Beaujolais (relaxed tastings) make a pleasant detour for drivers. The most scenic and interesting section lies between Macon and Villefranche-sur-Saône, a few minutes west of A-6 on D-68. The route runs from the Maconnais wine region and the famous village of Pouilly-Fuisse, south through Beaujolais' most important villages: Chiroubles, Fleurie, and Julienas. Look for *Route de Beaujolais* signs and expect to get lost a few times. For an amazing introduction to this region's wines, visit **Hameau du Vin** in Romanche-Thorins. The king of Beaujolais, Georges DuBoeuf, has constructed the perfect introduction to wine at his wine museum, which immerses you into the life of a wine-maker with impressive models, exhibits, films, and videos. You'll be escorted from the beginning of the vine to present-day wine-making, with a focus on Beaujolais wines (€11.50, includes small tasting and free English headphones, daily June–Sept 9:00–18:00, Oct–May 10:00–17:00; in Romanche-Thorins, look for signs to Hameau du Vin, then *La Gare*, and look for the old train station-turned-winery; tel. 03 85 35 22 22). Lyon's TI has information on afternoon bus excursions to the Beaujolais (€32, includes 2 tastings).

LYON

Straddling the Rhône and Saône Rivers between Burgundy and Provence, Lyon has been among France's important cities since pre-Roman times. Today, overlooked Lyon is one of France's big-city surprises. After Paris, it's the most historic and culturally important city in France. You get two distinctly different-feeling cities: The *molto* Italian cobbled alleys, Renaissance mansions, and colorful facades of Vieux Lyon; and the more staid but classy, Parisian-feeling shopping streets of Presqu'ile.

Planning Your Time

Lyon makes a handy day visit for train travelers, as many trains pass through Lyon and both stations have baggage lockers, but those who invest a night here can experience the most renowned cuisine in France at pleasing prices.

If you have a day here, start it on Fourvière Hill (take the funicular near St. Jean Cathedral in Vieux Lyon to Fourvière) and visit the Gallo-Roman Museum, Roman Theater, and Basilique Notre-Dame before catching the funicular or walking down to Vieux Lyon. Have lunch in Vieux Lyon and explore the covered passageways called *traboules* (see "Sights—Vieux Lyon," below), then cross over to the Presqu'île for museums and shopping. Finish your day across the Rhône River at the Resistance museum (take subway or walk 25 min from place Bellecour). Many of Lyon's important sights are closed on Mondays or Tuesdays, or both.

Drivers connecting Lyon with southern destinations should consider the scenic detour via the Ardeche Gorges (see "Transportation Connections—Lyon," below), and those connecting to Burgundy should consider visiting Brancion (see "Sights—Between Burgundy and Lyon," above) and cruising the Beaujolais wine route.

Orientation

Lyon may be France's second-largest city, but it feels manageable. Most sightseeing is near the Saône River and can be done on foot. If you stick to the sights listed below, you won't need more than the funicular and a few subway rides to help you get around.

Lyon's sights are concentrated in three adjacent areas: Fourvière Hill is to the west, with its white Basilique Notre-Dame glimmering over the city; historic Vieux Lyon lies just below on the west bank of the Saône; and the Presqu'île (home to all my recommended hotels) sits across the Saône River to the east. Huge place Bellecour lies in the middle of the Presqu'île.

Tourist Information: The well-equipped TI and SNCF ticket office share space on the southeast corner of place Bellecour (Mon–Sat 9:00–18:00, until 19:00 mid-June–mid-Sept, Sun 10:00–18:00, tel. 04 72 77 69 69). The good English-language map, which has museum information and a good enlargement of central Lyon, is free. Pick up the free leaflet on Vieux Lyon (shows good walking routes) and a schedule of events and concerts (ask about concerts in the Roman Theater).

The TI sells a useful **museum pass** for serious sightseers (1 day/€15, 2 days/€25, 3 days/€30, under 18 half-price; includes all museums, a day pass on Métro/bus system, and a walking tour of Lyon with live guide or audioguide). The handy **audioguide** (€6) offers good, self-guided walking tours, though I prefer the **live guided walks** (€9, English-language tours depart Wed–Mon from TI at St. Jean Métro/funicular station, no need to reserve—just show up, bilingual tours available off-season). The well-done

€6 *World Heritage Excursions* **guidebook**, sold at the TI, describes interesting self-guided walking tours (Vieux Lyon and Presqu'ile North walks are best).

Arrival in Lyon

By Train: Two train stations serve Lyon: Perrache and Part-Dieu. Many trains stop at both, and through trains connect the two stations every 10 minutes. Both are well-served by Métro, bus, and taxi and have lockers and baggage-checking services, making Lyon an easy stopover visit for train travelers.

The Perrache station is more central and within a 20-minute walk of place Bellecour (leave the station following signs to place Carnot, then cross place Carnot and walk straight up pedestrian rue Victor Hugo). Or take the Métro (direction: Laurent Bonnevay) two stops to Bellecour and follow *sortie rue République* signs. The Resistance museum is one stop away from Perrache station on the T-2 tramway (see "Getting around Lyon," below, for Métro and tramway tips).

To get to the city center from the Part-Dieu station, follow *sortie Vivier Merle* signs to the Métro, take it toward Stade de Gerland, transfer at Saxe-Gambetta to the Gare de Vaise route, get off at Bellecour, and follow signs for *sortie rue République* (see "Getting around Lyon," below, for Métro help).

Figure €9–12 to **taxi** from either train station to the hotels listed near place Bellecour.

By Car: The city center is fairly easy to navigate, though you'll encounter traffic on the surrounding freeways. From the freeways, follow signs to *Centre-ville* and *Presqu'ile* and then follow *place Bellecour* signs. Park in the lots under place Bellecour or place des Celestins (yellow P means parking lot) or get advice from your hotel. The TI's map has all public car parks well identified.

By Plane: Lyon's airport, Saint-Exupery (tel. 08 26 80 08 26, toll call-€0.15/min, www.lyon.aeroport.fr), has two flights per hour to Paris' Charles de Gaulle airport and 12 TGVs per day from downtown Paris, and is served by flights from most European capitals. Three shuttles per hour run from the airport to both train stations (€8.20 one-way, €14.60 round-trip, return ticket good for 2 months, tel. 04 72 68 72 17). Allow €45 for a taxi (€55 after 19:00).

Getting around Lyon

Lyon has a user-friendly public transit system, with two flashy streetcar lines (tramways T-1 and T-2), four underground Métro lines (A, B, C, and D), an extensive bus system and two helpful funiculars. The subway, while similar to Paris' Métro in many ways (e.g., routes are signed by *direction* for the last stop on the line), Lyon's Métro system is highly automated, cleaner, and less crowded. There are no turnstiles and no obvious ticket windows. Efficient ticket machines (coins only, change given) are located near the platforms (1 ride-€1.40, 10 rides-€10.60, 1 day-€3.80, funicular round-trip-€2.10). Buy your ticket (firmly push top button for 1 ticket, then put your coins in), validate it by punching it in a nearby chrome machine, and you're in business (tramway users validate on the trams). Study the wall maps to be sure of your direction; ask a local if you're not certain. Your ticket is good for one hour of travel including transfers between Métro, tramways, buses, and funiculars.

Sights—Fourvière Hill

▲▲**Gallo-Roman Museum (Musée de la Civilisation Gallo-Romaine)**—Constructed in the hillside with views of the Roman Theater, this museum makes Lyon's importance in Roman times clear. Lyon was the military base that Julius Caesar used to conquer Gaul (much of modern-day France). Admire the bronze chariot from the seventh century B.C. (yes, that's B.C.) and get oriented at the model of Roman Lyon. Your visit continues downhill past Gallo-Roman artifacts allowing you to piece together life in Lyon during the Roman occupation, including 2,000-year-old lead pipes, a speech by Claudius (translated into English), Roman coins, models of Roman theaters complete with moving stage curtains, and haunting funeral masks (€4, free on Thu, open Tue–Sun 10:00–18:00, until 17:00 Nov–Feb, closed Mon, rooms begin closing 20 min early, helpful English explanations, tel. 04 72 38 81 90).

Basilique Notre-Dame de Fourvière—In the late 1800s, the bishop of Lyon vowed to build a magnificent tribute to God if the Prussians left his city alone (the same reason and vow that built the Sacré-Coeur in Paris). The whipped-cream exterior is neo-everything, and the interior screams "overdone," though the mosaics are impressive and depict key historic scenes. Don't miss the chapel below or the panoramic views from behind the church (basilica open daily 6:00–19:00, Mass held several times a day, ask for schedule, in English the first Sun of the month in the adjoining "old chapel").

Observatory Tower—Climb 278 steps of the northeast tower for an even better lookout, including an excellent orientation table and a chance to see Lyon's two grand rivers flowing to their confluence (€2, April–Sept Wed–Sun 10:00–12:00 & 14:00–18:30, closed Mon–Tue; Oct–March Sat–Sun 13:30–17:30, closed Mon–Fri).

Lyon

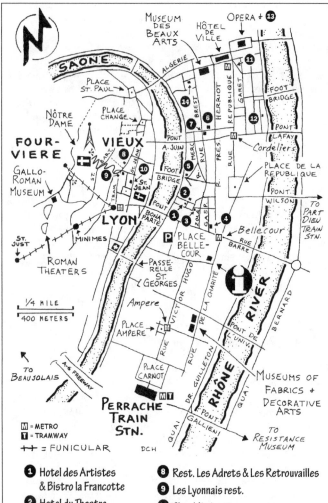

1. Hotel des Artistes & Bistro la Francotte
2. Hotel du Theatre
3. Hotel Colbert
4. Hotel Globe et Cecil
5. Hotel St. Antoine
6. Hotel Moderne
7. Hotel de Bretagne
8. Rest. Les Adrets & Les Retrouvailles
9. Les Lyonnais rest.
10. Chez Mimi rest.
11. Rue G. Verdi
12. Rest. Brunet & Au Pave de Viande
13. Les Muses rest.
14. Café des Federations

Sights—Vieux Lyon (Old Lyon)

▲*Traboules* (Covered Passageways)—Lyon is the Florence
of France, offering the best concentration of well-preserved
Renaissance buildings in the country. From the 16th to the 19th
centuries, Lyon was king of Europe's silk industry; at one point, it
hummed with more than 18,000 looms. The fine buildings of the
old center were designed by Italians and financed by the silk industry. Pastel courtyards, lovely loggias, and delicate arches line the
passageways *(traboules)* connecting these buildings. The serpentine
traboules provided shelter when silk was being moved from one
stage to the next, and would provide handy cover for the French
Resistance in World War II. Several of Lyon's 315 *traboules* are
open to the public (press top button next to street-front door to
release door when entering; push lit buttons to illuminate dark
walkways; pull lever sideways at door handle when leaving; please
respect residents' peace when wandering through). The TI's leaflet
of Vieux Lyon has all the *traboules* and courtyards marked, though
some are periodically closed. As you wander Vieux Lyon, look for
plaques next to doors giving a history of the building and *traboule*.
Snoop the courtyards at #26 and #28 rue St. Jean, and, as you walk
through Lyon's longest *traboule* at #27 rue de Boeuf (push buttons
as you go for mood lights), you'll understand why Lyon made an
ideal center for the Resistance.

Cathedral of St. Jean—Stand as far back as you can in the square
for the best view. This took 300 years to build and transcends
Romanesque and Gothic styles. This cathedral does not soar like
northern French cathedrals from the same period; influenced by
their Italian neighbors, churches in southern France are typically
less vertical than those in the north. Inside, you'll find a few beautiful stained-glass windows and an unusual astrological clock with
an underwhelming performance at 12:00, 14:00, 15:00, and 16:00
(cathedral open Mon–Fri 8:00–12:00 & 14:00–19:30, Sat–Sun
14:00–17:00, Mass at 9:00 and 19:00 weekdays, at 8:30 and 10:30
on Sun). The €0.75 English leaflet is overkill, and the treasury
is of little interest. Check out the ruins predating the cathedral
outside the left transept.

Gadagne Museum—This houses a puppet museum (covering
Lyon's famous Guignol puppets) and a Lyon history museum,
neither of which is ready for prime time (€4, Wed–Mon 10:45–
18:00, closed Tue, place du Petit College).

Sights—On or near Lyon's Presqu'ile

From the Perrache station to place des Terreaux, the Presqu'ile is
Lyon's shopping spine, with thriving pedestrian streets and stores in
all shapes and price ranges. Join the parade of shoppers on sprawling

rue de la République (north of place Bellecour), peruse the *bouchons* (characteristic bistros) of rue Mercière, and relax at a café on place des Terreaux. You'll also find these interesting museums:

▲**Museum of Fine Arts (Musée des Beaux Arts)**—Located around the peaceful courtyard of a former abbey, this fine-arts museum has an impressive collection ranging from Egyptian antiquities to medieval armor to Impressionist paintings. If you need a classical art fix, you'll love it; if you're short on time and going to Paris, it's skippable (€4, Wed–Mon 10:30–18:00, closed Tue, some rooms close 12:00–14:00, pick up museum layout on entering, great café-terrace, picnic-perfect courtyard, 20 place des Terreaux, Métro: Hôtel de Ville).

Museums of Fabrics and Decorative Arts (Musées des Tissus et des Arts Décoratifs)—These special-interest museums are well-organized and help you to understand Lyon's historic importance, but provide no English explanations. The Musée des Tissus held my interest with a tour of Lyon's important silk industry, including beautiful displays of silk from Napoleon's throne room to dresses, hats, and other clothing. The Musée des Arts Décoratifs is a large manor home decorated with period furniture and art objects (€4.60 covers both museums, Tue–Sun 10:00–17:30, closed Mon, Decorative Arts Museum closes 12:00–14:00, 34 rue de la Charité, Métro: Bellecour).

▲▲**Resistance and Deportation Center (Centre d'Histoire de la Resistance et de la Déportation)**—Located near Vichy, capital of the French puppet state and near neutral Switzerland, Lyon was the center of French Resistance from 1942 to 1945. This well-done museum, once used as a Nazi torture chamber, uses austere concrete backdrops, headsets, many videos, reconstructed rooms, and, it seems, anything they can get their hands on to help you understand how the Resistance came to be and what life was like for its members. Excellent English explanations throughout provide a good history lesson, and the headsets help, but you need to move slowly with your headset and stand near the remote signal boxes, or you'll feel like you're decoding your own enemy messages. Those with less time should focus on the TV monitors—the film describing the deportation is in a re-created train boxcar (€4, Wed–Sun 9:00–17:30, closed Mon–Tue, 15-min walk from Perrache station, cross pont Gallieni and walk 3 blocks to 14 avenue Berthelot; or, easier, take T-2 to Centre Berthelot—1 stop from Perrache—or the Métro to Jean Mace and walk back 3 blocks toward the river).

Sleeping in Lyon
(€1 = about $1, country code: 33, zip code: 69002)
Hotels in Lyon are a steal compared to those in Paris. Weekends are generally discounted in this city that thrives on business travel.

Skip the hotels near either train station. All hotels listed below are on the Presqu'ile; the first five are on or near the intimate place des Celestins, two blocks north of place Bellecour (Métro: Bellecour). Hotels have elevators unless otherwise noted, and air-conditioning is a godsend when it's hot. A **launderette** is at 7 rue Mercière (daily 6:00–21:00).

Sleeping on or near Place des Celestins

HIGHER PRICED

Hôtel des Artistes***, ideally located right on place des Celestins, is red-velvet plush, comfortable, professional, and the best value in its price range (Sb-€66–97, Db-€75–103, basic buffet breakfast-€8.50, CC, air-con, 8 rue Gaspard-Andre, tel. 04 78 42 04 88, fax 04 78 42 93 76, e-mail: hartiste@clubinternet.fr, SE).

Hôtel Globe et Cecil*** is the most elegant of my listings, offering refined comfort in tastefully decorated rooms, but with strange hallways (Sb-€90–107, Db-€122–126, includes buffet breakfast, CC, air-con, 21 rue Gasparin, tel. 04 78 42 58 95, fax 04 72 41 99 06, www.globeetcecilhotel.com).

MODERATELY PRICED

Comfort Hôtel Saint Antoine** is a well-situated and sufficiently comfortable modern hotel almost on the Saône River, with modern, well-appointed rooms, Internet access, air-conditioning, and fair rates (Sb-€55–69, Db-€58–74, extra bed-€9, buffet breakfast-€7, CC, 1 rue du Port du Temple, tel. 04 78 92 91 91, fax 04 78 92 47 37, www.hotel-saintantoine.fr).

LOWER PRICED

Hôtel du Théâtre**, across the small square from Hôtel des Artistes, is an artsy place with frumpy rooms in all sizes and shapes, some with sliver showers, none particularly luxurious. Those overlooking the place des Celestins tend to be larger and are worth the extra cost. Expect laid-back owners and many stairs (S-€34, Sb-€49–52, Db-€52–60, extra bed-€8, breakfast-€6, CC, no elevator, 10 rue de Savoie, entrance on back side of place des Celestins, tel. 04 78 42 33 32, fax 04 72 40 00 61, www.hoteldutheatre .online.fr, reservations by fax or telephone only).

Hôtel Colbert**, just off place des Celestins, is immaculate, well-located, and warmly run by Sebastian and Véronique. Bright, cheery rooms on the streetside are larger, but come with street noise (Sb-€55, Db-€60, CC, good buffet breakfast-€7, 4 rue des Archers, tel. 04 72 56 08 98, fax 04 72 56 08 65, www.hotel-colbert.com).

Sleeping near Place des Terreaux

These hotels are about 10 to 15 blocks north of place Bellecour; use Métro Cordeliers for both.

LOWER PRICED

Hôtel Moderne** is a reasonable value, with pleasant pastel rooms and a cheery lobby in the heart of the shopping area (Sb-€45–49, Db-€51–55, CC, 15 rue Dubois, tel. 04 78 42 21 83, must reserve by fax, fax 04 72 41 04 40, www.hotelmodernelyon.com).

Hôtel de Bretagne* is the best one-star value I could find, with tight and tidy rooms and good beds but tired carpeting (Sb-€35, Db-€42, Tb-€48, Qb-€51, CC, no elevator, 10 rue Dubois, tel. 04 78 37 79 33, fax 04 72 77 99 92).

Eating in Vieux Lyon

With an abundance of excellent restaurants in all price ranges, it's hard to go wrong—unless you order *tripes* (cow stomach) or come on a Sunday, when almost all restaurants close. Look for these classics: *quenelles* (large dumplings), roasted chicken from Bresse, and *salade lyonnaise* (lettuce, ham, and poached eggs).

Bouchons are small bistros that evolved from the days when mama would feed the silk workers. Vieux Lyon is a *bouchon* bazaar, though the rue Mercière on the Presqu'ile also offers many good places. Here are a few to get you started (all are closed Sun):

The epicenter of restaurant activity in Vieux Lyon is place Neuve St. Jean—compare the crowds and sift through their menus. **Les Adrets** is nearby, cozy, and good (€20 *menu*, 30 rue de Boeuf, tel. 04 78 38 24 30). At 38 rue de Boeuf, **Les Retrouvailles** offers an excellent €20 *menu*, a charming dining room, and a terrific overall experience. A block south, **Les Lyonnais** is cheaper, lighthearted, and locally popular, with photo portraits of loyal customers lining the walls (€18 *menu*, 1 rue Tramssac, tel. 04 78 37 64 82).

For a salad or quiche and a glass of wine with ambience, consider **Chez Mimi**'s small café one block from the cathedral (inside can be smoky, 66 rue St. Jean).

Eating on the Presqu'ile

The zinc bar bistro **La Francotte** is good for a relaxing drink or a meal and is handy to many hotels (closed Sun, 8 place des Celestins).

Near the opera, these two fine places go unnoticed by tourists (both closed Sun–Mon): The cozy, traditional *bouchon* **Restaurant Brunet** (€15 *menu*, 23 rue Claudia, tel. 04 78 37 44 31) and the more formal **Au Pave de Viande** (€15 *menu*, 15 rue Claudia, tel. 04 78 37 23 89).

For lunch or dinner with an exceptional view, ride the elevator to the seventh floor of the Opera House to **Les Muses de l'Opéra** (€16 dinner *menu*, tel. 04 72 00 45 58). For relaxed outdoor dining, window-shop the *bouchons* lining rue Giuseppe Verdi.

Café des Federations is a venerable institution worth a stop for the traditional Lyonnais ambience and good wine selection (€24 *menu*, closed Sun and Aug, 8 rue Major-Martin, tel. 04 78 28 26 00).

Transportation Connections—Lyon

After Paris, Lyon is France's most important rail hub. Train travelers will find this gateway to the Alps, Provence, the Riviera, and Burgundy an easy stopover. Two main stations serve Lyon (Part-Dieu and Perrache). Most trains officially depart from Part-Dieu, though many stop at Perrache, and trains run between the stations every 10 minutes. Double-check which station your train departs from.

By train to: Paris (20/day, 2 hrs), **Dijon** (14/day, 2 hrs), **Beaune** (13/day, 2 hrs, many change in Macon), **Avignon** (24/day, 14 to TGV station in 1.5 hrs, 10 to main station in 2.5 hrs), **Arles** (20/day, 2.5 hrs, most change in Avignon, Marseille, or Nîmes), **Nice** (9 day, 5 hrs, many change in Avignon, Marseille, or Valence, night train), **Annecy** (17/day, 2 hrs, most change in Aix les Bains), **Venice** (7/day, 11–13 hrs, most change in Geneva and Milan, night train), **Rome** (4/day, 12 hrs, at least 1 change in Milan, night train), **Florence** (3/day, 10 hrs), **Geneva** (10/day, 2 hrs), **Barcelona** (1 day train, 7 hrs, change in Perpignan; 2 night trains).

Drivers: En route to Provence, consider a three-hour detour through the spectacular Ardeche Gorge; exit the A-6 autoroute at Privas and follow the villages of Aubenas, Vallon Pont d'Arc (offers kayak trips), and Pont St. Esprit. En route to Burgundy, consider a Beaujolais detour (see "Sights—Between Burgundy and Lyon," above).

ALSACE AND NORTHERN FRANCE

The French province of Alsace stands like a flower-child referee between Germany and France. Bounded by the Rhine on the east and the softly rolling Vosges Mountains on the west, this is a lush land of Hansel and Gretel villages, sprawling vineyards, and I-could-live-here cities. Food and wine are the primary industry, topic of conversation, and perfect excuse for countless festivals.

Alsace has changed hands several times between Germany and France because of its location, natural wealth, naked vulnerability—and the fact that Germany thinks the mountains are the natural border, while France thinks it's the Rhine River. Having been a political pawn for 1,000 years, Alsace has a hybrid culture: Locals who swear do so bilingually, and the local cuisine features sauerkraut with fine wine. If you're traveling in December, come here for France's most celebrated Christmas markets and festivals.

Strasbourg is a big-city version of Colmar, worth a stop for its grand cathedral. The humbling battlefields of Verdun and the bubbly vigor of Reims in northern France are closer to Paris than Alsace, and follow logically only if your next destination is Paris.

Planning Your Time

Set up in or near Colmar. Allow most of a day for Colmar and a full afternoon for the Wine Road *(Route du Vin)*. If you have one day, wander Colmar's sights until after lunch and then set out for the *Route du Vin*. Urban Strasbourg has a soaring cathedral and a thriving center city. If you can spare an extra half-day, spend it there, but with limited time, skip it. Reims and Verdun are doable by car as stops between Paris and Colmar—if you're speedy. Train travelers with only one day between Colmar and Paris must choose Reims or Verdun.

Alsace to Champagne

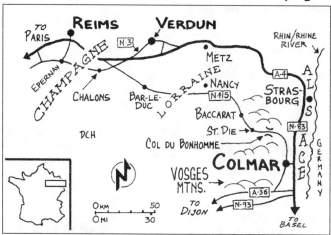

Getting around Alsace

Frequent trains link Colmar and Strasbourg (2/hr, 30 min). Buses and minivan excursions radiate from Colmar to villages along the *Route du Vin*, and you can rent bikes in Colmar and Turckheim if you prefer to pedal (for details on all of these options, see "Route du Vin," below).

Cuisine Scene—Alsace

Alsatian cuisine is a major tourist attraction in itself. The German influence is obvious: sausages, potatoes, onions, and sauerkraut. Look for *choucroute garni* (sauerkraut and sausage—although it seems a shame to eat it in a fancy restaurant), the more traditionally Alsatian *baeckeanoffe* (potato, meat, and onion stew), *rösti* (an oven-baked potato-and-cheese dish), fresh trout, and foie gras. At lunch, or for a lighter dinner, try a *tarte à l'oignon* (like an onion quiche, but better) or *tarte flambée* (like a thin-crust pizza with onion and bacon bits). If you're picnicking, buy some stinky Munster cheese. Dessert specialties are *tarte Alsacienne* (fruit tart) and *glace Kugelhopf* (a light cake mixed with raisins, almonds, dried fruit, and cherry liqueur).

Remember, restaurants serve only during lunch (11:30–14:00) and dinner (19:00–21:00, later in bigger cities); cafés serve food throughout the day.

Alsatian Wines

Alsatian wines are named for their grapes, unlike in Burgundy or Provence, where wines are commonly named after villages, or in

Bordeaux, where wines are often named after châteaux. White wines dominate in the Alsace. The following wines are made entirely of that grape variety: Sylvaner (fairly light, fruity, and inexpensive), Riesling (more robust than Sylvaner, but drier than the German style you're probably used to), Gewürztraminer (spicy, with a powerful bouquet; good with pâtés and local cheeses), Muscat (very dry, with a distinctive bouquet and taste; best as a before-dinner wine), Tokay/Pinot Gris (more full-bodied than Riesling, but fine with many local main courses), Pinot Noir (the local red is overpriced; very light and fruity, generally served chilled), and the tasty Crèmant d'Alsace (the region's good and inexpensive champagne). You'll also see *eaux-de-vie*, powerful fruit-flavored brandies; try the *framboise* (raspberry) flavor.

COLMAR

Colmar is a well-pickled old place of 70,000 residents, offering a few heavyweight sights in a warm, midsize-town package. Historic beauty was usually a poor excuse for being spared the ravages of World War II, but it worked for Colmar. The American and British military were careful not to bomb the half-timbered old burghers' houses, characteristic red- and green-tiled roofs, and cobbled lanes of Alsace's most beautiful city.

Today, Colmar thrives with colorful, half-timbered buildings, impressive art treasures, and German tourists. Schoolgirls park their rickety horse carriages in front of the city hall, ready to give visitors a clip-clop tour of old town. Antique shops welcome browsers, and hotel managers hurry down the sleepy streets to pick up fresh croissants in time for breakfast.

Orientation

Assume you will get lost, as there isn't a straight street in Colmar. Thankfully, most streets are pedestrian-only, and it's a lovely town to be lost in. Navigate by the high church steeples and the helpful signs directing visitors to the various sights. For tourists, the town center is place Unterlinden (a 15-min walk from the train station), where you'll find the TI, Colmar's most important museum, and a huge and handy Monoprix supermarket/department store. Every city bus starts or finishes on place Unterlinden.

Colmar is most crowded from May through September. Weekends are busiest (reserve ahead). The impressive music festival fills hotels the first two weeks of July, and the local wine festival rages for 10 days in early August. Open-air markets bustle next to the Dominican and St. Martin churches on Thursdays and Saturdays.

Tourist Information: The TI is next to the Unterlinden Museum on place Unterlinden. Pick up the excellent city map describing a good walking tour of Colmar, a *Route du Vin* map, information on bike rental, and *Colmar Actualités*, a booklet with bus schedules. Get information about concerts and festivals in Colmar and in nearby villages, and ask about Colmar's Folklore Tuesdays (with folk dancing at 20:30 every Tue mid-May–mid-Sept on place de l'Ancienne). Bikers should get a map of the bike routes (*Le Haut-Rhin à Velo* map, €5.50, suggests routes with estimated timings). The TI also reserves hotel rooms and has *chambres d'hôte* listings for Colmar and the region (April–Oct Mon–Sat 9:00–18:00, until 19:00 July–Aug, Sun 10:00–14:00; Nov–March Mon–Sat 9:00–12:00 & 14:00–18:00, Sun 10:00–14:00, tel. 03 89 20 68 92, www.ville-colmar.fr). A public WC is 20 meters/65 feet left of the TI.

Tours: The TI organizes walking tours of the old town (€4, July–Aug Tue, Thu, Fri, and Sun at 11:00; Sat and Sun only the rest of year, call ahead for times, usually held in the mornings). Private guides are also available through the TI (about €80 for 3 hours). For minivan tours of the *Route du Vin*, see "Getting around the Wine Road," below.

Arrival in Colmar

By Train: To reach the center from the station (15-min walk, bag check available), walk straight out past Hôtel Bristol, turn left on avenue de la République, and keep walking. Buses #1, #2, and #3 all go from the station to the TI (about €1, pay driver). Allow €8 for a taxi to a hotel in central Colmar. The bus stops here for *Route du Vin* villages.

By Car: Follow signs to *Centre-ville*, then *place Rapp*. There's a huge pay parking garage under place Rapp, and (for now) free lots at *parking du Musée Unterlinden* (across from Primo 99 hotel) and off the ring road near Hôtel St. Martin (follow signs from ring road to *Parking de la Vieille Ville*). Several hotels have private parking, and those that don't can advise you where to park.

Helpful Hints

Internet Access: Try Planet Café (3 rue Mercière, opposite Pfister House, tel. 03 89 24 45 07) and Infr@reseau (near TI at 12 rue du Rempart, tel. 03 89 23 98 45).

Laundry: You'll find a launderette near the recommended Maison Jund *chambre d'hôte* at 1 rue Ruest, just off the pedestrian street rue Vauban (usually open daily 8:00–21:00).

Market Days: Markets take place Thursdays on place de l'Ancienne Douane (mornings only; same square also hosts a flea market first and third Fri); Thursdays on place des Dominicains (all day, no produce); and Saturdays on place St. Joseph (mornings only).

Taxis: At the station, call 03 89 41 40 19; otherwise, call 03 89 80 71 71 or 06 09 42 60 75.

Bike Rental: Kiosque Colmarvelo is the cheapest around, with the most extensive hours (€3/half day, €5/full day, bikes come with basket and lock, baby seat upon request, in kiosk stand at 4 avenue République on place Rapp, near carousel, tel. 03 89 41 37 90).

Car Rental: Try Europcar (4 rue Timken, ZI Nord, tel. 03 89 20 85 70) or Avis (49 avenue 1ere Armée Francaise, tel. 03 89 23 21 82).

Self-Guided Tour of Colmar's Old Town

This walk works day or night. Look for handy information plaques with English explanations at various points throughout.

The importance of 15th- to 17th-century Colmar is clear as you wander its pedestrian-friendly old center, decorated with 45 buildings classified as historic monuments. In the Middle Ages, most of Europe was fragmented into chaotic little princedoms and dukedoms. Merchant-dominated cities, natural proponents of the formation of large nation-states, banded together to form "trading leagues" (the World Trade Organizations of their day). The Hanseatic League was the superleague of northern Europe. Prosperous Colmar was a member of a smaller league of 10 Alsatian cities, called the Decapolis (founded 1354).

Start your tour at the old **Customs House** (Koifhus). Here, delegates of the Decapolis would meet to sort out trade issues, much like the European Union does in nearby Strasbourg today. Walk under its archway to place de l'Ancienne Douane and face the Bartholdi statue—arm raised, à la *Statue of Liberty*—and do a 360-degree spin to appreciate a gaggle of gables. This was the center of business activity in Colmar, with trade routes leading from here to several major European cities. Today, it's the festive site of outdoor wine-tastings on many summer evenings. The soaring, half-timbered commotion of higgledy-piggledy rooftops on the other side of the fountain marks the **Tanners' Quarters**. These 17th- and 18th-century rooftops competed for space in the sun to dry their freshly tanned hides; the nearby river channel got rid of the waste products. Walk to the end of Petite rue des Tanneurs (*not* rue des Tanneurs), turn right, and take the first left along the stream. On your right is the old market hall (fish, produce, and other products were brought here by flat-bottomed boat). Cross the canal and turn right on rue de la Poissonnerie (the fisherman's street), and you'll enter **La Petite Venise** quarter, a bundle of Colmar's most colorful houses lining the small canal. This tourist-popular area is romantic at night, with a fraction of the tourists. That beautiful building hanging over the water is the four-star Hôtel Maréchal (see "Sleeping in Colmar," below).

Cross the bridge, take the second right on Grande Rue, and stroll to **Chez Hanzi** restaurant on the rue des Marchands (Merchants' Street), back near the old Customs House. Overhanging roofs such as these were a medieval tax dodge. Since houses were taxed on square footage at street level, owners would expand tax-free up and over the street. Walk up rue des Marchands, and in two blocks you'll come face-to-face with the **Pfister House** (Maison Pfister), a richly decorated merchant's house from 1537. The external spiral staircase turret and painted walls illustrate the city folk's taste for Renaissance humanism (the wine shop on the ground floor is Colmar's best). The man carved into the side of the building next door (to the left) was a drape maker; he's shown holding a bar, Colmar's measure of about one meter. (In the Middle Ages, it was common for cities to have their own units of length.) One more block on the left is the **Bartholdi Museum** (described below). A passage to the right leads to Colmar's golden **Cathédrale St. Martin,** with its lone tower (two were planned), then find your way up rue des Serruriers (Locksmiths' Street) to the **Dominican Church** (worth entering, described below). Compare the soaring St. Martin Cathedral with this low-slung, sober structure that perfectly symbolizes Dominican austerity; both were built at the same time. Continue up rue des Boulangers (Bakers' Street), and then make a hard right down rue des Têtes. The **House of Heads** on the right is Colmar's other famous merchant's house. It was built in 1609 and is decorated with 105 faces and masks. Angle down the rue de l'Eau (Water Street) for a shortcut to the TI and the Unterlinden Museum.

Sights—Colmar

▲▲▲**Unterlinden Museum**—Colmar's touristic claim to fame is one of my favorite museums in Europe. Its extensive yet manageable collection ranges from Roman Colmar to medieval wine-making exhibits, and from traditional wedding dresses to paintings that give vivid insight into the High Middle Ages.

The highlight of the museum (and, for me, the city) is Grünewald's gripping *Isenheim Altarpiece*, actually a series of three different paintings on hinges that pivot like shutters (study the little model on the wall, explained in English). Designed to help people in a medieval hospital endure horrible skin diseases (such as St. Anthony's Fire, later called rye ergotism) long before the age of painkillers, it's one of the most powerful paintings ever produced.

Colmar

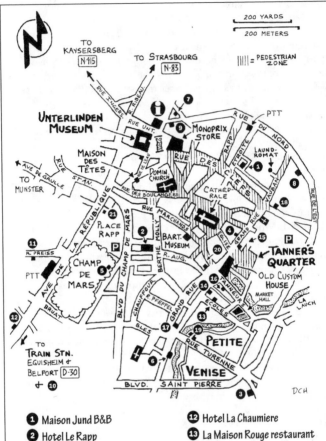

1 Maison Jund B&B
2 Hotel Le Rapp
3 Hotel Turenne
4 Hotel St. Martin
5 Hotel Mercure (Champs de Mars)
6 Hotel Marechal
7 Primo 99
8 Hotel Ibis
9 Hotel Mercure (Unterlinden)
10 To Hotel Bristol
11 Hotel Kyriad

12 Hotel La Chaumiere
13 La Maison Rouge restaurant
14 La Taverne restaurant
15 Winstub Schwendi
16 Creperie Tom Pouce
17 Café-Patisserie Salon de The
18 La Ville de Paris restaurant
19 Winstubs
20 Au Fer Rouge Restaurant
21 Bike Rental

Stand as if you were a medieval peasant in front of the center-piece and let the agony and suffering of the Crucifixion drag its fingers down your face. The point—Jesus' suffering—is drilled home: the weight of his body bending the crossbar, his elbows pulled from their sockets by the weight of his dead body, his mangled feet, the grief on Mary's face. In hopes that the intended viewers (the hospital's patients) would know that Jesus understood their suffering, he was even painted to appear as if he, too, had a skin disease. Study the faces and the Christian symbolism.

The three scenes of the painting changed with the seasons of the church year. The happy ending—a psychedelic explosion of Resurrection joy—is the spiritual equivalent of jumping from the dentist's chair directly into a Jacuzzi. The last two panels, showing the meeting of St. Paul the hermit and St. Anthony, are the product of a fertile imagination and the stuff of which nightmares are made.

There's more to the museum. Ringing the peaceful cloister is a fine series of medieval church paintings and sculpture, and a room filled with old winepresses. Downstairs, you'll find Roman and prehistoric artifacts. The upstairs rooms contain local and folk history, with everything from medieval armor to old-time toys (€7, price includes helpful audioguide, May–Oct daily 9:00–18:00, Nov–April Wed–Mon 9:00–12:00 & 14:00–17:00, closed Tue, tel. 03 89 41 89 23).

▲▲**Dominican Church**—Here's another medieval mindblower. In Colmar's Eglise des Dominicains, you'll find Martin Schongauer's angelically beautiful *Virgin in the Rosebush* holding court center stage, dating from 1473 but looking as if it were painted yesterday. Here, Mary is shown as a welcoming mother. Jesus clings to her, reminding the viewer of the possibility of an intimate relationship with Mary. The Latin on her halo reads: "Pick me also for your child, O very Holy Virgin." Rather than telling a particular Bible story, this is a general scene . . . designed to meet the personal devotional needs of any worshiper. Here, nature is not a backdrop. Mary and Jesus are encircled by it. Schongauer's robins, sparrows, and goldfinches bring extra life to an already impressively natural rosebush. The contrast provided by the simple Dominican setting heightens the flamboyance of this late-Gothic masterpiece. Dominican churches were intentionally austere, symbolic of their zeal to purify their faith and compete with the growing popularity of 13th-century heretical movements, such as Catharism, whose message was a simpler faith (€1.30, April–Dec daily 10:00–13:00 & 15:00–18:00, closed Jan–March). This Dominican austerity is more apparent after a visit to Colmar's fancier, and Franciscan, St. Martin's Cathedral.

Bartholdi Museum—This little museum recalls the life and work of the local boy who gained fame by sculpting the *Statue of Liberty*. Several of his statues grace Colmar's squares (€4, March–Dec Wed–Mon 10:00–12:00 & 14:00–18:00, closed Tue and Jan–Feb, in heart of old town at 30 rue des Marchands).

Sleeping in Colmar
(€1 = about $1, country code: 33, zip code: 68000)

Sleep Code: **S** = Single, **D** = Double/Twin, **T** = Triple, **Q** = Quad, **b** = bathroom, **s** = shower only, **CC** = Credit Cards accepted, **no CC** = Credit Cards not accepted, **SE** = Speaks English, **NSE** = No English, ***** = French hotel rating system (0–4 stars).

To help you sort easily through these listings, I've divided the rooms into three categories based on the price for a standard double room with bath:

Higher Priced—Most rooms more than €90.
Moderately Priced—Most rooms €90 or less.
Lower Priced—Most rooms €50 or less.

Hotels are fairly expensive and jammed on weekends in May, June, September, and October. Plan ahead. July and August are busy, but there are always rooms—somewhere. Should you have trouble finding a room in Colmar (the TI can help), look in a nearby village where small hotels and bed-and-breakfasts are plentiful; see my recommendations under "Sleeping in Eguisheim," below.

HIGHER PRICED

Hôtel St. Martin***, near the old Customs House, is a family-run place that began as a coaching inn (since 1361). It's small, with traditional yet well-equipped rooms woven into its antique frame. Half of its 24 rooms are in the annex, opposite a peaceful court-yard. While just as comfortable, these cheaper rooms have showers instead of tubs and no elevator or air-conditioning. Eighteen new rooms are planned for 2003 (Sb-€61–105, Db-€69–121, most about €96, Tb-€113–133, CC, free public parking nearby at *Parking de la Vieille Ville*, 38 Grand Rue, tel. 03 89 24 11 51, fax 03 89 23 47 78, www.hotel-saint-martin.com, Winterstein family SE).

Mercure Hôtels (Unterlinden and Champs de Mars)***: You can sleep comfortably in either of these chain hotels for about the same price as Hôtel St. Martin, but without a hint of the Old World (Sb-€91–105, Db-€99–112, CC, air-con, some rooms non-smoking, elevators, easy parking). The Champs de Mars Mercure is located in a park near place Rapp (2 avenue de la Marne, tel. 03 89 21 59 59, fax 03 89 21 59 00, e-mail: h1225@accor-hotels.com). The other Mercure, near the Unterlinden Museum, is a little less expensive (5 rue Golbery, tel. 03 89 41 71 71, fax 03 89 23 82 71, e-mail: h0978@accor-hotels.com).

Hôtel Maréchal**** provides Colmar's most famous and most characteristic digs in the heart of La Petite Venise, with plush rooms and professional service (standard Db-€85–125, Db with whirlpool tub-€115–215, suite Db-€245, CC, 4 place des Six Montagnes Noirs, tel. 03 89 41 60 32, fax 03 89 24 59 40, www.hotel-le-marechal.com). Their well-respected restaurant will melt a romantic's heart; you will be encouraged to dine here (*menus* from €30, reserve ahead).

MODERATELY PRICED

Hôtel Le Rapp**, just off place Rapp, is the best-located two-star hotel in town, with 42 just-large-enough rooms, a small basement pool, sauna, Turkish bath, and an indoor/outdoor bar-café. It's well-run, English-speaking, and family-friendly, with a big park one block away (Sb-€50–52, Db-€66–76, good buffet breakfast-€7.50, CC, elevator, 1 rue Berthe-Molley, tel. 03 89 41 62 10, fax 03 89 24 13 58, www.rapp-hotel.com). Its restaurant serves a classy Alsatian *menu* with impeccable service (closed Fri).

Hôtel Turenne** is sharp and a good value, with 83 rooms in a historic building. It's a 10-minute walk from the city center, a 15-minute walk from the train station, and is located on a busy street with easy parking. Rooms are well-appointed, but some have tight bathrooms. A third of the rooms are non-smoking (Sb-€42, Db-€56–62, Tb-€64, family-friendly studios-€100, CC, parking-€5.50, elevator for 1 wing, cozy bar, from train station walk straight out to avenue Raymond Poincaré, turn left on rue des Americains, 10 route du Bale, tel. 03 89 21 58 58, fax 03 89 41 27 64, www.turenne.com, SE).

Hôtel Ibis**, on the ring road, sells hospital-white, efficient comfort with pleasant rooms but small bathrooms (Sb-€54, Db-€58, CC, parking-€6, 11 rue St. Eloi, tel. 03 89 41 30 14, fax 03 89 24 51 49).

LOWER PRICED

Maison Jund offers my favorite budget beds in Colmar. This ramshackle yet magnificent half-timbered home, the home of an easygoing wine-maker, feels like a medieval tree house soaked in wine and filled with flowers. The rooms are simple but adequately comfortable, spacious, and equipped with kitchenettes. Most rooms are generally available only April to mid-September, though two rooms are rented year-round (D-€27, Db/Tb-€32–39, no breakfast served, CC, 12 rue de l'Ange, tel. 03 89 41 58 72, fax 03 89 23 15 83, e-mail: martinjund@hotmail.com). Leave your car at the lot across from the Primo 99 hotel, walk from Unterlinden Museum past Monoprix, and veer left on rue des Clefs, left on rue Etroite, and right on rue de l'Ange. This is not a hotel, so there is no real reception, though friendly Myriam (SE) seems to be around, somewhere, most of the time.

Primo 99**, near Unterlinden Museum, is an efficient, bright, nothing-but-the-plastic-and-concrete-basics place to sleep for those who consider ambience a four-letter word (S/D/T-€27, Sb-€43, Db-€46–52, Tb-€57, Qb-€62, CC, 5 rue des Ancêtres, free parking in big square in front, rooms held until 18:30 if you call, friendly staff, tel. 03 89 24 22 24, fax 03 89 24 55 96, www.hotel-primo.com, SE). Half the beds have footboards— a problem if you're taller than six foot two.

Sleeping near the Train Station

MODERATELY PRICED

Hôtel Bristol*** couldn't be closer to the station and, in spite of its Best Western plaque, has some character, with pleasant public spaces and good—if pricey—rooms (Db-€73–120, most Db about €89, CC, 7 place de la Gare, tel. 03 89 23 59 59, fax 03 89 23 92 26, www.grand-hotel-bristol.fr).

LOWER PRICED

La Chaumière* , on a big street two blocks from the station, is above and behind a truly French café and has been run by gentle Madame Servor for 40 years. Most of its modest, good-value rooms surround a courtyard off the street (S/D-€28, Sb/Db-€38–43, breakfast-€5, CC, parking-€4, walk straight out of the station and turn left on avenue de la République to #74, tel. 03 89 41 08 99, SE a smidgen).

Kyriad Hôtel** is a modern chain hotel and a reasonable value (Sb-€36, Db-€47–50, Tb-€61, buffet breakfast-€6, CC, elevator, 1 rue de la Gare, turn left immediately when leaving station and walk 10 min, tel. 03 89 41 34 80, fax 03 89 41 27 84, e-mail: kyriadcolmar@aol.com).

Eating in Colmar

(Also see "Eating in Eguisheim," below.)

La Maison Rouge has warm ambience and is good for reasonably priced, traditional Alsatian cuisine (€15.25 and €20 *menus*, try the endive salad and *tarte flambée forestière*, closed Sun, 9 rue des Ecoles, tel. 03 89 23 53 22).

La Taverne is nearby and serves *tartes flambées* and other regional specialties to appreciative locals (closed Sat at lunch and all Sun, 2 impasse de la Maison Rouge, tel. 03 89 41 70 33).

Winstub Schwendi has wood-cozy ambience and is

German-pub-lively. Try one of their robust Swiss *rösti* plates (€8.50–10, facing old Custom House at 3 Grand Rue).

Crêperie Tom Pouce serves inexpensive crêpes and salads with atmosphere (daily, 10 rue des Tanneurs).

La Ville de Paris is closer to the Unterlinden Museum, friendly, and affordable, serving traditional Alsatian dishes (€17.50 *menu*, place Jeanne d'Arc, tel. 03 89 24 53 15).

Hôtel Restaurant le Rapp is a traditional place to savor a slow, elegant meal served with grace and fine Alsatian wine (*menus* start at €15.25, great *baeckeanoffe*, good salads, closed Fri, air-con, 1 rue Berthe-Molley, tel. 03 89 41 62 10, SE).

Au Fer Rouge, in one of Colmar's oldest and most charac-teristic buildings, is a serious, worthwhile splurge. This is where locals go for a truly special occasion (€50–80 for dinner, reserve ahead, 52 Grand Rue, tel. 30 89 41 37 24, fax 03 89 23 82 24).

For canalfront dining, head into La Petite Venise to the photo-perfect bridge on rue Turenne, where you'll find two lively **Winstubs** (both cheap and fun for *tartes flambées*). On the other side of the bridge lies the **Café-Pâtisserie Salon de Thé,** with tasty quiches, *tarte flambées*, and salads (to take out or eat there, closed Mon, open until 22:00, until 19:00 off-season, on place des Six Montagnes Noires).

Picnics: The Monoprix department store/supermarket is across from the Unterlinden Museum and next to the TI (Mon–Sat 8:30–20:00, closed Sun).

Transportation Connections—Colmar
By train to: Strasbourg (hrly, 50 min), **Reims** (6/day, 6 hrs, changes in Strasbourg or Mulhouse and Metz or Chalon), **Beaune** (6/day, 4–5 hrs, changes in Besançon, Mulhouse, or Beflort and Dijon), **Paris'** Gare de l'Est (12/day, 5.5 hrs, change in Strasbourg, Dijon, or Mulhouse), **Amboise** (8/day, 9 hrs, via Paris), **Basel**, Switzerland (13/day, 1 hr), **Karlsruhe**, Germany (10/day, 2.5 hrs, best with change in Strasbourg; from Karlsruhe, it's 90 min to Frankfurt, 3 hrs to Munich).

ROUTE DU VIN (THE WINE ROAD)
Alsace's *Route du Vin* is an asphalt ribbon tying 145 kilometers/ 90 miles of vineyards, villages, and feudal fortresses into an understandably popular tourist package. The generally dry, sunny climate has made for good wine and happy tourists since Roman days. Colmar and Eguisheim are ideally located for exploring the 30,000 acres of vineyards blanketing the hills from Marlenheim to Thann. If you have only a day, focus on towns within easy striking range of Colmar. Top stops are Eguisheim, Kaysersberg,

Hunawihr, Ribbeauvillé, and the too-popular Riquewihr. As you tour this region, you'll see storks' nests on many church spires and city halls, thanks to a campaign to reintroduce the birds to this area (the big nests weigh over 1,000 pounds). Get a map of the *Route du Vin* from any TI.

Most towns have wineries that give tours (some charge a fee). The modern cooperatives at Eguisheim, Bennwihr, Hunawihr, and Ribbeauvillé, created after the destruction of World War II, provide a good look at a more modern and efficient method of production. Try the tasty Muscat and Gewürztraminer wines. Crèmant, the Alsatian "champagne," is very good—and much cheaper. The French term for headache, if you really get "Alsaced," is *mal à la tête*.

Getting around the Wine Road

Pick up a Michelin regional map before heading out.

By Bus: Public buses connect Colmar's train station with most of the villages along the *Route du Vin*. The schedules are fairly convenient but close to nonexistent on Sunday (Mon–Sat schedules from Colmar to Eguisheim: 6/day, 5 min; to Kaysersberg: hrly, 30 min; to Riquewihr, Bennwihr, Hunawihr, and Ribbeauvillé: 6/day, 30–45 min; to Turckheim: 6/day, 20 min). Get schedules from the TI and buy tickets from the driver (about €2–3 from Colmar to most Route du Vin villages).

By Minivan Tour: At **Les Circuits d'Alsace**, friendly Jean-Claude Werner leads day trips in a comfortable minivan. His tours are informative and include a variety of sights. Wine-tastings can be arranged on request (half-day tours-€47–50, full-day tours-€95, CC, reserve ahead through Colmar TI and be picked up there, or reserve directly with Jean-Claude and be picked up at your hotel, office is across from Colmar train station at 6 place de la Gare, open Mon–Fri 9:00–12:30 & 14:00–18:30, Sat 9:00–13:00, tel. 03 89 41 90 88, cellular 06 88 40 21 02, www.alsace-travel.com).

By Bike: The Wine Road's more-or-less-level terrain makes biking a reasonable option (see "Helpful Hints," page 438), for bike rental in Colmar or, to save yourself the ride out of Colmar, you can rent a bike in Turckheim (84 Grand Rue, tel. 03 89 27 06 36). Turckheim, Kaysersberg, Riquewihr, and Hunawihr make good biking destinations (figure 90 min to Kaysersberg, get advice and a good map from a bike shop and avoid major roads—except for those you use to leave Colmar, see directions under "By Car," below).

By Car: To reach the Wine Road north of Colmar, leave Colmar from the station following signs to Epinal. In Wintzen-heim, follow signs to Turckheim, then find D-10 *(Route du Vin)*

Alsace's Wine Road

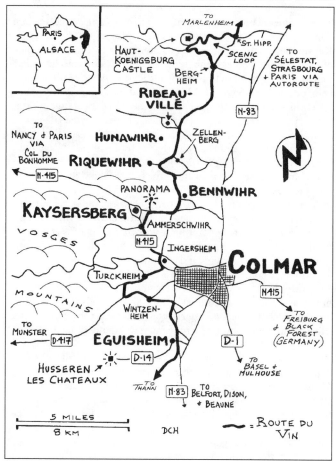

to Ingersheim (Kaysersberg is a short detour from here), Riquewihr, Hunawihr, Ribbeauvillé, and Château de Haut-Koenigsbourg. Look for *Route du Vin* signs. For Eguisheim, leave Colmar on N-83 toward Beflort.

By Foot: Generally well-signed walking trails connect *Route du Vin* villages through the vineyards (get info at local TIs), and hikers can climb to the higher ruined castles of the Vosges Mountains (Eguisheim and Ribbeauvillé are good bases). Kaysersberg to Riquewihr is a good 90-minute walk (return by bus, see "Kaysersberg," below).

Sights along the Wine Road, North of Colmar

These sights are listed from south to north.

Turckheim—This pleasant town, with a small castle, is just enough off the beaten path to be overlooked.

Kaysersberg—Albert Schweitzer's hometown offers a cute jumble of 15th-century homes, though its boutique-filled main drag can be tourist-swamped. The **TI** is inside Hôtel de Ville near the town's main entry (Mon–Sat 8:30–12:00 & 13:00–17:30, tel. 03 89 78 22 78, clean WCs under the arch next to TI). Walkers should pick up the free *sentier viticole* map for navigating between wine villages on foot and bus schedules from their destination village back to Colmar. Serious walkers can buy the €9 trail map (see "Walking Trails from Kaysersberg," below).

Climb the **castle tower** (near the TI) for the view, stroll down the main drag to the **St. Croix church** (worth a peek for its 400-year-old altarpiece, open daily, closes at 18:00), then find the stork's nest near the fortified town bridge. **Dr. Schweitzer's house** is small and disappointing, with scattered photos and no English (€2, Easter–Oct daily 9:00–12:00 & 14:00–18:00, closed Nov–Easter, 126 rue Général de Gaulle).

If you decide to bed down in Kaysersberg, do so at the spotless **Hôtel L'Arbre Vert****, where you get three stars for the price of two and tastefully decorated rooms (Sb-€55, Db-€57–66, in high season half pension preferred but not obligatory, across from Albert Schweitzer house at 1 rue Haute du Rempart, tel. 03 89 47 11 51, fax 03 89 78 13 40).

Walking Trails from Kaysersberg: Well-marked trails depart from the TI and lead through vineyards to other *Route du Vin* towns (walk under arch next to TI and find trail signs). For an easy 90-minute walk to Riquewihr (where buses can take you back to Colmar), go to the next village (Kientzheim), find the bike trail *(piste cyclable)* that departs from behind Hôtel de Ville, and follow the train until you see signs for the *Sentier Viticole* (marked with a red cross), which you can follow all the way to Riquewihr.

Alsatian Panorama at WWII Monument—This remarkable viewpoint, easiest to reach by car, is at the WWII monument and military cemetery (also called Negrophile Nationale or Cimitière Militaire). The spectacular setting, best at sunset, houses a monument to the American divisions that helped liberate Alsace in World War II (find the American flag), a beautiful cemetery for French and North African soldiers who died for the cause, and a brilliant panorama over the southern section of the *Route du Vin* and into Germany.

To find this poorly marked place, go to Sigolsheim (between Kaysersberg and Bennwihr). The road to the monument leaves from the town center (look for French flags at Pierre Sparr winery and follow small signs to Cimitière Militaire or Negrophile Nationale). After you check out the monument to the Americans, take the small road to the top to find the viewpoint and cemetery.

Riquewihr—Overly picturesque, this walled village is crammed with tourist shops, cafés, galleries, cobblestones, and flowers. Try the excellent wine-tasting and tour at Caves Dopff et Irion (Cour du Château, tel. 03 89 47 92 51, **TI** tel. 03 89 47 80 80).

Zellenberg—This town has an impressive setting and is worth a quick stop for the views from either side of its narrow perch.

Hunawihr—This bit of wine-soaked Alsatian cuteness is far less visited than its more famous neighbors and comes complete with a 16th-century fortified church that today is shared by Catholics and Protestants (the Catholics are buried next to the church; the Protestants are buried outside the church wall). Park below the church in the village at the sheltered picnic tables and follow the trail up to the church, then loop back through the village. Kids will enjoy Hunawihr's small stork park (Parc des Cygognes, April–Nov daily 10:00–12:00 & 14:00–18:00, closed Oct–March, other animals take part in the afternoon shows). You'll find a few *chambres d'hôte* and a good wine cooperative in Hunawihr. Eat well at **Winstub Suzel** near the church (closed Tue, 2 rue de l'Eglise, tel. 03 89 73 30 85).

Ribbeauvillé—Come here to hike. Two brooding castles hang above this pleasant town, seldom visited by Americans. The steep castle trail leaves from the top of the town (at Hôtel Trois Châteaux, park in city lot here). Allow 45 minutes one-way, or just climb 10 minutes for a view over the town.

Château de Haut-Koenigsbourg—If you haven't yet visited an Alsatian castle, here's your chance. Strategically situated on a rocky spur high above the flat Rhine plain, it protected passage between Alsace and Lorraine for centuries (fantastic views, on a clear day you can see the Black Forest and on a really clear day, the Alps). Rebuilt in the early 20th century, this well-furnished castle illustrates Germanic influence in Alsatian history. There's little English, so you need the informative 90-minute audioguide (€7, free first Sun of month, audioguide-€4, June–Aug daily 9:30–18:00, April–May and Sept 9:30–17:00, March and Oct 9:45–16:30, Nov–Feb closed 12:00–13:00, about 15 min north of Ribbeauvillé above St. Hippolyte, consider the longer scenic route via Thannenkirch).

EGUISHEIM

Just a few kilometers south of Colmar's suburbs (a flat and easy bike ride on busy roads), this circular, flower-festooned little wine town is nearly too cute. It's ideal for a relaxing lunch and makes a good small-town base for exploring Alsace. It's a cinch by car (easy parking) and accessible by bus (6/day, 10 min, departs Colmar's train station).

The helpful **TI** (on the street that bisects Eguisheim) has information on accommodations, festivals, walks in the vineyards, and hikes into the Vosges (April–Sept Mon–Fri 9:00–12:00 & 13:30–18:00, Sat until 17:30, Sun 10:00–12:00 only; Oct–March Mon–Fri 9:00–12:00 & 14:00–18:00, Sat until 16:00, closed Sun, 22 Grand Rue, tel. 03 89 23 40 33, www.ot-eguisheim.fr).

Eguisheim is best explored by walking around its narrow circular road (rue des Remparts) and then cutting through the middle. Visit the colorful church and one of Eguisheim's countless cozy **wineries** or the big and modern **Wine Cooperative** (Wolfberger, Cave Vinicole d'Eguisheim, daily 8:00–12:00 & 14:00–18:00, tours and tastings available, 6 Grand Rue, tel. 03 89 22 20 20).

Views over Eguisheim: If you have a car, follow signs up to Les Husseren and Les 5 Châteaux, then walk 20 minutes to the **ruined castle towers** for a good view of the Vosges above and vineyards below. Without wheels, find any path through vineyards above Eguisheim for nice views (the TI has a free map, *Canton de Wintzenheim en balade*). For a good 90-minute round-trip walk, start at the campground at the eastern end of town and continue on the road past the Stork Park (to the right of camping entrance), then find the *Sentier Viticole* signs (marked with red circles). Follow this *Sentier Viticole* road up to the stop sign (main road here), turn left, and look for the path on the right up into the vineyards. Follow signs through the vineyards to the village of Hussern, then double back to Eguisheim.

Sleeping in Eguisheim
(€1 = about $1, country code: 33, zip code: 68420)

Chambres d'Hôte

While none of the owners speak English, they're creative at communicating. Please remember to cancel if you reserve a room and can't use it.

MODERATELY PRICED

Your Alsatian grandmother, **Madame Hertz-Meyers,** welcomes you with big rooms in a mansion surrounded by vineyards, only 75 meters/250 feet from the village center. Rooms in the main house are perfect for families and better than her two modern apartments (Sb-€40, Db-€51–56, Tb-€72, includes breakfast, no CC, 3 rue Riesling; look for sign *Albert-Hertz, Dégustation-Vente*, walk into courtyard, and ring bell on left side of house;

check-in after 18:00 unless otherwise prearranged by fax, tel.
03 89 23 67 74, fax 03 89 23 99 23).

LOWER PRICED
It's hard to imagine a better location, more comfortable rooms,
or a more charming owner than **Monique Freudenreich**, who is
learning English (Db-€40, includes breakfast, no CC, 1 block
from TI, 4 cour Unterlinden, tel. & fax 03 89 23 16 44). Formal
Madame Dirringer's five comfortable rooms have big beds and
face a traditional courtyard (Db-€31–33, breakfast-€5, no CC,
11 rue Riesling, tel. 03 89 41 71 87). **Madame Alleman** has simple,
traditional rooms above her gift shop and bakery (Db-€28–31,
breakfast-€5, no CC, 28 Grande Rue, tel. 03 89 41 40 25, fax 03 89
49 24 47). Gentle **Madame Bombenger**'s modern home has nice
views into the vineyards and over Eguisheim (Db-€42, includes
breakfast, CC, 3 rue de Trois Pierres, tel. & fax 03 89 23 71 19).

Hotels
Hotels are a good value here, although most care more about
their restaurants than their rooms.

HIGHER PRICED
Overlooking the village, the modern yet tasteful **Hôtel St.
Hubert***** offers polished comfort, an indoor pool and sauna,
vineyards out your window, and free pickup at Colmar's train
station if reserved in advance (Db-€75–95, extra bed-€16, 4 of
the 12 rooms have terraces, buffet breakfast-€9.50, CC, 6 rue
des Trois Pierres, tel. 03 89 41 40 50, fax 03 89 41 46 88, www
.hotel-st-hubert.com, e-mail: hotel.st.hubert@wanadoo.fr).

MODERATELY PRICED
The picturesque **Auberge Alsacienne***** is a good value, with
small, tastefully designed rooms and rental bikes for guests
(Db-€50–60, Tb-€69, CC, 12 Grand Rue, tel. 03 89 41 50 20,
fax 03 89 23 89 32).

    The snazzy **Hostellerie du Château*****—part art gallery,
part hotel—is ideally located in front of the church and provides
stylish, contemporary luxury (Sb-€63, Db-€76–88, extra bed-
€15.25, breakfast-€9, CC, 2 place du Château St. Leon IX, tel.
03 89 23 72 00, fax 03 89 41 63 93).

LOWER PRICED
The five cozy rooms above **Auberge du Rempart** are a good value
(Db-€46–49, breakfast-€5, CC, 3 rue des Rempart Sud, near TI, tel.
03 89 41 16 87, fax 03 89 41 06 50, www.auberge-du-rempart.fr.st).

Eating in Eguisheim

Auberge de Trois Châteaux is cozy and good (26 Grand Rue, tel. 03 89 23 70 61). The recommended **Auberge Alsacienne** offers fine meals (2 courses-€18.50, 3 courses-€24.50), and the recommended **Auberge du Rempart** has good *tarte flambée* and outdoor tables surrounding a fountain (closed Mon, closed Sun off-season; for address and tel. of both, see "Sleeping in Eguisheim," above). **Le Pavillon Gourmand** is at the top of the town and is the place to go for a special meal (*menus* €13–28, closed Tue–Wed, 101 rue Rempart Sud, tel. 03 89 24 36 88).

STRASBOURG

Strasbourg is urban Alsace at its best, and it feels like a giant Colmar with water. It's one of France's most livable big cities, with generous space devoted to pedestrians, bike lanes, meandering waterways, and a young, lively population of university students and Eurocrats. Situated on the west bank of the Rhine River, Strasbourg provides the ultimate blend of Franco-Germanic culture, architecture, and ambience. Since 1949, Strasbourg has been home to the European Parliament, sharing administrative responsibilities for the European Union with Brussels, Belgium. Strasbourg is a fine day trip from Colmar or a handy stop en route to Paris. Plan on three hours, starting at Strasbourg's dazzling cathedral (try to be here by 12:15 for the clock's best performance, see below) and ending with La Petite France (for lunch).

Tourist Information: There are two TIs. One is at the train station (outside and 1 floor down, June–Sept daily 9:00–18:00; April–May and Oct daily 9:00–12:30 & 13:30–17:30; Nov–March Mon–Sat 9:00–12:30 & 13:30–16:30, closed Sun). The main office is at 17 place de la Cathédrale (daily 9:00–19:00, tel. 03 88 52 28 28, www.strasbourg.com). Buy the €1 city map (which describes a decent walking tour in English) or spring for the €6 audioguide covering the cathedral and old city, which includes a cute little map of the route (allow 90 min).

Arrival in Strasbourg

By Train: After stopping by the station TI (baggage check available), walk 15 pleasant minutes to the cathedral. Walk past Hôtel Vendôme up rue Marie Kuss, cross the river, and continue straight on rue 22 November to place Kleber. Cross place Kleber and turn right on rue des Grandes Arcades and follow that spire. (Return to the station via the La Petite France neighborhood.) A sleek tram runs from the station one floor below the TI (€1.10, Tram A, direction: Illkirch) to the Grande Rue stop, two blocks from the cathedral (return to the station, *Gare Central*, from same stop, direction: Hautpierre).

By Car: Follow *Centre-ville/Cathédrale* signs and park as close to the center as you can. Parking lots are well-marked—place Gutenberg and place du Château are most convenient, though the larger Austerlitz lot works fine.

Helpful Hints

U.S. Consulate: It's at 15 rue d'Alsace (tel. 03 88 32 67 27, fax 03 88 23 07 17).

Airport: The user-friendly Strasbourg-Entzheim airport (tel. 03 88 64 67 67) has frequent and often inexpensive flights to Paris and is easily accessible via tram and shuttle bus.

Sights—Strasbourg

▲▲**Strasbourg Cathedral (Cathédrale de Notre-Dame)**— Stand in front of Hôtel de la Cathédrale and crane your neck up. If this church makes an impression today, with its single soaring spire and pink sandstone color, imagine the impact it had on medieval peasants. The delicate Gothic style of the cathedral (begun in 1176, not finished until 1429) is another Franco-German mixture that somehow survived the French Revolution, the Franco-Prussian war, World War I, and World War II.

As you enter, notice the sculpture over the left portal (complacent, spear-toting Virtues getting revenge on those nasty Vices). Enter and walk about halfway down the center. The stained glass on the lower left shows various rulers of Strasbourg, while the stained glass on your right is the Bible for the poor (read: illiterate). A beautiful organ hangs above. Walk to the choir and stare at the stained-glass image of Mary; find the European Union flag at the top. In the right transept is a high-tech, 15th-century **astronomical clock** (restored in 1883) that gives a ho-hum performance every 15 minutes, better on the half-hour, best at 12:30 (arrive by 12:00 outside the right transept, buy your €1 ticket, then enter and hear an explanation of its workings; beware of pickpockets). For €3, you can climb 330 steps to the top of the narthex for an amazing view (access on right side of cathedral, cathedral open daily 7:00–11:35 & 12:40–19:00; tower open daily April–Sept 9:00–17:00, Oct–March 9:00–16:00).

Before leaving this area, stroll the impressive network of pedestrian streets that connect the cathedral with the huge place Kleber (home to various outdoor markets depending on the day of the week).

Museums near the Cathedral—These museums, all close to the cathedral, are interesting only for aficionados with a full day in Strasbourg, and they're all free the first Sunday of the month. The Palais Rohan houses three museums: the **Museum of Decorative Arts** (big, boring rooms with red velvet chairs), the

Museum of Fine Arts (modest but well-presented collection of paintings from Middle Ages to Baroque), and the **Archaeological Museum**, the best of the three, with an excellent presentation of Alsatian civilization over the millennia and English explanations (€3 per museum, €6 for all 3, Wed–Mon 10:00–18:00, closed Tue, 2 place du Château). The **Museum of the Cathedral** (Musée de l'Oeuvre Notre-Dame) has many artifacts from the cathedral but no English explanations (€3, Tue–Sun 10:00–18:00, closed Mon, 3 place du Château). The **Museum of Alsace**'s (Musée Alsacien) costumes and cultural exhibits are a good presentation of local traditions, with many stairs and walkways connecting furnished rooms in traditional homes (€3, Wed–Mon 10:00–18:00, closed Tue, across river from tourist boat dock at 23 quai St. Nicholas).

Boat Ride on the Ill River—Do a loop trip on the Ill River and get a different perspective on the city (€6.40, €6.80 at night, 70 min, English commentary via live guide or audioguide, boats depart 2/hr, April–Oct 9:30–21:00, May–Sept until 22:00, Nov–March 10:30–13:00 & 14:30–16:00, dock is 2 blocks outside cathedral's right transept, where rue Rohan meets the river).

La Petite France—Historic home to Strasbourg's tanners, this delightful area is laced with canals, grand half-timbered homes, cobblestones, and tourists. From the cathedral, walk to place Gutenberg, then follow rue Gutenberg, which turns into the pedestrian-only Grande Rue. Turn left off Grand Rue onto rue des Bouchers, and drop down to the river at the bridge. Wander deep—the best cafés line the canal on quai de la Bruche at the far end, and the small parks that lie between the canals are picnic- and siesta-perfect (cross bridge at rue des Moulins to reach the parks). Climb the grassy wall (Barrage Vauban) for a great view back over Strasbourg's medieval towers, city center, and water-ways. The glass structure behind you is the new modern-art museum (interesting more for its architecture than its collection). From here, it's a 10-minute walk back to the station (with river on your left, cross the third bridge and find rue Marie Kuss).

Sleeping in Strasbourg
(€1 = about $1, country code: 33, zip code: 67000)
You'll find a handy launderette near both listed hotels on Rue des Veaux.

HIGHER PRICED
Hôtel Cathédrale*, comfortable and stylish, lets you stare point-blank from your room at the cathedral (Db without view-€65–100, larger Db with view-€120–130, extra person-€15.50, breakfast buffet-€9.50, CC, air-con, elevator, Internet access, free

bicycles can be reserved for up to 2 hrs, laundry service, parking-€15 by reservation, 12 place de la Cathédrale, tel. 03 88 22 12 12, fax 03 88 23 28 00, www.hotel-cathedrale.fr, SE).

MODERATELY PRICED
Hôtel des Suisses**, across from the cathedral's right transept and off place du Château, is a quiet, dark, central, and solid two-star value (Sb-€45–55, Db-€59–69, Tb-€79–89, breakfast-€7, CC, elevator, 2 place de la Rape, tel. 03 88 35 22 11, fax 03 88 25 74 23, www.hotel-suisse.com, SE).

Eating in Strasbourg
Skip the touristy restaurants on the cathedral place and consider these nearby places: **Chez Yvonne** has a tradition of good food, pleasant staff, and reasonable prices (10 rue du Sanglier, tel. 03 88 32 84 15). **Au Tire Bouchon** costs a bit more, but is smaller and more intimate (daily, 5 rue des Tailleurs de Pierre, tel. 03 88 23 10 73).

In La Petite France, **Maison des Tanneurs,** located right on the river in a 16th-century building, is a big, snazzy place with dining rooms on two levels and an outside terrace (allow €35 for dinner, closed Sun–Mon, 42 rue du Bain aux Plantes, tel. 03 88 32 79 70).

Transportation Connections—Strasbourg
Strasbourg makes a good side-trip from Colmar or stop on the way to or from Paris.

By train to: Colmar (hrly, 50 min), **Paris'** Gare de l'Est (14/day, 4.5 hrs, 6 require changes), **Karlsruhe**, Germany (16/day, 1.5 hrs, 11 with change in Appenweier), **Basel**, Switzerland (hrly, 2 hrs).

VERDUN
Little remains in Europe today to remind us of World War I, but Verdun provides a fine tribute to the million-plus lives lost in the battles fought here. While the lunar landscape of World War I is now forested over, countless craters and trenches are visible. Millions of live bombs lie in vast cordoned-off areas. Drive through the eerie moguls surrounding Verdun, stopping at melted-sugar-cube forts and plaques marking where towns once existed. With two hours and a car, or a full day and a bike (and a strong heart), you can see the most stirring sights and appreciate the tremendous scale of the battles. The town of Verdun is not your destination, but a starting point for your visit into the nearby battlefields.

Tourist Information: The TI is on place Nation (May–Sept daily 8:30–18:30, Oct–April closed 12:00–14:00 and at 18:00, tel. 03 29 86 14 18).

Arrival in Verdun

By Train: Walk straight out of the station and down avenue Garibaldi to the town center.

By Car: Follow signs to *Centre-ville*, place Nation, and Porte Chatel; you'll pass the TI just before crossing the river.

Getting around the Verdun Battlefield

The TI has good maps of the battlefields. French-language **mini-van tours** of the battle sites are available June through September and leave the TI around 14:00 (€23 guides usually speak some English, and English handouts are available). You can rent a bike opposite Verdun's train station at **Cycles Flavenot** (tel. 03 29 86 12 43). To reach the battlefields by car or bike (about 30 km/ 18.5 miles round-trip), take D-112 from Verdun (look for signs to Douaumont) and then take D-913 to Douaumont.

The battlefield remains are situated on two sides of the Meuse River; the *rive droite* has more sights. By following signs to Fort Douaumont and the Ossuaire, you'll pass Musée Fleury.

Sights—Verdun

▲▲**Battlegrounds**—The most compelling sights are Mémorial-Musée de Fleury, l'Ossuaire, and Fort Douaumont. Start with **Mémorial-Musée de Fleury**, built around an impressive re-creation of a battlefield, with hard-hitting photos, weapon displays, and a worthwhile 15-minute movie narrated in English with headphones (€3, March–Dec 9:00–18:00, until 17:00 in winter). The museum is built on the site of a village (Fleury) that was obliterated during the fighting.

L'Ossuaire is the tomb of 130,000 French and Germans whose last homes were the muddy trenches of Verdun (March–early Sept daily 9:00–18:00, early Sept–Feb closes 12:00–14:00 and at 17:30). Look through the low windows for a bony memorial to those whose political and military leaders asked them to make the "ultimate sacrifice" for their countries. Enter the monument and experience a humbling and moving tribute. Ponder a war that left half of all Frenchmen aged 15 to 30 dead or wounded. Climb the tower for a territorial view (€1) and don't miss the thought-provoking 20-minute film (€2.50, €3 includes tower, closed Nov–March; theater in basement, ask for English version). The little €0.30 coin-op picture boxes in the gift shop are worth a look if you don't visit Mémorial-Musée de Fleury (turn through all of the old photos before time expires).

Before leaving, walk to the cemetery and listen for the eerie buzz of silence and peace. You can visit the nearby **Tranchée des Baionnettes**, where an entire company of soldiers was

Verdun

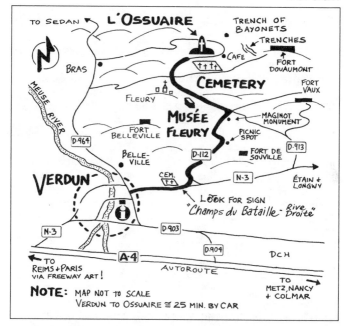

buried alive in their trench (the soldiers' bayonets remained above ground until recently).

The nearby **Fort Douaumont** was a strategic command center for both sides at various times. It's more interesting from the outside than the inside (walk on top and notice the round, iron-gun emplacements that could rise and revolve). A walk inside (€2.50) completes the picture, with long, damp corridors and a German memorial on the spot where 1,600 Germans were killed by a single blast. Halfway between l'Ossuaire and Fort Douaumont (on either side of the road) are clearly visible trenches. *Village Détruit* signs indicate where villages were entirely destroyed; only monuments remain to mark their existence.

Citadelle Souterraine—This is a disappointing train ride through the tunnels of the French Command in downtown Verdun. While it tries to re-create the Verdun scene, it's not worth your time.

Transportation Connections—Verdun

By train to: Colmar (5/day, 4–6 hrs, best with changes in Metz and Strasbourg), **Reims** (4/day, 3 hrs, most with change in Chalon), **Paris'** Gare de l'Est (5/day, 3 hrs, change in Metz or Chalon).

REIMS

Deservedly famous for its cathedral and champagne, contemporary Reims (pron. ramce) is a prosperous, modern city. Rebuilt after being leveled in World War I, Reims is 90 minutes from Paris by car or train and makes a good day trip or handy stop for travelers en route elsewhere. Most sights of interest (champagne caves included) are within a 20-minute walk from the cathedral.

To best experience contemporary Reims, wander the thriving shopping streets between the cathedral and the train station; rue de Vesle, rue Condorcet, and place d'Erlon are best.

Tourist Information: The TI is outside the cathedral's left transept (Easter–mid-Oct Mon–Sat 9:00–19:00, Sun 10:00–18:00; mid-Oct–Easter Mon–Sat 9:00–18:00, Sun 11:00–17:00, free map shows champagne caves, Internet access available, public WCs across street, tel. 03 26 77 45 25, www.tourisme.fr/reims). Ask about tours of the cathedral in English (usually 14:30 Sat–Sun, summer only) and skip the €7.65 audioguide tour.

Arrival in Reims

By Train: Walk straight out of the station (baggage check available) and through the park, cross the huge boulevards Joffre and Foch, and stroll up the pedestrian place Drouet d'Erlon. Turn left on rue Condorcet, then right on rue Talleyrand to reach the cathedral (15 min). Most buses leaving from the front of the station (station side of the street) will take you close to the cathedral (€0.75, verify with driver, get off at stop Grand Theatre).

By Car: Follow *Centre-ville* and *Cathédrale* signs and park on the street approaching the cathedral (rue Libergier) or in the well-signed *Parking Cathédrale* structure.

Sights—Reims

▲▲▲**Cathedral**—The cathedral of Reims is a glorious example of Gothic architecture, with the best west portal (inside and outside) anywhere. (Since medieval churches always face east, you enter the west portal.) Clovis, the first king of the Franks, was baptized here in A.D. 496 (thus determining France's religion). Ever since, Reims' cathedral has served as the coronation place of French kings and queens. Self-assured Joan of Arc led a timid Charles VII here to be coronated in 1429. This event rallied the French around their king to push the English out of France and end the Hundred Years' War. The cathedral houses many treasures, great medieval stained glass, and a luminous set of Marc Chagall stained-glass windows from 1974 that somehow fit well into this ancient stone structure. Informative English explanations are provided along the right aisle and offer sufficient historical detail (including the Chagall windows) for most travelers (daily 7:30–19:30).

Palais de Tau—This former Archbishop's Palace houses artifacts from the cathedral (mostly tapestries and stone statues) in impressive rooms—these guys lived well. There is sadly little English information, and while I enjoyed seeing eye to eye with the original statues from the cathedral's facade—particularly the huge Goliath that hangs above the entry's rose window—this museum isn't worth the time for most (€5.50, Tue–Sun May–Aug 9:30–18:30, Sept–April 9:30–12:30 & 14:00–17:30, closed Mon).

▲**Champagne Tours**—Reims is the capital of the Champagne region. While the bubbly stuff's birthplace was closer to Epernay, you can tour a champagne cave right in Reims. All charge for tastings and are open daily; the last tours usually depart about an hour before midday and afternoon closings. All but the four listed below must be reserved in advance to visit.

Mumm is closest to the train station and offers three kinds of worthwhile visits. The "traditional" (€5, 1 hr) includes a good 10-minute video explaining the history of Mumm and the champagne-making process, a tour of the cellars where 25 million bottles are stored, and a small museum of old champagne-making contraptions. The tour ends with a glass of Cordon Rouge. The "enological visit" offers all that, plus a "guided" tasting at the end (€12 for 2 types, €16 for 3 types, 1.5 hrs). You can also add a "vineyard visit" by minivan (€25, 3 hrs), but only by reservation in advance (daily March–Sept 9:00–11:00 & 14:00–17:00, Oct–Feb weekend afternoons, tel. 03 26 49 59 70, www.champagne-mumm.com). Mumm is four blocks left out of the train station, on the other side of place de la République at 34 rue du Champs de Mars. Don't go in #29 on the left-hand side of the street as shown on the city map; the visits are in the building on the right, #34, at the end of the courtyard. Follow signs for *Visites des Caves*.

The next three places cluster near each other about 25 minutes by foot southeast of the cathedral (from behind cathedral's right transept, walk down rue de l'Université, then rue de Barbatre; figure €7 for a one-way taxi from the train station). **Taittinger** does a great job of trying to convince you they're the best. After seeing their movie (in comfortable theater seats), follow your guide down into some of the five kilometers/three miles of chilly chalk caves, many dug by ancient Romans. Popping corks signal when the tour's done and the tasting's begun (€5.50, includes tasting, 1 hr, Mon–Fri 9:30–12:00 & 14:00–16:30, Sat–Sun 9:00–11:00 & 14:00–17:00, Dec–Feb closed weekends, 9 place St. Nicaise, tel. 03 26 85 84 33, www.taittinger.com). **Piper Heidsieck** offers a short, Disneyesque train-ride tour and tasting (€6.50 for 1 sample

Reims

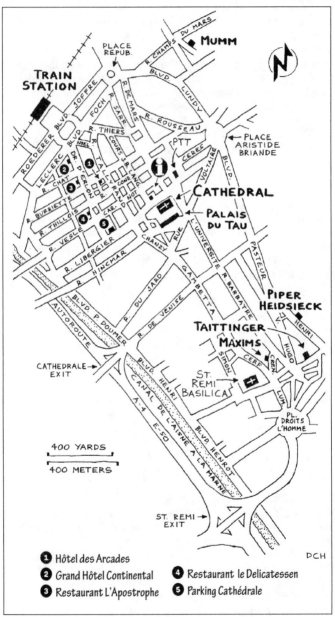

1. Hôtel des Arcades
2. Grand Hôtel Continental
3. Restaurant L'Apostrophe
4. Restaurant le Delicatessen
5. Parking Cathédrale

DCH

of champagne, €10 for 3, daily 9:00–11:45 & 14:00–17:00, Jan–
Feb closed Tue–Wed, 1 block beyond Taittinger up boulevard
Victor Hugo to 51 boulevard Henri-Vasnier, tel. 03 26 84 43 44,
www.piper-heidsieck.com). **Maxim's** is nearby and less famous,
with a we-try-harder attitude and the cheapest tasting. Their
€4.60, 50-minute tour includes a film, a tour of their cellars,
and a tasting of three different champagnes (open through lunch,
daily 10:00–19:00, last tour departs at 18:00, 17 rue des Créneaux,
tel. 03 26 82 70 67).

Sights—Near Reims
Epernay—Champagne purists may want to visit Epernay (26 km/
16 miles away, well-connected to Paris and Reims), where the
granddaddy of champagne houses, **Moët et Chandon**, offers
tours (€6.50 with tasting, daily 9:30–11:30 & 14:00–16:30, tel.
03 26 51 21 00). According to the story, it was near here in about
1700 that the monk Dom Perignon, after much fiddling with
double fermentation, stumbled onto this bubbly treat. On that
happy day, he ran through the abbey shouting, "Brothers, come
quickly . . . I'm drinking stars!"
Route de la Champagne—Drivers can joyride through the
scenic and prestigious vineyards just south of Reims. Follow
D-9 south to Cormontreuil, then Louvois, then Bouzy, to see
the chalky soil and vines that produce Champagne's costly
wines. Many of the villages have small hotels if you'd like to
sleep surrounded by vineyards.

Sleeping in Reims
(€1 = about $1, country code: 33, zip code: 51100)
It's hard to differentiate between the scads of hotels lining the vast
pedestrian place Drouet d'Erlon.

MODERATELY PRICED
Grand Hôtel Continental*** is a business hotel offering reasonable
three-star comfort, pleasant public spaces, and frequent specials
(Db-€53–100, Tb/Qb-€100–165, buffet breakfast-€9, CC, elevator,
laundry service, parking-€5, 93 place Drouet d'Erlon, tel. 03 26 40
39 35, fax 03 26 47 51 12, www.grandhotelcontinental.com, friendly
owner Philippe SE).

LOWER PRICED
The modern and friendly **Hôtel des Arcades**** is a simple, solid
value (Sb-€39, Db-€42–45, Tb-€45, breakfast-€6, CC, elevator,
parking-€6, 16 passage Sube, off rue Condorcet in mall opposite
merry-go-round, tel. 03 26 88 63 74, fax 03 26 40 66 56).

Eating in Reims

Le Delicatessen is a welcoming place serving lowbrow meals in a relaxed setting, with your choice of vegetable side dishes. Ask for the cozy non-smoking *(non-fumeur)* section in the back, and you'll feel like you're dining in grandma's living room (€12 *plats du jour*, closed Sun, on place Drouet d'Erlon at 3 rue Théodore Dubois, tel. 03 26 06 00 11). **L'Apostrophe** wins the snazziness contest, with a library-like interior and lively bar scene in the rear (look for their specials, 59 place Drouet d'Erlon, tel. 03 26 79 19 89).

Transportation Connections—Reims

By train to: Epernay (12/day, 30 min), **Verdun** (4/day, 3 hrs, most with change in Chalon), **Paris'** Gare de l'Est (12/day, 1.5 hrs), **Colmar** (6/day, 6 hrs, several changes).

APPENDIX

"La Marseillaise"

There's a movement in France to soften the lyrics of their national anthem. Sing it now…before it's too late.

Allons enfants de la Patrie, (Let's go, children of the fatherland,)
Le jour de gloire est arrivé. (The day of glory has arrived.)
Contre nous de la tyrannie (The blood-covered flag of tyranny)
L'étendard sanglant est levé. (Is raised against us.)
L'étendard sanglant est levé. (Is raised against us.)
Entendez-vous dans les campagnes
  (Do you hear these ferocious soldiers)
Mugir ces féroces soldats? (Howling in the countryside?)
Qui viennent jusque dans nos bras (They're nearly in our grasp)
Egorger vos fils et vos compagnes.
  (To slit the throats of your sons and your women.)
Aux armes citoyens, (Grab your weapons, citizens,)
Formez vos bataillons, (Form your battalions,)
Marchons, marchons, (March on, march on,)
Qu'un sang impur (So that their impure blood)
Abreuve nos sillons. (Will fill our trenches.)

French History in an Escargot Shell

Around the time of Christ, Romans "Latinized" the land of the Gauls. With the fifth-century fall of Rome, the barbarian Franks and Burgundians invaded. From this unique mix of Latin and Celtic cultures evolved today's France.

While France wallowed with the rest of Europe in medieval darkness, it got a head start in its development as a nation-state. In 507, Clovis established Paris as the capital of his Christian Merovingian dynasty. Clovis and the Franks would eventually become Louis and the French. Charles Martel stopped the spread of Islam by beating the Spanish Moors at the Battle of Poitiers. And Charlemagne, the most important of the "Dark Age" Frankish kings, was crowned Holy Roman Emperor by the pope in 1800. Charles the Great presided over the "Carolingian Renaissance" and effectively ruled a vast-for-the-time empire.

The Treaty of Verdun (843), which divided Charlemagne's empire among his grandsons, marks what could be considered the birth of Europe. For the first time, a treaty was signed in vernacular languages (French and German) rather than in Latin. While this split established a Franco/Germanic divide, it also heralded an age of fragmentation. While petty princes took the reigns, the Frankish king ruled only Ile-de-France, a small region around Paris.

Vikings, or Norsemen, settled in what became Normandy. Later, in 1066, these "Normans" invaded England. The Norman king, William the Conqueror, consolidated his English domain, accelerating the formation of modern England. But his rule also muddied the political waters between England and France, kicking off a centuries-long struggle between the two nations.

In the 12th century, Eleanor of Aquitaine (a separate country in southwest France) married Louis VII, king of France, bringing Aquitaine under French rule. They divorced, and she married Henry of Normandy, soon-to-be Henry II of England. This marital union gave England control of a huge swath of land from the English Channel to the Pyrenees. For 300 years, France and England would struggle over control of Aquitaine. Any enemy of the French king would find a natural ally in the English king.

In 1328, a French king (Charles IV) died without a son. The English king (Edward III) was his nephew and naturally was interested in the throne. The French resisted. This pitted France, the biggest and richest country in Europe, against England, which had the biggest army. They fought from 1337 to 1453 in what was modestly called the Hundred Years' War.

Regional powers from within France sided with England. Burgundy actually took Paris, captured the royal family, and recognized the English king as heir to the French throne. England controlled France from the Loire north, and things looked bleak for the French king.

Enter Joan of Arc, a 16-year-old peasant girl driven by religious voices. France's national heroine left home to support the dauphin Charles VII (boy prince, heir to the throne but too young to rule). Joan rallied the French, ultimately inspiring them to throw out the English. In 1430, Joan was captured by the Burgundians, who sold her to the English, who convicted her of heresy and burned her at the stake in Rouen. But the inspiration of Joan of Arc lived on, and by 1453, English holdings on the Continent had dwindled to the port of Calais.

By 1500, a strong centralized France had emerged with borders similar to today's borders. Her kings (from the Renaissance François I through the Henrys and all those Louises) were model divine monarchs, setting the standards for absolute rule in Europe.

Outrage over the power plays and spending sprees of the kings, coupled with the modern thinking of the Enlightenment—whose leaders were the French *philosophes*—led to the French Revolution (1789) and the end of the Old Regime and its notion that some are born to rule while others are born to be ruled.

But the excesses of the Revolution led to the rise of Napoleon, who ruled the French empire as a dictator until his excesses

ushered him into a South Atlantic exile. The French settled on
a compromise role for their ruler. The modern French king was
himself ruled by a constitution. Rather than dress in leotards and
powdered wigs, he went to work in a suit with a briefcase.

The 20th century spelled the end of France's reign as a military and political superpower. Devastating wars with Germany
in 1870, 1914, and 1940 and the loss of her colonial holdings left
France with not quite enough land, people, or production to be
a top player on a global scale.

France in the 21st century is the cultural capital of Europe
and a leader in the push to integrate Europe into one unified economic power. When that happens, Paris will once again emerge
as a superpower capital.

Contemporary Politics in France

The key political issues in France today are high unemployment
(about 9 percent), a steadily increasing percentage of ethnic
minorities, and the need to compete in a global marketplace.
The challenge is to address these issues while maintaining the
generous social benefits the French expect from their government. As a result, national policies seem to conflict with each
other (e.g., France supports the lean economic policies of the
European Union but recently reduced the French workweek
to 35 hours).

The unification of Europe has been powered by France and
Germany. The 15-member European Union is busy dissolving
borders, freeing up trade, and dealing with cross-border issues
from air quality to air traffic.

French national politics are fascinating. While only two
parties dominate American politics, France has five major parties.
From left to right, these include the reformed Communists (PCF—
Parti Communiste Française), the moderate Socialists (PS—Parti
Socialiste), the aristocratically conservative UDF (Union pour la
Démocratie Française), the center-right RPR (Rassemblement
pour la République), and the racist and isolationist Front National.
In general, the UDF and RPR split the conservative middle ground,
and the Socialists dominate the liberal middle ground. But in France,
unlike in the United States, informal coalitions are generally necessary for any party to "rule."

At the fringes, you'll read about the Front National party, led
by Jean-Marie Le Pen. Le Pen's "France for the French" platform
calls for the expulsion of ethnic minorities and broader police
powers. Although the Front National has a staunch voter base of
about 12 percent, the recent rise in unemployment and globaliza-
tion worries have increased its following somewhat. In the 2002

presidential primary, 16 candidates (a new record) vied for office, and Le Pen's loyal following put him in second place—ahead of the Socialist party candidate Lionel Jospin (who had been prime minister), but behind conservative incumbent Jacques Chirac. While Chirac won the regular election easily, Le Pen has been able to nudge the political agenda to the right. On the far left, the reformed Communists are still trying to recover from the fall of the Soviet Union and might not survive into another election due to an ever-dwindling following.

While the French president is elected by popular vote every seven years, he is more of a figurehead than his American counterpart. The more powerful prime minister is elected by the parliament (Assemblée Nationale) and confirmed by the new president. With five major parties, a single majority is rare—it takes a coalition to elect a prime minister. Currently, the right is working together better than the left, as the president (Jacques Chirac) and prime minister (Jean-Pierre Raffarin) are both conservatives.

Let's Talk Telephones

Dialing Direct

Here's a primer on making direct phone calls. For information specific to France, see "Telephones" in the introduction.

Making Calls within a European Country: About half of all European countries use area codes (like we do); the other half uses a direct-dial system without area codes.

To make calls within a country that uses a direct-dial system (France, Belgium, Czech Republic, Denmark, Italy, Portugal, Norway, Spain, and Switzerland), you dial the same number whether you're calling across the country or across the street.

In countries that use area codes (such as Austria, Britain, Finland, Germany, Ireland, Netherlands, and Sweden), you dial the local number when calling within a city, and you add the area code if calling long-distance within the country.

Making International Calls: You always start with the international access code (011 if you're calling from America or Canada, or 00 from Europe), then dial the country code of the country you're calling (see chart below).

What you dial next depends on the phone system of the country you're calling. If the country uses area codes, drop the initial zero of the area code, then dial the rest of the number.

Countries that use direct-dial systems (no area codes) vary in how they're accessed internationally by phone. For instance, if you're making an international call to the Czech Republic, Denmark, Italy, Norway, Portugal, or Spain, simply dial the international access code, country code, and phone number. But if you're calling France, Belgium, or Switzerland, drop the initial zero of the phone number.

International Access Codes
When dialing direct, first dial the international access code of the country you're calling from. For the United States and Canada, it's 011. Virtually all European countries use "00" as their international access code; the only exceptions are Finland (990) and Lithuania (810).

Country Codes
After you've dialed the international access code, dial the code of the country you're calling.

Austria—43	Greece—30
Belgium—32	Ireland—353
Britain—44	Italy—39
Canada—1	Morocco-212
Czech Rep.—420	Netherlands—31
Denmark—45	Norway—47
Estonia—372	Portugal—351
Finland—358	Spain—34
France—33	Sweden—46
Germany—49	Switzerland—41
Gibraltar—350	United States—1

Telephone Directory
Useful Phone Numbers and Addresses
Emergency: Dial 17 for police
Emergency Medical Assistance: 15
Train Schedules and Reservations: tel. 08 36 35 35 35
Directory Assistance: 12 (some English spoken)
Train (SNCF) Information: tel. 08 36 35 35 35
  (some English usually spoken)

Consulates/Embassies
U.S. Consulate: Open Mon–Fri 9:00–12:30 & 13:00–15:00, 2 rue St. Florentin, 75008, Paris. Mo: Concorde, tel. 01 43 12 22 22, www.amb-usa.fr/consul/consulat.htm.
U.S. Embassy: 2 avenue Gabriel (to the left as you face Hôtel Crillon), 75008, Paris. Mo: Concorde, tel. 01 43 12 22 22.
Canadian Consulate and Embassy: 35 avenue Montaigne, 75008, Paris. Mo: Franklin-Roosevelt, tel. 01 44 43 29 00.

European Calling Chart

Just smile and dial, using this key:
AC = Area Code, LN = Local Number.

European Country	Calling long distance within...	Calling from the U.S.A./ Canada to...	Calling from another European country to...
Austria	AC (Area Code) + LN (Local Number)	011 + 43 + AC (without the initial zero) + LN	00 + 43 + AC (without the initial zero) + LN
Belgium	LN	011 + 32 + LN (without initial zero)	00 + 32 + LN (without initial zero)
Britain	AC + LN	011 + 44 + AC (without initial zero) + LN	00 + 44 + AC . (without initial zero) + LN
Czech Republic	LN	011 + 420 + LN	00 + 420 + LN
Denmark	LN	011 + 45 + LN	00 + 45 + LN
Estonia	LN	011 + 372 + LN	00 + 372 + LN
Finland	AC + LN	011 + 358 + AC (without initial zero) + LN	00 + 358 + AC (without initial zero) + LN
France	LN	011 + 33 + LN (without initial zero)	00 + 33 + LN (without initial zero)
Germany	AC + LN	011 + 49 + AC (without initial zero) + LN	00 + 49 + AC (without initial zero) + LN
Gibraltar	LN	011 + 350 + LN	00 + 350 + LN From Spain: 9567 + LN
Greece	LN	011 + 30 + LN	00 + 30 + LN

European Country	Calling long distance within...	Calling from the U.S.A./ Canada to...	Calling from another European country to...
Ireland	AC + LN	011 + 353 + AC (without initial zero) + LN	00 + 353 + AC (without initial zero) + LN
Italy	LN	011 + 39 + LN	00 + 39 + LN
Morocco	LN	011 + 212 + LN (without initial zero)	00 + 212 + LN (without initial zero)
Netherlands	AC + LN	011 + 31 + AC (without initial zero) + LN	00 + 31 + AC (without initial zero) + LN
Norway	LN	011 + 47 + LN	00 + 47 + LN
Portugal	LN	011 + 351 + LN	00 + 351 + LN
Spain	LN	011 + 34 + LN	00 + 34 + LN
Sweden	AC + LN	011 + 46 + AC (without initial zero) + LN	00 + 46 + AC (without initial zero) + LN
Switzerland	LN	011 + 41 + LN (without initial zero)	00 + 41 + LN (without initial zero)
Turkey	AC (if no initial zero is included, add one) + LN	011 + 90 + AC (without initial zero) + LN	00 + 90 + AC (without initial zero) + LN

- The instructions above apply whether you're calling a fixed phone or cell phone.
- The international access codes (the first numbers you dial when making an international call) are 011 if you're calling from the U.S.A./Canada, or 00 if you're calling from virtually anywhere in Europe. Finland and Lithuania are the only exceptions. If calling from either of these countries, replace the 00 with 990 in Finland and 810 in Lithuania.
- To call the U.S.A. or Canada from Europe, dial 00 (unless you're calling from Finland or Lithuania), then 1 (the country code for the U.S.A. and Canada), then the area code and number. In short, 00 + 1 + AC + LN = Hi, Mom!

Paris Information
Tourist Information: tel. 08 92 68 31 12
  (recorded info with long menu)
American Church: tel. 01 40 62 05 00
American Hospital: tel. 01 46 41 25 25

Lost or Stolen Credit Cards
Visa: tel. 0800 9011 79
MasterCard: tel. 0800 90 1387
American Express: tel. 01 47 77 72 00
Diners Club: tel. Call USA collect (001-702-797-5532)

Cheap Flights within Europe
Access Voyages: 6 rue Pierre Lescot, 75001,
  Paris. Mo: Chatelet, tel. 01 44 76 84 50.
Any Way: 46 rue des Lombards, 75001,
  Paris. Mo: Chatelet or Hôtel de Ville, tel. 01 40 28 00 74.
Cash & Go: 34 avenue des Champs-Elysées, 75008,
  Paris. Mo: Franklin D. Roosevelt, tel. 01 53 93 63 63.

Festivals in France
This is just a partial list. For specific info and dates, contact the national TIs (listed in Introduction) and visit www.whatsgoingon .com, www.festivals.com, and www.franceguide.com.

January	Monte Carlo Motor Rally, Monaco
Jan–Feb	Carnival Celebrations, best in Nice
May	Festival de Versailles (arts);
	Cannes Film Festival Monaco Grand Prix;
	Ascension Day (religious procession);
	Festival Jeanne d'Arc (pageants), Rouen
June	Festival du Marais (arts), Paris
July	Bastille Day (July 14—fireworks, celebrations everywhere);
	Grand Parade du Jazz, Nice;
	Festival d'Avignon (arts), Avignon;
	Tour de France (ends in Paris);
	Les Tombées de la Nuit (arts festival), Rennes;
	Beaune International Music Festival;
	Fête de la Musique (July 17—free concerts celebrating summer solstice)
September	Fête d'Automne (arts festival), Paris;
	Wine harvest festivals in many towns
November	Les Trois Glorieuses (wine auction and festival), Beaune
December	Christmas Market, Strasbourg

2003

	JANUARY					
S	M	T	W	T	F	S
			1	2	3	4
5	6	7	8	9	10	11
12	13	14	15	16	17	18
19	20	21	22	23	24	25
26	27	28	29	30	31	

	FEBRUARY					
S	M	T	W	T	F	S
						1
2	3	4	5	6	7	8
9	10	11	12	13	14	15
16	17	18	19	20	21	22
23	24	25	26	27	28	

	MARCH					
S	M	T	W	T	F	S
						1
2	3	4	5	6	7	8
9	10	11	12	13	14	15
16	17	18	19	20	21	22
23/30 24/31	25	26	27	28	29	

	APRIL					
S	M	T	W	T	F	S
		1	2	3	4	5
6	7	8	9	10	11	12
13	14	15	16	17	18	19
20	21	22	23	24	25	26
27	28	29	30			

	MAY					
S	M	T	W	T	F	S
				1	2	3
4	5	6	7	8	9	10
11	12	13	14	15	16	17
18	19	20	21	22	23	24
25	26	27	28	29	30	31

	JUNE					
S	M	T	W	T	F	S
1	2	3	4	5	6	7
8	9	10	11	12	13	14
15	16	17	18	19	20	21
22	23	24	25	26	27	28
29	30					

	JULY					
S	M	T	W	T	F	S
		1	2	3	4	5
6	7	8	9	10	11	12
13	14	15	16	17	18	19
20	21	22	23	24	25	26
27	28	29	30	31		

	AUGUST					
S	M	T	W	T	F	S
					1	2
3	4	5	6	7	8	9
10	11	12	13	14	15	16
17	18	19	20	21	22	23
24/31	25	26	27	28	29	30

	SEPTEMBER					
S	M	T	W	T	F	S
	1	2	3	4	5	6
7	8	9	10	11	12	13
14	15	16	17	18	19	20
21	22	23	24	25	26	27
28	29	30				

	OCTOBER					
S	M	T	W	T	F	S
			1	2	3	4
5	6	7	8	9	10	11
12	13	14	15	16	17	18
19	20	21	22	23	24	25
26	27	28	29	30	31	

	NOVEMBER					
S	M	T	W	T	F	S
						1
2	3	4	5	6	7	8
9	10	11	12	13	14	15
16	17	18	19	20	21	22
23/30	24	25	26	27	28	29

	DECEMBER					
S	M	T	W	T	F	S
	1	2	3	4	5	6
7	8	9	10	11	12	13
14	15	16	17	18	19	20
21	22	23	24	25	26	27
28	29	30	31			

Climate

First line, average daily low temperature; second line, average daily high; third line, days of no rain.

	J	F	M	A	M	J	J	A	S	O	N	D
Paris												
	34°	34°	39°	43°	49°	55°	58°	58°	53°	46°	40°	36°
	43°	45°	54°	60°	68°	73°	76°	75°	70°	60°	50°	44°
	14	14	19	17	19	18	19	18	17	18	15	15
Nice												
	35°	36°	41°	46°	52°	58°	63°	63°	58°	51°	43°	37°
	50°	53°	59°	64°	71°	79°	84°	83°	77°	68°	58°	52°
	23	22	24	23	23	26	29	26	24	23	21	21

Numbers and Stumblers

- Europeans write a few of their numbers differently than we do. 1 = 1 , 4 = 4 , 7 = 7 . Learn the difference or miss your train.
- In Europe, dates appear as day/month/year, so Christmas is 25/12/03.
- Commas are decimal points and decimals commas. A dollar and a half is $1,50 and there are 5.280 feet in a mile.
- When pointing, use your whole hand, palm down.
- When counting with fingers, start with your thumb. If you hold up your first finger to request one item, you'll probably get two.
- What Americans call the second floor of a building is the first floor in Europe.
- Europeans keep the left "lane" open for passing on escalators and moving sidewalks. Keep to the right.

Metric Conversion (approximate)

1 inch = 25 millimeters
1 foot = 0.3 meter
1 yard = 0.9 meter
1 mile = 1.6 kilometers
1 centimeter = 0.4 inch
1 meter = 39.4 inches
1 kilometer = .62 mile
32 degrees F = 0 degrees C
82 degrees F = about 28 degrees C
1 ounce = 28 grams
1 kilogram = 2.2 pounds
1 quart = 0.95 liter
1 square yard = 0.8 square meter
1 acre = 0.4 hectare

Basic French Survival Phrases

English	French	Phonetics
Good day.	**Bonjour.**	bohn-zhoor
Mrs. / Mr.	**Madame / Monsieur**	mah-dahm / muhs-yur
Do you speak English?	**Parlez-vous anglais?**	par-lay-voo ahn-glay
Yes. / No.	**Oui. / Non.**	wee / nohn
I understand.	**Je comprends.**	zhuh kohn-prahn
I don't understand.	**Je ne comprends pas.**	zhuh nun kohn-prahn pah
Please.	**S'il vous plaît.**	see voo play
Thank you.	**Merci.**	mehr-see
I'm sorry.	**Désolé.**	day-zoh-lay
Excuse me.	**Pardon.**	par-dohn
(No) problem.	**(Pas de) problème.**	(pah duh) proh-blehm
It's good.	**C'est bon.**	say bohn
Goodbye.	**Au revoir.**	oh vwahr
one / two	**un / deux**	uhn / duh
three / four	**trois / quatre**	twah / kah-truh
five / six	**cinq / six**	sank / sees
seven / eight	**sept / huit**	seht / weet
nine / ten	**neuf / dix**	nuhf / dees
How much is it?	**Combien?**	kohn-bee-an
Write it?	**Ecrivez?**	ay-kree-vay
Is it free?	**C'est gratuit?**	say grah-twee
Included?	**Inclus?**	an-klew
Where can I buy / find...?	**Où puis-je acheter / trouver...?**	oo pwee-zhuh ah-shuh-tay / troo-vay
I'd like / We'd like...	**Je voudrais / Nous voudrions...**	zhuh voo-dray / noo voo-dree-ohn
...a room.	**...une chambre.**	ewn shahn-bruh
...the bill.	**...l'addition.**	lah-dee-see-ohn
...a ticket to ___.	**...un billet pour ___.**	uhn bee-yay poor
Is it possible?	**C'est possible?**	say poh-see-bluh
Where is...?	**Où est...?**	oo ay
...the train station	**...la gare**	lah gar
...the bus station	**...la gare routière**	lah gar root-yehr
...tourist information	**...l'office du tourisme**	loh-fees dew too-reez-muh
Where are the toilets?	**Où sont les toilettes?**	oo sohn lay twah-leht
men	**hommes**	ohm
women	**dames**	dahm
left / right	**à gauche / à droite**	ah gohsh / ah dwaht
straight	**tout droit**	too dwah
When does this open / close?	**Ça ouvre / ferme à quelle heure?**	sah oo-vruh / fehrm ah kehl ur
At what time?	**À quelle heure?**	ah kehl ur
Just a moment.	**Un moment.**	uhn moh-mahn
now / soon / later	**maintenant / bientôt / plus tard**	man-tuh-nahn / bee-an-toh / plew tar
today / tomorrow	**aujourd'hui / demain**	oh-zhoor-dwee / duh-man

When using the phonetics, try to nasalize the n sound.

For more user-friendly French phrases, check out *Rick Steves' French Phrase Book and Dictionary* or *Rick Steves' French, Italian & German Phrase Book and Dictionary*.

Faxing Your Hotel Reservation

Use this handy form for your fax or find it online at
www.ricksteves.com/reservation. Photocopy and fax away.

One-Page Fax

To: _____ @ _____
                    hotel   *fax*

From: _____ @ _____
                    name   *fax*

Today's date: ____ /_____ /____
                     day   month   year

Dear Hotel _____,

Please make this reservation for me:

Name: _____

Total # of people: _____   # of rooms: _____   # of nights: _____

Arriving: ____ /_____ /____ My time of arrival (24-hr clock): _____
              day   month   year

(I will telephone if I will be late)

Departing: ____ /_____ /____
                day   month   year

Room(s): Single___ Double___ Twin___ Triple___ Quad___

With: Toilet___ Shower___ Bath___ Sink only___

Special needs: View___ Quiet___ Cheapest___ Ground Floor___

Credit card: Visa___ MasterCard___ American Express___

Card #: _____

Expiration date:_____

Name on card: _____

You may charge me for the first night as a deposit. Please fax, e-mail, or
mail me confirmation of my reservation, along with the type of room
reserved, the price, and whether the price includes breakfast. Please also
inform me of your cancellation policy. Thank you.

_____
Signature

_____
Name

_____
Address

_____
City   *State*   *Zip Code*   *Country*

_____
E-mail Address

Road Scholar Feedback for FRANCE 2003

We're all in the same travelers' school of hard knocks. Your feedback helps us improve this guidebook for future travelers. Please fill this out (or use the online version at www.ricksteves.com/feedback), attach more info or any tips/favorite discoveries if you like, and send it to us. As thanks for your help, we'll send you our quarterly travel newsletter free for one year. Thanks! **Rick**

Of the recommended accommodations/restaurants used, which was:

Best _____

      Why? _____

Worst _____

      Why? _____

Of the sights/experiences/destinations recommended by this book, which was:

Most overrated _____

      Why? _____

Most underrated _____

      Why? _____

Best ways to improve this book:

_____

_____

I'd like a free newsletter subscription:

_____ Yes   _____ No   _____ Already on list

_____
Name

_____
Address

_____
City, State, Zip

_____
E-mail Address

    Please send to: ETBD, Box 2009, Edmonds, WA 98020

INDEX

FREE-SPIRITED TOURS FROM

Rick Steves

Great Guides

Big Buses

Small Groups

No Grumps

Best of Europe ■ Village Europe ■ Eastern Europe ■ Turkey ■ Italy ■ Village Italy ■ Britain
Spain/Portugal ■ Ireland ■ Heart of France ■ South of France ■ Village France ■ Scandinavia
Germany/Austria/Switzerland ■ London ■ Paris ■ Rome ■ Venice ■ Florence ■ Prague

Looking for a one, two, or three-week tour that's run in the Rick Steves style? Check
out Rick Steves' educational, experiential tours of Europe.

Rick's tours include much more in the "sticker price" than mainstream tours.
Here's what you'll get with a Europe or regional Rick Steves tour ...

- **Group size:** Your tour group will be no larger than 26.

- **Guides:** You'll have two guides traveling and dining with you on your fully guided
  Rick Steves tour.

- **Bus:** You'll travel in a full-size bus, with plenty of empty seats for you to spread
  out and read, snooze, enjoy the passing scenery, get away from your spouse, or
  whatever.

- **Sightseeing:** Your tour price includes all group sightseeing. There are no hidden
  extra charges.

- **Hotels:** You'll stay in Rick's favorite small, characteristic, locally-run hotels in
  the center of each city, within walking distance of the sights you came to see.

- **Price and insurance:** Your tour price is guaranteed for 2003. Single travelers
  do not pay an extra supplement (we have them room with other singles).
  ETBD includes prorated tour cancellation/ interruption protection coverage at
  no extra cost.

- **Tips and kickbacks:** All guide and driver tips are included in your tour price.
  Because your driver and guides are paid salaries by ETBD, they can focus on
  giving you the best European travel experience possible.

Interested? Call (425) 771-8303 or visit www.ricksteves.com for a free copy of
Rick Steves' 2003 Tours booklet!

Rick Steves' Europe Through the Back Door

130 Fourth Avenue North, PO Box 2009, Edmonds, WA 98020 USA
Phone: (425) 771-8303 ■ Fax: (425) 771-0833 ■ www.ricksteves.com

FREE TRAVEL GOODIES FROM

Rick Steves

EUROPEAN TRAVEL NEWSLETTER

My *Europe Through the Back Door* travel company will help you travel better *because* you're on a budget—not in spite of it. To see how, ask for my 64-page *travel newsletter* packed full of savvy travel tips, readers' discoveries, and your best bets for railpasses, guidebooks, videos, travel accessories and free-spirited tours.

2003 GUIDE TO EUROPEAN RAILPASSES

With hundreds of railpasses to choose from in 2003, finding the right pass for your trip has never been more confusing. To cut through the complexity, visit www.ricksteves.com for my online *2003 Guide to European Railpasses*. Once you've narrowed down your choices, we give you unbeatable prices, including important extras with every Eurailpass, **free:** my 90-minute *Travel Skills Special* video or DVD and your choice of one of my 24 guidebooks.

RICK STEVES' 2003 TOURS

We offer 20 different one, two, and three-week tours (200 departures in 2003) for those who want to experience Europe in Rick Steves' Back Door style, but without the transportation and hotel hassles. If a tour with a small group, modest family-run hotels, lots of exercise, great guides, and no tips or hidden charges sounds like your idea of fun, ask for my 48-page 2003 Tours booklet.

YEAR-ROUND GUIDEBOOK UPDATES

Even though the information in my guidebooks is the freshest around, things do change in Europe between book printings. I've set aside a special section at my website (www.ricksteves.com/update) listing *up-to-the-minute changes* for every Rick Steves guidebook.

Visit www.ricksteves.com to get your...

- ☑ **FREE EUROPEAN TRAVEL NEWSLETTER**
- ☑ **FREE 2003 GUIDE TO EUROPEAN RAILPASSES**
- ☑ **FREE RICK STEVES' 2003 TOURS BOOKLET**

Rick Steves' Europe Through the Back Door

130 Fourth Avenue North, PO Box 2009, Edmonds, WA 98020 USA
Phone: (425) 771-8303 ■ Fax: (425) 771-0833 ■ www.ricksteves.com

Free, fresh travel tips, all year long.

Britain is Back!

London Sights ■ Offbeat Brits ■ Britain with Kids
Rick's Thrifty Fifty Travel Tips
This Land is Euro Land
Unrest Making You Restless?
New Venice and Florence Guidebooks
Travel Tips from our Road Scholars
Handy New Travel Kits and Day Bags

Visit **www.ricksteves.com**
to get Rick's free
64-page newsletter... and more!